Greek Islands

THE ROUGH GUIDE

D0110871

There are more than one hundred Rough Guide titles
covering destinations from Amsterdam to Zimbabwe

Forthcoming titles include

Bangkok • Barbados • Japan • Jordan • Syria

Rough Guide Reference Serics

Classical Music • European Football • The Internet • Jazz
Opera • Reggae • Rock Music • World Music

Rough Guide Phrasebooks

Czech • French • German • Greek • Hindi & Urdu • Indonesian • Italian
Mandarin Chinese • Mexican Spanish • Polish • Portuguese
Russian • Spanish • Thai • Turkish • Vietnamese

Rough Guides on the Internet
http://www.roughguides.com

ROUGH GUIDE CREDITS

Text editor: Helena Smith
Series editor: Mark Ellingham
Editorial: Martin Dunford, Jonathan Buckley, Samantha Cook, Jo Mead, Kate Berens, Amanda Tomlin, Ann-Marie Shaw, Paul Gray, Sarah Dallas, Chris Schüler, Julia Kelly, Caroline Osborne, Kieran Falconer, Judith Bamber, Olivia Eccleshall, Orla Duane (UK); Andrew Rosenberg (US)
Picture research: Eleanor Hill

Production: Susanne Hillen, Andy Hilliard, Judy Pang, Link Hall, Nicola Williamson, Helen Ostick
Cartography: Melissa Flack, Maxine Burke
Online editors: Alan Spicer (UK); Geronimo Madrid (US)
Finance: John Fisher, Celia Crowley, Neeta Mistry
Marketing & Publicity: Richard Trillo, Simon Carloss, Niki Smith (UK); Jean-Marie Kelly, SoRelle Braun (US)
Administration: Tania Hummel, Alexander Mark Rogers

ACKNOWLEDGEMENTS

The **editor** would like to thank Judy Pang, Nicola Williamson and Eleanor Hill; at Rough Guides; Rosemary Morlin for proofreading; and MicroMap (Romsey, Hants) for cartography.

Marc Dubin thanks Persephone Papayriakoú, Manolis and Maria on Thássos; the Papasotiriou family on Límnos; George & Barbara Ballis, Jennifer Yiannakou and Melinda on Lésvos; Markos Kostalas and Theodhore Spordhilis on Khíos; Terena at Horiatopoulos Tours on Sámos; Alexis and Dhionysia Zikas on Kós, Christine Sakelaridhes on Khálki and Baz Ward for Tílos updates; and Andrew Stoddart at Hellenic Bookservice, for the thorough bibliographic search.

Nick Edwards thanks Martin Burne, Geraldine Cassidy on Kéa; Maria Koureli on Mílos; Vassilis Tzavaras on Mílos and elsewhere; Anne Collins, Vassilis, Melissa and Ruth on Síros; and Catherine McLaughlin on Ándros.

John Gill thanks Helena Smith and Jonathan Buckley; Iannis Tranakas; Stephan Jaskulowski; Lia Mathioudaki and the Corfu NTOG; Judith Mackrell and Mitzi Rogers; Towering Inferno; Mrs Pat Stubbs; the Vassilas and Petrou families of Paxos; Maria Gazi and brother Yioryios of Nidhrí; Yioryios Moraitis of Kioni; Mr Messaris and Mrs Vassilikis of the Argostóli NTOG; Barbara Salisbury; and KTEL staff and drivers everywhere.

John Hartle thanks Fanis Gavalas on Iráklia; Kathleen Gika on Íos; and Sharon Turner on Tínos.

PUBLISHING INFORMATION

This second edition published March 1998 by Rough Guides Ltd, 1 Mercer St, London WC2H 9QJ. Distributed by the Penguin Group:
Penguin Books Ltd, 27 Wrights Lane, London W8 5TZ
Penguin Books USA Inc., 375 Hudson Street, New York 10014, USA
Penguin Books Australia Ltd, 487 Maroondah Highway, PO Box 257, Ringwood, Victoria 3134, Australia
Penguin Books Canada Ltd, 10 Alcorn Avenue, Toronto, Ontario, Canada M4V 1E4
Penguin Books (NZ) Ltd, 182–190 Wairau Road, Auckland 10, New Zealand
Typeset in Linotron Univers and Century Old Style to an original design by Andrew Oliver.
Printed in England by Clays Ltd, St Ives PLC
Illustrations in Part One and Part Three by Edward Briant.
Illustrations on p.1 and p.415 by Henry Iles.

The publishers and authors have done their best to ensure the accuracy and currency of all the information in The Rough Guide to the Greek Islands, however, they can accept no responsibility for any loss, injury, or inconvenience sustained by any traveller as a result of information or advice contained in the guide.

Greek Islands

THE ROUGH GUIDE

written and researched by

Mark Ellingham, Marc Dubin, Natania Jansz and John Fisher

with additional contributions by

John Chapple, Nick Edwards, Geoff Garvey, John Gill, John Hartle, Diana Louis and Julia Tweed

THE ROUGH GUIDES

We set out to do something different when the first Rough Guide was published in 1982. Mark Ellingham, just out of university, was travelling in Greece. He brought along the popular guides of the day, but found they were all lacking in some way. They were either strong on ruins and museums but went on for pages without mentioning a beach or taverna. Or they were so conscious of the need to save money that they lost sight of Greece's cultural and historical significance. Also, none of the books told him anything about Greece's contemporary life – its politics, its culture, its people, and how they lived.

So with no job in prospect, Mark decided to write his own guidebook, one which aimed to provide practical information that was second to none, detailing the best beaches and the hottest clubs and restaurants, while also giving hard-hitting accounts of every sight, both famous and obscure, and providing up-to-the-minute information on contemporary culture. It was a guide that encouraged independent travellers to find the best of Greece, and was a great success, getting shortlisted for the Thomas Cook travel guide award, and encouraging Mark, along with three friends, to expand the series.

The Rough Guide list grew rapidly and the letters flooded in, indicating a much broader readership than had been anticipated, but one which uniformly appreciated the Rough Guide mix of practical detail and humour, irreverence and enthusiasm. Things haven't changed. The same four friends who began the series are still the caretakers of the Rough Guide mission today: to provide the most reliable, up-to-date and entertaining information to independent-minded travellers of all ages, on all budgets.

We now publish 100 titles and have offices in London and New York. The travel guides are written and researched by a dedicated team of more than 100 authors, based in Britain, Europe, the USA and Australia. We have also created a unique series of phrasebooks to accompany the travel series, along with an acclaimed series of music guides, and a best-selling pocket guide to the Internet and World Wide Web. We also publish comprehensive travel information on our web site:

and http://www.roughguides.com

HELP US UPDATE

We've gone to a lot of effort to ensure that this new edition of The Rough Guide to the Greek Islands is accurate and up-to-date. However, things change – places get "discovered", opening hours are notoriously fickle, restaurants and rooms raise prices or lower standards, extra buses are laid on or off. If you feel we've got it wrong or left something out, we'd like to know, and if you can remember the address, the price, the time, the phone number, so much the better.

We'll credit all contributions, and send a copy of the next edition (or any other Rough Guide if you prefer) for the best letters. Please mark letters: "Rough Guide Greek Islands Update" and send to:
Rough Guides, 1 Mercer St, London WC2H 9QJ, or
Rough Guides, 375 Hudson St, 9th floor, New York NY 10014.
Or send email to: mail@roughguides.co.uk
Online updates about this book can be found on Rough Guides' website at http://www.roughguides.com

THE AUTHORS

Mark Ellingham and **Natania Jansz** wrote the original edition of this book – the first ever Rough Guide – in 1981. They couldn't believe their good fortune in being paid by a publisher to spend time roaming around Classical ruins and medieval castles, and island-hopping in the Aegean. Mark continued writing Rough Guides and still works for the company as Series Editor. He is currently spending most of his time developing publication of the guides on the Internet but would be happier roaming the ruins, etc. Natania divides her time between Clinical Psychology and writing; she has edited the Rough Guide special, *More Women Travel*. Natania and Mark have a toddler, Miles, who rates Greek food (and sand) high on his list of life's good things.

John Fisher has also been involved with Rough Guides from the start. One of the original authors of the Greek guide, he has since written ten numerous other Rough Guide titles including the *Rough Guide to Crete*. Between travels, John can usually be found chained to a desk at Rough Guide HQ in London. He lives in south London with his wife and two young sons.

Marc Dubin first arrived in Greece in 1978, able to ask only for yoghurts, and the loo, in the local tongue. Since 1981 he has returned yearly, thereby acquiring fluency in Greek, and from 1989 onwards has lived part-time on the island of Sámos, where he recently restored an old cottage. Marc writes regularly for various publications on topics as diverse as Greek cuisine, music and backcountry trekking. When not in Greece, he lives in London or ranges across the Mediterranean in the course of updating his other *Rough Guides*: Turkey, Cyprus, and the Pyrenees.

READERS' LETTERS

We'd like to thank the readers of previous editions, who took time to write in with comments and suggestions. For this edition, we were helped by letters from:

Loretta Alborghetti, Helen Allce, Jim Dainbridge, Rev. and Mrs R. J. Blakeway-Phillips, Monica Bradley, Michael Davies, Sonia Barr, Nigel Burtt, Cathy and Steven Butler, M. Colman, Alison-Louise Conn, Marie Demetriou, Bridget Deutsch, David and Yvette Dickinsin, Constantine Dimaros, Arnulf Elvevold, Marit Erikksson, Emma Gervasio, Barbara Goulden, C.J. Hardy, Nicholas Harvey, R.A. Hine, Suzanne Ince, Sue Kennedy, Udo Kock, Paul Lawlor, Kevin McCarthy, R.E. Miller, Stephen Minta, Mr Nielsen, Zena L. Polin, Christopher Price, Caroline Read, Julian Richards, David and Wendy Rumsey, Philip Ryan, Carola Scupham, Christopher Stocks, Brian Storey, Pippa Todd, Steven White, Leslie Whitehouse, Adrian Whittaker and Deena Omar, Bill Wier, Christine Winter, David Wright and Carolyn Smith.

CONTENTS

PART THREE CONTEXTS 415

LIST OF MAPS

MAP SYMBOLS

Railway	⌂ Cave
Road	⛰ Viewpoint
Minor road	♦ Refuge
----- Path	▲ Campsite
– – – Ferry route	◉ Hotel
Waterway	▪ Restaurant
–––– Chapter division boundary	✕ Airport
––•–•• International boundary	⍓ Lighthouse
⌘ Mosque	ⓘ Information office
✡ Synagogue	⊠ Post office
+ County church	ⓒ Telephone
⌐ Monastery or convent	Ⓜ Metro station
♖ Castle	★ Bus stop
∴ Ruins	▇ Building
▲ Peak	⊞ Church
⌃⌃ Mountains	⁺⁺⁺ Christian cemetery
⌇ Marshland	▨ Park
⍦ Waterfall	▨ National park
♦ Ancient site	▇ Pedestrianised area
	▨ Beach

PLACE NAMES: A WARNING!

The art of rendering Greek words in Roman letters is in a state of chaos. It's a major source of confusion with **place names**, for which seemingly each local authority and each map-maker uses a different system. The word for "saint", for instance, one of the most common prefixes, can be spelt Áyios, Ágios, or Ághios. And, to make matters worse, there are often two forms of a name in Greek – the popularly used *dhimotikí*, and the old "classicizing" *katharévoussa*. Thus you will see the island of Spétses written also as Spétsai, or Khalkídha, the capital of Évvia, as Halkís (or even Chalcís, on more traditional maps). Throw in the complexities of Greek grammar – with different case-endings for names – and the fact that there exist long-established English versions of Classical place names, which bear little relation to the Greek sounds, and things get even more complicated.

In this book, we've used a modern and largely phonetic **system**, with Y rather than G for the Greek gamma, Kh (not H or Ch) for Greek khi, and DH rather than D for delta, in the spelling of all modern Greek place names. We have, however, retained the accepted "English" spellings for the **ancient sites**, and for familiar places like Athens (Athiná in modern Greek). We have also accented (with an acute) the stressed letter of each word; getting this right in pronunciation is vital in order to be understood.

INTRODUCTION

I t would take a lifetime of island-hopping to really get to know the well over a
hundred permanently inhabited Greek **islands**, let alone the countless smaller gull-
roosts which dot the Aegean and Ionian seas. At the right time of year or day, they
conform remarkably to their fantastic travel-poster image; any tourist board would
give their eyeteeth for the commonplace vision of purple-shadowed islands floating on
a cobalt-and-rose horizon.

Island **beaches** come in all shapes, sizes and consistencies, from discrete crescents
framed by tree-fringed cliffs straight out of a Japanese screen painting, to deserted,
mile-long gifts deposited by small streams, where you could imagine enacting Crusoe
scenarios among the dunes. But inland there is always civilization, whether the tiny
cubist villages of the remoter outposts, or burgeoning resorts as cosmopolitan – and
brazen – as any in the Mediterranean.

What amazes most first-time visitors is how, despite the strenuous efforts of developers and arsonists, this environment has not yet been utterly destroyed. If you're
used to the murky waters of the open Mediterranean as sampled in Spain, Israel or
southern France, then the Aegean will come as a revelation, with thirty-to-forty-foot
visibility the norm. This relative lack of pollution is proclaimed at certain beach-
fronts by tourist-board signs bestowing "Golden Starfish" or EU-ratified "Blue Flag"
awards on the place; patently self-congratulatory, but with basis in fact at many
coves, where live starfish or octopi curl up to avoid you, and dover sole or rays skit-
ter off across the bottom.

The sea is also a **water-sports** paradise: the joys of snorkelling and kayaking are
on offer to the untrained, and some of the best windsurfing areas in the world beck-
on. Yacht charter, whether bare-boat or skippered, is now big business, particularly
out of Rhodes, Kálymnos, Lefkádha, Póros and Piraeus; the Greek islands are rated
on a par with the Caribbean for quality sailing itineraries. And for the months when
the sea is too cold or the weather too blustery, many islands – not necessarily the
largest ones – offer superb hiking on surviving mule trails between hill villages, or up
the highest summits.

Although more protected than the Greek mainland from invasions, the various
island groups have been subjected to a staggering variety of foreign influences.
Romans, Arabs, Byzantines, crusading Knights of Saint John, Genoese, Venetians,
French, English, Italians and Ottomans have all controlled numbers of the islands since
the time of Alexander the Great. The high tide of empire has left behind countless
monuments: frescoed Byzantine churches and monasteries, the fortified Venetian capitals of the Cyclades and the Ionians, the more conventional castles of the Genoese and
Knights in the northeast Aegean and Dodecanese, Ottoman bridges and mosques, and
the Art Deco or mock-Renaissance edifices of the Italian Fascist administration.

Constructions from many of these eras is often juxtaposed with – or even superimposed on – the cities and temples of ancient Greece, which provide the foundation in all
senses for claims of an enduring Hellenic cultural identity down the centuries; museums, particularly on Crete, Sámos, Rhodes and Límnos, amply document the archeological evidence. But it was medieval Greek peasants, fisherman and shepherds, working without an indigenous ruling class to impose models of taste, who most tangibly
and recently contributed to our idea of Greekness with their songs and dances, costumes, weaving and vernacular architecture, some unconsciously drawing on ancient
antecedents. Much of this has vanished in recent decades, replaced by an avalanche of

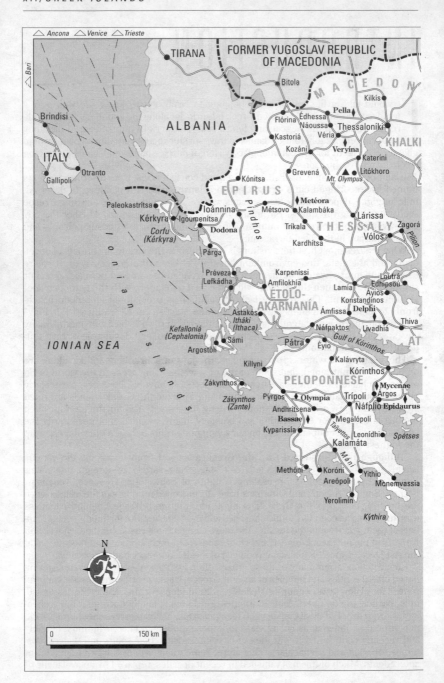

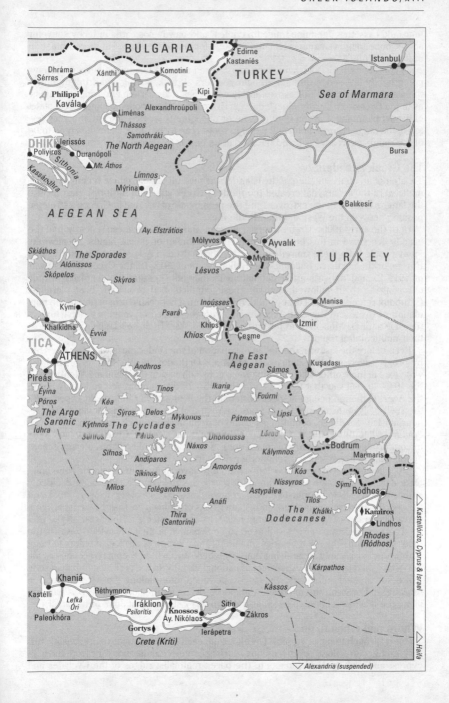

bouzouki cassettes, "genuine museum copies" and bawdy postcards in tacky souvenir shops, but enough remains in isolated pockets for visitors to marvel at its combination of form and function.

Of course, most Greek-island visits are devoted to more hedonistic pursuits: always going lightly dressed, swimming in balmy waters at dusk, talking and drinking under the stars until 3am. Such pleasures amply compensate for certain enduring weaknesses in the Greek tourism "product": don't arrive expecting orthopedic mattresses, state-of-the-art plumbing, Cordon-Bleu cuisine or obsequious service. Except at a very few top-of-the-range resorts, hotel and pension rooms can be box-like, campsites tend to be of the rough-and-ready sort, and the food at its best is fresh and simply presented.

The Greek islanders

To attempt an understanding of the islanders, it's useful to realize how recent and traumatic were the events that created the modern Greek state and **national character** – the latter a balance of the extrovert and the pessimistic partly due to Greece's strategic position between the West and the Middle East.

Until the early 1900s, Crete, the east Aegean and the Dodecanese – nearly half the islands described in this book – remained in Ottoman or Italian hands. Meanwhile, many people from these "unredeemed" territories lived in Asia Minor, Egypt, western Europe or the northern Balkans. The Balkan Wars of 1912–13, the Greco-Turkish war of 1919–22 and the organized population exchanges – essentially regulated ethnic cleansing – which followed each of these conflicts had profound, brutal effects. Orthodox refugees from Turkey suddenly made up a noticeable proportion of the population of Crete and the east Aegean, and with the forced or voluntary departure of their Levantines, Muslims and Jews (during World War II), these islands gradually lost their multicultural traits.

Even before the last war, the Italian occupation of the Dodecanese was characterized by progressively stricter suppression of Greek Orthodox identity, but in general the war years in most other island groups were not so dire as on the mainland. Neither was the 1946–49 civil war that followed, nor the 1967–74 dictatorship, felt so keenly out in the Aegean, though benign neglect was about the best many islands could expect until the 1960s. Given the chance to emigrate to Australia, Canada or Africa, many entrepreneurial islanders did so, continuing a trend of depopulation which ironically had accelerated earlier this century, following political union with the Greek mainland. The uncomfortably close memory of catastrophe, a continuing reality of misrule and scarce opportunity at home spurred yet another diaspora.

The advent of **tourism** in the 1960s arguably saved a number of islands from complete desolation, though local attitudes towards this deliverance have been decidedly ambivalent. It galls local pride to have become a class of seasonal service personnel, and the encounter between outsiders and villagers has often been corrosive to a deeply conservative rural society. Though younger Greeks are adaptable as they rake in the proceeds at resort areas, tourists still need to be sensitive in their behaviour towards the older generation. The mind boggles imagining the reaction of black-clad elders to nude bathing, or even scanty apparel, in a country where the Orthodox church remains an all-but-established faith and the guardian of national identity. In the presence of Italian-style expresso bars and autotellers, it's easy to be lulled into thinking that Greece became thoroughly European the moment it joined the EU – until a flock of sheep is paraded along the main street at high noon, or the 1pm ferry shows up at 3pm, or not at all.

Where and when to go

There is no such thing as a typical Greek island; each has its distinctive personality, history, architecture, flora – even a unique tourist clientele. Landscapes vary from the lush cypress-and-olive-swathed Ionians to the bare, minimalist ridges of the Cyclades and

Dodecanese, by way of subtle gradations between these extremes in the Sporades and northeast Aegean. Setting aside the scars from a few unfortunate man-made developments, it would be difficult to single out an irredeemably ugly island; all have their adherents and individual appeal, described in the chapter or section introductions.

Most islands and their inhabitants are far more agreeable, and resolutely Greek, outside the busiest period of early July to late August, when the crowds of foreigners, **soaring temperatures** and the effects of the infamous **meltémi** can detract considerably from enjoyment. The meltémi is a cool, fair-weather wind which originates in high-pressure systems over the far north Aegean, gathering steam as it travels southwards and assuming near-gale magnitude by the time it reaches Crete. North-facing coasts there, and throughout the Cyclades and Dodecanese, bear the full brunt; its howling is less pronounced in the north or east Aegean, where continental landmasses provide some shelter for the islands just offshore.

You won't miss out on **warm weather** if you come between late May and mid-June – when a wide variety of garden produce and fish is still available – or September, when the sea is warmest for swimming. During October you will probably hit a week's stormy spell, but for much of that month the "little summer of Áyios Dhimítrios", the Greek equivalent of **Indian summer**, prevails. While the choice of restaurants and nightlife in autumn can be limited, the light is softer: going out at midday becomes a pleasure rather than an ordeal. The most reliable venues for late autumn or early winter breaks are Rhodes and relatively balmy southeastern Crete, where swimming in December is not unheard of.

December to March are the **coldest** and least comfortable months, particularly on the Ionian islands, simply the rainiest patch in Greece from November onwards. The high peaks of northerly or lofty islands wear a brief mantle of **snow** around the turn of the year, with Crete's mountainous spine staying covered into April. Between January and April the glorious lowland **wildflowers** begin to bloom, beginning in the south Aegean. Early arrivals should keep in mind that travelling a few islands north or south often means the difference between tourist facilities open or still shut, as well as blos-

AVERAGE TEMPERATURES AND RAINFALL

	Jan			March			May			July			Sept			Nov		
	°F		Rain	°F		Rain	°F		Rain	°F		Rain	°F		Rain	°F		Rain
	Max	Min	days	Max	Min	days	Max	Min	days	Max	Min	days	Max	Min	days	Max	Min	days
Crete (Khaniá)	60	46	17	64	48	11	76	56	5	86	68	0	82	64	3	70	54	10
Cyclades (Mýkonos)	58	50	14	62	52	8	72	62	5	82	72	0.5	78	68	1	66	58	9
North Greece (Khalkidhikí)	50	36	7	59	44	9	77	58	10	90	70	4	83	64	5	60	47	9
Ionian (Corfu)	56	44	13	62	46	10	74	58	6	88	70	2	82	64	5	66	52	12
Dodecanese (Rhodes)	58	50	15	62	48	7	74	58	2	86	70	0	82	72	1	68	60	7
Sporades (Skiáthos)	55	45	12	58	47	10	71	58	3	82	71	0	75	64	8	62	53	12
East Aegean (Lésvos)	54	42	11	60	46	7	76	60	6	88	70	2	82	66	2	64	50	9

soms gone or yet to bloom. April weather is notoriously unreliable, though the air is crystal-clear and the landscape green – a photographer's dream. May is more settled, though the sea is still a bit cool for prolonged dips.

Other factors that affect the timing of a Greek island visit have to do with the level of tourism and the related amenities provided. Service standards, particularly in tavernas, invariably slip under peak-season pressures, and room rates are at their highest from July to September. If you can only visit during mid-summer, reserve a package well in advance, or plan an itinerary off the beaten track, gravitating towards islands with sparser ferry connections and/or no airport. Between November and April, you have to contend with pared-back ferry schedules (and almost nonexistent hydrofoil departures), plus skeletal facilities when you arrive. However, you will find fairly adequate services to the more populated islands, and at least one hotel and taverna open in the port or main town of all but the tiniest isles.

PART ONE

THE
BASICS

GETTING THERE FROM BRITAIN

It's about 2000 miles from London to most points in Greece, so for most visitors flying to the Greek islands is the only viable option. There are direct flights to a variety of Greek destinations from all the major British airports. Flying time varies from three hours (Corfu) to almost four hours (Rhodes) and the cost of charter flights is reasonable – sample return fares to Athens from London in midsummer start from around £160 (Manchester £180, Glasgow £200), but there are always bargains to be had. Easter and Christmas are also classed as high seasons, but outside these periods flights can be snapped up for as little as £120 return. Costs can also be highly competitive if you buy a flight as part of an all-in package: see pp.5–6 for details of holiday operators.

Road or **rail** alternatives take a minimum of three days but are obviously worth considering if you plan to visit Greece as part of an extended trip through Europe.

BY PLANE

Most of the cheaper flights from Britain to Greece are **charters**, which are sold either with a package holiday or as a flight-only option. The flights have fixed and unchangeable outward and return dates, and often a maximum stay of one month.

For longer stays or more flexibility, or if you're travelling out of season (when few charters are available), you'll need a **scheduled** flight. As with charters, these are offered under a wide variety of fares, and are again often sold off at discount by agents. Useful sources for discounted flights are the classified ads in the travel sections of newspapers like the *Independent*, *Guardian*, *Observer* and *Sunday Times*. Teletext is also worth checking, while your local travel agent shouldn't be overlooked.

Although **Athens** remains the prime destination for cheap fares, there are also **direct flights** from Britain to **Thessaloníki**, **Kalamáta**, **Kavála** and **Préveza** on the Greek mainland (most of these near several islands), and to the islands themselves of **Crete**, **Rhodes**, **Corfu**, **Lésvos**, **Límnos**, **Páros**, **Zákynthos**, **Kefallonía**, **Skiáthos**, **Sámos** and **Kós**. And with any flight to Athens, you can buy a **domestic connecting flight** (on the national carrier, Olympic) at an advantageous discount to one of three dozen or so additional Greek mainland and island airports.

SCHEDULED FLIGHTS

The advantages of scheduled flights are that they can be pre-booked well in advance, have longer ticket validities and involve none of the above restrictions on charters. However, many of the cheaper APEX and SuperAPEX fares do have an advance-purchase and/or minimum-stay requirements, so check conditions carefully. Scheduled flights also usually operate during the day.

As with charters, discount fares on scheduled flights are available from most high-street travel **agents**, as well as from a number of specialist flight and student/youth agencies. Many discount scheduled fares have an advance-purchase requirement, varying from 7 to 21 days.

The biggest choice of scheduled flights is with the Greek national carrier **Olympic Airways**, and **British Airways**; both fly direct from London Heathrow to Athens (Olympic three times daily, BA twice daily) and also to Thessaloníki (Olympic four times a week, BA once daily). **Virgin Airways** also has a daily service (twice daily in summer) to Athens. All these airlines offer a range of special fares and even in July and August can come up with deals as low as £160 return, plus tax; more realistically, though, you'll pay around £250–325 return for a scheduled flight. You'll also be able to book onward connections to various Greek islands; Olympic has a

AGENTS AND OPERATORS

Argo Tours, 100 Wigmore St, London W1H 9DR (☎0171/331 7000). Designated consolidator for Olympic, BA and Virgin.

Campus Travel, 52 Grosvenor Gardens, London SW1 (☎0171/730 3402); 541 Bristol Rd, Selly Oak, Birmingham (☎0121/414 1848); 39 Queen's Rd, Clifton, Bristol (☎0117/929 2494); 5 Emmanuel St, Cambridge (☎0223/324283); 53 Forrest Rd, Edinburgh (☎0131/668 3303); 166 Deansgate, Manchester (☎0161/273 1721); 105–106 St Aldates, Oxford OX1 1DD. (☎01865/242067). Student/youth travel specialists, with branches also in YHA shops and on university campuses all over Britain. Campus usually has its own student/youth charter flights to Athens during the summer.

STA Travel, 86 Old Brompton Rd, London W7 (☎0171/361 6161); 25 Queen's Rd, Bristol (☎0117/294399); 38 Sidney St, Cambridge (☎01223/66966); 75 Deansgate, Manchester (☎0161/834 0668); and personal callers at 117 Euston Rd, London NW1; 88 Vicar Lane, Leeds;

36 George St, Oxford; and offices at the universities of Birmingham, London, Kent and Loughborough. Discount fares, with particularly good deals for students and young people.

Trailfinders, 42–50 Earls Court Rd, London W8 6FT (☎0171/938 3366); 194 Kensington High St, London, W8 7RG (☎0171/938 3939/☎0171/938 3444); 215 Kensington High St, London W6 6BD (transatlantic and European ☎0171/937 5400); 58 Deansgate, Manchester M3 2FF (☎0161/839 6969, first and business class ☎0161/839 3434); 254–284 Sauchiehall St, Glasgow G2 3EH (☎0141/353 2224); 22–24 The Priory, Queensway, Birmingham B4 6BS (☎0121/236 1234); 48 Corn St, Bristol BS1 1HQ (☎0117/929 9000). One of the best-informed and most efficient agents for independent travellers; all branches open daily until 6pm, Thurs until 7pm.

Travel Bug, 597 Cheetham Hill Rd, Manchester (☎0161/721 4000). Large range of discounted tickets.

AIRLINES

Balkan Airlines, 322 Regent St, London W1 (☎0171/637 7637).

British Airways, 156 Regent St, London W1 (☎0345/222111).

Czech Airlines, 72 Margaret St, London W1 (☎0171/255 1898).

LOT Polish Airlines, 313 Regent St, London W1R 7PE (☎0171/580 5037).

Malev Hungarian Airlines, 10 Vigo St, London W1X 1AJ (☎0171/439 0577).

Olympic Airways, 11 Conduit St, London W1 (☎0171/409 3400).

Virgin Airways, Virgin Megastore, 14–16 Oxford St, London W1 (☎01293/747747).

slight edge in convenience for this, with both inbound international and onward domestic flights using the same, Olympic-only terminal in Athens. Flights from British regional airports route through Heathrow in the first instance.

East European airways like CSA, Balkan, Malev and LOT can be cheaper – £120 one way, £240 return for much of the year – but nearly always involve delays, with connections in (respectively) Prague, Sofia, Budapest and Warsaw. It is not always possible to book discount fares direct from these airlines, and you'll often pay no more by going through an agent (see box above).

CHARTER FLIGHTS

Travel agents throughout Britain sell **charter flights** to Greece, which usually operate from

May to October; late-night departures and early-morning arrivals are common. Even the high-street chains frequently promote "flight-only" deals, or discount all-inclusive holidays, when their parent companies need to offload their seat allocations. In any case, phone around for a range of offers. Charter airlines include Britannia, Excalibur and Monarch, but you can only book tickets on these through travel agents.

The greatest variety of **flight destinations** tend to be from London Gatwick and Manchester. In summer, if you book in advance, you should have a choice of most of the dozen Greek regional "international" airports listed above. Flying from elsewhere in Britain (Birmingham, Cardiff, Glasgow or Newcastle), or looking for last-minute discounts, you'll find options more limited, most commonly to Athens, Corfu, Rhodes, Kós and Crete.

It's worth noting that **non-EU nationals** who buy charter tickets to Greece must buy a return ticket, to return after no fewer than three days and no more than four weeks, and must accompany it with an **accommodation voucher** for at least the first few nights of their stay – check that the ticket satisfies these conditions or you could be refused entry. In practice, the "accommodation voucher" has become a formality; it has to name an existing hotel but you're not expected to use it (and probably won't be able to if you try).

The other important condition regards travel to **Turkey** (or any other neighbouring country). If you travel to Greece on a charter flight, you may visit another country only as a day trip; if you stay overnight, you will invalidate your ticket. This rule is justified by the Greek authorities because they subsidize charter airline landing fees, and are therefore reluctant to see tourists spending their money outside Greece. Whether you buy that excuse or not, there is no way around it, since the Turkish authorities clearly stamp all passports, and the Greeks usually check them. The package industry on the east Aegean and Dodecanese islands bordering Turkey, however, does some-

times prevail upon customs officials to back-date re-entry stamps when bad weather strands their tour groups overnight in Anatolia.

Student/youth charters are allowed to be sold as one-way flights only. By combining two one-way charters you can, therefore, stay for over a month. Student/youth charter tickets are available to anyone under 26, and to all card-carrying full-time students under 32.

Finally, remember that **reconfirmation** of return charter flights is vital and should be done at least 72 hours before departure.

PACKAGES AND TOURS

Virtually every British **tour operator** includes Greece in its programme, though with many of the larger groups you'll find choices limited to the established resorts – notably the islands of Rhodes, Kós, Crete, Skiáthos, Zákynthos and Corfu. If you buy one of these at a last-minute discount, you may find it costs little more than a flight – and you can use the accommodation offered as much or as little as you want. For a rather more low-key and genuinely "Greek" resort, however, it's better to book your holiday through one of the smaller **specialist agencies** listed below.

SPECIALIST PACKAGE OPERATORS

VILLA OR VILLAGE ACCOMMODATION

These companies are all fairly small scale operations, offering competitively priced packages with flights and often using more traditional village accommodation. They make an effort to offer islands without overdeveloped tourist resorts, using high-quality facilities.

Argo Travel, 100 Wigmore St, London W1H 9DR (☎0171/331 7070). Attractive properties in the Cyclades, Spétses, Póros, Sámos and Lésvos.

CV Travel, 43 Cadogan St, London SW3 2PR (☎0171/581 0851 or 0171/584 8803). Quality villas on Corfu and Paxí.

Corfu à la Carte, The Whitehouse, Bucklebury Alley, Cold Ash, Newbury, Berks RH16 9NN (☎01635/201 140). Selected beach and rural cottages on Corfu, Paxí, Skópelos, Sými and Skiáthos.

Direct Greece, Oxford House, 182 Upper Richmond Rd, Putney, London, SW15 2SH (☎0181/785 4000). Moderately priced studios

and villas at mainland Parga and on Crete, Lefkádha, Zákynthos, Lésvos, Khálki and Rhodes.

Elysian Holidays, 16 High Street, Tenterden, Kent TN30 6AP (☎01580/766599, fax 765416). Small company recently expanded from Volissós, Khíos to include Pátmos, Sýros and Évvia.

Grecofile/Filoxenia, Sourdock Hill, Barkisland, Halifax, West Yorkshire HX4 0AG (☎01422/375999).Tailor-made itineraries and specialist packages to several unspoiled islands.

Greek Islands Club, 66 High St, Walton-on-Thames, Kent KT12 1BU (☎01932/220477). Holidays on the Ionian islands, Skiáthos, Skópelos, Alónissos, Santórini, Mýkonos, Páros, Sýros, Crete, Ídhra and Spétses.

Greek Sun Holidays, 1 Bank St, Sevenoaks, Kent TN13 1UW (☎01732/740317). Respected, experienced outfit with a variety of packages, including fly-drive, in the Cyclades, Dodecanese and northeast Aegean.

Continues over

Laskarina Holidays, St Marys Gate, Wirksworth, Derbyshire DE4 4DQ (☎01629/822203). Top-end villas and apartments on Lipsí, Tílos, Kálymnos, Léros, Sými, Khálki, Alónissos, Skópelos and Spétses; consistently high marks for service.

Simply Crete/Simply Ionian, Chiswick Gate, 598–608 Chiswick High Rd, London W4 5RT (☎0181/995 9323). High-quality apartments, villas and small hotels on Crete and the Ionian islands.

Skiathos Travel, 4 Holmesdale Rd, Kew Gardens, Richmond, Surrey TW9 3J2 (☎0181/940 5157).Packages to the Sporades; some flight-only deals.

Sunvil Holidays, Sunvil House, 7–8 Upper Square, Old Isleworth, Middlesex TW7 7BJ (☎0181/568 4499 or 0181/847 4748). Another company highly rated for service, with featured properties on Corfu, Lefkádha, Skiáthos, Skópelos, several Cyclades, Límnos, Khíos and western Crete.

HIKING TOURS

All the operators below run trekking groups, which generally consist of ten to fifteen people, plus an experienced guide. The walks tend to be day-hikes from one or more bases, or point-to-point treks staying in village accommodation en route; camping is not usually involved.

Explore Worldwide, 1 Frederick St, Aldershot, Hampshire GU11 1LQ (☎01252/344161). Easy-to-moderate organized treks on Évvia, Crete, Tínos, Páros and Náxos; also kaïki sailing expeditions.

Ramblers Holidays, Longcroft House, Fretherne Rd, Welwyn Garden City, Herts AL8 6PQ (☎01707/331133).Walking tours on Évvia, Crete, Sámos, Pátmos, Khíos, Rhodes and Corfu.

Trekking Hellas, Filellínon 7, 105 57 Athens (☎30/1/33 10 323).Trekking in western Crete, easier walks on Ándhros, Tínos and Itháki.

Waymark Holidays, 44 Windsor Rd, Slough SL1 2EJ (☎01753/516477). Spring and autumn walking holidays on Sámos, Náxos and Mílos.

NATURE AND WILDLIFE

Marengo Guided Walks, 17 Bernard Crescent, Hunstanton PE36 6ER (☎01485/532710). Spring and autumn botanical outings in northern Lésvos, Thássos, Sámos and southern Crete, led by a trained botanist.

Peregrine Holidays, 40/41 South Parade, Summertown, Oxford OX2 7JP (☎01865/511642).Natural history tours on Corfu and Crete; the emphasis on each tour is on wildlife, though combined with visits to archeological sites.

SAILING

Dinghy sailing, yachting and windsurfing holidays based on small flotillas of four- to six-berth yachts start at around £350 per person per week off-season. Sailing holidays can be flotilla- or shore-based. If you're a confident sailor and can muster a group of people, it's possible simply to charter a yacht from a broker; the Greek National Tourist Organization has lists of companies.

The Moorings, Bradstowe House, Middle Wall, Whitstable, Kent CT5 1BF (☎01227/776 677). Operates charters out of Athens, Corfu and Kós.

Sunsail The Port House, Port Solent, Portsmouth, Hampshire PO6 4TH (☎01705/222222).Tuition in dinghy sailing, yachting and windsurfing. Flotilla clubs based at Lefkádha, Kefalloniá, Kós and Skiáthos.

MIND AND BODY

Skyros Centre, 92 Prince of Wales Rd, London NW5 3NE (☎0171/267 4424). Holistic health, fitness and "personal growth" holidays on the island of Skýros, as well as writers' workshops.

BY TRAIN

Travelling by **train** from Britain to Greece takes around three and a half days and fares work out more expensive than flights. However, with a regular ticket stopovers are possible – in France, Switzerland and Italy – while with an InterRail or Eurail train pass you can take in Greece as part of a wider rail trip around Europe.

ROUTES

The most practical route from Britain takes in France, Switzerland and **Italy** before crossing on the ferry from Bari or Brindisi to Pátra (Patras). Book seats well in advance, especially in summer (for ferry information, see the box on p.9).

Until the outbreak of civil war, the route through **former Yugoslavia** was the most popular; this is still problematic, and probably best avoided. A more rambling alternative from Budapest runs via **Bucharest and Sofia to Thessaloníki**, which is advised as your first stop in Greece since Athens is nearly nine hours further on the train.

TICKETS AND PASSES

Regular train tickets from Britain to Greece are not good value. London to Athens costs at least £380 return. If you are **under 26**, you can get a **BIJ ticket**, discounting these fares by around 25 percent; these are available through Eurotrain and Wasteels (see box below for addresses). Both regular and BIJ tickets have two months' return validity, or can be purchased as one-ways, and the Italy routes include the ferry crossing. The tickets also allow for stopovers, so long as you stick to the route prescribed.

Better value by far is to buy an **InterRail pass**, available to anyone resident in Europe for six months. You can buy it from British Rail (or any travel agent), and the pass offers unlimited travel on a zonal basis on up to 25 European rail networks. The only extras you pay are supplements on certain express trains, plus half-price fares in Britain (or the country of issue) and on the cross-Channel ferries. The pass includes the ferry from Brindisi in southern Italy to Pátra in Greece. There are several types: to reach Greece from the UK you'll need a pass valid for at least two zones (£209 for a month), though if you're intending to travel further in Europe you might invest in an all-zone card for £275; Greece is zoned with Italy, Turkey and Slovenia.

Finally, anyone over 60 and holding a British Rail Senior Citizen Railcard, can buy a **Rail Europe Senior Card** (£5 for a year). This gives up to thirty percent reductions on rail fares throughout Europe and thirty percent off sea crossings.

RAIL TICKET OFFICES

Eurotrain, 52 Grosvenor Gardens, London SW1 (☎0171/730 3402).

International Rail Centre, Victoria Station, London SW1 (☎0990/848 848).

Wasteels, Victoria Station, London SW1 (☎0171/834 7066).

BUS TICKET OFFICES

National Express Eurolines, 52 Grosvenor Gardens, London SW1 (☎0990/808080).

BY BUS

With charter flights at such competitive rates, it's hard to find good reasons for wanting to spend three or four days on a bus to Greece. However, it's still a considerably cheaper option than taking the train.

National Express Eurolines (bookable through any National Express office; see box opposite) is reliable, comfortable in bus terms, and pricey (£200–220 return). These days, other operators are thin on the ground, but even so it pays to be very wary about going for the cheapest company unless you've heard something about them. There have been a string of accidents in recent years with operators flouting the terms of their licence, and horror stories abound of drivers getting lost or their coaches being refused entry.

The route is either Belgium, Germany and Austria, or via France and Italy and then a ferry across to Greece. Stops of about twenty minutes are made every five or six hours, with the odd longer break for roadside café meals.

BY CAR

If you have the time and inclination, driving to Greece can be a pleasant proposition. Realistically, though, it's really only worth considering if you have at least a month to spare, are going to stay in Greece for an extended period, or want to take advantage of various stopovers en route.

It's important to plan ahead. The Automobile Association (AA) provides a comprehensive service offering general advice on all facets of driving to Greece and the names and addresses of useful contact organizations. Their European Routes Service (contact AA on ☎01256/20123 or your local branch) can arrange a detailed print-out of a route to follow. Driving licence, vehicle registration documents and insurance are essential; a green card is no longer required, but you will probably want a top-up to your basic policy for European-wide coverage – otherwise only the statutory minimum protection applies in other EU countries.

The most popular route is down through France and Italy to catch one of the Adriatic ferries. A much longer alternative through Eastern Europe (Hungary, Romania and Bulgaria) is just about feasible, and there is the option of taking a car on the ferry from Croatia.

LE SHUTTLE AND THE FERRIES

Le Shuttle operates trains 24 hours a day, carrying cars, motorcycles, buses and their passengers, and taking 35 minutes between Folkestone and Calais. At peak times, services operate every fifteen minutes, making advance bookings unnecessary; during the night, services still run hourly. Through trains connect London with Paris in just over three hours. Return fares from May to August cost around £280–310 per vehicle (passengers included), with discounts in the low season; passenger fares from London to Paris cost £95–155 return, depending on when you book.

The alternative cross-Channel options for most travellers are the ferry or hovercraft links between Dover and Calais or Boulogne (the quickest and cheapest routes), Ramsgate and Dunkerque, or Newhaven and Dieppe.

Ferry prices vary according to the time of year and, for motorists, the size of your car. The Dover–Calais/Boulogne runs, for example, start at about £180 return low season, £220 return high season for a car with up to five passengers. Foot passengers should be able to cross for about £50 return year round; taking a motorbike costs from £80–90 return.

CROSS-CHANNEL INFORMATION

Hoverspeed, (☎01304/240101). To Boulogne and Calais.

Le Shuttle, Customer Services Centre Information and ticket sales (☎0990/353535).

P&O European Ferries, Dover (☎01304/203388); Portsmouth (☎01705/772244); London (☎0990/980 980). To Calais.

Sally Line, Ramsgate, Kent (☎0990/595522). To Dunkerque.

Stena Sealink Line, Ashford (☎0990/353535). To Calais and Dieppe.

VIA ITALY

Heading for western Greece or the Ionian islands, it has always made most sense to drive via Italy – and whatever your final destination, taking a ferry on the final leg makes for a more relaxed journey. Initial routes down to Italy through France and Switzerland are very much a question of personal taste. One of the most direct is Calais–Reims–Geneva–Milan and then down the Adriatic coast to the Italian port of your choice. Even on the quickest autoroutes

(with their accompanying tolls), the journey will involve two overnight stops.

Once in Italy, there's a choice of five ports. Regular car and passenger ferries link Ancona, Bari and Brindisi with Igoumenítsa (the port of Epirus in western Greece) and/or Pátra (at the northwest tip of the Peloponnese and the closest port to Athens). Most sail via the island of Corfu, and a few call at several other Ionian islands en route to Pátra; you can stop over at no extra charge if you get these stops specified on your ticket. Generally, these ferries run year round, but services are greatly reduced out of season. Ferries also sail – less frequently – from Trieste and Venice. For more details see the box on p.9.

Note that crossing to Igoumenítsa is substantially cheaper than to Pátra; the cheapest of all the crossings are from Brindisi to Igoumenítsa. However, drivers will discover that the extra cost in Italian fuel – around double the British price – offsets the routes' savings over those from Bari or Ancona; the shipping companies are well aware of this and set their prices accordingly.

In summer, it is essential to book tickets a few days ahead, especially in the peak July–August season. During the winter you can usually just turn up at the main ports (Ancona, Bari, Brindisi, Igoumenítsa/Corfu), but it's still wise to book in advance, certainly if you are taking a car or want a cabin. A few phone calls before leaving are, in any case, advisable, as the range of fares and operators (from Brindisi especially) is considerable; if you do just turn up at the port, spend some time shopping around the agencies.

VIA HUNGARY, ROMANIA AND BULGARIA

Avoiding former Yugoslavia involves a pretty substantial diversion through Hungary, Romania and Bulgaria. This is not a drive to contemplate unless you actively want to see some of the countries en route – it's too exhausting and too problematic. However, it's all easier than it was, with visas simpler to obtain at the borders, if you haven't arranged them in advance.

From Budapest, the quickest route through Romania is via Timisoara, then to head towards Sofia in Bulgaria and on across the Rila mountains to the border at Kulata. Once at the Greek border, it's a three- to four-hour drive to Thessaloníki or Kavála. Bear in mind that road conditions are often poor and border crossings difficult. Contact the respective embassies and the AA for more advice.

FERRIES FROM ITALY

Note: all timings are approximate.

From Ancona: Marlines, Strintzis, ANEK and Minoan to Igoumenítsa (23–25hr) and Pátra (30hr); daily or nearly so year-round. Strintzis, Minoan and ANEK via Corfu and/or Igoumenítsa; Marlines only via Igoumenítsa. Most sailings 8–10pm, but there are a number of afternoon departures. Superfast is just that, direct to Pátra in 21hr almost daily year-round; Minoan offers high-speed craft on the same line in 22hr. Most departures in the afternoon, but a few in the late evening.

From Bari: Ventouris to Pátra direct (20hr), nearly daily departures year-round, July–Aug calls alternate days at Kefalloniá; to Igoumenítsa (12hr) slightly less frequent; Marlines to Igoumenítsa (13hr) daily in season, 4 weekly out. All sailings 7–11pm.

From Brindisi: Adriatica to Corfu, Igoumenítsa (11hr) and Pátra (20hr) year-round; direct to Pátra (17hr) summer only. Fraglines to Corfu/Igoumenítsa (11hr) almost daily March–Oct; Agoudimos to Igoumenítsa most days March–late Oct (10hr); Adria to Igoumenítsa (9hr) daily June–Sept. Hellenic Mediterranean Lines to Corfu/Igoumenítsa (11hr), 3–7 weekly March–Oct; Kefalloniá (13–15hr), alternate days June–Sept; Ithaki, Paxí and Zákynthos, variable mid July–early Sept; Strintzis almost daily March–Oct to Corfu and/or Igoumenítsa (9–10hr); Minoan to Corfu/Igoumenítsa, 4–7 weekly year-round (11hr). Most ferries leave Brindisi 9–11pm, but Minoan, Strintzis and (occasionally) Hellenic Mediterranean offer 9–10am departures. There's always at least one daily boat in winter, except between Christmas and New Year's Eve.

From Trieste: ANEK to Igoumenítsa, Corfu and Pátra (33–35hr). One weekly in winter, four weekly in summer, departing variable hours.

From Venice: Strintzis, Fri–Sat only to Corfu, Igoumenítsa and Pátra (37hr); Minoan to same ports 3–7 weekly (37hr); twice weekly May–Sept calls at Kefalloniá also. Departures about 5pm.

UK AGENTS

Serena Holidays, 40 Kenway Rd, London SW5 (☎0171/373 6548). For Adriatica Lines.

Viamare Travel Ltd, Graphic House, 2 Sumatra Rd, London NW6 (☎0171/431 4560). Agents for Agoudimos, ANEK, Fragline, Jadrolinija, Marlines, Medlink, Strintzis, Superfast, Ventouris, Vergina. Also for Salamis and Poseidon Lines, which sail Pireas–Rhodes or Crete–Limassol–Haifa, and vice-versa.

SAMPLE FARES

Prices below are one-way high/low season fares; port taxes (£3–5 per person in each direction) are not included. Note that substantial reductions apply on most lines for both InterRail or Eurail pass-holders, and for those under 26. Slight discounts are usually available on return fares. Many companies now allow you to sleep in your van on board; ask about reduced "camping" fares.

Igoumenítsa from Bari or Brindisi: deck class £18–£32/£13–£15; car from £21–£35/£13–£17.

Pátra from Bari or Brindisi: deck class £30–£32/£15–£23; car from £35–£46/£17–£23.

Patra from Ancona: deck class £34–£50/£27–£36; car from £65–£75/£34–£38.

Patra from Venice: deck class £42/£31; car from £76/£37.

Patra from Trieste: deck class £40/£29; car from £71/£35.

GETTING THERE FROM IRELAND

Summer charters operate from Dublin and Belfast to Athens and there are additional ser-

vices to Mýkonos, Rhodes, Crete and Corfu. A high-season charter from Dublin to Athens costs upwards of IR£200 return, while a week's package on one of the above islands costs from IR£440 per person for two weeks.

Year-round **scheduled services** with Aer Lingus and British Airways operate from both Dublin and Belfast via Heathrow to Athens, but you'll find them pricey compared with charters. Youth and student fares are offered by USIT (see below for address).

Travelling to London in the first place to pick up a cheap charter from there may save you a little money, but on the whole it's rarely worth the time and effort. For the record, budget flights to London are offered by British Midland, Aer Lingus and Ryan Air; while buying a Eurotrain boat and train ticket may also slightly undercut plane fares.

FLIGHT AGENTS IN IRELAND

Balkan Tours, 37 Ann St, Belfast BT1 4EB (☎01232/246795). Direct charter flights.

Joe Walsh Tours, 8–11 Baggot St, Dublin (☎01/676 3053). General budget fares agent.

Thomas Cook, 118 Grafton St, Dublin (☎01/677 1721). Mainstream package holiday and flight agent, with occasional discount offers.

Trailfinders, 4/5 Dawson Street, Dublin 2 (☎01/677 7888).

USIT Branches at: Aston Quay, O'Connell Bridge, Dublin 2 (☎01/679 8833); 10–11 Market Parade, Cork (☎021/270 900); Fountain Centre, College St, Belfast (☎01232/324073). Student and youth specialist.

AIRLINES

Aer Lingus, 41 Upper O'Connell St, Dublin (☎01/844 4777); 46–48 Castle St, Belfast (☎01232/314844); 2 Academy St, Cork (☎021/274331).

British Airways, 9 Fountain Centre, College St, Belfast (☎0345/222111); in Dublin, contact Aer Lingus.

GETTING THERE FROM NORTH AMERICA

Only a few carriers fly directly to Athens from North America, and nobody offers direct flights to any of the Greek islands. Most North Americans choose to travel to a gateway European city, and pick up a connecting flight on from there with an associated airline. If you have time, you may well discover that it's cheaper to arrange the final Greece-bound leg of the journey yourself, in which case your only criterion will be finding a suitable and good-value North America–Europe flight; for details of onward flights from the UK, see "Getting There from Britain" p.3.

The Greek national airline, Olympic Airways, only flies out of New York (JFK), Boston, Montreal and Toronto, though the airline can offer reasonably priced add-on flights within Greece, especially to the Greek islands, leaving from the same Athens terminal that you will fly into.

Another option to consider is picking up a flight to Europe and making your way to Greece by train, in which case a Eurail Pass makes a reasonable investment – all the details are covered below. For details of train routes, see "Getting There from Britain".

SHOPPING FOR TICKETS

Discount ticket outlets – advertised in the Sunday travel sections of major newspapers – come in several forms. Consolidators buy up blocks of tick-

ets that airlines don't think they'll be able to sell at their published fares, and unload them at a discount. Many advertise fares on a one-way or "open jaw" basis, enabling you to fly into one European city and out from another without penalty. Consolidators normally don't impose advance purchase requirements (although in busy times you should book ahead just to be sure of getting a ticket), but they do often charge very stiff fees for date changes. Discount agents also deal in blocks of tickets offloaded by the airlines, but they typically offer a range of other travel-related services like insurance, rail passes, youth and student ID cards, car rentals and tours. These agencies tend to be most worthwhile for students and under-26s, who can benefit from special fares and deals. Travel clubs are another option – most charge an annual membership fee, which may be worth it for their discounts on air tickets and car rental. Some agencies specialize in charter flights, which may be even cheaper than anything available on a scheduled flight, but again there's a trade-off: departure dates are fixed, and withdrawal penalties are high (check the refund policy). Student/youth fares can sometimes save you money, though again the best deals are usually those offered by seat consolidators advertising in Sunday newspaper travel sections.

Don't automatically assume that tickets purchased through a travel specialist will be cheapest – once you got a quote, check with the airlines and you may turn up an even better deal. In addition, exercise caution and never deal with a company that demands cash up front or refuses to accept payment by credit card.

For destinations not handled by discounters – which applies to most regional airports – you'll have to deal with airlines' published fares. The cheapest of these is an APEX (Advance Purchase Excursion) ticket, which carries certain restrictions. For instance, you may be expected to book – and pay – at least 21 days before departure, keep to a minimum/maximum limit on your stay, and be liable to penalties if you change your schedule. On transatlantic routes there are also winter Super APEX tickets, sometimes known as "Eurosavers" – slightly cheaper than ordinary APEX, they limit your stay to between 7 and 21 days. Some airlines also issue Special APEX tick-

AIRLINES IN NORTH AMERICA

Air Canada (Canada, call directory inquiries, ☎1-800/555-1212, for local toll-free number; US toll-free number is ☎1-800/776-3000).
Air France (☎1-800/237-2747; Canada, ☎1-800/667-2747).
Alitalia (☎1-800/223-5730).
British Airways (US, ☎1-800/247-9297; Canada, ☎1-800/668-1059).
Canadian Airlines (Canada, ☎1-800/665-1177; US, ☎1-800/426-7000).
Czech Airlines (☎1-800/223-2365; 212/765-6022; Montreal ☎ 1-800/561-5171; Toronto ☎1-800/641-0641).

Delta Airlines (☎1-800/241-4141).
Iberia (US, ☎1-800/772-4642; Canada, ☎1-800/423-7421).
KLM (US, ☎1-800/374-7747; Canada, ☎1-800/361-5073).
LOT Polish Airlines (☎1-800/223-0593).
Lufthansa (☎1-800/645-3880).
Olympic Airways (☎1-800/223-1226; 212/838-3600).
Sabena (☎1-800/955-2000).
Swissair (☎1-800/221-4750).
United Airlines (☎1-800/538-2929).

ets to those under 24, often extending the maximum stay to a year.

Note that fares are heavily dependent on season, and are highest from June–September; they drop either side of this, and you'll get the best deals during the low season, November–February (excluding Christmas). Note that flying on weekends ordinarily adds $50 or so to the round-trip fare; price ranges quoted in the sections below assume midweek travel.

FLIGHTS FROM THE USA

The twice-weekly non-stop flights to Athens out of New York and Boston on Olympic start at around US$760 round-trip in winter, rising to around $1080 in summer for a maximum thirty-day stay with seven-day advance purchase. Delta has a daily direct service from New York to Athens for the same APEX fare; likewise United, Swissair, Sabena and Iberia, although their flights are via European gateway cities. United also flies to Athens from Washington DC for a high/low season rate of around $1140/$820.

As with the service from the Eastern cities, the stiff competition between the different airlines dictates that fares to Athens from the Mid-west or West Coast are virtually identical: high/low season fares on Olympic, Delta, United, Iberia and so on start at $1180/$860 from Chicago or $1330/$1010 from LA, San Francisco or Seattle. With little else to choose between the major carriers, you might look into the stopover time at the different European gateway cities, as these can

sometimes be overnight; check with your ticket agent.

At the time of writing, LOT Polish Airlines have a special deal on their round-trip, low-season APEX fares from the US to Athens via Warsaw ($596 from New York, $656 from Chicago, $846 from LA). Since it's possible that similar offers may be made in the future (including comparative reductions on their high-season fares), it's certainly worth contacting them.

FLIGHTS FROM CANADA

As with the US, air fares from Canada to Athens vary tremendously depending upon where you start your journey. Olympic flies non-stop out of Montreal and Toronto twice a week for a scheduled fare of CDN$1268 round-trip in winter or CDN$1751 in summer.

KLM operates several flights a week to Athens via Amsterdam, from Toronto, Montreal, Vancouver and Edmonton. From Toronto, expect to pay around CDN$1050 in low season, CDN$1750 in high season; and from Vancouver CDN$1470 (low) or CDN$2170 (high). Travellers from Montreal can also try the European carriers Air France, Alitalia, British Airways, Iberia, Lufthansa and Swissair all of which operate several flights a week to Athens via major European cities. One unlikely source for good deals is Czech Airlines, which flies out of Montreal to Athens via Prague for CDN$840 (low) or CDN$1240 (high).

Finally, Air Canada flying in conjunction with European carriers, quotes the following low/high

DISCOUNT TRAVEL COMPANIES

Air Brokers International, 323 Geary St, Suite 411, San Francisco, CA 94102 (☎1-800/883-3273). Consolidator.

Air Courier Association, 191 University Boulevard, Suite 300, Denver, CO 80206 (☎303/278-8810). Courier flight broker.

Airhitch, 2472 Broadway, Suite 200, New York, NY 10025 (☎212/864-2000). Standby-seat broker. For a set price, they guarantee to get you on a flight as close to your preferred destination as possible, within a week.

Council Travel, Head Office: 205 E 42nd St, New York, NY 10017 (☎1-800/226-8624; 1-888 COUNCIL; 212/822-2700). Student travel organization with sixty branches in the US.

Educational Travel Center, 438 N Frances St, Madison, WI 53703 (☎1-800/747-5551). Student/youth discount agent.

Encore Travel Club, 4501 Forbes Blvd, Lanham, MD 20706 (☎1-800/444-9800). Discount travel club.

Interworld Travel, 800 Douglass Rd, Miami, FL 33134 (☎305/443-4929). Consolidator.

Last Minute Travel Club, 132 Brookline Ave, Boston, MA 02215 (☎1-800/LAST MIN). Travel club specializing in standby deals.

Moment's Notice, 425 Madison Ave, New York, NY 10017 (☎212/486-0503). Discount travel club.

New Frontiers/Nouvelles Frontières, Head offices: 12 E 33rd St, New York, NY 10016 (☎1-800/366-6387; 212/779-0600); 1001 Sherbrook East, Suite 720, Montreal, Quebec H2L 1L3 (☎514/526-8444). French discount travel firm. Other branches in LA, San Francisco and Quebec City.

Now Voyager, 74 Varick St, Suite 307, New York, NY 10013 (☎212/431-1616). Courier flight broker.

STA Travel, Head office: 48 East 11th St, New York, NY 10003 (☎1-800/777-0112). Worldwide specialist in independent travel with branches in the Los Angeles, San Francisco and Boston areas.

TFI Tours International, Head office: 34 W 32nd St, New York, NY 10001 (☎1-800/745-8000). Consolidator; other offices in Las Vegas, San Francisco, Los Angeles and Miami.

Travac, Head office: 989 6th Ave, New York NY 10018 (☎1-800/872-8800). Consolidator and charter broker; has another branch in Orlando.

Travel Avenue, 10 S Riverside, Suite 1404, Chicago, IL 60606 (☎1-800/333-3335). Discount travel agent.

Travel Cuts, Head office: 187 College St, Toronto, Ontario M5T 1P7 (☎1-800/667-2887; 1-888/238-2887; 416/979-2406). Canadian student travel organization with branches all over the country.

Travelers Advantage, 3033 S Parker Rd, Suite 900, Aurora, CO 80014 (☎1-800/548-1116). Discount travel club.

UniTravel, 1177 N Warson Rd, St Louis, MO 63132 (☎1-800/325-2222). Consolidator.

Worldtrek Travel, 111 Water St, New Haven, CT 06511 (☎1-800/243-1723). Discount travel agency.

Worldwide Discount Travel Club, 1674 Meridian Ave, Miami Beach, FL 33139 (☎305/534-2082). Discount travel club.

---

season fares to Athens: from Toronto/Montreal around CDN$1150/CDN$1485, and from Vancouver around CDN$1570/CDN$1860.

RAIL PASSES

A Eurail Pass is not likely to pay for itself if you're planning to stick to Greece, though it's worth considering if you plan to travel to Greece across Europe from elsewhere. The pass, which must be purchased before arrival in Europe, allows unlimited free train travel in Greece and sixteen other countries. The Eurail Youthpass (for under-26s) costs US$365 for 15 days, $587 for one month or $832 for two months; if you're 26 or over you'll have to buy a first-class pass, available in 15-day ($522), 21-day ($678), one-month ($838), two-month ($1188) and three-month ($1468) increments.

This, too, comes in under-26/first-class versions: ten days, $431/$616 and fifteen days, $568/$812. If you're travelling in a group of two or more, you might also want to consider the Eurail Saverpass. This costs $444 for fifteen consecutive days, $576 for 21; $712 for a month; $1010 for two months or $1248 for three. And there's also a Flexi Saverpass at $524 for ten days or $690 for 15.

RAIL CONTACTS IN NORTH AMERICA

CIT Tours, 9501 W Devon Ave, Suite 502, Rosemont, IL 60018 (☎1-800/223-7987).

Online Travel, 9501 W Devon Ave, Suite 502, Rosemont, IL 60018 (☎1-800/660-5300)

Rail Europe, 226 Westchester Ave, White Plains, NY 10604 (☎1-800/438-7245).

ScanTours, 3439 Wade St, Los Angeles, CA 90066 (☎1-800/223-7226).

SPECIALIST TOUR OPERATORS

USA

Adriatic Tours, 691 West 10th St, San Pedro, CA 90731 (☎1-800/262-1718). City highlights tours and cruise vacations.

Archeological Tours, 271 Madison Ave, New York, NY 10016 (☎212/986-3054). Specialist archeological tours.

Astro Tours, 2359 East Main St, Columbus, OH 43209 (☎1-800/543-7717; 614/237-7798).Cruise packages to the Greek islands.

Brendan Tours, 15137 Califa St, Van Nuys, CA 91411 (☎1-800/421-8446). City highlights, cruise packages and car rental.

Caravan Tours Inc, 401 N Michigan Ave, Suite 2800, Chicago, IL 60611 (☎1-800/621-8338). All kinds of packages covering the entire country.

Classic Adventures, PO Box 153, Hamlin, NY 14464-0153 (☎1-800/777-8090). Trekking, biking and walking tours in June and September, covering archeological sites and coastal trips.

Classic Holidays, 350 Park St, Suite 204, North Reading, MA 01864 (☎1-800/752-5055). Packages from 8 to 21 days, group tours and cruises.

Cloud Tours Inc, 645 Fifth Ave, New York, NY 10022 (☎1-800/223-7880). Affordable escorted tours and Mediterranean cruises.

Different Strokes Tours, 1841 Broadway, New York, NY 10023 (☎1-800/668 3301). Customized tours for gay/lesbian travellers.

Educational Tours and Cruises, 9 Irving St, Medford, MA 02155 (☎1-800/275-4109). Custom-designed tours to Greece and the islands, specializing in art, history, food and wine, ancient drama, painting and birdwatching.

Elderhostel, 75 Federal St, Boston, MA 02110 (☎617/426-8056) Educational and activity programs for senior travellers (companions may be younger).

Globus and Cosmos Tours, 5301 South Federal Circle, Littleton, CO 80123 (☎1-800/221-0090). Offers a variety of city and island packages.

Guaranteed Travel, 83 South St, Morristown, NJ 07963 (☎201/540-1770). Specializes in "Greece-Your-Way" independent travel.

Hellenic Adventures, 4150 Harriet Ave South, Minneapolis, MN 55409 (☎1-800/851-6349; 612/827-0937). A vast range of small group and independent tours: cultural, historical, horseback riding, hiking, wilderness, culinary and family oriented.

Homeric Tours, 55 E 59th St, New York, NY 10017 (☎1-800/223-5570). All-inclusive tours from 9–23 days, as well as cruises and charter flights.

Insight International Tours, 745 Atlantic Ave, Suite 720, Boston, MA 02111 (☎1-800/582-8380). General Greek vacations.

ST Cultural Tours, 225 W 34th St, New York, NY 10122 (☎1-800/833-2111; 212/563-1202). A wide range of package and independent educational tours.

Triaena Travel, 850 Seventh Ave, New York, NY 10019 (☎1-800/223-1273; 212/245-3700). Packages, cruises, apartments and villas.

Valef Yachts, Box 391, Ambler, PA 19002 (☎1-800/223-3845; 215/641-1624). Yachting trips and charters.

CANADA

Adventures Abroad, 20800 Westminter Highway; Suite 2148, Richmond, BC V6V 2W3 (☎1-800/665-3998; 604/303-1099). General operator, offering group and individual tours and cruises.

Auratours, 1470 Peel St, Suite 252, Montreal, Quebec H3A 1TL (☎1-800/363-0323). General operator, offering group and individual tours and cruises.

Worldwide Adventures, 36 Finch Ave West, Toronto, Ontario M2N 2G9 (☎1-800/387-1483; 416/221-3000). General operator, offering group and individual tours and cruises.

GETTING THERE FROM AUSTRALIA & NEW ZEALAND

It's fairly easy to track down flights from Australia to Athens, less so from New Zealand, but given the prices and most people's travel plans, you'll probably do better looking for some kind of Round-the-World ticket that includes Greece. If London is your first destination in Europe, and you've picked up a reasonably good deal on a flight there, it's probably best to wait until you reach the UK before arranging your onward travel to Greece; see "Getting there from Britain" p.3 for all the details.

Fares are seasonally adjusted with low season from mid-January to the end of February, October to November; high season mid-/end May, June to August, December to January and shoulder seasons the rest of the year. Tickets purchased direct from the airlines tend to be expensive; travel agents offer much better deals on fares and have the latest information on limited specials, round-the-world fares and stopovers. The best discounts are through **Flight Centres** and **STA**, who can also advise on visa regulations.

FLIGHTS FROM AUSTRALIA

Cheapest fares to Athens **from Australia** are with Olympic Airways from A$1700 low season, while Alitalia via Rome, Aeroflot via Moscow and Thai Airways via Bangkok all start around A$1850. In addition Singapore Airlines have a good connecting service to Athens from $1899. Qantas and British Airways offer a free return flight within Europe for A$2499–3099 which differs only slightly from their "Global Explorer" Pass (A$2599–3199), a **Round-the-World** fare that allows six stopovers worldwide wherever these two airlines fly to (except South America). Also worth considering is Garuda's A$1550 fare from Sydney, Brisbane or Cairns via Jakarta or

AIRLINES IN AUSTRALIA AND NEW ZEALAND

☎0800 numbers are toll free, but apply only if dialled outside the city in the address.

Aeroflot, Australia (☎02/9262 2233). Twice weekly flights from Sydney to Athens via transfers in Moscow and Bangkok.

British Airways, Australia (☎02/9258 3300); New Zealand (☎09/356 8690). Daily flights to London from major Australasian cities: code share with Qantas to offer their "Global Explorer" RTW fare.

Garuda, Australia (☎02/334 9944 or 1-800/800 873); New Zealand (☎09/366 1855). Several flights weekly from Australian and New Zealand cities to London, Frankfurt and Amsterdam via either a transfer or stopover in Denpasar/Jakarta.

Olympic Airways S.A., Australia (☎02/9251 2044); no NZ office. Twice weekly flights to Athens from Sydney and Melbourne, with onward connections to other Greek destinations.

Qantas Australia (☎13 1211); New Zealand (☎09/357 8900 and 0800/808 767). Daily flights to London from major Australasian cities: code share with British Airways to offer their "Global Explorer" RTW fare.

Singapore Airlines, Australia (☎13 1011); New Zealand (☎09/379 3209). Daily flights to Athens from Brisbane, Sydney, Melbourne, Perth and Auckland via Singapore.

Thai Airways Australia (☎13 1960); New Zealand (☎09/377 3886). Three flights a week to Athens via either a transfer or stopover in Bangkok from Brisbane, Sydney, Melbourne, Perth and Auckland.

DISCOUNT TRAVEL AGENTS IN AUSTRALIA & NEW ZEALAND

Anywhere Travel, 345 Anzac Parade, Kingsford, Sydney (☎02/9663 0411).

Brisbane Discount Travel, 260 Queen St, Brisbane (☎07/3229 9211).

Budget Travel, 16 Fort St, Auckland, plus branches around the city (☎09/3660061 and 0800/808 040).

Destinations Unlimited, 3 Milford Rd, Auckland (☎09/373 4033).

Flight Centres Australia: 82 Elizabeth St, Sydney, plus branches nationwide (☎13 1600), 205 Queen St, Auckland (☎09/309 6171), plus branches nationwide. Good discounts on fares.

Northern Gateway, 22 Cavenagh St, Darwin (☎08/8941 1394).

STA Travel, Australia: 702 Harris St, Ultimo, Sydney; 256 Flinders St, Melbourne; other offices in state capitals and major universities (nearest branch ☎13 1776, fastfare telesales ☎1300/360 960); 10 High St, Auckland (☎09/309 0458, fast-fare telesales ☎09/366 6673), plus branches in Wellington, Christchurch, Dunedin, Palmerston North, Hamilton and at major universities. World Wide Web site: *www.statravelaus.com.au*; email: *traveller@statravelaus.com.au*. Fare discounts for students and under 26s.

Thomas Cook, Australia: 175 Pitt St, Sydney; 257 Collins St, Melbourne; plus branches in other state capitals (local branch ☎13 1771; Thomas Cook Direct telesales ☎1800/063 913); 96 Anzac Ave, Auckland (☎09/379 3920). Travellers' cheques, bus and rail passes.

SPECIALIST TOUR OPERATORS IN AUSTRALIA & NEW ZEALAND

Adventure World, 73 Walker St, North Sydney (☎02/956 7766); 8 Victoria Ave, Perth (☎09/221 2300). Agents for a vast array of international adventure travel companies that operate trips to mainland Greece and islands.

Australians Studying Abroad, 1/970 High St, Armadale, Melbourne (☎03/9509 1955 and 1800/645 755). Study tours exploring Greek culture and art.

Grecian Mediterranean Holidays, 49 Ventnor Ave, West Perth (☎09/321 3930). A good selection of mainland and island holidays.

Grecian Tours Travel, 237a Lonsdale St, Melbourne (☎03/663 3711). Offers a variety of accommodation, and sightseeing tours.

House of Holidays, 298 Clayton Rd, Clayton, Victoria (☎03/543 5800). Greek specialist with a wide selection of holidays.

Kompas Holidays, 71 Grey St, Brisbane (☎07/3846 4006 and 1800/269 968); 115 Pitt St, Sydney (☎02/231 1277). City stopovers, sightseeing tours, cruises, traditional accommodation and yacht charter. Booking through travel agents only.

Kyrenia Travel Services, 92 Goulburn St, Sydney (☎02/9283 2144). Mainland and island accommodation, land tours and island hopping.

Peregrine Adventures, 258 Lonsdale St, Melbourne (☎03/9663 8611), plus offices in Brisbane, Sydney, Adelaide and Perth. Walking and cycling trips visiting historical towns and monuments.

Travel Market, 11th floor, 141 Queen St, Brisbane (☎07/3210 0323). Individually tailored holidays in the Greek Islands, for a range of budgets.

Denpasar to various European cities, from where you could pick up a cheap onward flight or continue **overland** to Athens.

FLIGHTS FROM NEW ZEALAND

From New Zealand, the best deals to Athens are with Thai Airlines via Bangkok from $2399, and Singapore Airlines via Singapore and Alitalia via Rome, both for around NZ$2499. United Airlines fly via Los Angeles, Washington and Paris starting at NZ$2599, and there's a very versatile offer with Lufthansa for $2899, who can route you through anywhere that Air New Zealand or Qantas fly – including Los Angeles, Singapore, Sydney, Hong Kong or Tokyo – for a stopover. British Airways/Qantas can get you to Europe, but not Athens, for $2699, so again you're better off with their Global Explorer Pass (see above) from NZ$3089. **Departure tax** from Athens is $42.

DEPARTURE POINTS: ATHENS, PIREÁS & MAIN PORTS

As detailed in the "Getting There" sections, you may well find yourself travelling to the islands via Athens. This is not necessarily a hardship. The Greek capital is, admittedly, no holiday resort, with its concrete architecture and air pollution, but it has modern excitements of its own, as well as superlative ancient sites. A couple of nights' stopover will allow you to take in the Acropolis, Ancient Agora and major museums, wander around the old quarter of Pláka and the bazaar area, and sample some of the country's best restaurants and clubs. And a morning flight into Athens would allow you time to take a look at the Acropolis and Pláka, before heading down to the port of Pireás (Piraeus) to catch one of the overnight ferries to Crete or the Dodecanese.

Not all the islands are accessible from Pireás, so we've given brief accounts of other useful mainland ports below.

ATHENS

Athens **airport** – Ellinikón – has two separate terminals: west (*dhitikó*) which is used by Olympic Airways (both national and international), and east (*anatolikó*) which is used by all the other airlines. The terminals are on opposite sides of the runway, so you have to drive halfway round the perimeter fence to get from one to the other. Olympic buses connect the two regularly from around 6am to midnight; taxis are available, too, and should cost no more than 2000dr. Both terminals have money exchange facilities, open 24 hours at the east terminal, 7am to 11pm at the west one; the west terminal also has automatic cash machines that accept Visa, Mastercard, Cirrus and Plus cards. Insist on some small denomination notes for paying for your bus ticket or taxi ride.

It's about 9km to **central Athens** or to the ferry port of **Pireás** (Piraeus). The easiest way to travel is by **taxi**, which should cost around 1000–1500dr, depending on traffic. Make sure that the meter is switched on, as new arrivals are often charged over the odds. You may find that you have fellow passengers in the cab: this is permitted, and each drop-off will pay the full fare. If you're happy to carry your bags around, you could also travel in by **bus**. Bus #091 connects both terminals with the centre of Athens (Omónia and Sýndagma squares). In theory, the bus runs every 30 minutes from 5.30am to 11.30pm, and every hour from 11.30pm to 5.30am. Tickets cost 170dr; 200dr between 1.30 and 5.30am. Bus #19 runs from both airport terminals to Pireás, allowing you to get straight to the ferries. It runs about every hour between 6am and 9.20pm. Tickets again cost 170dr (200dr from midnight to 5.30am). Take the bus to the end of the route, Platía Karaïskáki, which fronts the main harbour, and a line of ferry agencies.

All international **trains** arrive at the Stathmós Laríssis, just to the northwest of the city centre. There are hotels in this area or you can take yellow trolley bus (#1) immediately outside to reach Sýndagma square.

If you are just spending the day in Athens, and want to **store your baggage**, you can do so for 200dr per piece at Pacific Ltd, Nikis 24 – just off Sýndagma (Mon–Sat 7am–8pm, Sun 7am–2pm). You can also store bags here longer term if you want to take the minimum to the islands.

ACCOMMODATION AND EATING

Finding **accommodation** in Athens not a problem except at the very height of summer – though it's always best to phone ahead. A small selection of places are listed below, or you can book more upmarket rooms through the main EOT tourist office (Mon–Fri 9am–7pm, Sat 9am–2pm; ☎33 10 437 or 33 10 562 or 33 10 565) at 2 Amerikas Street, just up from Stadiou, which can also supply you with maps of the city.

For a quick stay, **Pláka**, the oldest quarter of the city, is the best area. It spreads south of Sýndagma square, is in easy walking range of the Acropolis, and has lots of outdoor restaurants and cafés. It's possible to stay in the port of Pireás, too, though there's no real need, and you might as well make the most of your time in Athens. All the listings below are in Pláka; price categories are for a double room in high season:

4000–6000dr
George's Guest House, Níkis 46 (☎32 26 474).
John's Place, Patróou 5 (☎32 29 719).
Thisseus Hostel, Thisséos 10 (☎32 45 960).

6000–8000dr

Dioskouri, Pittákou 6 (☎32 48 165).
Kouros, Kódhrou 11 (☎32 27 431).
Student Inn, Kidhathinéon 18 (☎32 44 808).

8000–16,000dr

Acropolis House, Kódhrou 6 (☎32 22 344).
Adonis, Kódhrou 3 (☎32 49 737).
Nefeli, Iperídhou 16 (☎32 28 044).

Pláka is bursting with touristy **restaurants**, most very pleasantly situated but poor value. Three with nice sites and good food are *Kouklis* (Tripíodhon 14), *O Platanos* (Dhioyénous 4) and *Iy Klimataria* (Klepsídhras 5). *Eden* (Liossíou 12) is a decent vegetarian restaurant.

THE CITY AND SIGHTS

Central Athens is a compact, easily walkable area. Its hub is **Sýndagma Square** (Platía Sintágmatos), flanked by the Parliament buildings, banks and airline offices, and, as mentioned, the National Bank with the Tourist Office. Pretty much everything you'll want to see in a fleeting visit – the Acropolis, Pláka, the major museums – is within 20–30 minutes' walk of here. Just east of the square, too, are the **National Gardens** – the nicest spot in town for a siesta.

Walk south from Sýndagma, along Níkis or Filellínon streets, and you'll find yourself in Pláka, the surviving area of the nineteenth-century, pre-Independence, village. Largely pedestrianized, it is a delightful area just to wander around – and it is the approach to the Acropolis. For a bit of focus to your walk, take in the fourth-century BC **Monument of Lysikrates**, used as a study by Byron, to the east, and the Roman-era **Tower of the Winds** (Aéridhes), to the west. The latter adjoins the Roman forum. Climb north from the Tower of the Winds and you reach **Anafiótika**, with its whitewashed Cycladic-style cottages (built by workers from the island of Anáfi) and the eclectic **Kanellópoulos Museum** (Tues–Sun 8.30am–3pm; 500dr).

Head north from the Roman Forum, along Athinás or Eólou streets, and you come to an equally characterful part of the city – the **bazaar** area, which shows Athens in its Near Eastern lights. **Monastiráki Square** is worth a look, too, with its Turkish mosque. On Sundays a genuine **Flea Market** sprawls to its west, out beyond the tourist shops promoted as "Athens Flea Market".

Even with a few hours to spare between flight and ferry, you can take in a visit to the **Acropolis** (April–Sept daily 8am–6.30pm; Oct–March Mon–Fri 8am–4.30pm, Sat & Sun 8am–2.30pm; site and museum 2000dr, Oct–March free on Sun). The complex of temples, rebuilt by Pericles in the Golden Age of the fifth century BC, is focused on the famed Parthenon. This, and the smaller Athena Nike and Erechtheion temples are given context by a small museum housing some of the original statuary left behind by Lord Elgin.

If you have more time, make your way down to the **Theatre of Dionysos**, on the south slope (daily 8.30am–2.45pm; 500dr), and/or to the Ancient (Classical Greek-era) **Agora** (south-eastern entrance down the path from the Areopagus; northern entrance on Adhrianoú; Tues–Sun 8.30am–2.45pm; 1200dr), presided over by the Doric **Thiseion**, or Temple of Hephaestus.

Athens' major museum is the **National Archeological Museum** (Patissíon 28; Mon 12.30–7pm, Tues–Fri 8am–7pm, Sat & Sun 8.30am–7pm; 2000dr). Its highlights include the Mycenean (Odyssey-era) treasures, Classical sculpture, and, upstairs, the brilliant Minoan frescoes from Thíra (Santoríni).

Two other superb museums are the **Benáki** (scheduled to re-open in 1998), a fascinating personal collection of ancient and folk treasures, and the **Goulandris Museum of Cycladic and Ancient Greek Art** (Mon, Wed–Fri 10am–4pm, Sat 10am–3pm; 600dr, free Sat), with its wonderful display of figurines from the Cycladic island civilization of the third millennium BC.

PIREÁS

Pireás (Piraeus), the port of Athens, is the last stop on the single-line **metro**, which you can board at Platía Viktorías, Omónia or Monastiráki squares. The journey takes about 25 minutes – trains run from 6am to midnight – and there's a flat fare of 100dr. If you're travelling by rail from Pátra, the train continues through Athens down to Pireás. **Taxis** cost around 1500dr from the city centre or the airport.

You can buy **ferry tickets** from agencies at the harbour in Pireás, or in central Athens (there are several outlets on Leóforos Amalías, which runs south of Sýndagma square). Wherever you buy tickets, make sure you ask around the agencies and get a ferry that makes a reasonably direct run to your island destination. There may be little choice to obscure islands, but ferries to the Cyclades and Dodecanese can take very different routes.

For the Argo-Saronic islands, you may prefer to take a "Flying Dolphin" **hydrofoil** from the Zéa Marina – a taxi ride (or bus #8) from the metro. These are twice as fast and around twice the cost. Tickets can be bought in advance in Athens – worth doing in high season – or an hour before departure at the quay.

OTHER MAINLAND PORTS

Although Pireás has a wide choice of ferry and hydrofoil connections, certain islands can (or must) be reached from other ports on the mainland. Below is a quick run-through of the more important and useful.

Note also that there are two islands – **Évvia** (northeast of Athens) and **Lefkádha** in the Ionian islands – that require no ferry, and can be reached by bus, and in Évvia's case also by train.

ALEXANDRHÓUPOLI

The third northern port (6hr by bus from Thessaloníki) has regular ferries to Samothráki. It's a somewhat unenticing place to stay.

IGOUMENÍTSA

Many ferries from Italy call at Igoumenítsa, stopping at Corfu en route. There are regular shuttles across to **Corfu**, plus daily hops to **Páxi**, augmented in summer by hydrofoils. Hotels are plentiful as nobody stays more than a night.

LÁVRIO

This tiny port, south of Athens (and reachable by bus from the Mavromatéon terminal; 1hr) has daily ferries to **Kéa**, the closest of the Cyclades.

KAVÁLA

The main port of northern Greece (3hr by bus from Thessaloníki) offers fast access to **Thássos**, either direct, or from the nearby shuttle point at Keramotí. There are also links to **Samothráki**, **Límnos** and other **northeast Aegean** islands. The city has a characterful harbour area but hotels are in short supply. Try booking ahead at the *Akropolis* (☎051/223 543), *Panorama* (☎051/228 412) or *Esperia* (☎051/229 621).

KYLLÍNI

This small port, south of Pátra (buses), is the main departure point for the Ionian island of **Zákynthos**, and in summer has boats to **Kefalloniá**. Little point in staying, if you time things right.

KÝMI

This is technically an island port – on Évvia (see Chapter Six) – but is mentioned here as it is the main port for the island of **Skýros** in the Sporades. Kými can be reached by Athens by bus.

NEÁPOLI

A small, undistinguished port at the southern foot of the Peloponnese, with ferry and hydrofoil connections to **Kýthira**, and local boats to the islet of **Elafónissos**. It can be reached by hydrofoil in summer from the Argo-Saronic islands.

PÁRGA AND ASTAKÓS

These two small ports, south of Igoumenítsa, have daily ferries to, respectively, **Páxi** and **Itháki** in the Ionian. Párga is a busy, pleasant resort.

PÁTRA (PATRAS)

Pátra is the major port of the Peloponnese, and the only real rival to Pireás in terms of traffic. It has ferry connections with Italy and with the main **Ionian islands**. Easiest access from Athens is on the train (Statmós Peloponíssou terminal; 4hr). The city itself is uninteresting, so plan on moving out the same day, if possible. Reasonable budget hotels include the *El Greco*, Ayíou Andhréou 145 (☎061/272 931), *Atlanta* Ayíou Andhréou 16 (☎061/277 502), and *Nicos* (☎061/623 757).

RÁFINA

Another small port near Athens (again reachable by bus from the Mavromatéon terminal; 40min). Connections are to the **Cyclades**, **Dodecanese**, **northeast Aegean** and nearby **Évvia**.

THESSALONÍKI

The northern capital has useful if pricey summer hydrofoils to **Skíathos**, **Skópelos** and **Alónissos** in the Sporades. Also regular ferries to these and **north-east Aegean** islands. It's worth exploring the Byzantine churches and Archeological Museum (with Philip of Macedon's tomb treasure). Hotels are plentiful if mostly uninspiring.

VÓLOS AND ÁYIOS KONSTANDÍNOS

Vólos is a large port city – modern and rather grim – in Thessaly, in central Greece. It is easiest reached from Athens by bus (Mavromatéon terminal; 4hr). Ferries and hydrofoils run regularly to the Sporades – **Skíathos**, **Skópelos** and **Alónissos**. Try to complete your journey the same day. **Áyios Konstandínos** is an alternative port for the **Sporades**, again with buses from Athens (Mavromatéon terminal; 2hr 30min).

YÍTHIO

This elegant Peloponnese town has ferries most days to the isolated Ionian island of **Kýthira**. It's a 5–6hr haul here by bus (Kifissóu 100 terminal) from Athens, changing at Spárti. Budget hotels in town include the *Kondoyannis*, Vassileos Pávlou 19 (☎0733/22 518), *Koutsouris*, junction Larysiou and Moretti (☎0733/22 321) and *Kranae*, Vassiléos Pávlou 15 (☎0733/22 011).

TRAVELLERS WITH DISABILITIES

It is all too easy to wax lyrical over the attractions of Greece: the stepped, narrow alleys, the ease of travel by bus and ferry, the thrill of clambering around the great archeological sites. It is almost impossible, on the other hand, for the able-bodied travel writer to see these attractions as potential hazards for anyone who has difficulty in walking, is wheelchair-bound or suffers from some other disability.

However, don't be discouraged. It is possible to enjoy an inexpensive and trauma-free holiday in Greece if some time is devoted to gathering **information** before arrival. Much existing or readily available information is out of date – you should always try to double-check. A number of addresses of contact organizations are published below. The Greek National Tourist Office is a good first step as long as you have specific questions to put to them; they publish a useful questionnaire which you could send to hotels or owners of apartment/villa accommodation.

PLANNING A HOLIDAY

There are **organized tours** and **holidays** specifically for people with disabilities; many companies in Britain will advise on the suitability of holidays or villas advertised in their brochures. If you want to be more independent, it's perfectly possible, provided that you do not leave home with the vague hope that things will turn out all right, and that "people will help out" when you need assistance. This cannot be relied on. You must either be completely confident that you can

manage alone, or travel with an able-bodied friend (or two).

It's important to become an authority on where you must be self-reliant and where you may expect help, especially regarding transport and accommodation. For example, to get between the terminals at Athens airport, you will have to fight for a taxi; it is not the duty of the airline staff to find you one.

It is also vital to **be honest** – with travel agencies, insurance companies, companions and, above all, with yourself. Know your limits and make sure others know them. If you do not use a wheelchair all the time but your walking capabilities are limited, remember that you are likely to need to cover greater distances while travelling (often over tougher terrain and in hotter weather) than you are used to. If you use a wheelchair, have it serviced before you go, and carry a repair kit.

Read your travel **insurance** small print carefully to make sure that people with a pre-existing medical condition are not excluded. And use your travel agent to make your journey simpler: **airlines** or bus companies can cope better if they are expecting you, with a wheelchair provided at airports and staff primed to help. A **medical certificate** of your fitness to travel, provided by your doctor, is also extremely useful; some airlines or insurance companies may insist on it.

Make a **list** of all the facilities that will make your life easier while you are away. You may want a ground-floor room, or access to a large elevator; you may have special dietary requirements, or need level ground to enable you to reach shops,

USEFUL CONTACTS

National Tourist Organization of Greece: See p.31 for addresses. Offers general advice on terrain and climate. They have nothing specific for disabled visitors except a brief list of hotels which may be suitable.

GREECE

Association Hermes, Patriárkhou Grigoríou tou Pémptou 13, 165 42 Aryiroúpolis, Athens (☎01/99 61 887). Can advise disabled visitors to Greece.

Lavinia Tours, Egnatía 101, 541 10 Thessaloníki (☎031/240 041). Evyenia Stravropoulou will advise disabled visitors and has tested many parts of Greece in her wheelchair. She also organizes tours within Greece.

UK

Holiday Care Service, 2nd floor, Imperial Buildings, Victoria Rd, Horley, Surrey RH6 7PZ (☎01293/774535). Publishes a fact sheet, and also runs a useful "Holiday Helpers" service for disabled travellers.

Mobility International, 228 Borough High St, London SE1 1JX (☎0171/403 5688). Issues a quarterly newsletter on developments in disabled travel.

Opus 23, Sourdock Hill, Barkisland, Halifax, West Yorkshire HX4 0AG (☎01422/375999). Part of Grecofile; will advise on and arrange independent holidays, or trips for those with carers.

RADAR, 12 City Forum, 250 City Rd, London EC1V 8AF (☎0171/250 3222). They publish fact sheets and an annual guide to international travel for the disabled.

Tripscope, The Courtyard, Evelyn Rd, London W4 5JL (☎0181/994 9294). Transport advice to most countries for all disabilities.

NORTH AMERICA

Directions Unlimited, 720 N Bedford Rd, Bedford Hills, NY 10507 (☎1-800/533-5343). Tour operator specializing in custom tours for people with disabilities.

Jewish Rehabilitation Hospital, 3205 Place Alton Goldbloom, Montreal, PQ H7V 1R2 (☎514/688-9550, ext 226). Guidebooks and travel information.

Mobility International USA, PO Box 10767, Eugene, OR 97440 (Voice & TDD: ☎503/343-1284). Information and referral service, access guides, tours and exchange programs. Annual membership $20 (includes quarterly newsletter).

Society for the Advancement of Travel for the Handicapped (SATH), 347 5th Ave, New York, NY 10016 (☎212/447-7284). Non-profit travel-industry referral service that passes queries on to its members as appropriate; allow plenty of time for a response.

Travel Information Service, Moss Rehabilitation Hospital, 1200 West Tabor Rd, Philadelphia, PA 19141 (☎215/456-9600). Telephone information and referral service.

Twin Peaks Press, Box 129, Vancouver, WA 98666; ☎206/694-2462 or ☎1-800/637-2256).Publisher of the Directory of Travel Agencies for the Disabled ($19.95), listing more than 370 agencies worldwide; Travel for the Disabled ($14.95); and the Directory of Accessible Van Rentals and Wheelchair Vagabond ($9.95), loaded with personal tips.

AUSTRALIA AND NEW ZEALAND

ACROD (Australian Council for Rehabilitation of the Disabled), PO Box 60, Curtin, ACT 2605 (☎02/6282 4333).

Disabled Persons Assembly, 173–175 Victoria St, Wellington (☎04/811 9100).

---

beaches, bars and places of interest. You should also keep track of all your other special needs, making sure, for example, that you have extra supplies of drugs – carried with you if you fly – and a prescription including the generic name in case of emergency. Carry spares of any kind of drug, clothing or equipment that might be hard to find in Greece; if there's an association representing people with your disability, contact them early in the planning process.

VISAS AND RED TAPE

UK and all other EU nationals need only a valid passport for entry to Greece; you are no longer stamped in on arrival or out upon departure, and in theory at least enjoy uniform civil rights with Greek citizens. US, Australian, New Zealand, Canadian and most non-EU Europeans receive mandatory entry and exit stamps in their passports and can stay, as tourists, for ninety days.

If you are planning to **travel overland**, you should check current visa requirements for Hungary, Romania and Bulgaria, Slovenia and Croatia at their closest consulates; transit visas for most of these territories are at present issued at the borders, though at a higher price than if obtained in advance at a local consulate.

GREEK EMBASSIES ABROAD

Australia 9 Turrana St, Yarralumla, Canberra, ACT 2600 (☎02/6273-3011).
Britain 1a Holland Park, London W11 3TP (☎0171/221 6467).
Canada 76–80 Maclaren St, Ottawa, ON K2P 0K6 (☎613/238-6271).
Ireland 1 Upper Pembroke St, Dublin 2 (☎01/767254).
New Zealand 5–7 Willis St, PO Box 27157, Wellington (☎04/473 7775).
USA 2221 Massachusetts Ave NW, Washington DC 20008 (☎202/939-5800).

VISA EXTENSIONS

If you wish to stay in Greece for longer than three months, you should officially apply for an **extension**. This can be done in the larger cities like Athens, Thessaloníki, Pátra, Rhodes and Iráklion through the Ipiresía Allodhapón (Aliens' Bureau); prepare yourself for concerted bureaucracy. In remoter locations you visit the local police station, where staff are apt to be more co-operative.

Unless you are of Greek descent, visitors from **non-EU** countries are currently allowed only one six-month extension to a tourist visa, which costs 11,000dr. In theory, **EU nationals** are allowed to stay indefinitely but, at the time of writing, must still present themselves every six months or every year, according to whether they have a non-employment resident visa or a work permit; the first extension is free, but you will be charged for subsequent extensions. In all cases, the procedure should be set in motion a couple of weeks before your time runs out and, if you don't have a work permit, you will be required to present pink, personalized bank **exchange receipts** (see "Costs, Money and Banks: Currency Regulations" p.28) totalling at least 500,000dr for the preceding three months, as proof that you have sufficient funds to support yourself without working. Possession of unexpired credit cards, a Greek savings account passbook or travellers' cheques can to some extent substitute for the pink receipts.

Certain individuals get around the law by leaving Greece every three months and re-entering a few days later, ideally via a different frontier post, for a new tourist stamp. However, with the recent flood of Albanian and ex-Yugoslavian refugees into the country, and a smaller influx of east Europeans looking for work, security and immigration personnel don't always look very kindly on this practice.

If you **overstay** your time and then leave under your own power – ie are not deported – you'll be given a 22,000dr spot fine upon departure, effectively a double-priced retroactive visa extension – no excuses will be entertained except perhaps a doctor's certificate stating you were immobilized in hospital.

CUSTOMS REGULATIONS

For EU citizens travelling between EU countries, limits on goods already taxed have been relaxed enormously. However, **duty-free allowances** are as follows: 200 cigarettes or 50 cigars, two litres of still table wine or one litre of spirits, and 50ml of perfume.

Exporting **antiquities** from Greece without a permit is a serious offence; **drug smuggling**, it goes without saying, incurs severe penalties.

INSURANCE

British and other EU nationals are officially entitled to free medical care in Greece (see "Health" p.25) upon presentation of an E111 form, available from most post offices. "Free", however, means admittance only to the lowest grade of state hospital (known as a yenikó nosokomío), and does not include nursing care or the cost of medications. In practice, hospital staff tend to greet E111s with uncomprehending looks, and you may have to request reimbursal by the NHS upon your return home. If you need prolonged medical care, you should make use of private treatment, which is expensive.

Some form of **travel insurance**, therefore, is advisable – and essential for **North Americans** and **Australasians**, whose countries have no formal health care agreements with Greece (other than allowing for free emergency trauma treatment). For medical claims, keep receipts, including those from pharmacies. You will have to pay for all private medical care on the spot (insurance claims can be processed if you have hospital treatment) but it can all be (eventually) claimed back. Travel insurance usually provides cover for the loss of baggage, money and tickets, too. If you're thinking of renting a moped or motorbike in Greece, or engaging in water sports, make sure the policy covers motorbike accidents and "hazardous" sports, which most don't without a supplemental payment.

EUROPEAN COVER

In Britain, there are a number of low-cost **specialist insurance companies** including Endsleigh, 97–107 Southampton Row, London WC1 (☎0171/436 4451), Campus Travel, 52 Grosvenor Gardens, London SW1 (☎0171/730 3402), and Columbus, 17 Devonshire Square, London EC2 (☎0171/375 0111). At all of these you can buy two weeks' basic cover in Greece for around £20, £30 for a month.

Most **banks** and **credit card** issuers also offer some sort of holiday insurance, often automatic if you pay for the holiday with a card. In these circumstances, it's vital to check what the policy actually covers – usually only death and/or dismemberment.

NORTH AMERICAN COVER

Before buying an insurance policy, check that you're not already covered. **Canadians** are usually covered for medical mishaps overseas by their provincial health plans. Holders of official student/teacher/youth cards are entitled to accident coverage and hospital in-patient benefits. **Students** will often find that their student health coverage extends during the vacations and for one term beyond the date of last enrolment. Bank and credit cards (particularly American Express) often have certain levels of medical or other insurance included, and travel insurance may also be included if you use a major credit or charge card to pay for your trip. **Homeowners'** or **renters'** insurance often covers theft or loss of documents, money and valuables while overseas, though conditions and maximum amounts vary from company to company.

After exhausting the possibilities above, you might want to contact a specialist **travel insurance** company; your travel agent can usually recommend one, or see the box opposite. Policies are comprehensive (accidents, illnesses, delayed or lost luggage, cancelled flights, etc), but maximum payouts tend to be meagre. Premiums vary, so shop around. The best deals are usually to be had through student/youth travel agencies. The policy offered by STA, for instance, comes with or without medical cover. Rates are $110/$85 for one month, $165/$120 for two, and rise by $55/$35 for each extra month.

Most North American travel policies apply only to items lost, stolen or damaged while in the custody of an identifiable, responsible third party – hotel porter, airline, luggage consignment, etc. Even in these cases you will have to contact the local police within a certain time limit to have a complete report made out so that your insurer can process the claim. Note also that very few insurers will arrange on-the-spot payments in the event of a major expense or loss; you will usually be **reimbursed** only after going home.

COVER FOR AUSTRALIA AND NEW ZEALAND

Travel insurance is available from most **travel agents** (see p.16) or direct from **insurance companies**, for periods ranging from a few days to a year or even longer. Most policies are similar in premium and coverage – but if you plan to indulge

TRAVEL INSURANCE COMPANIES IN NORTH AMERICA

Access America, PO Box 90310, Richmond, VA 23230 (☎1-800/284-8300).

Carefree Travel Insurance, PO Box 9366, 100 Garden City Plaza, Garden City NY 11530 (☎1-800/323-3149).

Travel Assistance International, 1133 15th St NW, Suite 400, Washington, DC 20005 (☎1-800/821-2828).

Travel Guard, 1145 Clark St, Stevens Point, WI 54481 (☎1-800/826-1300).

Travel Insurance Services, 2930 Camino Diablo, Suite 300, Walnut Creek, CA 94596 (☎1-800/937-1387).

in **high-risk activities** such as mountaineering, bungy jumping or scuba diving, check the policy carefully to make sure you'll be covered.

A typical policy for Greece will cost: A$100/NZ$110 for 2 weeks, A$170/NZ$190 for 1 month, A$250/NZ$275 for 2 months. Try Cover More, 9/32 Walker St, North Sydney (☎02/9202 8000 & 1800/251 881), and Ready Plan, 141 Walker St, Dandenong, Melbourne (☎03/9791 5077 & 1800/337 462); 10/ 63 Albert St, Auckland (☎09/379 3208).

INSURANCE REPORTS

In all cases of loss or theft of goods, you will have to contact the local police to have a **report** made out so that your insurer can process the claim. This can occasionally be a tricky business in Greece, since many officials simply won't accept that anything could be stolen on their turf, or at least don't want to take responsibility for it. Moreover, there have been enough fraudulent claims in recent years to make the police justifiably wary. Be persistent, and if necessary enlist the support of the local **tourist police** or tourist office.

HEALTH

There are no required inoculations for Greece, though it's wise to have a typhoid-cholera booster, and to ensure that you are up to date on tetanus and polio. Don't forget to take out travel insurance (see "Insurance" above), so that you're covered in case of serious illness or accidents.

The **water** is safe pretty much everywhere, though you will come across shortages or brackish supplies on some of the drier or more remote islands. Bottled water is widely available if you're cautious.

SPECIFIC HAZARDS

The main health problems experienced by visitors have to do with over-exposure to the sun, and the odd nasty from the sea. To combat the former, don't spend too long in the sun, wear a hat plus loose, long sleeves, and drink plenty of fluids in the hot months to avoid any danger of **sunstroke**; remember that even hazy sun can burn. For sea-wear, a pair of goggles for swimming and footwear for walking over wet rocks are useful.

HAZARDS OF THE DEEP

In the sea, you may have the bad luck to meet an armada of **jellyfish**, especially in late summer; they come in various colours and sizes ranging from purple "pizzas" to invisible, minute creatures. Various over-the-counter remedies are sold in resort pharmacies; baking soda or ammonia also help to lessen the sting. The welts and burning usually subside of their own accord within a few hours; there are no deadly man-of-war species in Greek waters.

Less vicious but more common are black, spiky **sea urchins**, which infest rocky shorelines year-round; if you step on or graze one, a needle (you can crudely sterilize it by heat from a cigarette lighter) and olive oil are effective for removing spines; if you don't extract them, they'll fester.

The worst maritime danger – fortunately very rare – seems to be the **weever fish** (*dhrakéna*), which buries itself in tidal zone sand with just its poisonous dorsal and gill spines protruding. If you tread on one the sudden pain is unmistakably excruciating, and the **venom** is exceptionally potent. Consequences can range up to permanent paralysis of the affected area, so the imperative first aid is to immerse your foot in water as hot as

you can stand. This serves to degrade the toxin and relieve the swelling of joints and attendant pain.

Somewhat more common are **stingrays** (Greek names include *platý, selákhi, vátos* or *trígona*), who mainly frequent bays with sandy bottoms where they can camouflage themselves. Though shy, they can give you a nasty lash with their tail if trodden on, so shuffle your feet a bit when entering the water.

SANDFLIES, MOSQUITOES AND SNAKES

If you are sleeping on or near a **beach**, it's wise to use insect repellent, either lotion or wrist/ankle bands, and/or a tent with a screen to guard against **sandflies**. Their bites are potentially dangerous, carrying visceral leishmaniasis, a rare parasitic infection characterized by chronic fever, listlessness and weight loss.

Mosquitoes (*kounóupia*) are less worrying – in Greece they don't carry anything worse than a vicious bite – but they can be infuriating. The best solution is to burn pyrethrum incense coils (*spíres* or *fidhákia* in Greek); these are widely and cheaply available, though smelly. Better if you can get them are the small electrical devices (trade name Vape Net) which vaporize an odourless insecticide tablet; many "rooms" proprietors supply them routinely. Insect repellents such as Autan are available from most general stores and kiosks.

Adders (*okhiés*) and **scorpions** (*skorpí*) are found in Greece, though both are shy; just take care when climbing over dry-stone walls where snakes like to sun themselves, and don't put hands/feet in places, like shoes, where you haven't looked first.

PHARMACIES AND DRUGS

For **minor complaints** it's enough to go to the local **farmakío**. Greek pharmacists are highly trained and dispense a number of medicines which elsewhere could only be prescribed by a doctor. In the larger towns there'll usually be one who speaks good English. Pharmacies are generally closed in the evenings and on Saturday mornings, but are supposed to have a sign on their door (in English) referring you to the nearest open alternative.

Homeopathic and herbal remedies are quite widely available, with homeopathic pharmacies in many of the larger towns identified by the characteristic green-cross sign.

If you regularly use any form of **prescription drug** you should bring along a copy of the prescription together with the generic name of the drug – this will help should you need to replace it, and will also avoid possible problems with customs officials. In this context, it's worth being aware that codeine is banned in Greece. If you import any, you just might find yourself in serious trouble, so check labels carefully; it's the core ingredient of Panadeine, Veganin, Sopadein, Codis and Empirin-Codeine, to name just a few common compounds.

Contraceptive pills are more readily available every year, but don't count on local availability, except in the large towns; unfortunately abortion is still the principal form of birth control. **Condoms**, however, are inexpensive and ubiquitous – just ask for *profylaktiká* (the more slangy *plastiká* or slightly vulgar *kapótes* are even better understood) at any pharmacy or corner *períptero* (kiosk); the pill, too, can be obtained over-the-counter from larger *farmakía*.

Lastly, **hay fever** sufferers should be prepared for the early Greek pollen season, at its height from April to June. Pharmacists stock tablets and creams, but it's cheaper to come prepared. Commercial antihistamines like Triludan are difficult to find in smaller towns, and local brands can cost upwards of £10/$16 equivalent for a pack of ten.

DOCTORS AND HOSPITALS

You'll find English-speaking **doctors** in any of the bigger towns or resorts; the tourist police, travel agents, hotel staff or even your consulate should be able to come up with some names if you have any difficulty.

For an **ambulance**, phone ☎166. In **emergencies**, treatment is given free in **state hospitals** – for cuts, broken bones, etc – though you will only get the most basic level of nursing care. Greek families routinely take in food and bedding for relatives, so as a tourist you'll be at a severe disadvantage. Somewhat better are the ordinary state-run outpatient clinics (*yatría*) attached to most public hospitals and also found in rural locales. These operate on a first-come, first-served basis, so go early; usual hours are 8am to noon.

Don't forget to obtain **receipts** for the cost of all drugs and medical treatment; without them, you won't be able to claim back the money on your travel insurance.

POLICE, TROUBLE AND HARASSMENT

In an emergency, dial ☎100 for the police and ☎171 for the tourist police; in a medical emergency, dial ☎166 for an ambulance.

As in the past, Greece remains one of Europe's safest countries, with a low crime rate and a deserved reputation for honesty. If you leave a bag or wallet at a café, you'll most likely find it scrupulously looked after, pending your return. Similarly, Greeks are relaxed about leaving possessions unlocked or unattended on the beach, in rooms or on campsites.

However, in recent years there has been a large increase in **theft** and **crimes** (perpetrated largely by Albanian refugees) in the cities and resorts, so it's wise to lock things up and treat Greece like any other European destination. Following are also a few pointers on offences that might get you into trouble locally, and some advice on **sexual harassment** – all too much a fact of life given the classically Mediterranean machismo of the culture.

SPECIFIC OFFENCES

The most common causes of a brush with authority are nude bathing or sunbathing, and camping outside an authorized site.

Nude bathing is legal on only a very few beaches (on Mýkonos, for example), and is deeply offensive to the more traditional Greeks – exercise considerable sensitivity to local feeling and the kind of place you're in. It is, for example, very bad etiquette to swim or sunbathe nude within sight of a church. Generally, if a beach has become fairly established for nudity, or is well secluded, it's highly unlikely that the police will come charging in. Where they do get bothered is if they feel a place is turning into a "hippie beach" or nudity is getting too overt on mainstream tourist stretches. Most of the time, the only action will be a warning, but you can officially be arrested straight off – facing up to three days in jail and a stiff fine.

Topless (sun)bathing for women is technically legal nationwide, but specific locales often opt out of the "liberation" and post signs to that effect, which should be heeded.

Very similar guidelines apply to **camping rough** – though for this you're still less likely to incur anything more than a warning to move on. The only real risk of arrest is if you are told to clear off and fail to do so. In either of the above cases, even if the police do take any action against you, it's more likely to be a brief spell in their cells than any official prosecution.

Incidentally, any sort of **disrespect** towards the Greek state or Orthodox Church in general, or Greek civil servants in particular, may be construed as offences in the most literal sense, so it's best to keep your comments on how things work (or not) to yourself. Every year a few foreign louts find themselves in deep trouble over a drunken indiscretion.

Drug offences are treated as major crimes, particularly since there's a growing local use and

addiction problem. The maximum penalty for "causing the use of drugs by someone under 18", for example, is life imprisonment and at least a 10-million-drachma fine. Theory is by no means practice, but foreigners caught in possession of small amounts of grass do get long jail sentences, if there's evidence that they've been supplying others.

If you get arrested for any offence, you have a right to contact your **consulate** who will arrange a lawyer for your defence. Beyond this, there is little they can, or in most cases will, do. There are honorary British consulates on Rhodes, Crete and Corfu, but otherwise the closest bona fide UK diplomatic representation to most islands is in Athens or Thessaloníki.

SEXUAL HARASSMENT

Many women travel independently in Greece without being harassed or feeling intimidated. Greek **machismo**, however, is strong, if less upfront than in, for example, southern Italy. Most of the hassle you are likely to get is from a small minority of Greeks, known as *kamákia* (fish harpoons) who migrate to the main resorts and towns in summer in pursuit of "liberated, fun-loving" tourists.

Indigenous Greeks, who become increasingly protective of you as you become more of a fixture in any one place, treat these outsiders with contempt. Their obvious stake-outs are beach bars and discos. Words worth remembering as unambiguous response include "*pápsteh*" (stop it), "*afístemeh*" (leave me alone) and "*fíyeteh*" (go away), the latter intensified if followed by *"dhró-mo!"* (road, as in "Hit the road!").

Hitching is not advisable for lone women travellers, but **camping** is generally not a problem, though away from recognized sites it is often wise to attach yourself to a local family by making arrangements to use nearby private land. In the more remote mountains and inland areas you may feel more uncomfortable travelling alone. The intensely traditional Greeks may have trouble understanding why you are unaccompanied, and might not welcome your presence in their exclusively male kafenía – often the only place where you can get a drink. Travelling with a man, you're more likely to be treated as a *xéni*, a word meaning both (female) stranger and guest.

Lone men need to be aware of one long-established racket in the port towns of the more populous islands. You may be approached by dubious gents offering to take you for a drink in a nearby bar. This is invariably staffed with hostesses (not really hookers) who convince you to treat them to drinks. At the end of the day you'll be landed with an outrageous bill, some of which goes for the hostess's "commission"; physical threats are brought to bear on reluctant payers.

COSTS, MONEY AND BANKS

The costs of living in Greece have spiralled during the years of EU membership: the days of renting a house for a few thousand drachmas a week are long gone, and food prices at corner shops now differ little from those of other member countries. However, outside the established resorts, travel in the country remains reasonably priced, with the cost of restaurant meals, accommodation and public transport less expensive than anywhere in northern or western Europe except Portugal.

Prices depend on where and when you go. The cities and tourist resorts are usually more expensive and costs increase in July, August and at Easter. **Solo travellers** invariably spend more than if they were sharing food and rooms; an additional frustration is the relative lack of single rooms. **Students** with an International Student Identity Card (ISIC) can get fifty percent discount off admission fees at most archeological sites and museums. Those over 65 can rely on site-admission discounts of twenty-five to thirty percent. These, and other occasional discounts, tend to be more readily available to EU nationals. A FIYTO card (available to non-students) has fewer benefits. Both cards are available from student/youth travel agencies.

SOME BASIC COSTS

In most places you can get by on a **budget** of £20–24/US$32–38.50 a day, which will get you a share of a double room in basic accommodation, breakfast, picnic lunch, a ferry or bus ride and a simple taverna meal. Camping would cut costs marginally. On £29–32/$46–51 a day you could live quite well, and share the cost of renting a motorbike or a small car.

Domestic Aegean **ferries**, a main unavoidable expense, are quite reasonably priced, helped by government subsidies to preserve remote island communities. A deck-class ticket from Pireás, the port of Athens, to Crete or Sámos, both twelve-to-fourteen-hour trips, costs about £12/US$18. For half the cost, there are dozens of closer islands in reach.

The simplest double **room** can generally be had for £11–17/$17.50–27 a night, depending on the location and the plumbing arrangements.

Organized **campsites** cost little more than £2/US$3.25 per person, with similar charges per tent and perhaps 25 percent more for a campervan. With discretion you can camp for free in the more remote, rural areas, though read the warning under "Police, Trouble and Harassment", p.26.

A very basic taverna **meal** with local wine costs around £6/US$10 a head. Add a better bottle of wine, seafood, or more careful cooking, and it could be up to £10/US$16 a head; you'll rarely pay more than that. Sharing seafood, Greek salads and dips is a good way to keep costs down in the better restaurants, but even in the most developed of resorts with inflated "international" menus you'll usually be able to find a more earthy but decent taverna where the locals eat.

CURRENCY

The Greek currency is the **drachma** (*dhrakhmí*), and the exchange rate is currently around 460dr to the pound sterling or 280dr to the US dollar.

The most common **notes** in circulation are those of 100, 200, 500, 1000, 5000 and 10,000 drachmas (*dhrakhmés*), while **coins** come in denominations of 5, 10, 20, 50 and 100dr; you might come across 1dr and 2dr coins, and 50dr bills, too, though they're rarely used these days. In practice, shopkeepers rarely bother with differences of under 10dr – whether in your favour or theirs.

BANKS AND EXCHANGE

Greek **banks** are normally open Mon–Thurs 8.30am–2pm, Fri 8.30am–1.30pm. Certain branches in the major cities and tourist centres are open extra hours in the evenings and on Saturday mornings for exchanging money, while outside these hours larger hotels and travel agencies can often provide this service, albeit sometimes with hefty commissions. Always take your passport with you as proof of identity and be prepared for at least one long queue: usually you have to line up once to have the transaction approved and again to pick up the cash.

The safest and easiest way to carry money is as **travellers' cheques**. These can be obtained from banks (even if you don't have an account) or from offices of Thomas Cook and American Express; you'll pay a commission of between one and two percent. When exchanging money in Greece using travellers' cheques, a flat-rate **commission** of

400–800dr is charged, so it's not a good idea to change really small amounts. You can cash the cheques at most banks and post offices.

Small-denomination foreign bank notes are also extremely useful. Since the freeing up of all remaining currency controls in 1994, a number of authorized **bureaux** for exchanging foreign cash have emerged in Athens and other major tourist centres. When changing small amounts, choose outfits charging a percentage commission (usually one percent) rather than a high flat minimum.

Alternatively, most British banks can issue current account holders with a **Eurocheque** card and chequebook, with which you can pay for things in some shops and withdraw drachmas from cash machines or Greek banks. An annual or biannual fee is payable for this service, plus a two percent processing charge on the debit facility (subject to a minimum), but there's no commission extracted at the Greek bank counter. The current limit is 45,000dr per cheque.

Exchanging money at the **post office** has some considerable advantages in Greece. You miss out on the queues at banks, and small islands and villages without banks almost all have a post office. Commissions levied for both cheques and cash tend, at about 300dr per transaction, to be much lower than at banks. If you have a UK-based Girobank account, you can use your chequebook to get money at remote post offices.

Finally, there is no need to change foreign currency into drachmas **before arrival** unless you're coming in at some ungodly hour to one of the remoter land or sea frontier posts, or on a Sunday. Airport arrival lounges will always have an exchange booth for passengers on incoming international flights.

CREDIT CARDS AND CASH DISPENSERS

Major credit cards are not accepted by the cheaper hotels and tavernas, but they're useful – indeed almost essential – for renting cars, for example, for buying Olympic Airways tickets, and for souvenirs.

If you run short of money, you can get an over-the-counter cash advance on a **credit card**, but be warned that the minimum amount is 15,000dr. The Emborikí Trápeza (Commercial Bank) handles Visa, and the Ethnikí Trápeza (National Bank) services Mastercard customers. However, there is usually a two percent credit-card charge, often unfavourable rates and always interminable delays while transaction approval is sought by telex.

It is far easier to use the ample and growing network of Greek **cash dispensers** – don't forget the PIN numbers for your various debit and credit cards. The most useful and well distributed are those of the National Bank/Ethniki Trapeza, which take Cirrus and Mastercard; the Commercial Bank/Emboriki Trapeza, which accepts Plus and Visa; and the Trápeza Pastes/Credit Bank, which accepts Visa and American Express. In the larger airports the Commercial and National banks often have cash dispensers in the arrivals hall. These days, almost any island with more a population of more than a few thousand – and/or substantial tourist traffic – will have at least one cash dispenser.

EMERGENCY CASH

All told, learning and using the PIN numbers for your various cards is the quickest and least expensive way of securing moderate amounts of emergency funds from home. But in an emergency, you can arrange to have **money sent** from abroad to a bank in Greece. Receiving funds via telex takes a minimum of three days and often up to six days, so be prepared for delays. From the UK, a bank charge of three percent, or minimum £17, maximum £35, is levied. Bank drafts can also be sent, with higher commission rates.

Funds can also be sent via Western Union Money Transfer (☎0800/833833 in the UK,

1-800/325-6000 in North America). Fees depend on the destination and the amount being transferred, but as examples, wiring £400–500 should cost around £37, while $1000 will cost around $75. The funds should be available for collection at Western Union's local representative (often Trapeza Ergasias/Ergo Bank) within minutes of being sent. The American Express MoneyGram (☎1-800/543-4080 in North America) is now only available to American Express cardholders.

CURRENCY REGULATIONS

Since 1994, Greek currency restrictions no longer apply to Greek nationals and other EU-member citizens, and the drachma is freely convertible. Arcane rules may still apply to arrivals from North America, Australia or non-EU European countries, but you'd have to be extremely unlucky to fall foul of them.

If, however, you have any reason to believe that you'll be acquiring large quantities of drachmas – from work or sale of goods – declare everything on arrival, then request (and save) pink, personalized **receipts** for each exchange transaction. Otherwise you may find that you can only re-exchange a small sum of drachmas on departure; even at the best of times many banks stock a limited range of foreign notes – your best bet is often the exchange booth in airport arrivals (not departures). These pink receipts are also essential for obtaining a visa extension (see "Visas and Red Tape" p.22).

INFORMATION AND MAPS

The **National Tourist Organization of Greece** (Ellinikós Organismós Tourismoú, or EOT; GNTO abroad) maintains offices in most European capitals, plus major cities in North America and Australia (see box for addresses). It publishes an impressive array of free, glossy, regional pamphlets, which are good for getting an idea of where you want to go, even if the actual text should be taken with an occasional spoonful of salt. Also available from the EOT are a reason-able fold-out map of Greece and a large number of brochures on special interests and festivals.

TOURIST OFFICES

In Greece, you will find **EOT offices** in most of the larger towns and resorts. The principal Athens office is at Amerikís 2, just up from Stadhíou. Here, in addition to the usual leaflets, you can pick up weekly **schedules** for the inter-island **ferries** – not 100 percent reliable, but useful as a guideline. The EOT staff are themselves very helpful for advice on **ferries,** and **bus** departures to the various ports of Attica.

Where there is no EOT office, you can get information (and often a range of leaflets) from municipally run tourist offices or from the **Tourist Police**. The latter are basically a branch (often just a single delegate) of the local police. They can sometimes provide you with lists of rooms to let, which they regulate.

MAPS

Maps are an endless source of confusion and sometimes outright disinformation in Greece. Each cartographic company seems to have its own peculiar system of transcribing Greek letters

---

GREEK NATIONAL TOURIST OFFICES ABROAD

Australia
51 Pitt St, Sydney, NSW 2000 (☎02/9241 1663).

Britain
4 Conduit St, London W1R 0DJ (☎0171/734 5997).

Canada
1300 Bay St, Upper Level, Toronto, ON M5R 3K8 (☎416/968-2220); 1223 rue de la Montagne, H3G 1Z2, Montreal, Quebec (☎514/871-1535).

Denmark
Copenhagen Vester Farimagsgade 1,2 DK 1606-Kobenhavn V (☎325-332).

Netherlands
Leidsestraat 13, NS 1017 Amsterdam (☎20/254-212).

Norway
Ovre Stottsgate 15B, 0157 Oslo 1 (☎2/426-501).

Sweden
Grev Turigatan 2, PO Box 5298, 10246 Stockholm (☎8/679 6480).

USA
645 Fifth Ave, New York, NY 10022 (☎212/421-5777); 168 North Michigan Ave, Chicago, IL (☎312/782-1084); 611 West 6th St, Los Angeles, CA(☎213/626-6696).

If your home country isn't listed here, apply to the embassy.
Note that there are no Greek tourist offices in Ireland or New Zealand.

MAP OUTLETS

UK
London
National Map Centre, 22–24 Caxton St, SW1H
0QU (☎0171/222 2466); Stanfords, 12–14 Long
Acre, WC2E 9LP (☎0171/836 1321); Daunt Books,
83 Marylebone High Street, London W1M 3DE
(☎0171/224 2295). The Travel Bookshop, 13–15
Blenheim Crescent, London W11 2EE
(☎0171/229 5260).

Glasgow
John Smith and Sons, 57–61 St Vincent St
(☎0141/221 7472).

Maps by mail or phone order are available from
Stanfords (☎0171/836 1321).

USA
Chicago
Rand McNally, 444 N Michigan Ave, IL 60611;
(☎312/321-1751).

New York
The Complete Traveler Bookstore, 199 Madison
Ave, NY 10016; (☎212/685-9007). Rand McNally,
150 E 52nd St, NY 10022; (☎212/758-7488).
Traveler's Bookstore, 22 W 52nd St, NY 10019;
(☎212/664-0995).

San Francisco
The Complete Traveler Bookstore,
3207Fillmore St, CA 92123; (☎415/923-1511);
Rand McNally, 595 Market St, CA 94105;
(☎415/777-3131).

Santa Barbara
Map Link Inc., 30 S La Patera Lane, Unit 5, Santa
Barbara CA 93107 (☎805/692-6777 or fax 962
0884).

Seattle
Elliot Bay Book Company, 101 S Main St, WA
98104; (☎206/624-6600).

Washington DC
The Map Store Inc., 1636 Ist NW, Washington,
DC 20006 (☎ 202/628-2608).

Note: Rand McNally now has more than twenty
stores across the US; call ☎1-800/333-0136 (ext
2111) for the address of your nearest store, or for
direct mail maps.

CANADA
Montreal
Ulysses Travel Bookshop, 4176 St-Denis;
(☎514/843-9447).

Toronto
Open Air Books and Maps, 25 Toronto St, M5R
2C1; (☎416/363-0719).

Vancouver
World Wide Books and Maps, 736a Granville St
V6Z 1G3; (☎604/687-3320).

AUSTRALIA
Sydney
Travel Bookshop, 20 Bridge St (☎02/9241 3554).

Melbourne
Bowyangs, 372 Little Bourke St (☎03/9670 4383).

Adelaide
The Map Shop, 16a Peel St (☎08/8231 2033).

Perth
Perth Map Centre, 891 Hay St (☎08/9322 5733).

NEW ZEALAND
Auckland
Specialty Maps, 58 Albert St (☎09/307 2217).

---

into English – and these, as often as not, do not
match the transliterations on the road signs.

The most reliable **road maps** of Greece are the
two Geo Center maps "Greece and the Islands" and
"Greek Islands/Aegean Sea", which together cover
the country at a scale of 1:300,000. The single-sided
fold-up Freytag-Berndt 1:650,000, with an index, is
very nearly as good. Despite recent revisions and
updating, Michelin #980 remains a third choice. All
these are widely available in Britain and North
America, though less easily in Greece; see the list
of map outlets below. Freytag-Berndt also publishes a series of more detailed maps on various
regions of Greece, such as the Peloponnese and the

Cyclades; these are best bought overseas from specialist outlets, though in Greece they are re-jacket-
ed and distributed by Efstathiadis.

Maps of **individual islands** are more easily
available on the spot, and while most are wildly
inaccurate or obsolete, with strange hieroglyphic
symbology, a rare few are reliable and up-to-date.

HIKING/TOPOGRAPHICAL MAPS

Hiking/topographical maps, subject to uneven
quality and availability, are gradually improving.
Road Editions (41 Ilía Ilíou St, 117 43 Athens ☎ 92
96 541) have produced a series of maps with the
co-operation of the **Army Geographical Service**

(*Yeografikí Ipiresía Stratoú*); these are available only in Athens. The YIS source maps are, unfortunately, unreliable in the matter of trails and new roads, but extremely accurate for natural features and village positions. If you want to obtain these for certain islands (see below), visit the YIS at Evelpídhon 4, north of Aréos Park in Athens, on Monday, Wednesday or Friday from 8am to noon only. All foreigners must leave their passport with the gate guard; EU citizens may proceed directly to the sales hall, where efficient, computerized transactions take just a few minutes. Other nationals will probably have to go upstairs for an interview;

if you don't speak reasonably good Greek, it's best to have a Greek friend get them for you.

As of writing, topographic maps covering Crete, the Dodecanese, the east Aegean, Skýros and northern Corfu are still off-limits to all foreigners, as well as Greeks. With matters unsettled across the Balkans, previous plans to lift such restrictions have been shelved indefinitely. A German company, **Harms**, has released a series of five maps at 1:80,000 scale which cover Crete from west to east and show, with poor-to-middling accuracy, many hiking routes – the only thing available until and unless the YIS declassifies this area.

GETTING AROUND

Island-hopping is an essential feature of a Greek holiday; the ferry network – supplemented in season by hydrofoils – is extensive, and will eventually get you to any of the inhabited isles. Planes are expensive, at three to four times the cost of a deck-class ferry ticket and almost twice as much as first or cabin class. They are, however, useful for saving time at the start of finish of a visit, providing critical links between smaller islands and Athens, Thessaloníki, Rhodes and Crete. Once on the islands themselves, buses provide basic connections, which most tourists choose to supplement by renting a moped, motorbike or car.

FERRIES

There are three different varieties of boat carrying passengers (and usually vehicles) around the islands: medium-sized to large **ordinary ferries** (which operate the main services), **hydrofoils** (run by Ceres "Flying Dolphins", Ilio Lines and Dodecanese Hydrofoils, among several companies), and local **kaïkia** (small boats which do short hops and excursions in season). Costs are very reasonable on the longer journeys, though proportionately more expensive for shorter, inter-island connections. Short-haul lines with monopolies – for example Alexandhroúpoli–Samothráki and Kými–Skýros – are invariably overpriced.

We've indicated most of the **ferry connections**, both on the maps (see pp.62–63 for a general picture) and in the "Travel Details" at the end of each chapter. Don't take our listings as exhaustive or wholly reliable, however, as schedules are notoriously erratic, and be aware that we have given details essentially for departures between June and September. **Out-of-season** departure frequencies are severely reduced, with many islands connected only once or twice a week. However, in spring or autumn those ferries that do operate are often compelled by the transport ministry to call at extra islands, making possible some interesting connections.

The most reliable, up-to-date information is available from the local **port police** (*limenarkhío*), which maintains offices at Pireás

(☎01/42 26 000) and on or near the harbours of all fair-sized islands. Smaller places may only have a *limenikós stathmós* (marine post), often just a single room with a VHF radio. Their officers rarely speak much English, but keep complete schedules posted – and, meteorological report in hand, are the final arbiters of whether a ship will sail or not in stormy weather conditions. *Apagorevtikó*, or obligatory halt of all seaborne traffic, is applied when winds exceed of Force 7 on the Beaufort scale; hydrofoils tend to be grounded with anything in excess of Force 6.

REGULAR FERRIES

On most ferry routes, your only consideration will be getting a boat that leaves on the day, and for the island, that you want. However, when sailing from **Pireás**, the port of Athens, to the Cyclades or Dodecanese islands, you should have quite a range of choice and may want to bear in mind a few of the factors below.

Most importantly, bear in mind that **routes** taken and the speed of the boats vary enormously. Before buying a ticket it's wise to establish how many stops there'll be before your island, and the estimated time of arrival. Especially in high season, early arrival is critical in getting what may be a very limited stock of accommodation.

The boats themselves have improved somewhat recently – just about the only ferry you might want to avoid if you have the choice are the malodourous *Áyios Rafael*, in the north Aegean. You will more often than not encounter a former English Channel or Scandinavian fjord ferry, rechristened and enjoying a new (and often final) lease of life in the Aegean.

Regular ferry **tickets** are, in general, best bought on the day of departure, unless you need to reserve a cabin berth or space for a car. Buying tickets in advance will tie you down to a particular ferry at a particular time – and innumerable factors can make you regret that, most obviously bad weather. There are only three periods of the year – March 23–25, the week before and after Easter, and mid-August – when ferries need to be booked at least a couple of days in advance. Following cases in 1996 of captains loading ferries to double their rated capacity, obligatory, computerized advance ticketing was to be universally introduced as from 1997 – but in the end this failed to happen. Until further notice (probably 1999), you can still buy a ticket once on board

with no penalty, despite what travel agents may tell you. Ticket prices for each route are currently set by the transport ministry and should not differ among ships or agencies.

The cheapest class of ticket, which you'll probably automatically be sold, is **deck class**, variously called *tríti* or *gámma*. This gives you the run of most boats except for the upper-class restaurant and bar. It's often well worth the few thousand extra drachmas for a **cabin bunk**, especially if you can share with friends; first-class cabin facilities usually cost scarcely less than a plane flight and are not terrific value – the only difference between first and second being the presence of a bathroom in the cabin.

Occasionally, with non-computerized companies, you will be sold a cabin berth at an intermediate port only to find that they are "full" when the boat arrives. Pursers will usually not refund you the difference between a cabin and third class. Your first- or second-class fare entitles you to a bunk, and this is clearly stated (in Greek) on the verso of your ticket. Make a scene if necessary until you are accommodated – there are almost always cabins in the bilge, set aside for the crew but generally unused, where you can sleep.

Motorbikes and **cars** get issued extra tickets, in the latter case up to four times the passenger fare. This obviously limits the number of islands you'll want to take a car to – it's really only worth it for the larger ones like Crete, Rhodes, Khíos, Lésvos, Sámos or Kefalloniá. Even with these, unless you're planning a stay of more than four days, you may find it cheaper to leave your car in Pireás or Thessaloníki and rent another on arrival.

Most ferries sell a limited range of **food**, though it tends to be overpriced and mediocre in quality. Honourable exceptions are the decent, reasonable meals served on the ferries to Crete, and the DANE Dodecanese ferries. On the short hops in the Argo-Saronic, Cyclades and Sporades, it is well worth stocking up with your own provisions.

HYDROFOILS

Hydrofoils – more commonly known as *dhelfínia* (after the Ceres "Flying Dolphins") – are roughly twice as fast (and at least twice as expensive) as ordinary ferries. They're a useful alternative to regular ferries if you are pushed for time; networks seem to be growing each year, so it's worth asking about services, even if they are not mentioned in this guide. Their drawback is that they were originally designed for cruising on placid Russian or Polish rivers, and are quite literally out of their depth on the Aegean; thus they are extremely sensitive to bad weather, and not for the seasick-prone. Most of these services don't operate – or are heavily reduced – from October to June and are also prone to arbitrary cancellation if not enough passengers turn up.

At present, hydrofoils operate among the **Argo-Saronic islands** close to Athens, down the east coast of the Peloponnese to Monemvassía and **Kýthira**, among the **Sporades** (Évvia, Skýros, Skiáthos, Skópelos and Alónissos), between Thessaloníki, Vólos and Áyios Konstandínos on the mainland to the Sporades and northern Évvia, between Kavála and **Thássos**, between Alexandhroúpoli and Samothráki plus occasionally Límnos, among certain of the **Cyclades** (Ándros, Tínos, Mýkonos, Páros, Náxos, Amorgós, the minor islets, Íos, Thíra – and Crete), and in the **Dodecanese** among Rhodes, Kós, Kálymnos, Léros and Pátmos, with regular forays up to Sámos or less often over to Tílos and Níssyros. The principal **mainland ports** are Zea and Flísvos marinas in Pireás, Rafína, Vólos, Áyios Konstandínos, Kavála, Thessaloníki and Alexandhroúpoli.

Schedules and **tickets** for the Ceres company, which operates the far-flung "Flying Dolphin" lines, are available in Athens from Filellínon 3, off Platía Sýndagma (☎01/32 44 600); in Pireás from Ceres Hydrofoils, Aktí Themistokléous 8 (☎01/12 80 001, fax 12 83 626); in Vólos from Tsoulos, Andonopoúlou 9–11 (☎0421/39 786); and in Thessaloníki from Kriti Travel, Íonos Dhragoúmi 1 (☎031/547 454). The main offices of Mamidhakis-Dodecanese Hydrofoils are Platía Kýprou 6, Ródhos (☎0241/24 000), while Ilios Lines are at Goúnari 2, Pireás (☎42 24 980). In the past, only Ceres has issued seasonal schedule booklets in advance, and run approximately in accordance with them.

KAÏKIA AND OTHER SMALL FERRIES

In season **kaïkia** (caiques) and small ferries of a few hundred tonnes' displacement sail between adjacent islands and to a few of the more obscure ones. These can be extremely useful and often very pleasant, but are no cheaper than mainline services. Indeed if they are technically **tourist agency charters**, and not passenger lines controlled by the transport ministry, they tend to be

quite expensive, with pressure to buy return fares (one-ways are almost always available). We have tried to detail the more regular links in the text, though many, inevitably, depend on the whims of local boat-owners. The only firm information is to be had from the quayside travel agency handling specific craft. Kaïkia and small ferries, despite appearances, have a good safety record; indeed it's the larger, overloaded car-ferries that have in the past run into trouble.

DOMESTIC FLIGHTS

Olympic Airways and its subsidiary Olympic Aviation operate most **domestic flights** within Greece. They cover a fairly wide network of islands and larger towns, though most routes are to and from Athens, or the northern capital of Thessaloníki. **Schedules** can be picked up at Olympic offices abroad (see "Getting There" sections pp.3–14) or through their branch offices or representatives in Greece, which are maintained in almost every town or island of any size.

Fares, including domestic airport tax of about £8.50/$14, usually work out around three to four times the cost of an equivalent bus or ferry journey, but on certain inter-island hauls poorly served by boat (Rhodes–Kastellórizo or Kárpathos–Sitía, for example), you might consider this time well bought. For obscure reasons, flights between Athens and Mílos, Kýthira and Préveza (for Lefkádha) are slightly better value per air mile, so take advantage.

Although airline operation is deregulated in Greece, thus far the only **private companies** to successfully challenge the Olympic monopoly are Air Greece and Kriti Air, which run internal flights from Athens to major destinations like Corfu, Rhodes and Crete. These generally undercut the equivalent Olympic Airlines flights by quite a margin, though departure frequencies tend to be sparse.

Island flights are often full in peak season; if they're part of your plans, **reserve** at least a week in advance. Domestic air tickets are **non-refundable** but you can change your flight details, space permitting, as late as a day before your original intended departure, without penalty.

Like ferries, flights can be **cancelled** in bad weather, since many services are on small, 30- to 68-seat turbo-prop planes that won't fly in strong winds or conditions of poor visibility. That said, a flight on a Dornier puddle-jumper is recommended at least once; you fly low enough to pick out every island feature.

The small aircraft also mean that a 15-kilo domestic baggage **weight limit** is fairly strictly enforced; if, however, you've just arrived from overseas, or purchased your ticket outside Greece, you are allowed the 23-kilo standard international limit. All services operated on the domestic network are **non-smoking**.

ISLAND GROUND TRANSPORT

Most islands have some kind of bus service, but most visitors prefer to rent a two- or four-wheeled vehicle; even if you just do so for a day, you will get the measure of a small island, and work out where you want to be based.

BUSES

Bus services on the **major routes** are highly efficient and frequent. On **secondary roads** they're less regular, but even the most remote villages will be connected – at least on weekdays – by a school or market bus to the provincial capital. As these often leave shortly after dawn, an alarm clock can be a useful travel aid. Coming in the opposite direction, these local buses usually leave the county town at about 2pm. On the **islands** there are usually buses to connect the port and main town for ferry arrivals or departures.

The network is nationally run by a single syndicate known as the **KTEL** (Kratikó Tamío Ellinikón Leoforíon). In medium-sized island towns there can be several scattered terminals for services in different directions (as at Iráklion, Crete) or separate terminals for suburban and long-distance routes (Khíos, Mytilíni), so make sure you have the right station for your departure.

Buses are amazingly **prompt** as a rule, so be there in plenty of time for scheduled departures. On smaller rural/island routes, it's generally first-come, first-served with some standing allowed, and tickets dispensed on board by an *ispráktoros* or conductor.

MOTORBIKES, MOPEDS AND BIKES

The cult of the **motorcycle** is highly developed in Greece, presided over by a jealous deity apparently requiring regular human sacrifice. Accidents among both foreign and local bikers are routine occurrences, with annual fatalities edging into two figures on the busier islands. Some pack-

age companies have even taken to warning clients in print against renting them, not coincidentally to make more money on group excursions, but with caution and common sense – and an eye to increasingly enforced regulations – riding a bike on a island should be a lot safer than piloting one through New York or London.

Many tourists come to grief on rutted dirt tracks or astride mechanically dodgy machines. In other cases **accidents** are due to attempts to cut corners, in all senses, by riding two to an underpowered scooter simply not designed to propel such a load. Don't be tempted by this apparent economy – you won't regret getting two separate mopeds, or one powerful 125cc bike to share – and remember that you're likely to be charged an exorbitant sum for any repairs if you crash. Above all, make sure your **travel insurance policy** covers motorcycle accidents.

One worthwhile precaution is to wear a **crash helmet** (*kránio*); most rental outfits will offer you one, and some will make you sign a waiver of liability if you refuse it. Helmet-wearing is in fact required by law, and more and more riders are having to comply as police set up roadblocks to catch offenders. Reputable establishments demand a full motorcycle driving licence for any engine over 75cc, and you will usually have to leave your passport as security.

Mopeds and small motor scooters, known in Greek as **papákia** (little ducks) after their characteristic noise, are good transport for all but the hilliest islands. They're available for rent on most islands, at any minimally developed resort. Motorcycles and scooters cost around 4000dr a day and upwards, mopeds about 3000dr. These specimen rates can be reduced with bargaining outside of peak season, or if you negotiate for a longer period of rental.

Before riding off, make sure you check the bike's mechanical state, since many are only cosmetically maintained and repaired. Bad brakes and worn spark plugs are the most common defects; dealers often keep the front brakes far too loose, with the commendable intention of preventing you going over the handlebars. If you break down it's your responsibility to return the machine, so take down the phone number of whoever rents it to you in case it gives out in the middle of nowhere; better agencies may offer a free retrieval service.

As far as **models** go, the three-speed Honda 50 and its clones the Suzuki Townmate and

Yamaha Birdie are the favourites; gears are shifted with an easy-to-learn left-foot pedal action, and (very important) they can be push-started if the ignition fails. These can carry two, though if you have a choice, the Cub 70–90cc series gives more power at nominal extra cost. A larger Vespa scooter is more comfortable on long trips, with capacious baskets, but has less stability, especially off paved surfaces. The Suzuki Address and its clones, though also comfortable for 30-km trips, is thirsty on fuel and most models cannot be push-started. Smaller but surprisingly powerful Piaggio Si or Monte Carlo models can take one person almost everywhere, carry two baskets or bags and are automatic action. Bungy cords (*khtapódhi* or "octopus" in slang) for tying down bundles are available on request.

If you intend to stay for some time in the warmer months, it's well worth considering the **purchase** of a moped or motorbike once in Greece. They are relatively inexpensive to run or repair, don't cause problems with passport stamps, can be taken on the ferries very cheaply, and can be resold easily upon departure.

Incidentally, the smallest grade of **mopeds** and **scooters** consume **mix**, a red- or green-tinted fuel dispensed from a transparent cylindrical device. This contains a minimum of three-percent two-stroke oil by volume; when unavailable, you brew it up yourself by adding to super-grade fuel the necessary amount of separately bottled two-stroke oil (*ládhi dhýo trokhón* in Greek). It's wise to err on the generous side – say five percent – or you risk the engine seizing up.

CYCLING

Cycling on the islands is not such hard going as you might imagine (except in mid-summer), especially on one of the mountain bikes that are rapidly supplanting the old boneshakers at rental outfits; they rarely cost more than 2000dr a day. You do, however, need steady nerves, as roads are generally narrow with no verges or bike lanes (except on Kós), and many Greek drivers consider bicycles a lower form of life.

If you have your own mountain or touring bike, you might consider taking it along by **plane** (it's free if within your 23-kilo allowance). Once in Greece you should be able to take a bike for free on most of the **ferries**, and with a little persuasion on the roof of **buses**. Any spare parts you might need, however, are best brought along, since most **specialist bike shops** are on the mainland.

DRIVING

Cars have obvious advantages for getting to the more inaccessible parts of larger islands, but this is one of the more expensive countries in Europe to **rent a car**. If you drive **your own vehicle** to and through Greece, via EU member states, you no longer require a Green Card. In accordance with recent directives, **insurance** contracted in any EU member state is valid in any other, but in many cases this is only third party cover – the statutory legal minimum. Competition in the industry is so intense, however, that many UK insurers will throw in full, pan-European cover for free or for a nominal sum, up to sixty days; shop around if necessary.

Upon arrival with EU number plates, your EU passport should no longer get a carnet stamp, and the car is in theory free to circulate in the country until its road tax or insurance expires. Other nationalities will get a non-EU car entered in their passport; the **carnet** normally allows you to keep a vehicle in Greece for up to six months, exempt from road tax. It is difficult, though not impossible, to leave the country without the vehicle; the nearest customs post will seal it for you (while you fly back home for a family emergency, for example) but you must find a Greek national to act as your guarantor, and possibly pay storage.

CAR RENTAL

Car rental on the Greek islands starts at £180/US$290 a week in high season for the smallest model, including unlimited mileage, tax and insurance. Tour operators' and local agents' brochures threaten alarming rates of £220/$350 for the same period but, except in August, no rental company expects to fetch that price for a car. Outside peak season, at the smaller **local outfits**, you can sometimes get terms of about £25/$40 per day, all inclusive, with better rates for three days or more. Open jeeps, an increasingly popular extravagance, begin at about £35/$55 per day, rising to £55/$90 at busy times. Except in the largest island port towns, rental cars can be unavailable between late October and late April, since insurance policies may only be paid for the six summer months.

Note that brochure prices in Greece almost never include tax, **collision damage waiver** (CDW) and personal insurance. CDW in particular is absolutely vital, as the cover included by law in the basic rental fee is inadequate, so check the fine print on your contract. Be wary of the ham-

CAR RENTAL AGENCIES

UK		Europe by Car	☎1-800/223-1516;
Avis	☎0990/900500.		212/245-1713.
Budget	☎0800/181181.	Hertz	☎1-800/654-3001;
Europcar/InterRent	☎0345/222525.		in Canada ☎1-800/263-0600.
Hertz	☎0990/996699.	National	☎1-800/CAR RENT.
Holiday Autos	☎0990/300400.	Thrifty	☎1-800/367-2277.
Transhire	☎0171/978 1922.		
Thrifty	☎ 0990/168238.	**AUSTRALIA**	
		Avis	☎1800/225 533.
USA		Budget	☎13 2727.
Alamo	☎1-800/522-9696.	Hertz	☎13 3039.
Auto Europe	☎1-800/223-5555.		
Avis	☎1-800/331-1084.	**NEW ZEALAND**	
Budget	☎1-800/527-0700.	Avis	☎09/526 2847.
Camwell Holiday Autos	☎1-800/422-7737.	Budget	☎09/375 2222.
Dollar	☎1-800/800-6000.	Hertz	☎09/309 0989.

mering cars get on dirt tracks: damage to tyres, windscreen and the underside of the vehicle are nearly always excluded from coverage. All agencies will want either a credit card or a large cash **deposit** up front; minimum age requirements vary from 21 to 25. In theory an **International Driving Licence** is also needed, but in practice European, Australasian and North American ones are honoured.

In **peak season**, you may get a better price by booking through one of the **foreign companies** that deal with local firms than if you negotiate for rental in Greece itself. One of the most competitive companies, which can arrange for cars to be picked up at most airports, is Holiday Autos; Transhire is another (see box above for phone numbers). Most package operators can also offer car rental in Greece, though their rates are generally higher than the specialist rental agents. **In Greece**, Payless, European, Thrifty, and Just are reliable medium-sized companies with branches on many islands; all tend to be cheaper than (and just as reputable) as the biggest international operators Budget, Europcar, Hertz and Avis. Specific local recommendations are given in the guide.

In terms of available **models**, the more competitive companies tend to offer the Subaro M80 or Vivio, the Fiat Cinquecento and the Suzuki Alto 800 as A-group cars, and Opel (Vauxhall) Corsa, Nissan Micra or Fiat Uno/Punto in the B-group. The Suzuki Alto 600, Fiat Panda or Seat Marbella should be avoided if at all possible. The standard four-wheel-drive options are Suzuki jeeps, mostly open – great for bashing down rutted tracks.

DRIVING IN GREECE

Greece has the highest **accident rate** in Europe after Portugal, and many of the roads can be quite perilous – asphalt can turn into a one-lane surface or a dirt track without warning on the smaller routes. Uphill drivers insist on their right of way, as do those first to approach a one-lane bridge – headlights flashed at you mean the opposite of what they mean in the UK or North America, signifying that the driver is coming through or overtaking.

Wearing a **seatbelt** is compulsory and children under ten are not allowed to sit in the front seats. First-aid kits are mandatory. If you are involved in any kind of accident it's illegal to drive away, and you can be held at a police station for up to 24 hours. If this happens, ring your consulate immediately, in order to get a lawyer (you have this right). Don't make a statement to anyone who doesn't speak, and write, very good English.

Tourists with proof of AA/RAC or similar membership are given free road assistance from ELPA, the Greek equivalent, which runs **breakdown services** based in Corfu, Rhodes and Crete, plus many smaller, loosely affiliated garages. In an **emergency** ring their road assistance service on ☎104, anywhere in the country. Many car rental companies have an agreement with ELPA's competitors, Hellas Service and Express Service, but they're prohibitively expensive to summon on your own – it costs over 25,000dr to enrol you as an "instant member" in their scheme.

Petrol/gasoline currently costs 225–240dr a litre for unleaded (*amólyvdhi*) or super. Most stations close at 7 or 8pm sharp, and nearly as many are shut all weekend, so keep a full jerrycan at all times. Filling stations run by international companies (BP, Mobil and Shell) usually take credit cards; Greek chains like EKO, Mamidhakis and Elinoil are just beginning to, with swipe readers in use.

TAXIS

Greek **taxis** are among the cheapest in Western Europe and well worth making use of (though see the caveats in "Travelling via Athens and Pireás" on p.17, and on p.27).

Use of the metre is supposedly mandatory, though on a few islands like Kálymnos and Léros there are taxis covering set routes for a fixed price. Elsewhere, Tariff "1" applies within city or town limits, with Tariff "2" (double rate) applying outside them or between midnight and 5am. The flag falls at 200dr throughout the country. There are also surcharges for entering a ferry harbour (currently 100dr), leaving an airport (200dr), and per large bag (50dr). For a week or so before and after Christmas and Easter, a *filodhórima* or bonus is levied. If you summon a taxi by phone, the metre starts running from the moment the driver begins heading towards you, with an additional "rendezvous" charge applicable. All of this may legitimately bump up the fare from the basic meter reading of about 1700dr per ten rural kilometres.

ACCOMMODATION

There are huge numbers of beds for tourists on the Greek islands, and most of the year you can rely on turning up pretty much anywhere and finding a room – if not in a hotel, then in a private house or block of rooms (the standard island accommodation). Only from mid-July to early September, the country's high season, are you likely to experience problems. At these times, it is worth striking off the standard tourist routes, turning up at each new place early in the day, and taking whatever is available in the hope

that you will be able to exchange it for something better later on.

HOTELS

Hotels are **categorized** by the tourist police from "Luxury" down to the almost extinct "E-class", and all except the top category have to keep within set price limits. Letter ratings are supposed to correspond to facilities available, though in practice categorization can depend on such factors as location within a resort and "influence" with tourism authorities. D-class usually have attached baths, while in C-class this is mandatory, along with a bar or breakfast area. The additional presence of a pool and/or tennis court, rooftop in cities if necessary, will attract a B-class rating, while A-class hotels must have a bar, restaurant and extensive common areas. Often they, and the De Luxe outfits (essentially self-contained complexes), back on to a beach.

In terms of **food**, C-class are only required to provide the most rudimentary of continental breakfasts – you may choose not to take, or pay for it – while B-class and above will usually offer some sort of buffet breakfast including cheese, cold cuts, sausages, eggs, and so on. With some outstanding exceptions, lunch or supper at hotel restaurants will be bland and poor value.

ROOM PRICES

All establishments listed in this book have been **price-coded** according to the scale outlined below. The rates quoted represent the **cheapest available room** in high season; all are prices for a double room, except for category ①, which are per person rates for hostels. Out of season, prices can drop by up to fifty percent, especially if you negotiate rates for a stay of three or more nights. Single rooms, where available, cost around seventy percent of the price of a double.

Rented private rooms on the islands usually fall into the ② or ③ categories, depending on their location and facilities, and the season; a few in the ④ category are more like plush self-catering apartments. They are not generally available from late October to the beginning of April, when only hotels tend to remain open.

You should expect rooms in all ① and most ② accommodation to be without private bath, though there may a basic washbasin in the room. In the ③ category and above there are usually private facilities. Some of the cheap places will also have more expensive rooms including en suite facilities – and vice versa, especially in the case of singles tucked in less desirable corners of the building.

Prices for rooms and hotels should by law be **displayed** on the back of the door of your room, or over the reception desk. If you feel you're being overcharged at a place which is officially registered, threatening to report it to the tourist office or police – who will generally adopt your side in such cases – should be enough to elicit compliance. Small amounts over the posted price may be legitimately explained by municipal tax or out-of-date forms. Occasionally you may find that you have bargained so well, or arrived so far out of season, that you are actually paying less than you're supposed to.

① 1400–2000dr	③ 6000–8000dr	⑤ 12,000–16,000dr
② 4000–6000dr	④ 8000–12,000dr	⑥ 16,000dr and upwards

ROOMS

The most common island accommodation are privately let **rooms** – *dhomátia* in Greek. These are regulated and officially divided into three classes (A down to C), according to facilities. These days the bulk of them are in new, purpose-built low-rise buildings, but a few are still actually in people's homes, where you'll occasionally be treated to disarming hospitality.

Dhomátia are usually better value than hotels, and in general spotlessly clean. At their (now vanishing) simplest, you'll get a bare, concrete room, with a hook on the back of the door and toilet facilities (cold water only) outside in the courtyard. At the fancier end of the scale, they are modern, fully furnished places with an en-suite, marble-clad bathroom and a fully equipped kitchen shared by the guests. Between these two extremes you may find that there's choice of rooms at various prices (they'll usually show you the most expensive first). Price and quality are not necessarily directly linked: always ask to see the room before agreeing to take it and settling on the price.

Hot water is more reliably provided by an electric boiler than by rooftop solar units, which tend to run out or cool off by sunset; "rooms" proprietors either jealously guard the boiler controls or entrust you with its workings. The "I" position is usually on, with a glow-light indicator on the tank; never leave the switch on while bathing, you risk electric shock and/or burning out the heating element.

Areas to look for rooms, and suggestions for the best options, are again included in the guide. But as often as not, the rooms find you: owners descend on ferry or bus arrivals to fill any space they have, sometimes waving photos of the premises. In smaller places you'll often see rooms advertised – sometimes in German (zimmer); the Greek signs to look for are "Enikiazómena Dhomátia" or "Enikiázonteh Dhomátia". In the more developed resorts where package clients predominate, dhomátia owners will often demand that you stay at least three days, or even a week.

In **winter**, from November to early April, private rooms are closed pretty much across the board to keep the hotels in business. There's no point in traipsing about hoping to find exceptions – most rooms owners obey the system very strictly. If they don't, the owners will find you themselves and, watching out for hotel rivals, guide you back to their place.

It has become standard practice for rooms proprietors to ask to keep your **passport** – ostensibly "for the tourist police", but in reality to prevent you skipping out with an unpaid bill. Some owners may be satisfied with just taking down the details, as in hotels, and they'll almost always return documents once you get to know them, or if you need them for another purpose.

VILLAS AND LONG-TERM RENTALS

The easiest – and usually most economical – way to arrange a **villa rental** is through one of the package holiday companies detailed on p.5. They represent some superb places, from simple to luxury, and costs can be very reasonable, especially if shared between several people. On the islands, a few local travel agents arrange villa rentals, though these are mostly places the overseas companies gave a miss on or couldn't fill. Out of season, you can sometimes get a good deal on villa or apartment rental for a month or more by asking around locally, though in these days of EU convergence and the increasing desirability of Greece as a year-round residence, "good deal" means anything under 45,000dr for a large studio (garsoniéra) or small one-bedroom flat.

HOSTELS AND MONASTERIES

The Greek islands are not exactly packed with **youth hostels** (*xenón neótitos* in the singular) – just three on Thíra, about a half dozen on Crete, many of them non-IYHF-affiliated – but these tend to be fairly easy-going affairs: slightly run-down and a far cry from similar north-European institutions. Some offer **roofspace**, providing a mattress and a pleasantly cool night under the stars. Competition from low-budget rooms means that they are not as cost-effective as elsewhere in Europe. Charges for a dormitory bed are around £3–5/US$5–8 a night; most hostels have a curfew of 11pm or midnight.

Greek **monasteries** and **convents** have a tradition of putting up travellers (of the appropriate sex). On the larger islands, this is still a customary – if steadily decreasing – practice, used mostly by villagers on pilgrimage; on the smaller islands dominated by tourism, monasteries tend to be unstaffed, and if they do provide cell-keys to travellers (as on Sífnos), it's on a fee basis.

Accordingly, you should always ask locally about the prevailing policy before heading out to a monastery or convent for the night. Also, dress modestly – shorts for men and women, and short skirts are total anathema – and try to arrive early in the evening, not later than 8pm or sunset (whichever is earlier).

CAMPING

Official campsites on the islands range from ramshackle compounds to highly organized and rather soulless complexes run by the EOT (Greek Tourist Organisation). Cheap, casual places cost from £2/US$3.50 a night per person, as much again for a tent and perhaps £3/$5 for a campervan; at the larger sites, though, it's not impossible for two persons and one tent to add up almost to the price of a basic room. The Greek Camping Association, Solonós 102, 106 80 Athens (☎01/36 21 560), publishes a booklet covering most officially recognized Greek campsites and the facilities they offer; it's available from EOT offices.

Generally, you don't have to worry about leaving tents or **baggage** unattended at campsites; Greeks are very honest. The main risk, sadly, comes from other campers, and from Albanians camping rough.

Camping rough – outside authorized campsites – is such an established element of Greek travel that few people realize that it's officially illegal. Since 1977, however, it has been forbidden by a law originally promulgated to harass Gypsies, and increasingly the regulations are enforced.

If you do camp rough, it is vital to exercise sensitivity and discretion. Obviously the police crack down on people camping (and littering) on or near popular tourist **beaches**, particularly when a large community of campers develops. Off the beaten track, however, and particularly in **rural inland areas**, nobody is very bothered. During high season, when everything – even campsites – may be full, attitudes towards freelance camping are more relaxed, even in the most touristy places. At such times the best strategy is to find a sympathetic taverna willing to guard small valuables and let you use their facilities in exchange for regular patronage.

EATING AND DRINKING

Greeks spend a lot of time socializing outside their homes, and sharing a meal is one of the chief ways of doing it. The atmosphere is always relaxed and informal, and pretensions (and expense-account prices) are rare outside of the more developed islands. Greeks are not prodigious drinkers – what tippling they do is mainly to accompany food – though in the resorts a whole range of bars and pubs have sprung up, principally to cater to tourists.

BREAKFAST, PICNIC FARE AND SNACKS

Greeks don't generally eat **breakfast** and the only egg-and-bacon kind of places are in resorts where foreigners congregate; they can be quite good value (1100–1600dr), especially where there's competition. More indigenous alternatives include yoghurts at a *galaktopolío* (milk bar), or cheese pies and pretzel rings from a street stall (see "Snacks" below).

Picnic fare is good, cheap and easily available at bakeries and *manávika* (fruit-and-veg stalls). **Bread**, alas, is often of minimal nutritional value and inedible within a day of purchase. It's well worth paying the bit extra at the bakery (*foúrnos*) for *olikís* (wholemeal), *sikalísio* (rye), *oktásporo* (eight-grain), or even *polýsporo* (multigrain), the latter types commonly baked where Germans or Scandinavians are about. When buying **olives**, go for the fat Kalamáta or Ámfissa ones; they're more expensive, but tastier. **Fétta**

cheese is ubiquitous – often, ironically, imported from Holland or Denmark, though local batches are usually better and not much dearer. The goat's-milk variety can be very dry and salty, so it's wise to taste before buying. If you have access to a fridge, dunking the cheese overnight in a plastic container with water will solve both problems. Another palatable cheese is the expensive gruyère-type *graviéra*.

Despite EU membership, and growing personal incomes and exotic tastes, Greece imports very little garden produce from abroad, aside from bananas. **Fruit** in particular is relatively expensive and available only by locale and season, though in the more cosmopolitan spots it's possible to find such far-away delicacies as avocados (Cretan ones are excellent). Reliable picnic fruits include *yiarmádhes*, giant peaches appearing in August and early September, and *krystália*, tiny hard green pears which ripen a month later and, despite appearances, are heavenly. Greece also has a booming kiwifruit industry, and while the first crop in October coincides with the end of the tourist season, the harvest carries over into the following May. Salad **vegetables** are more reasonably priced; besides the enormous, red-ripe tomatoes (June–Sept), there is a bewildering array of spring (April–May) greens, including rocket, dill, enormous spring onions and Kos lettuce. Useful expressions in the market include *éna tétarto* (250g) and *misó kiló* (500g).

Traditional **snacks** can be one of the distinctive pleasures of Greek eating, though increasingly edged out by an obsession with *tóst* (toasted sandwiches) and other western junk food at nationwide chains such as Goody's (burgers), Roma Pizza and Theios Vanias (baked pastries) – somewhat the less insipid for being homegrown. However, small independently produced **kebabs** (souvlákia) are widely available, and in most larger towns and resorts you'll find *yíros* – doner kebab with chips-and-sauce garnish in thick, doughy pita bread that's closer to an Indian nan.

Other common snacks include *tyrópites* (cheese pies) and *spanokópita* (spinach pie), which can usually be found at the baker's, as can *kouloúria* (crispy baked pretzel rings sprinkled with sesame seeds) and *voutímata* (dark biscuits heavy on molasses, cinnamon and butter).

RESTAURANTS

Greek cuisine and **restaurants** are simple and straightforward. There's no snobbery about eating out; everyone does it and it's still reasonably priced – 2800–3600dr per person for a substantial meal with house wine.

In choosing a restaurant, the best strategy is to go where the Greeks go. And they go late: 2pm to 3pm for **lunch**, 9pm to 11pm for **dinner**. You can eat earlier, but you're likely to get indifferent service and cuisine if you frequent establishments catering to the tourist schedule. Chic appearance is not a good guide to quality; often the more ramshackle, traditional outfits represent the best value. One good omen is the waiter bringing a carafe of refrigerated water, unbidden, rather than pushing you to buy bottled stuff.

In busy resort areas, it's wise to keep a wary eye on the **waiters**, who are inclined to urge you into ordering more than you want and then bring things you haven't ordered. They often don't actually write anything down and may work out the bill by examining your empty plates. Although cash-register receipts are now legally required in all establishments, these are often only for the grand total, and any itemized tabs, will be in totally illegible Greek scribble. Where prices are printed on menus, you'll be paying the right-hand (higher) of the two columns, inclusive of all taxes and usually service charge, although a small tip (150–200dr) is standard practice for the lad who lays the table, brings the bread and water, and so on. **Bread** costs extra, but consumption is not obligatory; so much Greek bread is inedible sawdust that there's no point in paying for it unless you're just using it as a scoop for dips.

Children are always welcome, day or night, at family tavernas, and Greeks anyway don't mind if they play tag between the tables or chase the **cats** – mendicant packs of which you should not feed, as signs often warn you.

ESTIATÓRIA

There are two basic types of restaurant: the **estiatório** and the **taverna**. Distinctions between the two are slight, though the former is more commonly found in towns and tends to have the slightly more complicated dishes termed **mayireftá** (literally, "cooked").

An *estiatório* will generally feature a variety of such oven-baked **casserole** dishes: *moussakás*, *pastítsio*, stews like *kokinistó* and *stifádho*,

yemistá (stuffed tomatoes, courgettes or peppers), the oily vegetable casseroles called *ladherá*, and oven-baked meat and fish. Usually you go into the kitchen and point at the desired steam trays to choose these dishes.

Batches are cooked in the morning and then left to stand, which is why *mayireftá* food is often **lukewarm** or even cold. Greeks don't mind this (most actually believe that hot food is bad for you), and dishes like *yemistá* are actually enhanced by being allowed to cool off and stand in their own juice. Similarly, you have to specify if you want your food with little or no oil (*khorís ládhi*), but once again you will be considered a little strange since Greeks regard olive oil as essential to digestion (and indeed it is one of the least pernicious oils to ingest in large quantities).

Desserts (*epidhórpia* in formal Greek) of the pudding-and-pie variety don't exist at *estiatória*, and yoghurt or cheese only occasionally. Fruit, however, is always available in season; watermelon, melon and grapes are the summer standards. Autumn treats worth asking after include *kydhóni* or *akhládhi stó foúrno*, baked quince or pear with some sort of syrup or nut topping.

TAVERNAS

Tavernas range from the glitzy and fashionable to rough-and-ready cabins set up under a reed canopy, behind a beach. Really primitive ones have a very limited (often unwritten) menu, but the more established will offer some of the main *mayireftá* dishes mentioned above as well as standard taverna fare. This essentially means **mezédhes** (hors d'oeuvres) and **tis óras** (meat and fish fried or grilled to order).

Since the idea of courses is foreign to Greek cuisine, starters, main dishes and **salads** often arrive together unless you request otherwise. The best thing is to order a selection of mezédhes and salads to share, in true Greek fashion. Waiters encourage you to take the *khoriátiki* salad – the so-called Greek salad, with *fétta* cheese – because it is the most expensive one. If you only want tomato, or tomato and cucumber, ask for *domatosaláta* or *angourodomáta*. *Lákhano* (cabbage) and *maroúli* (lettuce) are the typical winter and spring salads.

The most interesting **starters** are *tzatzíki* (yoghurt, garlic and cucumber dip), *melitzanosaláta* (aubergine/eggplant dip), *kolokithákia tiganitá* (courgette/zucchini slices fried in batter) or *melitzánes tiganités* (aubergine/eggplant slices fried in batter), *yígandes* (white haricot beans in vinaigrette or hot tomato sauce), *tyropitákia* or *spanakópittes* (small cheese or spinach pies), *okhtapódhi xydháto* (octopus vinaigrette) and *mavromátika* (black-eyed peas).

Among **meats**, *souvláki* (shish kebab) and *brizóles* (chops) are reliable choices. In both cases, pork (*khirinó*) is usually better-quality and cheaper than veal (*moskharísio*). The best souvláki, though not often available, is lamb (*arnísio*). At **psistariés** (grills), meaty lamb shoulder chops (*kopsídha*) are more substantial than the scrawny rib chops called *païdhákia*; roast lamb (*arní psitó*) and roast kid (*katsíki*) are **estiatório** fare. *Keftédhes* (meatballs), *biftékia* (a sort of hamburger) and the spicy sausages called *loukánika* are cheap and good. *Kotópoulo* (chicken), especially grilled, is also usually a safe bet.

Seaside tavernas also offer **fish**, though the choicer varieties, such as *barboúnia* (red mullet), *fangrí* (sea bream), *tsipoúra* (gilt-head bream) and *lavráki* (sea bass) are expensive, and less tasty if farmed (usually the case). The price is usually quoted by the kilo, which should not be much more than double the street-market rate, so if squid is 2500dr/kilo at the fishmonger's, that sum should fetch you two 250gm portions. The standard procedure is to go to the glass cooler and pick your own. The cheapest widely available fish are *gópes* (bogue) and *marídhes* (tiny whitebait, eaten head and all, ideally rolled in salt and sprinkled with lemon).

Cheaper **seafood** (*thalassiná*) such as *kalamarákia* (fried baby squid) and *okhtapódhi* (octopus) are a summer staple of most seaside tavernas, and occasionally *mýdhia* (mussels), *kydhónia* (cherrystone clams) and *garídhes* (small prawns) will be on offer at reasonable prices. Keep an eye, however, on freshness – mussels in particular are a common cause of stomach upsets or even mild poisoning.

Summer visitors get a relatively poor choice of fish, much of it frozen: drag-net-trawling is prohibited from late May to late October, when only lamp-lure, purse-seining and multi-hook line methods are allowed. During these warmer months, such few fish as are caught tend to be smaller and dry-fleshed, and are thus served with butter sauce.

As in *estiatória*, traditional tavernas offer fruit rather than sticky desserts, though nowadays these too are often available, along with coffee, in places frequented by foreigners.

SPECIALIST TAVERNAS – AND VEGETARIANS

Some tavernas specialize in a particular type of food: *psarotavérnes*, for example, feature fish, and *psistariés* serve spit-roasted lamb, pork or goat (generically termed *kondosoúvli*), grilled chicken (*kotópoulo skáras*) or *kokorétsi* (grilled offal roulade) – often plonked straight on your table on a sheet of waxed paper. A handful of other tavernas offer **game** (*kinígi*): rabbit, quail or turtle dove in the autumn.

If you are **vegetarian**, you may be in for a hard time, and will often have to assemble a meal from various mezédhes. Even the standbys of yoghurt with honey, *tzatzíki* and Greek salad begin to pall after a while, and many of the supposed "vegetable" dishes on menus are cooked in stock or have pieces of meat added to liven them up. Wholly or largely vegetarian restaurants are slowly on the increase in touristy areas; this guide highlights them where appropriate.

WINES

Both *estiatória* and tavernas will usually offer you a choice of bottled **wines**, and many have their own house variety: kept in barrels, sold in bulk by the quarter-, half- or full litre, and served either in glass flagons or brightly coloured tin "monkey-cups" called *kantária*. Not as many tavernas stock their own wine as once did, but it's worth asking whether they have wine *varelísio* (barrelled) or *khíma* (in bulk). Non-resinated wine is frequently more than decent. **Retsína** – pine-resinated wine, a slightly acquired taste – is also usually better straight from the barrel, though the bottled Yeoryiadhi brand from Thessaloníki is excellent.

Among the more common bottled wines, Cambas, Boutari Lac des Roches, the Rhodian CAIR products, and the Cretan Logado are good inexpensive whites, while Boutari Nemea is perhaps the best mid-range red. If you want something better but still moderately priced, Tsantali Agioritiko makes an excellent white or red, Boutari has a fine Special Reserve red, and the Macedonian vintner Carras does both excellent whites and reds. In addition, there are various premium micro-wineries whose products are currently fashionable: Hatzimikhali, Athanasiadhi, Skouras and Lazaridhi, for which you can expect to pay in excess of 4500dr a bottle.

A FOOD AND DRINK GLOSSARY

Basics

Aláti	Salt	O logariazmós	The bill
Avgá	Eggs	Psári(a)	Fish
(Khorís) ládhi	(Without) oil	Psomí	Bread
Khortofágos	Vegetarian	Olikís	Wholemeal bread
Katálogo/lísta	Menu	Sikalísio	Rye bread
Kréas	Meat	Thalassiná	Seafood
Lakhaniká	Vegetables	Tyrí	Cheese
Méli	Honey	Yiaoúrti	Yoghurt
Neró	Water	Zákhari	Sugar

Cooking terms

Akhnistó	Steamed	Sto foúrno	Baked
Pastó	Dry-marinated in salt	Tiganitó	Pan-fried
Psitó	Roasted	Tis óras	Grilled/fried to order
Saganáki	Rich red sauce; also fried cheese	Yakhní	Stewed in oil and tomato sauce
Skáras	Grilled	Yemistá	Stuffed (squid, vegetables, etc)
Sti soúvla	Spit roasted		

Soups and starters

Avgolémono	Egg and lemon soup	Krítamo	Rock samphire
Dolmádhes	Stuffed vine leaves	Mavromátika	Black-eyed peas
Fasoládha	Bean soup	Melitzanosaláta	Aubergine/eggplant dip
Florínes	Canned red Macedonian peppers	Revithokeftédhes	Chickpea (garbanzo) patties
		Skordhaliá	Garlic dip
Kápari	Pickled caper leaves	Soúpa	Soup
Kopanistí,	Spicy cheese purée	Taramosaláta	Cod roe paté
khtypití, tyrosaláta		Tzatzíki	Yoghurt and cucumber dip

Vegetables

Angináres	Artichokes	Koukiá	Broad fava beans
Angoúri	Cucumber	Maroúli	Lettuce
Ánitho	Dill	Melitzána	Aubergine/eggplant
Bámies	Okra, ladies' fingers	Papoutsákia	Stuffed aubergine/eggplant
Bouréki, bourekákia	Courgette/zucchini, potato and cheese pie	Patátes	Potatoes
		Piperiés	Peppers
Briám	Ratatouille	Pligoúri, pinigoúri	Bulgur wheat
Domátes	Tomatoes	Radhíkia	Wild chicory
Fakés	Lentils	Rízi/Piláfi	Rice (usually with sáltsa – sauce)
Fasolákia	French/string beans		
Khoriátiki (saláta)	Greek salad (with olives, fétta, etc)	Rókka	Rocket greens
		Saláta	Salad
Khórta	Greens (usually wild)	Spanáki	Spinach
Kolokithákia	Courgette/zucchini	Yígandes	White haricot beans

Fish and seafood

Astakós	Aegean lobster	Galéos	Dogfish, hound shark
Atherína	Sand smelt	Garídhes	Shrimp, prawns
Bakaliáros	Cod	Gávros	Mild anchovy
Barbóuni	Red mullet	Glóssa	Sole
Fangrí	Common bream	Gópa	Bogue

Continues over

Kalamarákia	Baby squid	*Platýs*	Skate, ray
Karavídhes	Crayfish	*Sardhélles*	Sardines
Kalamária	Squid	*Sargós*	White bream
Kefalás	Axillary bream	*Selákhi*	Skate, ray
Kolíos	Club mackerel	*Synagrídha*	Dentex
Koutsomoúra	Goatfish (small *barboúni*)	*Skathári*	Black bream
Kydhónia	Cherrystone clams	*Skoumbrí*	Atlantic mackerel
Lakérdha	Light-fleshed premium tuna	*Soupiá*	Cuttlefish
Marídhes	Whitebait	*Tsipoúra*	Gilt-head bream
Melanoúri	Saddled bream	*Vátos*	Skate, ray
Mýdhia	Mussels	*Xifías*	Swordfish
Okhtapódhi	Octopus		

Meat and meat-based dishes

Arní	Lamb	*Moussakás*	Aubergine, potato and meat pie with bechamel topping
Biftéki	Hamburger		
Brizóla	Pork or beef chop	*Païdhákia*	Lamb rib chops
Keftédhes	Meatballs, with egg and breadcrumbs	*Pastítsio*	Macaroni baked with meat
		Patsás	Tripe and trotter soup
Khirinó	Pork	*Salingária*	Garden snails
Kokorétsi	Liver/offal roullade, spit-roasted	*Sykóti*	Liver
Kopsídhia	Lamb shoulder chops	*Soutzoukákia*	Mincemeat rissoles/beef patties
Kotópoulo	Chicken	*Stifádho*	Meat stew with tomato
Kounélli	Rabbit	*Youvétsi*	Baked clay casserole of meat and short pasta
Loukánika	Spicy home made sausages		
Moskhári	Veal		

Sweets and dessert

Baklavás	Honey and nut pastry	*Kréma*	Custard
Bougátsa	Salt or sweet cream pie served warm with sugar and cinammon	*Loukoumádhes*	Dough fritters in honey syrup and sesame seeds
		Pagotó	Ice cream
Galaktobóureko	Custard pie	*Pastélli*	Sesame and honey bar
Karydhópita	Walnut cake	*Rizógalo*	Rice pudding
Khalvás	Sweetmeat, sesame or semolina		

Fruit and nuts

Akhládhia	Big pears	*Kerásia*	Cherries	*Pepóni*	Melon
Aktinídhia	Kiwifruit	*Krystália*	Miniature pears	*Portokália*	Oranges
Fistíkia	Pistachio nuts	*Kydhóni*	Quince	*Rodhákino*	Peach
Fráoules	Strawberries	*Lemóni*	Lemon	*Sýka*	(Dried) figs
Karpoúzi	Watermelon	*Míla*	Apples	*Stafýlia*	Grapes

Cheese

Fétta	Salty, white cheese	*Kasséri*	Medium-sharp cheese
Graviéra	Gruyère-type hard cheese	*Mizíthra*	Sweet cream cheese
Katsikísio	Goat cheese	*Próvio*	Sheep cheese

Drinks

Bíra	Beer	*Krasí*	Wine	*Portokaládha*	Orangeade
Boukáli	Bottle	*Áspro*	White	*Potíri*	Glass
Gála	Milk	*Kókkino/mávro*	Red	*Stinyássas!*	Cheers!
Galakakáo	Chocolate milk	*Kokkinélli/rozé*	Rosé	*Tsaï*	Tea, black
Gazóza	Generic fizzy drink	*Lemonádha*	Lemonade	*Tsaï vounoú*	"Mountain"
Kafés	Coffee	*Metalikó neró*	Mineral water		(sage) tea

CAFÉS, CAKE SHOPS AND BARS

The Greek eating and drinking experience encompasses a variety of other places beyond restaurants. Most importantly, there is the institution of the **kafenío**, found in every town, village and hamlet in the country. In addition, you'll come across **ouzerís**, **zakharoplastía** and **barákia**.

THE KAFENÍO

The **kafenío** (plural, kafenía) is the traditional Greek coffee shop or café. Although its main business is Greek coffee – prepared *skéto* or *pikró* (unsweetened), *métrio* (medium) or *glykó* (sweet) – it also serves spirits such as oúzo (aniseed-based spirit), brandy (Metaxa or Botrys brand, in three grades), beer, tea (either mountain sage tea or British-style) and soft drinks. Another refreshing drink sold in cafés is *kafés frappé*, a sort of iced instant coffee with or without milk and sugar – uniquely Greek despite its French-sounding name. Like Greek coffee, it is always accompanied by a welcome glass of cold water. Standard fizzy soft drinks are also sold in kafenía.

Usually the only edibles available are *glyká koutalioú* (sticky, syrupy preserves of quince, grape, fig, citrus fruit or cherry), and the old-fashioned *ipovrýkhio*, which is a piece of mastic submerged in a glass of water like a submarine, which is what the word means in Greek.

Like tavernas, kafenía range from the plastic and sophisticated to the old-fashioned, spit-on-the-floor variety, with marble or brightly painted wood tables and straw-bottomed chairs. An important institution everywhere in Greece, they form the pivot of life in the country villages. You get the impression that many men spend most of their waking hours there. Greek women are rarely to be seen in the more traditional places – and foreign women may sometimes feel uneasy or unwelcome in these establishments. Even in holiday resorts, you will find there is at least one café that the local men have reserved for themselves.

Some kafenía close at siesta time, but many remain open from early in the morning until late at night. The chief socializing time is 6–8pm, immediately after the *mikró ípno* or siesta. This is the time to take your pre-dinner oúzo, as the sun begins to sink and the air cools down.

OÚZO, MEZÉDHES AND OUZERÍS

Oúzo and the similar *tsípouro* (Thássos) and *tsikoudhiá* (Crete), are simply **spirits** of up to 48 per-

cent alcohol, distilled from grape-mash residue left over from wine-making, and then flavoured with herbs such as anise or fennel. There are nearly a score of brands, with the best reckoned to be from Lésvos, Sámos and Tírnavos on the mainland; the bad ones are spiked with molasses or grain alcohol to "fortify" them. Mini (after the mini-skirted lass on the label), is a common, very dry variety.

When you order, you will be served two glasses: one with the oúzo, and one full of water, to be tipped into your oúzo until it turns a milky white. You can drink it straight, but its strong, burning taste is hardly refreshing.

Until the 1980s, every oúzo you ordered was automatically accompanied by a small plate of **mezédhes**, on the house: bits of cheese, cucumber, tomato, a few olives, sometimes octopus or even a couple of small fish. Unfortunately these days you have to ask, and pay, for them.

Though confined to the better resorts and select neighbourhoods of the bigger island towns, one kind of drinking establishment specializes in oúzo and mezédhes. These are called an **ouzerí** (same in the Greek plural) or *ouzádhiko* – *tsipourádhiko* in the north Aegean –and are well worth trying for the marvellous variety of mezédhes they serve (though of late numbers of mediocre tavernas have appropriated the name). At the genuine article, several plates of mezédhes plus drinks will effectively substitute for a more involved meal at a taverna (though it usually works out to be more expensive, if you have a healthy appetite). Faced with the often bewilderingly varied menu, you might opt for the *pikilía* (medley) available in several sizes, the largest usually heavy on seafood.

SWEET SHOPS AND MILK BARS

Similar to the kafenío is the **zakharoplastío**. A cross between a café and patisserie, it serves coffee, alcohol, yoghurt and honey, and sticky cakes. The better establishments offer an amazing variety of pastries, cream and chocolate confections, honey-soaked Middle Eastern sweets like *baklavás*, *kataïfi* (honey-drenched "shredded wheat"), *loukoumádhes* (deep-fried batter puffs dusted with cinnamon and dipped in syrup); *galaktoboúreko* (custard pie), and so on.

If you want a stronger slant towards dairy products and away from pure sugar, seek out a *galaktopolío*, where you'll often find *rizógalo* (**rice pudding** – better than English canned variety), *kréma* (custard) and locally made *yiaoúrti* (yoghurt), best if it's *próvio* (from sheep's milk).

Ice cream, sold principally at the gelaterie which have swept over Greece of late (Dhodhoni is a posh chain), can be very good and almost indistinguishable from Italian prototypes. A scoop (*baláki*) costs 200–300dr; you'll be asked if you want it in a cup (*kypelláki*) or a cone (*khonáki*), and whether you want toppings like *santí* (whipped cream). By contrast, the mass-produced Delta or Evga brands are pretty average. A sign reading *pagotó politikó* or *kaïmáki* means that the shop concerned makes its own Turkish-style ice cream – as good as or better than the usual Italian – and the proprietors are probably of Asia Minor or Constantinopolitan descent.

Both *zakharoplastía* and *galaktopolía* are more family-oriented places than the kafenío, and many also serve a basic **continental breakfast** of méli mé voútyro (honey poured over a pat of butter) or jam (all kinds are called *marmeládha* in Greek; ask for *portokáli* – orange – if you want proper marmalade) with fresh bread or *friganiés* (melba-toast-type slivers). You are also more likely to find proper (*evropaïkó*) tea and non-Greek coffee. Nescafé has become the generic term for all instant coffee, regardless of brand; in resorts smart proprietors have taken to offering filter coffee, dubbed *gallikós* (French).

BARS – AND BEER

Bars (*barákia* in the plural), once confined to towns, cities and holiday resorts, are now found all over Greece, especially in pedestrian areas. They range from clones of Parisian cafés or Spanish bodegas to seaside cocktail bars, or imitation English "pabs" (sic), with videos running all day. At their most sophisticated, however, in the largest cities and resorts, they can hold their own against close equivalents in Spain or London; they are well-executed theme venues in ex-industrial premises or Neoclassical houses, with western (currently techno) soundtracks.

Formerly operating from mid-afternoon to dawn, most *barákia* now shut by 2 or 3am, depending on the municipality; during 1994 they were required by the Ministry of Public Order to make an admission/cover charge which included the first drink. Met with a wave of street demos and other mass civil disobedience, this decree is presently in abeyance but could be revived at any time.

For this and other reasons, drinks are invariably more expensive than at a café. *Barákia* are, however, the most likely to stock a **range of beers**, which in Greece are 98 percent foreign label made under licence, since the indigenous Fix brewery closed in 1984. Two new brands appeared in 1996–97 – Pils Hellas, akin to Heineken (see below), but less bitter; and Mythos, in light green bottles, a well-regarded, tart lager put out by the Boutarivintners. Kronenberg and Kaiser are the best available premium labels, the former in both light and dark varieties; since 1993 a tidal wave of even pricier, imported German beers such as Bitburger and Warstein has washed over the bigger resorts. Amstel and Henninger are the two ubiquitous cheapies, rather bland but inoffensive. A possible compromise in both palate and expense is the sharper-tasting Heineken, universally referred to as a "prássini" by bar and taverna staff after its green bottle.

COMMUNICATIONS

POSTAL SERVICES

Post offices are open Monday to Friday from 7.30am to 2pm, though certain main branches have hours through the evening and on Saturday morning. They exchange money in addition to handling mail.

Airmail letters from the mainland take three to six days to reach the rest of Europe, five to ten days to get to North America, and a bit longer for Australia and New Zealand. Allow an extra day or two when sending from an island without an airport. Aerogrammes are slightly faster, while for a modest fee (about 500dr) you can use **express service** (*katepígonda*). **Registered** (*systiméno*) delivery is also available, but it is quite slow unless coupled with express service. If you are sending large parcels home, note that these should and often can only be dealt with in large provincial or county capitals. This way your bundle will be in Athens, and on an international flight, within a day.

For a simple letter or card, a **stamp** (*grammatósima*) can also be purchased at a *períptero* (corner kiosk). However, the proprietors charge ten percent commission and never seem to know the current international rates. Ordinary **post boxes** are bright yellow, express boxes dark red; if you are confronted by two slots, "*Esoterikó*" is for domestic mail, "*Exoterikó*" for overseas.

The **poste restante/general delivery** system is reasonably efficient, especially at the post offices of larger towns. Mail should be marked poste restante, with your surname underlined, and addressed to the main post office of whichever town you choose. It will be held for a month and you'll need your passport to collect it.

PHONES

Making calls is relatively straightforward, though **OTE** (*Organismós Tiliepikinoníon tis Elládhos*, the state-run telecom) provides some of the worst service in the EU – at about the highest rates. **Call boxes**, invariably sited at the noisiest street corners, work only with phone cards (in three sizes: 100, 500 and 1000 units), bought from kiosks, OTE offices and newsagents. Not surprisingly, the largest ones represent the best value.

If you won't be around long enough to use up a phone card, it's probably easier to make local calls from a *períptero*, or **street kiosk**. Here the phone may be connected to a meter (if not, there'll be a sign saying *móno topikó*, "local only"), and you pay after you have made the call. Local, one-unit calls are cheap enough (20dr for six minutes, three minutes if the exchange is digital), but long-distance ones add up quickly (see below). There are a growing number of digital (*psifiakó*) exchanges, but most are still pulse-analogue (*palmikó*); when dialling long distance on the latter, you must wait for a characteristic series of six electrical crunches after the country or Greek area code before proceeding. Other options for calling include **counter coin phones** in bars and hotel lobbies; these take 10, 20, 50 and 100 drachma coins and, unlike the street phone boxes, can be rung back. Most of them are made in northern Europe and bear instructions in English. Avoid making long-distance calls from a hotel-room phone, as a fifty percent surcharge will be slapped onto the already steep rates.

For **international** (*exoterikó*) calls, it's better to use either card phones or visit the nearest OTE office, where there may be a digital booth reserved for overseas calls only; make your call and pay afterwards. **Reverse charge** (collect) or person-to-person calls can also be made here, though connections are not always immediate; be prepared to wait.

Increasingly, however, OTE offices are less and less in the business of providing metered calls, with most booths converted to card-phones and opening hours shortened. In the biggest cities

PHONING GREECE FROM ABROAD

Dial the international access code (given below)
+ 30 (country code) + area code (minus initial 0, see below) + number.

Australia ☎0011
Canada ☎011
Ireland ☎010

New Zealand ☎00
UK ☎00
USA ☎011

PHONING ABROAD FROM GREECE

Dial the country code (given below) + area code (minus initial 0) + number.

Australia ☎0061
Canada ☎001
Ireland ☎00353

New Zealand ☎0064
UK ☎0044
USA ☎001

GREEK PHONE CODES

Athens ☎01	Kós ☎0242	Pátmos ☎0247
Corfu ☎0661	Lefkádha ☎0645	Rhodes ☎0241
Khaniá ☎0821	Mobiles ☎093 & ☎094	Santoríni ☎0286
Iráklion ☎081	Mýkonos ☎0289	Skiáthos ☎0427
Kálymnos ☎0243	Náxos ☎0285	Thássos ☎0593
Kefalloniá ☎0674	Páros ☎0284	Zákynthos ☎0695

USEFUL TELEPHONE NUMBERS

Operator ☎131 (Athens only)
Operator ☎132 (Domestic)
Operator ☎161 (International)
Medical emergencies ☎166
Police emergency ☎100

Speaking clock ☎141
Tourist police ☎171
Fire brigade, urban ☎199
Forest fires ☎191
ELPA road assistance ☎104

there will be at least one branch open 24 hours, while elsewhere schedules are more commonly 7am–10pm or even 8am–3pm. In a few resorts there are OTE Portakabin booths keeping odd but useful schedules like 2–10pm. Outgoing **faxes** can also be sent from OTE offices, post offices and some travel agencies – at a price. Receiving a fax may also incur a small charge.

Calls will **cost**, very approximately, £2 for three minutes to all EU countries and most of the rest of Europe, or US$5 for the same time to North America or Australasia. **Cheap rates**, such as they are, apply from 3pm to 5pm and 9pm to 8am daily, plus all weekend, for calls within Greece; overseas off-peak periods are variable, but for Europe fall between 10pm and 8am.

For details of **phone codes** and **useful numbers**, see the box on above.

British Telecom, as well as North American long-distance companies like AT&T, MCI and Sprint, all enable their customers to make **credit-card calls** from Greece, but only back to the home country. There are now a few local-dial numbers with some providers, such as BT, which enable you to connect to the international network for the price of a one-unit call, and then charge the call to your home number – usually cheaper than the alternatives.

Mobile users should note that only GSM phones will work in Greece, over one of two networks. The Greeks, incidentally, are very keen on them, and they've become an obligatory fashion accessory among certain classes.

THE MEDIA

British newspapers are fairly widely available in Greece for 450–600dr, 800–900dr for Sunday editions. You'll find day-old copies of *The Independent* and *The Guardian*'s European edition, plus some of the tabloids, in all the resorts as well as in major island towns. **American** and **international** alternatives include the turgid *USA Today* and the more readable *International Herald Tribune*; *Time* and *Newsweek* are also widely available.

Among monthly **magazines**, the late lamented *Athenian* folded in 1997 after 23 years, with a successor, *Atlantis*, rising less than phoenix-like from the ashes. Slightly better is the expensive, glossy bi-monthly *Odyssey*, produced by and for wealthy diaspora Greeks and little different from an in-flight magazine.

GREEK PUBLICATIONS

Currently the only local **English-language** Greek newspaper is the *Athens News* (250dr, daily except Mon), in colour with good features and Balkan news, available in most resorts.

Many Greek papers are funded by **political groups**, which tends to decrease the already low quality of Greek dailies. Among these, only the centrist *Kathemerini* – whose former proprietor Helen Vlakhos attained heroic status for her defiance of the junta – approaches the standards of a major European newspaper. *Eleftherotypia*, once a PASOK mouthpiece, now aspires to more independence and has links with the UK's *Guardian*; *Avriani* has taken its place in the PASOK cheerleading section. *Ta Nea* is mostly known for its extensive small ads. On the **Left**, *Avyi* is the Eurocommunist forum with literary leanings, while *Rizospastis* acts is the organ for the KKE (unreconstructed Communists). *Ethnos* became notorious some years back by receiving covert KGB funding to act as a disinformation bulletin. At the opposite end of the political spectrum, *Apoyevmatini* generally supports the **centre-right** Néa Dhimokratía party, while *Estia*'s no-photo format and reactionary politics are both stuck somewhere at the turn of the century. The **ultra-nationalist** lunatic fringe is staked out by *Stokhos* ("Our Goal: Greater Greece. Our Capital: Constantinople").

Among **magazines** which are not merely translations of overseas titles, *Takhydhromos* is the respectable news-and-features weekly; *Ena* is more sensationalist, *Klik* a crass rip-off of *The Face*, and *To Pondiki* (The Mouse) a satirical weekly revue in the same vein as Britain's *Private Eye* – its famous covers are spot-on and accessible to anyone with minimal Greek. More specialized niches are occupied by low-circulation titles such as *Adhesmatos Typos* (a slightly rightist, muckraking journal) and *Andi*, somewhat in the mould of Britain's *New Statesman and Society*.

RADIO

If you have a **radio**, playing dial roulette can be rewarding. Greek music programmes are always accessible (if variable in quality) despite the language barrier, and since abolition of the government's former monopoly of wavelengths, regional stations have mushroomed; the airwaves are now positively cluttered, as every sizable town sets up its own studio and transmitter.

The **BBC World Service** can be picked up on short-wave frequencies throughout Greece, the most common ones are 15.07 and 12.09 Mhz.

TV

Greece's two central, government-controlled **TV stations**, ET1 and ET2, nowadays lag behind private channels – Mega-Channel, New Channel, Antenna, Star and Seven-X – in the ratings. Programming on all stations tends to be a mix of soaps (especially Italian, Spanish and Latin-American), game shows, westerns, B-movies and sports. All foreign films and serials are broadcast in their original language, with Greek subtitles. Except for Seven-X, which begins at 7pm, and Mega (a 24-hour channel), the main channels broadcast from breakfast time until the small hours.

Numerous **cable** and **satellite channels** are received, including Sky, CNN, MTV, Super Channel and French Canal Plus and Italian Rai Due. The range available depends on the area (and hotel) you're in.

OPENING HOURS AND PUBLIC HOLIDAYS

It is virtually impossible to generalize about Greek opening hours, except to say that they change constantly. The traditional timetable starts at a relatively civilized hour, with shops opening between 8.30am and 9.30am, and runs through until lunchtime, when there is a long break for the hottest part of the day. Things (except banks) may then reopen in the mid- to late afternoon.

Tourist areas tend to adopt a slightly more northern timetable, with certain shops and offices, as well as the most important archeological sites and museums, usually open throughout the day.

BUSINESS AND SHOPPING HOURS

Most **government agencies** are open to the public from 8am to 2pm. In general, however, you'd be optimistic to show up after 1pm expecting to be served the same day. **Private businesses** or service providers are apt to operate on a 9am–6pm schedule. If someone is actually selling something, then they are more likely to follow a split shift as detailed below.

Shopping hours during the hottest months are theoretically Monday, Wednesday and Saturday from approximately 9am to 2.30pm, and Tuesday, Thursday and Friday from 8.30am to 2pm and 6 to 9pm. During the cooler months with shorter daylight hours, the morning schedule shifts slightly forward, the evening trade thirty minutes or even a full hour back. However, there are so many **exceptions** to these rules by virtue of holidays and professional idiosyncrasy that you can't count on getting anything done except

from Monday to Friday, between 9.30am and 1pm. It's worth noting that **delis** and **butchers** are not allowed to sell fresh meat during the afternoon (though some flout this rule); similarly **fishmongers** are only open in the morning, as are **pharmacies**, which additionally are shut on Saturday.

All of the above opening hours will be regularly thrown out of sync by the numerous **public holidays** and **festivals**. The most important, when almost everything will be closed, are listed in the box below.

ANCIENT SITES AND MONASTERIES

All the major **ancient sites** are now fenced off and, like most **museums**, charge admission fees ranging from a token 400dr to a whopping 2000dr, with an average fee of around 800dr. At most of them reductions of twenty-five to thirty percent apply to senior citizens, and fifty percent to students with proper identification. In addition, entrance to all state-run sites and museums is **free** to all EU nationals on Sundays and public holidays outside of peak season – non-EU nationals are unlikely to be detected as such unless they go out of the way to advertise the fact.

Opening hours vary from site to site. As far as possible, individual times are quoted in the text, but bear in mind that these change with exasperating frequency, and at smaller sites may be subject to the whim of a local keeper. The times quoted are generally summer hours, which operate from around late April to the end of September. Reckon on similar days but later opening and earlier closing in winter.

PUBLIC HOLIDAYS

January 1	May 1
January 6	Whit Monday (50 days after Easter; see below)
March 25	August 15
First Monday of Lent (Feb or March; see below)	October 28
Easter weekend (April or May; see below)	December 25–26

VARIABLE RELIGIOUS FEASTS

	Lent Monday	Easter Sunday	Whit Monday
1998	March 2	April 19	June 8
1999	Feb 22	April 11	May 31

Smaller sites generally close for a long lunch and **siesta** (even where they're not supposed to), as do **monasteries**. The latter are generally open from 9am to 1pm and 5 to 8pm (3.30 to 6.30pm in winter) for limited visits. Most monasteries and important churches impose a fairly strict dress code for visitors; no shorts on either sex, with women expected to cover their arms and wear skirts; the necessary wraps are sometimes provided on the spot.

FESTIVALS AND CULTURAL EVENTS

Many of the big Greek popular festivals have a religious basis so they're observed in accordance with the Orthodox calendar. Give or take a few saints, this is similar to the regular Catholic liturgical year, except for Easter, which can fall as much as three weeks to either side of the western festival. Other festivals are cultural in nature, with the highlight for most people being to catch a performance of classical drama in one of the country's ancient theatres. There's also a full programme of cinema and modern theatre, at its best in Athens, but with something on offer in even the smallest town at some point during the year.

EASTER

Easter is by far the most important festival of the Greek year – infinitely more so than Christmas – and taken much more seriously than it is anywhere in western Europe. From Wednesday of Holy Week until the following Monday, the state radio and TV networks are given over solely to religious programmes.

The **festival** is an excellent time to be in Greece, both for its beautiful religious ceremonies and for the days of feasting and celebration that follow. The mountainous island of **Ídhra** with its alleged 360 churches and monasteries is the prime Easter resort, but unless you plan well in advance you have no hope of finding accommodation at that time. Probably the best idea is to make for a medium-sized village where, in most cases, you'll be accepted into the community's celebration. Other famous Easter celebrations are held at Corfu, Pyrgí on Khíos, Ólymbos on Kárpathos and Pátmos.

The first great public ceremony takes place on **Good Friday** evening as the Descent from the Cross is lamented in church. At dusk the *Epitáfios*, Christ's funeral bier, lavishly decorated by the women of the parish, leaves the sanctuary and is paraded solemnly through the streets. In many places, Crete especially, this is accompanied by the burning of effigies of Judas Iscariot.

Late **Saturday** evening sees the climax in a majestic *Anástasis* mass to celebrate Christ's triumphant return. At the stroke of midnight all the lights in every crowded church are extinguished, and the congregation plunged into the darkness which envelops Christ as He passes through the underworld. Then there's a faint glimmer of light behind the altar screen before the priest appears, holding aloft a lighted taper and chanting "*Avtó to Fós . . .*" (This is the Light of the World). Stepping down to the level of the parishioners, he touches his flame to the unlit candle of the nearest worshipper intoning "*Dévthe, lévethe Fós*" (Come, take the Light). Those at the front of the congregation and on the aisles do the same for their neighbours until the entire church – and the courtyard outside with its inevitable overflow of worshippers – is ablaze with burning candles and the miracle re-affirmed.

Even the most committed atheist is likely to find this moving. The traditional greeting, as fireworks explode all around you in the street, is "*Khristós Anésti*" (Christ is risen), to which the response is "*Alithós Anésti*" (Truly He is Risen). In the week up to Easter Sunday you should wish people a Happy Easter: "*Kaló Páskha*"; on or after the day, you say "*Khrónia Pollá*" (Many Happy Returns).

Worshippers then take the burning **candles** home through the streets, and it brings good fortune to the house if they arrive still burning. On reaching the front door it is common practice to make the sign of the cross on the lintel with the flame, leaving a black smudge visible for the rest of the year. The Lenten fast is traditionally broken early on Sunday morning with a meal of *mayerítsa*, a soup made from lamb tripe, rice and lemon. The bulk of the lamb will be roasted on spits for Sunday lunch, and festivities often take place through the rest of the day.

The Greek equivalent of **Easter eggs** are hard-boiled eggs (painted red on Holy Thursday), which are baked into twisted, sweet bread-loaves (*tsouréki*) or distributed on Easter Sunday. People rap their eggs against their friends' eggs, and the owner of the last uncracked egg is considered lucky.

THE FESTIVAL CALENDAR

Most of the other Greek festivals are celebrations of one or another of a multitude of **saints**; the most important are detailed on p.55. A village or church bearing the saint's name is a sure sign of celebrations – sometimes right across the town or island, sometimes quiet, local and consisting of little more than a special liturgy and banners adorning the chapel in question. Saints' days are also celebrated as name days; if you learn that it's an acquaintance's name day, you wish them "*Khrónia Pollá* " (Many Happy Returns). Also detailed on p.55 are a few more **secular** holidays, most enjoyable of which are the pre-Lenten carnivals.

In addition to the specific dates mentioned, there are literally scores of **local festivals**, or **paniyíria**, celebrating the patron saint of the main village church. With hundreds of possible name-saints' days (calendars list two or three, often arcane, for each day) you're unlikely to travel around Greece for long without stumbling on something.

It is important to remember the concept of the **paramoní**, or **eve of the festival**. Most of the events listed below are celebrated on the night before, so if you show up on the morning of the date given you will very probably have missed any music, dancing or drinking.

January 1
New Year's Day (*Protokhroniá*) in Greece is the feast day of Áyios Vassílios, and is celebrated with church services and the baking of a special loaf, vassilópitta, in which a coin is embedded, bringing its finder good luck throughout the year. The traditional New Year greeting is "*Kalí Khroniá*".

January 6
Epiphany (*Ayía Theofánia, Fóta* for short), when the *kalikántzari* (hobgoblins) who run riot on earth during the twelve days of Christmas are rebanished to the nether world by various rites of the Church. The most important of these is the blessing of baptismal fonts and all outdoor bodies of water. At seaside locations, the priest traditionally casts a crucifix into the deep, with local youths competing for the privilege of recovering it.

Pre-Lenten carnivals
These – known in Greek as *Apokriátika* – span three weeks, climaxing during the seventh weekend before Easter. If you're en route to the Ionian islands, consider a halt to take in the **Pátra Carnival**, which with its parades and costume parties, is one of the largest and most outrageous in the Mediterranean, with events from January 17 until "Clean Monday", the last day of Lent. On the last Sunday before Lent there's a grand chariot parade, with the city's large **gay population** in conspicuous participation. The Ionian islands themselves, especially Kefanloniá, are also good for Carnival, while the outrageous **Goat Dance** is enacted on Skýros in the Sporades.

March 25
Independence Day and the feast of the **Annunciation** (Evangelismós in Greek) is both a religious and a national holiday, with on the one hand military parades and dancing to celebrate the beginning of the revolt against Turkish rule in 1821, and on the other church services to honour the news being given to Mary that she was to become the Mother of Christ. There are major festivities on Tínos, Ídhra (Hydra) and many other places, particularly near any monastery or church named Evangelístria or Evangelismós.

April 23
The feast of St George (Áyios Yeóryios), the patron of shepherds, is a big rural celebration, with much feasting and dancing at associated shrines and towns. Good island venues include Skýros, for which George is patron saint, and Asigonía, a major pastoral centre in the mountains of Crete. If April 23 falls before Easter, ie during Lent, the festivities are postponed until the Monday after Easter.

May 1
May Day is the great urban holiday when townspeople traditionally make for the countryside for picnics, returning with bunches of wild flowers. Wreaths are hung on their doorways or balconies until they are burned on Midsummer's eve. There are also large demonstrations by the Left, claiming the Ergatikí Protomayiá (Working-Class First of May) as their own.

May 21
The feast of Áyios Konstandínos (St Constantine) and his mother, Ayía Eléni (St Helen), widely celebrated as the name day for two of the more popular Christian names in Greece.

June 29
The feast of Áyios Pétros and Áyios Pávlos (Peter and Paul). Two more commonly celebrated name days.

July 17
The feast of Ayía Marína is a big event in rural areas, as she's an important protector of crops. The eponymous port on Léros will also be en fête. Between this celebration and mid-September there are religious festivals every few days, and between these, secular holidays and the heat, most business comes to a standstill.

July 18–20
The feast of Profítis Ilías (the Prophet Elijah) is widely observed at the countless hill- or mountain-top shrines of Profítis Ilías.

July 26
The feast of Ayiá Paraskeví, with big village festivals across the Aegean.

August 6
The feast of the Metamórfosis (Transfiguration) provides another excuse for celebrations, particularly at Khristós village on Ikaría.

August 15
The Apokímisis tis Panayías (Assumption of the Blessed Virgin Mary). As at Easter, this is a day when people traditionally return to their home village, and in most places there will be no accommodation available on any terms. Even some Greeks will resort to sleeping in the streets. There is a great pilgrimage to Tínos, and major festivities at Páros, at Ayiássos on Lésvos, and at Ólymbos on Kárpathos.

August 29
Feast of the Beheading of John the Baptist (Ayios Ioánnis Pródhromos).

September 8
The Yénisis tis Panayías (Birth of the Virgin Mary) sees special services in churches dedicated to the event (with major festivals 24hr beforehand), and a double cause for rejoicing on Spétses where they also celebrate the anniversary of the Battle of the Straits of Spétses, which took place on September 8, 1822. A re-enactment of the battle takes place in the harbour, followed by fireworks and feasting well into the night.

September 14
A last major summer festival, the **Ípsosis tou Stavroú** (Exaltation of the Cross), keenly observed on Khálki.

September 26
Feast of St John the Evangelist (Áyios Ioánnis O Thelógos).

October 26
The Feast of Áyios Dhimitrios (St Demetrius), is another popular name day. New wine is traditionally tapped on this day, a good excuse for general inebriation.

October 28
Ókhi Day, the year's major patriotic shindig – a national holiday with parades, folk dancing and feasting to commemorate Metaxas's apocryphal one-word reply to Mussolini's 1940 ultimatum: "Okhi!" (No!).

November 8
Another popular name day, **the feast of the Archangels Michael and Gabriel** (Mikhaïl and Gavriïl, or Taxiárkhon), with rites at the numerous rural monasteries and chapels named after them – particularly on Sými and Lésvos.

December 6
The feast of Áyios Nikólaos (St Nicholas), the patron of seafarers, who has many chapels dedicated to him.

December 25

A much less festive occasion than Greek Easter, **Christmas** (*Khristoúyenna*) is still an important religious feast celebrating the birth of Christ, and in recent years it has started to take on more of the trappings of the Western Christmas, with decorations, Christmas trees and gifts. December 26 is not Boxing Day as in England but the **Sýnaxis tis Panayías**, or Meeting of the Virgin's Entourage.

December 31

New Year's Eve (*Paramoní Protokhroniá*), when, as on the other twelve days of Christmas, children go door-to-door singing the traditional *kálanda* (carols), receiving money in return. Adults tend to sit around playing cards, often for money. The *vassilópitta* is cut at midnight (see January 1).

CULTURAL FESTIVALS

As well as religious festivals, Greece has a full range of **cultural festivals, including a few on the more popular islands**. A leaflet entitled "Greek Festivals", available from GNTO offices abroad, includes details of smaller, **local festivals** of music, drama and dance, which take place on a more sporadic basis.

MAJOR FESTIVALS

Island-based events include:

Itháki Music Festival (July).

Iráklion Festival (early Aug).

Lefkádha Arts Jamboree (Aug).

Réthymnon Renaissance Fair (Aug)–Sept.

Santoríni Music Festival (Aug–Sept).

Rhodes Festival (Aug–Oct).

Sými Festival (late June–late Sept).

CINEMA

Greek **cinemas** show a large number of American and British movies, always in the original soundtrack with Greek subtitles. They remain affordable, currently 1600–1800dr depending on location and plushness of facilities, and in summer a number set up outside. An **outdoor movie** (cheaper at 1500dr) is worth catching at least once for the experience alone, though it's best to opt for the early screening (about 9pm) since the sound on the 11pm show gets turned down or even off to avoid complaints of noise from ad-jacent residences.

SPORTS AND OUTDOOR PURSUITS

The Greek seashore offers endless scope for water sports, with windsurfing-boards for rent in most resorts and, less reliably, waterskiing and parasailing facilities. Inland, the great attraction lies in hiking; often the smaller, less developed islands are better for this than larger islands comprehensively criss-crossed by roads.

As far as spectating goes, the twin Greek obsessions are **football** (soccer) and **basketball**, with **volleyball** a close third in popularity.

WATER SPORTS

The years since the mid-1980s have seen a massive growth in the popularity of **windsurfing** in Greece. The country's bays and coves are ideal for beginners, and boards can be rented in literally hundreds of resorts. Particularly good areas, with established schools, include the islands of

Lefkádha, Zákynthos, Náxos, Sámos, Lésvos, Kós Corfu and Crete. You can almost always pay for an initial period of instruction, if you've not tried the sport previously. Rates are very reasonable – about £6/US$10 an hour.

Waterskiing is available at a number of the larger resorts, and a fair few of the smaller ones too. By the crippling rental standards of the ritzier parts of the Mediterranean it is a bargain, with twenty minutes' instruction often available for around £8–10/$13–16. At many resorts, **parasailing** (*parapént* in Greek) is also possible; rates start at £10/$16 a go.

A combination of steady winds, appealing seascapes and numerous natural harbours have long made Greece a tremendous place for **sailing**. Holiday companies offer all sorts of packaged and tailor-made cruises (see p.5 & p.6 in "Getting There"). In Greece, boats and dinghies are rented out by the day or week at many resorts. Spring and autumn are the most pleasant and least expensive seasons; *meltémi* winds make for pretty nauseous sailing between late June and early September, and summer rates for the same craft can be three times as high as shoulder-season prices. For more details, pick up the. informative brochure "Sailing the Greek Sea" from GNTO offices, or contact the Hellenic Yachting Federation, Aktí Navárkhou Koundourióti 7, 185 34 Pireás (☎01/41 37 351, fax 31 119).

Because of the potential for pilfering submerged antiquities, **scuba diving** is severely restricted, its legal practice confined to certain coasts around Crete, Kálymnos, Mýkonos and most of the Ionian islands. For more information, contact the Union of Greek Diving Centres (☎01/92 29 532 or 41 18 909), or request the information sheet "Regulations Concerning Underwater Activities" from the nearest branch of the GNTO/EOT.

WALKING

Greeks are just becoming used to the notion that anyone should want to **walk** for pleasure, yet if you have the time and stamina it is probably the single best way to see the islands. This guide indicates some of the best walking routes on a number of islands; for more detail, you may want to acquire a specific **hiking guidebook** – see p.458. See also p.32 for details of hiking maps available, and p.6 for details of companies offering walking holidays on the islands.

FOOTBALL AND BASKETBALL

Football (soccer) is far and away the most popular sport in Greece – both in terms of participating and watching. The most important (and most heavily sponsored) teams are Panathanaïkós and AEK of Athens, Olympiakós of Pireás, and PAOK of Thessaloníki – all of which have fan clubs out on the islands. Other major teams in the provinces include Lárissa and the Cretan Ofí. If you're interested, matches (usually played on Wednesdays and Sundays) are easy enough to catch from September to May. In mid-autumn you might even see one of the Greek teams playing European competition. The Greek national team qualified for the 1994 World Cup in some style, and then proceeded to lose all their three games heavily and returned from the USA without scoring a goal.

The nation's **basketball** team is one of the continent's strongest and won the European Championship in 1987 – cheered all the way with enormous enthusiasm. At club level, many of the football teams maintain basketball squads.

FINDING WORK

Since Greece's full accession to the European Union in 1993, a citizen of any EU state has (in theory) the right to work in Greece. In practice, however, there are a number of bureaucratic hurdles to overcome. Formerly the most common job for foreigners was teaching English in the numerous private cramming academies (*frondistíria*) but lately severe restrictions have been placed on the availability of such positions for non-Greeks, and you will more likely be involved in a commercial or leisure-orientated-trade.

DOCUMENTATION FOR LEGAL EMPLOYMENT

If you plan to work **for someone else**, you first visit the nearest Department of Employment and collect two forms: one an employment application which you fill in, the other for the formal offer of work by your prospective employer. Once these are vetted, and revenue stamps (*khartósima*, purchased at kiosks) applied, you take them to the Alien's Bureau (*Ipiresía Allodhapón*) or, in its absence, the central police station to support your application for a residence permit (*ádhia paramonís*), which additionally requires your passport, two photographs, more *khartósima* and a stable address (not a hotel). Permits are given for terms of three or six months (white cards), one year (green triptych booklets) or even five years (blue booklets) if they've become well acquainted with you. For one- or five-year permits, a health examination at the nearest public hospital is required, to screen for TB, syphilis and HIV.

As a **self-employed** professional, you must satisfy the requirements of the Greek state with equivalent qualifications to native Greeks plying the same trade. You should also befriend a good accountant, who will advise you on which of the several varieties of incorporation are to your advantage; trading under a fictitious name is much more expensive tax-wise than doing business as a private person. You will also need to sign on with TEBE, the Greek National Insurance Scheme for self-employed people (similar to Class 4 DSS contributions in the UK). If you are continuing to contribute to a social insurance scheme in a country which has reciprocal agreements with Greece (all EU states do), this must be proved in writing – a tedious and protracted process.

Once you're square with TEBE, you visit the tax office to be issued a **tax number** (abbreviated "ahphi-mi" in Greek), which must be used in all transactions. You will be required to prepare receipt and invoice books with your tax number professionally printed on them, or have a rubber stamp made up for applying that number to every sheet. The tax office will also determine which rate of VAT (commonly "phi-pi-ah") you should pay for each kind of transaction; VAT returns must be filed every two months, which is where the friendly accountant who chose your incorporation type comes in handy again.

The self-employed tend to be issued one- or five-year residence permits, and they are supposed to be free of charge. EU nationals who do not wish to work in Greece, but still need a residence permit (eg for setting up a savings account) will still get a "white" pass gratis, but must present evidence of financial solvency; personalized pink exchange receipts, travellers' cheques or credit cards are all considered valid proofs.

At the present time, **non-EU nationals** who wish to work in Greece do so surreptitiously, with the ever-present risk of denunciation to the police and instant deportation. Having been forced to accept large numbers of EU citizens intending to find jobs in an existing climate of rising unemployment, the Greek immigration authorities are cracking down hard on any suitable targets, be they Albanian, African, Swiss or North American. That old foreigners' standby, teaching English, is now available only to TEFL certificate- holders, preferably Greek, non-EU nationals of Greek descent, and EU nationals in that order. If you are a non-EU foreign national of Greek descent, you are termed *omólogos* (returned Greek diaspora member) and in fact have tremendous employment and residence rights – you can, for example, open your very own *frondistírio* without any qualifications (this is painfully evident in the often appalling quality of English instruction in Greece).

SHORT-TERM WORK

Short-term work in Greece is always on an unofficial basis and for this reason it will generally be where you can't be seen by the police or you're badly paid – or, more often, both. The influx early in the 1990s of over 300,000 Albanians, Poles, Yugoslavs, Russian Greeks and assorted other refugees from the upper Balkans has resulted in a surplus of unskilled labour and severely depressed wages. Note that **youth hostels** are a good source of information on temporary work – indeed a few may even offer you a job themselves, if you turn up at the right time.

TOURISM-RELATED WORK

Most tourists working casually in Greece find jobs in **bars** or **restaurants** around the main resorts. Women will generally find these jobs easier to obtain than men – who should generally count themselves lucky to get work washing up. "Trained" chefs, however, sometimes fare better.

If you're waiting or serving, most of your wages will probably have to come from tips but you may well be able to get a deal that includes free food and lodging; evening-only hours can be a good shift, leaving you a lot of free time. The main drawback may be the machismo and/or chauvinist attitudes of your employer. (Ads in the local press for "girl bar staff" are certainly best ignored; see "Sexual Harassment" on p.27).

Corfu, with its big British slant, is an obvious choice for bar work; Rhodes, Crete, Skiáthos, Páros, Íos and Santoríni are also promising. Start looking, if you can, around April or May; you'll get better rates at this time if you're taken on for a season.

On a similar, unofficial level you might be able to get a sales job in **tourist shops** on Corfu, Ídhra, Rhodes or Crete, or (if you've the expertise) helping out at one of the **windsurfing** schools that have sprung up all around the coast.

Perhaps the best type of tourism-related work, though, is that of courier/greeter/group co-ordinator for a **package holiday company**. All you need is EU nationality and language proficiency compatible with the clientele, though knowledge of Greek is an advantage. English-only speakers are pretty well restricted to places with a big British package trade, namely Crete, Rhodes, Skiáthos and the Ionian islands.

Many such staff are recruited through ads in newspapers issued outside Greece, but it's by no means unheard of to be hired on the spot in April or May. A big plus, however you're taken on, is that you're usually guaranteed about six months of steady work, and that if things work out you may be re-employed the following season with contract and foreign-currency wages

from the home company, not from the local affiliate.

Outside the tourist season there can be building/painting/signpainting work preparing for the influx; ask around at Easter time. **Yacht marinas** can also prove good hunting-grounds though less for the romantic business of crewing, than scrubbing down and repainting. Again, the best possibilities are likely to be on Rhodes, Corfu, or Kálymnos.

SELLING AND BUSKING

You may do better by working for yourself. Travellers report rich pickings during the tourist season from **selling jewellery** on island beaches, or on boats – trinkets from Asia are especially popular with Greeks. Once you've managed to get the stuff past the customs officials (who will be sceptical, for instance, that all those trinkets are presents for friends), there rarely seem to be problems with the local police, though it probably pays to be discreet.

Busking can also be quite lucrative. Playing on pedestrianized platías of major island towns like Réthymnon or Rhodes, it's possible to make around 3000dr in a two-hour session. At resorts, you might just strike luckier if you've talent, since western-style pubs there occasionally hire foreign musicians for gigs.

DIRECTORY

BARGAINING This isn't a regular feature of life, though you'll find it possible with private rooms and some hotels out of season. Similarly, you may be able to negotiate discounted rates for vehicle rental, especially for longer periods. Services such as shoe, watch and camera repair don't have iron-clad rates, so use common sense when assessing charges (written estimates are not routine practice).

CHILDREN Kids are worshipped and indulged in Greece, perhaps to excess, and present few problems when travelling. Baby foods and nappies/diapers are ubiquitous and reasonably priced, plus concessions are offered on most forms of transport. Private rooms establishments and luxury hotels are more likely to offer some kind of babysitting service than the mid-range, C-class hotels.

DEPARTURE TAX This is levied on all international ferries – currently 1500dr per person and per car or motorbike. To non-EU states (Turkey, Egypt and Israel), it's 4000–5000dr per person depending on the port of departure, sometimes arbitrarily levied twice, on both entry and exit. There's also an airport departure tax of £8.50 equivalent (currently 3800dr) for destinations less than 750 miles away, £17/7600dr if it's further, but this is always included in the price of the ticket – there's no collection at the airport itself.

ELECTRICITY Voltage is 220 volt AC throughout the country. Wall outlets take double round-pin plugs as in the rest of continental Europe. Three-to-two-pin adapters should be purchased beforehand in the UK, as they can be difficult to find locally; the standard five-amp model permits operation of a hair dryer. North American appliances will require both a step-down transformer and a plug adapter (easy to find in Greece).

FILMS Fuji and Agfa print films are reasonably priced and easy to have processed – you practically trip over "One Hour Foto" places in resorts; Kodachrome and Ektachrome slide films can be purchased, again at typical UK prices, in larger towns, but regardless of what you're told, all processing orders are sent to Athens – wait until you get home.

GAY LIFE For men, overtly gay behaviour in public remains taboo in rural areas, and only visible at certain resorts like Ídhra, Rhodes or Mýkonos, still the most popular European gay resort after Ibiza in Spain. Erissós on Lésvos, the birthplace of Sappho, is (appropriately) an international mecca for lesbians. Homosexuality is legal over the age of 17, and (male) bisexual behaviour common but rarely admitted. Greek men are terrible flirts, but cruising them is a semiotic minefield and definitely at your own risk – references in gay guides to male cruising grounds should be treated sceptically. "Out" gay Greeks are rare, and "out" local lesbians rarer still; foreign same-sex couples will be regarded in the provinces with some bemusement but accorded the standard courtesy as foreigners.

LAUNDRIES *Plindíria* in Greek, they're beginning to crop up in most of the main resort towns; sometimes an attended service wash is available for little or no extra charge over the basic cost of 1300–1500dr per wash and dry. Otherwise, ask rooms owners for a *skáfi* (laundry trough), a bucket (*kouvás*), or the special laundry area often available; they freak out if you use bathroom washbasins, Greek plumbing and wall-mounting being what they are.

PERÍPTERA These are street-corner kiosks, or sometimes a hole-in-the-wall shopfront. They sell everything from pens to disposable razors, stationery to soap, sweets to condoms, cigarettes to plastic crucifixes – and are often open when nothing else is.

TIME As throughout the EU, Greek summer time begins at 4am on the last Sunday in March, when the clocks go forward one hour, and ends at 4am the last Sunday in October when they go back. Be alert to this, as scores of visitors miss planes, ferries, etc, every year – the change is not well publicized. Greek time is thus always two hours ahead of Britain. For North America, the difference is seven hours for Eastern Standard Time, ten hours for Pacific Standard Time, with an extra hour plus or minus for those weeks in April and October when one place is on daylight savings and the other isn't. A recorded time message (in Greek) is available by dialling ☎141.

TOILETS Public toilets are usually in parks or squares, often subterranean; otherwise try a bus station. Except in areas frequented by tourists, public toilets tend to be pretty filthy – it's best to use those in restaurants and bars. Remember that throughout Greece, you drop paper in the adjacent wastebins, not in the bowl.

USEFUL THINGS TO BRING An alarm clock (for early buses and ferries), a torch (especially if you camp out), mosquito repellent, sunscreen with a high SPF (15 or above, generally unavailable in Greece), and ear plugs for noisy ferries and hotels.

PART TWO

THE

GUIDE

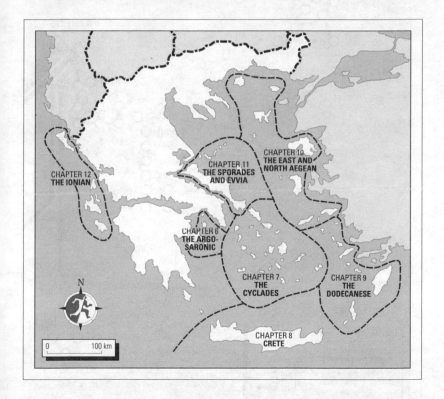

CHAPTER 12
THE IONIAN

CHAPTER 11
THE SPORADES
AND EVVIA

CHAPTER 10
THE EAST AND
NORTH AEGEAN

CHAPTER 6
THE ARGO-
SARONIC

CHAPTER 7
THE
CYCLADES

CHAPTER 9
THE
DODECANESE

CHAPTER 8
CRETE

N

0   100 km

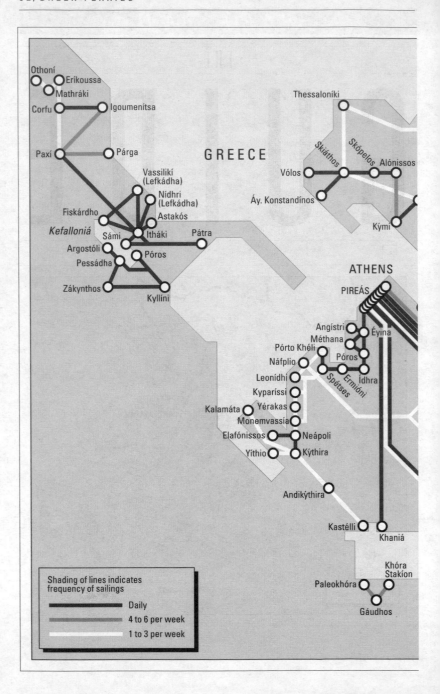

Othoní
Eríkoussa
Mathráki
Corfu — Igoumenítsa
Paxí — Párga

GREECE

Thessaloníki
Skiáthos Skópelos
Vólos — Alónissos
Áy. Konstandínos
Kými

Vassilikí (Lefkádha)
Nídhri (Lefkádha)
Fiskárdho — Astakós
Kefaloniá
Sámi — Itháki — Pátra
Argostóli — Póros
Pessádha
Zákynthos
Kyllíni

ATHENS
PIREÁS

Angístri — Éyina
Méthana
Pórto Khéli — Póros
Náfplio — Ídhra
Leonídhi — Ermióni
Kyparíssi — Spétses
Kalamáta — Yérakas
Monemvassía
Elafónissos — Neápoli
Yíthio — Kýthira

Andikýthira

Kastélli — Khaniá

Khóra Stakíon
Paleokhóra
Gáudhos

Shading of lines indicates frequency of sailings

— Daily
— 4 to 6 per week
— 1 to 3 per week

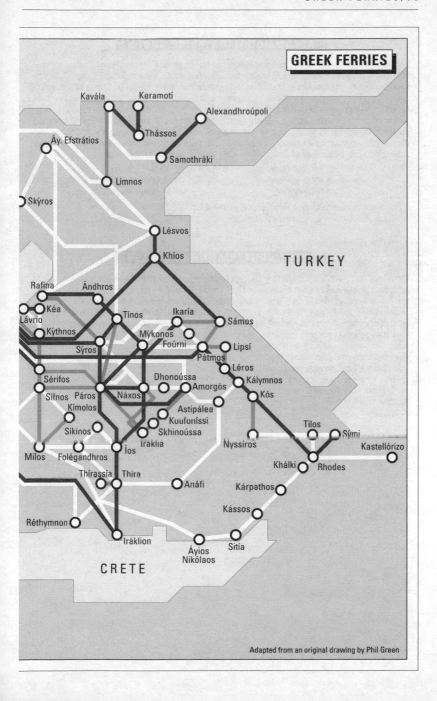

GREEK FERRIES

Adapted from an original drawing by Phil Green

ACCOMMODATION PRICE CODES

Throughout the book we've used the following **price codes** to denote the cheapest available room in high season; all are prices for a double room, except for category ①, which represents per person rates. Out of season, rates can drop by up to fifty percent, especially if you are staying for three or more nights. Single rooms, where available, cost around seventy percent of the price of a double.

Rented private rooms on the islands usually fall into the ② or ③ categories, depending on their location and facilities, and the season; a few in the ④ category are more like plush self-catering apartments. They are not generally available from late October through to the beginning of April, when only hotels tend to remain open.

① 1400–2000dr		④ 8000–12,000dr
② 4000–6000dr		⑤ 12,000–16,000dr
③ 6000–8000dr		⑥ 16,000dr and upwards

For more accommodation details, see pp.39–41.

FERRY ROUTES AND SCHEDULES

Details of ferry routes, together with approximate journey times and frequencies, are to be found at the end of each chapter in the "travel details" section. Please note that these are for general guidance only. Ferry schedules change with alarming regularity and the only information to be relied upon is that provided by the port police in each island harbour. Ferry agents in Pireás and on the islands are helpful, of course, but keep in mind that they often represent just one ferry line and won't neccessarily inform you of the competition. Be aware, too, that ferry services to the smaller islands tend to be pretty skeletal from mid-September through to May.

In many island groups, ferries are supplemented by Flying Dolphin hydrofoils – which tend to be twice as quick and twice the price. Most of the major hydrfoil routes are operated from May to early September, with lesser ones sometimes running to July and August only.

CHAPTER ONE

THE ARGO-SARONIC

The rocky, volcanic chain of **Argo-Saronic** islands, most of them barely an olive's throw from the Argolid, differ to a surprising extent not just from the mainland but from one another. Less surprising is their massive popularity, with Éyina (Aegina) especially becoming something of an Athenian suburb at weekends.

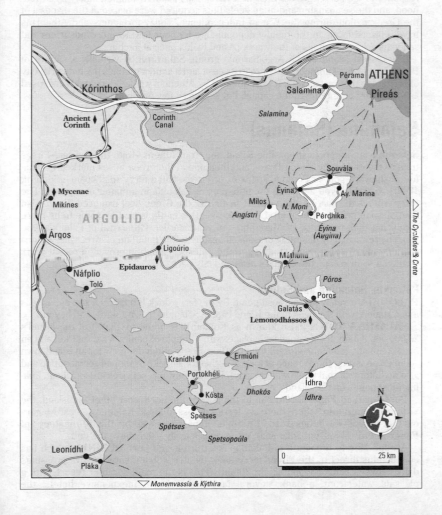

Ídhra (Hydra), Póros and Spétses are not far behind in summer, though their visitors tend to be predominantly cruise- and package-tourists. More than any other group, these islands are at their best out of season, when populations fall dramatically and the port towns return to quiet, provincial-backwater life.

Éyina, important in antiquity and more or less continually inhabited since then, is the most fertile of the group, famous for its pistachio nuts, as well as for one of the finest ancient temples in Greece. Its main problem – the crowds – can be escaped by avoiding weekends, or taking the time to explore its satellite isles, **Angístri** and **Moní**.

The three southerly islands, **Spétses**, **Ídhra** and **Póros**, are pine-cloaked and relatively infertile. They were not really settled until medieval times, when refugees from the mainland – principally Albanian Christians – established themselves here. In response to the barrenness of their new home the islanders adopted piracy as a livelihood, and the seamanship and huge fleets thus acquired were placed at the disposal of the Greek nation during the War of Independence. Today foreigners and Athenians have replaced locals in the rapidly depopulating harbour towns, and windsurfers and sailboats are faint echoes of the warships and kaïkia once at anchor.

The closest island of the Argo-Saronic group, **Salamína**, is virtually a suburb of Pireás, just over a kilometre offshore to its east, and it almost touches the industrial city of Mégara to the west as well. It is frequented by Athenian weekenders and is also used as a base for commuting to the capital, but sees very few foreign visitors.

Salamína (Salamis)

Salamína is the quickest possible island hop from Athens. Take the Kyfissia–Pireás train to the end of the line in Pireás and then one of the green buses marked Pérama to the shipyard port of Pérama, just west of Pireás, and a ferry (daily 5am–midnight; 120dr) will whisk you across to the little port of Paloukía in a matter of minutes. The ferry crosses the narrow strait where, in 480BC, the Greek fleet trounced the Persian fleet, despite being outnumbered three to one; this battle is said by some to be more significant than the battle of Marathon, ten years earlier. On arrival in Paloukía, you won't be rewarded by desirable or isolated beaches – the pollution of Pireás and Athens is a little too close for comfort although the water has much improved in recent years – but you soon escape the capital's *néfos* and city pace.

Paloukía, Salamína and Selínia

PALOUKÍA is really just a transit point. By the ferry dock is a taverna and opposite is a bus station, with services to the island capital Salamína Town (3km), and beyond.

SALAMÍNA TOWN (also known as Kouloúri) is home to 18,000 of the island's 23,000 population. It's a ramshackle place, with a couple of banks, a fish market and an over-optimistic (and long-closed) tourist office. Pretty much uniquely for an island town – and emphasizing the absence of tourists – there is no bike or moped rental outlet, and also no hotel (not that you'd want to stay). Fortunately, bus services are excellent, linking most points on the island.

Buses marked **Faneroméni** run to the port at the northwest tip of the island, the **Voudoro peninsula**, where there are ferries across to Lákki Kalomírou, near Mégara on the Athens–Kórinthos road. En route it passes close by the **Monastery of Faneroméni** (6km from Salamína), rather majestically sited above the gulf.

Around 6km to the south of Paloukía is a third island port, **SELÍNIA**, which has connections direct to the Pireás ferry dock (winter 9.30am, summer five crossings daily between 8am–2.30pm; 330dr; 30min). This is the main summer resort, with a pleasant waterfront, a bank, several tavernas and two inexpensive hotels, the

Akroyali (☎01/46 73 263; ②) and *Votsalakia* (☎01/46 71 334; ③). Selínia can be reached direct by bus from Paloukía.

Eándio and the south

South from Salamína Town, the road edges the coast towards Eándio (6km; regular buses). There are a few tavernas along the way, but the sea vistas are not inspiring. **EÁNDIO**, however, is quite a pleasant village, with a little pebble beach and the island's best **hotel**, the *Gabriel* (☎01/46 62 275; ④), owned by poet and journalist Giorgos Tzimas, who can be prevailed upon to recite a poem or two. The hotel overlooks the bay, whose waters are returning to health.

Two roads continue from Eándio. The one to the southeast runs to the unassuming village resorts of Peráni and Paralía (both around 4km from Eándio). The more interesting route is southeast to Kanákia (8km from Eándio; no buses), over the island's pine-covered mountain, and passing (at around 5km) a monastery – dedicated, like almost all Salamína churches, to Áyios Nikólaos. At the monastery you could turn off the road (left) along a track to the harbour and small-scale resort of Peristéria (5km). This is a much more attractive settlement than the littered beach and scruffy huts of Kanákia itself.

Éyina (Aegina)

Given its current population of a little over 10,000, it seems incredible that **Éyina** (Aegina) was a major power in Classical times – and a rival to Athens. It carried on trade to the limits of the known world, maintained a sophisticated silver coinage system (the first in Greece) and had prominent athletes and craftsmen. However, during the fifth century BC the islanders made the political mistake of siding with their fellow Dorians,

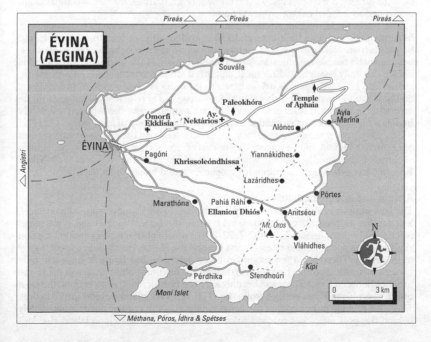

the Spartans, which Athens seized on as an excuse to act on a long-standing jealousy; her fleets defeated those of the islanders in two separate sea battles and, after the second, the population was expelled and replaced by more tractable colonists.

Subsequent history was less distinguished, with the familiar central Greece pattern of occupation – by Romans, Franks, Venetians, Catalans and Turks – before the War of Independence brought a brief period as seat of government for the fledgling Greek nation. These days, the island is most famous for its **pistachio orchards**, whose thirsty trees lower the water table several feet annually; hence the notices warning you of the perennial water crisis.

Athenians regard Éyina as a beach annexe for their city, being the closest place to the capital most of them would swim at, though for tourists it has a monument as fine as any in the Aegean in its beautiful fifth-century BC **Temple of Aphaia**. This is located on the east coast, close to the port of **Ayía Marína**, and if it is your primary goal, you'd do best to take one of the ferries or hydrofoils which run directly to that port in season. If you plan to stay, then make sure your boat will dock at **Éyina Town**, the island capital. Ferries and hydrofoils also stop at **Souvála**, a Greek weekend retreat between the two ports devoid of interest to outsiders. Hydrofoils, incidentally, are far more frequent, run from the same quay in Pireás as the conventional boats, and cost hardly any more for this particular destination.

Éyina Town

A solitary column of a Temple of Apollo beckons as your ferry or hydrofoil steams around the point into the harbour at **ÉYINA TOWN**. The island's capital, it makes an attractive base, with some grand old buildings from the time (1826–28) when it served as the first capital of Greece after the War of Independence. And for somewhere so close to Athens, it isn't especially overrun by foreign tourists, nor are accommodation prices unduly inflated except on weekends.

The **harbour** is workaday rather than picturesque, but is nonetheless appealing: fishermen talk and tend their nets, and kaïkia loaded with produce from the mainland bob at anchor. North of the port, behind the small town beach, the rather weatherbeaten Apollo temple column stands on a low hill that was the ancient acropolis and is known, logically enough, as **Kolóna** (Column). Around the temple are rather obscure **ruins** (daily 8.30am–3pm; 500dr), only worth it for the sweeping view from Moní islet on the south to the mainland shore on the northwest. There is a small museum in the grounds. On the north flank of Kolóna hill there's an attractive bay with a small, sandy **beach** – the best spot for swimming in the immediate vicinity of the town.

The town's other sights, such as they are, are the frescoed thirteenth-century church of **Ómorfi Ekklisía**, fifteen minutes' walk east of the port, and a house in the suburb of Livádhi, just to the north, where a plaque recalls the residence of **Nikos Kazantzakis**, when he was writing his most celebrated book, *Zorba the Greek*.

Arrival and accommodation

The **bus station** is also on the recently refurbished Platía Ethneyersías, with an excellent service to most villages on the island, while the largest moped and cycle rental place – Sklavenas Rent-a-Car (☎0297/22 892), which also rents open-sided cars at slightly above normal island rates – is just beyond the pink corner building immediately to the north. There are a few mountain bikes available, but Éyina is large and hilly enough to make motorized cycles worthwhile for anything other than a pedal to the beaches between Éyina Town and Pérdhika. Three **banks** line the waterfront; the **post office** is on Platía Ethneyersías; while the **OTE** lies well inland beyond the cathedral. There's a **tourist police** post in the same building as the regular police, immediately behind the post office but reached from Leonárdhou Ladhá. Aegina Island Holidays

(☎0297/26 430) on the waterfront, offers excursions to the Epidavros theatre festival and handles tickets for the Sea Falcon Hydrofoils.

Good inexpensive **accommodation** can be found in the rooms rented by Andonis Marmarinos at Leonárdhou Ladhá 30 (☎0297/22 954; ④); they're spotless, fairly but though not en suite. For more comfort try the *Hotel Marmarinos* nearby at no. 24, run by a branch of the same family (☎0297/23 510; ④). Across the street, *Hotel Artemis* (☎0297/25 195; ④) is appealingly set in a pistachio orchard. The slightly fancier but no more expensive *Areti* (☎0297/23 593; ④) and *Avra* (☎0297/22 303; ④) hotels are on the seafront between Platía Ethneyersías and Kolóna, where ocean views compensate for the traffic noise. Next to the *Avra* is the inexpensive and friendly *Plaza Hotel* (☎0297/25 600; ③).

Eating and entertainment

Perhaps the best **food** in town is to be had at the newly opened *En Agini* restaurant in a courtyard in Spiro Rodi street just below the huge St Nikolas church. The food is of high quality, and the prices reasonable. Directly behind the fish market is a particularly good and inexpensive seafood **taverna**, the *Psarotaverna Agora*, with outdoor seating on the cobbles in summer. Similar in concept, though not quite as good value, is *Ta Vrekhamena*, a little hole-in-the-wall on Leonárdhou Ladhá just seaward from the police station, offering a very limited menu of bulk wine, ouzo and grilled octopus. Next to the *Hotel Areti*, the small *Lekkas* is excellent for no-nonsense meat grills by the waterside. At the other end of the block next to the Plaza Hotel is *Floisvos*, offering food grilled over charcoal on tables by the sea. At the south end of the quay, by the Alpha Trapeza Pisteos (Credit Bank), *Maridhaki* is a less carnivorous traditional place, dishing up the usual Greek oven standards. For a mild blowout, try Petros's *Ippokambos* on the road alongside the football ground on the corner with the old prison; it's superb for mezédhes.

In terms of **nightlife**, Éyina Town boasts two summer·**cinemas**, the Olympia near the football grounds before the *Miranda* hotel and the new Akroyiali at the end of Éyina harbour on the Pérdhika road, which shows quality foreign films; the winter cinema, the Titina, is by the park with the medieval tower-house, a block below OTE. On the corner of Aiándos and Piléos, the *Belle Epoque* bar is worth a visit for its ornate turn-of-the-century architecture. Nightclubs and discos are mostly to be found across the island in Ayía Marína but the *Eltiana* nightclub is just behind the Ávra beach

The Temple of Aphaia

The Doric **Temple of Aphaia** (Mon–Fri 8.30am–7pm, Sat & Sun 8.30am–3pm; 800dr) lies 12km east of Éyina Town, among pines that are tapped to flavour the local retsina, and beside a less aesthetic radio mast. It is one of the most complete and visually complex ancient buildings in Greece, with superimposed arrays of columns and lintels evocative of an Escher drawing. Built early in the fifth century BC, or possibly at the end of the sixth century, it predates the Parthenon by around sixty years. The dedication is unusual: Aphaia was a Cretan nymph who had fled from the lust of King Minos, and seems to have been worshipped almost exclusively on Éyina. As recently as two centuries ago the temple's pediments were intact and virtually perfect, depicting two battles at Troy. However, like the Elgin marbles they were "bought" from the Turks – this time by Ludwig of Bavaria, which explains their current residence in the Munich Glyptothek museum.

There are buses to the temple from Éyina Town, or you could walk from Ayía Marína along the path that takes up where Kolokotróni leaves off, but the best approach is by rented motorbike, which allows you to stop at the monastery of Áyios Nektários, and the island's former capital of Paleokhóra.

Áyios Nektários and Paleokhóra

Áyios Nektários, a whitewashed modern convent situated around halfway to the Temple of Aphaia, was named in honour of the Greek Orthodox Church's most recent saint, who died in 1920 and was canonized in 1962. A huge church belonging to the convent was recently completed on the main road below. Opposite the convent car park a partly paved road leads up into the hills towards the seventeenth-century convent of Khryssoleóndissa – primarily worth seeing for its views.

Paleokhóra, a kilometre or so further east, was built in the ninth century as protection against piracy, but it failed singularly in this capacity during Barbarossa's 1537 raid. Abandoned in 1827 following Greek independence, Paleokhóra is now utterly deserted, but possesses the romantic appeal of a ghost village. You can drive right up to the site: take the turning left after passing the new large church and keep going about 400m. Some twenty of Paleokhóra's reputed 365 churches and monasteries – one for every saint's day – remain in recognizable state, and can be visited, but only those of Episkopí (locked), Áyios Yeóryios and Metamórfosis (on the lower of the two trails) retain frescoes of any merit or in any state of preservation. Little remains of the town itself; when the islanders left, they simply abandoned their houses and moved to Éyina Town.

The East: Ayía Marína and Pórtes

The island's major package resort of **AYÍA MARÍNA**, 15km from Éyina Town, lies on the east coast of the island, south of the Aphaia Temple ridge. The concentrated tackiness of its jam-packed high street is something rarely seen this side of Corfu: signs for Guinness, burger bars and salaciously named ice creams and cocktails. The beach is packed and overlooked by constantly sprouting, half-built hotels, and the water is not good. It's really only worth coming here for connections to Pireás. There are some five ferries a day in season, with departures in the morning and late in the afternoon, and now the Sea Falcon Line hydrofoils (☎0297/26 430) link both Ayía Marína and Souvála with Pireás.

Beyond the resort, the paved road continues south 8km to **PÓRTES**, a pokey, low-key shore hamlet, dramatically set with a cliff on the north and wooded valleys behind. Among the uneasy mix of new summer villas-in-progress (no short-term accommodation) and old basalt cottages are scattered two or three tiny fish **tavernas** and snack bars, with a functional beach between the two fishing anchorages. Soon the road deteriorates to a steep, rough dirt track climbing to the village of Anitséou, just below a major saddle on the flank of Mount Óros. A small taverna, *The Hunter's Inn* (☎0297/40 210), tucked away above the village, serves home cooked food and locally baked bread at weekends, and is run by English-speaking Greeks returned from abroad. The road surface improves slightly as it forges west towards the scenic village of **Pakhiá Rákhi**, almost entirely rebuilt in traditional style by foreign owners. From here, a sharp descent leads to the main west-coast road at Marathóna (for which see opposite), or a longer, paved and tree-lined route back to Éyina Town.

Mount Óros

Just south of the saddle between Pahiá Ráhi and Anitséou, mentioned above, are the massive foundations of the shrine of **Ellaníou Dhiós**, with the monastery of Taxiárkes squatting amid the massive masonry. The 532m summit of **Mount Óros**, an hour's walk from the highest point of the road, is capped by the modern Chapel of the Ascension, and has views across the entire island and over much of the Argo-Saronic Gulf.

A few other **paths** cross the largely roadless, volcanic flanks of Óros from Vlakhídhes. Amazingly in this bulldozer-mad country, one to **Sfendhoúri** hamlet still survives, initially marked by white paint dots. Sfendhoúri itself has a road link with Pérdhika (see opposite). Gerald Thompson's *A Walking Guide to Aegina*, available locally, describes in detail a series of walks across the range of mountains and wooded valleys between Mount Oros and the Aphaias temple and down to the port of Souvala, all avoiding main roads.

The West: Marathóna, Pérdhika and Moní islet

The road due south of Éyina Town running along the west coast of the island is served by regular buses (8–10 daily). **MARATHÓNA**, 5km from Éyina, constitutes the only sandy-beach resort on the west coast and is tolerable enough, with its clutch of rooms and tavernas along the shore.

PÉRDHIKA, 9km along and the end of the line, is more scenically set on its little bay and certainly has the best range of non-packaged accommodation on the island, besides the main town. There are **rooms**, and the *Hotel Hippocampus* (☎0297/61 363; ③). On the pedestrianized esplanade overlooking the water are a dozen **tavernas**; the best is *Argyris To Proreo*, which boasts log-cabin-like decor. At the head of the bay by the bus stop is the *Votsitsanos* taverna and bar running the length of the small beach and shaded by eucalyptus trees.

The only other diversion at Pérdhika is a trip to **Moní islet** just offshore (300dr one way; 10min; several departures daily). There was once an EOT-run campsite on Móni, but this is now abandoned and derelict. There are no facilities on the islet and most of it is fenced off as a nature conservation area. It's really only worth the trip for a swim in wonderfully clear water, as Pérdhika bay itself is of dubious cleanliness and has very small beaches.

Angístri

Angístri, a half-hour by boat from Éyina, is small enough to be overlooked by most island-hoppers, though it's now in many foreign holiday brochures. The island fosters an uneasy coexistence between Athenian and German old-timers, who bought property here years ago, and British newcomers on package trips. Beaches, however,

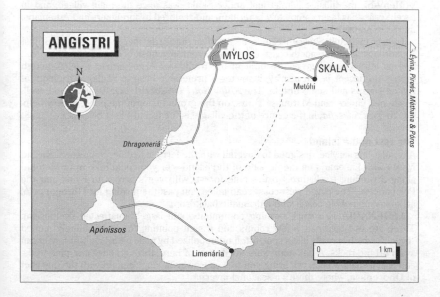

remain better and less crowded than on Éyina, and out of season the pine-covered island succumbs to a leisurely village pace, with many islanders still making a living from fishing and farming. Headscarves worn by the old women indicate the islanders' Albanian ancestry, and until recently they still spoke *Arvanítika* – a dialect of medieval Albanian with Greek accretions – amongst themselves.

The Angístri dock in Éyina Town, separate from the main harbour, is directly opposite the *Ethniki Trapeza* (National Bank). **Boats** from Éyina and Pireás call at both the main villages, Skála and Mílos. **From Pireás**, a direct ferry runs at least twice daily in season, once a day out of season: the journey takes two hours. From Éyina (departures from the fish market harbour), there are boats four or five times a day in season, twice a day out of season.

Skála and Mýlos

The essentially modern resort of **SKÁLA** is dominated by dreary modern apartment buildings and hotels with little to distinguish or commend them; they tend to face either inland or the windswept north side of the peninsula over which Skála is rapidly spreading. The popular town beach, the island's only sandy one, nestles against the protected south shore of this headland, below an enormous church that is the local landmark. Between the beach and the ferry dock are two **hotels** with a bit more going for them position-wise: the *Akti* (☎0297/91 232; ④) and the *Anayennisis* (☎0297/91 332; ④); on summer weekends you would be well advised to reserve ahead at one of these. The tavernas here are pretty nondescript. Both **mopeds** and **mountain bikes** are available for rent at slightly inflated rates (even compared with Éyina); Limenária, the end of the trans-island road, is only 8km distant, so in cooler weather you can comfortably cross Angístri on foot or by bike. A road to the left of the harbour leads within fifteen minutes to the *Angistri Club*, with a disco-bar on the rocks above the sea. From there, it's another ten minutes' walk to a secluded **pebble beach** backed by crumbling cliffs and pine-covered hills; along with Dhragoneriá (see below), this is the best the island has to offer, and is clothing-optional.

Metókhi, the hillside hamlet just above Skála, was once the main village, and in recent years has been completely bought up and restored by foreigners and Athenians; there are no facilities.

Utterly overbuilt Skála threatens in the near future to merge with **MÝLOS**, just 1500m west along the north coast. Once you penetrate a husk of new construction, you find an attractive village centre built in the traditional Argo-Saronic style. Although there's no decent beach nearby, it makes a preferable base to Skála, with plenty of rented **rooms** and some **hotels**. The *Milos Hotel* (☎0297/91 241; ④) is a good, well-positioned choice, and Maroussa Tours, on the ground floor of the hotel, is very helpful. *Ta Tria Adherfia*, in the centre of the village, is the island's best taverna.

The rest of the island

A regular bus service, designed to dovetail with the ferry schedule, connects Skála and Mýlos with Limenária on the far side of the island – or you could hike from Metókhi along a winding track through the pine forest, with views across to Éyina and the Peloponnese. The paved west-coast road takes you past the turning for **Dhragoneriá**, an appealing pebble beach with a dramatic backdrop.

LIMENÁRIA is a small farming community, still largely unaffected by tourism. There are two tavernas, a few rooms and a sign pointing to a misleadingly named "beach", which is really just a spot, often monopolized by male naturists, where you can swim off the rocks. A half-hour walk northwest of here, through olive and pine trees, and past a shallow lake, will bring you to a causeway linking Angístri with the tiny islet of **Dhoroússa**, where there's a seasonal taverna.

Póros

Separated from the mainland by a 350-metre strait, **Póros** ("the ford") only just counts as an island. But qualify it does and, far more than the other Argo-Saronic Gulf islands, it is package tour territory, while its proximity to Pireás also means a weekend invasion by Athenians. Unspoiled it isn't, and the beaches are few and poor, especially compared with neighbouring Ídhra and Spétses. The island town has a bit of character though, and the topography is interesting. Póros is in fact two islands, **Sferiá** (which shelters Póros Town) and the more extensive **Kalávria**, separated from each other by a shallow engineered canal.

In addition to its regular ferry and hydrofoil connections with Pireás and the other Argo-Saronics, Póros has frequent boats shuttling across from the mainland port of **Galatás** in the Peloponnese: there's a car ferry every twenty minutes. This allows for some interesting excursions – locally to the lemon groves of Limonódhassos, Ancient Troezen near Trizíni, and the nearby Devil's Bridge. Further afield, day-trips to Náfplio or to performances of ancient drama at the great theatre of Epidaurus are possible by car, or by taking an excursion, available through travel agents in Póros Town (see below).

Póros Town

Ferries from the Argo-Saronics or from Galatás drop you at **PÓROS**, the only town on the island, which rises steeply on all sides of the tiny volcanic peninsula of Sferiá. The harbour and town are picturesque, and the cafés and the waterfront lively. There are no special sights, save for a little **archeological museum** (Mon–Sat 9am–3pm; free) with a display on the mainland site of Troezen.

Near the boat dock is Hellenic Sun Travel, which has a large number of rooms available (☎0298 25 901/3; ③–⑥). Just back from the waterfront are three other **travel agents**:

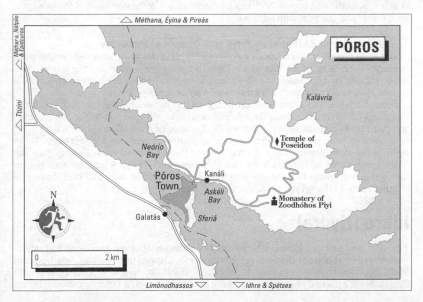

Marinos Tours (☎0298/23 423), sole agents for the Flying Dolphin hydrofoils, Family Tours (☎0298/23 743) and Saronic Gulf Travel (☎0298/24 555). All these agencies **exchange money**, sell island **maps**, arrange **accommodation** in rented rooms, and handle **tours** off the island. If you want to look around on your own, the quieter and preferable places are in the streets back – and up – from the clocktower, although prices are generally on the high side. Here you'll find two reasonable hotels; *Dimitra* (☎0298/22 697; ④) and *Latsi* (☎0298/22 392; ④). Most of the other hotels are across the canal on Kalávria. Camping is not encouraged anywhere on the island and there is no official campsite.

Down on the quayside, good-value **restaurants** include *Grill Oasis* and *Mouragio*, at the far end away from the ferry dock. The *Amvrosia*, up behind the small post office square, serves good fresh fish, and the *Kypos* restaurant beyond it on the left is well worth a visit. Up in town nearer the clocktower, the *Dimitris* taverna is run by a butcher and, unsurprisingly, has good meat. The *Akroyiali*, on the right hand side of the road some 300m down the shore to the left after the Naval Cadet's Training School, is a good family fish taverna with a fine view back over the town.

Additional facilities around the waterfront include a couple of **moped** and **bicycle** rental outlets (you can take either across on boats to the mainland), a **bank**, **post office**, and the helpful **tourist police** (☎0298/22 462; mid-May–Sept).

Kalávria

Most of Póros's **hotels** are to be found on Kalávria, the main body of the island, just across the canal beyond the Naval Cadets' Training School. They stretch for two kilometres or so on either side of the bridge, with some of those to the west ideally situated to catch the dawn chorus – the Navy's marching band. If you'd rather sleep on, head beyond the first bay where the fishing boats tie up. Here, on **Neório Bay** 2km from the bridge, is the pleasant *Hotel Pavlou* (☎0298/22 734; ⑤).

Alternatively, turn right around **Askéli Bay**, where there is a group of posh hotels and villas facing good clear water, if not much in the way of beaches. The best island beach is **Kanáli**, which usually charges admission – a reflection both of Póros's commercialism and the premium on sand.

The Monastery of Zoödhókhou Piyís and Temple of Poseidon

At the end of the four-kilometre stretch of road around Askéli is the simple eighteenth-century **Monastery of Zoödhókhou Piyís**, whose monks have fled the tourists and been replaced by a caretaker to collect the admission charges. It's a pretty spot, with a couple of summer tavernas under the nearby plane trees.

From here you can either walk up across to the far side of the island through the pines and olives, or bike along the road. Either route will lead you to the few columns and ruins that make up the sixth-century BC **Temple of Poseidon** – though keep your eyes open or you may miss them; look for a small white sign on a green fence to the right of the road coming from the monastery. Here Demosthenes, fleeing from the Macedonians after taking part in the last-ditch resistance of the Athenians, took poison rather than surrender to the posse sent after him. A road leads on and back down in a circular route to the "grand canal".

Ídhra (Hydra)

The port and town of **Ídhra**, with its tiers of substantial stone mansions and white-walled, red-tiled houses climbing up from a perfect horseshoe harbour, is a beautiful spectacle. Unfortunately, thousands of others think so, too, and from Easter until September it's packed to the gills. The front becomes one long outdoor café, the hotels are full and the discos flourish. Once a fashionable artists' colony, established in the 1960s as people restored the grand old houses, it has experienced a predictable meta-morphosis into one of the more popular (and expensive) resorts in Greece. But this acknowledged, a visit is still to be recommended, especially if you can get here some time other than peak season.

Ídhra Town

The waterfront of **ÍDHRA TOWN** is lined with mansions, most of them built dur-ing the eighteenth century, on the accumulated wealth of a remarkable merchant fleet of 160 ships which traded as far afield as America and, during the Napoleonic Wars, broke the British blockade to sell grain to France. Fortunes were made and the island also enjoyed a special relationship with the Turkish Porte, governing itself, paying no tax, but providing sailors for the Sultan's navy. These conditions naturally attracted Greek immigrants from the less-privileged mainland, and by the 1820s the town's population stood at nearly 20,000 – an incredible figure when you reflect that today it is under 3000. During the War of Independence, Hydriot merchants provided many of the ships for the Greek forces and inevitably many of the commanders.

The **mansions** of these merchant families, designed by architects from Venice and Genoa, are still the great monuments of the town. If you are interested in seeking them out, a town map is available locally – or ask the tourist police (see p.31) for help in locating them. On the western waterfront, and the hill behind, are the **Voulgaris** mansion, with its interesting interior, and the **Tombazis** mansion, used as a holiday hostel for arts students. Higher up, the **Koundouriotis** mansion was once the proud home of George Koundouriotis, a wealthy shipowner who fought in the War of Independence and whose great grandson, Pavlos Koundouriotis, was president of Greece in the 1920s. On the eastern waterfront are the **Kriezis** mansion, the **Tsamados** mansion, now the national merchant navy college which you can visit between lectures, and the **Spiliopoulous** mansion.

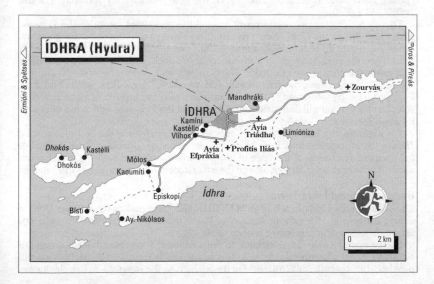

ÍDHRA FESTIVALS

On the second or third weekend in June, Ídhra Town celebrates the **Miaoulia**, in honour of Admiral Andreas Miaoulis whose **fire boats**, packed with explosives, were set adrift upwind of the Turkish fleet during the War of Independence. The highlight of the celebrations is the burning of a boat at sea as a tribute to the sailors who risked their lives in this dangerous enterprise.

On an altogether more peaceful note, the **International Puppet Theatre Festival** takes place here at the end of July, and appeals to children of all ages.

Ídhra is also reputedly hallowed by no less than 365 churches – a total claimed by many a Greek island, but here with some justice. The most important is the cathedral of **Panayía Mitropóleos**, built around a courtyard down by the port, and with a distinctive clocktower.

Practicalities

The town is small and compact, but away from the waterfront the streets and alleyways are steep and finding your way around can be difficult. There are several **banks** along the waterfront, and the **tourist police** (☎0298/52 205; daily mid-May–mid-Oct, 9am–10pm) are on Votsi, opposite the **OTE**.

There are a number of **pensions** and **hotels** along, or just behind, the waterfront in Ídhra town, often charging up to a third more than usual island rates. Some of the restaurants along the waterfront act as agents for the outlying pensions and hotels, which could save you time and footwork; better still, phone ahead and book. *Hotel Amarylis* at Tombazi 15 (☎0298/53 611; ④) is a small hotel with comfortable rooms and private facilities, or there are a couple of beautifully converted old mansions, *Pension Angelika*, Miaouli 42 (☎0298/52 202; ⑤) and *Hotel Hydra*, at Voulgari 8 (☎0298/52 102; ⑤). On the waterfront, but entered from Miaouli, is the slightly run-down but very welcoming *Hotel Sofia* (☎0298/52 313; ③). Of the new pensions, try *Antonio's*, Harami (☎0298/53 227; ④).

There's no shortage of **restaurants** around the waterfront, of which the *Veranda Restaurant* (below the *Hotel Hydra*) has stunning views of the sunset, but for good tavernas you would do well to head a little inland. *The Garden* taverna, known for good meat, is on the road heading up from the hydrofoil dock, with the equally good *Kseri Elia* down the narrow street outside *The Garden*'s wall. Above the *Amarylis Hotel* is the small *Barba Dimas* taverna, which has wonderful mezédhes, snails and fish. Farther up on the same road, *To Kryfo Limani* is a pleasant taverna in a small garden. A bit farther yet you will find good home cooking at the *Yeitoniko*, which has tables on its small verandah.

For **nightlife**, the long-established *Kavos* above the harbour is the best disco, while *Heaven* has impressive views from its hillside site. *Amalour*, straight up from the hydrofoil dock and *Hydronetta* at the edge of town towards Kamíni are lively and play foreign music. The very popular *Sirocco*, also on the waterfront in Ídhra town, plays Greek music.

Beaches around Ídhra Town

The island's only sandy beach is at **MANDHRÁKI**, 2km east of Ídhra Town along a concrete track; it's the private domain of the *Miramare Hotel* (☎0298/52 300; ⑥), although the windsurfing centre is open to all.

On the opposite side of the harbour, to the southeast, a coastal path leads around to **KAMÍNI**, about a twenty-minute walk. Just as you reach Kamíni on the right is a small pension, *Antonia* (☎0298/52 481; ④) On the left, across the street, Eléni Petrolékka has a rival pension (☎0298/52 701; ④), with just two studio flats. Also on the left is the *Kondylenia* restaurant, with fresh fish and a wonderful view of the sunset. About ninety yards up the dry streambed to the left is *Christina's*, a fine traditional Greek fish taverna. Continuing along the water on the unsurfaced mule track you'll come to **Kastéllo**, another small, rocky beach with the ruins of a tiny fort.

Thirty minutes' walk beyond Kamíni (or a boat ride from the port) will bring you to **VLYKHÓS**, a small hamlet with two tavernas, **rooms** and a historic nineteenth-century bridge. The first taverna is *Maria's*, a bit inland and well shaded for lunch. The second is *Marina's*, set on the rocks over the water. Both of these restaurants can call a water taxi to whisk you back to town. **Camping** is tolerated here (though nowhere else closer to town) and the swimming in the lee of an offshore islet is good. Further out is the island of **Dhokós**, only seasonally inhabited by goatherds and people tending their olives.

The interior and south coast

There are no motor vehicles of any kind on Ídhra, except for two lorries to pick up the rubbish, and no surfaced roads away from the port: the island is mountainous and its interior accessible only by foot or donkey. The net result of this is that most tourists don't venture beyond the town, so with a little walking you can find yourself in a quite different kind of island. The pines devastated by forest fires in 1985 are now recovering.

Following the streets of the town upwards and inland you reach a path which winds up the mountain, in about an hour's walk, to the **Monastery of Profítis Ilías** and the **Convent of Ayía Efpraxía**. Both are beautifully situated; the nuns at the convent (the lower of the two) offer hand-woven fabrics for sale. Further on, to the left if you face away from the town, is the **Monastery of Ayía Triádha**, occupied by a few monks (no women admitted). From here a path continues east for two more hours to the cloister of **Zourvás** in the extreme east of the island.

The donkey path continues west of Vlíkhos to **Episkopí**, a high plateau planted with olives and vineyards and dotted by perhaps a dozen summer homes (no facilities). An inconspicuous turning roughly half an hour below leads to Mólos Bay, sea-urchin infested and reportedly recently purchased by foreigners who don't welcome visitors, and to the more pleasant farming hamlet of **Kaoumíti**. From Episkopí itself faint tracks lead to the western extreme of the island, on either side of which the bays of **Dísti** and **Áyios Nikólaos** offer solitude and good swimming. Bísti has a pebble beach with good rocks for swimming off at one side. Ayios Nikólaos has a small sand beach. Any point on the coast can be reached by the water taxis, which will drop you off and then pick you up again at any time you arrange.

The best cove of the many on the south coast is **Limióniza** (beyond Ayía Triádha), with a pebble beach and pine trees.

Spétses (Spetsai)

Spétses was the island where John Fowles once lived and which he used, thinly disguised as Phraxos, as the setting for *The Magus*. It is today very popular with well-to-do Athenians and with foreigners, and seems to have risen above the bad reputation an unhealthy proportion of cheap package tours and "lager louts" blighted it with in the 1980s. The architecture of Spétses Town is characterful and distinguished, if less dramatic than that of Ídhra. And, despite a bout of forest-fire devastation in 1990, the landscape described by Fowles is still to be seen: "away from its inhabited corner [it is] truly haunted . . . its pine forests uncanny". Remarkably, at Spétses's best beach, Áyii Anáryiri, development has been limited to a scattering of holiday villas.

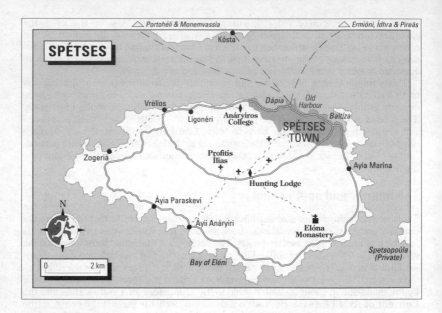

Spétses Town

SPÉTSES TOWN is the island's port – and its only settlement. It shares with Ídhra the same history of late eighteenth-century mercantile adventure and prosperity, and the same leading role in the War of Independence, which made its foremost citizens the aristocrats of the newly independent Greek state. Pebble-mosaic courtyards and streets sprawl between 200-year-old mansions, whose architecture is quite distinct from the Peloponnesian styles across the straits. Though homeowners may bring private cars onto the island, their movement inside the town limits is prohibited. A few taxis supplement the horse-drawn buggies, whose bells ring cheerfully night and day along the long waterfront, though animal welfare activists are justifiably worried by the condition of some of the horses by summer's end. Otherwise, motorbikes are the preferred mode of transport.

The sights are principally the majestic old houses and gardens, the grandest of which is the magnificent Mexis family mansion, built in 1795 and now used as the **local museum** (Tues–Sun 8.30am–2.30pm; 400dr), housing a display of relics from the War of Independence that includes the bones of the Spetsiot admiral-heroine Lascarina Bouboulina. Bouboulina's home, to the rear of the cannon-studded main harbour known on the island as the Dápia, has been made into a **museum** (daily 10am–7pm; 1000dr) by her descendants and is well worth visiting. Guided tours (30 min) are given in English several times a day.

Just outside the town, Fowles aficionados will notice **Anáryiros College**, a curious Greek re-creation of an English public school where the author was employed and set part of his tale; it is now vacant, save for the occasional conference or kids' holiday programme. Like the massive Edwardian **Hotel Possidonion**, another *Magus* setting, on the waterside, it was endowed by Sotirios Anáryiros, the island's great nineteenth-century benefactor. An enormously rich self-made man, he was also responsible for planting the pine forest that now covers the island. His former house, behind the *Hotel Roumani*, is a monument to bad taste, decked out like a Pharaoh's tomb.

Perhaps more interesting than chasing *Magus* settings though, is a walk east from the Dápia. En route, you pass the smaller "old harbour", still a well protected mooring, and the church of **Áyios Nikólaos** with its graceful belfry and some giant pebble mosaics. At the end of the road you reach the **Baltíza** inlet where, among the sardine packed yachts, half a dozen boatyards continue to build kaïkia in the traditional manner; it was one of these that recreated the *Argo* for Tim Severin's re-enactment of the "Jason Voyage".

Practicalities

A good way to get around the island is by bike and, despite the hills, you can reach most points or make a circuit without too much exertion. Several reliable **bike and moped** rental outlets are scattered through town.

All kinds of **accommodation** are available in Spétses Town, though the *Possidonion*, where kings and presidents have slept, no longer operates as a hotel. Be warned that prices are inflated in high season, but the town is smaller and less steep than Ídhra, so hunting around for a good deal is not such hard work. If you don't fancy pounding the streets yourself, try Alasia Travel (☎0298/74 098) or Melédon Tourist and Travel Agency (☎0298/74 497), both by the Dápia. Two simple but comfortable places are *Faros* (☎0298/72 613; ④) and *Stelios* (☎0298/72 971; ③). Good, though less central options are *Studios Orlof* near Ayía Marína beach and *Makis/Costas Studios* in Kounoupítsa, west of the Dápia. Few places stay open all year – exceptions include the central *Pension Alexandris* (☎0298/72 211; ④) and the *Klimis Hotel* (☎0298/74 497; ④), a quiet and pleasant place.

In Spétses Town, **food** and **drink** tend to be a bit on the pricey side. Among the best options are *Roussos*, 300m east of the Dápia just beyond Klimis; the Bakery Restaurant, about 100m up from the Dápia; and *Lazaros's Taverna*, another 300m beyond it. For fish, go to the long established *Patralis* on the water at Kounoupítsa beyond the Spetses Hotel; *Siora's* in the Old Harbour is also good but expensive and crowded. The ouzerí *Byzantino*, also on the Old Harbour, is popular, too.

By day, *Stambolisos To Kafenio*, beyond the Flying Dolphin office at the Dápia, remains steadfastly traditional. By night, clubbers head for *Figaro* in the Old Harbour, and the places at the other end of town around Kounoupítsa. Few of these places shut until the fishermen are setting out.

Spétses has a couple of good **craft shops**: *Pityousa* and *O Palios Eleonas* (behind the *Hotel Soleil*) offer some attractive original work.

Around the island

For **swimming** you need to get clear of the town. Beaches within walking distance are at **Ayía Marína** (twenty minutes east, with the very pleasant *Paradise* restaurant), at various spots beyond the **old harbour**, and several other spots half an hour away in either direction. The tempting islet of **Spetsopoúla**, just offshore from Ayía Marína, is unfortunately off-limits: it's the private property of the heirs of shipping magnate Stavros Niarchos.

For heading further afield, you'll need to hire a **bike** or **moped**, or use the **kaïkia** rides from the Dápia, which run to beaches around the island in summer. A very expensive alternative are **waterboat taxis**, though they can take up to ten people. **Walkers** might want to go over the top of the island to Áyii Anáryiri; forest fire has ravaged most of the pines between Ayía Marína and Áyii Anáryiri, though happily they are growing back. The route out of town starts from behind *Lazaros's Taverna*.

West from Spétses Town

Heading west from the Dápia around the coast, the road is paved or in good condition almost all around the island. The forest stretches from the central hills right down to the shore and it makes for a beautiful coastline with little coves and rocky promontories, all shaded by trees. *Panas* taverna at Ligoneri provides wonderful respite from the bustle of town. You can swim below and then have lunch or dinner under the pines.

Vréllos is one of the first places you come to, at the mouth of a wooded valley known locally as "Paradise", which would be a fairly apt description, except that, like so many of the beaches, it becomes polluted every year by tourists' rubbish. However, the entire shore is dotted with coves and in a few places there are small tavernas – there's a good one at **Zogeriá**, for instance, where the scenery and rocks more than make up for the inadequate little beach.

Working your way anti-clockwise around the coast towards Áyii Anáryiri you reach **Áyia Paraskeví** with its small church and beach – one of the most beautiful coves on Spétses and an alternate stop on some of the kaïki runs. There's a basic beach café here in summer. On the hill above is the house John Fowles used as the setting for *The Magus*, the **Villa Yasemiá**. It was once owned by the late Alkis Botassis, who claimed to be the model for the *Magus* character – though Fowles denies "appropriating" anything more than his "outward appearance" and the "superb site" of his house.

Áyii Anáryiri

Áyii Anáryiri, on the south side of the island, is the best, if also the most popular, beach: a beautiful, long, sheltered bay of fine sand. Gorgeous first thing in the morning, it fills up later in the day, with bathers, windsurfers and, at one corner, speedboat-driving waterski instructors. On the right-hand side of the bay, looking out to sea, there's a sea cave, which you can swim to and explore. There's a good taverna on the beach and, just behind, *Tasso's*, run by one of the island's great eccentrics.

travel details

Ferries

From the central harbour at **Pireás** at least 4 boats daily run to Ayía Marína (1hr) and 11 to Éyina (1hr 30min); 1–2 daily to Skála and Mílos (2hr); 4 daily to Póros (3hr 30min); 1–2 daily to Ídhra (4hr 30min) and Spétses (5hr 30min). About 4 connections daily between Éyina and Póros; 4–5 daily between Éyina and Angístri; from Angístri about 4 weekly to Paleá Epídhavros, far less frequently to Póros and Méthana.

Most of the ferries stop on the mainland at Méthana (between Éyina and Póros) and Ermióni (between Ídhra and Spétses); it is possible to board them here from the Peloponnese. Some continue from Spétses to Pórto Khéli. There are also constant boats between Póros and Galatás (10min) from dawn until late at night, and boat-taxis between Spétses and Pórto Khéli.

NB There are more ferries at weekends and fewer out of season (although the service remains good); for Éyina and Póros they leave Pireás most frequently between 7.30am and 9am, and 2pm and 4pm. Do not buy a return ticket as it saves no money and limits you to one specific boat. The general information number for the Argo-Saronic ferries is ☎01/41 75 382.

Flying Dolphin hydrofoils

Approximately hourly services from the central harbour at Pireás to **Éyina** only 6am–8pm in season, 7am–5pm out of season (40min).

All hydrofoils going beyond Éyina leave from the **Zea Marina**: 4–15 times daily to Póros (1hr), Ídhra (1hr 40min), and Spétses (2–2hr 30min). All these times depend upon the stops en route, and frequencies vary with the season.

Éyina is connected with the other three islands twice a day; Póros, Ídhra and Spétses with each other 3–5 times daily. Some hydrofoils also stop at Méthana and Ermióni and all of those to Spétses continue to Porto Khéli (15min more). This is a junction of the hydrofoil route – there is usually one a day onwards to Toló and Náfplio (and vice versa; 30 and 45min) in season and another (almost year-round) to Monemvassía (2hr). The Monemvassía hydrofoil continues 2–4 times a week to the island of Kýthira.

NB Services are heavily reduced out of season, though all the routes between Pórto Khéli and Pireás still run. Hydrofoils are usually twice as fast and twice as expensive as ordinary boats, though to Éyina the price is little different. You can now buy round trip tickets to destinations in the Argo-Saronic Gulf. In season, it's not unusual for departures to be fully booked for a day or so at a time.

Details and tickets available from the Ceres Pireás ticket office at Ákti Themistokléous 8 (☎01/42 80 001, number perennially engaged). The Ceres Athens office at Filellínon 3 (☎01/32 44 600) is more convenient if you are in Athens. Tickets can also be bought at the departure quays on Aktí Tselépi in Pireás and at Zéa.

CHAPTER TWO

THE CYCLADES

Named after the circle they form around the sacred island of Delos, the **Cyclades** (Kykládhes) is the most satisfying Greek archipelago for island-hopping. On no other group do you get quite such a strong feeling of each island as a microcosm, each with its own distinct traditions, customs and path of modern development. Most of these self-contained realms are compact enough to walk around in a few days, giving you a sense of completeness and identity impossible on, say, Crete or most of the Ionian islands.

The islands do share some features however, the majority of them (Ándhros, Náxos, Sérifos and Kéa excepted) being arid and rocky; most also share the "Cycladic" style of brilliant-white, cubist architecture. The extent and impact of tourism, though, is markedly haphazard, so that although some English is spoken on most islands, a slight detour from the beaten track – from Íos to Síkinos, for example – can have you groping for your Greek phrasebook.

But whatever the level of tourist development, there are only two islands where it has come completely to dominate their character: **Íos**, the original hippie-island and still a paradise for hard-drinking backpackers, and **Mýkonos**, by far the most popular of the group, with its teeming old town, selection of nude beaches and sophisticated clubs and gay bars. After these two, **Páros**, **Sífnos**, **Náxos**, and **Thíra** (Santoríni) are currently the most popular, with their beaches and main towns drastically overcrowded at the height of the season. To avoid the hordes altogether – except in August, when nearly everywhere is overrun and escape is impossible – the most promising islands are **Síkinos**, **Kímolos** or **Anáfi**, or the minor islets around Náxos. For a different view of the Cyclades, visit **Tínos** and its imposing pilgrimage church, a major spiritual centre of Greek Orthodoxy, or **Sýros** with its elegant townscape, and (like Tínos), large Catholic minority. Due to their closeness to Athens, adjacent **Kýthnos** and **Kéa** are predictably popular – and relatively expensive – weekend havens for Greeks. The one

---

ACCOMMODATION PRICE CODES

Throughout the book we've used the following **price codes** to denote the cheapest available room in high season; all are prices for a double room, except for category ①, which represents per person rates. Out of season, rates can drop by up to fifty percent, especially if you are staying for three or more nights. Single rooms, where available, cost around seventy percent of the price of a double.

Rented private rooms on the islands usually fall into the ② or ③ categories, depending on their location and facilities, and the season; a few in the ④ category are more like plush self-catering apartments. They are not generally available from late October through to the beginning of April, when only hotels tend to remain open.

① 1400–2000dr	④ 8000–12,000dr
② 4000–6000dr	⑤ 12,000–16,000dr
③ 6000–8000dr	⑥ 16,000dr and upwards

For more accommodation details, see pp.39–41.

major ancient site is **Delos** (Dhílos), certainly worth making time for; the commercial and religious centre of the Classical Greek world, it's visited most easily on a day trip, by kaïki or jet boat from Mýkonos.

When it comes to **moving on**, many of the islands – in particular Mílos, Páros, Náxos and Thíra – are handily connected with Crete (easier in season), while from Tínos, Mýkonos, Sýros, Páros, Náxos, Thíra or Amorgós you can reach many of the Dodecanese by direct boat. Similarly, you can regularly get from Mýkonos, Náxos, Síros and Páros to Ikaría and Sámos (in the eastern Aegean – see p.284 and p.296).

One consideration for the timing of your visit is that the Cyclades often get frustratingly **stormy**, particularly in early spring or late autumn, and it's also the group worst affected by the *meltémi*, which blows sand and tables about and with ease throughout much of July and August. Delayed or cancelled ferries are not uncommon, so if you're heading back to Athens to catch a flight leave yourself a day or two's leeway.

Kéa (Tziá)

Kéa is the closest of the Cyclades to the mainland, and is extremely popular in summer, and at weekends year-round, with Athenians. Their impact is mostly confined to certain small coastal resorts, leaving most of the interior quiet, although there is a preponderance of expensive apartments and villas, and not as many good tavernas as you might expect because so many visitors self-cater. Midweek, or outside peak season, Kéa is a more enticing destination, with its rocky, forbidding perimeter and inland oak and almond groves.

As ancient Keos, the island and its strategic well-placed harbour supported four cities – a pre-eminence that continued until the nineteenth century when Sýros became the main Greek port. Today tourists account for the sea traffic – regular ferry connections with Lávrio on the mainland (only a ninety-minute bus ride from Athens), plus useful hydrofoils and ferries to and from Zéa, Kýthnos and Rafína.

The northwest coast: Korissía to Otziás

The small northern ferry and hydrofoil port of **KORISSÍA** has fallen victim to uneven expansion and has little beauty to lose; if you don't like its looks upon disembarking, try to get a bus to Písses (16km), Otziás (6km) or Ioulidha (6km). Buses usually meet the boats; from July until August there's a regular fixed schedule around the island, but at other times they can be very elusive. There are just four **taxis** on Kéa, and two motorbike rental outfits, which are more expensive than on most islands, though Nikos Laliótis (☎0288/21 485), 200m along the road to Khóra, has much better prices than the harbour shop.

There's a list of rooms in the seafront tourist information office, and the kindly agents for the Flying Dolphin hydrofoils (To Stegadhi gift shop) sell maps and guides, and can phone around in search of **accommodation**. The best choices are *Nikitas* pension (☎0288/21 193; ④), open all year and very friendly, *Pension Korissia* (☎0288/21 484; ④), well inland along the stream bed, *Iy Tzia Mas* (☎0288/21 305; ④), right behind the best end of the otherwise uninspiring port beach, and the somewhat noisy *Karthea* (☎0288/21 204; ④), which does, however, boast single rooms and year-round operation – and a cameo appearance in recent Greek history. When the junta fell in July 1974, the colonels were initially imprisoned for some weeks in the then-new hotel, while the recently restored civilian government pondered what to do with them; Kéa was then so remote and unvisited that the erstwhile tyrants were safely out of reach of a vengeful populace. For **eating**, *Iy Akri* is the best of a small bunch, while *O Kostas* near the jetty

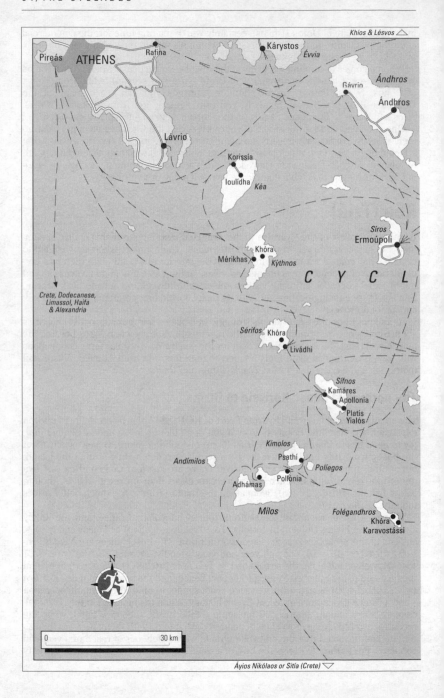

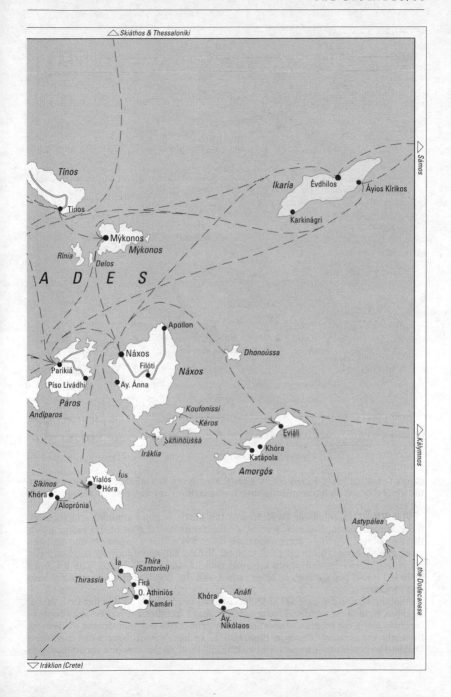

△ Skiáthos & Thessaloníki

△ Sámos

Tínos

Tínos

Ikaría Évdhilos Áyios Kírikos

Karkinágri

Mýkonos

Mýkonos

Rínia

Delos

A D E S

Apóllon

Dhonoússa

Náxos

Parikiá

Filóti

Náxos

Píso Livádhi

Ay. Ánna

Páros

Koufoníssi

Andíparos

Kéros

Skhinoússa

Eviáli

Iráklia

Khóra

Katápola

△ Kálymnos

Amorgós

Íos

Síkinos

Yialós

Khóra

Hóra

Aloprónia

Astypálea

Ía

Thíra
(Santoríni)

△ the Dodecanese

Thirassía

Firá

O. Athiniós

Khóra Anáfi

Kamári

Ay.
Nikólaos

▽ Iráklion (Crete)

is functional but fairly decent. There's good swimming at **Yialiskári**, a small, eucalyptus-fringed beach on the headland above Korissía; the *Yialiskari* rooms (☎0288/21 197; ⑤) enjoy a good view.

VOURKÁRI, a couple of kilometres to the north, is more compact and arguably more attractive than Korissía, serving as the favourite hangout of the yachting set; there's no real beach or accommodation here. Three fairly expensive and indistinguishable **tavernas**, serve up good seafood dishes, and there's a very good ouzerí – *Strofi tou Mimi* – located where the road cuts inland towards Otziás. The few **bars** include *Vinylio*, popular with an older crowd, and the slightly more happening *Kouros* and *Prodhikos*.

Another 4km to the east, **OTZIÁS** has a small beach that's a bit better than that at Korissía, though more exposed to prevailing winds; facilities are limited to a couple of tavernas and a fair number of apartments for rent. Kéa's only functioning monastery, the eighteenth-century **Panayía Kastrianí**, is an hour's walk along a dirt road from Otziás. The hostel at the monastery (☎0288/21 348; ②) is the cheapest accommodation deal on the island, albeit rather basic and isolated. Although more remarkable for its fine setting on a high bluff than for any intrinsic interest, from here you can take the pleasant walk on to the island capital, Ioulídha, in another two hours.

Ioulídha

IOULÍDHA, ancient Ioulis, was the birthplace of the renowned early fifth-century BC poets Simonides and Bacchylides. With its numerous red-tiled roofs, Neoclassical buildings and winding flagstoned paths, it is by no means a typical Cycladic village, but, beautifully situated in an amphitheatric fold in the hills, is architecturally the most interesting settlement on the island. Accordingly it has "arrived" in recent years, with numerous trendy bars and bistros much patronized on weekends. The **Archeological Museum** (Tues–Sun 8.30am–3pm; free) displays finds from the four ancient city-states of Kéa, although the best items were long ago spirited away to Athens. The lower reaches of the town stretch across a spur to the **Kástro**, a tumbledown Venetian fortress incorporating stones from an ancient temple of Apollo. Fifteen minutes' walk northeast, on the path toward Panayía Kastrianí, you pass the **Lion of Kea**, a sixth-century BC sculpture carved out of the living rock. Six metres long and two metres high, the imposing beast has crudely powerful haunches and a bizarre facial expression. There are steps right down to the lion, but the effect is most striking from a distance.

There are two **hotels** in Ioulídha, quieter than anything down in Korissía, and both much in demand: the somewhat pokey *Filoxenia* (☎0288/22 057; ③) is perched above a shoe shop and has no en-suite plumbing and saggy beds; the more comfortable *Ioulis* (☎0288/22 177; ④) up in the kástro has superb views from its terrace and west-facing rooms.

You're spoiled for choice in the matter of **eating** and **drinking**, with quality generally higher here than near Korissía. *Iy Piatsa*, just as you enter the lower town from the car park, has a variety of tasty dishes, while *To Kalofagadhon* up on the platía enjoys great views and is the best place for a full-blown meat feast. Further up there is good standard fare on the terrace of *To Steki tis Tzias*. The aptly named *Panorama* serves up pastries and coffee and is a good place to watch the sun set, while after-dark action seems to oscillate between such bars as *Kamini*, *Leon* and, best of all, *Mylos*. A newly opened kéndro, *Ta Pedhia Pezi* (which means "the guys are playing"), a few kilometres out off the road towards Písses is terrific for a full-on bouzoúki night. An **OTE**, **post office** and **bank agent** round up the list of amenities.

The south

About 8km southwest of Ioulídha, reached via a mix of tracks and paths, or by mostly paved road, the crumbling Hellenistic watchtower of **Ayía Marína** sprouts dramatically from the grounds of a small nineteenth-century monastery. Beyond, the paved main road twists around the dramatically scenic head of the lovely agricultural valley at **PÍSSES**, emerging at a large and little-developed beach. There are three tavernas behind, plus a pleasant **campsite**, *Camping Kea*, which has good turfy ground and also runs the studios (☎0288/31 302; ④) further inland. The pension above the taverna (☎0288/31 301; ③) is the best deal around. Of the tavernas, the best is *To Akroyiali*, with a good range and excellent rosé wine.

Beyond Písses, the asphalt – and the bus service – peters out along the 5km south to **KOÚNDOUROS**, a sheltered, convoluted bay popular with yachters; there's a taverna behind the largest of several sandy coves, none cleaner or bigger than the beach at Písses. The luxury *Kea Beach* hotel (☎0288/31 230; ⑤) sits out on its own promontory with tennis courts and pool, and there is a hamlet of dummy windmills; built as holiday homes, they are "authentic" right down to their masts, thatching and stone cladding. At the south end of the bay, *Manos* taverna and rooms (☎0288/31 214; ③) is by far the best value, with TV in all rooms. If you want to base yourself on this side of the island it's worth noting that the hydrofoil stops at the *Kea Beach* hotel. A further 2km south at **Kambí**, there's a nice little beach and a good taverna, *To Kambi*.

Besides the very scant ruins of ancient Poiessa near Písses, the only remains of any real significance from Kéa's past are fragments of the temple of Apollo at **ancient Karthaia**, tucked away on the southeastern edge of the island above Póles Bay, with an excellent deserted twin beach that's easiest reached by boat. Otherwise, it's a good three hour round-trip walk from the hamlet of Stavroudháki, some way off the lower road linking Koúndouros, Khávouna and Káto Meriá. Travelling by motorbike, the upper road, which more directly plies between Písses and Káto Meriá, is worth following as an alternative return along the island's summit to Ioulídha; it's paved between Ioulídha and Káto Meriá, and the entire way affords fine views, over the thousands of magnificent oaks which constitute Kéa's most distinctive feature.

Kýthnos (Thermiá)

Though perhaps the dullest and certainly the most barren of the Cyclades, a short stay on **Kýthnos** is a good antidote to the exploitation likely to be encountered elsewhere. Few foreigners bother to visit – the island is quieter than Kéa, even in midsummer – while the inhabitants (except in more commercialized Mérikhas) are overtly friendly. All these factors compensate for the paucity of specific diversions: it's a place where Athenians come to buy land for villas, go spear-fishing, and sprawl on generally mediocre beaches without having to jostle for space. You could use it as a first or, better, last island stop; there are weekly ferry connections with Kéa, more frequent services to and from Sérifos, Sífnos and Mílos, as well as seasonal hydrofoils to Kéa, Zéa and Rafína.

Mérikhas and around

In good weather boats dock on the west coast at **MÉRIKHAS**, a rather functional ferry and fishing port with most of the island's facilities. This fact almost obliges you to stay here, and makes Mérikhas something of a tourist ghetto, but it's redeemed by proximity to the island's best beaches. The closest beach of any repute is **Episkopí**, a 500m stretch of averagely clean grey sand with a single taverna, thirty minutes' walk north of the town; you can shorten this considerably by sticking to coast-hugging trails and tracks below the road. Far better are the adjacent beaches of **Apókroussi**, which has a canteen, and **Kolóna**, the latter essentially a sandspit joining the islet of Áyios Loukás to Kýthnos. They lie about an hour's walk northwest of Episkopí, and are easiest reached by boat-trip from the harbour. Camping is generally tolerated, even on Martinákia beach, the nearest to Mérikhas, which has an eponymous taverna.

Accommodation proprietors often meet the ferries, and a relative abundance of rooms makes for good bargaining opportunities. Few places have sea views, one exception being the *Kythnos Hotel* (☎0281/32 092; ③) near the ferry dock. Behind the seafront, *Pension Yiasemi* (☎0281/32 248; ④) is a decent choice; studios there and elsewhere can be good value too. The best **restaurants** are *To Kandouni*, furthest from the ferry, a tasty grill with tables right by the water and specialities like *sfougato*, and *Yialos*, about halfway along the seafront, which has a good section of salads and dips. Among purveyors of a modest nightlife, by far the friendliest and liveliest place is *To Vyzantio*, just back from the water, whose animated owner plays varied rock music. *Remezzo*

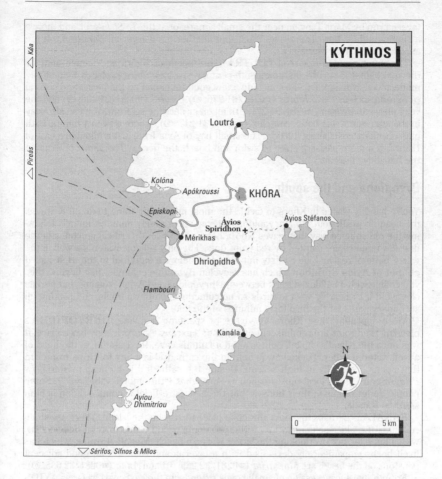

behind the beach has a fine location and plays good music, and eclectic Greek folk music can be heard at the modern *New Corner*, 100m along the road to Dhriopídha.

The **bus service**, principally to Loutrá, Khóra, Dhryopídha and Kanála, is reasonably reliable, in season at least; the only motorbike rental is through the main Milos Express ticket agency and is noticeably more expensive than on many islands. The Cava Kythnos shop doubles as the official **National Bank** outlet (exchange all day), and is the agent for hydrofoil tickets and the boat to Kéa.

Khóra and Loutrá

KHÓRA is 6km northeast of Mérikhas, set in the middle of the island. Tilting south off an east–west ridge, and laid out to an approximate grid plan, it's an awkward blend of Kéa-style gabled roofs, Cycladic churches with dunce-cap cupolas, and concrete monsters. Khóra supports the main **OTE** branch, and a **post office** (open only until noon); at present the closest accommodation is at Loutrá (see p.90). You can **eat** at the taverna run by Maria Tzoyiou near the small square, or at the *To Steki* grill, and there's a single outdoor **bar**, *Apokalypsi*. You'll find another good taverna, *Paradisos*, on the approach road from Mérikhas.

The much-vaunted resort of **LOUTRÁ** (3km north of Khóra and named after its thermal baths) is scruffy, its nineteenth-century spa long since replaced by a sterile modern construction. Facilities include a few good **tavernas** on the beach and several **pensions** such as *Porto Klaras* (☎0281/31 276; ④), *Delfini* (☎0281/31 430; ③) and the very pleasant *Meltemi* (☎0281/31 271; ④), all on or near the seafront. You can also stay in the state-run *Xenia* baths complex (☎0281/31 217; ④), where a twenty-minute bath plus check-up costs about 1000dr. The small bay of Ayía Iríni, just a kilometre east of Loutrá, is a more pleasant place to swim and boasts the decent *Trehandiri* taverna on the hill above the bay.

Dryopídha and the south

You're handily placed in Khóra to tackle the most interesting thing to do on Kýthnos: the beautiful **walk** south to Dhryopídha. It takes about ninety minutes, initially following the old cobbled way that leaves Khóra heading due south; critical junctions in the first few minutes are marked by red paint dots. The only reliable water is a well in the valley bottom, reached after thirty minutes, just before a side trail to the triple-naved **chapel of Áyios Sprídhon** which has recycled Byzantine columns. Just beyond this, you collide with a bulldozed track between Dhryopídha and Áyios Stéfanos, but purists can avoid it by bearing west towards some ruined ridgetop windmills, and picking up secondary paths for the final forty minutes of the hike.

More appealing than Khóra by virtue of spanning a ravine, **DHRYOPÍDHA**'s pleasing tiled roofs are reminiscent of Spain or Tuscany. A surprisingly large place, it was once the island's capital, built around a famous cave, the Katafíki, at the head of a well watered valley. Tucked away behind the cathedral is a tiny **folklore museum** that opens erratically in high season. Beside the cathedral is a cheap psistariá, *Ly Pelagra* and a good local ouzerí called *O Apithanos* ("the unbelievable guy"). Some people do let rooms in their houses, but the nearest official accommodation is 6km south at Kanála.

KANÁLA is perhaps the most attractive place to stay on the island. There are some rooms in the older settlement up on the promontory and a fine taverna, *Louloudhas*, with a huge terrace overlooking the larger western beach, **Megáli Ámmos**, which has itself been sympathetically developed with a taverna and rooms. Two good adjacent pensions on the beach are *Margarita* (☎0281/32 265; ④) and *Anna* (☎0281/32 035; ④).

From Kanála, a succession of small coves extends up the east coast as far as **ÁYIOS STÉFANOS**, a small coastal hamlet with two high season tavernas opposite a chapel-crowned islet linked by a causeway to the body of the island. Southwest of Dhryopídha, reached by a turning off the road to Kanála, **Flamboúri** is the most presentable beach on the west coast. The double bay of **Ayíou Dhimitríou** at the extreme southern tip of the island is reached over a rough road, and is not really worth the effort, although there are now two restaurants and rooms to rent in high season.

Sérifos

Sérifos has long languished outside the mainstream of history and modern tourism. Little has happened here since the legendary Perseus returned with the Gorgon's head, in time to save his mother Danaë from being ravished by the local king Polydectes. Many would-be visitors are deterred by the apparently barren, hilly interior which, with the stark, rocky coastline, makes Sérifos appear uninhabited until your

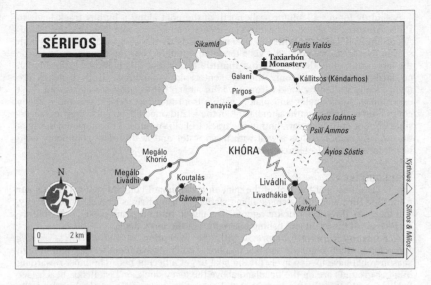

ferry turns into Livádhi bay. The island is recommended for serious **walkers**, who can head for several small villages and isolated coves in the little-explored interior. Modern Serifots love seclusion, and here, more than anywhere else in the Cyclades, you will find farmsteads miles from anywhere, with only a donkey path to their door. Everyone here seems to keep livestock, and to produce their own wines, and many also cultivate the wild **narcissus** for the export market.

Few islanders speak much English, and many have a deserved reputation of being slow to warm to outsiders; one suspects that the locals still don't quite know what to make of the hordes of northern Europeans who descend on the place for the brief but intense July and August season. American yachties drop anchor here in some numbers as well, to take on fresh water which, despite appearances, Sérifos has in abundance.

Livádhi and the main beaches

Most visitors stay in the port, **LIVÁDHI**, set in a wide greenery-fringed bay and handy for most of the island's beaches. The usually calm bay here is a magnet for island-hopping yachts, whose crews chug to and fro in dinghies all day and night. It's not the most attractive place on Sérifos – and to stay here exclusively would be to miss some fine walks – but Livádhi and the neighbouring cove of Livadhákia are certainly the easiest places to find rooms and any other amenities you might need, all of which are very scarce elsewhere.

Unfortunately, the long **beach** at Livádhi is nothing to write home about: the sand is hard-packed and muddy, and the water weedy and prone to intermittent jellyfish flotillas – only the far northeastern end is at all usable. Walk uphill along the street from the *Mylos* bakery, or over the southerly headland from the cemetery, to reach the neighbouring, far superior **Livadhákia**. This golden-sand beach, shaded by tamarisk trees, offers snorkelling and other watersports, one rather average taverna and some furtive nudism. If you prefer more seclusion, five minutes' stroll across the headland to the south brings you to the smaller **Karávi** beach, which is cleaner and almost totally naturist, but has no shade or facilities.

A slightly longer 45-minute walk north of the port along a bumpy track leads to **Psilí Ámmos**, a sheltered, white-sand beach considered the best on the island. Accordingly, it's popular, with two rival tavernas, both of which tend to be full in high season. Naturists are pointed – via a ten-minute walk across the headland – towards the larger and often deserted **Áyios Ioánnis** beach, but this is rather exposed with no facilities at all, and only the far south end is inviting. Both beaches are theoretically visited by kaïkia from Livádhi, as are two nearby sea-caves, but don't count on it. Additionally, and plainly visible from arriving ferries, two more sandy coves hide at the far southeastern flank of the island opposite an islet; they are accessible on foot only, by a variation of the track to Psilí Ámmos. The more northerly of the two, **Áyios Sóstis**, has a well with fresh water and is the most commonly used beach for secluded freelance camping.

Practicalities

The **OTE** office is at the foot of the quay in Livádhi, and you can rent a **bike** or **car** from Blue Bird next to the single filling station, or from Krinas Travel above the jetty, and there are three **boat-ticket agents**. The public **bus stop** and posted schedule are at the base of the yacht and fishing boat jetty, not the ferry dock.

Accommodation proprietors – with the exception of the *Coralli Camping Bungalows*, which regularly sends a minibus – don't always meet ferries, and in high season you'll have to step lively off the boat to get a decent bed. The most rewarding hunting grounds are on the headland above the ferry dock, or Livadhákia beach (see below); anything without a sea view will be a notch cheaper. Up on the headland, the *Pension Cristi* (☎0281/51 775; ④) has an excellent, quiet position overlooking the bay; the nearby *Areti* (☎0281/51 479; ④) is a little snootier for the same price. Alternatively, down in the flatlands, the relatively inexpensive seafront *Kyklades Hotel* (☎0281/51 553; ④) has the important virtues of year-round operation and kindly management, though the bay-view rooms get some traffic noise. The new *Hotel Anna* (☎0281/51 666; ④) by the yacht harbour is another fall-back, while the cheapest rooms in Livádhi are next to each other at the far end of the bay: *Margarita* (☎0281/51 321; ③) and *Adonios Peloponnisos* (☎0281/51 113; ③).

Livadhákia, ten to fifteen minutes' walk south, offers more nocturnal peace, choice and quality, though it has a more touristy feel and the mosquitoes are positively ferocious – bring insecticide coils or make sure your room is furnished with electric vapour pads. One of the oldest and largest complexes of rooms and apartments, close to the beach and with verdant views, is run by Vaso Stamataki (☎0281/51 346; ④). Newer and higher-standard choices include the *Helios Pension* (☎0281/51 066; ③), just above the road as you arrive at Livadhákia and, further along, the *Medusa* (☎0281/51 127; ④). Cheaper are the rooms in adjacent buildings just after *Helios*, run by two sisters, Yioryia (☎0281/51 336; ③) and Mina (☎0281/51 545; ③) – the latter place has sea views. Further along is *Dhorkas* (☎0281/51 422; ④) and right by the beach above a restaurant, is *O Alexandros* (☎0281/51 119; ④). Near the built up area, beside one of only two public access tracks to the beach and behind the best patch of sand, *Coralli Camping Bungalows* (☎0281/51 500; ⑤) has a restaurant, bar, shop and landscaped camping area, but no prizes for a warm welcome.

A makeshift road runs the length of the Livádhi seafront, crammed with restaurants, shops, and all the services you might need. At the strategic southerly crossroads, the *Mylos* bakery has exceptionally good cheese pies and wholegrain bread; a butcher and a handful of fruit shops and **supermarkets** are scattered along the beach, while there's a **pharmacy** at the foot of the quay.

You'll pay through the nose for **eating** in the obvious places near the quay in Livádhia (although *Mokkas* fish taverna is friendly and good value); walk up the beach, and meals get less expensive and more authentically Greek. The two best traditional tavernas are the busy *Stamatis*, and the welcoming restaurant under the *Hotel Cyclades*. At the extreme far northeast end of the beach, *Sklavenis* (aka *Margarita's*) has loyal adherents to its down-home feel and courtyard seating, but many find the food overly deep-fried and too pricey. Closer to the yacht harbour, *Meltemi* is a good – if slightly expensive – ouzerí, something out of the ordinary for the island. For crepes and ice cream, try *Meli*, in the commercial centre by the port police.

Nightlife is surprisingly lively, though few establishments stay in business more than two consecutive seasons. The main cluster is about a third of the way along the seafront and includes the westernized *Vitamin C*, *Karnayio* and *Agria Menta*, as well as the skiládhiko-style bouzoúki joint *AlterEgo*, and a smaller bar with a pool table named *Aiolos*.

Buses connect Livádhi with Khóra, 2km away, some ten times daily, but only manage one or two daily trips to Megálo Livádhia, Galaní, and Kállitsos. You may well want to walk, if you're travelling light; it's a pleasant if steep forty minutes up a cobbled way to Khóra, with the *kalderími* leading off from a bend in the road about 300m out of Livádhia. By the beginning of October, you'll have no choice, since the bus – like nearly everything else – ceases operation for the winter.

Khóra

Quiet and atmospheric **KHÓRA**, teetering precariously above the harbour, is one of the most spectacular villages of the Cyclades. The best sights are to be found on the town's borders: tiny churches cling to the cliff edge, and there are breathtaking views across the valleys below. At odd intervals along its alleyways you'll find part of the old castle making up the wall of a house, or a marble statue leaning incongruously in one corner. A pleasant diversion is the hour-long **walk** down to **Psilí Ámmos**: start from beside Khóra's cemetery and aim for the lower of two visible pigeon towers, and then keep close to the phone wires, which will guide you towards the continuation of the double-walled path descending to a bend in the road just above the beach.

Among two or three **tavernas**, the nicest place is *Iy Piatsa*, a tiny establishment near the church on the upper square serving local dishes such as wild fennel fritters; *Stavros* just east of the bus-stop platía, is consistent and can arrange beds too. The island's **post office** is found in the lowest quarter, and a few more expensive **rooms** for rent lie about 200m north of town, on the street above the track to the cemetery.

The north

North of Khóra, the island's high water table sometimes breaks the surface to run in delightful rivulets swarming with turtles and frogs, though in recent years many of the open streams seem to have dried up. Reeds, orchards, and even the occasional palm tree still take advantage of the unexpected moisture, even if it's no longer visible. This is especially true at **KÁLLITSOS** (Kéndarhos), reached by a ninety-minute path from Khóra, marked by fading red paint splodges along a donkey track above the cemetery. Once at Kállitsos (no facilities), a paved road leads west within 3km to the fifteenth- to seventeenth-century **monastery of Taxiarkhón**, designed for sixty monks but presently home only to one of the island's two parish priests, one of a dying breed of farmer-fisherman monks. If he's about, the priest will show you treasures in the monastic church, such as an ivory-inlaid bishop's throne, silver lamps from Egypt (to where many Serifots emigrated), and the finely carved *témblon*.

As you loop back towards Khóra from Kállitsos on the asphalt, the fine villages of Galaní and Panayía (named after its tenth-century church) make convenient stops. In **GALANÍ** you can get simple **meals** at the central store, which also sells excellent, tawny-pink, sherry-like wine; its small-scale production in the west of the island is highly uneconomic, so you'll find it at few other places on Sérifos. Below the village, trails lead to the remote and often windswept beach of **Sikaminiá**, with no facilities and no camping allowed; a better bet for a local swim is the more sheltered cove of **Platýs Yialós** at the extreme northern tip of the island, reached by a partly-paved track (negotiable by moped) that branches off just east of Taxiarkhón. The beach now has a taverna and a number of rooms and seems set for further development. The church at **Panayía** is usually locked, but comes alive on its feast day of Ksilopanayía (August 16). Traditionally the first couple to dance around the adjacent olive tree would be the first to marry that year, but this led to unseemly brawls – so the priest always goes first these days.

The southwest

A little way south of Panayía, you reach a junction in the road. Turn left to return to Khóra, or continue straight towards **Megálo Khorió** – the site of ancient Sérifos, but with little else to recommend it. **Megálo Livádhi**, further on, is a remote and quiet beach resort 8km west of Khóra, with two tavernas and some rooms. Iron and copper ore were once exported from here, but cheaper African deposits sent the mines into decline and today most of the idle machinery rusts away, though some gravel-crushing still goes on. There is a monument at the north end of the beach to four workers killed during a protest against unfair conditions in 1916. An alternate turning just below Megálo Khorió leads to the small mining and fishing port of **Koutalás**, a pretty if shade-less sweep of bay with a church-tipped rock, and a tiny beach – it has become rather a ghost settlement and the workers' restaurants have all closed down. The winding track from here back to Livádhi is easy to drive or walk along, passing the more attractive **Gánema** beach, which has a taverna of the same name.

Sífnos

Sífnos is a more immediately appealing island than its northern neighbours: prettier, more cultivated and with some fine architecture. This means that it's also much more popular, and extremely crowded in July or August, when rooms are very difficult to find. Take any offered as you land, come armed with a reservation, or, best of all, time your visit for June or early in September, though bear in mind that most of the trendier bars and the souvenir shops will be shut for the winter by the middle of the latter month. In keeping with the island's somewhat upmarket clientele, freelance camping is forbidden (and the two designated sites are substandard), while nudism is tolerated only in isolated coves. The locals tend, if anything, to be even more dour and introverted than on Sérifos.

On the other hand, Sífnos' modest size – no bigger than Kýthnos or Sérifos – makes it eminently explorable. The **bus service** is excellent, most of the roads quite decent and there's a network of paths that are fairly easy to follow. Sífnos has a strong tradition of pottery and was long esteemed for its distinctive cuisine, although most tourist-orientated cooking is average at best. However, the island's shops and greengrocers are well stocked in season.

Ferry connections have improved in recent years, keeping pace with the island's increasing popularity. The main lines head south, via Kýmolos to Mílos, with occasional extensions to Thíra, Crete and select Dodecanese, or north, via Sérifos and Kýthnos to Pireás. The only links with the central Cyclades are provided by the weekly visits of the Páros Express, currently on Sunday, which gets you to Páros or Sýros rather late at night; there are occasional connections on the Ilios Lines hydrofoil in the summer months.

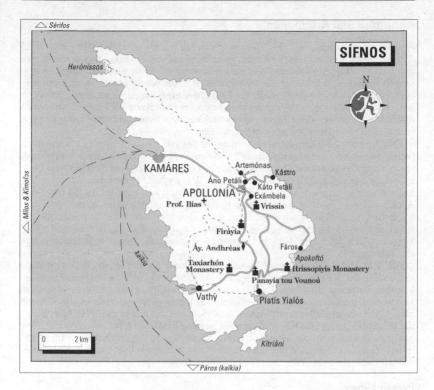

Kamáres

KAMÁRES, the island's port, is tucked away at the foot of high, bare cliffs in the west which enclose a beach. A busy, fairly downmarket resort with concrete blocks of villas edging up to the base of the cliffs, Kamáres' seafront crammed with bars, travel agencies, ice-cream shops and fast-food places. You can store luggage at the semi-official **tourist office**, Aegean Thesaurus, while hunting for a room (proprietors tend not to meet boats) – they also change money and can advise on bed availability throughout the island.

Accommodation is relatively expensive, though bargaining can be productive outside peak season. Try the rooms above the Katzoulakis Tourist Agency near the quay, as well as the reasonable *Hotel Stavros* (☎0284/31 641; ④), just beyond the church; the good but expensive *Voulis Hotel* (☎0284/32 122; ⑤) lies across the bay. The **campsite** around the bay is rather lacking in shade but has adequate facilities; it is attached to the good value *Korakis* rooms (☎0284/32 366; ④).

The best **restaurants** are the *Meropi*, ideal for a pre-ferry lunch or a more leisurely meal, the *Boulis* with its collection of huge retsina barrels, the *Kamares* ouzomezedhopolio and the *Kapetan Andreas* fish taverna. Kamáres also boasts a fair proportion of the island's **nightlife**: try the *Collage Bar* for a sunset cocktail, and move on to the *Mobilize Dancing Club* or the *Cafe Folie*. The best place to hire a moped is at *Diónysos*, next to *Mobilize Dancing Club*, which is run by the amiable mechanic's son.

Apollonía and Artemónas

A steep twenty-minute bus ride (hourly service until late at night) takes you up to **APOLLONÍA**, the centre of the Khóra, an amalgam of three hilltop villages which have merged over the years into one continuous community. With white buildings, flower-draped balconies, belfries and pretty squares, it is eminently scenic, though not self consciously so. On the platía itself, the **Folk Museum** (open on request; 2000dr) is well worth a visit. Most of the exhibits celebrate a certain Kyría Tseleméndi, who wrote a famous local recipe book (fragments of which are kept here), and there's also an interesting collection of textiles, laces, artwork, costumes and weaponry.

Radiating out from the platía is a network of stepped marble footways and the main pedestrian street, flagstoned Odhós Styliánou Prókou, which is lined with shops, churches and restaurants. The garish, cakebox cathedral of **Áyios Spíridhon** is nearby, while the eighteenth-century church of **Panayía Ouranoforía** stands in the highest quarter of town, incorporating fragments of a seventh-century BC temple of Apollo and a relief of St George over the door. **Áyios Athanásios**, next to Platía Kleánthi Triandafílou, has frescoes and a wooden *témblon*. Some 3km southeast, a short distance from the village of Exámbela, you'll find the active monastery of **Vrýssis** which dates from 1612 and is home to a good collection of religious artefacts and manuscripts.

ARTEMÓNAS, fifteen minutes south of Apollonía on foot, is worth a morning's exploration for its churches and elegant Venetian and Neoclassical houses alone. **Panayía Gourniá** (key next door) has vivid frescoes, the clustered-dome church of **Kokhí** was built over an ancient temple of Artemis (also the basis of the village's name), and seventeenth-century **Áyios Yeóryios** contains fine icons. Artemónas is also the point of departure for **Kherónissos**, an isolated hamlet with two tavernas and a few potteries behind a deeply indented, rather bleak bay at the northwestern tip of the island. There's a motorable dirt track there – and occasional boat trips from Kamáres, though these are only worth the effort on calm days.

Practicalities

The **bank**, **post office**, **OTE** and **tourist police** are all grouped around Apollonía's central platía. Most of the village's **rooms** establishments are along the road towards Fáros, and thus a bit noisy; the *Margarita* (π0284/31 701; ④) is comfortable and fairly representative. If you want quieter premises with a better view, be prepared to pay more: your best bet is to look on the square for the main branch of the excellent travel agency, Aegean Thesaurus (π0284/31 151, fax 31 145), which can book you into more expensive rooms (③–④). They also sell a worthwhile package consisting of an accurate topographical map, bus/boat schedules and a short text on Sífnos for a few hundred drachmas. Near the central platía, there's the late-arrival fall-back *Sofia* (π0284/31 238; ③), though most people find somewhere else the next day, as it's a rather cheerless 1970s construction; the *Galini*, 400m south, up in Katavatí (π0284/31 011; ③), is preferable.

In Khóra there are still a bare handful of quality **tavernas**, the doyen of which is the *Liotrivi* up in Artemónas, which has moved from the old oil-press suggested by its name to extended new premises on the village square. Next to the post office in Apollonía, *Iy Orea Sifnos* has standard fare and a flower-decked garden; *To Apostoli to Koutouki* in the backstreets is also reasonable.

Nightlife in Apollonía tends to be dominated by the thirty-something crowd which, having dined early by Greek-island standards, lingers over its oúzo until late. The central *Argo* music bar features the currently fashionable mix of rock early on and Greek pop later; the *Kivotos* club out of town features live skíládhiko, while gentler rembétika can be heard at Aloni.

The east coast

Most of Sífnos' coastal settlements are along the less precipitous eastern shore, within a modest distance of Khóra and its surrounding cultivated plateau. These all have good bus services, and a certain amount of food and accommodation, Kástro being far more appealing than the touristy resorts of Platís Yialós and Fáros.

Kástro

An alternative east-coast base which seems the last place on Sífnos to fill up in season, **KÁSTRO** can be reached on foot from Apollonía in 35 minutes, all but the last ten on a clear path beginning at the *Hotel Anthoussa* and threading its way via Káto Petáli hamlet. Built on a rocky outcrop with an almost sheer drop to the sea on three sides, the ancient capital of the island retains much of its medieval character. Parts of its boundary walls survive, along with a full complement of sinuous, narrow streets graced by balconied, two-storey houses and some fine sixteenth- and seventeenth-century churches with ornamental floors. Venetian coats-of-arms and ancient wall-fragments can still be seen on some of the older dwellings; there are remains of the ancient acropolis (including a ram's head sarcophagus by one of the medieval gates), as well as a small **archeological museum** (Tues–Sat 9am–3pm, Sun 11am–2pm; free) installed in a former Catholic church in the higher part of the village.

Among the several rooms establishments, the newly modernized *Aris* apartments (☎0284/31 161; ④) have something for most budgets and are open all year. The *Star* and *Zorbas* are the obvious tavernas to try out, while the *Sierra Maestra* café-bar, run by an old hippy, is suitably laid back and has a fantastic view. On the edge of town, the *Castello* disco-bar is a livelier hang-out. There's nothing approximating a beach in Kástro; for a swim you have to walk to the nearby rocky coves of **Serália** (to the southeast, and with more rooms) and **Paláti**. You can also hike – from the windmills on the approach road near Káto Petáli – to either the sixteenth-century monastery of **Khryssostómou**, or along a track opposite to the cliff face that overlooks the church of the **Eptá Martíres** (Seven Martyrs); nudists sun themselves and snorkel on and around the flat rocks below.

Platís Yialós

From Apollonía there are almost hourly buses to the resort of **PLATÍS YIALÓS**, some 13km distant, near the southern tip of the island. Despite claims to be the longest beach in the Cyclades, the sand can get very crowded at the end near the watersport facilities rental. Diversions include a pottery workshop, but many are put off by the ugly *Platys Yialos* hotel at the southern end of the beach, and the strong winds which plague it. **Rooms** are expensive, although the comfortable *Pension Angelaki* (☎0284/71 28; ④), near the bus stop, is more reasonably priced. The *Hotel Eurosini* (☎0284/71 353; ⑤) is comfortable, and breakfast is included in the price. The local **campsite** is rather uninspiring: a stiff hike inland, shadeless, and on sloping, stony ground. Among several fairly pricey **tavernas** are the straightforward *To Steki* and *Bus Stop*.

A more rewarding walk uphill from Platís Yialós brings you to the convent of **Panayía to Vounoú** (though it's easy to get lost on the way without the locally sold map); the caretaker should let you in, if she's about.

Fáros and around

Less crowded beaches are to be found just to the northeast of Platís Yialós (though unfortunately not directly accessible along the coast). **FÁROS**, again with regular bus links to Apollonía, makes an excellent fall-back base if you don't strike it lucky elsewhere. A small and friendly resort, it has some of the cheapest **accommodation** on the island, and a few early-evening **tavernas**, the best of which is *To Kyma*. The closest beaches are not up to much: the town strand itself is muddy, shadeless and crowded, and the one to the northeast past the headland not much better. Head off in the opposite direction, however, through the older part of the village, and things improve at **Glyfó**, a longer, wider beach favoured by naturists and snorkellers.

Continuing from Glyfó, a fifteen-minute cliffside path leads to the beach of **Apokoftó**, with the good *Lembessis* taverna, and, up an access road, the *Pension Flora* (☎0284/71 278; ③) which has superb views. The shore itself tends to collect seaweed, however, and a rock reef must be negotiated to get into the water. Flanking Apokoftó to the south, marooned on a sea-washed spit and featuring on every EOT poster of the island, is the disestablished, seventeenth-century **Khryssopiyís monastery**, whose cells are rented out in summer (☎0284/31 255; ②) – other rooms are available if the cells are full in high season. According to legend, the cleft in the rock appeared when two village girls, fleeing to the spit to escape the attentions of menacing pirates, prayed to the Virgin to defend their virtue.

The interior and Vathý

Apollonía is a good base from which to start your explorations of remoter Sífnos. You can rent **bikes** at Moto Apollo, beside the BP station on the road to Fáros, but the island is best explored on foot.

Taking the path out from Katavatí (the district south of Apollonía) you'll pass, after a few minutes, the beautiful empty **monastery of Firáyia** and – fifteen minutes along the ugly new road – the path climbing up to **Áyios Andhréas**, where you'll be rewarded with tremendous views over the islands of Sýros, Páros, Íos, Folégandhros and Síkinos. Just below the church is an enormous Bronze-Age archeological site.

Even better is the all-trail walk to Vathý, around three hours from Katavatí and reached by bearing right at a signed junction in Katavatí. Part-way along you can detour on a conspicuous side trail to the **monastery of Profítis Ilías**, on the very summit of the island, with a vaulted refectory and extensive views.

Vathý

A fishing village on the shore of a stunning funnel-shaped bay, **VATHÝ** is the most attractive and remote base on the island and, remarkably, the new road doesn't seem to be leading to extra development. There are still just a few rooms places, the best deals probably being at *Manolis* taverna (②), or those attached to the tiny **monastery of the Archangel Gabriel**. Unusually, camping rough is positively encouraged by the locals, a reflection of their friendly attitude towards outsiders. For **food**, *Manolis* does excellent grills and has a fascinating gyrating clay oven in the courtyard, *Iy Okeanidha* has good mezédhes such as chickpea balls and cheesy aubergine patties, while *To Tsikali* behind the monastery is cheaper but less varied.

Now that there are regular buses (8 daily in high season, 2 daily at other times) the kaïkia no longer run from Kamáres. It is possible to walk to Platýs Yiálos in ninety minutes, but the path is not well marked. At the far end of the bay a traditional pottery still functions.

Mílos

Mílos has always derived prosperity from its strange geology. Minoan settlers were attracted by obsidian, and other products of its volcanic soil made the island – along with Náxos – the most important of the Cyclades in the ancient world. Today the quarrying of barite, perlite and porcelain brings in a steady revenue, but has left deep and unsightly scars on the landscape. The rocks, however, can be beautiful in situ: on the left as your ferry enters Mílos Bay, two outcrops known as the Arkoúdhes (Bears) square off like sumo wrestlers. Off the north coast, accessible only by excursion boat,

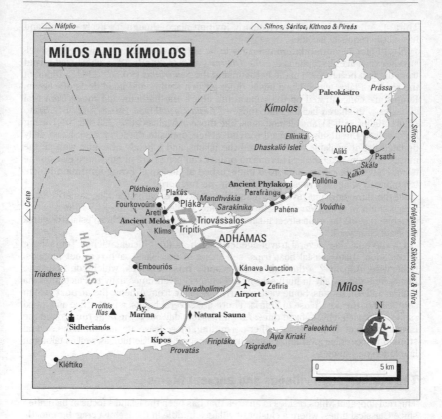

the Glaroníssia (Seagull Isles) are shaped like massed organ pipes, and there are more weird formations on the southwest coast at Kléftiko. Inland, too, you frequently come across strange, volcanic outcrops, and thermal springs burst forth.

The landscape has been violated, but as with most weathered volcanic terrain, Mílos is incredibly fertile; away from the summits of **Profítis Ilías** in the southwest and lower hills in the east, a gently undulating countryside is intensively cultivated to produce grain, hay and orchards. The island's domestic architecture, with its lava-built, two-up-and-two-down houses, is reminiscent of Níssyros, while parts of the coast, with their sculpted cliffs and inlets, remind some visitors of Cyprus.

Yet the drab whole is less than the sum of the often interesting parts; Mílos is not and never will become another Santoríni, despite a similar geological history, and is probably the better for it. The locals are reconciled to a very short tourist season lasting from late June to early September, and make most of their money during late July and August, when prices are rather high.

Adhámas

The main port of **ADHÁMAS**, known as Adhámandas to locals, was founded by Cretan refugees fleeing a failed rebellion in 1841. Despite sitting on one of the Mediterranean's best natural harbours (created by a volcanic cataclysm similar to, but earlier than,

Thira's), Adhámas is not a spectacularly inviting place, though it's lively enough and has all the requisite facilities.

Most hotel **accommodation** manages to be simultaneously noisy, viewless and relatively expensive. Exceptions are the *Delfini* (☎0287/22 001; ⑤), a short way inland from the first beach north of the harbour, and the *Semiramis* (☎0287/ 22 117; ⑤) left of the road to Pláka, which has a lovely quiet garden setting and good deals off-season. Rooms are concentrated on the conical hill above the harbour, and range from real cheapies with shared facilities like those of *Anna Gozadhinou* (☎0287/ 22 364; ②), to smart studios with TV and all mod cons, like those of Mallís (☎0287/22 612; ⑤). During high season the highly organized **tourist office** opposite the ferry dock has a daily updated list of available rooms around the island, and a handy brochure with all the numbers at any given time. There is no proper campsite here or anywhere else on the island, but freelance camping goes undisturbed at the small **Frangomnímata** beach, ten minutes' walk northwest by the French war memorial.

Of the three adjacent **tavernas** along the seafront towards the long tamarisk-lined beach south of town, *Navagio* is the best value, while close to the jetty *Flisvos* is reasonable. Just off the main street inland, *Ta Pitsounakia* is a good cheap psistariá with a pleasant courtyard.

On the quayside, several travel agencies such as the efficient Vichos Tours have information about coastal boat trips, sell maps of the island, and rent out mopeds. Otherwise, Adhámas is the hub of the island's **bus services**, which run hourly to Pláka, nine times daily in high season to Pollónia, seven times daily to Paleokhóri via Zefíria, and to Provatás. Some visitors arrive by plane from Athens: the **airport** is 5km southeast of the port, close to Zefíria. There are several banks, a post office and a taxi rank with a posted list of fixed rates. An unmissable day out is the **boat tour** round the island on one of three boats; weather permitting, these leave at 9am and make several stops at inaccessible swimming spots like the magnificent Kléftiko, as well as taking in late lunch on Kímolos.

The northwestern villages and ancient Melos

The real appeal of Mílos resides in an area that has been the island's focus of habitation since Classical times, where a cluster of villages huddle in the lee of a crag 4km northwest of the harbour.

PLÁKA (MÍLOS) is the largest of these communities and is the official capital of the island, a status borne out by the presence of the hospital, **OTE**, **post office**, a part-time **bank** and three **motorbike rental** outfits along the approach road. Unfortunately, Pláka's **rooms** are housed in three or four modern blocks overlooking this busy boulevard, and prompt few thoughts of staying. But a number of ouzería have opened up in recent years, making it a real **eating** paradise: highly recommended are *Arkhondoula*, *Dhiporto* and *To Kastro* up in the centre of the village, as well as *Plakiani Gonia* on the approach road.

The attractive village of **TRYPITÍ** (meaning "perforated" in Greek), which takes its name from the cliffside tombs of the ancient Melian dead nearby, covers a long ridge a kilometre south of Pláka. Despite semi-desolation (many houses are for sale), it probably makes the best base if you're after a village environment, with its three modest **rooms** establishments, two of which are just down the steep street from the tiny platía below the main church. Here also the modest *Kafenio Iy Hara* does simple **meals**, and has a fantastic view of the vale of Klíma (see opposite); more elaborate and expensive fare is available at the *Methismeni Politia* ouzerí, at the top of the road to the catacombs. From Trypití, it's possible to walk more or less directly down to Adhámas via Skinópi on the old *kalderími*, which begins on the saddle linking Trypití with the hamlet of Klimatovoúni.

TRIOVÁSSALOS and its twin **PÉRAN TRIOVÁSSALOS** are more workaday, less polished than Pláka or Trypití. There are "rooms to rent" signs out here as well, but they'll inevitably be noisier. Péran also offers the idiosyncratic taverna *O Khamos* (which means "chaos"), and a naive pebble mosaic in the courtyard of **Áyios Yeóryios church** – created in 1880, the mosaic features assorted animal and plant motifs.

Local sites – and the coast

Pláka boasts **two museums** of moderate interest. Behind the lower car park, at the top of the approach boulevard through the newer district, the **archeological museum** (Tues–Sun 8.30am–3pm; 500dr) contains numerous obsidian implements, plus a whole wing of finds from ancient Phylakopi (see p.103) whose highlights include a votive lamp in the form of a bull and a rather Minoan-looking terracotta goddess. Labelling is scant, but isn't really needed for a plaster cast of the most famous statue in the world, the *Venus de Milo*, the original of which was found on the island in 1820 and appropriated by the French; her arms were knocked off in the melée surrounding her abduction. Up in a mansion of the old quarter, the **Folklore Museum** (Tues–Sat 10am–2pm & 6–9pm, Sun 10am–2pm; 400dr) offers room re-creations but is otherwise a Greek-labelled jumble of impedimenta pertaining to milling, brewing, cheese-making, baking and weaving, rounded off by old engravings, photos and mineral samples.

A stairway beginning near the police station leads up to the old Venetian **Kástro**, its slopes clad in stone and cement to channel precious rainwater into cisterns. Near the top looms the enormous chapel of **Panayía Thalassítra**, where the ancient Melians made their last stand against the Athenians before being massacred in 416 BC. Today it offers one of the best views in the Aegean, particularly at sunset in clear conditions.

From the archeological museum, signs point you towards the **early Christian catacombs** (Tues–Sun 8am–8pm; free), 1km south of Pláka and just 400m from Trypití village; steps lead down from the road to the inconspicuous entrance. Although some 5000 bodies were buried in tomb-lined corridors which stretch some 200m into the soft volcanic rock, only the first 50m are illuminated and accessible by boardwalk. They're worth a look if you're in the area, but the adjacent ruins of **ancient Melos**, extending down from Pláka almost to the sea, justify the detour. There are huge Dorian walls, the usual column fragments lying around and, best of all, a well preserved Roman **amphitheatre** (unrestricted access) some 200m west of the catacombs by track, then trail. Only seven rows of seats remain intact, but these evocatively look out over Klíma to the bay. Between the catacombs and the theatre is the signposted spot where the *Venus de Milo* was found; promptly delivered to the French consul for "safekeeping" from the Turks, this was the last the Greeks saw of the statue until a copy was belatedly forwarded from the Louvre in Paris.

At the very bottom of the vale, **KLÍMA** is the most photogenic of several fishing hamlets on the island, with its picturesque boathouses tucked underneath the principal living areas. There's no beach to speak of, and only one place to stay – the impeccably sited *Panorama* (☎0287/21 623; ⑤), whose restaurant currently seems to be resting on its laurels.

Pláthiena, 45 minutes' walk northwest of Pláka, is the closest proper beach, and thus is vastly popular in summer. There are no facilities, but the beach is fairly well protected and partly shaded by tamarisks. Head initially west from near the police station on the marked footpath towards **ARETÍ** and **FOURKOVOÚNI**, two more cliff-dug, boathouse-hamlets very much in the Klíma mould. Although the direct route to Pláthiena is signposted, it's no longer to go via Fourkovoúni; both hamlets are reached by side turnings off the main route, which becomes a jeep track as you approach Fourkovoúni. By moped, access to Pláthiena is only from Plakés, the northernmost and smallest of the five northwestern villages.

The south

The main road to the south of the island splits at **Kánava junction**, an unrelievedly dreary place at first glance owing to the large power plant here. But opposite this, indicated by a rusty sign pointing seaward, is the first of Mílos' **hot springs**, which bubble up in the shallows and are much enjoyed by the locals.

Taking the left or easterly fork leads to **ZEFÍRIA**, hidden among olive groves below the bare hills; it was briefly the medieval capital until an eighteenth-century epidemic drove out the population. Much of the old town is still deserted, though some life has returned, and there's a magnificent seventeenth-century church.

South of here it's a further 8km down a winding road to the coarse-sand beach of **Paleokhóri**. Actually a triple strand totalling about 800m in length and unarguably the island's best, clothing is optional at the westerly cove, where steam vents heat both the shallow water and the rock overhangs onshore. There are a number of places to stay, such as the inland *Broutsos Studios* (☎01/34 78 425; ⑤), and the *Artemis* restaurant (☎0287/31 221; ④) nearer the beach, but the best value are Panayiota Vikelli's rooms (☎0287/31 228; ④). Apart from the *Artemis*, there are a couple of other tavernas including the new *Pelagos*, which has a large raised patio.

The westerly road from Kánava junction leads past the airport gate to **Khivadholímni**, considered to be the best beach on Mílos bay itself. Not that this is saying much: Khivadholímni is north-facing and thus garbage-prone, with shallow sumpy water offshore although there is a taverna, a disco bar and a sizeable community of campers during the summer. It's better to veer south to **Provatás**, a short but tidy beach, closed off by colourful cliffs on the east. Being so easy to get at, it hasn't escaped some development: there are two-room establishments plus, closer to the shore, a new luxury complex. The best value for food and accommodation is the *Maistrali* (☎0287/31 206; ③).

Some 2km west of Provatás, you'll see a highway sign for **Kípos** just before the asphalt fizzles out. Below and to the left of the road, a small **medieval chapel** dedicated to the Kímisis (Assumption) sits atop foundations far older – as evidenced by the early Christian reliefs stacked along the west wall and a carved, cruciform baptismal font in the *ieron* behind the altar screen. At one time a spring gushed from the low tunnel-cave beside the font – sufficiently miraculous in itself on arid Mílos. Several kilometres before Provatás, a road forks east through a dusty white quarry to the trendy and popular beach of **Firipláka**, beautifully set but sadly dominated in high summer by a noisy canteen pumping out techno. Further east, **Tsigrádho** beach is accessible by boat, or by the novel means of a rope hanging down a crevice in the cliff face.

For the most part **Khálakas**, the southwestern peninsula centred on the wilderness of 748-metre Profítis Ilías, is uninhabited and little built upon, with the exception of the **monastery of Sidherianós**. The roads are memorable, if a little tiring, and several spots are worth making the effort to see. **Emboriós** on the east side of the peninsula has a fine little beach and a great local taverna with a few cheap rooms (☎0287/21 389; ④). On the mostly rugged west coast, **Triádhes** is one of the finest and least spoilt beaches in the Cyclades, but you'll have to bring your own provisions. **Kléftiko** in the southwest corner is only reachable by boat, but repays the effort to get there with its stunning rock formations, semi-submerged rock tunnels, and colourful coral.

The north coast

From either Adhámas or the Pláka area, good roads run roughly parallel to the **north coast** which, despite being windswept and largely uninhabited, is not devoid of interest. **Mandhrákia**, reached from Péran Triovássalos, is another boathouse settlement, and **Sarakíniko**, to the east, is a sculpted inlet with a sandy sea bed and a summer beach café. About 8km from Adhámas, the little hamlet of **Pákhena**, not shown on many maps, has a cluster of rooms and a small beach – the best value rooms are *Terry's* (☎0287/22 640; ④). About a kilometre beyond this, the remains of three superimposed Neolithic settlements crown a small knoll at **Filakopí** (ancient Phylakopi); the site was important archeologically, but hasn't been maintained and is difficult to interpret. Just before the site is another one of Milos' coastal wonders: the deep-sea inlet of **Papafránga**, set in a ravine and accessible through a gap in the cliffs.

Pollónia

POLLÓNIA, 12km northeast of Adhámas, must be the windiest spot on the island, hence the name of its longest-lived and best **bar**, *Okto Bofor* (meaning "Force 8 gales"), near the church. The second resort on Mílos after Adhámas, it is, not surprisingly, immensely popular with windsurfers. Pollónia is essentially a small harbour protected by a storm-lashed spit of land on the northeast, where self-catering units are multiplying rapidly, fringed by a long but narrow, tamarisk-fringed beach to the rear, and closed off on the south by a smaller promontory on which the tiny original settlement huddles. Besides the town beach, the only other convenient, half-decent beach is at **Voúdhia**, 3km east, where you will find more of the island's hot springs, although it is effectively spoiled by its proximity to huge mining works, which lend it the desolate air of a *Mad Max* scene.

On the quay are a row of four **tavernas**, the best of these being *Kapetan Nikolaos* (aka *Koula's*; open year-round) and *Araxovoli* with an unusual menu. Inland and south of here you'll find another concentration of **accommodation**, more simple rooms and fewer apartments, most with the slight drawback of occasional noise and dust from quarry trucks. Among the newest and highest-quality units here are the *Kapetan Tasos Studios* (☎0287/41 287; ③), with good views of the straits between Mílos and Kímolos. Up behind the quay, *Corina* (☎0287/41 209; ④) is a more reasonable option, as is *Flora* (☎0287/41 249; ④) on the road towards the spit, which also rents out bikes. Pollónia has no bank or post office, but there is a helpful **travel agency**, Blue Waters (☎0287/41 442), which can change money, rent cars, book accommodation and sell ANEK ferry tickets (services to Sitía on Crete). A **motorbike rental** place behind the beach, and a well-stocked **supermarket**, completes the list of amenities. There is a huge map fixed on a metal frame near the bus stop, which shows all the facilities and gives telephone numbers.

Getting to Kímolos (see below) may be the main reason you're here. Either the Tria Adhelfia or one other kaïki makes the trip daily year-round at 6.45am and 2pm, returning from Kímolos an hour later; during high season, there are five crossings a day.

Kímolos

Of the three islets off the coast of Mílos, Andímilos is home to a rare species of chamois, Políegos has more ordinary goats, but only **Kímolos** has any human habitation. Volcanic like Mílos, with the same little lava-built rural cottages, it profits from its geology and used to export chalk (*kimolía* in Greek) until the supply was exhausted. Still a source of fuller's earth, the fine dust of this clay is a familiar sight on the island, where mining still outstrips fishing and farming as an occupation. Rugged and barren in the interior, there is some fertile land on the southeast coast where low-lying wells provide water, and this is where the population of about eight hundred is concentrated.

Kímolos is sleepy indeed from September to June, and even in August sees hardly any visitors. This is probably just as well, since there are fewer than a hundred beds on the whole island, and little in the way of other amenities.

Psathí and Khóra

Whether you arrive by ferry, or by kaïki from Pollónia, you'll dock at the hamlet of **PSATHÍ**, pretty much a non-event except for the excellent *To Kyma* **taverna** midway along the beach. The laissez-faire attitude towards tourism is demonstrated by the fact that there are no rooms here, but equally, nobody minds if you sleep on the small beach. **Ferry tickets** are sold only outside the expensive café at the end of the jetty, an hour or so before the anticipated arrival of the boat; the Pollónia kaïki comes and goes unremarked from the base of the jetty five times a day in summer. There is no bus on the island, but at the time of writing a licence had been obtained for a taxi, and only a driver was required.

Around the bay there are a few old windmills and the dazzlingly white **KHÓRA** perched on the ridge above them. Unsung – and neglected, although there are plans to reconstruct it and build government rooms – is the magnificent, two-gated **kástro**, a fortified core of roughly the same design as those at Andíparos and Síkinos; the perimeter houses are intact but its heart is a jumble of ruins. Just outside the kástro on the north stands the conspicuously unwhitewashed, late-sixteenth-century church of **Khryssóstomos**, the oldest and most beautiful on the island. It takes fifteen minutes to walk up to the surprisingly large town, passing the recommended *Villa Maria* (☎0287/51392; ④) about five minutes along the way and nearer to Psathí; you'll also find accommodation, managed by Margaro Petraki (☎0287/51 314; ②), tucked away in the rather unglamourous maze of backstreets. The aptly named *Panorama*, near the east gate of the kástro, is the most elaborate and consistently open **taverna**, and there are a couple of basic psistariés. Self-catering is an easy proposition – and may be a necessity before June or after August – with a well-stocked supermarket, produce stalls and a butcher. Finally, there's a friendly **OTE** office behind Khryssóstomos church, a boat agency and a **post office** which does exchange. By 1998 the small archeological **museum** (Tues–Sun 8am–2pm), currently on the road into Khóra, should have moved to more spacious premises near the church; its collection comprises pottery from the Geometric to the Roman period.

Around the island

During summer at least, the hamlet of **ALYKÍ** on the south coast is a better bet for staying than Psathí and Khóra; it only takes about thirty minutes to walk there on the paved road that forks left just before the *Villa Maria*. Alikí is named after the salt pan which sprawls between a rather mediocre beach with no shade or shelter, and has a pair of **rooms** – *Sardis* (☎0287/51 458; ④) and *Passamihalis* (☎0287/51 340; ③) – and simple **tavernas**. You can stroll west one cove to **Bonátsa** for better sand and shallow water, though you won't escape the winds. Passing another cove you come to the even more attractive beach of Kalamítsi, with better shade and the good little taverna and rooms of Ventourís (☎093/611685; ③). To the east, between Alikí and Psathí, the smaller, more secluded beach of **Sténda** is better for camping.

The 700m coarse-sand beach of **Elliniká** is 45 minutes' walk west of Alikí: starting on the road, bear left – just before two chapels on a slope – onto a narrower track which runs through the fields at the bottom of the valley. Divided by a low bluff, the beach is bracketed by two capes and looks out over Dhaskalió islet, and tends to catch heavy weather in the afternoon; there are no facilities here.

Another road leads northeast from Khóra to a beach and radioactive springs at **Prássa**, 7km away. The route takes in impressive views across the straits to Políegos and there are several shady peaceful coves where you could camp out. Innumerable goat tracks invite exploration of the rest of the island; in the far northwest, on Kímolos' summit, are the ruins of an imposing Venetian fortress known as **Paleókastro**. The local community has plans to open an official campsite at Klíma Bay 2km northeast of Khóra, once it has relocated the rubbish dump that currently befouls the place.

Ándhros

Ándhros, the second largest and northernmost of the Cyclades, has a number of fine features to offer the visitor, although you have to search them out. Thinly populated but prosperous, its fertile, well-watered valleys have attracted scores of Athenian holiday villas whose red-tiled roofs and white walls stand out among the greenery. Some of the more recent of these have robbed many of the villages of life and atmosphere, turning them into scattered settlements with no nucleus, and have created a weekender mentality manifest in noisy Friday and Sunday evening traffic jams at the ferry dock. The island neither needs, nor welcomes, independent travellers, and it can be almost impos-

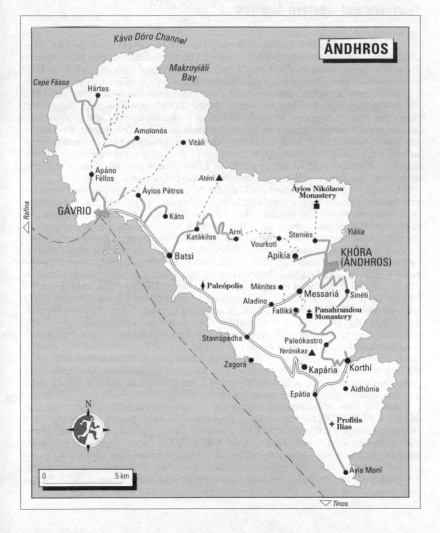

sible to get a bed in between the block-bookings during high season. On the positive side, the permanent population is distinctly hospitable; traditionally working on ships, they are only too happy to practise their English on you. Together with some of the more idiosyncratic reminders of the Venetian period, such as the *peristereónes* (pigeon towers) and the *frákhtes* (dry-stone walls, here raised to the status of an art form), it is this friendliness that lends Ándhros its charm.

Ferries connect the island with Rafína on the mainland, only an hour from Athens on the bus, and you can loop back onto the central Cycladic routes via Mýkonos or Sýros. The bus service is poor, and you'd be well advised to consider renting a bike to tour the sights – otherwise you'll face a lot of walking.

Northern and western Ándhros

All ferries and catamarans arrive at the main port, **GÁVRIO**, a nondescript place whose dirty, windswept beach is usually deserted. The sea in the enclosed harbour is so murky that even the wildfowl aren't interested. A converted dovecote houses a sporadically functioning **tourist office**, and the ferry **ticket agent** only opens half an hour before boats arrive. There's also a part-time **bank**, and a **post office** on the waterfront.

The cheapest **accommodation** is in the clean and reasonable *Galaxy* (☎0282/71 228; ④) or the *Bati* rooms behind the beach (☎0282/71 010; ④); *Camping Andros*, 2km down the road, has decent facilities, including a swimming pool and a good café. **Restaurants** worth trying include the good if basic estiatório *Tria Asteria*, the *Vengera* taverna with its nice leafy courtyard 100m inland, and the smart new *Trehandiri* ouzerí opposite the catamaran dock. **Nightlife** revolves around the *Idhroussa* and *Tropical* bars, or at livelier outdoor places on Áyios Pétros beach several kilometres south, where the *Marabou* taverna frequently features live guitar music.

The road north begins behind the *Hotel Gavrion Beach*. Around 3km northwest are two beaches named **Fellós**: one with holiday villas and a taverna, the other hidden beyond the headland and popular with freelance campers. Beyond Ápano Fellós, the countryside is empty except for a few hamlets inhabited by the descendants of medieval Albanians who settled here and in southern Évvia several hundred years ago.

Most traffic heads 8km south down the coast, past the excellent *Yiannouli* taverna, to **BATSÍ**, the island's main package resort, with large hotels and bars around its fine natural harbour. The beautiful though crowded beach curves round the port, and the sea is cold, calm and clean (except near the taxi park). **Hotels** range from the cheap but seedy *Avra* (☎0282/41 216; ②), through the comfortable *Chryssi Akti* (☎0282/41 236; ⑤) with TV and air conditioning, to the very upmarket *Aneroussa Beach Hotel* (☎0282/41 045; ⑥), south of town past the Stivári area towards Áyia Marína Beach. There are plenty of rooms, and good food can be had at *O Stamatis*, an old place with a nice atmosphere, or at *Ta Kavouria*, which specializes in fish – both are near the harbour. Further out at **Stivári**, a pleasant café/taverna, *Stivari Gardens*, is run by an English woman. For **nightlife** there are five bars, mostly featuring the standard foreign/Greek musical mix, although *Diva* plays some psychedelic sounds. Finally, there are two banks where you can change money.

From Batsí you're within easy walking distance of some beautiful inland villages. At **KÁTO KATÁKILOS**, one hour inland, three **tavernas** host "Greek nights" organized in Bátsi; a rough track leads to **ATÉNI**, a hamlet in a lush, remote valley, as yet unvisited by the dreaded donkey safaris. **ANO KATÁKILOS** has a couple of undervisited tavernas with fine views across the village. A right-hand turning out of Katákilos heads up the mountain to **ARNÍ**, whose lone taverna is often shrouded in mist. Another rewarding trip is to a well-preserved, 20-metre-high **Classical tower** at Áyios Pétros, 5km from Gávrio or 9km coming from Batsí.

South of Batsí along the main road are Káto and Áno Apróvato. **Káto** has rooms, a café and a path to a quiet beach, while nearby is the largely unexplored archeological site of **Paleópolis**.

Khóra and around

A minimal bus service links the west coast with **KHÓRA** or **ÁNDHROS** town, 35km from Gávrio. With its setting on a rocky spur cutting across a huge bay, the capital is the most attractive place on the island. Paved in marble and schist from the still-active local quarries, the buildings around the bus station are grand nineteenth-century affairs, and the squares with their ornate wall fountains and gateways are equally elegant. The hill quarters are modern, while the small port acts as a yacht supply station, and below are the sands of Parapórti – a fine beach, if a little exposed to the *mellémi* winds in summer.

The few **hotels** in town are on the expensive side, and tend to be busy with holidaying Greeks: try the *Aigli* (☎0282/22 303; ④), opposite the big church on the main walkway. Most rooms are clustered behind the long **Nimboúrio** beach north of town, and range from good cheap old-style family guesthouses like those of Firiou (☎0282/22 921; ③) or Pandazi (☎0282/22 777; ③), to modern apartments such as *Alkioni Inn* (☎0282/24 522; ⑥), as well as the seasonal **campsite**. For **eating**, most cafés are up in Khóra, although the restaurant right by the bus station is good, and there's a decent psistariá on the main drag. The nicest taverna is *O Nonas*, tucked away at the town end of the beach behind the ugly *Xenia* hotel. Up in Khóra there's the *Rock Café* for a **drink**, but the epicentre of nightlife is the two-storey *Vecera*, a thumping disco halfway along the beach. There's an **OTE**, post office and bank around town, a couple of travel agents and three moped rentals, two behind the beach, and one on the road to Gavrio.

From the square right at the end of town you pass through an archway and down to windswept **Platía Ríva**, with its statue of the unknown sailor scanning the sea. Beyond lies the thirteenth-century Venetian **Kástro**, precariously joined to the mainland by a narrow-arched bridge, which was damaged by German munitions in World War II. The **Modern Art Museum** (Wed–Sun 10am–2pm, also 6–8pm in summer; 1000dr) has a sculpture garden and a permanent collection that includes works by Picasso and Braque, as well as temporary exhibits. Don't be discouraged by the stark modern architecture of the **Archeological Museum** (Tues–Sun 8.30am–3pm; 500dr); it turns out to be well laid out and labelled with instructive models. The prize items on view are the fourth-century "Hermes of Ándhros", reclaimed from a prominent position in the Athens archeological museum, and the "Matron of Herculaneum".

Hiking inland and west from Ándhros, the obvious destination is **MÉNITES**, a hill village just up a green valley choked with trees and straddled by stone walls. The church of the **Panayía** may have been the location of a Temple of Dionysus, where water was turned into wine; water still flows continuously from the local rocks. Nearby is the medieval village of **MESSARIÁ**, with the deserted twelfth-century Byzantine church of **Taxiárkhis** below and the pleasantly shady *Platanos* taverna. The finest monastery on the island, **Panakhrándou**, is only an hour's (steep) walk away, via the village of Fallíká; reputedly tenth-century, it's still defended by massive walls but occupied these days by just three monks. It clings to an iron-stained cliff southwest of Khóra, to which you can return directly with a healthy two- to three-hour walk down the creek valley, guided by red dots. There is a wonderful taverna, *Pertesis*, at Strapouriés, which boasts a view all the way down to the coast and excellent food.

Hidden by the ridge directly north of Khóra, the prosperous nineteenth-century village of **STENIÉS** was built by the vanguard of today's shipping magnates, and today you can splash out at the good fish tavernas here. Just below, at Yiália, there's a small pebble beach with a café and watersports facilities. Beyond Steniés is **APIKÍA**, a tidy little village which bottles Sariza-brand mineral water for a living; there are a few **tavernas** and a very limited number of **rooms**, as well as the new luxury hotel *Dighi Sarisa* (☎0282/23 799 or 23 899; ⑥), just below the spring itself. The road is now asphalted up to Vourkotí and even past this point is quite negotiable via Arní to the west coast. There are some stunning views all along this road but bike riders need to take care when the *meltémi* is blowing – it can get dangerously windy.

Southern Ándhros

On your way south, you might stop at **Zagorá**, a fortified Geometric town – unique in having never been built over – that was excavated in the early 1970s. Located on a desolate, flat-topped promontory with cliffs falling away on three sides, it's worth a visit for the view alone. With your own transport, the sheltered cove of Sinéti is also worth a detour.

The village of **KORTHÍ**, the end of the line, is a friendly though nondescript village set on a large sandy bay, cut off from the rest of the island by a high ridge and so relatively unspoiled – and pleasant enough to merit spending the night at *Pension Rainbow* (☎0282/61 344; ③) or at the austere-looking *Hotel Korthion* (☎0282/61218; ④). There are also several good seafood **restaurants**. You could also take in the nearby convent of **Zoödhókhou Piyís** (open to visitors before noon), with illuminated manuscripts and a disused weaving factory.

To the north is **PALEÓKASTRO**, a tumbledown village with a ruined Venetian castle – and a legend about an old woman who betrayed the stronghold to the Turks, then jumped off the walls in remorse, landing on a rock now known as "Old Lady's Leap". In the opposite direction out of Korthí are **AÏDHÓNIA** and **KAPÁRIA**, dotted with pigeon towers (*peristereónes*) left by the Venetians.

Tínos

Tínos still feels one of the most Greek of the larger islands. A few foreigners have discovered its beaches and unspoiled villages, but most visitors are Greek, here to see the church of **Panayía Evangelístria**, a grandiose shrine erected on the spot where a miraculous icon with healing powers was found in 1822. A Tiniote nun, now canonized as Ayía Pelayía, was directed in a vision to unearth the relic just as the War of Independence was getting underway a timely coincidence which served to underscore the links between the Orthodox Church and Greek nationalism. Today, there are two major annual pilgrimages, on March 25 and August 15, when, at 11am, the icon bearing the Virgin's image is carried in state down to the harbour over the heads of the faithful.

The Ottoman tenure here was the most fleeting in the Aegean. **Exóbourgo**, the craggy mount dominating southern Tínos and surrounded by most of the island's sixty-odd villages, is studded with the ruins of a Venetian citadel which defied the Turks until 1715, long after the rest of Greece had fallen. An enduring legacy of the long Venetian rule is a persistent Catholic minority, which accounts for almost a third of the population, and a sectarian rivalry said to be responsible for the numerous graceful belfries scattered throughout the island – Orthodox and Catholic parishes vying to build the tallest. The sky is pierced, too, by distinctive and ornate dovecots, even more in evidence here than on Ándhros. Aside from all this, the inland village architecture is striking and there's a flourishing folk-art tradition which finds expression in the abundant local marble. The islanders have remained open and hospitable to the relatively few foreigners and the steady stream of Greek visitors who touch down here, and any mercenary inclinations seem to be satisfied by booming sales in religious paraphernalia to the faithful.

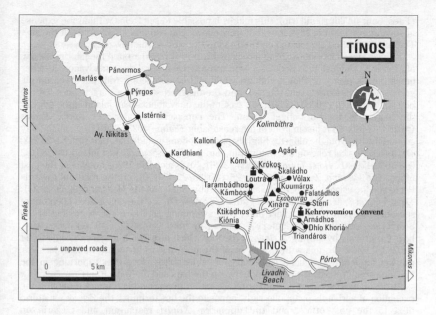

Tínos Town and the southern beaches

At **TÍNOS** town, trafficking in devotional articles certainly dominates the streets leading up from the busy waterfront to the Neoclassical **church** (daily 8am–8pm) which towers above. Approached via a massive marble staircase, the famous **icon** inside is all but buried under a dazzling mass of gold and silver *tammata* (votive offerings); below is the crypt (where the icon was discovered) and a mausoleum for the sailors drowned when the Greek warship *Elli*, at anchor off Tínos during a pilgrimage, was torpedoed by an Italian submarine on August 15, 1940. Museums around the courtyard display more objects donated by the faithful (who inundate the island for the two big yearly festivals), as well as icons, paintings and work by local marble sculptors

The shrine aside – and all the attendant stalls, shops and bustle – the port is none too exciting, with just scattered inland patches of nineteenth-century buildings. You might make time for the **Archeological Museum** (Tues–Sun 8.30am–3pm; 500dr) on the way up to the church, whose collection includes a fascinating sundial from the local Roman Sanctuary of Poseidon and Amphitrite (see p.110).

Practicalities

Ferries dock at any of three different **jetties**; this can depend on weather conditions. There are at least three boats a day from Pireás and four from Rafína, with connections to Ándhros, Mýkonos, Páros and Sýros. When you're leaving, ask your ticket agent which jetty to head for. **Buses** leave from a small parking area in front of a cubbyhole-office on the quay, to Pánormos, Kalloní, Stení, Pórto and Kiónia (timetables available here; no buses after 7.30pm). A **moped** is perhaps a more reliable means of exploring – Vidalis, Zanáki Alavánou 16, is a good rental agency.

Windmills Travel (☎0283/ 23 398), on the front towards the new jetty, can help with information as well as hotel and **tour bookings**; they even have a book exchange. In season an excursion boat does day trips taking in Delos (see p.117) and Mýkonos

(Tues–Sun; 4000dr round trip); this makes it possible to see Delos without the expense of staying overnight in Mýkonos, but only allows you two and a half hours at the site. The **tourist police** are located on the road to the west of the new jetty.

To have any chance of securing a reasonably priced **room** around the pilgrimage day of March 25 (August 15 is hopeless), you must arrive several days in advance. At other times there's plenty of choice, though you'll still be competing with out-of-season pilgrims, Athenian tourists and the sick and the disabled seeking a miracle cure. Of the hotels, the *Eleana* (☎0283/22 561; ④), east of the quay about 400m inland at the edge of the bazaar, is a good budget option. The conspicuous waterfront *Yannis Rooms* (☎0283/22 515; ④) is just in front of the reasonable *Thalia* (☎0283/22811; ④), all the way around the bay from the old jetty. Slightly pricier options include the *Avra* (☎0283/22 242; ④), a Neoclassical relic on the waterfront, and the *Favie Souzane* just inland (☎0283/22 693 or 22 176; ④). *Hotel Tinion* (☎0283/22 261; ⑤) is a stylish 1920s hotel near the post office. The *Vyzantio*, Zanáki Alavánou 26 (☎0283/22 454; ④), on the road out towards Pórto and the villages, is not especially memorable but it and the *Meltemi* (☎0283/22 881; ⑤) at Filipóti 7, near Megalokháris (☎0283/22 881; ④), are the only places open out of season. Finally, there is a smart hotel with swimming pool near the beginning of the beach road east of the promontory – *Aeolos Bay Hotel* (☎0283/23 410; ⑥). Otherwise, beat the crowds by staying at *Tinos Camping* which also has a few nice rooms to let (☎0283/22 344; ②); follow the signs from the port, it's a ten-minute walk. A farmers' **market** for locally produced fruit and vegetables takes place every morning in the Palládha area (towards the new jetty between the bars and the waterfront).

As usual, most seafront **restaurants** are rather overpriced and indifferent, with the exception of a friendly psitopolio right opposite the bus terminal, the *Zefyros* estiatório next to the post office, and the upmarket *Xinari* restaurant and pizzaria on Evangelístrias. A cluster of places around the bazaar just to the left of Megalokháris as you face the church include *Palea Pallada* and *Peristereonas*, both of them reasonable. Tucked away in a small alley near the seafront off Evangelistrías, *Pigada* does a fine clay-pot moussaka, as well as some more unusual dishes, while *O Kipos*, further inland on the way to the church, has a pleasant garden setting. Wash down your meal with the island's very good barrelled retsina, which is available just about everywhere.

There are quite a few **bars**, mostly in a huddle near the new quay. *Fevgatos* has a pleasant atmosphere, and *Kala Kathoumena* is pretty lively with a mixture of international hits and Greek music.

Nearby beaches

Kiónia, 3km northwest (hourly buses), is the site of the **Sanctuary of Poseidon and Amphitrite** which was discovered in 1902; the excavations yielded principally columns (*kionia* in Greek), but also a temple, baths, a fountain, and hostels for the ancient pilgrims. The **beach** is functional enough, but it's better to walk past the large *Tinos Beach Hotel*, the last stop for the bus, and follow an unpaved road to a series of sandy coves beyond.

The beach beyond the headland east of town starts off rocky but improves if you walk 500 metres further along. Further east, **Pórto** (six buses daily) boasts two good beaches to either side of **Áyios Sóstis** headland, with a couple of good tavernas as well as rooms at the reasonably priced restaurant belonging to Akti Aegeou (☎0283/24 248; ⑥) on the first beach of Áyios Pandelímon. *Porto Tango* (☎0283/24 411; ⑥) is a good upmarket hotel here.

Northern Tínos

A good beginning to a foray into the interior is to take the stone stairway – the continuation of Odhós Ayíou Nikoláou – that passes behind and to the left of Evangelístria. This climbs for ninety minutes through appealing countryside to **KTIKÁDHOS**, a fine village with a good sea-view taverna, *Iy Dhrosia*. You can either flag down a bus on the main road or stay with the trail until Xinára (see "Around Exóbourgo" below).

Heading northwest from the junction flanked by Ktikádhos, Tripótamos and Xinára, there's little to stop for – except the fine dovecotes around Tarambádhos – until you reach **KARDHIANÍ**, one of the most strikingly set and beautiful villages on the island, with its views across to Sýros from amid a dense oasis. Nestled in the small sandy bay below is a fine little restaurant by the name of *Anemos*, which serves octopus stew and other dishes at good prices. Kardhianí has been discovered by wealthy Athenians and expatriates, and now offers the exotic *To Perivoli* taverna. **ISTÉRNIA**, just a little beyond, is not nearly so appealing but it does have a pension at the top of the village and a few cafés, perched above the turning for **Órmos Isterníon**, a comparatively small but overdeveloped beach.

Five daily buses along this route finish up at **PÝRGOS**, a few kilometres further north and smack in the middle of the island's marble-quarrying district. A beautiful village, its local artisans are renowned throughout Greece for their skill in producing marble ornamentation; ornate fanlights and bas-relief plaques crafted here adorn houses throughout Tínos. With an attractive shady platía, Pýrgos is popular in summer, but you should be able to find a **room** easily enough, and you have a choice of two **tavernas**, *Vinia* being the more elegant by far.

The marble products were once exported from **PÁNORMOS** (Órmos) harbour, 4km northeast, with its tiny but commercialized beach; there's little reason to linger, but if you get stuck there are rooms and some tavernas.

Around Exóbourgo

The ring of villages around **Exóbourgo** mountain is the other focus of interest on Tínos. The fortified pinnacle itself (570m), with ancient foundations as well as the ruins of three Venetian churches and a fountain, is reached by steep steps from **XINÁRA** (near the island's major road junction), the seat of the island's Roman Catholic bishop. Most villages in north central Tínos have mixed populations, but Xinára and its immediate neighbours are purely Catholic; the inland villages also tend to have a more sheltered position, with better farmland nearby – the Venetians' way of rewarding converts and their descendants. Yet **TRIPÓTAMOS**, just south of Xinára, is a completely Orthodox village with possibly the finest architecture in this region – and has accordingly been pounced on by foreigners keen to restore its historic properties.

At **LOUTRÁ**, the next community north of Xinára, there's an Ursuline convent and a good **Folk Art Museum** (summer only 10.30am–3.30pm; 300dr) in the old Jesuit Monastery here; to visit, leave the bus at the turning for Skaládho. From Krókos, which has a couple of scenically situated restaurants, it's a forty-minute walk to **VÓLAKAS** (Volax), one of the most remote villages on the island, a windswept oasis surrounded by bony rocks. Here, half a dozen elderly Catholic basketweavers fashion some of the best examples of that craft in Greece. There is a small **Folklore Museum** (free); you have to ask for it to be opened up.

At Kómi, 5km beyond Krókos, you can take a detour for **KOLYMBÍTHRA**, a magnificent double beach: one part wild, huge and windswept, the other sheltered and with a taverna and rooms, but no camping. The bus to Kalloní goes on to Kolymbíthra twice a day in season; out of season you'll have to get off at Kómi and walk 4km.

From either Skaládho or Vólakas you go on to Koúmaros, where another long stairway leads up to Exóbourgo, or skirt the pinnacle towards Stení and Falatádhos which appear as white speckles against the fertile Livádha valley. From Stení you can catch the bus back to the harbour (seven daily). On the way down, try and stop off at one of the beautiful settlements just below the important twelfth-century **convent of Kekhrovouníou**, where Ayía Pelayía had her vision. Particularly worth visiting are

DHÝO KHORIÁ with a fine main square where cave-fountains burble, and TRIANDÁROS which has a two good, reasonable **eating** places – *Iy Lefka* and *Eleni's* taverna, a tiny place at the back of the village. If you have your own transport, there are quite wide and fairly negotiable tracks down to some lovely secluded bays on the east of the island from the area of Steni. One such is **Santa Margarita**; given the lack of tourist development here, it's a good idea to take something to drink.

This is hardly an exhaustive list of Tiniot villages; armed with a map and good walking shoes for tackling the many old trails that still exist, you could spend days within sight of Exóbourgo and never pass through the same hamlets twice. Take warm clothing out of season, especially if you're on a moped, since the forbidding mountains behind Vólakas and the Livadhéri plain keep things noticeably cool.

Mýkonos

Originally visited only as a stop on the way to ancient Delos, **Mýkonos** has become easily the most popular (and the most expensive) of the Cyclades. Boosted by direct air links with Britain and domestic flights from Athens, an incredible 800,000 tourists pass through in a good year, producing some spectacular overcrowding in high summer on Mýkonos' 75 square kilometres. But if you don't mind the crowds, or – and this is a much more attractive proposition – you come out of season, the prosperous capital is still one of the most beautiful of all island towns, its immaculately whitewashed houses concealing hundreds of little churches, shrines and chapels.

The sophisticated nightlife is pretty hectic, amply stimulated by Mýkonos' former reputation as *the* gay resort of the Mediterranean – a title lost in recent years to places like Ibiza and Sitges in Spain; whatever, the locals take this comparatively exotic clientele in their stride. Unspoiled it isn't, but the island does offer excellent (if crowded) beaches, picturesque windmills and a rolling arid interior. An unheralded Mýkonian quirk is the legality of scuba diving, a rarity in Greece, and dive centres have sprung up on virtually every beach.

Mýkonos Town

Don't let the crowds put you off exploring **MÝKONOS TOWN**, the archetypal postcard image of the Cyclades. Its sugar-cube buildings are stacked around a cluster of seafront fishermen's dwellings, with every nook and cranny scrubbed and shown off. Most people head out to the beaches during the day, so early morning or late afternoon are the best times to wander the maze of narrow streets. The labyrinthine design was intended to confuse the pirates who plagued Mýkonos in the eighteenth and early nineteenth centuries, and it still has the desired effect.

You don't need any maps or hints to explore the convoluted streets and alleys of town; getting lost is half the fun. There are, however, a few places worth seeking out: coming from the ferry quay you'll pass the **Archeological Museum** (Tues–Sat 9am–3pm, Sun 9.30am–2.30pm; 400dr) on your way into town, which displays some good Delos pottery; the town also boasts a **Marine Museum** displaying various nautical artefacts including a lighthouse re-erected in the back garden (Tues–Sun 8.30am–3pm; 200dr). Alternatively, behind the two banks there's the **Library**, with Hellenistic coins and late medieval seals, or, at the base of the Delos jetty, the **Folklore Museum** (Mon–Sat 5.30–8.30pm, Sun 6.30–8.30pm; free), housed in an eighteenth-century mansion and cramming in a larger-than-usual collection of bric-a-brac, including a vast four-poster bed. The museum shares the same promontory as the old Venetian kástro, the entrance to which is marked by Mýkonos' oldest and best-known church, **Paraportianí**, which is a fascinating asymmetrical hodge-podge of four chapels amalgamated into one.

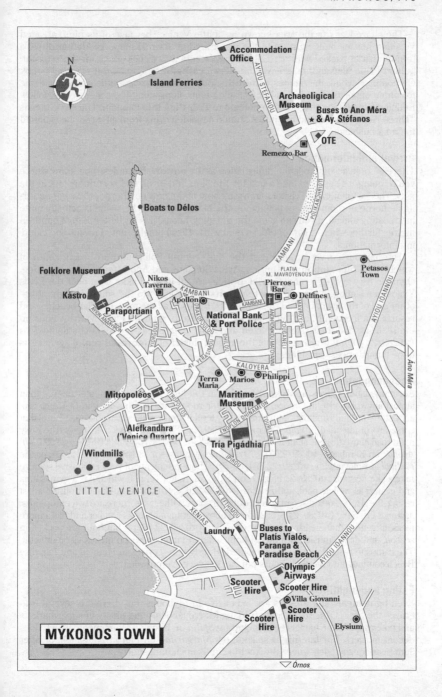

MÝKONOS TOWN

The shore leads to the area known as "Little Venice" because of its high, arcaded Venetian houses built right up to the water's edge. Its real name is **Alefkándhra**, a trendy district packed with art galleries, chic bars and discos. Back off the seafront, behind Platía Alefkándhra, are Mýkonos' two **cathedrals**: Roman Catholic and Greek Orthodox. Beyond, the famous **windmills** look over the area, a little shabby but ripe for photo opportunities. Instead of retracing your steps along the water's edge, follow Énoplon Dhinaméon (left off Mitropóleos) to **Tría Pigádhia** fountain. The name means "Three Wells", and legend has it that should a maiden drink from all three she is bound to find a husband.

Arrival and information

There is some accommodation information at the **airport**, but unless you know where you're going it's easier to take a taxi for the 3km into town, and sort things out at the jetty. The vast majority of visitors arrive by boat at the new northern **jetty**, where a veritable horde of room-owners pounce on the newly arrived. The scene is actually quite intimidating and so, if you can avoid the grasping talons, it is far better to go a hundred metres further where a row of offices deal with official hotels, rented rooms and camping information.

The harbour curves around past the dull, central Polikandhrióti beach; south of which is the **bus station** for Toúrlos, Áyios Stéfanos and Áno Méra. The **post office**, Olympic Airways office and **tourist police** are all in the Lákka area near the Platís Yialós bus station. A second **bus terminus**, for beaches to the south, is right at the other end of the town, beyond the windmills. Buses to all the most popular beaches and resorts run frequently, and till the early hours. **Taxis** go from Platía Mavroyénous on the seafront, and their rates are fixed and quite reasonable; try Mýkonos Radio Taxi (☎0289/22 400). It is also here that the largest cluster of **motorbike rental** agencies is to be found: prices vary little.

Accommodation

Accommodation **prices** in Mýkonos rocket in the high season to a greater degree than almost anywhere else in Greece. If you're after **rooms**, it's worth asking at *O Megas* grocery store on Andhroníkou Matoyiánni – they tend to know what's available. One **hotel** that comes recommended is *Villa Giovanni* (☎0289/22 485; ⑥), on Ayíou Ioánnou, the busy main road above the bus station. **In town**, try *Delfines* on Mavroyenous (☎0289/22 292; ⑥), *Apollon* on Kambani (☎0289/22 223; ⑤), *Maria* at Kaloyéra 18 (☎0289/24 212; ⑥), or the *Philippi* at Kaloyéra 25 (☎0289/22 294; ④–⑤). There are plenty of very expensive splurge hotels like *Elysium* (☎0289/23 952; ⑥) on Skholíou Kalón Tehnon which has a gym, sauna and jacuzzi as well as pool, and *Petasos* (☎0289/22608; ⑥) above Polikandhrióti. As a last resort, the *Apollo 2001* disco may rent out roof space. Otherwise, there are two **campsites**: *Mykonos Camping* (☎0289/24 578; 2,300dr) above Paranga beach is smaller and has a more pleasant setting than nearby *Paradise Camping* (☎0289/22 852) – but both are packed in season, and dance music from the 24-hour bars on Paradise Beach makes sleep difficult. The campsite restaurants are best avoided. Hourly bus services to Paranga and Paradise Beach continue into the early hours but can get very overcrowded.

Eating and nightlife

Even **light meals** and **snacks** are expensive in Mýkonos, but there are several bakeries – the best is *Andhrea's*, just off Platía Mavroyénous – and plenty of supermarkets and takeaways in the backstreets, including *Spilia* on Énoplon Dhinaméon, which does decent burgers. For **late-night** snacks, try *Margarita's* on Flórou Zouganéli, or after 3am head for the port, where the Yacht Club is open until sunrise.

The area around Kaloyéra is a promising place to head for a full **meal**. The *Edem Garden* at the top of Kaloyéra, is a popular gay restaurant with an adventurous menu, and *El Greco* at Tría Pigádhia is expensive but romantic. Alefkándhra can offer *La Cathedral*, by the two cathedrals on the platía, the pricey but well-sited *Pelican*, behind the cathedrals, the *Oasis Garden Restaurant* nearby on Mitropóleos, in a quiet garden with reasonable food, and *Spiro's* for good fish on the seafront. *Kostas*, also behind the two cathedrals, has competitive prices, a good selection including bar-relled wine (not easily found on Mýkonos) and friendly service. Less than fifty metres further along Mitropóleos, the small *Yiavroutas Estiatorio* is probably the least expensive and most authentically Greek place on the island, again with good bar-relled wine. There's something for most tastes in the Lákka (bus station) area: a vari-ety of salads at *Orpheas*, French cuisine at *Andromeda*, and Italian at *Dolce Vita*. Just behind the Town Hall is *Nikos' Taverna* – crowded, reasonable and recommended – and 1km north you can dine by a floodlit pool overlooking the cruise ships at the lux-ury *Hotel Cavo Tagoo*.

Nightlife in town is every bit as good as it's cracked up to be – and every bit as pricey. *Remezzo* (near the OTE) is one of the oldest bars, now a bit over the hill but a nice place to watch the sunset before the onslaught of the hilarious Greek dancing lessons. *Skandinavian Bar-Disco* is a cheap and cheerful party spot, as is the nearby *Irish Bar*, and there are more drinking haunts over in the Alefkándhra area. For classi-cal music, try *Kastro's* for an early evening cocktail, moving on later to the fairly swanky *Montparnasse*. *Bolero's* and *Piano Bar* both have live music, while *Le Cinema* is a newish club worth trying. The **gay** striptease and drag-show scene has shifted to the *Factory* by the windmills; *Manto* and adjacent bars are also popular.

The beaches

The closest **beaches** to town are those to the north, at **Toúrlos** (only 2km away but horrid) and **Áyios Stéfanos** (4km, much better), both developed resorts and connect-ed by a very regular bus service to Mýkonos. There are tavernas and rooms to let (as well as package hotels) at Áyios Stéfanos, away from the beach; *Nikos* taverna at the far end of the bay has a pleasant setting and good prices.

Other nearby destinations include southwest peninsula resorts, with undistin-guished beaches tucked into pretty bays. The nearest to town, 1km away, is **Mogáli Ammos**, a good beach backed by flat rocks and pricey rooms, but nearby Kórfos bay is disgusting, thanks to the town dump and machine noise. Buses serve **Órnos** – home to the Lucky Divers Scuba Club (☎0289/23 220) – and an average beach, and **Áyios Ioánnis**, a dramatic bay with a tiny, stony beach and a chapel.

The south coast is the busiest part of the island. Kaḯkia ply from town to all of its beaches, which are among the straightest on the island, and still regarded to some extent as family strands by the Greeks. You might begin with **Platýs Yialós**, 4km south of town, though you won't be alone: one of the longest-established resorts on the island, it's not remotely Greek any more, the sand is monopolized by hotels, and you won't get a room to save your life between June and September. **Psaroú**, next door, is very pret-ty – 150m of white sand backed by foliage and calamus reeds, crowded with sun-bathers. Facilities here include a diving club (☎0289/23 579), waterskiing and wind-surfer rental, but again you'll need to reserve well in advance to secure a room between mid-June and mid-September.

A dusty footpath beyond Platís Yialós crosses the fields and caves of the headland across the clifftops past *Mykonos Camping*, and drops down to **Paradise Beach**, a cres-cent of golden sand that is packed in season. Behind are the shops, self-service restau-rants and noisy 24-hour beach bars of *Paradise Camping*. The next bay east contains

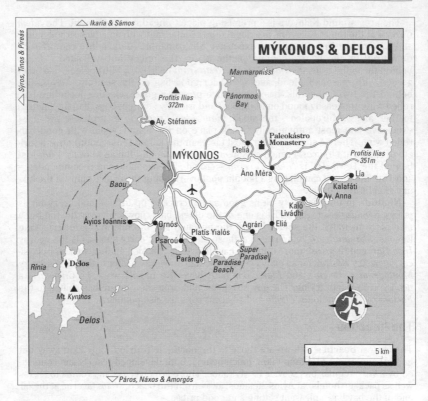

Super Paradise (officially "Plindhrí") beach, accessible by footpath or by kaïki. Once renowned as an exclusively gay, nudist beach, it's now pretty mixed, and a has a good, friendly atmosphere and a couple of tavernas.

Probably the **best beach** on Mýkonos, though, is **Elía**, the last port of call for the kaïkia. A broad, sandy stretch with a verdant backdrop, it's the longest beach on the island, though split in two by a rocky area. Almost exclusively nudist, it boasts an excellent restaurant, *Matheos*. If the crowds have followed you this far, one last escape route is to follow the bare rock footpath over the spur (look for the white house) at the end of Elía beach. This cuts upwards for grand views east and west and then winds down to **Kaló Livádhi** (seasonal bus service), a stunning beach adjoining an agricultural valley scattered with little farmhouses; even here there's a restaurant (a good one at that) at the far end of the beach. **Lía**, further on, is smaller but delightful, with bamboo windbreaks and clear water, plus another taverna.

The rest of the island

If time is limited, any of the beaches above will be just fine. There are others, though, away from Mýkonos Town, as well as a few other destinations worth making the effort for.

East of Elía, roughly 12km by road from the town, **Ayía Ánna** boasts a shingle beach and taverna, with the cliffs above granting some fine vistas; the place achieved its moment of fame as a location for the film *Shirley Valentine*. **Tarsaná**, on the other side of the isthmus, has a long, coarse sand beach, with watersports, a taverna and smart bungalows on offer. **Kalafáti**, almost adjacent, is more of a tourist community, its white-sand beach supporting a few hotels, restaurants and a disco. There's a local bus service from here to Áno Méra (see below), or you can jump on an excursion boat to **Tragoníssi**, the islet just offshore, for spectacular coastal scenery, seals and wild birds. The rest of the east coast is difficult – often impossible – to reach: there are some small beaches, really only worth the effort if you crave solitude, and the region is dominated by the peak of Profítis Ilías, sadly spoiled by a huge radar dome and military establishment. The **north coast** suffers persistent battering from the *meltémi*, plus tar and litter pollution, and for the most part is bare, brown and exposed. **Pánormos Bay** is the exception to this – a lovely, relatively sheltered beach, and one of the least crowded on the island, with a couple of decent tavernas.

From Pánormos, it's an easy walk to the only other settlement of any size on the island, **ÁNO MÉRA**, where you should be able to find a **room**. The village strives to maintain a traditional way of life: in the main square there's a proper kafenío and fresh vegetables are sold, ouzo and a local cheese are produced, and there's just one hotel. The taverna *Tou Apostoli to Koutouki* is popular with locals. The red-roofed church near the square is the sixteenth-century **monastery of Panayía Tourlianí**, where a collection of Cretan icons and the unusual eighteenth-century marble baptismal font are worth seeing. It's not far, either, to the late twelfth-century **Paleokástro monastery** (also known as Dárga), just north of the village, in a magnificent green setting on an otherwise barren slope. To the northwest are more of the same dry and wind-buffeted landscapes, though they do provide some enjoyable, rocky walking with expansive views across to neighbouring islands – stroll down to Áyios Stéfanos for buses back to the harbour.

Delos (Dhílos)

The remains of **ancient Delos**, Pindar's "unmoved marvel of the wide world", though skeletal and swarming now with lizards and tourists, give some idea of the past grandeur of this sacred isle a few sea-miles west of Mýkonos. The ancient town lies on the west coast on flat, sometimes marshy ground which rises in the south to **Mount Kínthos**. From the summit – an easy walk – there's a magnificent view across the Cyclades: the name of the archipelago means "those [islands] around [Delos]".

The first excursion boats to Delos leave Mýkonos daily at 8.30am (1600dr round trip), except Mondays when the site is closed. You have to return on the same boat but in season each does the trip several times and you can choose what time you leave. The last return is usually about 3pm, and you'll need to arrive early if you want to make a thorough tour of the site. In season a daily kaḯki makes return trips from the beaches (2500dr) with pick-up points at Paránga, Platís Yialós and Ornos, but only allows you three hours on the island. It's a good idea to bring your own food and drink as the tourist pavilion's snack bar is a rip-off.

Some history

Delos' ancient fame was due to the fact that Leto gave birth to the divine twins Artemis and Apollo on the island, although its fine harbour and central position did nothing to hamper development. When the Ionians colonized the island around 1000 BC it was already a cult centre, and by the seventh century BC it had become the commercial and religious centre of the **Amphictionic League**. Unfortunately Delos also attracted the attention of Athens, which sought dominion over this prestigious

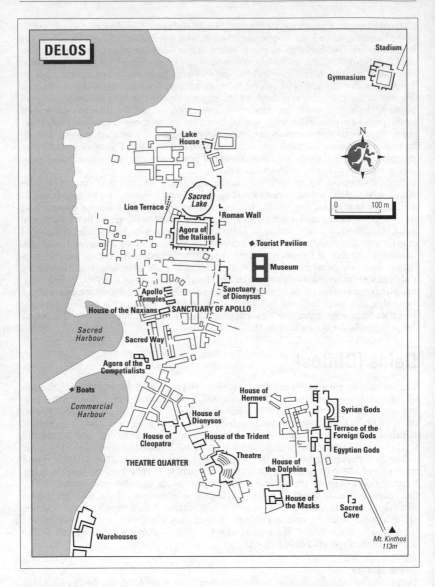

island; the wealth of the Delian Confederacy, founded after the Persian Wars to protect the Aegean cities, was harnessed to Athenian ends, and for a while they controlled the Sanctuary of Apollo. Athenian attempts to "purify" the island began with a decree that no one could die or give birth on Delos – the sick and the pregnant were taken to the islet of Rheneia – and culminated in the simple expedient of banishing the native population.

Delos reached its peak in the third and second centuries BC, after being declared a free port by its Roman overlords. In the end, though, its undefended wealth brought ruin: first Mithridates (88 BC), then Athenodorus (69 BC), plundered the treasures and the island never recovered. By the third century AD, Athens could not even sell it, and for centuries, every passing seafarer stopped to collect a few prizes.

The site

Tues–Sun 8.30am–3pm; 1200dr.

As you land, the Sacred Harbour is on your left, the Commercial Harbour on your right; and straight ahead is the **Agora of the Competialists**. Competialists were Roman merchants or freed slaves who worshipped the Lares Competales, the guardian spirits of crossroads; offerings to Hermes would once have been placed in the middle of the *agora*, their position now marked by a round and a square base. The **Sacred Way** leads north from the far left corner; it used to be lined with statues and the grandiose monuments of rival kings. Along it you reach three marble steps which lead into the **Sanctuary of Apollo**: much was lavished on the god, but the forest of offerings has been plundered over the years. On your left is the Stoa of the Naxians, while against the north wall of the House of the Naxians, to the right, a huge statue of Apollo stood in ancient times. In 417 BC the Athenian general Nicias led a procession of priests across a bridge of boats from Rheneia to dedicate a bronze palm tree; when it was later blown over in a gale it took the statue with it. Three **Temples of Apollo** stand in a row to the right along the Sacred Way: the Delian Temple, that of the Athenians, and the Porinos Naos, the earliest of them, dating from the sixth century BC. To the east towards the museum you pass the **Sanctuary of Dionysus**, with its marble phalluses on tall pillars.

The best finds from the site are in Athens, but the **museum** still justifies a visit. To the north is a wall that marks the site of the **Sacred Lake** where Leto gave birth, clinging to a palm tree. Guarding it are the superb **lions**, their lean bodies masterfully executed by Naxians in the seventh century BC; of the original nine, three have disappeared and one adorns the Arsenale at Venice. On the other side of the lake is the City Wall, built in 69 BC – too late to protect the treasures.

Set out in the other direction from the Agora of the Competialists and you enter the residential area, known as the **Theatre Quarter**. Many of the walls and roads remain, but there is none of the domestic detail that brings such sites to life. Some colour is added by the mosaics: one in the **House of the Trident**, and better ones in the **House of the Masks**, most notably a vigorous portrayal of Dionysus riding on a panther's back. The **Theatre** itself seated 5500 spectators, and, though much ravaged, offers some fine views. Behind the theatre, a path leads past the **Sanctuaries of the Foreign Gods** and up **Mount Kínthos** for more panoramic sightseeing.

Sýros

Don't be put off by first impressions of **Sýros**. From the ferry it looks grimly industrial, but away from the Neórion shipyard things improve quickly. Very much a working island with no real history of tourism, it is probably the most Greek of the Cyclades; there are few holiday trappings and what there is exists for the benefit of the locals. You probably won't find, as Herman Melville did when he visited in 1856, shops full of ". . . fez-caps, swords, tobacco, shawls, pistols, and orient finery . . .", but you're still likely to appreciate Sýros as a refreshing change from the beautiful people. Of course, outsiders do come to the island; in fact there's a thriving permanent foreign community, and the beaches are hardly undeveloped, but everywhere there's the underlying assumption that you're a guest of an inherently private people.

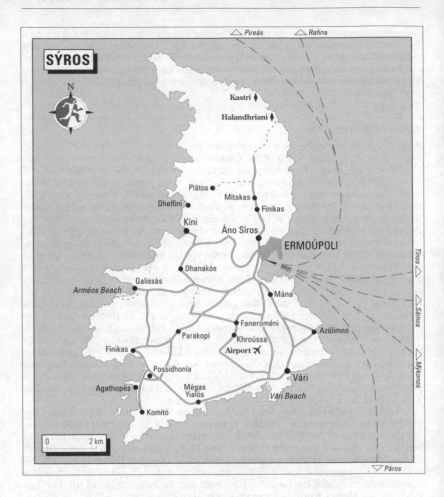

Ermoúpoli

The main town and port of **ERMOÚPOLI** was founded during the War of Independence by refugees from Psará and Khíos, becoming Greece's chief port in the nineteenth century. Although Pireás outran it long ago, Ermoúpoli is still the largest town in the Cyclades, and the archipelago's capital. Medieval Sýros was largely a Catholic island, but an influx of Orthodox refugees during the War of Independence created two distinct communities; almost equal in numbers, the two groups today still live in their respective quarters, occupying two hills that rise up from the sea.

Ermoúpoli itself, the **lower town**, is worth at least a night's stay, with grandiose buildings a relic of its days as a major port. Between the harbour and **Áyios Nikólaos**, the fine Orthodox church to the north, you can stroll through its faded splendour. The **Apollon Theatre** is a copy of La Scala in Milan and once presented a regular Italian opera season; today local theatre and music groups put it to good use. The long, central **Platía Miaoúli** is named after an admiral of the revolution whose statue stands there, and in the evenings the population parades in front of its arcaded kafenía, while the children ride the mechanical animals. Up the stairs to the left of the Town Hall is the small **Archeological Museum** (Tues–Sun 8.30am–3pm; free) with three rooms of finds from Sýros, Páros and Amorgós. To the left of the clock tower more stairs climb up to **Vrondádho**, the hill that hosts the Orthodox quarter. The wonderful church of the **Anástasi** stands atop the hill, with its domed roof and great views over Tínos and Mýkonos – if it's locked, ask for the key at the priest's house.

On the taller hill to the left is the intricate medieval quarter of **Áno Sýros**, with a clutch of Catholic churches below the cathedral of St George. There are fine views of the town below, and, close by, the **Cappuchin monastery of St Jean**, founded in 1535 to do duty as a poorhouse. It takes about 45 minutes of tough walking up Omírou to reach this quarter, passing the Orthodox and Catholic cemeteries on the way – the former full of grand shipowners' mausoleums, the latter with more modest monuments and French and Italian inscriptions (you can halve the walking time by taking a short cut on to the stair-street named Andhréa Kárga, part of the way along). Once up here it's worth visiting the local art and church exhibitions at the Vamvakeri **museum** (daily 10.30am–1pm & 7–10pm; 500dr), and the Byzantine museum attached to the monastery.

Arrival, facilities and accommodation

The **quayside** is still busy, though nowadays it deals with more tourist than industrial shipping; Sýros is a major crossover point on the ferry-boat routes. Also down here is the **bus station**, along with the **tourist police** and several **bike rental** places. Between them shops sell the *loukoumia* (Turkish delight) and *halvadhopita* (sweetmeat pie) for which the island is famed. **Odhós Khíou**, the market street, is especially lively on Saturday when people come in from the surrounding countryside to sell fresh produce.

Keeping step with a growing level of tourism, **rooms** have improved in quality and number in recent years; many are in garishly decorated, if crumbling, Neoclassical mansions. Good choices include *Kastro* rooms, Kalomenopóulou 12 (☎0281/88 064; ③), *Dream* on the seafront near the bus station (☎0281/84 356; ④), and the central rooms on Platía Miaoúli (☎0281/88 509; ④) and at *Paradise*, Omírou 3 (☎0281/83 204; ⑤). A notch up in price and quality is the well-sited *Hotel Hermes* (☎0281/83 011; ⑥) on Platía Kanári, overlooking the port or, for a slice of good-value opulence, try the *Xenon Ipatias* (☎0281/83 575; ⑨), beyond Áyios Nikólaos. At peak times the Team Work agency (on the waterfront) may be able to help with accommodation. For plusher places around town and hotels and rooms of all categories around the island there is a kiosk belonging to the Rooms and Apartments Association of Syros (☎0281/87 360) along the waterfront – turn right after disembarking.

Eating, drinking and nightlife

The most authentic and reasonably priced of the harbour **tavernas** is *Medusa*, at Ándhrou 3, a block in from the water; places actually on the quay, such as *1935*, tend to be more touristy and expensive. There are one or two exceptions, including the very reasonable *Caro D'Oro* which serves up casseroles and barrelled wine, and the popular *Psaropoula* ouzerí. Highly recommended for an Italian treat is *Il Giardino*, set in a beautifully restored villa opposite the *Apollon*. On Platía Miaoúli, the *Manousos* taverna is a good traditional place. Way up in Vrondádho, at Anastáseos 17, on the corner of Kalavrítou, the cooking at *Tembelis* makes up for the limited seating and grouchy service; *Folia*, at Athanasíou Dhiakoú 6, is more expensive but serves such exotica as rabbit and

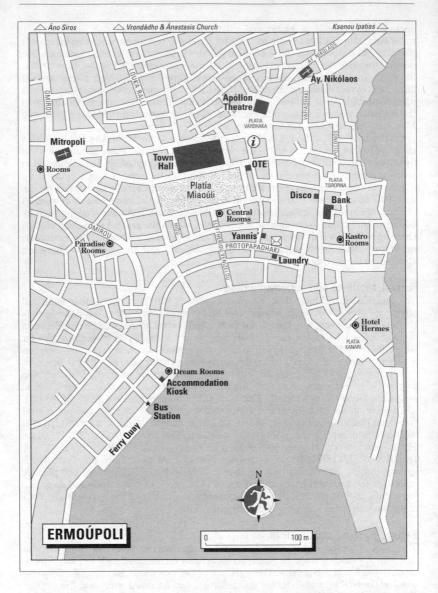

Áy. Nikólaos

Apóllon Theatre

PLATIA VARDHAKA

Mitropolí

Town Hall

OTE

Rooms

Platía Miaoúli

PLATIA TSIROPINA

Disco

Bank

Central Rooms

Kastro Rooms

Paradise Rooms

Yannis'

PROTOPAPADHAKI

Laundry

Hotel Hermes

PLATIA KANARI

Dream Rooms

Accommodation Kiosk

Bus Station

Ferry Quay

N

ERMOÚPOLI

0   100 m

pigeon. In Ano Sýros, the *Thea* taverna, signposted in Greek from the car park, is fine and affords the views its name would suggest; the *Iy Piatsa* ouzerí is also worth a try.

Incidentally, Sýros still honours its contribution to the development of **rembétika**; bouzoúki-great Markos Vamvakaris hailed from here and a platía in Áno Sýros has been named after him. **Taverna-clubs** such as *Lillis* (up in Áno Sýros) and *Rahanos*, with music on weekends, now take their place beside a batch of more conventional disco-clubs down near the Apollon Theatre. There are several other (often expensive) bouzoúki bars scattered around the island, mostly strung along routes to beach resorts. The seafront has a rash of lively **bars** – *Tramps* has a relaxed atmosphere and the most eclectic music. There's another cluster around the Platía Miaoúli: *Clearchos* piano bar is rather smooth, *Agora* has imaginative decor and a musical mix, while *Piramatiko* is best for up-to-date indie sounds. The big venue for night-owls is *Rodo*, a huge disco in a converted warehouse out past the Neórión shipyard opposite the turning to Vári. Finally, the newly opened *Aegean Casino* on the seafront features live music at the restaurant, and is open till 6am for those who have money to burn (and are sufficiently well-dressed).

Around the island

The main loop road (to Gallissás, Fínikas, Mégas Yialós, Vári and back), and the road west to Kíni, are good: **buses** ply the routes hourly in season, and run until late. Elsewhere, expect potholes – especially to the **north** where the land is barren and high, with few villages. The main route north from Áno Sýros has improved and is quite easily negotiable by bike; en route, the village of **Mýtikas** has a decent taverna just off the road. A few kilometres further on the road forks, with the left turn leading, after another left, to the small settlement of **Sirioúga** where there's an interesting cave to explore, or straight on to **Kámbos**, from where a path leads down to Lía Beach; the right fork eventually descends to the north-east coast after passing an excellent kafenío, *Sgouros*, with views across to Tínos.

The well-trodden route **south** offers more tangible and accessible rewards. Closest to the capital, fifteen minutes away by bus, is the coastal settlement of **KÍNI**. There are two separate beaches, the *Sunset Hotel* (☎0281/71 211; ③–④), with the excellent *Zalounis* taverna just below and, just away from the seafront, the *Hotel Elpida* (☎0281/71 224; ③). **GALISSÁS**, a few kilometres south, but reached by different buses, has developed along different lines. Fundamentally an agricultural village, it's been taken over in recent years by backpackers attracted by the island's only **campsites** (both have good facilities and send minibuses to all boats, but *Camping Yianna* has the advantage over *Two Hearts* of being closer to the sea) and a very pretty beach, more protected than Kíni's. This new-found popularity has created a surplus of unaesthetic **rooms**, which at least makes bargaining possible, and five bona fide hotels, of which the cheapest is *Petros* (☎0281/42 067; ③), though the *Benois* (☎0281/42 833; ⑤) is decent value, with buffet breakfast included. Amongst the many eating choices, *Diskovolos* and *Cavos*, overlooking the bay, are worth a try. Galissás' identity crisis is exemplified by the proximity of bemused, grazing dairy cattle, a heavy-metal music pub, and upmarket handicrafts shops. Still, the people are welcoming, and if you feel the urge to escape, you can rent a moped, or walk ten minutes past the headland to the nudist beach of **Arméos**, where there's fresh spring water and unofficial camping. Note that buses out are erratically routed; to be sure of making your connection you must wait at the high-road stop, not down by the beach. **Dhelfini** just to the north is also a fine beach, though it's slowly falling prey to the developers under the translated name of Dolphin Bay.

A pleasant one-hour walk or a ten-minute bus ride south from Galissás brings you to the more mainstream resort of **FÍNIKAS**, purported to have been settled originally by the Phoenicians (although an alternative derivation could be from *fínikas*, meaning "palm tree" in Greek). The beach is narrow and gritty, right next to the road but protected to some extent by a row of tamarisk trees; the pick of the hotels is the *Cyclades* (☎0281/42 255; ⑤), which also has an acceptable restaurant, though the *Amaryllis* rooms (☎0281/42 894; ③) are much cheaper. The *Panorama* restaurant on the seafront is recommended.

Fínikas is separated by a tiny headland from its neighbour **POSSIDHONÍA** (or Delagrazzia), a nicer spot with some idiosyncratically ornate mansions and a bright blue church right on the edge of the village. It's worth walking ten minutes further south, past the naval yacht club and its patrol boat to **Agathopés**, with a sandy beach and a little islet just offshore. Komitó, at the end of the unpaved track leading south from Agathopés, is nothing more than a stony beach fronting an olive grove. **Accommodation** around Possidhonía ranges from the luxurious and extremely expensive *Hotel Eleana* (☎0281/42 601; ⑥), reckoned by some to be the best in the Cyclades, to the cheerful *Elpida Pension* (☎0281/42 577; ③), while *Meltemi* is the best seafood taverna.

The road swings east to **MÉGAS YIALÓS**, a small resort below a hillside festooned with brightly painted houses. The long, narrow beach is lined with shady trees and there are pedal boats for hire. Of the **room** set-ups, *Mike and Bill's* (☎0281/43 531; ④) is a reasonable deal, and the pricier *Alexandra Hotel* (☎0281/42 540; ⑤) on the bay enjoys lovely views. **VÁRI** is more – though not much more – of a town, with its own small fishing fleet. Beach-goers are in a goldfish bowl, as it were, with tavernas and **rooms** looming right overhead, but it is the most sheltered of the island's bays, something to remember when the *meltémi* is up. The *Kamelo* hotel (☎0281/61 217; ⑤) provides the best value, and has TV in all the rooms. The adjacent cove of **AKHLÁDHI** is far more pleasant and boasts two small good-value hotels, including the *Emily* (☎0281/61400; ④) on the seafront, and has one taverna.

Páros and Andíparos

Gently and undramatically furled around the single peak of Profítis Ilías, **Páros** has a little of everything one expects from a Greek island – old villages, monasteries, fishing harbours, a labyrinthine capital – and some of the best nightlife and beaches in the Aegean. Parikía, the Khóra, is the major hub of inter-island ferry services, so that if you wait long enough you can get to just about any island in the Aegean. However, the island is almost as heavily touristy and expensive as Mýkonos: in peak season, it's touch-and-go when it comes to finding rooms and beach space. At such times, the attractive inland settlements or the satellite island of **Andíparos** handle the overflow. Incidentally, the August 15 festival here is one of the best such observances in Greece, with a parade of flare-lit fishing boats and fireworks delighting as many Greeks as foreigners, but it's a real feat to secure accommodation around this time.

Parikía and around

PARIKÍA sets the tone architecturally for the rest of Páros, with its ranks of typically Cycladic white houses punctuated by the occasional Venetian-style building and church domes. But all is awash in a constant stream of ferry passengers, and the town is relentlessly commercial. The busy waterfront is jam-packed with bars, restaurants, hotels and ticket agencies, while the maze of houses in the older quarter behind, designed to baffle both wind and pirates, has surrendered to an onslaught of chi-chi boutiques.

Just beyond the central clutter though, the town has one of the most architecturally interesting churches in the Aegean – the **Ekatondapilianí**, or "The One-Hundred-Gated". What's visible today was designed and supervised by Isidore of Miletus in the sixth century, but construction was actually carried out by his pupil Ignatius. It was so beautiful on completion that the master, consumed with jealousy, is said to have grappled with his apprentice on the rooftop, flinging them both to their deaths. They are portrayed kneeling at the column bases across the courtyard, the old master tugging at his beard in repentance and his rueful pupil clutching a broken head. The church was substantially altered after a severe earthquake in the eighth century, but its essen-

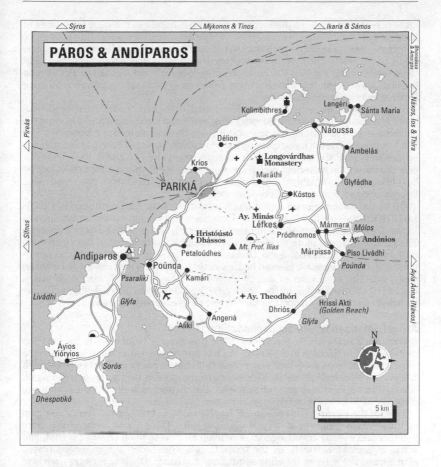

tially Byzantine aspect remains, its shape an imperfect Greek cross. Enclosed by a great wall to protect its icons from pirates, it is in fact three interlocking churches; the oldest, the chapel of Áyios Nikólaos to the left of the apse, is an adaptation of a pagan building dating from the early fourth century BC. To the right of the courtyard, the **Byzantine Museum** (daily 9am–1pm & 5.30–9.30pm; 500dr, free on Tues) displays a collection of icons. Behind Ekatondapilianí, the **Archeological Museum** (Tues–Sun 8.30am–2.30pm; 500dr) has a fair collection of antique bits and pieces, its prize exhibits being a fifth-century winged Nike and a piece of the *Parian Chronicle*, a social and cultural history of Greece up to 264 BC engraved in marble.

These two sights apart, the real attraction of Parikía is simply to wander the town itself. Arcaded lanes lead past Venetian-influenced villas, traditional island dwellings and the three ornate wall fountains donated by the Mavroyénnis family in the eighteenth century. The town culminates in a seaward Venetian **Kástro**, whose surviving east wall incorporates a fifth century round tower and is constructed using masonry pillaged from a temple of Athena. Part of the base of the temple is still visible next to the beautiful, arcaded church of Áyios Konstandínos, and Áyia Eléni crowns the highest point, from where the fortified hill drops sharply to the quay in a series of hanging gardens.

If you're staying in town, you'll want to get out into the surroundings at some stage, if only to the beach. The most rewarding **excursion** is the hour's walk along an unsurfaced road starting just past the museum up to **Áyii Anáryiri** monastery. Perched on the bluff above town, this makes a great picnic spot, with cypress groves, a gushing fountain and some splendid views.

There are **beaches** immediately north and south of the harbour, though none are particularly attractive when compared with Páros' best. In fact, you might prefer to avoid the northern stretch altogether: heading **south** along the asphalt road is a better bet. The first unsurfaced side track you come to leads to a small, sheltered beach; fifteen minutes further on is **PARASPÓROS**, with a reasonable **campsite** (☎0284/21 100) and beach near the remains of an ancient *asklepeion*. Continuing for 45 minutes (or a short hop by bus) brings you to arguably the best of the bunch, **AYÍA IRÍNI**, with good sand and a taverna next to a farm and shady olive grove.

Off in the same direction, but a much longer two-hour haul each way, is **PETALOÚDHES**, the so-called "Valley of the Butterflies", a walled-in oasis where millions of Jersey tiger moths perch on the foliage during early summer (June–Sept 9am–8pm; 200dr). The trip pays more dividends when combined with a visit to the eighteenth-century nunnery of **Khristoú stó Dhássos**, at the crest of a ridge twenty minutes to the north. Only women are allowed in the sanctuary, although men can get as far as the courtyard. The succession of narrow drives and donkey paths linking both places begins just south of Parikía, by the *Xenon Ery*. Petaloúdhes can be reached from Parikía by bus (in summer), by moped, or on an overpriced excursion by mule.

Arrival, information and accommodation

Ferries **dock** in Parikía by the windmill; the **bus stop** is 100m or so to the left. Bus routes extend to Náoussa in the north, Poúnda (for Andíparos) in the west, Alikí in the south, and Dhríos on the island's east coast (with another very useful service between Dhríos and Náoussa). Buses to Náoussa carry on running hourly through the night, while other services stop around midnight. The **airport** is around 12km from town, close to Alikí – from where ten daily buses run to Parikía.

Most of the island is flat enough for bicycle rides, but mopeds are more common and are available for rent at several places in town. Polos Tours is one of the more together and friendly **travel agencies**, issuing air tickets when Olympic is shut, and acting as agents for virtually all the boats. Luggage can be left at Santorineos Travel, 50m beyond Polos Tours (heading south along the front). Olympic Airways itself is at the far end of Odhós Probóne, while the **tourist police** occupy a building at the back of the seafront square.

As for **accommodation**, Parikía is a pleasant and central base, but absolutely mobbed in summer. You'll be met off the ferry by locals offering rooms, even at the most unlikely hours; avoid persistent offers of rooms or hotels to the north as they'll invariably be a long walk away from town. One of the best deals is to be had is at the *Pension Festos* on the back streets inland, managed by young Brits (☎0284/21 635; ④); it has beds in shared rooms making it a good choice for single travellers. Popular **hotels** include *Dina* (☎0284/21 325; ④) near Platía Veléntza, *Kontes* (☎0284/21 096; ⑤) near the harbour windmill and *Hotel Oasis* (☎0284/21 227; ③–④) on Prombóna, very close to the harbour. *Hotel Kypreou* (☎0284/21 383; ④) is a small family-run hotel on Prombóna, which, like *Oasis* and *Kontes*, stays open through the winter. A good upmarket choice is *Hotel Doukissa* (☎0284/22 442; ⑥) near the Archeological Museum, while *Irini Triadafilou* (☎0284/23 022; ③) has a few basic rooms within the kástro, some with good sea views.

Eating, drinking and nightlife

Many Parikía **tavernas** are run by outsiders operating under municipal concession, so year-to-year variation in proprietors and quality is marked. However, the following seem to be long-established and/or good-value outfits. Rock-bottom is the *Koutouki Thanasis*, which serves oven food for locals and bold tourists and lurks in a back street to the left of the (expensive) *Hibiscus*. Also in the picturesque backstreets are *Kyriakos Place* on Lohágou Grivári, which has seats out under a fine tree, and the *Garden of Dionysos* nearby. In the exotic department, *May Tey* serves average Chinese food at moderate markup, while Italian dishes can be found at *La Barca Rossa* on the seafront or *Bella Italia* across a waterfront square.

There is a welter of places of varying quality and prices along the **seafront** towards the bar enclave. Of these, *Asteras Grill House* is very good with some decent specials as well as the usual grilled meats. Down a backstreet just to the north of the harbour, *Nisiotissa* has a highly entertaining chef-proprietor and is rarely crowded; *Delfini*, on the first paved drive along the road to Poúnda, is long-established and famous for its Sunday barbecue with live music. There are a couple of specialist eating places: *The Happy Green Cow*, a friendly café with vegetarian and vegan food behind the National Bank, and *Wired Café*, a new Internet café on the market street running behind the kástro (2000dr per hour).

Parikía has a wealth of **pubs**, **bars** and low-key **discos**, not as pretentious as those on Mýkonos or as raucous as the scene on Íos, but certainly everything in between. The most popular cocktail bars extend along the seafront, all tucked into a series of open squares and offering competing but staggered (no pun intended) "Happy Hours", so that you can drink cheaply for much of the evening. *Kafenio O Flisvos*, about three-quarters of the way south along the front, is the last remaining traditional outfit among the rash of pizzerias, snack-bars, juice and ice-cream joints. A rowdy crowd favours the conspicuous *Saloon D'Or*, while the *Pirate Bar* features jazz and blues. *Evinos* and *Pebbles* are more genteel, the latter pricey but with good sunset views and the occasional live gig. The "theme" pubs are a bit rough and ready for some: most outrageous is the *Dubliner Complex*, comprising four bars, a snack section, disco and seating area.

Finally, a thriving cultural centre, *Arhilokhos* (near Ekatondapiliani) caters mostly to locals, with occasional **film** screenings – there are also two open-air cinemas, *Neo Rex* and *Paros*, where foreign films are shown in season.

Náoussa and around

The second port of Páros, **NÁOUSSA** was once an unspoiled, sparkling labyrinth of winding, narrow alleys and simple Cycladic houses. Alas, a rash of new concrete hotels and attendant trappings have all but swamped its character, though down at the small harbour, fishermen still tenderize octopuses by thrashing them against the walls. The local festivals – an annual Fish and Wine Festival on July 2, and an August 23 shindig celebrating an old naval victory over the Turks – are also still celebrated with enthusiasm; the latter tends to be brought forward to coincide with the August 15 festival of the Panayía. Most people are here for the local beaches (see p.128) and the relaxed nightlife; there's really only one sight, a **museum** (daily 9am–1.30pm & 7–9pm; free) in the monastery of Áyios Athanásios, with an interesting collection of Byzantine and post-Byzantine icons from the churches and monasteries around Náoussa.

Despite encroaching development, the town is noted for its nearby beaches and is a good place to head for as soon as you reach Páros. **Rooms** are marginally cheaper here than in Parikía; track them down with the help of the **tourist office** which is just over the bridge, west from the harbour. The *Sea House* (☎0284/52 198; ④) on the rocks above Pipéri beach was the first place in Náoussa to let rooms and has one of the best locations, and the *Manis Inn* (☎0284/51 744; ⑤) is an upmarket hotel with pool behind Pipéri beach; out of season you should haggle for reduced prices at the *Madaki* (☎0284/51 475; ④) and the *Stella* (☎0284/52 198; ④). There are two **campsites** in the vicinity: the relaxed and friendly *Naoussa* campsite (☎0284/51565), out of town towards Kolimbíthres (see below), and the newer *Surfing Beach* (☎0284/51 013) at Sánta Maria, northeast of Náoussa; both run courtesy mini-buses to and from Parikía.

Most of the harbour **tavernas** are surprisingly good, specializing in fresh fish and seafood; *O Barbarossas* ouzerí is the best of these. There are more places to eat along the main road leading inland from just beside the little bridge over the canal. *Zorbas*, with good barrelled unresinated wine, and the *Glaros* next door are both open 24 hours. **Bars** cluster around the old harbour: *Linardo* is the big dance spot, *Agosta* plays rock, *Camaron* and the *Pirate* bar play only Greek music, and *Pico Pico* also plays Greek music, with an emphasis on *nisiotiká*.

Local beaches

Pipéri **beach** is couple of minutes' walk west of Náoussa's harbour; there are other good-to-excellent beaches within walking distance, and a summer kaïki service to connect them. To the west, an hour's tramp brings you to **Kolymbíthres** (Basins), where there are three tavernas and the wind- and sea-sculpted rock formations from which the place draws its name. A few minutes beyond, **Monastíri** beach, below the abandoned Pródhromos monastery, is similarly attractive, and partly nudist. If you go up the hill after Monastíri onto the rocky promontory, the island gradually shelves into the sea via a series of flattish rock ledges, making a fine secluded spot for diving and snorkelling, as long as the sea is calm. Go northeast and the sands are better still, the barren headland spangled with good surfing beaches – **Langéri** is backed by dunes; the best surfing is at **Sánta María**, a trendy beach connected with Náoussa by road which also has a pleasant taverna named *Aristofanes*; and **Platiá Ámmos** perches on the northeastern tip of the island.

The northeast coast and inland

AMBELÁS hamlet marks the start of a longer trek down the **east coast**. Ambelás itself has a good beach, a small taverna, and some rooms and hotels, of which the *Hotel Christiana* (☎0284/51 573; ④) is excellent value, with great fresh fish, local wine in the restaurant and extremely friendly proprietors. From here a rough track leads south, passing several undeveloped stretches on the way: after about an hour you reach **Mólos** beach, impressive and not particularly crowded. **MÁRMARA**, twenty minutes further on, has rooms to let and makes an attractive place to stay, though the marble that the village is built from and named after has largely been whitewashed over.

If Mármara doesn't appeal, then serene **MÁRPISSA**, just to the south, might – a maze of winding alleys and ageing archways overhung by floral balconies, all clinging precariously to the hillside. There are rooms here too, and you can while away a spare hour climbing up the conical Kéfalos hill, on whose fortified summit the last Venetian lords of Páros were overpowered by the Ottomans in 1537. Today the monastery of **Áyios Andónios** occupies the site, but the grounds are locked; to enjoy the views over eastern Páros and the straits of Náxos fully, pick up the key from the priest in Máripissa before setting out. On the shore nearby, **PÍSO LIVÁDHI** was once a quiet fishing village, but has been ruined by rampant construction in the name of package tourism. The main reason to visit is to catch a (seasonal) kaïki to Ayía Ánna on Náxos; if you need to **stay** overnight here, *Hotel Andromache* (☎0284/41 387 or 42 565; ④) is a good place behind the beach. The *Captain Kafkis Camping* (☎0284/41 392) – a small quiet site – is out of town on the road up to Márpissa.

Inland

The road runs west from Píso Livádhi back to the capital. A medieval flagstoned path once linked both sides of the island, and parts of it survive in the east between Mármara and the villages around Léfkes. **PRÓDHROMOS**, encountered first, is an old fortified farming settlement with defensive walls girding its nearby monastery, while **LÉFKES** itself, an hour up the track, is perhaps the most beautiful and unspoiled settlement on Páros. The town flourished from the seventeenth century on, its population swollen by refugees fleeing from coastal piracy; indeed it was the island's Khóra during most of the Ottoman period. Léfkes' marbled alleyways and amphitheatrical setting are unparalleled and, despite the few rooms, a disco and a taverna on the outskirts, and the presence of two oversized hotels – the *Hotel Pantheon* (✆0284/41 646; ④), a large 1970s hotel at the top of the village and *Lefkes Village* (✆0284/41 827 or 42 398; ⑤), a very upmarket place just outside – the area around the main square has steadfastly resisted change; the central kafenío and bakery observe their siestas religiously.

Thirty minutes further on, through olive groves, is **KÓSTOS**, a simple village and a good place for lunch in a taverna. Any traces of path disappear at **MARÁTHI**, on the site of the ancient marble quarries which once supplied much of Europe. Considered second only to Carrara marble, the last slabs were mined here by the French in the nineteenth century for Napoleon's tomb. From Maráthi, it's easy enough to pick up the bus on to Parikía, but if you want to continue hiking, strike south for the monastery of **Áyios Minás**, twenty minutes away. Various Classical and Byzantine masonry fragments are worked into the walls of this sixteenth-century foundation, and the friendly couple who act as custodians can put you on the right path up to the convent of **Thapsaná**. From here, other paths lead either back to Parikía (two hours altogether from Áyios Minás), or on up to the island's summit for the last word in views over the Cyclades.

The south of the island

There's little to stop for south of Parikía until **POÚNDA**, 6km away, and then only to catch the ferry to Andíparos (see overleaf). What used to be a sleepy hamlet is now a concrete jungle, and neighbouring **ALIKÍ** appears to be permanently under construction. The **airport** is close by, making for lots of unwelcome noise; the sole redeeming feature is an excellent beachside restaurant, by the large tamarisk tree. The end of the southern bus route is at Angeriá, about 3km inland of which is the **convent of Áyii Theodhóri**. Its nuns specialize in weaving locally commissioned articles and are further distinguished as *paleomeroloyites*, or old-calendarites, meaning that they follow the medieval Orthodox (Julian) calendar, rather than the Gregorian one.

Working your way around the **south coast**, there are two routes east to Dhríos. Either retrace your steps to Angeriá and follow the (slightly inland) coastal jeep track, which skirts a succession of isolated coves and small beaches; or keep on across the foothills from Áyii Theodhóri – a shorter walk. Aside from an abundant water supply (including a duck pond) and surrounding orchards, **DHRÝOS** village is mostly modern and characterless, lacking even a well-defined platía. Follow the lane signed "Dhríos Beach", however, and things improve a bit.

Between here and Píso Livádhi to the north are several sandy coves – Khryssí Aktí (Golden Beach), Tzirdhákia, Mezádha, Poúnda and Logarás – prone to pummelling by the *meltémi*, yet all favoured to varying degrees by campers, and windsurfers making a virtue out of necessity. **KHRYSSÍ AKTÍ** is now thoroughly overrun with tavernas, room complexes and the whole range of watersports; there are also tavernas at Logarás, but other facilities are concentrated in Dhríos, which is still the focal point of this part of the island.

Andíparos

Andíparos was once quiet and unspoiled, but now the secret is definitely out. The waterfront is lined with new hotels and apartments, and in high season it can be full of the same young, international crowd you were hoping to leave behind on Páros. It has, however, has kept its friendly small island atmosphere and still has a lot going for it, including good sandy beaches and an impressive cave, and the rooms and hotels are less expensive than on Páros.

Most of the population of 800 live in the large low-lying northern **village**, across the narrow straits from Páros, the new development on the outskirts concealing an attractive traditional settlement around the kástro. A long, flagstoned pedestrian street forms its backbone, leading from the jetty to the Cycladic houses around the outer wall of the kástro, which was built by Leonardo Loredano in the 1440s as a fortified settlement safe from pirate raids: the Loredano coat of arms can still be seen on a house in the courtyard. The only way into the courtyard is through a pointed archway from the platía, where several cafés are shaded by a giant eucalyptus. Inside, more whitewashed houses surround two churches and a cistern built into the surviving base of the central tower.

Andíparos' **beaches** begin right outside town: Psaralíki just to the south with golden sand and tamarisks for shade is much better than Sifnéïko (aka "Sunset") on the opposite side of the island. Villa development is starting to follow the newly paved road down the east coast, but has yet to get out of hand. Glýfa, 4km down, is another good beach and, further south, Sóros has rooms and tavernas. On the west coast there are some fine small sandy coves at Áyios Yeóryios, the end of the road, and a long stretch of sand at Livádhia. Kaïki make daily trips round the island and, less frequently, to the uninhabited islet of Dhespotikó, opposite Áyios Yeóryios.

The great **cave** (summer daily 10.45am–3.45pm; 500dr) in the south of the island is the chief attraction for day-trippers. In these eerie chambers the Marquis de Nointel, Louis XIV's ambassador to Constantinople, celebrated Christmas Mass in 1673 while a retinue of 500, including painters, pirates, Jesuits and Turks, looked on; at the exact moment of midnight explosives were detonated to emphasize the enormity of the event. Although electric light and cement steps have diminished its mystery and grandeur, the cave remains impressive. Tour buses run from the port every half hour in season (1200dr return), giving you an hour to explore; out of season, bus services and opening hours are reduced and in winter you'll have to fetch the key for the cave from the village.

Practicalities

To get here, you have a choice of **boats** from Parikía (hourly; 40min), arriving at the jetty opposite the main street, or the car ferry from Poúnda (half-hourly; 10min), arriving 150m to the south. In season there's no need to use the car ferry unless you take a moped over or miss the last boat back to Parikía; the car ferry keeps running until midnight. The service to Parikía is reduced out of season and runs only once a day in winter.

There are plenty of **hotels** along the waterfront, including *Anargyros* (☎0284/61 204; ④), which has good rooms and air-conditioned apartments. More upmarket places to the north of the jetty include *Mantalena* (☎0284/61 206; ⑥) and *Artemis* (☎0284/61 460; ⑤), while inland there are some cheaper rooms as well as the *Hotel Galini* (☎0284/61 420; ⑤) to the left of the main street and next to a disco. The popular **campsite** (☎0284/61 221) is a ten-minute walk northeast along a track, next to its own nudist beach; the water here is shallow enough for campers to wade across to the neighbouring islet of Dhipló. For peace and quiet with a degree of comfort try *Studios Delfini* (☎093/275 911; ⑤) with its own taverna at Áyios Yeóryios.

The best of the waterfront **tavernas** is *Anargyros*, below the hotel of the same name. *Klimataria*, 100m inland to the left off the main street, has tables in a pleasant, shady garden, and *To Kastro* is one of the better restaurants outside the kástro. There are plenty of **bars** in the same area but the locals usually stick to the excellent *To Kendro* zakharoplastía in the eucalyptus-filled platía. For quiet music and views of the mountains try *Cafe Yam*, an outdoor café-bar near the Klimataria. A short-schedule **bank**, an **OTE** booth with morning and evening opening hours, a **post office**, a cinema and several **travel agents** round up the list of amenities.

Náxos

Náxos is the largest and most fertile of the Cyclades, and with its green and mountainous highland scenery seems immediately distinct from many of its neighbours. The difference is accentuated by the **unique architecture** of many of the interior villages: the Venetian Duchy of the Aegean, which ruled from the thirteenth to the sixteenth century, left towers and fortified mansions scattered throughout the island, while medieval Cretan refugees bestowed a singular character upon Náxos' eastern settlements.

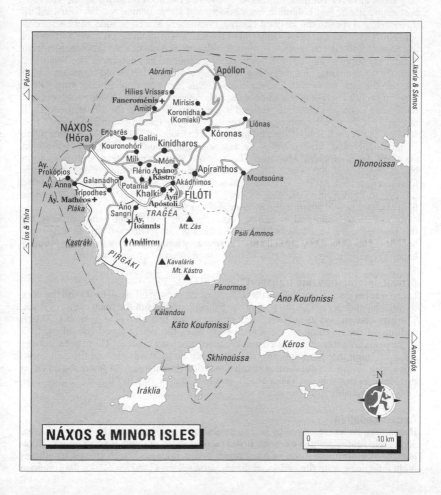

NÁXOS & MINOR ISLES

0   10 km

Today Náxos could easily support itself without tourism by relying on its production of potatoes, olives, grapes and lemons, but has thrown its lot in with mass tourism, so that parts of the island are now almost as busy and commercialized as Páros in season. But the island certainly has plenty to see if you know where to look: the highest mountains in the Cyclades, intriguing central valleys, a spectacular north coast, and marvellously sandy beaches in the southwest.

Náxos Town

A long causeway, built to protect the harbour to the north, connects **NÁXOS TOWN** (or Khóra) with the islet of Palátia – the place where, according to legend, Theseus abandoned Ariadne on his way home from Crete. The huge stone portal of a **Temple of Apollo** still stands there, built on the orders of the tyrant Lygdamis in the sixth century BC, but never completed. Most of the town's life goes on down by the crowded port esplanade or just behind it; back streets and alleys behind the harbour lead up through low arches to the fortified **Kástro**, from where Marco Sanudo and his successors ruled over the Cyclades. Only two of the kástro's original seven towers – those of the Sanudo and Glezos families – remain, although the north gate (approached from Apóllonos) survives as a splendid example of a medieval fort entrance. The Venetians' Catholic descendants, now dwindling in numbers, still live in the old mansions which encircle the site, many with ancient coats-of-arms above crumbling doorways. Other brooding relics survive in the same area: a seventeenth-century Ursuline convent and the Roman Catholic Cathedral, restored in questionable taste in the 1950s, though still displaying a thirteenth-century crest inside. Nearby is one of Ottoman Greece's first schools, the French School; opened in 1627 for Catholic and Orthodox students alike, its pupils included, briefly, Nikos Kazantzakis. The school building now houses an excellent **Archeological Museum** (Tues–Sun 8.30am–3pm; 500dr) with finds from Náxos, Koufoníssi, Keros and Dhonoússa, including an important collection of Early Cycladic figurines. Archaic and Classical sculpture, and pottery dating from Neolithic through to Roman times are also on display. On the roof terrace a Hellenistic mosaic floor shows a nereid surrounded by deer and peacocks.

As well as archeological treasures, Náxos has some very good sandal-makers: try the Markos store on Papavassilíou. The island is also renowned for its wines and liqueurs; a shop on the quay sells the *Prombonas* white and vintage red, plus *kitron*, a lemon firewater in three strengths (there's also a banana-flavoured variant).

Arrival, information and transport

Large **ferries** dock along the northerly harbour causeway; all small boats and the very useful Skopelitis ferry use the jetty in the fishing harbour, not the main car-ferry dock. The **bus station** is at its landward end: buses run five times a day to Apóllon (1000dr), and one of the morning services to Apóllon takes the newly paved coastal road via Engares and Ábrami, and is much quicker though not any cheaper. There are six buses a day to Apiranthos via Filoti, two of these going on to Moutsoúna on the east coast. Buses run (every 30min; 8am–midnight) to Áyios Prokopios, Ayía Ánna and as far as the Maragas campsite on Pláka beach, and four times a day to Pirgáki. Printed timetables are available from the bus station.

Accommodation

Rooms can be hard to come by and somewhat overpriced in the old quarter of Khóra, and single rooms are non-existent. If you come up with nothing after an hour of hunting, the southern extension of town offers better value, although there's significant night-time noise from the clubs and discos. *Litsa's Rooms* (☎0285/24 272; ⑤) comprise good new rooms and studios just to the south of the kástro, or try *Iliada Studios* (☎0285/23 303 or 24 277; ⑤) on the cliffs beyond Grotta Beach, with good views over the town and out to sea. *Panos Studios* (☎0285/26 078 or 22 087; ⑤) are reasonable, and are located near Áyios Yióryios beach.

Hotel choices include the *Panorama* on Afitrítis (☎0285/24 404; ④), the nearby *Anixis* (☎0285/22 112; ④), or, as a last resort, the *Dionyssos* (☎0285/22 331; ②) near the kástro, which also has dorm beds for 1500dr. Around the back of the kástro, is the friendly *Kastell* (☎0285/23 082; ④), and other options include: *Hotel Pantheon* (☎0285/24 335; ④), with a few rooms in a traditionally furnished house on Apollonos, going up to the kástro, *Hotel Anna* (☎0285/22 475; ④), a good family run hotel in the Grotta area north of the kástro which stays open through the winter; and *Hotel Galaxy* (☎0285/22 422; ⑥), an upmarket beach hotel with a pool, behind Áyios Yióryios beach.

Eating, drinking and nightlife

One of the best quayside breakfast bars is the *Bikini* creperie. Further along to the south are a string of relatively expensive but simple oven-food **tavernas** – *Iy Kali Kardhia* is typical, serving acceptable casserole dishes washed down with barrelled wine. Much better for the money are *Papagalos* in the new southern district, almost all the way to Áyios Yeóryios bay, and the good but pricey fish taverna *Karnayio* on the front. A hidden gem is *To Roupel*, a good old kafenío in the backstreets between the front and the kástro. *Cafe En Plo* and *Musique Café* are two reasonable places in the middle of the quay, both popular with locals; *Cafe Picasso*, near Papagalos, serves Mexican food, and is only open in the evenings. The *Elli Cafe Bar Restaurant* behind Grotta Beach is a little more expensive but serves really imaginative food, and *Portokali Club* on the headland to the south of town is a club, café and restaurant with good views over Áyios Yeóryios bay.

Much of the evening action goes on at the south end of the waterfront, and slightly inland in the new quarter. **Nightlife** tends more towards drinking places, though there is the lively *Ocean Club*, subsisting on pop-chart fodder, *Ole Club* towards the middle of the quay for dance music, and *Lakrindi Jazz Bar*, a tiny place on Apóllonos. There's also an open-air cinema, the Ciné Astra, on the road to the airport at the southern end of town. It's a fair walk out but the Ayía Anna bus stops here.

The southwestern beaches

The **beaches** around Náxos Town are worth sampling. For some unusual swimming just to the **north** of the port, beyond the causeway, **Grotta** is easiest to reach. Besides the caves for which the place is named, the remains of submerged Cycladic buildings are visible, including some stones said to be the entrance to a tunnel leading to the unfinished Temple of Apollo. The finest spots, though, are all **south** of town, the entire southwestern coastline boasting a series of excellent **beaches** accessible by regular bus. **ÁYIOS YEÓRYIOS**, a long sandy bay fringed by the southern extension of the hotel "colony", is within walking distance. There's a line of cafés and tavernas at the northern end of the beach, and a windsurfing school, plus the first of four **campsites**, whose touts you will no doubt have become acquainted with at the ferry jetty. This first campsite (*Camping Naxos* ☎0285/23 500) isn't recommended; *Maragas* and *Plaka* have far more attractive locations on Pláka beach (see p.134). A word of warning for campers: although this entire coast is relatively sheltered from the *meltémi*, the plains behind are boggy and you should bring along mosquito repellent.

Buses take you to **ÁYIOS PROKÓPIOS** beach, with reasonably priced hotels, rooms and basic tavernas, plus the relaxed *Apollon* campsite nearby. Or follow the busy road a little further to **AYÍA ÁNNA** (habitually referred to as "Ayi'Ánna"), a small resort where there are plenty of **rooms** and tavernas. *Bar Bagianni* on the road from

Áyia Ánna to Áyios Prokópios is a colourful and popular bar which serves vegetarian food, the sea-view *Hotel Ayia Anna* (☎0285/23 870; ④)) and adjacent *Gorgona* taverna are highly recommended. Away from the built-up area, the beach here is nudist, and the busy *Maragas* campsite (☎0285/24 552) thrives; it also has double rooms (②).

Beyond the headland stretch the five kilometres of **PLÁKA** beach, a vegetation-fringed expanse of white sand becoming built up with tavernas and rooms. Pláka **campsite** (☎0285/42 700), 700 metres down the beach is a good new site: small and quiet and away from the busier built up end of the beach. The *Hotel Orkos Village* (☎0285/75 321; ⑤) comprises apartments in an attractive location, on a hillside above the coast between Pláka beach and Mikrí Vígla.

For real isolation, go to the other side of Mikrí Vígla headland, along a narrow foot-path across the cliff edge, to **KASTRÁKI** beach; towards the middle of the beach *Areti* (☎0285/75 292; ④) has apartments and a restaurant. A few people camp around the taverna on the small headland a little further down. In summer this stretch, all the way from Mikrí Vígla down to Pirgáki, attracts camper vans and windsurfers from all over Europe. On the Aliko promontory to the south of Kastráki there is a small nudist beach.

From Kastráki, it's couple of hours' walk up to the castle of **Apalírou** which held out for two months against the besieging Marco Sanudo. The fortifications are relatively intact and the views magnificent. **PYRGÁKI** beach has a couple of tavernas and a few rooms; four kilometres further on is **Ayiássos** beach.

The rest of the **southern coast** – indeed, virtually the whole of the southeast of the island – is remote and mountain-studded; you'd have to be a dedicated and well-equipped camper/hiker to get much out of the region.

Central Náxos and the Tragéa

Although buses for Apóllon (in the north) link up the central Naxian villages, the core of the island – between Náxos town and Apíranthos – is best explored by moped or on foot. Much of the region is well off the beaten track, and can be a rewarding excursion if you've had your fill of beaches; Christian Ucke's *Walking Tours on Naxos*, available from bookshops in Náxos town, is a useful guide for hikers.

Out of Khóra, you quickly arrive at the neighbouring villages of **GLINÁDHO** and **GALANÁDHO**, forking respectively right and left. Both are scruffy market centres: Glinádho is built on a rocky outcrop above the Livádhi plain, while Galánadho displays the first of Náxos' fortified mansions and an unusual "double church". A combined Orthodox chapel and Catholic sanctuary separated by a double arch, the church reflects the tolerance both of the Venetians during their rule and of the locals to estab-lished Catholics afterwards. Continue beyond Glinádho to **TRÍPODHES** (ancient Biblos), 9km from Náxos Town. Noted by Homer for its wines, this old-fashioned agri-cultural village has nothing much to do except enjoy a coffee at the shaded kafenío. The start of a long but rewarding walk is a rough road (past the parish church) which leads down the colourful Pláka valley, past an old watchtower and the Byzantine church of Áyios Mathéos (mosaic pavement), and ends at the glorious Pláka beach (see above).

To the east, the twin villages of **SANGRÍ**, on a vast plateau at the head of a long val-ley can be reached by continuing to follow the left-hand fork past Galanádho, a route which allows a look at the domed eighth-century church of **Áyios Mámas** (on the left), once the Byzantine cathedral of the island but neglected during the Venetian period and now a sorry sight. Either way, **Káto Sangrí** boasts the remains of a Venetian castle, while **Áno Sangrí** is a comely little place, all cobbled streets and fragrant courtyards. Thirty minutes' stroll away, on a path leading south out of the village, are the partially reconstructed remains of a Classical temple of Demeter.

The Tragéa

From Sangrí the road twists northeast into the **Tragéa** region, scattered with olive trees and occupying a vast highland valley. It's a good jumping-off point for all sorts of exploratory rambling, and **KHALKÍ** is a fine introduction to what is to come. Set high up, 16km from the port, it's a noble and silent town with some lovely churches. The **Panayía Protóthronis** church, with its eleventh- to thirteenth-century frescoes, and the romantic **Grazia (Frangopoulos) Pýrgos**, are open to visitors, but only in the morning. Tourists wanting to stay here are still something of a rarity, although you can usually get a room in someone's house by asking at the store. The olive and citrus plantations surrounding Halkí are criss-crossed by paths and tracks, the groves dotted with numerous Byzantine chapels and the ruins of fortified *pirgi* or Venetian mansions. Between Khalkí and Akadhimí, but closer to the latter, sits the peculiar twelfth-century "piggyback" church of **Áyii Apóstoli**, with a tiny chapel (where the ennobled donors worshipped in private) perched above the narthex; there are brilliant thirteenth-century frescoes as well.

The road from Khalkí heads north to **MONÍ**. Just before the village, you pass the sixth-century monastery of **Panayía Dhrossianí**, a group of stark grey stone buildings with some excellent frescoes; the monks allow visits at any time, though you may have to contend with coach tours from Náxos Town. Moní itself enjoys an outstanding view of the Tragéa and surrounding mountains, and has three tavernas, and some rooms. A dirt road leads on to Kinídharos with the old marble quarry above the village; a few kilometres beyond a signpost points you down a rough track to the left, to **FLÉRIO** (commonly called Melanés). The most interesting of the ancient marble quarries on Náxos, this is home to two famous **koúri**, dating from the sixth century BC, that were left recumbent and unfinished because of flaws in the material. Even so, they're finely detailed figures, over five metres in length: one of the statues lies in a private, irrigated orchard; the other is up a hillside some distance above, and you will need to seek local guidance to find it.

From Flério you could retrace your steps to the road and head back to the Khóra via Míli and the ruined Venetian castle at Kouronohóri, both pretty hamlets connected by footpaths. If you're feeling more adventurous, ask to be directed south to the footpath which leads over the hill to the Potamiá villages. The first of these, **ÁNO POTAMIÁ**, has a fine taverna and a rocky track back towards the Tragéa. Once past the valley the landscape becomes craggy and barren, the forbidding Venetian fortress of **Apáno Kástro** perched on a peak just south of the path. This is believed to have been Sanudo's summer home, but the fortified site goes back further if the Mycenean tombs found nearby are any indication. From the fort, paths lead back to Khalkí in around an hour. Alternatively you can continue further southwest down the Potamiá valley towards Khóra, passing first the ruined **Cocco Pýrgos** – said to be haunted by one Constantine Cocco, the victim of a seventeenth-century clan feud – on the way to **MÉSO POTAMIÁ**, joined by some isolated dwellings with its twin village **KÁTO POTAMIÁ**, nestling almost invisibly among the greenery flanking the creek.

At the far end of the gorgeous Tragéa valley, **FILÓTI**, the largest village in the region, lies on the slopes of Mount Zas (or Zeus) which, at 1000m, is the highest point in the Cyclades. To get an idea of the old village, climb the steps up the hill from the platía, near to which the *Babulas Grill-Restaurant* (☎0285/31 426; ②) has rooms. A turning at the southern end of the village is signposted to the Pýrgos Himárou, a remote 20m Hellenistic watchtower, and Kalándou beach on the south coast; beyond the turning the road is unpaved. There are no villages in this part of the island so bring supplies if you're planning to camp. From the village, it's a round-trip walk of two to three hours to the summit of Zas, a climb which rewards you with an astounding panorama of virtually the whole of Náxos and its Cycladic neighbours. From the main Filóti–Apóllon road, take the side road towards Dhánakos until you reach a small chapel on the right, just beside the start of the waymarked final approach trail.

APÍRANTHOS, a hilly, winding 10km beyond, shows the most Cretan influence of all the interior villages. There are four small **museums** and two Venetian fortified mansions, while the square contains a miniature church with a three-tiered belltower. Ask to be pointed to the start of the spectacular path up over the ridge behind; this ends either in Moní or Kalóxilos, depending on whether you fork right or left respectively at the top. Cafés and tavernas on the main street look out over a terraced valley below. Rooms are available but are not advertised – ask in the cafés or in the embroidery shop. Apíranthos is good quiet place to stay for a few days, and being high in the mountains is noticeably cooler and greener than the coast.

Apíranthos has a beach annexe of sorts at **Moutsoúna**, 12km east. Emery mined near Apíranthos used to be transported here, by means of an aerial funicular, and then shipped out of the port. The industry collapsed and the sandy cove beyond the dock now features a growing colony of holiday villas. An unpaved road heads south along the coast to a remote sandy beach at Psilí Ámmos – ideal for self-sufficient campers, but you must take enough water. From here a track carries on to Panórmos beach in the southeastern corner of the island.

Northern Náxos

The route through the mountains from Apíranthos to Apóllon is very scenic, and the roads are in good condition all the way. Jagged ranges and hairpin bends confront you before reaching Kóronos, the halfway point, where a road off to the right threads through a wooded valley to **Liónas**, a tiny and very Greek port with a pebble beach. You'd do better to continue, though, past Skadhó to the remote, emery-miners' village of **KOMIAKÍ** which is a pleasing, vine-covered settlement – the highest village in the island and the original home of *kitron* liqueur.

Back on the main road, a series of slightly less hairy bends lead down a long valley to **APÓLLON** (Apóllonas), a small resort with two beaches: a tiny and crowded stretch of sand backed by cafés and restaurants, and a longer and quieter stretch of shingle, popular mainly with Greek families. If you are staying, try the friendly *Hotel Eolos* (☎0285/67 088; ③) overlooking the larger beach, or the *Hotel Adonis* (☎0285/67 060; ④) opposite. The only major attraction is a **koùros**, approached by a path from the main road just above the village. Lying in situ at a former marble quarry, this largest of Náxos's abandoned stone figures is just over ten metres long, but, compared with those at Flério, disappointingly lacking in detail. Here since 600 BC, it serves as a singular reminder of the Naxians' traditional skill; the famous Delian lions (see p.119) are also made of Apollonian marble. Not surprisingly, bus tours descend upon the village during the day, and Apóllon is now quite a popular little resort. The local festival, celebrated on August 29, is one of Náxos's best.

From Náxos town there is now a daily bus service direct to Apóllon (taking about an hour). It's easy to make a round trip by bus of the north coast and inland villages in either direction. The coastal road is spectacularly beautiful, going high above the sea for most of the way – it's more like parts of Crete or the mainland than other islands. Ten kilometres past the northern cape sprouts the beautiful **Ayía** *pirgos*, or tower, another foundation (in 1717) of the Cocco family. There's a tiny hamlet nearby, and, 7km further along, a track leads off to **Ábrami** beach, an idyllic spot with a family-run taverna and **rooms** to let, *Pension and Restaurant Efthimios* (☎0285/63 244; ③). Just beyond the hamlet of Khília Vrýssi is the abandoned **monastery of Faneroménis**, built in 1606. Nearby, there's another deserted beach, **Amíti**, and then the track leads inland, up the Engarés valley, to Engarés and Galíni, only 6km from Khóra. On the final stretch back to the port you pass a unique eighteenth-century Turkish fountain-house and the fortified monastery of **Ayíou Ioánnou Khryssostómou**, where a couple of aged nuns are still in residence. A footpath from the monastery and the road below lead straight back to town.

Koufoníssi, Skhinoússa, Iráklia and Dhonoússa

In the patch of the Aegean between Náxos and Amorgós there is a chain of six small islands neglected by tourists and by the majority of Greeks, few of whom have heard of them. **Kéros** – ancient Karos – is an important archeological site but has no permanent population, and **Káto Koufoníssi** is inhabited only by goatherds. However, the other four islands – **Áno Koufoníssi, Skhinoússa, Iráklia** and **Dhonoússa** – are all inhabited, served by ferry, and can be visited. Now just beginning to be discovered by Greeks and foreigners alike, the islets' increasing popularity has hastened the development of better facilities, but they're still a welcome break from the mass tourism of the rest of the Cyclades, especially during high season. If you want real peace and quiet – what the Greeks call *isykhia* – get there soon.

A few times weekly in summer a Pireás-based **ferry** – usually the *Apollon Express* or the tardy *Ergina* – calls at each of the islands, linking them with Náxos and Amorgós and (usually) Páros, Sýros, Sérifos and Sífnos. A kaïki, the *Skopelitis*, is a reliable daily fixture, leaving Náxos in mid-afternoon for relatively civilized arrival times at all the islets. Ilio Lines' hydrofoil calls on demand at all the islands (except Dhonoússa) on its twice-weekly foray to Amorgós; you must let the steward, if you're on the hydrofoil, or agent, if you're on the island, know if you want to be picked up or put down.

Koufoníssi and Kéros

Ano Koufoníssi is the most populous island of the group; there is a reasonable living to be made from fishing and, with some of the best beaches in the Cyclades, it is attracting increasing numbers of Greek and foreign holidaymakers. Small enough to walk round in a morning, the island can feel overcrowded in July and August.

The old single-street village of **KHÓRA**, on a low hill behind the harbour, is being engulfed by new room and hotel development, but still has a friendly, small-island atmosphere. A map by the jetty shows where to find all the island's **rooms**: *To Limani* (☎0285/71 851 or 71 450; ④) is a café with new rooms near the harbour; the popular restaurant and pension *Iy Melissa* (☎0285/71 454; ④) is on the main street; the new and upmarket *Hotel Aigaion* (☎0285/74 050 or 74 051; ⑤) is by the village beach; *To Akroyiali* (☎0285/71 685; ④) is on the front just beyond the beach; Yiorgia Kouveou has rooms at *Hondros Kavos* (☎0285/71 707; ④), to the east of the village; and the *Petros Club* (☎0285/71 728; ⑤) is in a quiet position inland, with excellent views.

Koufoníssi is noted for its fish **tavernas**; the *Karnayio* ouzerí on the bay to the west of the harbour is cheaper than most and has a fine array of seafood. The nearby *To Steki Tis Marias* is a good breakfast place and café with views over the narrow channel to Káto Koufoníssi. The most popular nightspot is *Soroccos*, an expensive café/bar on the front, while good alternatives include *Ta Kalamia*, with a quieter choice of music, and *Scholeio*, a creperie and bar. The OTE office and ticket agency are on the main street, and money can be changed at the post office (limited hours).

All the good beaches are in the southeast of the island, starting at **Fínikas**, a ten-minute walk from the village, where there are rooms, a self-service restaurant and a **campsite** (☎0285/71 683) with rather poor facilities. Fínikas is the first of a series of small bays and coves of gently shelving golden sand, some with low cliffs hollowed out into sea-caves. Further east, a path round a rocky headland leads to **Porí**, a much longer and wilder beach, backed by dunes and set in a deep bay. It can be reached more easily from the village by following a track heading inland through the low scrub-covered hills.

KÁTO KOUFONÍSSI, the uninhabited island to the southwest, has a seasonal taverna and some more secluded beaches; a kaïkia shuttles people across until late in the

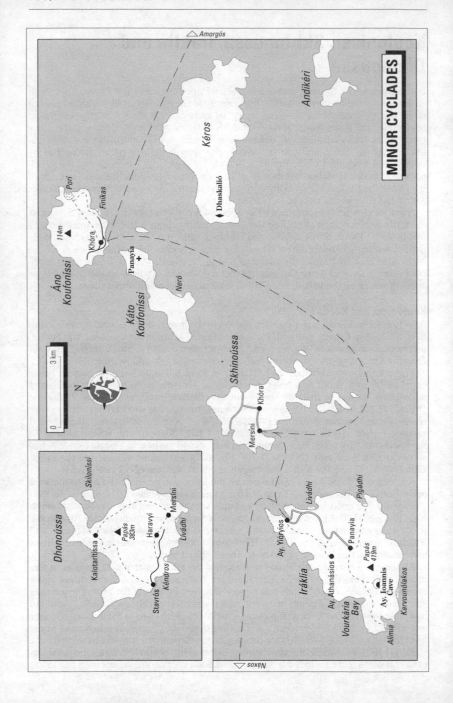

MINOR CYCLADES

Amorgós

Andikéri

Kéros

Dhaskalió

Pori

Finikas

Áno Koufoníssi

114m

Khóra

Panayia

Neró

Káto Koufoníssi

N

3 km

0

Skhinoússa

Khóra

Mersini

Dhonoússa

Skilóníssi

Kalotarítissa

Papás 383m

Haravyí

Mersíni

Livádhi

Stavrós

Kéndros

Iráklia

Ay. Yióryios

Livádhi

Pigádhi

Ay. Athanásios

Panayia

Papás 419m

Vourkária Bay

Ay. Ioánnis Cave

Alimiá

Karvounólakos

Náxos

evening. A festival is held here on August 15, at the church of the Panayía. The island of **Kéros** is harder to reach, but if there is a willing group of people keen to visit the ancient site, a boat and boatmen can be hired for around 15,000dr for the day.

Skhinoússa

A little to the west, the island of **Skhinoússa** is just beginning to awaken to its tourist potential, largely due to the energetic efforts being made in that direction by one Yiorgos Grispos.

Boats dock at the small port of Mirsíni, which has one pension (☎0285/71 157; ④) and a couple of cafés; a road leads up to **KHÓRA**, the walk taking just over ten minutes. As you enter the village, the well-stocked shop of the Grispos family is one of the first buildings on the left and the aforementioned Yiorgos is a mine of information. Indeed, he is personally responsible for the island's map and postcards, as well as being the boat/hydrofoil agent, having the OTE phone and selling the Greek and foreign press.

Accommodation is mostly in fairly simple rooms, such as *Pension Meltemi* (☎0285/71 195; ⑤), *Anesis* (☎0285/71180; ③), *Drossos* and *Nomikos* (no phone; both ④). The main concentration of **restaurants**, cafés and bars is along the main thoroughfare, including a lively ouzerí and, further along on the left, the pleasant *Schoinoussa* restaurant – another Grispos family venture.

There are no less than sixteen beaches dotted around the island and accessible by a lacework of trails. Freelance campers congregate on **Tsigoúri beach**, a little over five minutes from Khóra; the only other beach with any refreshments is **Almiros**, which has a simple canteen.

Iráklia

The westernmost of the minor Cyclades, **Iráklia** (pronounced Irakliá by locals) is a real gem, with an atmosphere reminiscent of the Greece of fifteen years ago, despite increasing visitor numbers.

Ferries and hydrofoils call at **ÁYIOS YEÓRYIOS**, a small but sprawling settlement behind a sandy tamarisk-backed beach. Irini Koveou (☎0285/71 448; ③) has a café-restaurant and rooms opposite the harbour, and more rooms and places to eat can be found along the old road to Livádhi beach. *Anna's Place* (☎0285/71 145; ④) provides the most upmarket accommodation, as well as a tourist shop with maps showing the route to a fine **cave** on the far side of the island. Theofanis Gavalas (☎0285/71 565; ②), Dhimítrios Stefanídhis (☎0285/71 484; ③), Alexandra Tournaki (☎0285/71 482; ③) and Angelos Koveos (☎0285/71 486; ④) all have rooms nearby. *O Pefkos* is a pleasant **taverna**, with tables shaded by a large pine tree, while the café/shop *Melissa* acts as the main ticket agency for ferries.

Livádhi, the best beach on the island, is a 15-minute walk past a taverna, whose friendly and animated proprietor usually meets ferries at the dock. The beach really is lovely, both deep and wide, with plenty of large bushes, a few trees for shade, and a crystalclear sea. The village of Livádhi, deserted since 1940, stands on the hillside above, its houses ruined and overgrown; among the remains are Hellenistic walls incorporated into a later building, and fortifications from the time of Marco Sanudo. Marietta Markoyianni (☎0285/71 252; ②) has the only rooms on the beach; *Zografos Rooms* (☎0285/71 946; ④), above the road to Panayía, has fine views but is rather remote.

PANAYÍA or **KHÓRA**, an unspoiled one-street village at the foot of Mount Papas, is another hour's walk inland along the newly paved road. It has a bakery, two café/shops and the excellent and cheap *O Kritikos* ouzerí, but no rooms. A track to the east heads down to Pigádhi, a rocky beach with sea urchins, at the head of a narrow inlet. To the west a track from the near deserted hamlet of **Áyios Athanásios** leads back to the port.

The **cave of Áyios Ioánnis** lies behind the mountain, at the head of a valley leading to Vourkaria bay. From Panayía, follow a signposted track west before zigzagging up to a saddle well to the north of the summit, with views over Skhinoússa, Koufoníssi, Kéros, Náxos and Amorgós; the path drops down to the south around the back of the mountain. A painted red arrow on the left indicates the turning to the cave, just over an hour from Panayía. A church bell hangs from a cypress tree above the whitewashed entrance, and inside there's a shrine, and the cave opens up into a large chamber with stalactites and stalagmites. It can be explored to a depth of 120m and is thought to be part of a much larger cave system, yet to be opened up; a festival is held here every year on August 18.

The main trail continues beyond the cave to a small sandy beach at **Alimía** but this can be reached more easily with the beach boat from Áyios Yeóryios. In season the boat sails daily to either Skhinoússa, Alimiá or the nearby pebble beach of Karvounólakos.

Dhonoússa

Dhonoússa is a little out on a limb compared with the others, and ferries and hydrofoils call less frequently. Island life centres on the pleasant port settlement of **STAVRÓS**, spread out behind the harbour and the village beach.

Rooms, most without signs, tend to be booked up by Greek holidaymakers in August; try Mikhalis Prasinos (☎0285/51 578; ③) with rooms along a lane behind the church, Dhimitris Prasinos ☎(☎0285/51 579; ③) with rooms open year-round near the *Iliovasilema* restaurant or Nikos Prasinos (☎0285/51 551; ④) who has good new studios above the rocks west of the harbour. *Ta Kymata* is the most popular of the four tavernas but *Meltemi* and *Iliovasilema* are also good. Nikitas Roussos (☎0285/51 648) has a **ticket agency** above the harbour and can change money and book rooms.

The hills around Stavrós are low and barren and scarred by bulldozed tracks, but a little walking is repaid with dramatic scenery and a couple of fine beaches. Freelance campers and nudists head for **Kéndros**, a long and attractive stretch of sand fifteen minutes to the east, although shade is limited and there are no facilities. A road is being built on the hillside above, replacing the donkey track to the farming hamlets of Kharavyí and Mersíni; these have more hens and goats in the streets than people, and there are no cafés, shops or rooms. **Mersíni** is an hour's walk from Stavrós and has a welcome spring beneath a plane tree, the island's only running water. A nearby path leads down to Livádhi, an idyllic white sand beach with tamarisks for shade. In July and August there's a daily beach boat from the port.

KALOTARÍTISSA in the north can still only be reached on foot or by boat – a track heading inland from Stavrós climbs a valley west of Papás, the island's highest point, before dropping down rapidly to the tiny village with a simple **taverna** and one room to rent (☎0285/51 562; ②). There are two small pebble beaches and a path that continues above the coast to Mersíni. It takes four to five hours to walk round the island.

Amorgós

Amorgós, with its dramatic mountain scenery and laid-back atmosphere, is attracting visitors in increasing numbers; most ferries and hydrofoils call at both Katápola in the southwest and Eyiáli in the northeast. The island can get extremely crowded in midsummer, the numbers swollen by French paying their respects to the film location of Luc Besson's *The Big Blue*, although few actually venture out to the wreck of the Olympia, at the island's west end, which figured so prominently in the movie. In general it's a low-key, escapist clientele, happy to have found a relatively large, interesting and uncommercialized island with excellent walking.

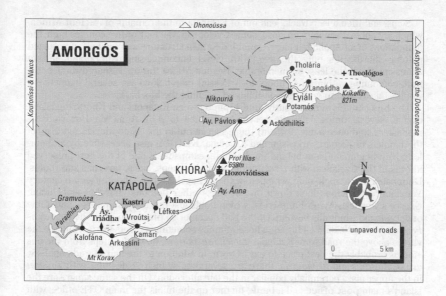

The southwest

KATÁPOLA, set at the head of a deep bay, is actually three separate hamlets: Katápola proper on the south flank, Rakhídhi on the ridge at the head of the gulf, and Xilokeratídhi along the north shore. There is a beach in front of Rahídhi, but the beach to the west of Katápola is better, though not up to the standards of Eyiáli. In season there is also a regular kaïki to nearby beaches at **Maltézi** and **Plákes** (400dr return) and a daily kaïki to the islet of **Gramboúsa** off the western end of Amorgós (2000dr return).

There are plenty of small **hotels** and **pensions** and, except in high summer when rooms are almost impossible to find, proprietors tend to meet those boats arriving around sunset – though not necessarily those that show up in the small hours. A good new place next to the beach at the western end of Katápola is *Eleni Rooms* (☎0285/71 543 or 71 628; ④). *Dhimitri's Place* in Rahídhi (③) is a compound of interconnecting buildings in an orchard, where rooms with bath and use of kitchen vary in price, depending on the season and the number of people. On the same road, *Angeliki Rooms* (☎0285/71 280; ③) is well-run, friendly and good value, as Angeliki doesn't put up her prices for August; the fancy *Hotel Minoa* (☎0285/71 480; ⑤) on the waterfront is considerably noisier. *Panayiotis Rooms* (☎0285/71 890; ④) in Xilokeratídhi is good value.

In Katápola proper, *Mourayio* is the most popular **taverna** in town; alternatively try the *Akrogiali* taverna. What **nightlife** there is focuses on a handful of cafés and pubs. A bar called *Le Grand Bleu* in Xilokeratídhi regularly shows *The Big Blue* on video but there are other less expensive and pretentious places to drink, *Ippokampos*, a café and bar on the front at Rakhídhi being a good choice.

Prekas is the one-stop **boat ticket agency**, and a new **OTE** stays open until 11pm. **Moped rental** is available at Corner Rentabike (☎0285/71 867), though the local bus service is more than adequate and walking trails delightful. The **campsite** (☎0285/71 802) is well signed between Rahídhi and Xilokeratídhi; in the latter district are three **tavernas**, of which the middle one – *Vitzentzos* – is by far the best.

Steps, and then a jeep track, lead out of Katápola to the remains of **ancient Minoa**, which are apt to disappoint up close: some Cyclopean wall four or five courses high, the foundations of an Apollo temple, a crumbled Roman structure and bushels of unsorted pottery shards. It's only the site, with views encompassing Khóra and ancient Arkessíni, that's the least bit memorable. Beyond Minoa the track soon dwindles to a trail, continuing within a few hours to Arkessíni (see below) via several hamlets – a wonderful **excursion** with the possibility of catching the bus back.

The **bus** shuttles almost hourly until 11pm between Katápola and Khóra, the island capital; several times daily the service continues to Ayía Ánna via Hozoviotíssas monastery, and once a day (9.45am) there's a run out to the "Káto Meriá", made up of the hamlets of Kamári, Arkessíni and Kolofána. **KHÓRA**, also accessible by an hour-long path beginning from behind the Rakhídhi campsite, is one of the best preserved khóras in the Cyclades, with a scattering of tourist shops, cafés, tavernas and rooms. Dominated by a rock plug wrapped with a chapel or two, the thirteenth-century Venetian fortifications look down on countless other bulbous churches – including Greece's smallest, **Áyios Fanoúrios**, which holds just three worshippers – and a line of decapitated windmills beyond. Of the half-dozen or so **places to stay**, the fanciest is *Pension Hora* (☎0285/71 110; ④), whose minibus sometimes meets ferries, outside the village above the road from Katápola. *Liotrivi* restaurant, down the steps from the bus stop, is probably the best place to **eat** in town. In addition to the pair of traditional tavernas, *Kastanis* and *Klimataria*, there are several noisy bistro-café-pubs, with *To Steki* in the upper plaza perennially popular in the late afternoon. On the same square are the island's main **post office** and a **bank**; further up the hill is the main OTE office, with somewhat limited opening hours.

From the top of Khóra, next to the helipad, a wide cobbled *kalderími* drops down to two major attractions, effectively short-cutting the road and taking little longer than the bus to reach them. Bearing left at an inconspicuous fork after ten minutes, you'll come to the spectacular **monastery of Khozoviotíssas** (daily 8am–1pm & 5–7pm; donation), which appears suddenly as you round a bend, its vast wall gleaming white at the base of a towering orange cliff. Only four monks occupy the fifty rooms now, but they are quite welcoming, considering the number of visitors who file through; you can see the eleventh-century icon around which the monastery was founded, along with a stack of other treasures. The foundation legend is typical for such institutions in outlandish places: during the Iconoclastic period a precious icon of the Virgin was committed to the sea by beleaguered monks at Khózova, somewhere in the Middle East, and it washed up safely at the base of the palisade here. The view from the katholikón's terrace, though, overshadows all for most visitors, and to round off the experience, visitors are ushered into a comfy reception room and treated to a sugary lump of *loukoúmi*, a fiery shot of *kitró* and a cool glass of water.

The right-hand trail leads down, within forty minutes, to the pebble **beaches** at **Ayía Ánna**. Skip the first batch of tiny coves in favour of the path to the westernmost bay, where naturists cavort, almost in scandalous sight of the monastery far above. As yet there are no tavernas here, nor a spring, so bring food and water for the day.

For alternatives to Ayía Ánna, take the morning bus out toward modern Arkessíni, alighting at Kamári hamlet (where there's a single taverna) for the twenty-minute path down to the adjacent beaches of **Notiná**, **Moúros** and **Poulopódhi**. Like most of Amorgós' south-facing beaches, they're clean, with calm water, and here, too, a fresh-water spring dribbles most of the year. The road is paved as far as Kolofana, where there is one place with rooms. From here unpaved roads lead to the western tip of the island, and remote beaches at Káto Kámbos and at Paradhísa, facing the islet of Gramuoussa.

Archeology buffs will want to head north from Kamári to Vroútsi, start of the over-grown hour-long route to **ancient Arkessini**, a collection of tombs, six-metre-high walls and houses out on the cape of Kastrí. The main path from Minoa also passes through Vroútsi, ending next to the well-preserved Hellenistic fort known locally as the "Pýrgos", just outside modern **ARKESSÍNI**. The village boasts a single taverna with rooms, and, more importantly, an afternoon bus back to Khóra and Katápola.

The northeast

The energetically inclined can walk the four to five hours from Khóra to Eyiáli. On the Khóra side you can start by continuing on the faint trail just beyond Khozoviótissas, but the islanders themselves, in the days before the road existed, preferred the more scenic and sheltered valley route through Terláki and Rikhtí. The two alternatives, and the modern jeep road, more or less meet an hour out of Khóra. Along most of the way, you're treated to amazing views of **Nikouriá islet**, nearly joined to the main island, and in former times a leper colony. The only habitations en route are the summer hamlet of **Asfodilídhi**, with well water but little else for the traveller, and **Potamós**, a double village you encounter on the stroll down towards Eyiáli bay.

EYIÁLI (Órmos), smaller than Katápola, is a delightful beachside place stuck in a 1970s time-warp. **Accommodation** includes *Hotel Pelagos* (☎0285/73 206; ④), a largish new hotel a short walk up from the harbour (near Akrogiali), *Nikitas* (☎0285/73 237; ④)) and *Akrogiali* (☎0285/73 249; ④), both above the harbour, and *Lakki* (☎0285/73 244; ②), which has a fine setting along the beach but a rather fierce management style. Overlooking the bay on the road up to Tholária is a luxury hotel with a swimming pool, the *Aegialis* (☎0285/73 107 or 73 393; ⑤). Behind the *Lakki* there is a very friendly official **campsite**, *Amorgos Camping* (☎0285/ 73 500). For **eating out**, try *To Limani* (aka *Katerina's*) on the single inland lane, packed until midnight by virtue of its excellent food and barrel wine. Other good options are the *Amorgialos* kafenío, right by the harbour which serves up octopus, and *Delear*, a smart beach bar with live music some evenings, and rather pricey drinks. A few seasonal music **bars**, such as *Selini*, attempt to compete with *Katerina's*.

The main Eyiáli **beach** is more than serviceable, getting less weedy and reefy as you stroll further north, the sand interrupted by the remains of a Roman building jutting into the sea. A trail here leads over various headlands to an array of clothing-optional bays: the first sandy, the second mixed sand and gravel, the last shingle. There are no facilities anywhere so bring along what you need.

Eyiáli has its own **bus service** up to each of the two villages visible above and east, with eight departures daily up and down (a timetable is posted by the harbour bus stop in town), but it would be a shame to miss out on the beautiful **loop walk** linking them with the port. A path starting at the far end of the beach heads inland and crosses the road before climbing steeply to **THOLÁRIA**, named after vaulted Roman tombs found around Vígla, the site of ancient Eyiáli. Vigla is on a hill opposite the village but there is little to see beyond the bases of statues and traces of city walls incorporated into later terracing. Another path winds down behind the hill to a tiny pebble beach at Míkrí Vlihádha far below. A handful of **taverna-cafés**, including a handsome wooden-floored establishment near the church, are more contemporary concerns, and there are now several places to stay, including some fairly fancy **rooms** (reserve through *Pension Lakki* in Eyiáli), the large and upmarket *Vigla* (☎0285/73 288; ⑤), and the *Thalassino Oneiro* (☎0285/73 345; ④), which has a fine restaurant and an extremely friendly owner. **LANGÁDHA** is another hour's walk along a path starting below Tholaria; to the left of the trail is the chapel of Astratios with an altar supported by the capital of a Corinthian column. Past here there are views down to the inlet of Megáli Vlihádha and, on a clear day, across to Ikaria to the north. The path descends through the village of Stroumbos, abandoned apart from three or four houses restored as holiday homes, and into a small gorge before climbing the steps up to Langádha. The place is home to a sizeable colony of expatriates – something reflected in the German-Greek cooking at *Nikos'* **taverna** at the lower end of the village, which also has some **rooms** (☎0285/73 310; ④), as does *Yiannis'* taverna.

Beyond Langádha, another rocky path leads around the base of the island's highest peak, the 821-metre-high **Kríkellos**, passing on the way the fascinating church of **Theológos**, with lower walls and ground plan dating to the fifth century. Somewhat easier to reach, by a slight detour off the main Tholária–Langádha trail, are the church and festival grounds of **Panayía Panokhorianí** – not so architecturally distinguished but a fine spot nonetheless.

Íos

No other island is quite like **Íos**, nor attracts the same vast crowds of young people, although attempts are being made to move the island's tourism upmarket; the island now enforces Greece's early closing laws (3am except Fri & Sat) and bars no longer stay open all night. The only real villages – **Yialós**, **Khóra** and **Mylopótamos** – are in one small corner of the island, and until recently development elsewhere was restricted by poor roads. As a result there are still some very quiet beaches with a few rooms to rent. Yialós has one of the best and safest natural harbours in the Cyclades and there is talk of building a new yacht marina.

Most visitors stay along the arc delineated by the port – at Yialós, where you'll arrive (there's no airport), in Khóra above it, or at the beach at Mylopótamos; it's a small area, and you soon get to know your way around. **Buses** constantly shuttle between Koumbára, Yialós, Khóra and Mylopótamos, with a daily service running roughly from 8am to midnight; you should never have to wait more than fifteen minutes, but at least

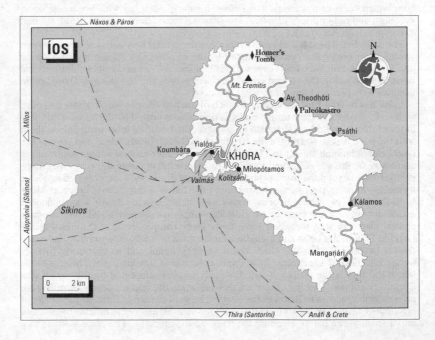

once try the short walk up (or down) the stepped path between Yialós and Khóra. Various travel offices run their own buses to the beaches at Manganári and Ayia Theodhóti; they sell return tickets only, and are a bit expensive. To rent your own transport, try Jacob's Car and Bike Rental (☎0286/91 047) in Yialós, and Vangelis Bike Rental (☎0286/91 919) in Khóra.

Despite its past popularity, **sleeping on the beach** on Íos is really worth avoiding these days. Crime and police raids are becoming more frequent as the island strains under the sheer impact of increasing youth tourism, and the police have been known to turn very nasty. They prefer you to sleep in the official campsites and, given the problem of theft, you should probably take their advice.

Yialós and Khóra

From **YIALÓS** quayside, **buses** turn around just to the left, while Yialós **beach** – surprisingly peaceful and uncrowded – is another five minutes' walk in the same direction. You might be tempted to grab a room in Yiálos as you arrive: owners meet the ferries, hustling the town's **accommodation**, and there are also a couple of kiosks by the jetty that will book rooms for you. At the far end of the beach is a plush option: *Ios Beach Bungalows* (☎0286/91 267; ⑤); *Galini Rooms* (☎0286/91 115; ④) down a lane behind the beach is a good quiet choice, if a little out of the way. There are more rooms on the stepped path from Yialós to Khóra although they can be noisy at night: the *Hotel-Bar Helios* (☎0286/91 500; ③) has a few simple, older rooms, the *Princess Sissy Hotel* (☎0286/91 244; ④) further up the steps towards Khóra is also reasonable, and *Ios Camping* (☎0286/91 329) has new management and has been improved recently, with a new swimming pool and café. Yialós has all the other essentials – accommodation kiosks, a reasonable supermarket (to the right of the bus stop), and a few **tavernas**. The *Octopus Tree*, a small kafenío by the fishing boats, serves cheap fresh seafood caught by the owner, while on the front heading towards the beach the *Waves Restaurant* does good Indian food. A twenty-minute stroll over the headland at **KOUMBÁRA**, there's a smaller and less crowded beach, with a taverna and a rocky islet to explore. The *Polydoros* taverna in Koumbára is one of the better places to eat on Íos, and is worth the bus ride.

KHÓRA (aka Íos Town) is a twenty-minute walk up behind the port, though you've got a better chance of getting something reasonable by haggling if you intend to stay for several days. The old white village is overwhelmed by the crowds of tourists in season, but with any number of arcaded streets and whitewashed chapels, it does have a certain charm.

Khóra divides naturally into two parts. The old town climbing the hillside to the left as you arrive is separated by an open space from newer development to the right. There are plenty of basic **rooms** in the old part (although the bars can make sleep difficult): *The Hotel Filippou* (☎0286/91 290; ④) is above the National Bank and next to the cathedral; *Yánnis Stratís* (☎0286/91 494; ②) has a few very simple rooms next door; and *Markos Pension* (☎0286/91 059; ④; ask for the ten percent discount for Rough Guide readers) with a poolside bar is one of the best choices in the new part. *Iliovassilema Rooms* (☎0286/91 997; ④) just out of town down a path past the Íos Club, is quiet and has fine views over the port, and the *Four Seasons Pension* (☎0286/91 308; winter 0286/ 92 081; ④) up a turning by Vangelis Bike Rental is also well away from the noise of the bars and clubs. The snack bar downstairs serves – bizarrely – a full Scottish breakfast.

What Khóra is still really about, though, is **nightlife**. Every evening the streets throb to music from ranks of competing discos and clubs – mostly free, or with a nominal entrance charge, though drinks tend to be expensive. Most of the smaller **bars** and pubs are tucked into the thronging narrow streets of the old village on the hill, offering

> A note of warning: bars on Íos are more expensive than they used to be, but still cheap compared with other islands. One way to keep prices down is to replace spirits with homemade alcohol, and Greeks call the resulting drinks **bombas** for obvious reasons. Beware of free drinks and cheap cocktails; a crackdown has been attempted but bombas are still around.

something for everyone – unless you just want a quiet drink. A welcome exception to the techno-pop dancing fodder can be found at the *Taboo* bar, run by two friendly brothers and featuring underground rock, eclectic decor and a clientele to match; *Pegasus* and the *Kahlua Bar* are also recommended. The larger **dancing clubs**, including the *Anjuna Club* which plays techno and trance music, and the *Disco Scorpion* are to be found on the main road to Mylopótamos. Finally the *Ios Club*, perched right up on the hill, plays quieter music, has reasonable food and is a good place to watch the sunset.

Eating is a secondary consideration but there are plenty of cheap and cheerful psistariés and take-away joints: sound choices include *Iy Folia*, near the top of the village, and the *Lord Byron* mezedhopoleio in an alley near the cathedral – it's open year round and tries hard to recreate a traditional atmosphere, with old rembétika music and some good and unusual Greek food.

Around the island

The most popular stop on the island's bus routes is **MYLOPÓTAMOS** (universally abbreviated to Mylópotas), the site of a magnificent beach and a mini-resort. There are two **campsites**: *Far Out* (☎0286/91 468), towards the far end of the beach, is more popular but can get very noisy and crowded, and *Stars* (☎0286/91302), by the road up to Khóra, is showing its age but is a bit quieter with more shade. At the far end of the bay *The Purple Pig* (☎0286/91 301; ④), a new Australian-run **backpackers' hotel** with beds in shared rooms (3500dr) and a café and bar, is a good alternative to the campsites and one of the best choices on Íos for single travellers. Across the road *Gorgona* (☎0286/91 307; ④) and *Dracos* (☎0286/91 281 or 91 010; ④) have reasonable rooms. *Dracos* also has a good taverna on its own little quay, serving freshly caught fish. The *Far Out Hotel* (☎0286/91 446 or 91 702; ⑤) on the road down from Khóra and the pricey *Ios Palace Hotel* (☎0286/91 269; ⑤) above the near end of the beach are the best upmarket choices. The *Harmony Restaurant* on the rocks beyond the *Ios Palace* is one of the better places to eat, serving pizzas and Mexican food. The restaurants and self-service cafés behind the beach are uninspiring, and only the *Faros Café* rates a mention for staying open through the night to cater for the crowds returning from Khóra in the early hours. Mylopótamos itself has surprisingly little in the way of nightlife.

From Yialós, daily boats depart at around 10am (returning in the late afternoon) to **MANGANÁRI** on the south coast, where there's a beach and a swanky hotel; you can also get there by moped. There's an expensive speedboat (4000dr return) from Yialós to Manganári, but most people go by bus (1500dr return). These are private buses run by travel agencies, leaving Yialós about 11am, calling at Khóra and Mylopótamos and returning later in the afternoon. Predominantly nudist, Manganári is the beach to come to for serious tans, although there's more to see, and a better atmosphere at **AYÍA THEODHÓTI** up on the east coast. There's a new paved road across the island to Ayía Theodhóti – the daily excursion bus costs 1000dr return. A couple of kilometres south of Ayía Theodhóti is a ruined Venetian castle which encompasses the ruins of a marble-finished town and a Byzantine church. In the unlikely event that the beach – a good one and mainly nudist – is too crowded, try the one at **PSÁTHI**, 14km to the southeast. Frequented by wealthy Athenians, this small resort has a couple of pricey tavernas, making it better for a day-trip than an extended stay. The road is very poor and not really safe for mopeds, although there are plans to improve it. Another island beach is at **KÁLAMOS**; get off the Manganári bus at the turning for Kálamos, which leaves you with a 4km walk.

Homer's "tomb" is the only cultural diversion on the island. The story goes that, while on a voyage from Sámos to Athens, Homer's ship was forced to put in at Íos, where the poet subsequently died. The tomb can be reached by moped along a safe new unpaved road (turning left from the paved road to Ayía Theódhoti 4.5km from Khóra). The town itself has long since slipped down the side of the cliff, but the rocky ruins of the entrance to a tomb remain, as well as some graves – one of which is claimed to be Homer's, but which in reality probably dates only to the Byzantine era.

Síkinos

Síkinos has so small a population that the mule-ride or walk up from the port to the village was only replaced by a bus late in the 1980s and, until the new jetty was completed at roughly the same time, it was the last major Greek island where ferry passengers were still taken ashore in launches. With no dramatic characteristics, nor any nightlife to speak of, few foreigners make the short trip over here from neighbouring Íos and Folégandhros or from sporadically connected Páros, Náxos, or Thíra. There is no bank on the island, but there is a **post office** up in Kástro-Khóra, near the **OTE**, and you can sometimes change cash at the store in Aloprónia.

Aloprónia and Kástro-Khóra

Such tourist facilities as exist are concentrated in the little harbour of **ALOPRÓNIA**, with its long sandy beach and the recent additions of an extended breakwater and jetty. More and more formal **accommodation** is being built here, but it's still possible to

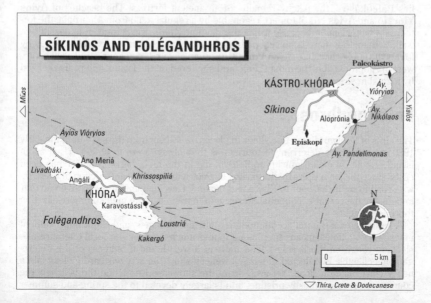

camp or just sleep out under the tamarisks behind the beach. For rooms, try *Flora* (π0286/51 214; ④), *Loukas* (π0286/51 076; ③) or the friendly *Sigalas* (π0286/51 233; ④) above the jetty; alternatively, the comfortable and traditional *Hotel Kamares* (π0286/51 234; ④) is more affordable than the conspicuous *Porto Sikinos* luxury complex (π0286/51 247; ⑥). *To Meltemi* **taverna** on the quay is the locals' hangout, while the fancier *Ostria* is affiliated with the *Hotel Kamares* and the *Loukas* has standard fare. The *Vrachos Rock Cafe* above the quay is where the kids hang out, while *Vengera* music bar on the opposite side of the bay is a smoother joint.

The double village of **KÁSTRO-KHÓRA** is served by the single island bus, which shuttles regularly from early morning till quite late in the evening between the harbour and here, though the route should soon be extended to Episkopí with the completion of the new road. On the ride up, the scenery turns out to be less desolate than initial impressions suggest. Draped across a ridge overlooking the sea, Kástro-Khóra makes for a charming day trip, and the lovely oil-press **museum** (July to mid-Sept 6.30–8.30pm; free), run privately by a Greek-American is definitely not to be missed. A partly ruined monastery, **Zoödhókhou Piyís** ("Spring of Life", a frequent name in the Cyclades), crowns the rock above; the architectural highlight of the place, though, is the central quadrangle of **Kástro**, a series of ornate eighteenth-century houses arrayed defensively around a chapel-square, their backs to the exterior of the village. The quality of rooms has improved, and both Markos Zagoreos (π0286/51 263; ③) and Haroula (π0286/51 212; ③) have competitive prices – the former has great views. A good selection of food is available, along with fine local wine, at both *Klimataria* and *Kastro*.

Around the island

West of Kástro-Khóra, an hour-plus walk (or mule ride) takes you through a landscape lush with olive trees to **Episkopí**, where elements of an ancient temple-tomb have been ingeniously incorporated into a seventh-century church – the structure is known formally as the **Iróön**. Ninety minutes from Kástro-Khóra, in the opposite direction, lies **Paleokástro**, the patchy remains of an ancient fortress. The beaches of **Áyios Yióryio** and **Áyios Nikólaos** are reachable by a regular kaïki from Aloprónia; the former is a better option because it has the daytime *Almira* restaurant. It is possible to walk to them, but there is no real path at the later stages. A more feasible journey by foot is the pebble beach at **Áyios Pandelímonas**: just under an hour's trail walk southwest of Aloprónia, it is the most scenic and sheltered on the island, and is also served by a kaïki in season.

Folégandhros

The cliffs of **Folégandhros** rise sheer in places over 300m from the sea – until the early 1980s as effective a deterrent to tourists as they always were to pirates. Used as an island of political exile right up until 1974, life in the high, barren interior has been eased since the junta years by the arrival of electricity and the construction of a lengthwise road from the harbour to Khóra and beyond. Development has been given further impetus by the recent exponential increase in tourism and the mild commercialization this has brought.

A veritable explosion in accommodation for most budgets, and slight improvement in ferry arrival times, means there is no longer much need for – or local tolerance of – sleeping rough on the beaches. The increased wealth and trendiness of the heterogeneous clientele is reflected in fancy jewellery shops, an arty postcard gallery and a newly constructed helipad. Yet away from the showcase Khóra and the beaches, the countryside remains mostly pristine, and is largely devoted to the spring and summer cultivation of barley, the mainstay of many of the Cyclades before the advent of tourism. Donkeys and donkey-paths are also still very much in evidence, since the terrain on much of the island is too steep for vehicle roads.

Karavostássi and around

KARAVOSTÁSSI, the rather unprepossessing port whose name simply means "ferry stop", serves as a last-resort base; it has several **hotels** but little atmosphere. Best value, if you do decide to stay is *Hotel Ailos* (☎0286/41 205; ④), while the *Poseidon* (☎0286/41 272; ⑤) throws in breakfast at its decent restaurant *To Kati Allo*, which means "Something Else". The *Vardia Bay* (☎0286/41 277; ⑤) above the harbour is extremely pricey, but has the excellent *Iy Kali Kardhia* below it, while the *Smyrna* ouzerí in a converted boathouse is nice for a drink. There are many buses a day in summer to Khóra, and three of those go on to Ano Meriá. Jimmy's motorbike rental (☎0286/41 448) has better prices than the one in Khóra.

The closest **beach** is the smallish, but attractive enough, sand-and-pebble **Vardhiá**, signposted just north over the headland. Some twenty minutes' walk south lies **Loustriá**, a rather average beach with tamarisk trees and the island's official **campsite** which is good and friendly, although the hot water supply can be erratic.

Easily the most scenic beach on Folégandhros, with an offshore islet and a 300m stretch of pea-gravel, is at **Katergó**, on the southeastern tip of the island. Most people visit on a boat excursion from Karavostássi or Angáli, but you can also get there on foot from the hamlet of Livádhi, a short walk inland from Loustriá. Be warned, though, that it's a rather arduous trek, with some nasty trail-less slithering in the final moments.

Khóra

The island's real character and appeal are to be found in the spectacular **KHÓRA**, perched on a cliff-top plateau some 45 minutes' walk from the dock; an hourly high-season **bus** service (6 daily spring/autumn) runs from morning until late at night. Locals and foreigners – hundreds of them in high season – mingle at the cafés and tavernas under the almond, flowering judas and pepper trees of the two main platías, passing the time unmolested by traffic, which is banned from the village centre. Toward the cliff-edge, and entered through two arcades, the defensive core of the medieval **kastro** is marked by ranks of two-storey houses, whose repetitive, almost identical stairways and slightly recessed doors are very appealing.

From the square where the bus stops, a zigzag path with views down to both coastlines climbs to the crag-top, wedding-cake church of **Kímisis Theotókou**, nocturnally illuminated to grand effect. Beyond and below it hides the **Khryssospiliá**, a large cave with stalactites, accessible only to proficient climbers; the necessary steps and railings have crumbled away into the sea, although a minor, lower grotto can still be visited.

Practicalities

Khóra's **accommodation** seems slightly weighted to favour hotels over rooms, with concentrations around the bus plaza at the east entrance to the village and at the western edge. Recommended rooms places include the purpose-built complex run by Irini Dekavalla (☎0286/41 235; ③), east of the bus stop. The nearby *Hotel Polikandia* (☎0286/41 322; ⑤) has an engaging proprietress and far lower rates than appearances suggest, especially off season. The most luxurious facilities are at the cliff-edge *Anemomilos Apartments* (☎0286/41 309; ⑥), immaculately appointed and with stunning views. The only hotel within the Khóra – the *Castro* (☎0286/41 230; ⑤) is a bit overpriced, despite recent renovation and undeniable atmosphere, with three rather dramatic rooms looking directly out on an alarming drop to the sea. At the western edge of Khóra near the police station, densely packed rooms outfits tend to block each other's views; the least claustrophobic is the long-established *Odysseas* (☎0286/41 276; ③), which also manages some attractive apartments near the *Anemomilos*. By the roadside on the way to Áno Meriá, the *Fani-Vevis* (☎0286/41 237; ④), in a Neoclassical mansion overlooking the sea, seems to function only in high season.

Khóra's dozen or so **restaurants** are surprisingly varied. The *Folegandhros* ouzerí in water-cistern plaza, is fun, if a bit eccentrically run. Breakfast can be enjoyed on the adjacent Platía Kondaríni at *Iy Melissa*, which does good fruit and yoghurt, omelettes and juices. *Iy Piatsa* has a nightly changing menu of well-executed Greek dishes, while their neighbour and local hangout *O Kritikos* is notable only for its grills. *Iy Pounda* near the bus stop is the most traditional place and has a small garden, while *Apanemo* at the far end of town has good food and a quieter setting, despite its proximity to the main bar area. Self-catering is an attractive option, with two well-stocked fruit shops and two supermarkets. Khóra is inevitably beginning to sprawl unattractively at the edges, but this at least means that the burgeoning **nightlife** – two dancing bars and a quantity of musical pubs and ouzerís – can be exiled to the north, away from most accommodation. *Methexis* plays mostly old rock, while *Greco* has more up-to-date sounds, and *Patitiri* features live rembétika. A combination **OTE/post office** (no bank) completes the list of amenities, though the single **ferry agent** also does money exchange as does the Italian-run Sottavento agency, which offers a wide range of services.

The rest of the island

Northwest of Khóra a narrow, cement road threads its way towards **ÁNO MERIÁ**, the other village of the island; after 4km you pass its first houses, clustered around the three churches of Áyios Pandelímonas, Áyios Yióryios and Áyios Andhréas. Four tavernas operate in high season only: *O Mimis* is about halfway along, and *Iy Sinandisi* is at the turning for Áyios Yeóryios beach, while *Barba Kostas* and *Iliovasilema*, at the far end of the sprawling village, complete the list. Several rooms are also available; particularly recommended are *Stella's* (☎0286/41 329; ②)

Up to six times a day in high season a **bus** trundles out here to drop people off at the footpaths down to the various sheltered beaches on the northwest shore of the island. Busiest of these is **Angáli** (aka Vathý), with five rather basic room outfits (no phones; all ②) and three equally simple summer-only tavernas, reached by a fifteen-minute walk along a dirt road from the bus stop.

Nudists are urged to take the paths which lead twenty minutes east or west to **Firá** or **Áyios Nikólaos** beaches respectively; the latter in particular, with its many tamarisks, coarse sand and view back over the island, is Katergó's only serious rival in the best-beach sweepstakes. At Áyios Nikólaos, a lone taverna operates up by the namesake chapel; Firá has no facilities at all. From the *Iliovasilema* taverna, a motorable track continues north to a point from where a 500m path takes you down to the pleasant little bay of Ambéli, which also has facilities.

Thíra (Santoríni)

As the ferry manoeuvres into the great caldera of **Thíra**, the land seems to rise up and clamp around it. Gaunt, sheer cliffs loom hundreds of feet above, nothing grows or grazes to soften the view, and the only colours are the reddish-brown, black and grey pumice striations layering the cliff face. The landscape tells of a history so dramatic and turbulent that legend hangs as fact upon it.

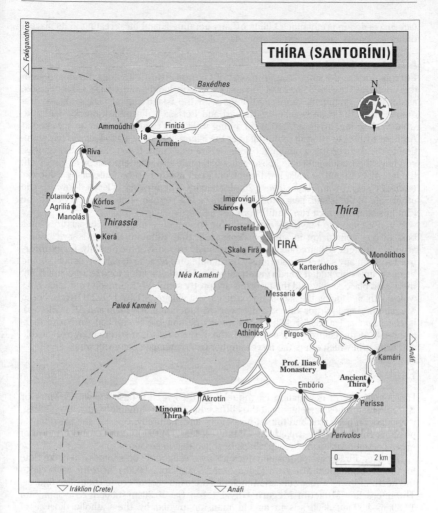

THÍRA (SANTORÍNI)

N

Folégandhros

Baxédhes

Ammoúdhi Finitiá
Ía Arméni

Ríva

Potamós Kórfos
Agriliá
Manolás *Thirassía*
Kerá

Imerovígli
Skáros

Thíra

Firostefáni
FIRÁ

Skala Firá

Monólithos

Karterádhos

Néa Kaméni

Paleá Kaméni

Messariá

Órmos
Athiniós Pírgos

Kamári

Prof. Ilias
Monastery

Ancient
Thíra

Embório

Akrotín

Minoan
Thíra

Períssa

Perívolos

0   2 km

Anáfi

▽ *Iráklion (Crete)*   ▽ *Anáfi*

From as early as 3000 BC the island developed as a sophisticated outpost of Minoan civilization, until around 1550 BC when catastrophe struck: the volcano-island erupted, its heart sank below the sea, and earthquakes reverberated across the Aegean. Thíra was destroyed and the great Minoan civilizations on Crete were dealt a severe blow. At this point the island's history became linked with legends of Atlantis, the "Happy Isles Submerged by Sea". Plato insisted that the legend was true, and Solon dated the cataclysm to 9000 years before his time – if you're willing to accept a mistake and knock off the final zero, a highly plausible date.

These apocalyptic events, though, scarcely concern modern tourists, who are here mostly to stretch out on the island's dark-sand beaches and absorb the peculiar, infernal atmosphere: as recently as a century ago, Thíra was still reckoned to be infested with vampires. Though not nearly so predatory as the undead, current visitors have in fact succeeded in pretty much killing off any genuine island life, creating in its place a rather expensive and stagey playground.

Arrival and departure

Ferries dock at the somewhat grim port of **Órmos Athiniós**; **Skála Firás** and **Ía** in the north are reserved for local ferries, excursion kaïkia and cruise ships. **Buses**, astonishingly crammed, connect Athiniós with the island capital Firá, and, less frequently, with the main beaches at Kamári and Périssa – disembark quickly and take whatever's going, if you want to avoid a long walk. You're also likely to be accosted at Athiniós by people offering rooms all over the island; it may be a good idea to pay attention to them, given the scramble for beds in Firá especially. If you alight at Skála Firás, you have the traditional route above you – 580 mule-shit-splattered steps to Firá itself. It's not that difficult to walk, but the intrepid can also go up by mule or by cable car (summer only 6.40am–10pm, every 20min; 800dr). The **airport** is located towards the other side of the island, near Monólithos; there is a regular shuttle bus service to the Firá bus station, which runs until 10pm.

When it comes to **leaving** – especially for summer/evening ferry departures – it's best to buy your ticket in advance. Note, too, that although the bus service stops around midnight, a shared taxi isn't outrageously expensive. Incidentally, **ferry information** from any source is notoriously unreliable on Thíra, so departure details should be quadruple-checked. If you do get stranded in Athiniós waiting for a ferry connection, there's no place to stay, and the tavernas are pretty awful. With time on your hands, it's well worth zigzagging the 3500m up to the closest village, **MEGALOKHÓRI**. Between Megalokhóri and Pýrgos village, quite near the junction of the main and Athiniós road, is *Hotel Zorbas* (☎0286/31 433; ⑥), with very personable Greek and American management. At the centre of Megalokhóri, the *Yeromanolis* is a surprisingly reasonable and tasty grill which offers the increasingly rare homemade Santoríni wine.

Firá

Half-rebuilt after a devastating earthquake in 1956, **FIRÁ** (also known as Thíra or Khóra) still lurches dementedly at the cliff's edge. With a stunningly attractive setting, it appears on postcards and tourist brochures and, naturally, you pay the price for its position. Busy with day-trippers in summer at least, initial impressions of Firá are of gross commercialism, and it is perhaps best avoided in season.

However, Firá's cliff-top position does justify a visit, and you should also make time for the **Archeological Museum** (Tues–Sun 8.30am–3pm; 800dr), near the cable car to the north of town, whose collection includes a curious set of erotic Dionysiac figures. The interesting **Museum Megaro Ghyzi** (Mon–Sat 10.30am–1.30pm & 5–8pm, Sun 10.30am–4.30pm; 350dr) is in an old mansion owned by the Catholic diocese of Santoríni and restored as a cultural centre. It has a good collection of old prints and maps as well as photographs of the town before and after the 1956 earthquake.

Practicalities

Caldera-side hotels and studios in **Firá** itself are expensive but there are plenty of rooms without caldera views at the back of town. Otherwise there are three **youth hostels** in the northern part of town, cheap, often full, but not too bad if you have your own bedding and sleep on the roof; the *Kamares* hostel (☎0286/24 472) on Erythroú Stavroú is the official hostel and the cheapest, but the other two hostels are better and also have reasonably priced double rooms. The *International Youth Hostel* (☎0286/22 387; ①) is across the alleyway from *Kamares* in a large old house: both are close to the bars and clubs and can be a bit noisy at night. *Kontohori Hostel* (☎0286/22 722 or 22

577; ①) is in a quiet location on the edge of town, down a turning off 25-Martiou, the road to Firostefáni and Ía.

FIROSTEFÁNI, between Firá and Imerovígli, is the best bet for reasonably priced rooms with views over the caldera. Rooms in Firostefáni of varying prices and standards include *Apartments Gaby* (☎0286/22 057; ④), *Stathis Rooms* (☎0286/22 835; ④), *Hotel Mylos* (☎0286/23 884; ④) and *Ioannis Roussos* (☎0286/22 511 or 22 862; ③). *Villa Haroula* (☎0286/24 226; ⑥) is a good new hotel on the road down to *Santorini Camping* (☎0286/22 944) at the back of town, which stays open with heating through the winter. You might try **KARTERÁDHOS**, a small village about twenty minutes' walk south of Firá, where there are rooms and the pleasant *Hotel Albatross* (☎0286/23 435, fax 23 431; ⑥), or Messariá, another 2km further, with some more expensive hotels.

Firá's **restaurants** are primarily aimed at the tourist market, but there are a few worth trying: the *Flame of the Volcano* is the last of the caldera-side restaurants heading north past the cable car station (towards Firostefáni) and is better and more reasonably priced than most, although you are still paying extra for the view. *Nikolas* on Erythroú Stavroú is an old-established and defiantly traditional taverna but it can be hard to get a table. Otherwise try *Koutouki* and *Bella Thira*, next to each other on 25-Martíou. As for **nightlife**, the places listed below are all on Erythroú Stavroú (walking south from the Kamares Youth Hostel), along with various other clubs and bars. *Enigma*, a soul disco, occupies a converted house and garden, the *Casablanca Club*, below *Kyra Thira* which is good jazz bar, is popular for dance music.

Theoskepasti Tours (☎0286/22 256 or 22 176) on 25-Martíou, next to the OTE, is helpful and is the only tourist agency in Firá with reliable information about ferries to Thirassía. **Buses** leave Firá from the just south of Platía Theotokopoúlou to Périssa, Perívolos, Kamári, Monólithos, Akrotíri, Athiniós and the airport. **Taxis** (☎0286/22 555) go from near the bus station. If you want to see the whole island in a couple of days a rented **moped** is useful; Moto Chris at the top of the road that leads down to *Santorini Camping* is particularly recommended.

The north

Once outside Firá, the rest of Santoríni comes as a nice surprise, although development is beginning to encroach. The volcanic soil is highly fertile, with every available space terraced and cultivated; wheat, tomatoes (most made into paste), pistachios and grapes are the main crops, all still harvested and planted by hand. The island's *visándo* and *nikhtéri* wines are a little sweet for many tastes but are among the finest produced in the Cyclades.

A satisfying – if demanding – approach to Ía, 12km from Firá in the northwest of the island, is to walk the stretch from **IMEROVÍGLI**, 3km out of Firá, using a spectacular footpath along the lip of the caldera; the walk takes around two hours. Imerovígli has a taverna and one moderate hotel, the *Katerina* (☎0286/22 708; ④) and if you carry on to Ía you'll pass Toúrlos, an old Venetian citadel on Cape Skáros, on the way. *Chromata* (☎0286/23 278; ⑥) at Imerovígli are smart and extremely expensive caldera-side villas that require booking well in advance.

ÍA was once a major fishing port of the Aegean, but it has declined in the wake of economic depression, wars, earthquakes and depleted fish stocks. Partly destroyed in the 1956 earthquake, the town has been sympathetically reconstructed, its pristine white houses clinging to the cliff face. Apart from the caldera and the village itself there are a couple of things to see, including a **Naval Museum** (9am–1pm & 5–8pm, closed Tues) and the very modest remains of a Venetian castle. With a **post office**, part-time **bank** and **bike-rental** office, Ía is a good, and quieter alternative to Firá. Much of the town's **accommodation** is in its restored old houses; expensive choices include the troglodytic *Hotel Lauda* (☎0286/71 157; ④), the *Hotel Anemones* (☎0286/71 342; ④), and the *Hotel Fregata* (☎0286/71 221; ④). The *Chelidonia Villas* (☎286/71 287; ⑤) are attractive restored cliff-side houses.

Quite near the bus terminal, also reachable by the main road that continues round to the back end of the village, is an excellent new hostel – the *Oia Youth Hostel* (☎0286/71 465; ①), with a terrace and shady courtyard, a good bar, clean dormitories and breakfast included. Recommended **restaurants** include *Petros* (for fish) and *Cafe Flora*, a friendly new place with reasonable prices; generally, the further you go along the central ridge towards the new end of Ía, the better value the restaurants. **Nightlife** revolves around sunset-gazing, for which people are bussed in from all over the island, creating traffic chaos; when this pales, there's *Strofi* rock-music bar.

Below the town, 200-odd steps switchback hundreds of metres down to two small harbours: **Ammoúdhi**, for the fishermen, and **Arméni**, where the excursion boats dock. Off the cement platform at Ammoúdhi you can swim past floating pumice and snorkel among shoals of giant fish, but beware the currents around the church-islet of Áyios Nikólaos. At Arméni, a single taverna specializes in grilled-octopus lunches. **FINIKIÁ**, 1km east of Ía, is a very quiet and traditional little village with a good restaurant – the expensive but varied *Finikias*. *Lotza Rooms* (☎0286/ 71 051; ③) are located in an old house in the middle of the village, while *Villa Agnadi* (☎0286/71 647; ⑥) comprises good apartments above the village, near the main road. Just north of Ía is **Baxédhes** beach, a quiet alternative to Kamári and Périssa (see below), with a few tavernas including the *Paradhisos*, which has good food and reasonable prices.

The east and south

Beaches on Santoríni, to the east and south, are bizarre – long black stretches of volcanic sand which get blisteringly hot in the afternoon sun. They're no secret, and in the summer the crowds can be a bit overpowering. Closest to Firá, **MONÓLITHOS** has a couple of tavernas but is nothing special. Further south, **KAMÁRI** has surrendered lock, stock and barrel to the package-tour operators and there's not a piece of sand that isn't fronted by concrete villas.

Nonetheless it's quieter and cleaner than most, with some beachfront **accommodation** including *Hotel Nikolina* (☎0286/31 702; ③), with basic but cheap rooms towards the southern end of the beach, as well as the *White House* (☎0286/31 441; ④), *Poseidon Hotel* (☎0286/31 698; ④) and the recommended *Sea Side Rooms* (☎0286/33 403; ③) further along the beach. *Kamari Camping* (☎0286/31 453) is a small and quiet municipal-run site with limited facilities, a fifteen-minute walk on the road out of Kamári.

Psistaria O Kritikos, a taverna-grill frequented by locals rather than tourists, is one of the best places to **eat** on the island. It's a long way out of Kamári on the road up to Messariá, and too far to walk, but the bus stops outside. There are plenty of cafés and restaurants behind the beach, though many are expensive or uninspired. *Saliveros*, in front of the *Hotel Nikolina*, has taverna food at reasonable prices, and *Almira*, next to *Sea Side Rooms*, is a smarter restaurant and only a little more expensive. Kamári is a family resort with little in the way of clubs and nightlife, but there is a good open-air **cinema** near the campsite, and in summer buses run until 1am so there's no problem getting back to Firá after seeing a film.

Things are scruffier at **PÉRISSA**, around the cape. Despite (or perhaps because of) its attractive situation and abundance of cheap rooms, it's noisy and crowded with backpackers. *Camping Perissa Beach* (☎0286/81 343) is right behind the beach and has plenty of shade but is also next to a couple of noisy late-night bars. There are two youth hostels on the road into Périssa: *Anna* (☎0286/82 182; ②) is fairly basic but better than the unofficial hostel across the road. There are plenty of cheap rooms in the same area and some upmarket hotels behind the beach including the smart and expensive *Hotel*

Veggara (☎0286/82 060; ⑥). The beach itself extends almost 7km to the west, sheltered by the occasional tamarisk tree.

Kamári and Périssa are separated by the Mésa Vounó headland, on which stood **ancient Thíra** (Tues–Sun 9am–3pm), the post-eruption settlement dating from the ninth century BC. Excursion buses go up from Kamári (2000dr), staying two hours at the site (ask at Kamári Tours behind the beach) but you can walk the **cobbled path** starting from the square by the Argo General Store. The path zigzags up to a white-washed church by a **cave**, containing one of Thira's few freshwater springs, before crossing over to meet the road and ending at a saddle between Mésa Vounó and Profítis Ilías, where a refreshments van sells expensive drinks. From here, the path to the site passes a chapel dating back to the fourth century AD before skirting round to the Temenos of Artemidoros with bas-relief carvings of a dolphin, eagle and lion representing Poseidon, Zeus and Apollo. From here the path follows the sacred way of the ancient city through the remains of the agora and past the theatre. Most of the ruins (dating mainly from Hellenistic and Roman times) are difficult to place, but the site is impressively large and the views are awesome. The site can also be reached by a path from Périssa, and either way it's an hour's walk.

Inland along the same mountain spine is the monastery of **Profítis Ilías**, now sharing its refuge with Greek radio and TV pylons and the antennae of a NATO station. With just one monk remaining to look after the church, the place only really comes to life for the annual Profítis Ilías festival, when the whole island troops up here to celebrate. The views are still rewarding, though, and from near the entrance to the monastery an old footpath heads across the ridge in about an hour to ancient Thíra. The easiest ascent is the thirty-minute walk from the village of Pýrgos.

PÝRGOS itself is one of the oldest settlements on the island, a jumble of old houses and alleys that still bear the scars of the 1956 earthquake. It climbs to another Venetian fortress crowned by several churches and you can clamber around the battlements for sweeping views over the entire island and its Aegean neighbours. By way of contrast **MESSARIÁ**, a thirty-minute stroll north, has a skyline consisting solely of massive church domes that lord it over the houses huddled in a ravine.

Akrotíri

Evidence of the Minoan colony that once thrived here has been uncovered at the other ancient site of **Akrotíri** (Tues–Sat 8.30am–3pm; 1200dr), at the southwestern tip of the island. Tunnels through the volcanic ash uncovered structures, two and three storeys high, first damaged by earthquake then buried by eruption; Professor Marinatos, the excavator and now an island hero, was killed by a collapsing wall and is also buried on the site. Only a small part of what was the largest Minoan city outside of Crete has been excavated thus far. Lavish frescoes adorned the walls, and Cretan pottery was found stored in a chamber; most of the frescoes are currently exhibited in Athens.

Akrotíri itself can be reached by bus from Firá or Périssa; the excellent *Glaros* taverna on the way to Kókkini Ámmos beach has excellent food and barrelled wine. Kókkini Ámmos is about 500m from the site and is quite spectacular with high reddish brown cliffs above sand the same colour (the name means "red sand"). There's a drinks stall in a cave hollowed into the base of the cliff. It's a better beach than the one below the site, but gets crowded in season.

The Kaméni islets and Thirassía

From either Firá or Ía, boat excursions and local ferries run to the charred volcanic islets of **Paleá Kaméni** and **Néa Kaméni**, and on to the relatively unspoiled islet of Thirassía, which was once part of Santoríni until shorn off by an eruption in the third century BC. At Paleá Kaméni you can swim from the boat to hot springs with sulphurous mud, and Néa Kaméni, with its mud-clouded hot springs features a demanding hike to a volcanically active crater.

The real attraction though, is **Thirassía**, the quietest island in the Cyclades. The views are as dramatic as any on Santoríni, and tourism has little effect on island life. The downside is that there is no sandy beach, no nightlife and nowhere to change money.

Most tour boats head for **Kórfos**, a stretch of shingle backed by fishermen's houses and high cliffs. It has a few tavernas, including *Tonio* which stays open when the day trippers have gone, but no rooms. From Kórfos a stepped path climbs up to **MANOLÁS**, nearly 200m above. Donkeys are still used for transport and stables can be seen in both villages. Manolás straggles along the edge of the caldera, an untidy but attractive small island village that gives an idea of what Santoríni was like before tourism arrived there. It has a bakery, a couple of shops and some indifferent tavernas that open only for the midday rush: the **restaurant** at the *Hotel Cavo Mare* (☎0286/29 176; ⑤) wins out by giving diners the use of the swimming pool. Dhimítrios Nomikós has **rooms** (☎0286/29 102; ②) overlooking the village from the south.

The best **excursion** from Manolás is to follow the unmade road heading south; about halfway along you pass the church of Profítis Ilías on a hilltop to the left. From here an old and overgrown trail descends through the deserted caldera-side village of **Kerá**, before running parallel with the road to the **Monastery of Kímisis** above the southern tip of the island. Minoan remains were excavated in a pumice quarry to the west of here in 1867, several years before the first discoveries at Akrotíri, but there is nothing to be seen today.

Ferries run to Thirassía four times a week in season and three times a week through the winter. There is no problem taking a car or rental bike over, but fill up with petrol first. Day trips take in Néa Kaméni and Paleá Kaméni but are expensive (5000dr) and only stay two or three hours on Thirassía. In Firá, Theoskepastí Tours (☎0286/22 256 or 22 176), next to the OTE office on 25-Martíou, is the only reliable source of ferry information, and its day trips allow you to take a vehicle over to Thirassía at no extra charge.

Anáfi

A ninety-minute boat ride to the east of Thíra, **Anáfi** is the last stop for ferries and hydrofoils, and something of a travellers' dead end, with only one weekly ferry on to the Dodecanese. Not that this is likely to bother most of the visitors, who intentionally come here for weeks in mid-summer, and take over the island's beaches with a vengeance.

At most other times the place seems idyllic, and indeed may prove too sleepy for some: there are no bona fide hotels, mopeds, discos or organized excursions, and donkeys are still the main method of transport in the interior. Anáfi, though initially enchanting, is a harsh place, its mixed granite/limestone core overlaid by volcanic rock spewed out by Thíra's eruptions. Apart from the few olive trees and vines grown in the valleys, the only plants that seem to thrive are prickly pears.

The harbour and Khóra

The tiny harbour hamlet of **ÁYIOS NIKÓLAOS** has a single taverna, *To Akroyiali*, with a few rooms (☎0286/61 218; ②), while *Dave's Cafe*, with straw umbrellas above the beach, is a colourful English-run drinking spot. Jeyzed Travel (☎0286/61 253, fax 61 352) can provide information as well as issuing ferry tickets, changing money and booking rooms. In August there are enough Greek visitors to fill all the rooms on the island and it's a good idea to book ahead. Most places to stay are in Khóra. In season a bus runs from the harbour every two hours or so from 9am to 11pm.

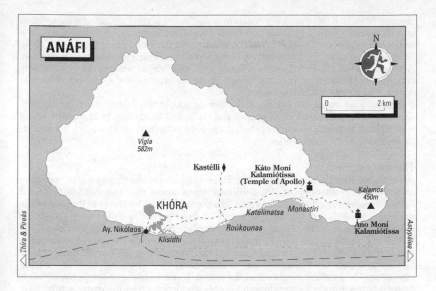

KHÓRA itself, adorning a conical hill overhead, is a stiff, 25-minute climb up the obvious old mule path which shortcuts the modern road. Exposed and blustery when the *meltémi* is blowing, Khóra can initially seem a rather forbidding ghost town. This impression is slowly dispelled as you discover the hospitable islanders taking their coffee in sheltered, south-facing terraces, or under the anti-earthquake barrel vaulting that features in domestic architecture here.

The modern, purpose-built **rooms** run by Kalliopi Halari (☎0286/61 271; ②) and Voula Loudharou (☎0286/61 279; ③), and those run by Margarita Kollidha (☎0286/61 292; ③) at the extreme east edge of the village, are about the most comfortable – and boast stunning views south the islets of Ftená, Pakhiá and Makriá, and the distinctive monolith at the southeastern corner of Anáfi. Somewhat simpler are the rooms of the Gavalas family (②), looking down over the village from the top of the mule path. Evening **diners** seem to divide their custom between the simple, welcoming *To Steki*, with reasonable food and barrel wine served on its terrace, and the more upmarket *Alexandhra's* on the central walkway with a bar upstairs. Otherwise there are shops, a bakery, a **post office** and an OTE station.

East along the coast: beaches and monasteries

The glory of Anáfi is a string of south-facing beaches starting under the cliffs at Áyios Nikólaos. Freelance campers head for **KLISÍDHI**, a short walk to the east of the harbour, where 200m of tan, gently shelving sand is pounded by gentle surf, and splendidly malopropic signs announce that "Nubbism is not allowed". Above the calamus-and-tamarisk oasis backing the beach there are two cafés and a taverna, including the *Kafestiatorion tis Margaritas* with popular rooms (☎0286/61 237; ③). The *Villa Apollon* on the hillside above has the island's most upmarket accommodation (☎0286/61 348; ④). Klisídhi can be reached by a new road but it's quicker to take the cliff-top path starting behind the power station at the harbour. East of here the beaches can only be reached by foot or boat.

From a point on the paved road just east of Khóra, the **main path** skirting the south flank of the island is signposted: "Kastélli – Paleá Khóra – Roúkouna – Monastíri". The primary branch of this trail roller-coasters in and out of several agricultural valleys that provide most of Anáfi's produce and fresh water. Just under an hour along, beside a well, you veer down a side trail to **Roúkounas**, easily the island's best beach, with some 500m of broad sand rising to tamarisk-stabilized dunes, which provide welcome shade. A single taverna, *To Papa*, operates up by the main trail in season; the suggestively craggy hill of **Kastélli**, an hour's scramble above the taverna, is the site both of ancient Anaphi and a ruined Venetian castle.

Beyond Roúkounas, it's another half hour on foot to the first of the exquisite half-dozen **Katelímatsa** coves, of all shapes and sizes, and 45 minutes to **Monastíri** beach – all without facilities, so come prepared. Nudism is banned on Monastíri, because of its proximity to the monasteries.

The monasteries

Between Katelímatsa and Kálamos, the main route keeps inland, past a rare spring, to arrive at the **monastery of Zoödhókhou Piyís**, some two hours out of Khóra. A ruined temple of Apollo is incorporated into the monastery buildings to the side of the main gate; according to legend, Apollo caused Anáfi to rise from the waves, pulling off a dramatic rescue of the storm-lashed Argonauts. The courtyard, with a welcome cistern, is the venue for the island's major festival, celebrated eleven days after Easter. A family of cheesemakers lives next door and can point you up the start of the spectacular onward path to **Kalamiótissa**, a little monastery perched atop the abrupt pinnacle at the extreme southeast of the island. It takes another hour to reach, but is eminently worthwhile for the stunning scenery and views over the entire south coast. Kalamiótissa comes alive only during its 7–8 September festival; at other times, you could haul a sleeping bag up here to witness the amazing sunsets and sunrises, with your vantage point often floating in a sea of cloud. There is no water up here, so bring enough with you. It's a full day's outing from Khóra to Kalamiótissa and back; you might wish to take advantage, in at least one direction, of the excursion **kaïki** that runs from Áyios Nikólaos to Monastiri (6 times daily in high season). There is also a slightly larger mail-and-supplies boat (currently Mon & Thurs 11am) which takes passengers to and from Thíra (Athiniós), supplementing the main-line ferries to Pireás.

travel details

Ferries

Most of the Cyclades are served by mainline ferries from **Pireás**, but there are also boats which depart from **Lávrio** (for Kéa and, less often, Kýthnos) and **Rafína**, which has become increasingly important of late, as work proceeds on the new international airport at nearby Spáta. At the moment there are regular services from Rafína to Ándhros, Tínos, Mýkonos, Sýros, Páros, Náxos and Amorgós, with less frequent sailings to the North and East Aegean. All three ports are easily reached by bus from Athens.

The frequency of sailings given below is intended to give an idea of services from April to October, when most visitors tour the islands. During the winter expect departures to be at or below the minimum level listed, with some routes

cancelled entirely. Conversely, routes tend to be more comprehensive in spring and autumn, when the government obliges shipping companies to make extra stops to compensate for numbers of boats still in dry dock.

By 1998 the long-awaited computerized booking system should be operational, and all agents will be required to issue computerized tickets. This move is designed to conform to EU regulations and prevent the overcrowding of ferries so common in the past. It means that in high season, certain popular routes may be booked up days in advance, so if you're visiting a few islands it is important to check availability on arrival in Greece, and book your outward and final pre-flight tickets well ahead. There is not usually so much problem with space between islands, as there is to and from Pireás.

Amorgós 5–6 ferries weekly to Náxos and Páros, some of these continuing to Rafína rather than Pireás; 4–5 to Sýros; 3–4 weekly to Tínos; 4 to Mýkonos; 2–3 weekly to Ándhros, Koufoníssi, Skhinoússa, Iráklia and Dhonoússa; 1–3 weekly to Astypálea; 1 weekly to Kálymnos and Kós.

Anáfi 3 weekly to Pireás (12hr 30min) via Thíra (1hr 30min), Íos, Náxos, Páros; 1 weekly to Sýros, Astypálea, Síkinos and Folégandhros; 2 weekly mail boats to Thíra (2hr).

Ándhros At least 3 daily to Rafína (2hr), Tínos (2hr), and Mýkonos; 4 weekly to Sýros; 1 weekly to Amorgós and the minor islets behind Náxos.

Dhonoússa 3–4 weekly to Amorgós; 1–3 weekly to Náxos; 1–2 weekly to Koufoníssi, Skhinoússa, Iráklia, Páros, Sýros, Pireás; 1 weekly to Mýkonos, Tínos, Astypálea, Pátmos, Lipsí, Léros, Kós, Níssyros, Tílos, Sými and Rhodes.

Íos At least 2 daily to Pireás (10hr), Páros (5hr), Náxos (3hr) and Thíra (2hr); 5–6 weekly to Síkinos and Folégandhros; 4 weekly to Crete; 1–3 weekly to Mílos, Kímolos, Sérifos, Sífnos and Kýthnos; 1 weekly to Tínos, Skiáthos and Thessaloníki; 2–3 weekly to Kárpathos and Kássos; 2 weekly to Rhodes.

Kéa 1–3 daily to Lávrio (1hr 30min); 2 weekly to Kýthnos.

Kímolos 2 daily kaïkia to Mílos (Pollónia) year-round, 5 in summer; 2–5 weekly to Mílos (Adhámas), Sífnos, Sérifos, Kýthnos, and Pireás (7hr); 1 weekly to Folégandhros, Síkinos and Thíra.

Kýthnos 4–12 weekly to Pireás (3hr 15min); 4–10 weekly to Sérifos, Sífnos, and Mílos; 2–4 weekly to Kímolos, Folégandhros, Síkinos, Íos and Lávrio.

Koufoníssi, Skhinoússa, Iráklia 2–3 weekly Náxos, 2 weekly to Mýkonos; 1–2 weekly to Páros, Sýros and Tínos; 1 weekly to Dhonoússa, Amorgós, Astypálea, Ándhros, Rafína and Pireás.

Mýkonos At least 2 daily to Pireás (5hr), Rafína (3hr 30min), Tínos (1hr), Ándhros (3hr 30min) and Sýros (2hr); 3–4 weekly to Amorgós; 3 weekly to Crete (Iráklion), Skiáthos and Thessaloníki; 2–3 weekly to Dhonoússa; 1–2 weekly to Koufoníssi, Skhinoússa and Iráklia; 1 weekly to Kýthnos, Kéa, Pátmos, Lipsí, Léros, Kós, Níssyros, Tílos, Sými and Rhodes; daily (except Monday) excursion boats to Delos.

Mílos At least daily to Pireás (8hr); 5–10 weekly to Sífnos (2hr), Sérifos and Kýthnos; 2–5 daily kaïkia or 4–6 weekly ferries to Kímolos; 2–3 weekly to Folégandhros, Síkinos, Íos and Thíra; 1–3 weekly to Crete (Iráklion or Sitía); 1 weekly to Náxos, Amorgós, Náfplio (Peloponnese), Kássos, Kárpathos, Khálki, Sými and Rhodes (Ródhos).

Náxos At least 3 daily to Pireás (8hr), Páros (1hr), Íos and Thíra; at least 1 daily to Sýros; 5–7 to Amorgós; 6 weekly to Crete (Iráklion); 5–7 weekly to Amorgós; 5–6 to weekly Tínos; 5 weekly to Síkinos and Folégandhros; 3–4 weekly to Ándhros and Rafína; 3–4 weekly to Anáfi; 3 to Rhodes; 2–6 weekly to Ikaría and Sámos; 2–3 weekly to Astypálea, Kássos, Kárpathos, Pátmos, Léros, Kálimnos, Kós, Skiáthos, Thessaloníki, Iráklia, Skhinoússa, Koufoníssi and Dhonoússa; 1 to Foúrni, Kýthnos, Kéa and Khálki.

Páros At least 3 daily to Pireás (7hr), Andíparos, Náxos, Íos, Thíra; at least 1 daily to Sýros and Tínos; daily to Iráklion (Crete); 3–6 weekly to Ikaría and Sámos; 5 weekly to Síkinos, Folégandhros and Amorgós; 4–5 weekly to Rafína; 3–5 weekly to Skiáthos and Thessaloníki; 3 weekly to Rhodes, Kárpathos; 2–3 weekly to Anáfi; 2 weekly to Sífnos, Sérifos, Foúrni, Pátmos, Léros, Kálymnos, Kós, Astypálea and Kássos; 1–3 weekly to Koufoníssi, Skhinoússa, Iráklia; 1 weekly to Vólos, Kéa, Kýthnos, Mílos, Kímolos and Khálki; at least hourly from Parikía to Andíparos in summer, dropping to 3 weekly in winter. There is also a car ferry from Poúnda to Andíparos at least hourly throughout the year.

Sérifos and Sífnos 5–12 weekly to Pireás (4hr 30min) and each other; 5–10 weekly to Mílos; 2–5 weekly to Kímolos; 2–3 weekly to Folégandhros, Sýkinos, Íos, and Thíra (Santoríni); once weekly to Sýros; once weekly to eastern Crete and select Dodecanese; daily (June–Aug) from Sífnos to Páros.

Síkinos and Folégandhros 2–6 weekly between each other, and to Pireás (10hr), Kýthnos, Sérifos, Sífnos and Mílos; 1–3 weekly to Íos, Thíra, Sýros, Páros, Náxos and Kímolos.

Sýros At least 2 daily to Pireás (4hr), Tínos (1hr), Mýkonos (2hr), Náxos, and Páros; 4 weekly to Rafína (3hr 30min), 2 weekly to Amorgós and the islets behind Náxos; 2 weekly to Íos, Síkinos, Folégandhros and Thíra; 2 weekly to Ikaría, Sámos and Astypálea; 1–2 weekly to Pátmos, Léros, Kálimnos, Kós, Níssyros, Tílos and Rhodes.

Thíra At least 3 daily to Pireás (10–12hr), Páros, Íos and Náxos; daily to Iráklion, Crete (5hr); 5–7 weekly to Síkinos and Folégandhros; 4 weekly to Anáfi, Sífnos and Mýkonos; 3–5 weekly to Sýros, Tínos, Skiáthos and Thessaloníki; 3–4 weekly to Mílos and Kímilos; 3 weekly to Kárpathos; 2–3 weekly to Sérifos; 2 weekly to Kássos; 2 weekly to Rhodes; 1 weekly to Astypálea, Khálki, Kýthnos and Vólos; 3–4 weekly to Thirassía (plus lots of expensive daily excursion boats in season); 2 weekly mail boats to Anáfi.

Tínos At least 2 daily to Pireás (5hr), Rafína (4hr), Ándhros, Sýros and Mýkonos; 5–6 weekly to Páros and Náxos; 4–5 weekly to Thíra and Iráklion (Crete); 3–5 weekly Skiáthos and Thessaloníki; 3–4 weekly to Amorgós; 1 weekly to Íos, Koufoníssi, Skhinoússa, Iráklia, Kéa, Kýthnos, Vólos, Pátmos, Lipsí, Léros, Kós, Níssyros, Tílos, Sými and Rhodes; also excursion boats calling at Delos and Mýkonos, 1 daily except Monday.

Other services

To simplify the lists above, certain strategic **hydrofoil** and **small-boat services** have been omitted. Of these, the *Skopelitis* plies daily in season between Mýkonos and Amorgós, spending each night at the latter and threading through all of the minor isles between it and Náxos, as well as Náxos and Páros (Píso Livádhi), in the course of a week. Note that, as well as being overcrowded and unreliable, this boat has no café or restaurant on board, so take provisions for what can be quite lengthy journeys. The Páros Express is actually a small car ferry based on Sýros (despite its name), which does a very useful weekly circle route linking that island with Páros, Náxos, Íos, Thíra, Síkinos, Folégandhros, Sífnos, Sérifos and Kýthnos. The Seajet catamaran – a small-capacity (and expensive) jet-boat (☎0294/22 888 for details), operates almost daily during summer out of Rafína and connects Sýros, Tínos, Mýkonos, Páros and Náxos. Ceres "Flying Dolphins" hydrofoils operate between Zéa (Pireás), Kéa and Kýthnos – twice daily Friday to Monday in high season, once daily mid-week. A new company, Speed Lines hydrofoils, is competing with Ilio Lines in the central and eastern Cyclades.

Flights

There are **airports** on **Páros**, **Mýkonos**, **Thíra**, **Sýros**, **Mílos** and **Náxos**. In season, or during storms when ferries are idle, you have little chance of getting a seat on less than three days' notice. The Athens–Mílos route is probably the best value for money; the other destinations seem deliberately overpriced, in a usually unsuccessful attempt to keep passenger volume manageable. Expect off-season (Oct–April) frequencies to drop by at least eighty percent.

Athens–Páros (4–5 daily; 45min)

Athens–Mýkonos (4–7 daily; 50min)

Athens–Thíra (4–8 daily; 1hr)

Athens–Sýros (2–3 daily; 35min)

Athens–Mílos (2 daily; 45min)

Athens–Náxos (2 daily; 45min)

Mýkonos–Thíra (2–3 weekly; 40min)

Mýkonos–Iráklion (Crete) (1 weekly; 1hr 10min)

Mýkonos–Rhodes (1 weekly; 1hr 10min)

Thíra–Iráklion (Crete) (1–2 weekly; 40min)

Thíra–Rhodes (3 weekly; 1hr).

CHAPTER THREE

CRETE

Crete (Kríti) is a great deal more than just another Greek island. In many places, especially in the cities or along the developed north coast, it doesn't feel like an island at all, but rather a substantial land in its own right – a mountainous, wealthy and surprisingly cosmopolitan one. But when you lose yourself among the mountains, or on the less-known coastal reaches of the south, it has everything you could want of a Greek island and more: great beaches, remote hinterlands and hospitable people.

In **history**, Crete is distinguished above all as the home of Europe's earliest civilization. It was only at the beginning of this century that the legends of King Minos and of a Cretan society that ruled the Greek world in prehistory were confirmed by excavations at **Knossós** and **Festós**. Yet the **Minoans** had a remarkably advanced society, the centre of a maritime trading empire as early as 2000 BC. The artworks produced on Crete at this time are unsurpassed anywhere in the ancient world, and it seems clear, that life on Crete in those days was good. This apparently peaceful culture survived at least three major natural disasters. Each time the palaces were destroyed, and each time they were rebuilt on a grander scale. Only after the last destruction, probably the result of an eruption of Thíra (Santoríni) and subsequent tidal waves and earthquakes, do significant numbers of weapons begin to appear in the ruins. This, together with the appearance of the Greek language, has been interpreted to mean that Mycenaean Greeks had taken control of the island. Nevertheless, for nearly 500 years, by far the longest period of peace the island has seen, Crete was home to a culture well ahead of its time.

The Minoans of Crete came probably originally from Anatolia; at their height they maintained strong links with Egypt and with the people of Asia Minor, and this position as meeting point and strategic fulcrum between east and west has played a major role in Crete's subsequent history. Control of the island passed from Greeks to Romans to Saracens, through the Byzantine Empire to Venice, and finally to Turkey for more than two centuries. During World War II, the island was **occupied** by the Germans and attained the dubious distinction of being the first place to be successfully invaded by paratroops.

ACCOMMODATION PRICE CODES

Throughout the book we've used the following **price codes** to denote the cheapest available room in high season; all are prices for a double room, except for category ①, which represents per person rates. Out of season, rates can drop by up to fifty percent, especially if you are staying for three or more nights. Single rooms, where available, cost around seventy percent of the price of a double.

Rented private rooms on the islands usually fall into the ② or ③ categories, depending on their location and facilities, and the season; a few in the ④ category are more like plush self-catering apartments. They are not generally available from late October through to the beginning of April, when only hotels tend to remain open.

① 1400–2000dr	④ 8000–12,000dr
② 4000–6000dr	⑤ 12000–16,000dr
③ 6000–8000dr	⑥ 16,000dr and upwards

For more accommodation details, see pp.39–41.

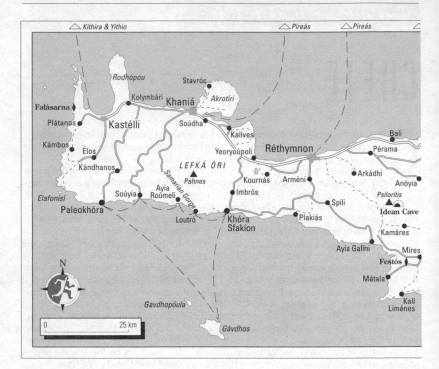

Today, with a flourishing **agricultural economy**, Crete is one of the few islands which could probably support itself without tourists. Nevertheless, **tourism** is heavily promoted. The northeast coast in particular is overdeveloped, and though there are parts of the south and west coasts that have not been spoiled, they are getting harder to find. By contrast, the high mountains of the interior are still barely touched, and one of the best things to do on Crete is to **rent a vehicle** and explore the remoter villages.

Where to go

Every part of Crete has its loyal devotees and it's hard to pick out highlights, but generally if you want to get away from it all you should head west, towards **Khaniá** and the smaller, less well connected places along the south and west coasts. It is in this part of the island that the White Mountains rise, while below them yawns the famous **Samarian Gorge**. The far east, around **Sitía**, is also relatively unscathed.

Whatever you do, your first main priority will probably be to leave **Iráklion** (Heraklion) as quickly as possible, having paid the obligatory, and rewarding, visit to the **archeological museum** and nearby **Knossós**. The other great Minoan sites cluster around the middle of the island: **Festós** and **Ayía Triádha** in the south (with Roman **Górtys** to provide contrast), and **Mália** on the north coast. Almost wherever you go, though, you'll find a reminder of the island's history, whether it's the town of **Gourniá** near the cosmopolitan resort of **Áyios Nikólaos**, the exquisitely sited palace of **Zákros** in the far east, or the lesser sites scattered around the west. Unexpected highlights include Crete's Venetian forts at **Réthymnon** and **Frangokástello**; its hundreds of fres-

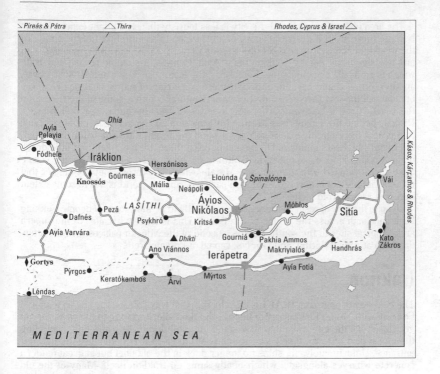

coed Byzantine churches, most famously at **Kritsá**; and, at Réthymnon and Khaniá, the cluttered old Venetian and Turkish quarters.

Climate

Crete has by far the longest summers in Greece, and you can get a decent tan here right into October and swim at least from May until November. Several annual harvests also make it a promising location for finding **casual work**. The cucumber green houses and pickling factories around Ierápetra have proved to be winter lifelines for many long-term Greek travellers. The one seasonal blight is the *meltémi*, which blows harder here and more continuously than anywhere else in Greece – the best of several reasons for avoiding an **August** visit.

IRÁKLION, KNOSSÓS AND CENTRAL CRETE

Many visitors to Crete arrive in the island's capital, **Iráklion** (Heraklion), but it's not a beautiful city, nor one where you'll want to stay much longer than it takes to visit the **archeological museum** and nearby **Knossós**. Iráklion itself, though it has its good points – superb fortifications, a fine market, atmospheric old alleys, and some interesting lesser museums – is for the most part an experience in survival: it's modern, raucous, traffic-laden and overcrowded.

The area immediately around the city is less touristy than you might expect, mainly because there are few decent beaches of any size on this central part of the coast. To the west, mountains drop straight into the sea virtually all the way to Réthymnon, with just two significant coastal settlements – **Ayía Pelayía**, a sizeable resort, and **Balí**, which is gradually becoming one. Eastwards, the main resorts are at least 40km away, at **Khersónissos** and beyond, although there is a string of rather unattractive developments all the way there. Inland, there's agricultural country, some of the richest on the island, Crete's best vineyards, and a series of wealthy but rather dull villages. Directly behind the capital rises **Mount Ioúktas** with its characteristic profile of Zeus; to the west the Psilorítis massif spreads around the peak of **Mount Ídha** (Psilorítis), the island's highest mountain. On the south coast there are few roads and little development of any kind, except at **Ayía Galíni** in the southwest, a nominal fishing village long since swamped with tourists, and **Mátala**, which has thrown out the hippies that made it famous and is now crowded with package-trippers. **Léndas** has to some extent occupied Mátala's old niche.

Despite the lack of resorts, there seem constantly to be thousands of people trekking back and forth across the centre of the island. This is largely because of the superb archeological sites in the south: **Festós**, second of the Minoan palaces, with its attendant villa at **Ayía Triádha**, and **Górtys**, capital of Roman Crete.

Iráklion

The best way to approach **IRÁKLION** is by sea: that way you see the city as it should be seen, with Mount Ioúktas rising behind and the Psilorítis range to the west. As you get closer, it's the city walls that first stand out, still dominating and fully encircling the oldest part of town; finally you sail in past the great **fort** defending the harbour entrance. Unfortunately, big ships no longer dock in the old port but at great modern concrete wharves alongside, which neatly sums up Iráklion itself. Many of the old parts have been restored from the bottom up, but they're of no relevance to the dust and noise that characterizes much of the city today. In recent times, however, Iráklion's administrators have been giving belated attention to dealing with some of the image problems, and large tracts of the centre are currently undergoing landscaping and refurbishment schemes designed to present a less daunting prospect to the visitor.

Orientation, arrival and information

Virtually everything you're likely to want to see in Iráklion lies within the walled city, and even here the majority of the interest falls into a relatively small sector, the northeastern corner. The most vital thoroughfare, **25-Avgoústou**, links the harbour with the commercial city centre. At the bottom it is lined with shipping and travel agencies and rental outlets, but as you climb these give way to banks, restaurants and stores. **Platía Venizélou** (or Fountain Square), off to the right, is crowded with cafés and restaurants; behind Venizélou is **El Greco Park**, with the OTE office and more bars, while on the opposite side of 25-Avgoústou are some of the more interesting of Iráklion's older buildings. Further up 25-Avgoústou, **Kalokerinoú** leads down to Khaniá Gate and westwards out of the city; straight ahead, **Odhós 1821** is a major shopping street, and adjacent 1866 is given over to the animated **market**. To the left,

The telephone code for Iráklion is ☎081

Dhikeosínis, heads for **Platía Eleftherías**, paralleled by the touristy pedestrian alley, Dhedhálou, the direct link between the two squares. The newly revamped Eleftherías is very much the traditional centre of the city, both for traffic, which swirls around it constantly, and for life in general; it is ringed by more expensive tourist cafés and restaurants and comes alive in the evening with crowds of strolling locals.

Points of arrival

Iráklion **airport** is right on the coast, 4km east of the city. The #1 bus leaves for Platía Eleftherías every few minutes from the car park in front of the terminal; buy your ticket (150dr) at the booth before boarding. There are also plenty of taxis outside (which you'll be forced to use when the buses stop at 10.30pm), and prices to major destinations are posted – it's about 1000dr to the centre of town.

There are three main **bus stations** and a small terminus. Services along the coastal highway to or from the **east** (Mália, Áyios Nikólaos, Sitía and so on) use the terminal just off the main road between the ferry dock and the Venetian harbour; the #2 local bus to Knossós runs from the city bus stop, adjacent to the east bus station. Main road services **west** (Réthymnon and Khaniá) leave from a terminal right next to the east bus station on the other side of the road. Buses for the **southwest** (Festós, Mátala or Ayía Galíni) and along the inland roads west (Tílissos, Anóyia) operate out of a terminal just outside Khaniá Gate, a very long walk from the centre along Kalokerinoú (or jump on any bus heading down this street). The **southeast** (basically Ierápetra and points en route) is served by a small terminus just outside the walls in Platía Kýprou at the end of Odhós Evans on Trikoúpi.

From the wharves where the **ferries** dock, the city rises directly ahead in steep tiers. If you're heading for the centre, for the archeological museum or the tourist office, cut straight up the stepped alleys behind the bus station onto Dhoúkos Bofór and to Platía Eleftherías; this will take about fifteen minutes. For accommodation though, and to get a better idea of the layout of Iráklion's main attractions, it's simplest to follow the main roads by a rather more roundabout route. Head west along the coast, past the major east-bound bus station and on by the Venetian harbour before cutting up towards the centre on 25-Avgoústou.

Information

Iráklion's **tourist office** (Mon–Fri 8am–2.30pm; ☎228 203, fax 226 020) is just below Platía Eleftherías, opposite the archeological museum at Zanthoudhídhou 1. The **tourist police** – more helpful than most – are on Dhikeosínis, halfway between Platía Eleftherías and the market.

Accommodation

Finding a **room** can be difficult in season. The best place to look for inexpensive rooms is in the area around Platía Venizélou, along Khandhákos and towards the harbour to the west of 25-Avgoústou. Other concentrations of affordable places are around El Greco park and in the streets above the Venetian harbour. Better hotels mostly lie closer to Platía Eleftherías, to the south of Platía Venizélou and near the east- and west-bound bus stations. The dusty park between the main bus station and the harbour is often crowded with the sleeping bags of those who failed to find, or couldn't afford, a room; if you're really hard up, crashing here is a possibility, but a pleasant environment it is not.

The **youth hostel** at Výronos 5 (☎286 281; ①), which has operated since 1963, is family run and very friendly and helpful, with plenty of space and up to fifty beds on the roof if you fancy sleeping out under the stars. In addition to dormitories, family and double rooms are also available; there are hot showers, breakfast (400dr) and

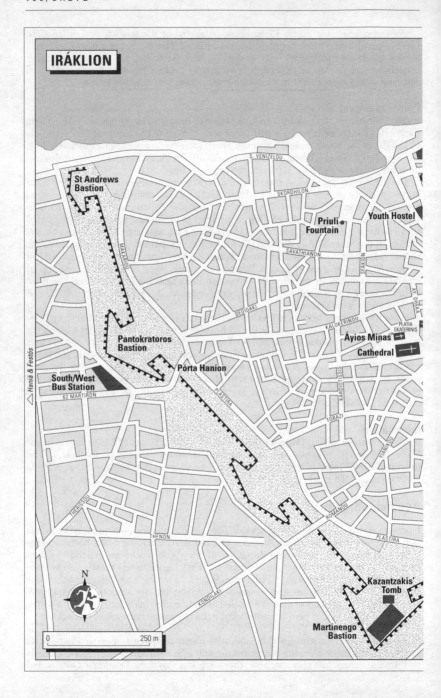

IRÁKLION

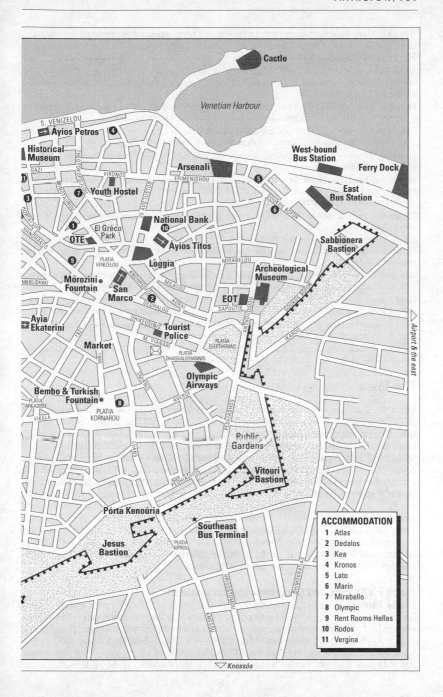

Castle

Venetian Harbour

S. VENIZELOU

Áyios Petros **4**

Historical
Museum

GAZI

West-bound
Bus Station

Ferry Dock

VIRONOS

Arsenáli

EPIMENIDHOU

5

East
Bus Station

3

Youth Hostel **7**

DOUKOS BOFOR

6

El Gréco
Park

National Bank

10

Sabbionera
Bastion

OTE **1**

Áyios Títos

9

PLATIA
VENIZELOU

MIRABELOU

Loggia

Môrozini
Fountain

San
Marco

MILATOU

KORAI

Archeological
Museum

Ayía
Ekaterini

DHIKEOSINIS

DHEDHALOU

2

EOT

SAPOUTIE

ANTHOULIDHOU

DOUKOS BOFOR

IKAROU

Airport & the east

Market

M. YIANARI

Tourist
Police

PLATIA
DHASKALOYIANNIS

PLATIA
ELEFTHERIAS

Bembo & Turkish
Fountain

PLATIA
ARKADIOU

8

AVEROF

Olympic
Airways

PEDHIADHOS

VIKELA

PLATIA
KORNAROU

EVANS

Public
Gardens

Vitouri
Bastion

PEDHIADHOS

Pórta Kenoúria

PLATIA
KIPROU

Southeast
Bus Terminal

Jesus
Bastion

DHIMOKRATIAS

KNOSSOU

MONOFATSIOU

ACCOMMODATION

1 Atlas
2 Dedalos
3 Kea
4 Kronos
5 Lato
6 Marin
7 Mirabello
8 Olympic
9 Rent Rooms Hellas
10 Rodos
11 Vergina

Knossós

TV. There are no **campsites** near to Iráklion. The nearest sites are both found to the east of the city – *Creta Camping* at Goúves (16km), and *Caravan Camping* at Hersonisos (28km).

Atlas, Kandanoléon 11 (☎288 989). A rather run-down old pension in a convenient but noisy alley between Platía Venizélou and El Greco park. There's a pleasant roof garden, and freshly squeezed orange juice for breakfast. ②.

Dedalos, Dhedhálou 15 (☎244 812, fax 224 391). Very centrally placed on the pedestrianized alley between Venizélou and Eleftherías. Decent balcony rooms with private bath. ③.

Lato, Epomenídhou 15 (☎228 103, fax 240 350). Stylish and luxurious hotel where the air-conditioned rooms have mini-bar, TV and sea-view balcony. Good value for the price. ⑥.

Kronos, Agaráthou 2, west of 25-Avgoústou (☎282 240, fax 285 853). Pleasant, modern hotel with sea view and baths in all rooms. ③.

Marin, Doukos Bofór 10, (☎288 582). Comfortable and good-value rooms with baths, overlooking the Venetian harbour; get a balcony room at the front for a great view. Very convenient for the bus stations and the archeological museum. ④.

Mirabello, Theotokopoúlou 20 (☎285 052, fax 225 852). Good-value, family-run place in a quiet street close to El Greco park. ③.

Olympic, Platía Kornárou (☎288 861, fax 222 512). Overlooking the busy platía and the famous Bembo and Turkish fountains. One of the many hotels built in the 1960s, but one of the few that has been refurbished. ⑤.

Rea, Kalimeráki 1 (☎223 638). A friendly, comfortable and clean hotel in quiet street. Some rooms with washbasin, others with own shower. One of the best of the cheaper hotels. ②.

Rent Rooms Hellas, Khándakos 24 (☎280 858, fax 284 442). Hostel-type place with simple doubles, and dormitory rooms favoured by younger travellers. Also has a roof garden and snack bar. ①.

Rent Rooms Vergina, Khortátson 32 (☎242 739). Basic but pleasant rooms (with washbasins) in quiet street around a courtyard with an enormous banana tree. ②.

Pension Rodos, Platía Áyios Títos (☎228 519). Homely no frills double and triple rooms place, on a picturesque square with a great breakfast bar next door. ②.

The Town

From the port, the town rises overhead, and you can cut up the stepped alleys for a direct approach to **Platía Eleftherías** (Liberty Square) and the **archeological museum**. The easiest way to the middle of things, though, is to head west along the coast road, past the main bus stations and the *arsenáli*, and then up 25-Avgoústou, which leads into **Platía Venizélou**. This is crowded with Iráklion's youth, patronizing outdoor cafés (marginally cheaper than those on Eleftherías), and with travellers who've arranged to meet in "Fountain Square". The recently restored **fountain** itself is not particularly spectacular at first glance, but on closer inspection is really a very beautiful work; it was built by Venetian governor Francesco Morosini in the seventeenth century, incorporating four lions which were some 300 years old even then. From the platía you can strike up Dhedhálou, a pedestrianized street full of tourist shops and restaurants, or continue on 25-Avgoústou to a major traffic junction. To the right, Kalokerinoú leads west out of the city, the **market** lies straight ahead, and Platía Eleftherías is a short walk to the left up Dhikeosínis.

Platía Eleftherías and the archeological museum

Platía Eleftherías is very much the traditional heart of the city: traffic swirls around it constantly, and in the evening strolling hordes jam its expensive cafés and restaurants. Most of Iráklion's more expensive shops are in the streets leading off the platía.

The **Archeological Museum** (Mon 12.30–6pm, Tues–Sun 8am–6pm; 1500dr, Sun free) is nearby, directly opposite the EOT office. Almost every important prehistoric and Minoan find on Crete is included in this fabulous, if bewilderingly large, collection. The museum tends to be crowded, especially when a guided tour stampedes through, but it's worth taking time over. You can't hope to see everything, nor can we attempt to describe it all (several good museum guides are sold here; the best probably being the glossy one by J.A. Sakellarakis) but highlights include the **town mosaics** in Room 2 (galleries are arranged basically in chronological order), the famous **inscribed disc** from Festós in Room 3 (itself the subject of several books), most of Room 4, especially the magnificent bull's head **rhyton** (drinking vessel), the **jewellery** in Room 6 (and everywhere) and the engraved **black vases** in Room 7. Save some of your time and energy for upstairs, where the **Hall of the Frescoes**, with intricately reconstructed fragments of the wall paintings from Knossós and other sites, is especially wonderful.

Walls and fortifications

The massive **Venetian walls**, in places up to fifteen metres thick, are the most obvious evidence of Iráklion's later history. Though their fabric is incredibly well preserved, access is virtually nonexistent. It is possible, just, to walk along them from St Anthony's bastion over the sea in the west, as far as the tomb of Nikos Kazantzakis, Cretan author of *Zorba the Greek*, whose epitaph reads: "I believe in nothing, I hope for nothing, I am free." At weekends, Iraklians gather here to pay their respects and enjoy a free view of the soccer matches played by the island's first-division team, OFI Crete, in the stadium below. If the walls seem altogether too much effort, the **port fortifications** are very much easier to see. Stroll out along the jetty (crowded with courting couples after dark) and you can get inside the sixteenth-century **castle** (Mon–Sat 8am–6pm, Sun 10am–3pm; 400dr) at the harbour entrance, emblazoned with the Venetian Lion of St Mark. Standing atop this, you can begin to understand how Iráklion (or Candia as it was known until the seventeenth century) withstood a 22-year siege before finally falling to the Ottomans. On the landward side of the port, the Venetian **arsenali** can also be seen, their arches rather lost amid the concrete road system all around.

Churches, icons and the Historical Museum

From the harbour, 25-Avgoústou will take you up past most of the rest of what's interesting. The **church of Áyios Títos**, on the left as you approach Platía Venizélou, borders a pleasant little platía. It looks magnificent principally because, like most of the churches here, it was adapted by the Turks as a mosque and only reconsecrated in 1925; consequently it has been renovated on numerous occasions. On the top side of this platía, abutting 25-Avgoústou, is the Venetian **City Hall** with its famous loggia, again almost entirely rebuilt. Just above this, facing Platía Venizélou, is the **church of San Marco**, its steps usually crowded with the overflow of people milling around in the platía. Neither of these last two buildings has found a permanent role in its refurbished state, but both are generally open to house some kind of exhibition or craft show.

Slightly away from the obvious city-centre circuit, but still within the bounds of the walls, there are a couple of lesser museums worth seeing if you have the time. First of these is the excellent collection of **icons** in the **church of Ayía Ekateríni** (Mon–Sat 10am–1pm, Tues, Thurs & Fri also 4–6pm; 500dr), an ancient building just below the undistinguished cathedral, off Kalokerinoú. The finest here are six large scenes by Mikhalis Damaskinos (a near-contemporary of El Greco) who fused Byzantine and Renaissance influences. Supposedly both Damaskinos and El Greco studied at Ayía Ekateríni in the sixteenth century, when it functioned as a sort of monastic art school.

The **Historical Museum** (Mon–Sat 9am–2pm; 500dr) is some way from here, down near the waterfront opposite the stark *Xenia* hotel. Its display of folk costumes and jumble of local memorabilia includes the reconstructed studies of both Nikos Kazantzakis and Emanuel Tsouderos (Cretan statesman and Greek prime minister). There's enough variety to satisfy just about anyone, including the only El Greco painting on Crete, *View of Mount Sinai and the Monastery of St Catherine*.

The beaches

Iráklion's **beaches** are some way out, whether east or west of town. In either direction they're easily accessible by public bus: #6 west from the stop outside the *Astoria* hotel in Platía Eleftherías; #7 east from the stop opposite this, under the trees in the centre of the platía.

Almyrós (or Amoudhári) to the west has been subjected to a degree of development, taking in a campsite, several medium-size hotels and one giant one (the *Zeus Beach*, in the shadow of the power station at the far end), which makes the beach hard to get to without walking through or past something built up.

Amnissós, to the east, is the better choice, with several tavernas and the added amusement of planes swooping in immediately overhead to land. This is where most locals go on their afternoons off; the furthest of the beaches is the best, although new hotels are encroaching here, too. Little remains here to indicate the once-flourishing port of Knossós aside from a rather dull, fenced-in dig. If you're seriously into antiquities, however, you'll find a more rewarding site in the small villa, known as **Nírou Kháni** (Tues–Sun 8.30am–3pm) at **Kháni Kokkíni**, the first of the full-blown resort developments east of Iráklion.

Eating

Big city as it is, Iráklion disappoints when it comes to eating. The cafés and tavernas of platías **Venizélou** and **Eleftherías** are essential places to sit and watch the world pass, but their food is expensive and mediocre. One striking exception is *Bougátsa Kirkor*, by the Morosini fountain in Venizélou, where you can sample authentic *bougátsa*; alternatively, try a plate of *loukoumádhes*, available from a number of cafés at the top of Dhikeosínis. The cafés and tavernas on **Dhedhálou**, the pedestrian alley linking the two main platías, are very run of the mill, persistent waiters enticing you in with faded photographs of what appears to be food.

A more atmospheric option is to head for the little alley, **Fotíou Theodhosáki**, which runs through from the market to Odhós Evans. It is entirely lined with the tables of rival taverna owners, certainly authentic and catering for market traders and their customers as well as tourists. Compared with some, they often look a little grimy, but they are by no means cheap, which can come as a surprise. Nearby, at the corner of Evans and Yiánari, is the long-established *Ionia* taverna, which is the sort of place to come to if you are in need of a substantial, no-nonsense feed, with a good range of Greek dishes.

A relaxed lunchtime venue in the **centre** of town is *Geroplantos* with tables on the leafy Platía Áyios Titos beside the church of the same name. Across from here is a stunning new bar *Pagopoleion* (Ice Factory), good for breakfast and snacks. It's the creation of photographic artist Chrissy Martiros, who has preserved a strident inscription on one wall, left by the Nazi occupiers who used local labour to run what was then Iráklion's only ice factory. Still near the centre, just off Eleftherías at **Platía Dhaskaloyiánnis** (where the post office is), are some inexpensive and unexceptional tavernas; the platía is however a pleasant and relaxing venue, if not for a meal then to sit at one of its cafés. Nearer Venizélou, try exploring some of the back streets to the east, off Dhedhálou and behind the loggia. The *Taverna Giovanni*, on the alley Korai parallel to Dhedhálou, is one of the better tavernas in Iráklion: a friendly lively place with a varied menu that uses fresh, good quality ingredients but with reasonable prices;

it also caters for vegetarians. Should you have a craving for non-Greek food, there is **Italian** at the pricey *Loukoulos* and **Chinese** at the *New China Restaurant*, both with leafy courtyards and both in the same street as the *Taverna Giovanni*. **Mexican** tacos and beers are on offer at *El Azteca*, Psaromilíngon 32, west of Khándhakos – a lively bar with similar establishments nearby.

The **waterfront** is dotted with fish tavernas with little to recommend them. Instead, walk across the road to *Ippokambus*, which specializes in mezédhes at moderate prices. It is deservedly popular with locals and is often crowded late into the evening: you may have to wait in line or turn up earlier than the Greeks eat. Even if you see no space it is worth asking as the owner may suddenly disappear inside the taverna and emerge with yet another table to carry further down the pavement.

For **snacks** and **takeaways**, there's a whole group of *souvláki* stalls clustering around 25-Avgoústou at the entrance to El Greco park, which is handy if you need somewhere to sit and eat. For cheese or spinach pies and other pastries, sweet or savoury, there are no shortage of zakharoplastía, such as the *Samaria* next to the Harley Davidson shop across from the park, and a couple of places at the park's southwest corner. If you want to buy your own food, the **market** on Odhós 1866 is the place to go; it's an attraction in itself, which you should see even if you don't plan to buy anything.

Drinking, nightlife and entertainment

Iráklion is a bit of a damp squib as far as **nightlife** goes, certainly when compared with many other towns on the island. If you're determined, however, there are a few city-centre possibilities, and plenty of options if all you want to do is sit and **drink**. In addition, there are a number of **cinemas** scattered about: check the posters on the boards by the tourist police office.

Bars

Bars tend to fan out into the streets around Khándhakos; among a number of new-style places, *Jasmin* is tucked in an alley mid-way down Khándhakos, and serves a variety of teas (including the Cretan *dhíktamo*) with easy jazz and rock as background music. At the beginning of Khándhakos is *Tasso's*, a popular hang-out for young hostellers, lively at night and with good breakfasts to help you recover in the morning; *Odysseia* Khándhakos 63); *El Azteca* (Psaromilíngon 32, west of Khándhakos), a Mexican bar serving tacos; *Utopia*, also on Khándhakos; and the nearby *Bonsai*.

The most animated place is a platía behind Dhedhálou (up from the *Giovanni*), where there are several trendy bars (including *Flash* and *Notos*) with outdoor tables, which are popular with students in term time. Enjoy a game of backgammon here during the day or early evening; later it can get extremely lively with many distractions. In and around **Platía Venizélou**, there are many bars, again some are very fashionable, with *De Facto* being one of the most popular. This is one of the new breed of kafenío emerging in Iráklion, attracting younger people: the drinks are **cocktails** rather than *raki*, the music is Western or modern Greek and there are prices to match. Another is the *Idaean Andron*, on Perdhikári around the corner from the *Selena* hotel, which has a good atmosphere, and there are more along Kandanoléon, off El Greco park.

Iráklion looks a great deal better than you'd expect from above, and there are fancier **rooftop places** above most of the restaurants in Platía Eleftherías, the *Cafe-Bar Dore* for example. This serves food as well, and while it's not exactly the sort of place to wear cut-offs and T-shirt, it's no more expensive than the restaurants on the platía below. Many hotels around the city have rooftop bars which welcome non-residents; those just above the bus stations and harbour, such as the *Alaira*, have particularly stunning views.

Clubs and discos

For **discos** proper, there is a large selection, even if they are all playing "techno" at the moment, interspersed with Greek music (not the Greek music you get for tourists). *Trapeza* is the most popular, down towards the harbour at the bottom of Doukos Bofor, below the archeological museum. *Makao* also has a following and is on the opposite side of the street to *Trapeza*, or try *Genesis* next door. Another cluster of nightclubs can be found on Ikárou, about a twenty-minute walk away. Retrace your steps towards the archeological museum, but before emerging onto Platía Eleftherías turn left downhill and follow the main road, Ikárou. Here you'll find the *Minoica*, the *Korus Club* and the *Athina*, all playing similar music and popular with young Iraklions.

Listings

Airlines Olympic, Platía Eleftherías (☎229 191), is the only airline with a permanent office in Iráklion. Charter airlines flying in to Iráklion mostly use local travel agents as their representatives.

Airport For airport information call ☎245 644. Bus #1 runs from Platía Eleftherías to the airport every few minutes.

Banks The main branches are on 25-Avgoústou, many of which have 24hr cash machines (not always working); there's also a VISA machine at Ergo Bank on Dhikeosínis.

Car and bike rental 25-Avgoústou is lined with rental companies, but you'll find cheaper rates on the backstreets; it's always worth asking for discounts. Good places to start include: Blue Sea, Kosma Zotou 7, near the bottom of 25-Avgoústou (☎241 097) for bikes; Eurocreta, Sapotie 2 (☎226 700) near the archeological museum for cars; Ritz in the *Hotel Rea*, Kalimeráki 1 (☎223 638) for cars; and Sun Rise, 25-Avgoústou 46 (☎221 609), for cars and bikes.

Ferry tickets Available from Minoan Lines (25-Avgoústou 78; ☎229 646), Kavi Club near the tourist office (☎221 166), or any of the travel agents listed below.

Hospital Most central is the hospital on Apollónion, southwest of Platía Kornárou, between Albér and Moussoúrou.

Laundry Washsalon, Khándhakos 18 (daily 9am–7pm).

Left luggage Offices in the east-bound and southwest bus stations (daily 6am–8pm; 200dr per bag per day), as well as commercial agencies at 25-Avgoústou (daily 7am–11pm; 450dr per bag per day) and Khándhakos 18 (open 24hrs; large locker 400dr per day). You can also leave bags at the youth hostel (even if you don't stay there) for 200–300dr per bag per day. If you want to leave your bag while you go off on a bike for a day or two, the rental company should be prepared to store it.

Newspapers and books For English-language newspapers and novels, as well as local guides and maps, Dhedhálou is the best bet. Planet International Bookstore behind Platía Venizélou at the corner of Khándhakos and Kydhonías, has a huge stock of English-language titles.

Pharmacies Plentiful on the main shopping streets – at least one is open 24hr on a rota basis: the others will have a sign on the door indicating which it is.

Post office Main office in Platía Dhaskaloyiánnis, off Eleftherías (Mon–Fri 7.30am–8pm). There's also a temporary office (a van) at the entrance to El Greco Park (daily 7.30am–7pm), handy for changing money.

Taxis Major taxi ranks in Platía Eleftherías and El Greco Park, or call ☎210 102 or 210 168. Prices displayed on boards at ranks.

Telephones The OTE head office is on the west side of El Greco Park; it's an efficient 24hr service, though expect long waits.

Travel agencies Budget operators and student specialists include the extremely helpful Blavakis Travel, Platía Kallérgon 8, just off 25-Avgoústou by the entrance to El Greco Park (☎282 541) and Prince Travel, 25-Avgoústou 30 (☎282 706). For excursions around the island, villa rentals and so on, the bigger operators are probably easier: Irman Travel, Dhedhálou 26 (☎242 527) or Creta Travel Bureau, 20–22 Epimenídhou (☎243 811). The latter is also the local American Express agent.

Knossós

KNOSSÓS, the largest of the **Minoan palaces**, reached its cultural peak more than 3000 years ago, though a town of some importance persisted here well into the Roman era. It lies on a low, largely man-made hill some 5km southeast of Iráklion; the surrounding hillsides are rich in lesser remains spanning 25 centuries, starting at the beginning of the second millennium BC.

Barely a hundred years ago the palace existed only in mythology. Knossós was the court of the legendary King Minos, whose wife Pasiphae bore the Minotaur, half-bull, half-man. Here the labyrinth was constructed by Daedalus to contain the monster, and youths were brought from Athens as human sacrifice until Theseus arrived to slay the beast, and with Ariadne's help, escape its lair. The discovery of the palace, and the interplay of these legends with fact, is among the most amazing tales of modern archeology. Heinrich Schliemann, the excavator of Troy, suspected that a major Minoan palace lay under the various tumuli here, but was denied the necessary permission to dig by the local Ottoman authorities at the end of the last century. It was left for Sir Arthur Evans, whose name is indelibly associated with Knossós, to excavate the site, from 1900 onwards.

The #2 local **bus** sets off every ten minutes from the Iráklion's city bus stop (adjacent to the east bus station), runs up 25-Avgoústou (with a stop by Platía Venizélou) and

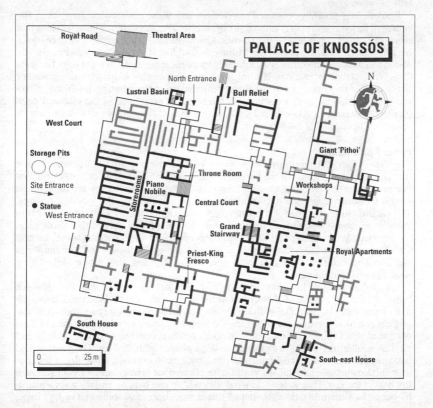

out of town on Odhós 1821 and Evans. At Knossós, outside the fenced site, is the *cara-vanserai* where ancient wayfarers would rest and water their animals. Head out onto the road and you'll find no lack of watering holes for modern travellers either – a string of rather pricey tavernas and tacky souvenir stands. There are several **rooms** for rent here, and if you're really into Minoan culture, there's a lot to be said for staying out this way to get an early start. Be warned that it's expensive and unashamedly commercial.

The Site

Daily: April–Sept 8am–6pm; Oct–March 8.30am–3pm; 1500dr.

As soon as you enter the **Palace of Knossós** through the West Court, the ancient ceremonial entrance, it is clear how the legends of the labyrinth grew up around it. Even with a detailed plan, it's almost impossible to find your way around the site with any success. The best advice is not to try; wander around for long enough and you'll eventually stumble upon everything. If you're worried about missing the highlights, you can always tag along with one of the constant guided tours for a while, catching the patter and then backtracking to absorb the detail when the crowd has moved on. You won't get the place to yourself, whenever you come, but exploring on your own does give you the opportunity to appreciate individual parts of the palace in the brief lulls between groups.

Knossós was liberally "restored" by Evans, and these restorations have been the source of furious controversy among archeologists ever since. It has become clear that much of Evans's upper level – the so-called *piano nobile* – is pure conjecture. Even so, his guess as to what the palace might have looked like is certainly as good as anyone else's, and it makes the other sites infinitely more meaningful if you have seen Knossós first. Without the restorations, it would be almost impossible to imagine the grandeur of the multi-storey palace or to see the ceremonial stairways, strange, top-heavy pillars and gaily painted walls that distinguish the site. For some idea of the size and complexity of the palace in its original state, take a look at the cutaway drawings (wholly imaginary but probably not too far off) on sale outside.

Royal Apartments

The superb **Royal Apartments** around the central staircase are not guesswork, and they are plainly the finest of the rooms at Knossós. Unfortunately, extensive renovations are currently taking place and these mean that the apartments are likely to be closed for some time, although glimpses can be had through the wooden railings. The **Grand Stairway** itself is a masterpiece of design: not only a fitting approach to these sumptuously appointed chambers, but also an integral part of the whole plan, its large well bringing light into the lower storeys. Light wells such as these, usually with a courtyard at the bottom, are a constant feature of Knossós and a reminder of just how important creature comforts were to the Minoans, and of how skilled they were at providing them.

For evidence of this luxurious lifestyle you need look no further than the **Queen's Suite**, off the grand **Hall of the Colonnades** at the bottom of the staircase. Here, the main living room is decorated with the celebrated **dolphin fresco** (a reproduction; the original is now in the Iráklion archeological museum) and with running friezes of flowers and abstract spirals. On two sides, it opens out onto courtyards that let in light and air; the smaller one would probably have been planted with flowers. The room would have been scattered with cushions and hung with plush curtains, while doors and further curtains between the pillars would have allowed for privacy, and for cool shade in the heat of the day. This, at least, is what they'd have you believe, and it's a very plausible scenario. Remember, though, that all this is speculation and some of it is pure hype;

the dolphin fresco, for example, was found in the courtyard, not the room itself, and would have been viewed from inside as a sort of *trompe l'oeil*, like looking through a glass-bottomed boat. Whatever the truth, this is an impressive example of Minoan architecture, the more so when you follow the dark passage around to the queen's **bathroom**. Here is a clay tub, protected behind a low wall (and again probably screened by curtains when in use), and the famous "flushing" toilet (a hole in the ground with drains to take the waste away – one flushed it by throwing a bucket of water down).

The much-pored over **drainage system** was a series of interconnecting terracotta pipes running underneath most of the palace. Guides to the site never fail to point these out as evidence of the advanced state of Minoan civilization, and they are indeed quite an achievement, in particular the system of baffles and overflows to slow down the runoff and avoid any danger of flooding. Just how much running water there would have been, however, is another matter; the water supply was, and is, at the bottom of the hill, and even the combined efforts of rainwater catchment and hauling water up to the palace can hardly have been sufficient to supply the needs of more than a small elite.

Going up the Grand Stairway to the floor above the queen's domain, you come to a set of rooms generally regarded as the **King's Quarters**. These are chambers in a considerably sterner vein; the staircase opens into a grandiose reception chamber known as the **Hall of the Royal Guard**, its walls decorated in repeated shield patterns. Immediately off here is the **Hall of the Double Axes**, believed to be have been the ruler's personal chamber, a double room that would allow for privacy in one portion while audiences were held in the more public section. Its name comes from the double-axe symbol carved into every block of masonry.

The Throne Room and the rest of the palace

Continuing to the top of the Grand Stairway, you emerge onto the broad **Central Court**. Open now, this would once have been enclosed by the walls of the buildings all around. On the far side, in the northwestern corner of the courtyard, is the entrance to another of Knossós's most atmospheric survivals, the **Throne Room**. Here, a worn stone throne sits against the wall of a surprisingly small chamber; along the walls around it are ranged stone benches, and behind there's a reconstructed fresco of two griffins. In all probability this was the seat of a priestess rather than a ruler (there's nothing like it in any other Minoan palace), but it may just have been an innovation wrought by the Mycenaeans, since it seems that this room dates only from the final period of Knossós's occupation. The Throne Room is now closed off with a wooden gate, but you can lean over this for a good view, and in the antechamber there's a wooden copy of the throne on which everyone perches to have their picture taken.

The rest you'll see as you wander, contemplating the legends of the place which blur with reality. Try not to miss the giant *pithoi* in the northeast quadrant of the site, an area known as the palace workshops; the storage chambers which you see from behind the Throne Room and the reproduction frescoes in the reconstructed room above it; the fresco of the Priest-King looking down on the south side of the central court, and the relief of a charging bull on its north side. This last would have greeted you if you entered the palace through its north door; you can see evidence here of some kind of gatehouse and a lustral bath, a sunken area perhaps used for ceremonial bathing and purification. Just outside this gate is the **theatral area**, an open space a little like a stepped amphitheatre, which may have been used for ritual performances or dances. From here the **Royal Road**, claimed as the oldest road in Europe, sets out. At one time, this probably ran right across the island; nowadays it ends after about a hundred yards in a brick wall beneath the modern road. Circling back around the outside of the palace, you get more idea of its scale by looking up at it; on the south side are a couple of small reconstructed Minoan houses which are worth exploring.

Beyond Knossós

If you have transport, the drive beyond Knossós can be an attractive and enjoyable one, taking minor roads through much greener country, with vineyards draped across low hills and flourishing agricultural communities. If you want specific things to seek out, head first for **MYRTIÁ**, an attractive village with the small **Kazantzakis Museum** (Mon, Wed & Sat 9am–1pm & 4pm–8pm, Tues & Fri 9am–1pm; 500dr) in a house where the writer's parents once lived. **ARKHÁNES**, at the foot of Mount Ioúktas, is a much larger place that was also quite heavily populated in Minoan times. None of the three archeological sites here is open to the public, but one of them, **Anemospília**, has caused huge controversy since its excavation in the 1980s: many traditional views of the Minoans, particularly that of Minoan life as peaceful and idyllic, have had to be rethought in the light of the discovery of an apparent human sacrifice. An excellent new museum (daily 8.30am–2.30pm, closed Tues; free) displays finds from this and other excavations. From Arhánes you can also drive to the top of Mount Ioúktas to enjoy the panoramic views. At **VATHÝPETRO**, south of the mountain, is a **Minoan villa** (Mon–Sat 8.30am–2pm; free), which once controlled the rich farmland south of Arkhánes. Inside a remarkable collection of farming implements was found, and a wine press. Substantial amounts of the farm buildings remain, and it's still surrounded by a vineyard three thousand five hundred years later – making it probably the oldest in Europe.

Southwest from Iráklion: sites and beaches

If you take a **tour** from Iráklion (or one of the resorts), you'll probably visit the **Górtys**, **Festós** and **Ayía Triádha** sites in a day, with a lunchtime swim at **Mátala** thrown in. Doing it by public transport, you'll be forced into a rather more leisurely pace, but there's still no reason why you shouldn't get to all three and reach Mátala within the day; if necessary, it's easy enough to hitch the final stretch. **Bus services** to the Festós site are excellent, with some nine a day to and from Iráklion (fewer run on Sunday), five of which continue to or come from Mátala; there are also services direct to Ayía Galíni. If you're arriving in the afternoon, plan to visit Ayía Triádha first, as it closes early.

The route to Áyii Dhéka

The road from Iráklion towards Festós is a pretty good one by the standards of Cretan mountain roads, albeit rather dull. The country you're heading towards is the richest agricultural land on the island, and right from the start the villages en route are large and business-like. In the largest of them, Ayía Varvára, there's a great rock outcrop known as the **Omphalos** (Navel) of Crete, supposedly the very centre of the island.

Past here, you descend rapidly to the fertile fields of the Messará plain, where the road joins the main route across the south near the village of **ÁYII DHÉKA**. For religious Cretans Áyii Dhéka is something of a place of pilgrimage; its name, "The Ten Saints", refers to ten early Christians martyred here under the Romans. In a crypt below the modern church you can see the martyrs' tombs. It's an attractive village to wander around, with several places to eat and even some **rooms** along the main road.

Górtys

Daily 8.30am–3pm; 800dr.

Within easy walking distance of Áyii Dhéka, either through the fields or along the main road, sprawls the site of **Górtys**, ruined capital of the Roman province that included not

Harbour, Éyina

Drydock for kaïkia, Parikía

Church in Kástro, Síkinos

The clear waters of Delos

The Sanctuary of Dionysos, Delos

Stairpath to Khóra, Sérifos

Large storage jar, Malia palace, Crete

West beach, Paleokhóra, Crete

A windmill at Toploú Monastery, Crete

PETER WILSON

Venetian houses, Réthymnon, Crete

only Crete but also much of North Africa. Cutting across the fields will give you some idea of the scale of this city, at its zenith in approximately the third century AD; an enormous variety of other remains, including an impressive **theatre**, are strewn across your route. Even in Áyii Dhéka you'll see Roman pillars and statues lying around in people's yards or propping up their walls.

There had been a settlement here from the earliest times, but the extant ruins date almost entirely from the Roman era. Only now is the site being systematically excavated, by the Italian School. At the main entrance to the fenced site, alongside the road, are the ruins of the still impressive **basilica of Áyios Títos**; the eponymous saint converted the island to Christianity and was its first bishop. Beyond this is the **Odeion** which houses the most important discovery on the site, the **Law Code**. These great inscribed blocks of stone were incorporated by the Romans from a much earlier stage of the city's development; they're written in an obscure early Greek-Cretan dialect, and in a style known as *boustrophedon* (ox-ploughed), with the lines reading alternately in opposite directions like the furrows of a ploughed field. At ten metres by three metres, this is reputedly the largest Greek inscription ever found. The laws set forth reflect a strictly hierarchical society: five witnesses were needed to convict a free man of a crime, only one for a slave; raping a free man or woman carried a fine of a hundred staters, violating a serf only five. A small **museum** in a loggia (also within the fenced area) holds a number of large and finely worked sculptures found at Górtys, more evidence of the city's importance.

Míres

Some 20km west of Górtys, **MÍRES** is an important market and focal point of transport for the Messará plain: if you're switching buses to get from the beaches on the south coast to the archeological sites or the west, this is where you'll do it. There are good facilities including a **bank**, a few **restaurants** and plenty of **rooms**, though there's no particular reason to stay unless you are waiting for a bus or looking for work (it's one of the better places for agricultural jobs). Heading straight for Festós, there's usually no need to stop.

Festós (Phaestos)

Daily 8am–6pm; 1200dr.

The **Palace of Festós** was excavated by the Italian, Federico Halbherr (also responsible for the early work at Górtys), at almost exactly the same time as Evans was working at Knossós. The style of the excavations, however, could hardly have been more different. Here, to the approval of most traditional archeologists, reconstruction was kept to an absolute minimum – it's all bare foundations, and walls which rise at most a metre above ground level. This means that despite a magnificent setting overlooking the plain of Messará, the palace at Festós is not as immediately arresting as those at Knossós or Mália. Much of the site is fenced off and, except in the huge central court, it's almost impossible to get any sense of the place as it was; the plan is almost as complex as at Knossós, with none of the reconstruction to bolster the imagination.

It's interesting to speculate why the palace was built halfway up a hill rather than on the plain below – certainly not for defence, for this is in no way a good defensive position. Psychological superiority over the peasants or reasons of health are both possible, but it seems quite likely that it was simply the magnificent view that finally swayed the decision. The site looks over Psilorítis to the north and the huge plain, with the Lasíthi mountains beyond it, to the east. Towards the top of Psilorítis you should be able to make out a small black smudge: the entrance to the Kamáres cave (see p.187).

On the ground closer at hand, you can hardly fail to notice the strong similarities between Festós and the other palaces: the same huge rows of storage jars, the great courtyard with

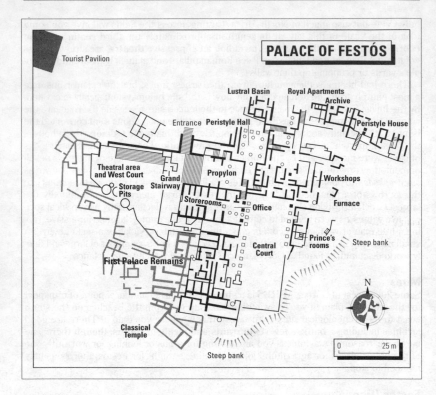

its monumental stairway, and the theatral area. Unique to Festós, however, is the third court-yard, in the middle of which are the remains of a **furnace** used for metalworking. Indeed, this eastern corner of the palace seems to have been home to a number of craftsmen, includ-ing potters and carpenters. Oddly enough, Festós was much less ornately decorated than Knossós; there is no evidence, for example, of any of the dramatic Minoan wall paintings.

The **Tourist Pavilion** at Festós serves drinks and food and also has a few beds, though these are very rarely available (thanks to advance bookings) and expensive when they are. The nearby village of **ÁYIOS IOÁNNIS**, along the road towards Mátala, has a few more **rooms**, including some at *Taverna Ayios Ioannis* (☎0892/42 006) which is also a good place to eat.

Ayía Triádha

Daily 8.30am–3pm; 500dr.

Some of the finest artworks in the museum at Iráklion came from **Ayía Triádha**, about a 45-minute walk (or a short drive) from Festós. No one is quite sure what this site is, but the most common theory has it as some kind of royal summer villa. It's smaller than the palaces, but if anything even more lavishly appointed and beautifully situated. In any event, it's an attractive place to visit, far less crowded than Festós, with a wealth of interesting little details. Look out in particular for the row of **stores** in front of what was apparently a marketplace, and for the remains of the **paved road** that once led down to the Gulf of Messará. The sea itself looks invitingly close, separated from the base of the hill only by Timbáki airfield (mainly used for motor racing these days), but if you try to drive down there, it's almost impossible to find your way around the unmarked dust tracks. There's a fourteenth-century **church** at the site, worth visiting in its own right for the remains of ancient frescoes.

Mátala

MÁTALA has by far the best-known **beach** in Iráklion province, widely promoted and included in tours mainly because of the famous **caves** cut into the cliffs above its beautiful sands. These are believed to be ancient tombs first used by Romans or early Christians, but more recently inhabited by a sizeable hippie community. You'll still meet people who will assure you that this is *the* travellers' beach on Crete. Not any more it isn't. Today, the town is full of package tourists and tries hard to present a respectable image; the cliffs are now cleared and locked up every evening.

A few people still manage to evade the security, or sleep on the beach or in the adjacent campsite, but on the whole the place has changed entirely. The last ten years have seen the arrival of crowds and the development of hotels, discos and restaurants to service them; early afternoon, when the tour buses pull in for their swimming stop, sees the beach packed to overflowing. If you're prepared to accept Mátala for what it is – a resort of some size – you'll find the place more than bearable. The town beach is beautiful, and if the crowds get excessive, you can climb over the rocks in about twenty minutes (past more caves, many of which are inhabited through the summer) to another excellent stretch of sand, known locally as "Red Beach". In the evening, when the trippers have gone, there are waterside bars and restaurants looking out over invariably spectacular sunsets.

The chief problems concern prices and crowds: rooms are both expensive and oversubscribed, food is good but not cheap. If you want **accommodation**, try looking up the little street to the left as you enter town, just after the *Zafiria* hotel (☎0892/45 112; ④), where there are several rooms for rent, such as *Matala View* (☎0892/45 114; ②), and *Pension Nikos* (☎0892/42 375; ②). If these are full, then everywhere closer in is likely to be, too, so head back out on the main road, or try the **campsite**, *Camping of Matala* (☎0892/45 720), next to the beach above the car park; *Kommos Camping* (☎0892/45 596), is a nicer site, but a few kilometres out of Mátala and reached by heading back towards Pítsidia and turning left along a signed track. There are places to **eat and drink** all over the main part of town. Also impossible to miss are most other facilities, including stores, currency exchange, car and bike rental, travel agents, post office, and an OTE office in a temporary building in the car park behind the beach.

Around Mátala: Pitsídhia and Kalamáki

One way to enjoy a bit more peace is to stay at **PITSÍDHIA**, about 5km inland. This is already a well-used option, so it's not quite as cheap as you might expect, but there are plenty of rooms, lively places to eat and even music bars. If you decide to stay here, the beach at **KALAMÁKI** is an alternative to Mátala. Both beaches are approximately the same distance to walk, though there is a much better chance of a bus or a lift to Mátala. Kalamáki itself is beginning to develop somewhat, with a number of rooms and a couple of tavernas, but so far it's a messy and unattractive little place. The beach stretches for miles, surprisingly wild and windswept, lashed by sometimes dangerously rough surf. At the southern end (more easily reached by a path off the Pitsídhia–Mátala road) lies **Kómmos**, once a Minoan port serving Festós and now the site of a major archeological excavation. It's not yet open to the public, but you can peer into the fenced-off area to see what's been revealed so far, which is pretty impressive: dwellings, streets, hefty stonework and even the ship sheds where repairs on the Minoan fleet were carried out.

Iráklion's south coast

South of the Messará plain are two more beach resorts, Kalí Liménes and Léndas, with numerous other little beaches along the coast in between, but nothing spectacular. **Public transport** is very limited indeed; you'll almost always have to travel via Míres (see p.177). If you have your own transport, the roads in these parts are all passable, but most are very slow going; the Kófinas Hills, which divide the plain from the coast, are surprisingly precipitous.

Kalí Liménes

While Mátala itself was an important port under the Romans, the chief harbour for Górtys lay on the other side of Cape Líthinon at **KALÍ LIMÉNES**. Nowadays, this is once again a major port – for oil tankers. This has rather spoiled its chances of becoming a major resort, and there's no paved road or proper facilities. Some people like Kalí Liménes: the constant procession of tankers gives you something to look at, there are a number of places offering **rooms** – the best is the *Karavovrousi Beach* (☎0892/42 197; ②), a kilometre or so east of the village – the coastline is broken up by spectacular cliffs and, as long as there hasn't been a recent oil spill, the beaches are reasonably clean and totally empty. But (fortunately) not too many share this enthusiasm.

Léndas

LÉNDAS, further east along the coast, is far more popular, with a couple of buses daily from Iráklion and a partly justified reputation for being peaceful (sullied by considerable summer crowds). Many people who arrive think they've come to the wrong place, as at first sight the village looks filthy, the beach is small, rocky and dirty, and the rooms are frequently all booked. A number of visitors leave without ever correcting that initial impression, but the attraction of Léndas is not the village at all but on the other (west) side of the headland. Here, there's an enormous, excellent sandy beach, part of it usually taken over by nudists, and a number of taverna/bars overlooking it from the roadside. The beach is a couple of kilometres from Léndas, along a rough track; if you're walking, you can save time by cutting across the headland. A considerably more attractive prospect than staying in Léndas itself is **camping** on the beach to the west of the village, or with luck getting a **room** at one of the few beach tavernas – try *Tsarakis* (☎0892/95 378; ②) for sea-view rooms. After you've discovered the beach, even Léndas begins to look more welcoming, and at least it has most of the facilities you'll need, including a shop which will change money and numerous places to eat.

Once you've come to terms with the place, you can also explore some less good but quite deserted beaches eastwards, and the scrappy remains of **ancient Lebena** on a hilltop overlooking them. There was an important *Asclepieion* (temple of the god Asclepios) here around some now-diverted warm springs, but only the odd broken column and fragments of mosaic survive in a fenced-off area on the village's northern edge.

East of Iráklion: the package-tour coast

East of Iráklion, the startling pace of **tourist development** in Crete is all too plain to see. The merest hint of a beach is an excuse to build at least one hotel, and these are outnumbered by the concrete shells of resorts-to-be. It's hard to find a room in this monument to the package-tour industry, and expensive if you do.

Goúrnes and Goúves

As a general rule, the further you go, the better things get: when the road detours all too briefly inland, the real Crete of olive groves and stark mountains asserts itself. You certainly won't see much of it at **GOÚRNES**, where there used to be a US Air Force base, or at nearby Kato Goúves, where there's a **campsite**, *Camping Creta* (☎0897/41 400), which will be quiet unless and until the Greek Air Force move in next door as planned. From here, however, you can head inland to the old village of **GOÚVES**, a refreshing contrast, and just beyond to the **Skotinó Cave**, one of the largest and most spectacular on the island (about an hour's walk from the coast).

Not far beyond Goúrnes is the turning for the direct route up to the Lasíthi plateau, and shortly after that you roll into the first of the big resorts, Hersónisos (or, more correctly, Límin Khersoníssou; Khersónisos is the village in the hills just behind, also overrun by tourists).

Khersónissos (Límin Khersoníssou)

KHERSÓNISSOS was once the port that served the Minoan city of Knossós, and was more recently just a small fishing village; today it's the most popular of Crete's package resorts. If what you want is plenty of bars, tavernas, restaurants and Eurodisco nightlife then come here. The resort has numerous small patches of sand beach between rocky outcrops, but a shortage of places to stay in peak season.

Along the modern seafront, a solid line of restaurants and bars is broken only by the occasional souvenir shop: in their midst you'll find a small pyramidal Roman **fountain** with broken mosaics of fishing scenes, the only real relic of the ancient town of Chersonesos. Around the headland above the harbour and in odd places along the seafront, you can see remains of Roman harbour installations, mostly submerged.

Beach and clubs excepted, the distractions of Khersónissos comprise **Lykhnostatis** (daily 9.30am–2pm; 1000dr), an open-air "museum" of traditional Crete, on the coast on the eastern edge of the town; a small **aquarium** just off the main road at the west end of town, opposite the *Hard Rock Cafe* (daily 10am–9pm; 800dr); the watersports paradise *Star Water Park* (admission free, charges for individual sports) at the eastern end of the resort; and a few kilometres inland, the slides, cascades and whirlpools of the newly opened and immense *Aqua Splash Water Park* (daily 10am–7pm; 3700dr, discounted rates after 2.30pm).

A short distance inland are the three **hill villages** of Koutoulafári, Piskopianó and "old" Khersónisos, which all have a good selection of tavernas, and are worth searching out for accommodation.

Practicalities

Khersónissos is well provided with all the back-up **services** you need to make a holiday go smoothly. Banks, bike and car rental, post office and OTE are all on or just off the main drag, as are the taxi ranks. **Buses** in either direction leave every thirty minutes.

Finding somewhere to stay can be difficult in July and August. Much of the **accommodation** here is allocated to package-tour operators and what remains is not that cheap. To check for availability of accommodation generally, the quickest and best option is to enquire at one of the many travel agencies along the main street, or ask at the helpful **tourist office** – officially housed on Yiaboudháki, just off the main street towards the harbour, but at the time of writing temporarily evicted to a small kiosk beside the newsstands in front of the church at the western end of the main street. Reasonably priced central options include the *Nancy* on Ayía Paraskevís (☎0897/22 212; ④), and *Virginia* on

Mákhis Krítis (☎0897/22 466; ②), but be prepared for a fair amount of noise. There are two good **campsites**, one at the eastern end of town, *Caravan Camping* (☎0897/22 025 or 24 718) which also has several reed-roofed bungalows, and *Hersonissos Camping* (☎0897/22 902 or 23 792), just to the west of town. The youth hostel was recently closed, and there are no current plans for a replacement.

Despite the vast number of **eating places**, there are few in Khersónissos worth recommending, and the tavernas down on the harbour front should be avoided. One of the few Greek tavernas that stands out is *Kavouri* along Arkhéou Theátrou, but it is fairly expensive, so it's better to head out of town on the Piskopianó road where, near the junction to Koutoulafári, the friendly *Fengari* taverna serves good Greek food at a reasonable price. Sitting at your table overlooking the street below you can marvel at the steady trek of clubbers heading down the hill to the bars and nightclubs of Khersónisos. The hill villages have the greatest selection of tavernas, particularly Koutoulafári, where you can have a relaxed evening amongst the narrow streets and small platías.

Khersónissos is renowned for its **nightlife**, and there's no shortage of it. Most of the better bars and clubs are along the main road. Especially popular are *La Luna*, with up-to-date music, and the *Hard Rock Café*, which has live music. *Aria*, a large glass-fronted disco, is the biggest on Crete. Other popular haunts include *Legend*, and the beach bar-disco pub *Pirates*, both at the eastern end of town, and, towards the harbour, *Camelot*, *Blackout* and *New York*. If you fancy a quiet drink then you have come to the wrong resort, but you could try *Kahluai Beach Cocktail Bar* or *Haris Ouzo* and *Raki Place* (beneath the *Hotel Virginia*). There is an open-air **cinema** at the *Creta Maris* hotel.

Stalídha

STALÍDHA is a Cinderella town, sandwiched in between its two louder, brasher and some would say uglier sisters, Mália and Khersónissos, but is neither quiet or undeveloped. This rapidly expanding beach resort, with more than sixty tavernas and bars and a few discos, can offer the best of both worlds with a friendlier and more relaxed setting, a better beach (and usual array of water sports) and very easy access to its two livelier neighbours. The town essentially consists of a single, relatively traffic-free street which rings the seafront for more than two miles, before the apartment blocks briefly become fewer and further, until the mass development of Mália begins.

Finding a place to stay can be difficult as **accommodation** is almost entirely in studio and apartment blocks which are booked by package companies in high season. Out of season, however, you may well be able to negotiate a very reasonable price for a studio apartment complete with swimming pool; ask in the central travel agencies first, as they will know what is available, and expect to pay at least 8000dr for two. Finding somewhere to **eat** is less difficult as there are plenty of rather ordinary tavernas, the best and most authentic being *Maria's* and the *Hellas Taverna*, both at the western end of the resort.

Stalídha is completely overshadowed by its neighbours when it comes to **nightlife**, though you can dance at *Bells* disco, on the main coast road, or at *Rhythm*, on the beach; the *Sea Wolf Cocktail Bar* and *Akti Bar* are near each other along the beach.

Mália

Much of **MÁLIA** is taken up by the package industry, so in peak season finding a place to stay is not always easy. You're best off, especially if you want any sleep, trying one of the numerous **rooms** and **pensions** (③) signposted in the old town, such as the *Esperia* (☎0897/31 086; ②). Tracking back from here, along the main Iráklion road, there are a number of reasonably priced **pensions** on the left including the *Argo* (☎0897/31 636; ④), though these can be noisy. If you really want to be in the centre of things, try *Kostas* (☎0897/31 485; ④), a family-run pension incongruously located behind the mini golf at the end of the beach road. Otherwise, on arrival visit one of the travel companies along the main road – for example, Foreign Office (☎0897/31 217) – to enquire about accommodation availability. To the east of town, the new **youth hostel** (☎0897/31 555; ①) is extremely pleasant, but should be booked in advance in high season.

Eating in Mália is unlikely to be a problem as **restaurants** jostle for your custom at every step, especially along the beach road. None of these are particularly good, but that's the price of mass production. The best places are around Platía Ayíou Dhimitríou, a pleasant square beside the church in the centre of the old town. Try a meal at *Kalesma, Yiannis, Kalimera* or *Petros*, after an aperitif at the *Ouzeri Kapilla*, where they serve excellent local wine from the wood. There are a number of other welcoming tavernas and very pleasant bars, including the *Stone House* and *Temple*, lining, or just off, the platía.

The beach road comes into its own at night, when the profusion of **bars**, **discos** and **clubs** erupt into a pulsating cacophony. *Zoo* is a relatively new club, and once past midnight, one of the internal walls parts to reveal an even larger dance area. The club's newest attraction, its body piercing studio (the only one in Crete), opens at 2am. *Zig Zag, Takis* and *Highway* are the other really popular clubs in Mália. *Desire*, along the beach road, concentrates on rock and has good-quality live music some nights. Unfortunately, a good night's clubbing and dancing is frequently spoiled by groups of drunken youths pouring out of the bars. The situation has got so bad that tour operators have threatened to pull out of the resort if action isn't taken to deal with the hooligans.

The Palace of Mália

Daily 8.30am–3pm; 800dr, Sun free.

Much less imposing than either Knossós or Festós, the **Palace of Mália**, 2km east of Mália town, in some ways surpasses both. For a start, it's a great deal emptier and you can wander among the remains in relative peace. While no reconstruction has been attempted, the palace was never reoccupied after its second destruction, so the ground plan is virtually intact. It's a great deal easier to comprehend than Knossós and, if you've seen the reconstructions there, it's easy to envisage this seaside palace in its days of glory. There's a real feeling of an ancient civilization with a taste for the good life, basking on the rich agricultural plain between the Lasíthi mountains and the sea.

From this site came the famous **gold pendant** of two bees (which can be seen in the Iráklion museum or on any postcard stand), allegedly part of a horde that was plundered and whose other treasures can now be found in the British Museum in London. The beautiful leopard-head axe, also in the museum at Iráklion, was another of the treasures found here. At the site, look out for the strange indented stone in the central court, which probably held ritual offerings, for the remains of ceremonial stairways, and for the giant *pithoi* which stand like sentinels around the palace. To the south and west, digs are still going on as a large town comes slowly to light, and these will soon be viewable via an overhead walkway, under construction at the time of writing.

Any passing **bus** should stop at the site, or you could even rent a **bike** for a couple of hours as it's a pleasant, flat ride from Mália town. Leaving the archeological zone and turning right, you can follow the road down to a lovely stretch of clean and relatively peaceful beach, backed by fields, scrubland and a single makeshift taverna,

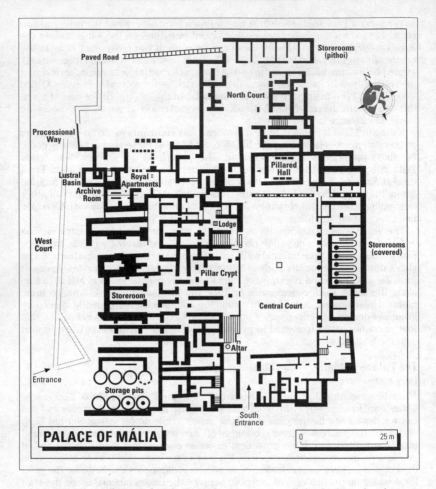

PALACE OF MÁLIA

Paved Road

North Court

Storerooms (pithoi)

Processional Way

Pillared Hall

Lustral Basin

Royal Apartments

Archive Room

Lodge

West Court

Storerooms (covered)

Pillar Crypt

Central Court

Storeroom

Altar

Entrance

Storage pits

South Entrance

0   25 m

which serves excellent fresh fish. From here you can walk back along the shore to Mália or take a bus (every thirty minutes in either direction) from the stop on the main road.

Sísi and Mílatos

Head **east** from the Palace of Mália, and it's not long before the road leaves the coast, climbing across the hills towards Áyios Nikólaos. If you want to escape the frenetic pace of all that has gone before, try continuing to **SÍSI** or **MÍLATOS**. These little shore villages are bypassed by the main road as it cuts inland, and are still very much in the early stages of the tourist industry, though both have several tavernas. Sísi, the more developed of the two, also has its first disco bar (*Minoa*), a large new holiday complex (*Kalimera Krita*) a couple of kilometres to the east, and even a post office – a sure sign of resort status. Accommodation in both is mainly in studios and apartments; it's best to ask in the travel agencies for details of availability. In Sísi there's also a small pension, *Elena* (②) just behind the harbour, and a **campsite** (☎0841/71 247), whilst in Mílatos, rooms can be found in the old village, 2km inland. The village beaches aren't great, but the resorts make for a refreshing change of pace, and there are some fine, deep aprons of sand in the rocky coves beyond the resort centres.

West of Iráklion: around Psilorítis

Most people heading west from Iráklion, speed straight out on the new **coastal highway**, nonstop to Réthymnon. If you're in a hurry this is not such a bad plan; the road is fast and spectacular, hacked into the sides of mountains which for the most part drop straight to the sea, though there are no more than a couple of places where you might consider stopping. By contrast, the old roads inland are agonizingly slow, but they do pass through a whole string of **attractive villages** beneath the heights of the Psilorítis range. From here you can set out to explore the **mountains** and even walk across them to emerge in villages with views of the south coast.

The coastal route towards Réthymnon

Leaving the city, the **new highway** runs behind a stretch of highly developed coast, where the hotels compete for shore space with a cement works and power station. As soon as you reach the mountains, though, all this is left behind and there's only the clash of rock and sea to contemplate. As you start to climb, look out for **Paleókastro**, beside a bridge which carries the road over a small cove; the castle is so weathered as to be almost invisible against the brownish face of the cliff.

Ayía Pelayía and Fódhele

Some 3km below the highway, as it rounds the first point, lies the resort of **AYÍA PELAYÍA**. It looks extremely attractive from above but, once there, you're likely to find the narrow, taverna-lined beach packed to full capacity; this is not somewhere to roll up without a reserved room, although the Pagosimo travel agency (☎081/811 402) can usually come up with something, even at the last minute. Out of season you might find a real bargain at an apartment and, despite the high season crowds, the resort maintains a dignity long since lost in Mália and Hersonisos, and even a certain exclusivity; a couple of Crete's most luxurious hotels, including the enormous *Paradise Creta* (☎0834/51 570, fax 51 151; ⑤) nestle on the headland just beyond the main town beach.

Not far beyond Ayía Pelayía, there's a turning inland to the village of **FÓDHELE**, allegedly El Greco's birthplace. A plaque from the University of Toledo acknowledges the claim and, true or not, the community has built a small tourist industry on that basis. There are a number of craft shops and some pleasant tavernas where you can sit outside along the river. A peaceful 1km walk (or drive) takes you to the spuriously titled "El Greco's house" and the picturesque Byzantine **church of the Panagia** (Mon–Fri 9.30am–5pm; free). None of this amounts to very much but it is a pleasant, relatively unspoiled village if you simply want to sit in peace for a while. A couple of **buses** a day run here from Iráklion, and there's the odd tour; if you arrive on a direct bus, the walk back down to the highway (about 3km), where you can flag down a passing service, is not too strenuous.

Balí and Pánormos

BALÍ, on the coast approximately halfway between Iráklion and Réthymnon, also used to be tranquil and undeveloped, and by the standards of the north coast it still is in many ways. The village is built around a couple of small coves, some 2km from the highway (a hot walk from the bus), and is similar to Ayía Pelayía except that the beaches are not quite as good and there are no big hotels, just an ever-growing proliferation of studios, apartment buildings, rooms for rent, and a number of "modest hotels" (brochure-speak). You'll have plenty of company here; the last and best beach, known as "Paradise", no longer really deserves the name; it's a beautiful place to splash about, surrounded by mountains rising straight from the sea, but there's rarely a spare inch on the sand.

Continuing along the coast, the last stop before you emerge on the flat stretch leading to Réthymnon is at **PÁNORMOS**. This makes a good stopover if you're in search of somewhere more peaceful and authentic. The small sandy beach can get crowded when boats bring day trippers from Réthymnon, but most of the time the attractive village remains relatively unspoiled, and succeeds in clinging to its Greek identity. There are several decent tavernas and rooms places, one large hotel and the very comfortable *Pension Lucy* (☎0834/51 212; ③).

Inland towards Mount Psilorítis

Of the **inland routes**, the old main road (via Márathos and Dhamásta) is not the most interesting. This, too, was something of a bypass in its day and there are few places of any size or appeal, though it's a very scenic drive. If you want to dawdle, you're better off on the road which cuts up to **Týlissos** and then goes via **Anóyia**. It's a pleasant ride through fertile valleys filled with olive groves and vineyards, a district (the Malevísi) renowned from Venetian times for the strong, sweet Malmsey wine.

Týlissos and Anóyia

TÝLISSOS has a significant archeological site (daily 9am–3pm; 500dr) where three Minoan houses were excavated; unfortunately, its reputation is based more on what was found here (many pieces in the Iráklion museum) and on its significance for archeologists than on anything which remains to be seen. Still, it's worth a look, if you're passing, for a glimpse of Minoan life away from the big palaces, and for the tranquillity of the pine-shaded remains.

ANÓYIA is a much more tempting place to stay, especially if the summer heat is becoming oppressive. Spilling prettily down a hillside close below the highest peaks of the mountains, it looks traditional, but closer inspection shows that most of the buildings are actually concrete; the village was destroyed during World War II and the local men rounded up and shot – one of the German reprisals for the abduction of General Kreipe. The town has a reputation as a **handicrafts** centre (especially for woven and woollen goods), skills acquired both through bitter necessity after most of the men had been killed, and in a conscious attempt to revive the town. At any rate it worked, for the place is thriving today – thanks, it seems, to a buoyant agricultural sector and the number of elderly widows keen to subject any visitor to their terrifyingly aggressive sales techniques.

Quite a few people pass through Anóyia during the day, but not many of them stay, even though there are some good pensions and rented rooms in the upper half of the town, including the *Kriti* (☎0834/31 048; ②), *Avis* (☎0834/31 360, fax 31 058; ②) and *Ariste* (☎0834/31 459; ③) which has en-suite rooms. The town has a very different, more traditional ambience at night, and the only problem is likely to be finding somewhere to **eat**: although there are plenty of snack bars and so-called tavernas, most have extremely basic menus, more or less limited to barbecued lamb which is the local speciality.

Mount Psilorítis and its caves

Heading for the mountains, a rough track leads 13km from Anóyia to the **Nídha plateau** at the base of Mount Psilorítis. Here there's a taverna that used to let rooms but seems now to have closed to the public altogether, though it's still used by groups of climbers. A short path leads from the taverna to the celebrated **Idhéon Ándhron** (Idean Cave), a rival of that on Mount Dhíkti (see overleaf) for the title of Zeus's birthplace, and certainly associated from the earliest of times with the cult of Zeus. There's a major archeological dig going on inside, which means the whole cave is fenced off, with a miniature railway running into it to carry all the rubble out. In short, you can see nothing.

The taverna also marks the start of the way to the top of **Mount Psilorítis** (2456m), Crete's highest mountain, a climb that for experienced, properly shod hikers is not at all arduous. The route is well marked with the usual red dots, and it should be a six- to seven-hour return journey to the chapel at the summit, although in spring, thick snow may slow you down.

If you're prepared to camp on the plateau (it's very cold, but there's plenty of available water) or can prevail on the taverna to let you in, you could continue on foot next day down to the southern slopes of the range. It's a beautiful hike, at least while the road they're attempting to blast through is out of sight, and also relatively easy, four hours or so down a fairly clear path to **VORÍZIA**. If you're still interested in caves, there's a more rewarding one above the nearby village of **KAMÁRES**, a climb of some three hours on a good path. Both Vorízia and Kamáres have a few **rooms** and some tavernas, at least one daily **bus** down to Míres, and alternate (more difficult) routes to the peak of Psilorítis if you want to approach from this direction.

EASTERN CRETE

Eastern Crete is dominated by **Áyios Nikólaos**, and while it is a highly developed resort, by no means all of the east is like this. Far fewer people venture beyond the road south to **Ierápetra** and into the eastern isthmus, where only **Sitía** and the famous beach at **Vái** ever see anything approaching a crowd. Inland, too, there's interest, especially on the extraordinary **Lasíthi** plateau, which is worth a night's stay if only to observe its abidingly rural life.

Inland to the Lasíthi plateau

Leaving the palace at Mália, the highway cuts inland towards **NEÁPOLI**, soon beginning a spectacular climb into the mountains. Set in a high valley, Neápoli is a market town little touched by tourism. There is one hotel, some rooms, a modern church and a couple of museums. Beyond the town, it's about twenty minutes before the bus suddenly emerges high above the Gulf of Mirabéllo and Áyios Nikólaos, the island's biggest resort. If you're stopping, Neápoli also marks the second point of access to the **Lasíthi Plateau**.

Scores of bus tours drive up here daily to view the "thousands of white-cloth-sailed windmills" which irrigate the high plain, and most groups will be disappointed. There are very few working windmills left, and these operate only for limited periods (mainly in June). This is not to say the trip is not justified, as it would be for the drive alone, and there are many other compensations. The plain is a fine example of rural Crete at work, every inch devoted to the cultivation of potatoes, apples, pears, figs, olives and a host of other crops; stay in one of the villages for a night or two and you'll see real life return as the tourists leave. There are plenty of easy rambles around the villages as well, through orchards and past the rusting remains of derelict windmills. You'll find rooms in the main town of **TZERMIÁDHO**, and at Áyios Konstandínos, Áyios Yeóryios – where you'll find a **folk museum**, and the friendly *Hotel Dias* (☎0844/31 207; ②) – and Psykhró.

Psykhró and the Dhiktean cave

PSYKHRÓ is much the most visited, as it's the base for visiting Lasíthi's other chief attraction, the birthplace of Zeus, the **Dhiktean Cave** (daily 8am–6.45pm, reduced hours off season; 800dr; watch out for slippery stones inside). In legend, Zeus's father, the Titan Kronos, was warned that he would be overthrown by a son and accordingly ate all his offspring; however, when Rhea gave birth to Zeus in the cave, she fed Kronos a stone and left the child concealed, protected by the Kouretes, who beat their shields outside to disguise his cries. The rest, as they say, is history (or at least myth). There's an obvious path running up to the cave from Psykhró and, whatever you're told, you don't have to have a guide if you don't want one, though you will need some form of illumination. On the other hand, it is hard to resist the guides, who do make the visit much more interesting, and they're not expensive if you can get a small group together (2000dr for up to ten people). It takes a Cretan imagination to pick out Rhea and the baby Zeus from the lesser stalactites and stalagmites.

Buses run around the plateau to Psykhró direct from Iráklion and from Áyios Nikólaos via Neápoli. Both roads offer spectacular views, coiling through a succession of passes guarded by lines of ruined windmills.

Áyios Nikólaos and around

ÁYIOS NIKÓLAOS ("Ag Nik" to the majority of its British visitors) is set around a supposedly bottomless **salt lake**, now connected to the sea to form an inner harbour. It is supremely picturesque and has some style and confidence, which it exploits to the full. The lake and port are surrounded by restaurants and bars, which charge above the odds, and whilst still very popular, some tourists are distinctly surprised to find themselves in a place with no decent beach at all.

There are swimming opportunities further north however, where the pleasant low-key resort of **Eloúnda** is the gateway to the mysterious islet of **Spinalónga**, and some great back country to the north – perfect to explore on a scooter. Inland from Áyios Nikólaos, **Kritsá**, with its famous church and textile sellers is a tour-bus mecca, but just a couple of kilometres away, the imposing ruins of **ancient Lató** are usually deserted.

Áyios Nikólaos practicalities

The greatest concentration of **stores** and **travel agents** are on the hill between the bridge and Platía Venizélou. The main **ferry agent** is LANE (☎0841/26 465 or 23 090) opposite the OTE (daily 7am–10pm in high season), on the corner of 25-Martíou and K Sfakianáki. The **post office** (Mon–Fri 7.30am–8pm, Sat 7.30am–2pm) is halfway up Koundoúrou. The **tourist office** (daily 8.30am–9.30pm; ☎0841/22 357, fax 82 534), situated between the lake and the port, is one of the best on the island for information about accommodation. To hire a scooter or mountain bike try Mike Manolis, 25-Maritíou (☎0841/24 940), near the OTE office. Good car deals are available at Club Cars, 28-Oktobríou 24, near the post office.

Accommodation

The town is no longer packed solid with tourists, so it is much easier to find a place to stay, though in the peak season you won't have so much choice. One thing in your favour is that there are literally thousands of **rooms**, scattered all around town. The tourist office normally has a couple of boards with cards and brochures about hotels and rooms, including their prices. If the prices seem very reasonable it is because they

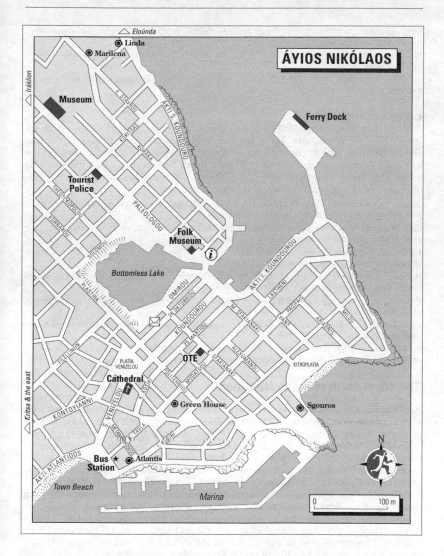

are for the low season. There is no longer a youth hostel, and the nearest **campsite** is *Gournia Moon*, 17km away (see p.191).

Atlantis, (☎0841/28 964) Nothing special but handy for the bus station; there's a snack bar below for breakfast. ②.

Green House, Modhátsou 15 (☎0841/22 025). Probably the best cheap place to stay in town; clean with shared facilities. ①.

Katerina, Stratigoú Kóraka 30 (☎0841/22 766). A pension close to the *Marilena* and another good choice in the same price bracket. ②.

Lida, Salamínos 3a (☎0841/22 130, fax 26 433). All the rooms in this friendly hotel have a shower, balcony and a partial seaview. ③.

Marilena, Érithrou Stavroú 14 (☎0841/22 681, fax 22 681). One of the cheaper pensions, this is excellent value. ③.

Sgouros, Kotroplatía (☎0841/28 931, fax 25 568). Modern hotel overlooking one of the town's beaches, and close to plenty of tavernas. ④.

Eating and drinking

At least when it comes to eating there's no chance of missing out, even if the prices are fancier than the restaurants. There are tourist-oriented **tavernas** all around the lake and harbour and little to choose between them, apart from the different perspectives you get on the passing fashion show. Have a **drink** here perhaps, or a mid-morning coffee and choose somewhere else to eat. The places around the Kiroplatía are generally fairer value, but again you are paying for the location.

Aouas, Paleológou 40. This taverna serves good, traditional Cretan food in and under a plant-covered trellised courtyard, and is reasonably cheap.

Café Migomis, Nikoláov Plastíra 22. Pleasant café high above the bottomless lake with a stunning view. Perfect place for breakfast, afternoon or evening drinks.

La Strada, just below the west side of Platía Venizélou. Authentic and good value pizza and pasta, should you fancy a change of cuisine.

Itanos, Kýprou 1, off the east side of Platía Venizélou. Popular with locals, this taverna serves Cretan food and wine, and has a terrace across the road opposite.

Pelagos, on Kóraka, just back off the lake behind the tourist office. A stylish fish taverna, serving good pricey food.

Ofou To Lo, Kitroplatía. Best of the moderately priced places on the seafront here: the food is consistently good.

To Ellinikon, just off the west side of Platía Venizélou. Great little traditional taverna run by the ebullient Yanna, who cooks up tasty country dishes accompanied by local wine and raki.

The coast north of Áyios Nikólaos

North of Áyios Nikólaos, the swankier hotels are strung out along the coast road, with upmarket restaurants, discos and cocktail bars scattered between them. **ELOÚNDA**, a resort on a more acceptable scale, is about 8km out along this road. Buses run regularly, but if you feel like renting a moped it's a spectacular ride, with impeccable views over a gulf dotted with islands and moored supertankers. Ask at the bookshop on the central square facing the sea, about the attractive seaview *Delfinia Apartments* (☎0841/41 641, fax 41 515; ③), or try the friendly *Pension Oasis* (☎0841/41 076, fax 41 218; ②) just off the square. Alternatively, one of the many travel agents around the main square, such as Olous Travel, can help with finding a room or apartment.

Just before the village a track (signposted) leads across a causeway to the "sunken city" of **Oloús**. There are restored windmills, a short length of canal, Venetian salt pans and a well preserved dolphin mosaic, but of the sunken city itself no trace beyond a couple of walls in about two feet of water. At any rate swimming is good, though there are sea urchins to watch out for.

From Eloúnda, kaïkia run to the fortress-rock of **Spinalónga**. As a bastion of the Venetian defence, this tiny islet withstood the Turkish invaders for 45 years after the mainland had fallen; in more recent decades, it served as a leper colony. As you watch the boat which brought you disappear to pick up another group, an unnervingly real sense of the desolation of those years descends. **PLÁKA**, back on the mainland, used to be the colony's supply point; now it is a haven from the crowds, with a small pebble beach and a couple of ramshackle tavernas. There are boat trips daily from Áyios Nikólaos to Oloús, Eloúnda and Spinalónga, usually visiting at least one other island along the way.

Inland to Kritsá and Lató

The other excursion everyone from Áyios Nikólaos takes is to **KRITSÁ**, a "traditional" village about 10km inland. Buses run at least every hour from the bus station, and despite the commercialization it's still a good trip: the local **crafts** (weaving, ceramics and embroidery basically, though they sell almost everything here) are fair value, and it's also a welcome break from living in the fast lane at "Ag Nik". In fact, if you're looking for somewhere to stay around here, Kritsá has a number of advantages: chiefly availability of **rooms**, better prices, and something at least approaching a genuinely Greek atmosphere; try *Argyro* (☎0841/51 174; ②) on your way to the village. There are a number of decent places to eat, too, or just to have a coffee and a cake under one of the plane trees.

On the approach road, some 2km before Kritsá, is the lovely Byzantine **church of Panayía Kyrá** (Mon–Sat 9am–3pm, Sun 9am–2pm; 800dr), inside which is preserved perhaps the most complete set of Byzantine frescoes in Crete. The fourteenth- and fifteenth-century works have been much retouched, but they're still worth the visit. Excellent (and expensive) reproductions are sold from a shop alongside. Just beyond the church, a surfaced road leads off towards the archeological site of **Lató** (Tues–Sun 8.30am–3pm; free), a Doric city with a grand hilltop setting. The city itself is extensive, but neglected, presumably because visitors and archeologists on Crete are concerned only with the Minoan era. Ruins aside, you could come here just for the views: west over Áyios Nikólaos and beyond to the bay and Oloús (which was Lató's port), and inland to the Lasíthi mountains.

The eastern isthmus

The main road south and then east from Áyios Nikólaos is not a wildly exciting one, essentially a drive through barren hills sprinkled with villas and above the occasional sandy cove. Five kilometres beyond a cluster of development at Kaló Khório, a track is signed on the right for the **Moní Faneroméni**. The track is a rough one and climbs dizzily skywards for 6km, giving spectacular views over the Gulf of Mirabélo along the way. The view from the monastery itself must be the among the finest in Crete. To get into the rather bleak looking monastery buildings, knock loudly. You will be shown up to the chapel, built into a cave sanctuary, and the frescoes are quite brilliant.

Gournia, Pakhia Ámmos and Mokhlos

Back on the coast road, it's another 2km to the site of **Gourniá** (Tues–Sun 8.30am–3pm; 500dr), slumped in the saddle between two low peaks. The most completely preserved **Minoan town**, its narrow alleys and stairways intersect a throng of one-roomed houses centred on a main square, and the house of the local ruler. Although less impressive than the great palaces, the site is strong on revelations about the lives of the ordinary people ruled from Knossós. Its desolation today (you are likely to be alone save for a dozing guard) only serves to heighten the contrast with what must have been a cramped and raucous community 3500 years ago.

It is tempting to cross the road here and take one of the paths through the wild thyme to the sea for a swim. Don't bother – the bay and others along this part of the coastline act as a magnet for every piece of floating detritus dumped off Crete's north coast. There is a larger beach, and rooms to rent, in the next bay along at **PAKHIÁ ÁMMOS**, about twenty minutes' walk, where there is also an excellent fish taverna, *Aiolus*; or in the other direction, there's the campsite of *Gournia Moon*, with its own small cove and a swimming pool.

This is the narrowest part of the island, and from here a fast new road cuts across the isthmus to Ierápetra in the south. In the north though, the route on towards Sitía is one of the most exhilarating in Crete. Carved into cliffs and mountain sides, the road teeters above the coast before plunging inland at Kavoúsi. Of the beaches you see below, only **MÓKHLOS** is at all accessible, some 5km below the main road. This sleepy village has a few rooms, a hotel or two and a number of tavernas; if you find yourself staying the night, try the rooms at *Limenaria* (☎0841/94 206; ②). Nearer Sitía the familiar olive groves are interspersed with vineyards, and in late summer the grapes, spread to dry in the fields and on rooftops, make an extraordinary sight in the varying stages of their slow change from green to gold to brown.

Sitía

SITÍA is the port and main town of the relatively unexploited eastern edge of Crete. It's a pleasant if unremarkable place, offering a plethora of waterside restaurants, a long sandy beach and a lazy lifestyle little affected even by the thousands of visitors in peak season. There's an almost Latin feel to the town, reflected in (or perhaps caused by) the number of French and Italian tourists, and it's one of those places you may end up staying longer than you intended. For entertainment, there's the **beach**, providing good swimming and windsurfing, and in town a mildly entertaining **folklore museum** (Tues–Sun 9.30am–2.30pm; Wed & Thurs also 6pm–8pm; 500dr), a Venetian fort and Roman fish tanks to explore, and an interesting **archeological museum** (Tues–Sun 8.30am–3pm; 500dr). Look out, too, for the town's resident pelican, Níkos, who has his own living quarters on the harbour quay.

Practicalities

There are plenty of cheap pensions and **rooms**, especially in the streets around the OTE, a good **youth hostel** (☎0843/22 693; ①) on the main road as it enters town, and rarely any problem about sleeping on the beach (though it is worth going a little way out of town to avoid any danger of being rousted by the police). For rooms, try *Pension Venus*, Kondhiláki 60 (☎0843/24 307; ②), *Hotel Arhontiko*, Kondhiláki 16 (☎0843/28 172; ②), and *Hotel Nora*, Rouseláki 31 (☎0843/23 017; ②) near the ferry port; if you have problems finding somewhere to stay, the **tourist police** at Anthéon 5 near the bus station (8.30am–7pm; ☎0843/23 590) may be able to help.

For **food**, the waterside places are rather expensive; the best value choices near here are the *Itanos Cafe* for mezédhes and *Creta House* serving traditional island dishes, both at the start of the beach road (Konstadínou Karamanlí). Authentic Belgian crepes are to be had at *Creperie Mike*, Elvenizélou 162, to the east of Zorbas. **Nightlife** centres on a few bars and discos near the ferry dock and out along the beach. The town's monster disco, *Planitarion*, attracts crowds from all over the east. It's a kilometre beyond the ferry port (see map), and is best reached by taxi. The one major excitement of the year is the August **Sultana Festival** – a celebration of the big local export, with traditional dancing and all the locally produced wine you can consume included in the entrance to the fairground.

Onward to Váï beach and Palékastro

Leaving Sitía along the beach, the Váï road climbs above a rocky, unexceptional coastline before reaching a fork to the **Monastery of Toploú** (daily 9am–1pm & 2pm–6pm; 700dr). The monastery's forbidding exterior reflects a history of resistance to invaders, but doesn't prepare you for the gorgeous flower-decked cloister within. The blue-robed monks keep out of the way as far as possible, but their cells and refectory are left discreetly on view. In the church is one of the masterpieces of Cretan art, the eighteenth-century icon *Lord Thou Art Great*. Outside you can buy enormously expensive reproductions.

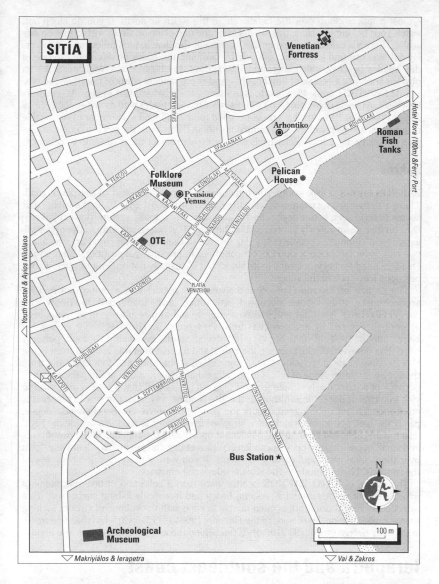

Vái beach itself features alongside Knossós or the Lasíthi plateau on almost every Cretan travel agent's list of excursions. Not surprisingly, it is now covered in sunbeds and umbrellas, though it is still a superb beach. Above all, it is famous for its palm trees, and the sudden appearance of the grove is indeed an exotic shock; lying on the fine sand in the early morning, the illusion is of a Caribbean island. As everywhere, notices warn that "Camping is forbidden by law", and for once the authorities seem to mean it

– most campers climb over the headlands to the south or north. If you do sleep out, watch your belongings since this seems to be the one place on Crete with crime on any scale. There's a café and an expensive taverna at the beach, plus toilets and showers. By day you can find a bit more solitude by climbing the rocks or swimming to one of the smaller beaches which surround Vaï. **Ítanos**, twenty minutes' walk north by an obvious trail, has a couple of tiny beaches and some modest ruins of the Classical era.

PALÉKASTRO, some 9km south, is in many ways a better place to stay. Although its beaches can't begin to compare, you'll find several modest places with rooms –notably *Hotel Hellas* (☎0843/61 240; ②) which provides good rooms and food – a number of reasonable restaurants, and plenty of space to camp out without the crowds; the sea is a couple of kilometres down a dirt track. Palékastro is also the crossroads for the road south to Zákros.

Zákros

ZÁKROS town is a little under 20km from Palékastro, at the end of the paved road. There are several tavernas and a hotel, the *Zakros* (☎0843/61 284; ③), in the village that seems to have seen better days. The Minoan palace is actually at Káto (lower) Zákros, 8km further down a newly paved road to the sea. Most buses run only to the upper village, but in summer, a couple every day do run all the way to the site. Part way along you can, if on foot, take a short cut through an impressive **gorge** (the "Valley of the Dead", named for ancient tombs in its sides) but it's usually not difficult to hitch if your bus does leave you in the village.

The **palace of Zákros** (Tues–Sun 8.30am–7pm; 500dr) was an important find for archeologists; it had been occupied only once, and abandoned hurriedly and completely. Later, it was forgotten almost entirely and as a result was never plundered or even discovered by archeologists until very recently. The first major excavation began only in 1960; all sorts of everyday objects (tools, raw materials, food, pottery) were thus discovered intact among the ruins, and a great deal was learned from being able to apply modern techniques (and knowledge of the Minoans) to a major dig from the very beginning. None of this is especially evident when you're at the palace, except perhaps in a particularly simple ground plan, so it's as well that it is also a rewarding visit in terms of the setting. Although the site is some way from the sea, in places it is often marshy and waterlogged: partly the result of eastern Crete's slow subsidence, partly the fault of a spring which once supplied fresh water to a cistern beside the royal apartments, and whose outflow is now silted up. Among the remains of narrow streets and small houses higher up, you can keep your feet dry and get an excellent view down over the central court and royal apartments. If you want a more detailed overview of the remains, buy the guide to the site on sale at the entrance.

The village of **KÁTO ZÁKROS** is little more than a collection of tavernas, some of which rent out rooms around a peaceful beach and minuscule fishing anchorage. It's a wonderfully restful place, but is often unable to cope with the volume of visitors seeking rooms in high season. You could try the *Poseidon* (☎0843/93 316; ③) which has fine views, and *Rooms George* (☎0843/93 316; ③), 200m behind the archeological site, is also good.

Ierápetra and the southeast coast

From Sitía, the route south is a cross-country roller-coaster ride until it hits the south coast at **MAKRYIALÓS**. This little fishing village has one of the best beaches at this end of Crete, with fine sand which shelves so gently you feel you could walk the 340km to Africa. Unfortunately, in the last few years it has been heavily developed, so while still a very pleasant place to stop for a swim or a bite, it's not somewhere you're likely to find a cheap room.

From here to Ierápetra there's little reason to stop; the few beaches are rocky and the coastal plain submerged under ranks of polythene-covered greenhouses. Beside the road leading into Ierápetra, are long but exposed stretches of sand, including the appropriately named "Long Beach", where you'll find a campsite, *Camping Koutsounari* (☎0842/61 213), which has plenty of shade.

Ierápetra

IERÁPETRA itself is a bustling modern supply centre for the region's farmers. It also attracts an amazing number of package tourists and not a few backpackers looking for work, especially out of season. The tavernas along the tree-lined front are scenic enough and the EU blue-flagged beach stretches a couple miles east. But as a town, most people find it pretty uninspiring. Although there has been a port here since Roman times, only the **Venetian fort** guarding the harbour and a crumbling minaret remain as reminders of better days. What little else has been salvaged is in the one-room **museum** (Tues–Sat 8.30am–3pm; 400dr) near the post office.

If you want to stay, head up Kazantzakís from the chaotic bus station, and you'll find **rooms** at the *Four Seasons* (☎0842/24 390; ③), or in the nearby *Cretan Villa*, Lakerda 16 (☎0842/26 522; ③), a beautiful 180-year-old house. More central, and also good value, is the *Hotel Ersi*, Platía Eleftherías 20 (☎0842/23 208; ②). You'll find places to **eat** and **drink** all along the waterfront (the better places being towards the Venetian fort); there is a clutch of bars and fast-food places along the central Kyrba, behind the promenade.

West from Ierápetra

Heading west from Ierápetra, the first stretch of coast is grey and dusty, the road jammed with trucks and lined with drab ribbon development. There are a number of small resorts along the beach, though little in the way of public transport. If travelling under your own steam, there is a scenic detour worth taking at Gra Ligiá: the road, on the right for Anatolí climbs to Máles, a village clinging to the lower slopes of the **Dhíkti range**. Here would be a good starting point if you want to take a walk through some stunning mountain terrain. Otherwise, the dirt road back down towards the coast (signposted Mýthi) has spectacular views over the Libyan Sea, and eventually follows the Mýrtos river valley down to Mýrtos itself.

Mýrtos and Árvi

MÝRTOS is the first resort that might actually tempt you to stop, and it's certainly the most accessible, just off the main road with numerous daily **buses** to Ierápetra and a couple direct to Iráklion. Although developed to a degree, it nonetheless remains tranquil and inexpensive, with lots of young travellers (many of whom sleep on the beach, to the irritation of locals). If you want a **room**, try *Rooms Angelos* (☎0842/51 106; ②), or *Nikos House* (☎0842/51 116; ②), though there are plenty of others. Just off the road from Ierápetra are a couple of excavated **Minoan villas** you might want to explore: Néa Mýrtos and Pýrgos.

After Mýrtos the main road turns inland towards Áno Viánnos, then continues across the island towards Iráklion; several places on the coast are reached by a series of rough sidetracks. That hasn't prevented one of them, **ÁRVI**, from becoming a larger resort than Mýrtos. The beach hardly justifies it, but it's an interesting little excursion (with at least one bus a day) if only to see the bananas and pineapples grown here and to experience the microclimate – noticeably warmer than neighbouring zones, especially in spring or autumn – that encourages them. For rooms you could try the central *Pension Gorguna* (☎0895/71 211; ②).

Beyond Árvi

Two more villages, **KERATÓKAMBOS** and **TSOÚTSOUROS**, look tempting on the map. Keratókambos has a rather stony beach and only basic rooms – the *Morning Star* taverna (☎0895/51 209; ②) is a good bet and the food is tasty too – but it's popular with Cretan day-trippers and great if you want to escape from the tourist grind for a spell. Tsoútsouros is developed and not really worth the tortuous thirteen-kilometre dirt road in.

If you hope to continue across the **south** of the island, be warned that there are no buses, despite completion of the road towards Mýres after years of work. It's an enjoyable, rural drive, but progress can be slow; there's very little traffic if you're trying to hitch.

RÉTHYMNON AND AROUND

The relatively low, narrow section of Crete which separates the Psilorítis range from the White Mountains in the west seems at first a nondescript, even dull part of the island. Certainly in scenic terms it has few of the excitements that the west can offer; there are no major archeological sites and many of the villages seem modern and ugly. On the other hand, **Réthymnon** itself is an attractive and lively city, with some excellent beaches nearby. And on the south coast, in particular around **Plakiás**, there are beaches as fine as any Crete can offer, and as you drive towards them the scenery and villages improve by the minute.

Réthymnon

In the past ten years or so, **RÉTHYMNON** has seen a greater influx of tourists than perhaps anywhere else on Crete, with the development of a whole series of large hotels extending almost 10km along the beach to the east. For once, though, the middle of town has been spared, so that at its heart Réthymnon remains one of the most beautiful of Crete's major cities (only Khaniá is a serious rival), with an enduringly provincial air. A wide sandy beach and palm-lined promenade border a labyrinthine tangle of Venetian and Turkish houses lining streets where ancient minarets lend an exotic air to the skyline. Dominating everything from the west, is the superbly preserved outline of the **fortress** built by the Venetians after a series of pirate raids had devastated the town.

The Town

With a **beach** right in the heart of town, it's tempting not to stir at all from the sands, but Réthymnon repays at least some gentle exploration. For a start, you could try checking out the further reaches of the beach itself. The waters, protected by the breakwaters in front of town have their disadvantages – notably crowds and dubious hygiene – but less sheltered sands stretch for miles to the east, crowded at first but progressively less so if you're prepared to walk a bit.

Away from the beach, you don't have far to go for the most atmospheric part of town, immediately behind the **inner harbour**. Almost anywhere here, you'll find unexpected old buildings, wall fountains, overhanging wooden balconies, heavy, carved doors and rickety shops, many still with local craftsmen sitting out front, gossiping as they ply their trades. Look out especially for the **Venetian loggia**, which houses a shop selling high quality and expensive reproductions of classical art; the **Rimóndi fountain**, another of the more elegant Venetian survivals; and the **Nerandzes mosque**, the best preserved in Réthymnon but currently closed for renovation. Simply by walking past these three,

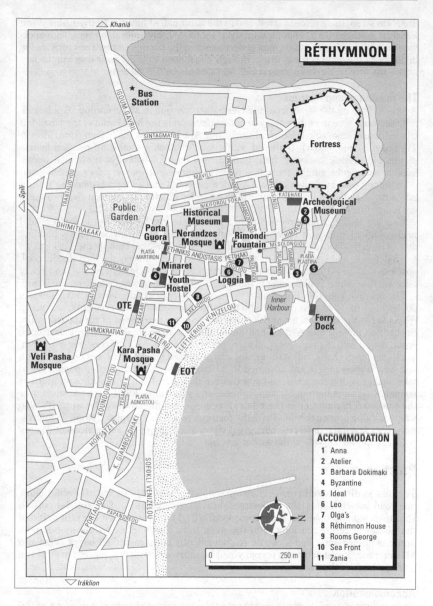

△ Khaniá

RÉTHYMNON

★ **Bus Station**

SINTAGMATOS

IGOUM. GAVRIL

HRANIALIDHOU

◁ Spili

Fortress

KORNAROU HAKIS

MAVILI

NIKIFOROU FOKA

KATEHAKI

Archeological Museum

MELISINOU

Public Garden

Historical Museum

Porta Guora

Nerándzes Mosque

Rimondi Fountain

DHIMITRAKAKI

PLATÍA MARTIRON

ETHNIKIS ANDISTASIS

PETIHAKI

Minaret

Youth Hostel

Loggia

DHASKALAKI

MOATSOU

YERAKARI K.

SOULIOU

PALEOLOGOU

ARKADHIOU

HIMARAS

MESOLONGIOU

DAMVERGI

SALAMINIS

PLATÍA PLASTIRA

OTE

DHIMOKRATIAS

V. KALERGI

ELEFTHERIOU VENIZELOU

Inner Harbour

Ferry Dock

Veli Pasha Mosque

Kara Pasha Mosque

KOUNDOURIOTOU

YERAKARI I.

PLATÍA AGNOSTOU

EOT

HORTATZI G.

K. GIAMBOUDHAKI

SOFOKLI VENIZELOU

F. PORTALIOU

PAPANDREOU

△ Iráklion

0   250 m

Z

ACCOMMODATION

1 Anna
2 Atelier
3 Barbara Dokimaki
4 Byzantine
5 Ideal
6 Leo
7 Olga's
8 Réthimnon House
9 Rooms George
10 Sea Front
11 Zania

you'll have seen many of the liveliest parts of Réthymnon. Ethnikís Andistásis, the street leading straight up from the fountain, is also the town's **market** area.

The old city ends at the Porta Guora at the top of Andistásis, the only surviving remnant of the city walls. Almost opposite are the quiet and shady **Public Gardens**. These are always a soothing place to stroll, and in the latter half of July, the **Réthymnon Wine Festival** is staged here. Though touristy, it's a thoroughly enjoyable event, with spectacular local dancing as the evening progresses and the barrels empty. The entrance fee includes all the wine you can drink, though you'll need to bring your own cup or buy one of the souvenir glasses and carafes on sale outside the gardens.

The museums and fortress

A little further up the street from the Nerandzes mosque at M Vernardou 28, a beautifully restored seventeenth-century Venetian mansion is the new home of the small but tremendously enjoyable **Historical and Folk Art Museum** (daily 9am–1pm, Mon & Tues also 6–8pm; 400dr). Gathered within four, cool, airy rooms are musical instruments, old photos, basketry, farm implements, an explanation of traditional bread-making techniques, smiths' tools, traditional costumes and jewellery, lace, weaving and embroidery, pottery, knives and old wooden chests. It makes for a fascinating insight into a fast disappearing rural (and urban) lifestyle, which had often survived virtually unchanged from Venetian times to the 1960s, and is well worth a look.

Heading in the other direction from the fountain you'll come to the fortress and **archeological museum** (Tues–Sun 8.30am–3pm; 500dr), which occupies a building almost directly opposite the entrance to the fortress. This was built by the Turks as an extra defence, and later served as a prison, but it's now entirely modern inside: cool, spacious and airy. Unfortunately, the collection is not particularly exciting, and really only worth seeing if you're going to miss the bigger museums elsewhere on the island.

The massive **Venetian Fortress** (Tues–Sun 8am–8pm; reduced hours out of season; 6000dr) is a must, however. Said to be the largest Venetian castle ever built, this was a response, in the last quarter of the sixteenth century, to a series of **pirate raids** (by Barbarossa among others) that had devastated the town. Inside now is a vast open space dotted with the remains of all sorts of barracks, arsenals, officers' houses, earthworks and deep shafts, and at the centre a large domed building that was once a church and later a **mosque**. It was designed to be large enough for the entire population to take shelter within the walls, and you can see that it probably was. Although much is ruined, it remains thoroughly atmospheric, and you can look out from the walls over the town and harbour, or in the other direction along the coast to the west. It's also worth walking around the outside of the fortress, preferably at sunset, to get an impression of its fearsome defences, plus great views along the coast and a pleasant resting point around the far side at the *Sunset* taverna.

Practicalities

The **bus station** in Réthymnon is by the sea to the west of town just off Periferiakós, the road which skirts the waterfront around the fortress. The **tourist office** (Mon–Fri 8am–5.30pm, Sat 9am–2pm; ☎0831/24 143) is across on the other side of the historical centre, backing onto the main town beach, close to the mobile post office (summer only) and a couple of conveniently sited cash dispensers (Visa and Mastercard). If you arrive by **ferry**, you'll be more conveniently placed, over at the western edge of the harbour.

Accommodation

There's a great number of places to stay in Réthymnon, and only at the height of the season are you likely to have difficulty finding somewhere, though you may get weary looking. The greatest concentration of **rooms** is in the tangled streets west of the inner harbour, between the Rimóndi fountain and the museums; there are also quite a few places on and around Arkadhíou and Platía Frakidháki. The cheapest beds in town are in the **youth hostel**, Tombázi 41 (☎0831/22 848; ①), where you can also sleep on the roof. It's large, clean, very friendly and popular, and there's food, showers, clothes-washing facilities and even a library, with books in various languages.

There are a couple of **campsites** 4km east of town; take the bus for the hotels (marked *Scaleta/El Greco*) from the long-distance bus station to get there. *Camping Elizabeth* (☎0831/28 694) is a pleasant, large site on the beach, with all facilities. Only a few hundred metres further east along the beach is *Camping Arkadia* (☎0831/28 825), a bigger and slightly less friendly site.

Anna, Katekháki (☎0831/25 586). Comfortable pension in a quiet position on the street that runs straight down from the entrance to the fortress to Melissinou. ④.

Atelier, Khimáras 32 (☎0831/24 440). Pleasant rooms close to *Rooms George*, run by a talented potter, who has her studio in the basement and sells her wares in a shop on the other side of the building. ③.

Barbara Dokimaki, Plastíra 14 (☎0831/22 319). Strange warren of a rooms place, with one entrance at the above address, just off the seafront behind the *Ideon*, and another on Dambergi; ask for the newly refurbished top-floor rooms, which have balconies. ③.

Byzantine, Vospórou 26 (☎0831/55 609). Excellent-value rooms in a renovated Byzantine palace. The tranquil patio bar is open to all, and breakfast is included in price. ④.

Ideon, Platía Plastíra 10 (☎0831/28 667, fax 28 670). Hotel with a brilliant position just north of the ferry dock; little chance of space in season, though. ⑤.

Leo, Vafé 2 (☎0831/26 197). Good hotel with lots of wood and a traditional feel; the price includes breakfast, and there's a good bar. ④.

Olga's Pension, Soulíou 57 (☎0831/53 206, fax 29 851). The star attraction at this very friendly pension on one of Rethimnon's most touristy streets is the resplendent flower-filled roof garden. ②.

Réthymnon Haus, V. Kornárou 1 (☎0831/23 923). Very pleasant rooms of a high standard in an old building just off Arkadhíou. Bar downstairs. ②.

Rooms George, Makedhonías 32 (☎0831/50 967). Decent rooms (some with fridge), near the archeological museum. ③.

Sea-Front Rent Rooms, Arkadhíou 159 (☎0831/51 981, fax 51 062). Rooms with sea views and balconies in an attractively refurbished mansion with ceiling fans and lots of wood. ③.

Zania, Pávlou Vlástou 3 (☎0831/28 169). Pension right on the corner of Arkadhíou by the old youth hostel building; a well-adapted old house, but only a few rooms. ③.

Eating and drinking

Immediately behind the town beach are arrayed the most touristy **restaurants**. One that maintains its integrity (and reasonable prices) is the *Samaria* taverna, almost opposite the tourist office. Around the inner **harbour**, there's a second, rather more group of expensive tavernas, specializing in fish, though as often as not the intimate atmosphere in these places is spoiled by the stench from the harbour itself: *O Zefyros* and *Seven Brothers* are two of the less outrageously pricey.

The cluster of kafenía and tavernas by the **Rimóndi fountain** and the newer places spreading into the surrounding streets generally offer considerably better value, and a couple of the old-fashioned kafenía serve magnificent yoghurt and honey. Places to try include *Kyria Maria* at Moskhovítou 20, tucked down an alley behind the fountain (after the meal, everyone gets a couple of delicious *tiropitákia* with honey on the house); *Agrimi*, a reliable standard on Platía Petikháki; and the *Zanfoti* kafenío overlooking the fountain which is relatively expensive, but a great place to people-watch over a coffee; and, for a slightly cheaper option *O Psaras* (the Fisherman), a simple, friendly taverna by the church on the corner of Nikiforou Foka and Koronaíou. A good lunchtime stop close to the archeological museum is *O Pontios*, Melissinoú 34, a simple place with tables outside and an enthusiastic female proprietor. Healthy, home-baked lunches can also be had at *Stella's Kitchen*, a simple café linked to Olga's Pension at Soulíou 55, where meals can be enjoyed up on the leafy roof garden. A noisier evening alternative is *Taverna O Gounos*, Koronéou 6 in the old town; the family who run it perform live *lyra* every night, and when things get really lively the dancing starts.

If you want takeaway food, there are numerous **souvláki** stalls, including a couple on Arkadhíou and Paleológou and another at Petikháki 52, or you can buy your own ingredients at the **market** stalls set up daily on Ethnikís Andistásis below the Porta Guora. There are small general stores scattered everywhere, particularly on Paleológou and Arkadhíou; east along the beach road you'll even find a couple of mini supermarkets. The **bakery** *I Gaspari* on Mesolongíou, just behind the Rimóndi fountain, sells the usual cheese pies, cakes and the like, and it also bakes excellent brown, black and rye bread. There's a good zakharoplastío, *N.A. Skartsilakos*, on Paleológou, just north of the fountain, and several more small cafés which are good for breakfast or a quick coffee.

Nightlife
Nightlife is concentrated in the same general areas as the tavernas. At the west end of Venizélou, in the streets behind the inner harbour, the overflow from a small cluster of noisy music bars – *Templum, 252, Dimmam* and *Venetianikoa* – begins to spill out onto the pavement as party-goers gather for the nightly opening of the *Fortezza Disco* in the inner harbour, which is the gliziest in town. Heading up Salamínos, a string of more subdued cocktail bars – *Memphis, Santan* and *Palmira* – cater for those in search of a quieter drink. The larger discos are mostly out to the east, among the big hotels, but *Venizelou* right by the inner harbour, is a touristy Cretan music and dancing place, with live performances every evening from 9.30pm.

Around Réthymnon

While some of Crete's most drastic resort development spreads ever eastwards out of Réthymnon, to the west a sandy coastline, not yet greatly exploited, runs all the way to the borders of Khaniá. But of all the short trips that can be made out of Réthymnon, the best known and still the most worthwhile is to the **Monastery of Arkádhi**.

Southeast to Arkádhi

The **Monastery of Arkádhi** (daily 8am–8pm; 300dr), some 25km southeast of the city and immaculately situated in the foothills of the Psilorítis range, is also something of a national Cretan shrine. During the 1866 rebellion against the Turks, the monastery became a rebel strongpoint in which, as the Turks gained the upper hand, hundreds of Cretan guerrillas and their families took refuge. Surrounded and, after two days of fighting, on the point of defeat, the defenders ignited a powder magazine just as the Turks entered. Hundreds (some sources claim thousands) were killed, Cretan and Turk alike, and the tragedy did much to promote international sympathy for the cause of Cretan independence. Nowadays, you can peer into the roofless vault where the explosion occurred and wander about the rest of the well-restored grounds. The sixteenth-century Rococo church survived, and is one of the finest Venetian structures left on Crete; other buildings house a small museum devoted to the exploits of the defenders of the (Orthodox) faith. The monastery is easy to visit by public bus or on a tour.

West to Yeoryoúpoli and beyond

Leaving Réthymnon to the west, the main road climbs for a while above a rocky coastline before descending (after some 5km) to the sea, where it runs alongside sandy **beaches** for perhaps another 7km. An occasional hotel offers accommodation, but on the whole there's nothing but a line of straggly bushes between the road and the windswept sands.

If you have your own vehicle, there are plenty of places you can stop at here for a swim, and rarely anyone else around – but beware of some very strong currents.

If you want to stay for any time, probably the best base is **YEORYOÚPOLI** at the far end, where the beach is cleaner, wider and further from the road. There's been a distinct acceleration in the pace of development at Yeoryoúpoli over the last few years and it's now very much a resort, packed with rooms to rent, small hotels, apartment buildings, tavernas and travel agencies; there's even a small land train to transport visitors along the sea front and on short excursions. But everything remains on a small scale, and the undeniably attractive setting is untarnished, making it a very pleasant place to pass a few days, as long as you don't expect to find many vestiges of traditional Crete. Most of the better rooms, including *Rent Rooms Stelios* (☎0825/61 308; ②), *Irene* (☎0825/61 278; ②) and *Cretan Cactus* (☎0825/61 027; ②), are away from the main platía along the road down towards the beach. More central possibilities include *Rooms Voula* (☎0825/61 359; ②) above a gift shop to the east of the platía, and the *Paradise Taverna* (☎0825/61 313; ③) off the southeast corner of the platía, which has rooms and is a good place to eat.

Within walking distance inland – though it can also be visited on the tourist train from Yeoryoúpoli – is **Kournás**, Crete's only lake, set deep in a bowl of hills and almost constantly changing colour. There are a few tavernas with rooms to rent along the shore here, or you could try for a bed in the nearby village of Moúri. A few kilometres uphill in Kournás village, the *Kali Kardia* taverna is a great place to sample the local lamb and sausages.

Beyond Yeoryoúpoli, the main road heads inland, away from a cluster of coastal villages beyond Vámos. It thus misses the Dhrápano peninsula, with some spectacular views over the sapphire Bay of Soudha, several quiet beaches and the setting for the film of *Zorba the Greek*. **Kókkino Khorió**, the movie location, and nearby **Pláka** are indeed postcard-picturesque (more so from a distance), but **Kefalás**, inland, outdoes both of them. On the exposed north coast there are good beaches at **Almyrídha** and **Kalýves**, and off the road between them. Both are fast developing into resorts in their own right; accommodation is mostly in apartments and rooms are scarce, although there are a few mid-range and more upmarket hotels, and a decent pension, *Katrina* (☎0825/38 775; ③), a short walk uphill from the centre of Almyrídha. With a string of good fish tavernas along the beach and a pleasantly refreshing sea breeze, Almyrídha makes an enjoyable lunch stop.

South from Réthymnon

There are a couple of alternative routes south from Réthymnon, but the main one heads straight out from the centre of town, an initially featureless road due south across the middle of the island towards **Ayía Galíni**. About 23km out, a turning cuts off to the right for **Plakiás** and **Mýrthios**, following the course of the spectacular Kourtaliótiko ravine.

Plakiás and the south coast

PLAKIÁS has undergone a major boom and is no longer the pristine village all too many people arriving here expect. That said, it's still quite low key, and there's a satisfactory beach and a string of good tavernas around the dock. There are hundreds of **rooms**, but at the height of summer you'll need to arrive early if you hope to find one; the last to fill are generally those on the road leading inland, away from the waterside. For rooms try *Christos's Taverna* (☎0832/31 871; ②) on the seafront, or the excellent balcony rooms at *Ipokambos* (☎0832/31 525; ②) slightly inland on the road to the **youth hostel** (☎0832/31 306; ①), which is 500m inland and signed from the seafront. The

beach is long and nobody is likely to mind if you sleep out on the southern section –
but Dhamnóni (see below) is far better if that's your plan.

Once you've found a room there's not a lot else to discover here. You'll find every
facility strung out around the waterfront, including a temporary post office, bike rental,
money exchange, supermarket and even a laundry. Places to eat are plentiful too. The
attractive **tavernas** on the waterfront in the centre are a little expensive; you'll eat
cheaper further inland – seek out *Medusa* taverna – or around the corner at one of the
tavernas facing west where *Sunset* taverna is the first in line.

Mýrthios

For a stay of more than a day or two, **MÝRTHIOS**, in the hills behind Plakiás, also
deserves consideration. It's no longer a great deal cheaper, but at least you'll find locals
still outnumbering the tourists and something of a travellers' scene based around
another popular **youth hostel** (☎0832/31 202; ①), with a friendly taverna and several
rooms for rent. The Plakiás bus will usually loop back through Mýrthios, but check;
otherwise, it's less than five minutes' walk from the junction. It takes twenty minutes to
walk down to the beach at Plakiás, a little longer to Dhamnóni, and if you're prepared
to walk for an hour or more, there are some entirely isolated coves to the west – ask for
directions at the hostel.

Dhamnóni

Some of the most tempting **beaches** in central Crete hide just to the east of Plakiás,
though unfortunately they're now a very poorly kept secret. These three splashes of
yellow sand, divided by rocky promontories, are within easy walking distance and
together go by the name **Dhamnóni**. At the first, Dhamnóni proper, there's a taverna
with showers and a wonderfully long strip of sand, but there's also a lot of new development including a number of nearby rooms for rent and a huge new Swiss timeshare
complex, which has colonized half of the main beach. At the far end, you'll generally
find a few people who've dispensed with their clothes, while the little cove which shelters the middle of the three beaches (barely accessible except on foot) is entirely nudist. Beyond this, **Ammoúdhi** beach has another taverna (with good rooms for rent)
and a slightly more family atmosphere.

Préveli and "Palm Beach"

Next in line comes **PRÉVELI**, some 6km southeast of Lefkóyia. It takes its name from
a **monastery** (daily 8am–7pm; 500dr) high above the sea which, like every other in
Crete, has a proud history of resistance, in this case accentuated by its role in the last
war as a shelter for marooned Allied soldiers awaiting evacuation off the south coast.
There are fine views and a monument commemorating the rescue operations, but little
else to see. The evacuations took place from **"Palm Beach"**, a sandy cove with a small
date-palm grove and solitary drink stand where a stream feeds a little oasis. The beach
usually attracts a summer camping community and is now also the target of day-trip
boats from Plakiás. Sadly, these two groups between them have left this lovely place
filthy, and despite a belated clean-up campaign it seems barely worth the effort. The
climb down from the monastery is steep, rocky and surprisingly arduous: it's a great
deal easier to come here by boat.

Spíli and Ayía Galíni

Back on the main road south, **SPÍLI** lies about 30km from Réthymnon. A popular coffee break for tours passing this way, Spíli warrants time if you can spare it. Sheltered
under a cliff are narrow alleys of ancient houses, all leading up from a platía with a

famous 24-spouted fountain. If you have your own transport, it's a worthwhile place to stay, peacefully rural at night but with several good **rooms** for rent. Try the *Green Hotel* (☎0832/22 225; ②) or the pleasant *Rooms Herakles* (☎0832/22 411; ②) just behind.

The ultimate destination of most people on this road is **AYÍA GALÍNI**. If heading here was your plan, maybe you should think again since this picturesque "fishing village" is so busy that you can't see it for the tour buses, hotel billboards and British package tourists. It also has a beach much too small for the crowds that congregate here. Even so, there are some saving graces – mainly some excellent restaurants and bars, plenty of rooms and a friendly atmosphere that survives and even thrives on all the visitors. Out of season, it can be quite enjoyable, and from November to April the mild climate makes it an ideal spot to spend the winter. A lot of long-term travellers do just that, so it's a good place to find work packing tomatoes or polishing cucumbers. If you want somewhere to stay, start looking at the top end of town, around the main road: the good-value *Hotel Minos* (☎0832/91 292; ②) with superb views is a good place to start, but there are dozens of possibilities, and usually something to be found even at the height of summer.

The coastal plain east of Ayía Galíni, hidden under acres of polythene greenhouses and burgeoning concrete sprawl, must be among the ugliest regions in Crete, and **Timbáki** the dreariest town. Since this is the way to Festós and back to Iráklion, however, you may have no choice but to grin and bear it.

The Amári Valley

An alternative route south from Réthymnon, and a far less travelled one, is the road which turns off on the eastern fringe of town to run via the **Amári Valley**. Very few buses go this way, but if you're driving it's well worth the extra time. There's little specifically to see or do (though hidden away are a number of frescoed Byzantine churches), but it's an impressive drive under the flanks of the mountains and a reminder of how, in places, rural Crete continues to exist regardless of visitors. The countryside here is delightfully green even in summer, with rich groves of olive and assorted fruit trees, and if you **stay** (there are rooms in Thrónos and Yerákari), you'll find the nights are cool and quiet. It may seem odd that many of the villages along the way are modern; they were systematically destroyed by the Germans in reprisal for the 1944 kidnapping of General Kreipe.

KHANIÁ AND THE WEST

The substantial attractions of Crete's westernmost quarter are all the more enhanced by its relative lack of visitors, and despite the now-rapid spread of tourist development, the west is likely to remain one of the emptier parts of the island. This is partly because there are no big sandy beaches to accommodate resort hotels, and partly because it's so far from the great archeological sites. But for mountains and empty (if often pebbly) beaches, it's unrivalled.

Khaniá itself is one of the best reasons to come here, perhaps the only Cretan city which could be described as enjoyable in itself. The immediately adjacent coast is relatively developed and not overly exciting; if you want beaches head for the south coast. **Paleokhóra** is the only place which could really be described as a resort, and even this is on a thoroughly human scale; others are emptier still. **Ayía Rouméli** and **Loutró** can be reached only on foot or by boat; **Khóra Sfakíon** sees hordes passing through but few who stay; **Frangokástello**, nearby, has a beautiful castle and the first stirrings of development. Behind these lie the **Lefká Óri** (White Mountains) and, above all, the famed walk through the **Gorge of Samariá**.

Khaniá

KHANIÁ, as any of its residents will tell you, is spiritually the capital of Crete, even if the nominal title passed (in 1971) to Iráklion. For many, it is also by far the island's most attractive city, especially if you can catch it in spring, when the Lefká Óri's snow-capped peaks seem to hover above the roofs. Although it is for the most part a modern city, you might never know it as a tourist. Surrounding the small outer harbour is a wonderful jumble of half-derelict **Venetian streets** that survived the wartime bombardments, and it is here that life for the visitor is concentrated. Restoration and gentrification, consequences of the tourist boom, have made inroads of late, but it remains an atmospheric place.

> The telephone code for Khaniá is ☎0821

Arrival, information and orientation

Large as it is, Khaniá is easy to handle once you've reached the centre; you may get lost wandering among the narrow alleys of the old city but that's a relatively small area, and you're never far from the sea or from some other obvious landmark. The **bus station** is on Kidhonías, within easy walking distance from the action – turn right out of the station, then left down the side of Platía 1866 and you'll emerge at a major road junction opposite the top of Hálidhon, the main street of the old quarter leading straight down to the Venetian harbour. Arriving by **ferry**, you'll anchor about 10km from Khaniá at the port of Soúdha: there are frequent buses which will drop you by the **market** on the fringes of the old town, or you can take a taxi (around 1500dr). From the **airport** (15km east of town on the Akrotíri peninsula) taxis (around 2500dr) will almost certainly be your only option, though it's worth a quick check to see if any sort of bus is meeting your flight. The **tourist office** is in the new town, just off Platía 1866 at Kriári 40 (Mon–Fri 7.30am–2.30pm).

Accommodation

There must be thousands of **rooms** to rent in Khaniá and, unusually, quite a few comfortable **hotels**. Though you may face a long search for a bed at the height of the season, eventually everyone does seem to find something.

There are two **campsites** within striking distance, the nearer being *Camping Khania* (☎31 138), some 4km west of Khaniá behind the beach, served by local bus (see p.211). The site is lovely, if rather basic – just a short walk from some of the better beaches. *Camping Ayía Marína* (☎68 596) lies about 8km west of Khaniá, on an excellent beach at the far end of Ayía Marína village. This is beyond the range of Khaniá city buses, so to get here by public transport you have to go from the main bus station. Check before turning up, because the site is earmarked for redevelopment.

Harbour area

Perhaps the most desirable rooms of all are those overlooking the **harbour**, which are sometimes available at reasonable rates: be warned that this is often because they're very noisy at night. Most are approached not direct from the harbourside itself but from Zambelíou, the alley behind, or from other streets leading off the harbour further around (where you may get more peace). The nicest of the more expensive places are here, too, usually set back a little so that they're quieter, but often with views from the upper storeys.

Amphora, Theotokopóulou 20 (☎ & fax 93 224). Large, traditional hotel, and beautifully renovated; worth the expense if you get a view, but probably not for the cheaper rooms with no view. ⑥.

Artemis, Kondhiláki 13 (☎92 802). One of many in this touristy street running inland from Zambelíu. ③.

Lucia, Akti Koundouriótou (☎90 302). Harbour-front hotel with balcony rooms; less expensive than you might expect for one of the best views in town. ③.

Meltemi, Angélou 2 (☎ 92 802). First of a little row of pensions in a great situation on the far side of the harbour; perhaps noisier than its neighbours, but ace views and a good café downstairs. ③.

Pension Lena, Theotokopoula 60 (☎ and fax 72 265). Charming rooms in an old wooden Turkish house restored by friendly German proprietor. Pleasant breakfast café below. ③.

Rooms Eleonora, Theotokúpoula 13 (☎50 011). One of several in the backstreets around the top of Angélou. ③.

Rooms George, Zambelíou 30 (☎88 715). Old building with steep stairs and eccentric antique furniture; rooms vary in price according to position and size. ②.

Rooms Stella, Angélou 10 (☎73 756). Creaky, eccentric old house above a ceramics shop, close to the *Lucia*, with plain, clean rooms. ③.

Theresa, Angélou 8 (☎40 118). Beautiful old house in a great position, with stunning views from roof terrace and some of the rooms; classy decor, too. A more expensive pension than its neighbours but deservedly so; unlikely to have room in season unless you book. ④.

The old town: east of Khálidhon

In the eastern half of the old town rooms are far more scattered, and in the height of the season your chances are much better over here. **Kastélli**, immediately east of the harbour, has some lovely places with views from the height. Take one of the alleys leading left off Kaneváro if you want to try these, but don't be too hopeful since they are popular and often booked up.

Fidias, Sarpáki 8 (☎52 494). Signposted from the cathedral, this favourite backpackers' meeting place is rather bizarrely run, but is an extremely friendly pension and has the real advantage of offering single rooms or fixing shares. ③.

Kastelli, Kanevárou 39 (☎ and fax 45 314). Not in the prettiest location, but a comfortable, modern, reasonably priced pension and very quiet at the back. The owner is exceptionally helpful and also has a few apartments and a beautiful house (for up to five people) to rent. ③.

Kydonia, Isódhion 15 (☎57 179). Between the cathedral platía and Platía Sindriváni, in the first street parallel to Khálidhon. Rather dark, but good value for so central a position. ③.

Lito, Episkópou Dhorothéou 15 (☎53 150). Pension very near the cathedral, in a street with several other options. ③.

Marina Ventikou, Sarpáki 40 (☎57 601). Small, personally run rooms place in a quiet corner of the old town. ③.

Monastiri, Ayíou Márkou 18, off Kanevárou (☎54 776). Pleasant rooms, some with a sea view in the restored ruins of a Venetian monastery. ③.

Nikos, Dhaskaloyiánnis 58 (☎54 783). One of a few down here near the inner harbour; relatively modern rooms all with shower. ②.

The City

Khaniá has been occupied almost continuously since Neolithic times, so it comes as a surprise that a city of such antiquity should offer little specifically to see or do. It is, however, a place which is fascinating simply to wander around, stumbling upon surviving fragments of city wall, the remains **ancient Kydonia** which is being excavated, and odd segments of Venetian or Turkish masonry.

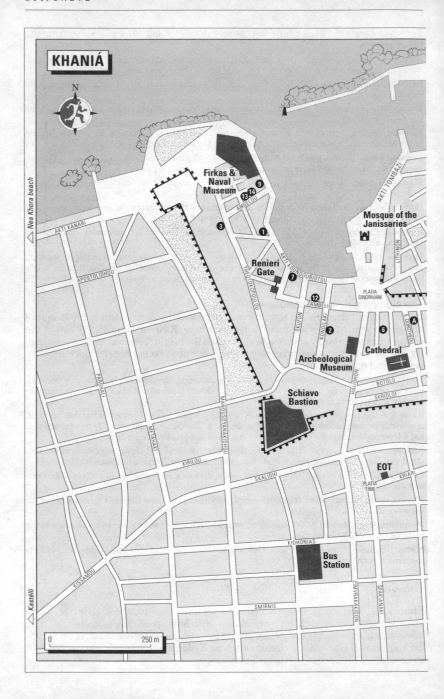

KHANIÁ

N

△ Nea Khora beach

△ Kastélli

Firkas & Naval Museum

Mosque of the Janissaries

AKTI TOMBAZI

LITHINON

AKTI KANARI

ANGELOU

❸

❶⯀

❶❸❶❹❾

Renieri Gate

AKTI KOUNDOURIOTOU

❼

PLATIA SINDRIVANI

THEOTOKOPOULOU

APOSTOLIDHOU

❶❷

ZAMBELIU

E. DOROTHEOU

❷

SKUFON

KONDILAKI

❻

Ⓐ

PARDHALI

Archeological Museum

Cathedral

MELANAKI

Schiavo Bastion

HALIDHON

BOTOLO

SKRIDLOF

MANUSOYANAKIDHOU

KIRILOU

SKALIDHI

EOT

PLATIA 1866

KRIARI

KISSAMOU

KIDHONIAS

Bus Station

ZIMVRAKAKIDHON

SFAKIANAKI

SMIRNIS

0   250 m

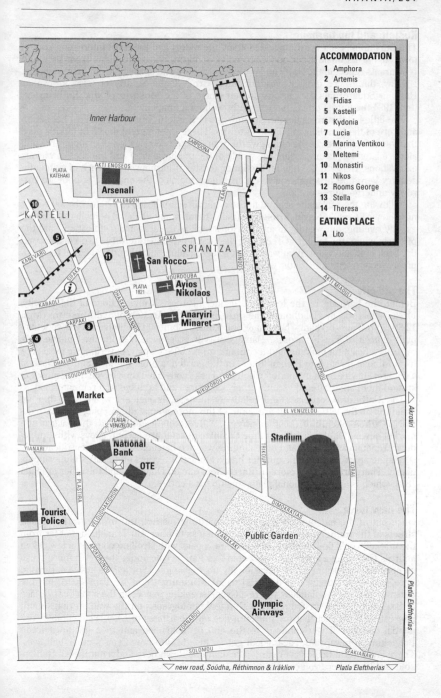

ACCOMMODATION

1 Amphora
2 Artemis
3 Eleonora
4 Fidias
5 Kastelli
6 Kydonia
7 Lucia
8 Marina Ventikou
9 Meltemi
10 Monastiri
11 Nikos
12 Rooms George
13 Stella
14 Theresa

EATING PLACE

A Lito

Inner Harbour

PLATIA KATEHAKI

AKTI ENOSEOS

Arsenali

KALERGON

KASTÉLLI

SIFAKA

SPIANTZA

San Rocco

VOURDOUBA

PLATIA 1821

Ayios Nikolaos

Anaryiri Minaret

KANEVARO

SIFAKA

SARPAKI

DHASKALOYIANNIS

KARAOLI

DHALIANI

TSOUDHERON

Minaret

Market

PLATIA S. VENIZELOU

National Bank

OTE

YIANARI

N. PLASTIRA

VELOUDHAKYDHON

Tourist Police

KALYDHONIOU

NIKOFOROU FOKA

EL VENIZELOU

TRIKOUPI

Stadium

DIMOKRATIAS

TZANAKAKI

Public Garden

KORNAROU

Olympic Airways

SOLOMOU

SFAKIANAKI

SARPDONA

KIDOU

MINOS

AKTI MIAOULI

KIPROU

KORAI

△ Akrotíri

△ Platía Eleftherías

▽ new road, Soúdha, Réthimnon & Iráklion   Platía Eleftherías ▽

Kastélli and the harbour

The **port** area is as ever the place to start, the oldest and the most interesting part of town. It's at its busiest and most attractive at night, when the lights from bars and restaurants reflect in the water and crowds of visitors and locals turn out to promenade. By day, things are quieter. Straight ahead from Platía Sindrivani (also known as Harbour Square) lies the curious domed shape of the **Mosque of the Janissaries**, until 1991 the tourist office, but currently without a function.

The little hill that rises behind the mosque is **Kastélli**, site of the earliest habitation and core of the Venetian and Turkish towns. There's not a great deal left, but it's here that you'll find traces of the oldest **walls** (there were two rings, one defending Kastélli alone, a later set encompassing the whole of the medieval city) and the sites of various excavations. Beneath the hill, on the inner (eastern) harbour, the arches of sixteenth-century **Venetian arsenals** survive alongside remains of the outer walls; both are currently undergoing restoration.

Following the esplanade around in the other direction leads to a hefty bastion which now houses Crete's **Naval Museum** (daily 10am–4pm; 400dr). The collection is not exactly riveting, but wander in anyway for a look at the seaward fortifications and the platform where the modern Greek flag was first flown on Crete (in 1913). Walk around the back of these restored bulwarks to a street heading inland and you'll find the best-preserved stretch of the outer walls.

The old city

Behind the harbour, lie the less picturesque but more lively sections of the old city. First, a short way up Hálidhon on the right, is Khaniá's **Archeological Museum** (Mon 12.30–7pm, Tues–Fri 8am–7pm, Sat & Sun 8.30am–3pm; 500dr) housed in the Venetian-built church of San Francesco. Damaged as it is, especially from the outside, this remains a beautiful building and it contains a fine little display, covering the local area from Minoan through to Roman times. In the garden, a huge fountain and the base of a minaret survive from the period when the Turks converted the church into a mosque; around them are scattered various other sculptures and architectural remnants.

The **Cathedral**, ordinary and relatively modern, is just a few steps further up Hálidhon on the left. Around it are some of the more animated shopping areas, particularly **Odhós Skrídhlof** (Leather Street), with streets leading up to the back of the market beyond. In the direction of the Spiántza quarter are ancient alleys with tumble-down Venetian stonework and overhanging wooden balconies; though gentrification is spreading apace, much of the quarter has yet to feel the effect of the city's modern popularity. There are a couple more **minarets** too, one on Dhaliáni, and the other in Platía 1821, which is a fine traditional platía to stop for a coffee.

The new town

Once out of the narrow confines of the maritime district, the broad, traffic-choked streets of the **modern city** have a great deal less to offer. Up Tzanakáki, not far from the market, you'll find the **Public Gardens**, a park with strolling couples, a few caged animals (including a few *kri-kri* or Cretan ibex) and a café under the trees; there's also an open-air auditorium which occasionally hosts live music or local festivities. Beyond here, you could continue to the **Historical Museum** (Mon–Fri 9am–1pm), but the effort would be wasted unless you're a Greek-speaking expert on the subject; the place is essentially a very dusty archive with a few photographs on the wall. Perhaps more interesting is the fact that the museum lies on the fringes of Khaniá's desirable residential districts. If you continue to the end of Sfakianáki and then go down Iróon Polytekhníou towards the sea, you'll get an insight into how Crete's other half lives. There are several (expensive) garden restaurants down here and a number of fashionable café-bars where you can sit outside.

The beaches

Khaniá's beaches all lie to the west of the city. For the packed **city beach**, this means no more than a ten-minute walk following the shoreline from the naval museum, but for good sand you're better off taking the local bus out along the coast road. This leaves from the east side of Platía 1866 and runs along the coast road as far as **Kalamáki beach**. Kalamáki and the previous stop, **Oasis beach**, are again pretty crowded but they're a considerable improvement over the beach in Khaniá itself. In between, you'll find emptier stretches if you're prepared to walk: about an hour in all (on sandy beach virtually all the way) from Khaniá to Kalamáki, and then perhaps ten minutes from the road to the beach if you get off the bus at the signs to *Aptera Beach* or *Camping Khania*. Further afield there are even finer beaches at **Ayía Marína** to the west, or **Stavrós** (see p.211) out on the Akrotíri peninsula (reached by KTEL buses from the main station).

Eating

You're never far from something to **eat** in Khaniá: in a circle around the harbour is one restaurant, taverna or café after another. All have their own character, but there seems little variation in price or what's on offer. Away from the water, there are plenty of slightly cheaper possibilities on Kondhiláki, Kanevárou and most of the streets off Khálidhon. For snacks or lighter meals, the cafés around the harbour on the whole serve cocktails and fresh juices at exorbitant prices, though breakfast (especially "English") can be good value. For more traditional places, try around the market and along Dhaskaloyiánnis (*Singanaki* here is a good traditional bakery serving *tyrópitta* and the like, with a cake shop next door). Fast food is also increasingly widespread, with numerous *souvláki* places on Karaolí; at the end of the outer harbour, near the naval museum; and around the corner of Plastíra and Yianári, across from the **market** (see "Listings" overleaf, for details of the market and supermarkets).

Anaplous, Sífaka 37. A couple of blocks west of Platía 1821, this is a popular new open-air restaurant inside a stylishly "restored" ruin of a Turkish mansion bombed in the war. Serves both mezédhes and full meals.

Boúyatsa, Sífaka 4. Tiny place serving little except the traditional creamy *bougátsa*: eat in or take away.

Dino's, inner harbour by bottom of Sarpidhóna. One of the best choices for a pricey seafood meal with a harbour view; *Apostolis*, almost next door, is also good.

Karnáyio, Platía Katekháki 8. Set back from the inner harbour near the port police. Not right on the water, but one of the best harbour restaurants nonetheless.

Lito, Episkópou Dhorothéou 15. Café/taverna with live music (usually Greek-style guitar), one of several in this street.

Meltemi, Angélou 2. Slow, relaxed place for breakfast, and where locals (especially expats) sit whiling the day away or playing *tavli*.

Neorion, Sarpidhóna. Café to sit and be seen in the evening; some tables overlook the harbour. Try an expensive but sublime lemon *graníta*.

Rudi's Bierhaus, Sífaka 24. Austrian Rudi Riegler's bar stocks more than a hundred of Europe's finest beers to accompany mezédhes.

Tamam, Zambelíou just before Renieri Gate. Young, fashionable place with adventurous Greek menu including much vegetarian food. Unfortunately only a few cramped tables outside, and inside it's very hot. Slow service.

Tasty Souvlaki, Khálidhon 80. Always packed despite being cramped and none-too-clean, which is a testimonial to the quality and value of the *souvláki*. Better to take away.

Taverna Ela, top of Kondhiláki. Live Greek music to enliven your meal in yet another roofless taverna townhouse.

Tholos, Agíon Dhéka 36. Slightly north of the cathedral, *Tholos* is another "restaurant in a ruin", this time Venetian/Turkish, with a wide selection of Cretan specialities.

To Dhiporto, Betólo 31, one block north of Skridhlóf. Long-established, very basic taverna amid all the leather shops. Multilingual menu offers such delights as "Pigs' Balls", or, more delicately, *Testicules de Porc*.

Vasilis, Platía Sindriváni. Perhaps the least changed of the harbourside cafés. Reasonably priced breakfasts.

Bars and nightlife

Khaniá's **nightlife** has more than enough venues to satisfy the most insomniac night-owls. Most of the clubs and disco bars are gathered in the area around the inner har-bour, whilst there are plenty of terrace bars along both harbour fronts with more scat-tered throughout the old quarter.

The smartest and newest places are on and around **Sarpidhóna**, in the far corner of the inner harbour: bars like *Fraise* on Sarpidóna; and late night disco-bars such as *Berlin Rock Café*, on Radimánthous, just around the corner at the top of Sarpidóna. Heading from here around towards the outer harbour, you'll pass others including the *Four Seasons*, a very popular bar by the port police, and then reach a couple of the older places including *Remember* and *Scorpio* behind the Plaza. *Fagotto*, Angélou 16, is a pleasant, laid-back jazz bar, often with live performers. **Discos** proper include *Ariadni*, on the inner harbour (opens 11.30pm, but busy later), and *Millenium*, a big, bright place on Tsoudherón behind the market, which doesn't really get going until 2am. Tucked down a passage near the Schiavo Bastion (Skalídhi and Khálidhon), *Anayennisi Club* is a new place that becomes frenetic after midnight.

A couple of places that offer more traditional entertainment are the *Café Kriti*, Kalergón 22, at the corner of Andhroyíou, basically an old-fashioned kafenío where there's **Greek music** and **dancing** virtually every night, and the *Firkas* (the bastion by the naval museum), with Greek dancing at 9pm every Tuesday – pricey but authen-tic entertainment. It's also worth checking for events at the open-air auditorium in the public gardens, and for performances in restaurants outside the city, which are the ones the locals will go to. Look for posters, especially in front of the market and in the little platía across the road from there.

For **films**, you should also check the hoardings in front of the market. There are open-air screenings at *Attikon*, on Venizélou out towards Akrotíri, about 1km from the centre, and occasionally in the public gardens.

Listings

Airlines Olympic, Tzanakáki 88 (Mon–Fri 9am–4pm; ☎57 701). There's a bus from here connect-ing with their flights. For airport information call ☎63 245.

Banks The main branch of the National Bank is directly opposite the market. Convenient smaller banks for exchange are next to the bus station, at the bottom of Kaneváro just off Platía Sindrivani, or at the top of Khálidhon. There are also a couple of exchange places on Khálidhon, open long hours, and a post-office van parked through the summer in the cathedral platía.

Bike and car rental Possibilities everywhere, especially on Khálidhon, though these are rarely the best value. For bikes and cars try Duke of Crete, Sífaka 3 (☎21 651), Skalídhi 16 (☎57 821) and branches in Ayía Marína and Plataniás (discount for cash); for cars try Tellus Rent a Car, Kaneváro 9, east of Platía Sindriváni (☎50 400, fax 91 716).

Boat trips Various boat trips are offered by travel agents around town, mostly round Soúdha Bay or out to beaches on the Rodhópou peninsula. Domenico's on Kanevárou offers some of the best of these.

Ferry tickets The agent for Minoan is Nanadakis Travel, Khálidhon 8 (☎23 939); the agent for ANEK is on Venizélou, right opposite the market (☎23 636).

Laundry There are three, at Kanevárou 38 (9am–10pm), Episkópou Dorothéou 7 and Áyii Dhéka 18; all do service washes.

Left luggage The bus station has a left luggage office.

Market and supermarkets If you want to buy food or get stuff together for a picnic, the market is the place to head for. There are vast quantities of fresh fruit and vegetables as well as meat and fish, bakers, dairy stalls and general stores for cooked meats, tins and other standard provisions. There are also several small stores down by the harbour platía which sell cold drinks and a certain amount of food, but these are expensive (though they do open late). A couple of large supermarkets can be found on the main roads running out of town, for instance Inka on the way to Akrotíri.

Post office The main post office is on Tzanakáki (Mon–Fri 7am–8pm, Sat 8am–2pm for exchange). In summer, there's a handy Portakabin branch set up in the cathedral platía.

Taxis The main taxi ranks are in the cathedral platía and, especially, Platía 1866. For radio taxis try ☎29 405 or ☎58 700.

Telephones OTE headquarters (daily 6am–midnight) is on Tzanakáki just past the post office. It's generally packed during the day, but often empty late at night.

Tourist police Kareskáki 44 (☎94 477). Town and harbour police are on the inner harbour.

Travel agencies For cheap tickets home try Bassias Travel, Skridhlóf 46 (☎44 295), very helpful for regular tickets too. They also deal in standard excursions. Other travel agents for tours and day trips are everywhere.

Around Khaniá: the Akrotíri and Rodhopoú peninsulas

Just north of Khaniá, the **Akrotíri peninsula** loops around to protect the Bay of Soúdha and a NATO military base and missile-testing area. In an ironic twist, the peninsula's northwestern coastline is fast developing into a luxury suburb; the beach of Kalathás, near Khorafákia, long popular with jaded Khaniotes, is surrounded by villas and apartments. **STAVRÓS**, further out, has not yet suffered this fate, and its **beach** is absolutely superb if you like the calm, shallow water of an almost completely enclosed lagoon. It's not very large, so it does get crowded, but rarely overpoweringly so. There's a makeshift taverna/souvláki stand on the beach, and a couple of tavernas across the road, but for accommodation you need to search slightly south of here, in the area around **Blue Beach**, where there are plenty of apartment buildings.

Inland are the **monasteries** of **Ayía Triádha** (daily 9am–2pm & 5–7pm; 300dr) and **Gouvernétou** (daily 9am–12.30pm & 4.30–7pm). The former is much more accessible and has a beautiful seventeenth-century church inside its pink-and-ochre cloister, though ongoing renovations have recently caused many of the monks to relocate and on occasions make the normally peaceful enclosure more like a building site. Beyond Gouvernétou, which is in a far better state of preservation and where traditional monastic life can still be observed, you can clamber down a craggy path to the abandoned ruins of the monastery of Katholikó and the remains of its narrow (swimmable) harbour.

West to Rodhopoú

The coast to the west of Khaniá was the scene of most of the fighting during the German invasion in 1941. As you leave town, an aggressive diving eagle commemorates the German parachutists, and at Máleme there's a big German cemetery; the Allied cemetery is in the other direction, on the coast just outside Soúdha. There are also beaches and considerable tourist development along much of this shore. At **Ayía Marína** there's a fine sandy beach, and an island offshore said to be a sea monster petrified by Zeus before it could swallow Crete. Seen from the west, its "mouth" still gapes open.

Between **Plataniás** and **Kolymbári** an almost unbroken strand unfurls, by no means all sandy, but deserted for long stretches between villages. The road here runs through mixed groves of calamus reed (Crete's bamboo) and oranges; the windbreaks fashioned from the reeds protect the ripening oranges from the *meltémi*. At Kolymbári, the road to Kastélli cuts across the base of another mountainous peninsula, **Rodhopoú**. Just off the main road here is a monastery, **Goniá** (daily 9am–2pm & 5–7pm; respectable dress), with a view most luxury hotels would envy. Every monk in Crete can tell tales of his proud ancestry of resistance to invaders, but here the Turkish cannon balls are still lodged in the walls to prove it, a relic of which the good fathers are far more proud than of any of the icons.

South to the Samarian Gorge

From Khaniá the **Gorge of Samariá** (May to mid-Oct; 1200dr for entry to the national park) can be visited as a day trip or as part of a longer excursion to the south. At over 16km, it's Europe's longest gorge and is startlingly beautiful. **Buses** leave Khaniá for the top at 6.15am, 7.30am, 8.30am and 1.30pm, and you'll normally be sold a return ticket (valid from Khóra Sfakíon at any time). It's well worth catching the early bus to avoid the full heat of the day while walking through the gorge, though be warned that you will not be alone – there are often as many as five coachloads setting off before dawn for the nail-biting climb into the White Mountains. There are also direct early-morning buses from Iráklion and Réthymnon, and bus tours from virtually everywhere on the island. Despite all the crowds, the walk is hard work, especially in spring when the stream is a roaring torrent. Early and late in the season, there is a danger of **flash floods**, which are not to be taken lightly: in 1993, a number of walkers perished when they were washed out to sea. If in doubt, phone the Khaniá Forest Service (☎0821/67 140) for information.

Omalós

One way to avoid the early start would be to stay at **OMALÓS**, in the middle of the mountain plain from which the gorge descends. There are some ordinary **rooms** for rent and a couple of surprisingly fancy **hotels**; try the *Neos Omalos* (☎0821/67 269; ③). But since the village is some way from the start of the track, and the buses arrive as the sun rises, it's almost impossible to get a head start on the crowds. Some people sleep out at the top (where there's a bar-restaurant and kiosks serving drinks and sandwiches), but a night under the stars here can be a bitterly cold experience. The one significant advantage to staying up here would be if you wanted to undertake some other climbs in the White Mountains, in which case there's a **mountain hut** (☎0821/24 647; ①) about ninety minutes' walk from Omalós or from the top of the gorge.

The gorge

The **Gorge** itself begins at the *Xilóskala*, or "wooden staircase", a stepped path plunging steeply down from the southern lip of the Omalós plain. Here, at the head of the track, opposite the sheer rock face of Mount Gíngilos, the crowds pouring out of the buses disperse rapidly as keen walkers march purposefully down while others dally over breakfast, contemplating the sunrise for hours. You descend at first through almost alpine scenery: pine forest, wild flowers and very un-Cretan greenery – a verdant shock in the spring, when the stream is also at its liveliest (and can at times be positively dangerous). Small churches and viewpoints dot the route, and about halfway down you pass the abandoned village of **Samariá**, now home to a wardens' station, with picnic facilities and filthy toilets. Further down, the path levels out and the gorge walls

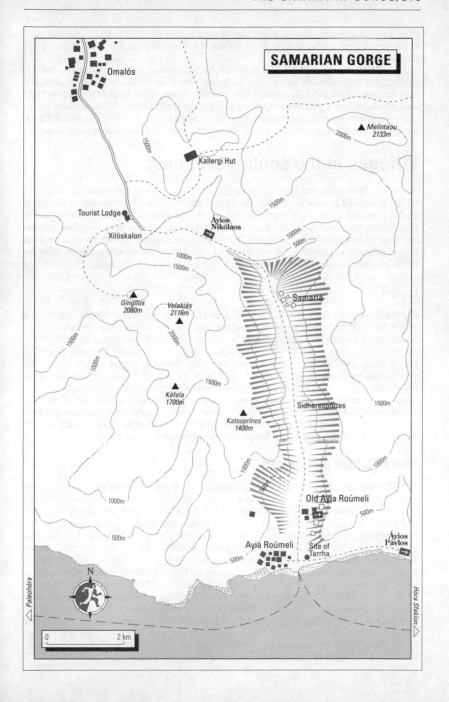

SAMARIAN GORGE

Omalós

Melíntaou
2133m

Kallergi Hut

Tourist Lodge

Áyios
Nikólaos

Xilóskalon

Samariá

Gíngilos
2080m

Volakiás
2116m

Sidherespóttes

Kéfala
1700m

Katsoprínes
1400m

Old Ayía Roúmeli

Áyios
Pávlos

Ayía Roúmeli

Site of
Tarrha

Paleohóra

Hóra Sfakíon

N

0   2 km

close in until at the narrowest point (the *Sidherespórtes* or "Iron Gates") one can practically touch both tortured rock faces at once, and, looking up, see them rising sheer
for almost a thousand feet.

At an average pace, with regular stops, the walk down takes five or six hours, and the
upward trek considerably longer. It's strenuous (you'll know all about it next day), the
path is rough, and solid shoes vital. On the way down, there is plenty of water from
springs and streams (except some years in September and October), but nothing to eat.
The park that surrounds the gorge is the only mainland refuge of the Cretan wild ibex,
the *kri-kri*, but don't expect to see one; there are usually far too many people around.

Villages of the southwest coast

When you finally emerge from the gorge, it's not long before you reach the village of
AYÍA ROUMÉLI, which is all but abandoned until you reach the beach, a mirage of
iced drinks and a cluster of tavernas with **rooms** for rent. If you want to get back to
Khaniá, buy your boat tickets now, especially if you want an afternoon on the beach; the
last boat (connecting with the final 6.30pm bus from Khóra Sfakíon) tends to sell out
first. If you plan to stay on the south coast, you should get going as soon as possible for
the best chance of finding a room somewhere nicer than Ayía Rouméli.

Loutró

For tranquillity, it's hard to beat **LOUTRÓ**, two-thirds of the way to Khóra Sfakíon, and
accessible only by boat or on foot. The chief disadvantage of Loutró is its lack of a real
beach; most people swim from the rocks around its small bay. If you're prepared to
walk, however, there are **deserted beaches** along the coast to the east. Indeed, if
you're really into walking there's a **coastal trail** through Loutró which covers the
entire distance between Ayía Rouméli and Khóra Sfakíon, or you could take the daunting zigzag path up the cliff behind to the mountain village of Anópoli. Loutró itself has
a number of **tavernas** and **rooms**, though not always enough of the latter. Call the *Blue
House* (☎0825/91 127) if you want to book ahead; this is also the best place to eat. There
is also space to **camp** out on the cape by a ruined fort, but due to a long history of problems, you should be aware that campers are not very popular in the village.

Khóra Sfakíon and beyond

KHÓRA SFAKÍON is the more usual terminus for walkers traversing the gorge, with
a regular boat service along the coast to and from Ayía Rouméli. Consequently, it's
quite an expensive and not an especially welcoming place; there are plenty of rooms
and some excellent tavernas, but for a real beach you should jump straight on the
evening bus going toward Plakiás. Plenty of opportunities for a dip present themselves
en route, one of the most memorable at **Frangokástello**, a crumbling Venetian attempt
to bring law and order to a district that went on to defy both Turks and Germans. Its
square, crenellated fort, isolated a few kilometres below a chiselled wall of mountains,
looks like it's been spirited out of the High Atlas or Tibet. The place is said to be haunted by ghosts of Greek rebels massacred here in 1829; every May, these *dhrossoulítes*
(dewy ones) march at dawn across the coastal plain and disappear into the sea near the
fort. The rest of the time Frangokástello is peaceful enough, with a superb beach and
a number of tavernas and rooms, but is somewhat stagnant if you're looking for things
to do. Slightly further east, and less influenced by tourism or modern life, are the attractive villages of **Skalotí** and **Rodhákino**, each with basic lodging and food.

Soúyia

In quite the other direction from Ayía Rouméli, less regular boats also head to **SOÚYIA** and on to Paleokhóra. Soúyia, until World War II merely the anchorage for Koustoyérako inland, is low key with a long, grey pebble beach and mostly modern buildings (except for a church with a sixth-century Byzantine mosaic as the foundation). Since the completion of the new road to Khaniá, the village has started to expand; even so, except in the very middle of summer, it continues to make a good fallback for finding a room or a place to camp, eating cheaply and enjoying the beach when the rest of the island is seething with tourists.

Kastélli and the western tip

Apart from being Crete's most westerly town, and the end of the main road, **KASTÉLLI** (Kíssamos, or Kastélli Kissámou as it's variously known) has little obvious attraction. It's a busy town with a rocky beach visited mainly by people using the boat that runs twice weekly to the island of Kýthira and the Peloponnese. The very ordinariness of Kastélli, however, can be attractive: life goes on pretty much regardless of outsiders, but there's every facility you might need. The **ferry agent's office** in Kastélli is right on the main platía (Xirouxákis; ☎0822/22 655), and nothing else is far away apart from the dock, a two-kilometre walk (or inexpensive taxi ride) from town.

Falásarna to Elafoníssi

To the west of Kastélli lies some of Crete's loneliest, and, for many visitors, finest coastline. The first place of note is ancient **Falásarna**, city ruins which mean little to the non-specialist, but they do overlook some of the best beaches on Crete, wide and sandy with clean water. There's a handful of tavernas and an increasing number of rooms for rent; otherwise, you have to sleep out, as many people do. This can mean that the main beaches are dirty, but they remain beautiful, and there are plenty of others within walking distance. The nearest real town is **Plátanos**, 5km up the recently paved road, along which there are a couple of daily buses.

Further south, the western coastline is still less discovered and the road is surfaced only as far as Kámbos; there's little in the way of official accommodation. **Sfinári** has several houses which rent rooms, and a quiet pebble beach a little way below the village. **Kámbos** is similar, but even less visited, its beach a considerable walk down a hill. Beyond them both is the **monastery of Khryssoskalítissa**, increasingly visited by

---

A ROUND TRIP

If you have transport, a circular drive from Kastélli, taking the coast road in one direction and the inland route through Élos and Topólia, makes for a stunningly scenic circuit. Near the ocean, villages cling to the high mountain sides, apparently halted by some miracle in the midst of calamitous seaward slides. Around them, olives ripen on the terraced slopes, the sea glittering far below. Inland, especially at **ÉLOS**, the main crop is the chestnut, whose huge old trees shade the village streets.

In **TOPÓLIA**, the chapel of Ayía Sofia is sheltered inside a cave which has been used as a shrine since Neolithic times. Cutting south from Élos, a paved road continues through the high mountains towards Paleokhóra. On a motorbike, with a sense of adventure and plenty of fuel, it's great: the bus doesn't come this way, villagers still stare at the sight of a tourist, and a host of small, seasonal streams cascade beside or under the asphalt.

tours from Khaniá and Paleokhóra now the road has been sealed, but well worth the effort for its isolation and nearby beaches; the bus gets as far as Váthy, from where the monastery is another two hours' walk away.

Five kilometres beyond Khryssoskalítissa, the road bumps down to the coast opposite the tiny uninhabited islet of **Elafonísi**. You can easily wade out to the islet with its sandy beaches and rock pools, and the shallow lagoon is warm and crystal-clear. It looks magnificent, but daily boat trips from Paleokhóra and coach tours from elsewhere on the island ensure that, in the middle of the day at least, it's far from deserted. Even bigger changes are now on the horizon here as Greek and German companies have bought up large tracts of land to create a monster tourist complex, although these plans are currently stalled, with developers in dispute with the government about how things should proceed. If you want to stay, and really appreciate the place, there are a couple of seasonal tavernas, but bring some supplies unless you want to be wholly dependent on them.

Kándhanos and Paleokhóra

Getting down to Paleokhóra by the main road, now paved the whole way, is a lot easier, and several daily buses from Khaniá make the trip. But although this route also has to wind through the western outriders of the White Mountains, it lacks the excitement of the routes to either side. **Kándhanos**, at the 58-kilometre mark, has been entirely rebuilt since it was destroyed by the Germans for its fierce resistance to their occupation. The original sign erected when the deed was done is preserved on the war memorial: "Here stood Kándanos, destroyed in retribution for the murder of 25 German soldiers".

When the beach at **PALEOKHÓRA** finally appears below it is a welcome sight. The little town is built across the base of a peninsula, its harbour on one side, the sand on the other. Above, on the outcrop, Venetian ramparts stand sentinel. These days Paleokhóra has become heavily developed, but it's still thoroughly enjoyable, with a main street filling with tables as diners spill out of the restaurants, and with a pleasantly chaotic social life. A good place to **eat** with some good imaginative vegetarian specials is *The Third Eye*, just out of the centre towards the sandy beach. There are scores of places to stay (though not always many vacancies) and there's also a fair-sized **campsite**; in extremis, the beach is one of the best to sleep out on, with showers, trees and acres of sand. Nearby discos and a rock'n'roll bar, or the soundtrack from the open-air cinema, combine to lull you to sleep. When you tire of Paleokhóra and the excellent windsurfing in the bay, there are excursions up the hill to Prodhrómi, for example, or along a five-hour coastal path to Soúyia.

You'll find a helpful **tourist office** (daily 9.30am–1pm & 5.30–9pm) in the town hall on Venizélos in the centre of town; they have full accommodation lists and a map (though you'll hardly need this). The **OTE**, **banks** and **travel agents** are all nearby; the **post office** is on the road behind the sandy beach. **Boats** run from here to Elafonísi, the island of Gávdhos, and along the coast to Soúyia and Ayía Rouméli.

Gávdhos

The island of **Gávdhos**, some fifty kilometres of rough sea south of Paleokhóra, is the most southerly landmass in Europe. Gávdhos is small (about 10km by 7km) and barren, but it has one major attraction: the enduring **isolation** which its inaccessible position has helped preserve. There are now a few package tours (travel agents in Paleokhóra can arrange a room if you want one), and there's a semi-permanent community of campers through the summer, but if all you want is a beach to yourself and a taverna to grill your fish, this remains the place for you.

travel details

Flights

Khaniá Several flights a day to Athens; one weekly to Thessaloníki.

Iráklion Many daily flights to Athens; 4 weekly to Rhodes; 2 weekly to Mýkonos; and 3 weekly to Thessaloníki.

Ferries

Áyios Nikólaos and Sitía 1–3 ferries a week to Kássos, Kárpathos, Khálki, Rhodes and the Dodecanese; 1–2 weekly to Thíra, Folégandhros, Mílos, Sífnos and Pireás.

Khaniá 1 or 2 ferries daily to Pireás (12hr).

Khóra Sfakíon 5 ferries daily to Loutró/Ayía Rouméli; 3 weekly to Gávdhos in season.

Iráklion 2 ferries daily to Pireás (12hr); 3 ferries weekly to Thessaloníki; at least one daily ferry to Thíra (4hr), also fast boats and hydrofoils (2hr 30min); daily ferries to Páros in season; most days to Mýkonos and Íos; at least twice weekly to Náxos, Tínos, Skýros, Skíathos, Kárpathos and Rhodes. Ferries to Ancona (Italy) twice weekly and Çeşme (Turkey) weekly; also weekly to Limassol (Cyprus) and Haifa (Israel).

Kastélli (Kíssamos) 1–3 ferries weekly to Kýthira, Yíthio (8hr), Monemvassía and Pireás.

Paleokhóra 3 boats a week in season to Gávdhos. Also daily sailings to Elafonísi and Soúyia.

Réthymnon 3 ferries a week to Pireás (12hr); weekly service and seasonal day trips to Thíra.

Buses

Áyios Nikólaos–Sitía (6 daily 6.30am–6pm; 2hr).

Khaniá–Réthymnon–Iráklion (30 daily 5.30am–9.30pm; 3hr total).

Khaniá–Khóra Sfakíon (3 daily 8.30am–2pm; 2hr).

Khaniá–Paleokhóra (5 daily 8.30am–5pm; 2hr).

Iráklion–Áyios Nikólaos (38 daily 6.30am–7.30pm; 1hr 30min).

Iráklion–Ierápetra (7 daily 7.30am–6.30pm; 2hr 30min).

Iráklion–Ayía Galíni (38 daily 6.30am–7pm; 2hr 15min).

Iráklion–Festós (9 daily 7.30am–5.30pm; 1hr 30min).

Kastélli–Khaniá (15 daily 5am–7.30pm; 1hr 30min).

Réthymnon–Spíli–Ayía Galíni (6 daily 6.30am–5pm; 45min–1hr 30min).

CHAPTER FOUR

THE DODECANESE

T he furthest Greek island group from the mainland, the **Dodecanese** (Dhodhekánisos) lie close to the Turkish coast – some, like Kós and Kastellórizo, almost within hailing distance of the shore. Because of this position, and their remoteness from Athens, the islands have had a turbulent history: they were the scene of ferocious battles between German and British forces in 1943–44, and were only finally included in the modern Greek state in 1948 after centuries of occupation by Crusaders, Ottomans and Italians. Even now the threat (real or imagined) of invasion from Turkey is very much in evidence. When you ask about the heavy military presence, many locals talk in terms of "when the Turks come", rarely "if".

Whatever the rigours of the various occupations, their legacy includes a wonderful blend of architectural styles and of Eastern and Western cultures. Medieval Rhodes is the most famous, but almost every island has some Classical remains, a Crusaders' castle, a clutch of traditional villages, and abundant grandiose public buildings. For these last the Italians, who occupied the islands from 1912 to 1943, are mainly responsible. In their determination to beautify the islands and turn them into a showplace for fascism they undertook public works, excavations and reconstruction on a massive scale; if historical accuracy was often sacrificed in the interests of style, only an expert is likely to complain. A more sinister aspect of the Italian administration was the attempted forcible Latinization of the populace: spoken Greek and Orthodox observance were banned in public from 1923 to 1943. The most tangible reminder of this policy is the (dwindling) number of older people who can still converse – and write – more fluently in Italian than in Greek.

Aside from this bilingualism, the Dodecanese themselves display a marked topographic and economic schizophrenia. The dry limestone outcrops of **Kastellórizo**, **Sými**, **Khálki**, **Kássos** and **Kálymnos** have always been forced to rely on the sea for their livelihoods, and the wealth generated by the maritime culture – especially in the nineteenth century – fostered the growth of attractive port towns. The sprawling, rel-

---

ACCOMMODATION PRICE CODES

,Throughout the book we've used the following **price codes** to denote the cheapest available room in high season; all are prices for a double room, except for category ①, which represents per person rates. Out of season, rates can drop by up to fifty percent, especially if you are staying for three or more nights. Single rooms, where available, cost around seventy percent of the price of a double.

Rented private rooms on the islands usually fall into the ② or ③ categories, depending on their location and facilities, and the season; a few in the ④ category are more like plush self-catering apartments. They are not generally available from late October through to the beginning of April, when only hotels tend to remain open.

① 1400–2000dr	④ 8000–12,000dr
② 4000–6000dr	⑤ 12,000–16,000dr
③ 6000–8000dr	⑥ 16,000dr and upwards

For more accommodation details, see pp.39–41.

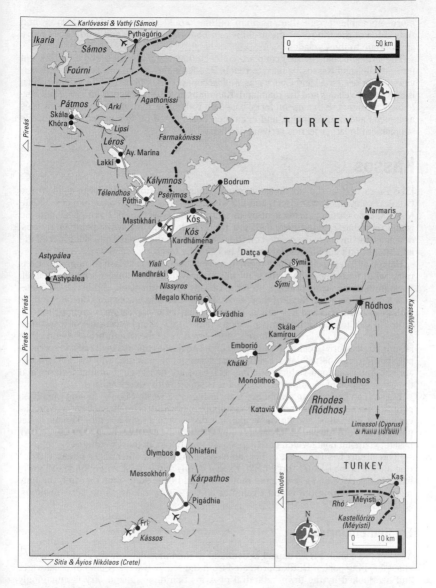

atively fertile giants, **Rhodes** (Ródhos) and **Kós**, have recently seen their traditional agricultural economies almost totally displaced by a tourist industry drawn by good beaches and nightlife, as well as the Aegean's most exciting historical monuments. **Kárpathos** lies somewhere in between, with a (formerly) forested north grafted on to a rocky limestone south; **Tílos**, despite its lack of trees, has ample water, though the green volcano-island of **Níssyros** does not. **Léros** shelters softer contours and more amenable terrain than its map outline would suggest, while **Pátmos** and **Astypálea** at the fringes of the archipelago boast architecture and landscapes more appropriate to the Cyclades.

The largest islands in the group are connected by regular ferries, and none (except for Astypálea and Kássos) is hard to reach. Rhodes is the main transport hub, with services to Turkey, Israel and Cyprus, as well as connections with Crete, the northeastern islands, the Cyclades and the mainland. Kálymnos and Kós are jointly an important secondary terminus, with a useful ferry based on Kálymnos, hydrofoil services using Kós as a focus and transfer point, and excursion boats based on Kós providing a valuable supplement to larger ferries arriving at uncivil hours.

Kássos

Like Psará islet in the northeast Aegean, **Kássos** contributed its large fleet to the Greek revolutionary war effort, and likewise suffered appalling consequences. In late May 1824, an Ottoman army sent by Ibrahim Pasha, Governor of Egypt, besieged the island; on June 7, aided perhaps by a traitor's tip as to the weak point in Kássos' defences, the invaders descended on the populated north-coastal plain, slaughtered the inhabitants, and put houses, farms and trees to the torch.

Barren and depopulated since then, numerous sheer gorges slash through lunar terrain, with fenced smallholdings of olives providing the only permanent relief. Springtime grain crops briefly soften the usually empty terraces, and livestock somehow survives on a thin furze of thornbush. Kássos attracts few visitors despite regular air links with Rhodes and Kárpathos. What remains of the population is grouped together in five villages facing Kárpathos, leaving most of the island accessible only to those on foot or on boat excursions. There's little sign here of the wealth brought into other islands by diaspora Greeks or tourists; crumbling houses and disused hillside terraces poignantly recall better days. Evidence of subsequent emigration to the US is widespread: American logo-T-shirts and baseball caps are de rigueur summer fashion, and the conversation of vacationing expatriates is spiked with Americanisms.

Kássos can be tricky to reach; Frý's anchorage just west of Boúka fishing port is so poor that passing ferries won't stop if any appreciable wind is up. In such cases, you disembark at Kárpathos and fly the remaining distance in a light aircraft. The air ticket plus a taxi fare to Kárpathos airport is comparable to the amount charged by Kárpathos-based excursion boats which can manoeuvre into Boúka in most weathers.

The airport lies 1km west of Frý, an easy enough walk, otherwise a cheap (400dr) ride on one of the island's three taxis. Except in July and August, when there's an unreliable bus service and a few rental motorbikes and boat excursions on offer, the only method of exploring the island's remoter corners is by hiking along fairly arduous, shadeless tracks.

Frý and Emboriós

Most of the capital **FRÝ's** appeal is confined to the immediate environs of the wedge-shaped fishing port of **Boúka**, protected from the sea by two crab-claws of breakwater and overlooked by the town cathedral of Áyios Spirídhon. Inland, Frý is engagingly unpretentious, even down-at-heel; no attempt has been made to prettify what is essentially a dusty little town poised halfway between demolition and reconstruction. **Accommodation** is found at the seafront hotels *Anagenissis* (☎0245/41 323, fax 41 036; ②) and, just behind, the less expensive *Anessis* (☎0245/41 201, fax 41 730; ②). The manager of the *Anagenessis* also has a few pricier apartments (④), and runs the all-in-one travel agency just below. Both hotels tend to be noisy owing to morning bustle on the waterfront – and the phenomenal number of small but lively **bars** in town, one right under the *Anessis*. During high season a few **rooms** operate; these tend to be in the suburb of Emboriós, fifteen minute's walk east, and also more expensive.

Perched overlooking the Boúka, *Iy Oraia Bouka* is easily the best of Frý's **tavernas**, and is reasonably priced. *To Meltemi* ouzerí, on the way to Emboriós, is an honourable runner-up. Shops in Frý, including two fruit stalls, are fairly well stocked for self-catering.

Frý's town **beach**, if you can call it that, is at **Ammouá** (Ammoudhiá), a thirty-minute walk beyond the airstrip along the coastal track. This sandy cove, just before the landmark chapel of Áyios Konstandínos, is often caked with seaweed and tar, but persevere five minutes more and you'll find much cleaner pea-gravel coves. Otherwise, it's worth shelling out for high-season boat excursions to far better beaches on a pair of islets visible to the northwest, **Armathiá** and **Makrá**. There are no amenities (nor shade) on either islet.

The interior

Kássos' inland villages cluster in the agricultural plain just inland from Frý, and are linked to each other by road; all, except the dull grid of Arvanitokhóri, are worth a passing visit, accomplishable by foot in a single day.

Larger in extent and more rural than Frý, **AYÍA MARÍNA**, 1500m inland and uphill, is most attractive seen from the south; one of its two belfried churches is the focus of the island's liveliest festival, on July 17. Just beyond the hamlet of Kathístres, a further 500m southwest, the cave of **Ellinokamára** is named for the Hellenistic wall partially blocking the entrance; from there a path continues another ninety minutes in the same direction to the larger, more natural cave of **Seláï**, with impressive stalactites. On the opposite side of the plain, **PANAYÍA** is famous for its now-neglected mansions – many of Kássos' wealthiest ship captains hailed from here – and the oldest surviving church on the island, the eighteenth-century **Panayía tou Yeóryi**. From **PÓLIO**, 2km above Panayía and site of the island's badly deteriorated medieval castle, a track leads southeast within ninety minutes to **Áyios Mámas**, one of two important rural monasteries.

Between Ayía Marína and Arvanitokhóri, a dirt track heads southwest from the paved road linking the two villages; having skirted the narrows of a fearsome gorge, you are unlikely to see another living thing aside from goats or an occasional wheeling hawk. After about an hour the Mediterranean appears to the south, a dull expanse ruffled only by the occasional ship bound for Cyprus and the Middle East. When you finally reach a fork, adopt the upper, right-hand turning, following derelict phone lines and (initially) some cement paving towards the rural monastery of **Áyios Yeóryios Khadhión**, 11km (3hr on foot) from Frý, and only frequented during its late-April festival time, and during mid-summer by the resident caretaker. There are a few open guest cells and cistern water here if you need to fill up canteens; the only other water en route is a well at the route's high point.

From the monastery it's another 3km – bikes can make it most of the way – to **Khélathros**, a lonely cove at the mouth of one of the larger, more forbidding Kassiote canyons. The sand-and-gravel beach itself is small and mediocre, but the water is pristine and – except for the occasional fishing boat – you'll probably be alone. The lower, left-hand option at the fork is the direct track to Khélathros, but this is only 2km shorter, and following severe storm damage, impassable to any vehicle and all but the most energetic hikers.

Kárpathos

A long, narrow island between Rhodes and Crete, wild **Kárpathos** has always been something of an underpopulated backwater, although it is the third largest of the Dodecanese. A mountainous spine, habitually cloud-capped, rises to over 1200 metres, and divides the more populous, lower-lying south from an exceptionally rugged north. Despite a magnificent windswept coastline of cliffs and promontories interrupted by little beaches, Kárpathos has succumbed surprisingly little to tourism. This has much to do with the appalling road system – rutted where paved, unspeakable otherwise – the paucity of interesting villages, and the often high cost of food, which offsets reasonable room prices.

Kárpathos hasn't the most alluring of interiors: the central and northern uplands were badly scorched by forest fires in the 1980s, and agriculture plays a slighter role than on any other Greek island of comparable size. Frankly, the Karpathians are too well off to bother much with farming – massive emigration to America and the resulting remittance economy has transformed Kárpathos into one of the wealthiest Greek islands. Most visitors come here for a glimpse of the traditional village life that prevails in the isolated north of the island, and for the numerous superb, secluded beaches. Although the airport can take direct international flights, only a few charters use it, and visitors are concentrated in a couple of resorts in the south.

Kárpathos' four Mycenean and Classical cities figure little in ancient chronicles. Alone of the major Dodecanese, the island was held by the Genoese and Venetians after the Byzantine collapse and so has no castle of the crusading Knights of Saint John, nor any surviving medieval fortresses of consequence. The Ottomans couldn't be bothered to settle or even garrison it; instead they left a single judge or *kadi* at the main town, making the Greek population responsible for his safety during the many pirate attacks.

Pigádhia (Kárpathos Town)

PIGÁDHIA, the capital, often known simply as Kárpathos, nestles at the south end of scenic Vróndi Bay, whose sickle of sand extends 3km northwest. The town itself, curling around the jetty and quay where ferries and excursion boats dock, is as drab as its setting is beautiful, an ever-increasing number of concrete blocks creating an air of a vast building site; by comparison the Italian-era port police building seems an heirloom. Although there's nothing special to see, Pigádhia does offer just about every facility you might need.

Practicalities

There's an **OTE** at the top end of Ethnikís Andistásis; Olympic Airways is on Apodhímon Karpathíon ("Street of the Overseas Karpathians"), at the corner of Mitropolítou; while the **post office** is on 28-Oktovríou, the main inland street running parallel to Apodhímon Kapathíon.

If you want to explore the island there are regular **buses** to Pilés, via Apéri, Voládha and Óthos, as well as to Ammopí, and a less regular service to Arkássa and Finíki. Set-rate, unmetered **taxis** aren't too expensive to get to these and other points (such as the airport) on the paved road system, but charge a fortune to go anywhere further afield. Outfits near the post office like Holiday (☎0245/22 813) or Circle (☎0245/22 690) rent **cars** at vastly inflated rates, while Hermes (☎0245/22 090) does **bike rental**. Be warned that the only fuel on the island is to be found just to the north and south of town, and the tanks on the small bikes are barely big enough to complete a circuit of the south, let alone head up north – which is, in any case, expressly forbidden by most outfits. For seagoing jaunts, **windsurfers** and **canoes** are rented from various stalls on Vróndi beach.

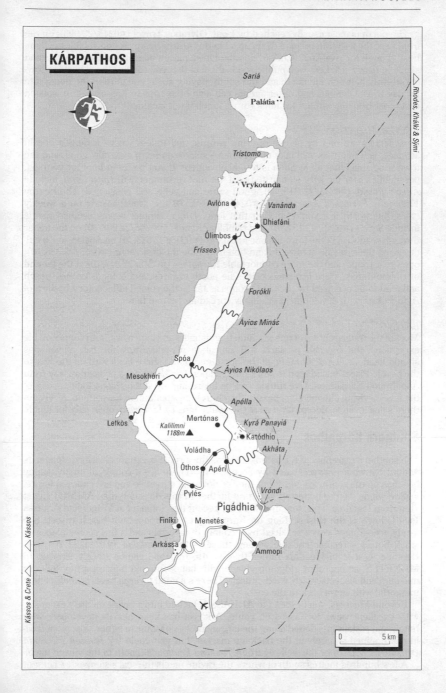

The north is most usually reached by **boat**. Olympos Travel (☎0245/22 993), on the front near the jetty, offers good deals on all-in **day-tours** (from around 4500dr to Ólymbos), though the rival boat (Chrisovalandou Lines; pay on board) is more attractive and stable in heavy sea. Less well-publicized is the fact that you can use these boats to travel **one-way** between the north and the south, paying about one-third of the going rate for day trips. Olympos and other agents can also offer trips to Kássos and to isolated east coast beaches without facilities (bring lunch if not included).

ACCOMMODATION

Most ferries are met by people offering **rooms**, and unless you've arranged one in advance, you might as well take up an offer – standards seem generally good, and the town is so small that no location is too inconvenient. If you prefer to hunt for yourself, possibilities near the jetty, signposted past the (not recommended) *Hotel Coral*, include *Anna's Rooms* (☎0245/22 313; ②), good value and very well positioned. The nearby *Vittoroulis Furnished Apartments* (☎0245/22 639; ④) are available only on a weekly basis, but worth it if you're staying that long. Other, simpler rooms establishments include *Sofia's* (☎0245/22 154; ②), the rambling *Konaki* (☎0245/22 908; ②) on the upper through-road west of the town hall, or *Filoxenia* (☎0245/22 623; ②) on Anastasíou, a cul-de-sac on the east side of town. Inland hotels include the basic *Avra* (☎0245/22 388; ②), open year-round, and the more comfortable *Karpathos* (☎0245/22 347; ③) at the far end of Dhimokratías. More luxurious places lie north towards, and behind, **Vróndi** beach and tend to be occupied by package groups as far as the ruined fifth-century basilica of **Ayía Fotiní**, with development gradually spreading beyond here.

EATING

Most of the waterfront **tavernas** are indistinguishable and expensive, with some notable exceptions: the *Olympia* psistariá will appeal to meat-lovers, while fish aficionados should head for *Iy Kali Kardhia*, at the north end of the shore boulevard on the way to the beach. Places inland tend to work out cheaper: try *Mike's*, up a pedestrian way from Apodhímon Karpathíon. Live **music** can be heard nightly at the *Halkia* kafenío, one of the few surviving old buildings next to the church on Apodhímon Karpathíon. At Vróndi there's just a single, decent taverna at the south end, *To Limanaki*, open only for lunch.

Southern Kárpathos

The southern extremity of Kárpathos towards the airport is extraordinarily desolate, its natural barrenness exacerbated by recent fires. There are a couple of empty, sandy beaches on the southeast coast, but they're not at all attractive and are exposed to prevailing winds. You're better off going no further in this direction than **AMMOPÍ**, just 7km from Pigádhia. This, together with the recent development at Vróndi and Arkássa (see below), is the closest thing on Kárpathos to a purpose-built beach resort: two sandy, tree-fringed coves serviced by a couple of tavernas and a few rooms places or small hotels – recommendable among these is the *Votsalakia* (☎0245/22 204; ③). Heading west from Pigádhia rather than south, the road climbs steeply 9km up to **MENETÉS**, an appealing ridgetop village with handsome old houses, a tiny folklore museum and a spectacularly sited church. There's a good taverna here, *Manolis*, and a memorial with views back to the east.

Beyond Menetés, you descend to **ARKÁSSA**, tucked into a ravine on the west coast, with excellent views to Kássos en route. Arkássa has been heavily developed, with hotels and restaurants dotted along the largely rocky coastline to either side; most facilities are aimed squarely at the package market, but you could try *Pension Filoxenia* (☎0245/61 341; ②) or the well-regarded *Taverna Petaloudha*, both in the village itself.

A few hundred metres south of where the ravine meets the sea, a signposted cement side road leads to the whitewashed chapel of Ayía Sofía, marooned amidst various remains of Classical and Byzantine Arkessia. These consist of several mosaic floors with geometric patterns, including one running diagonally under the floor of a half-buried chapel, emerging from the walls on either side. The Paleókastro headland beyond was the site of Mycenean Arkessia.

The tiny fishing port of **FINÍKI**, just a couple of kilometres north, offers a minuscule beach, occasional excursions to Kássos, three or four **tavernas** with seafood menus, and several **rooms** establishments lining the road to the jetty, including *Fay's Paradise* (☎0245/61 308; ③). The asphalt on the west-coast road currently runs out well short of the attractive resort of **LEFKÓS** (Paraliá Lefkoú). Although this is a delightful place for flopping on the beach, only three weekly buses call, and Lefkós marks the furthest point you can reach from Pighádhia on a small motorbike and return safely before running out of fuel. Your efforts will be rewarded by the striking landscape of cliffs, hills, islets and sandspits surrounding a triple bay. The *Sunlight Restaurant* has an enviable tamarisk-shaded position on the southern cove, and several **rooms** places dot the promontory overlooking the two more northerly, and progressively wilder, bays.

Back on the main road, you climb northeast through one of the few sections of pine forest not scarred by fire, to **MESOKHÓRI**. The village tumbles down towards the sea around narrow, stepped alleys; the access road ends at the top of town, where a snack bar constitutes the only tourist facility. Alternatively, you can carry on to Spóa, overlooking the east coast.

Central Kárpathos

The centre of Kárpathos supports a quartet of villages blessed with superb hillside settings and ample running water. In these settlements nearly everyone has "done time" in North America, then returned home with their nest eggs: New Jersey, New York and Canadian car plates tell you exactly where repatriated islanders struck it rich. West-facing **PYLÉS** is the most attractive, while **ÓTHOS**, noted for its red wine and a private ethnographic museum is the highest and chilliest, just below 1214-metre Mount Kalilímni and a huge wind turbine. On the east side of the ridge you find **VOLÁDHA** with its tiny Venetian citadel. From **APÉRI**, the largest, lowest and wealthiest settlement, you can drive 7km along a very rough road to the dramatic pebble beach of **Akháta**, with a spring but no other facilities.

Beyond Apéri, the road up the **east coast** is extremely rough in places, passing above beaches most easily accessible by boat trips from Pigádhia. **Kyrá Panayiá** is the first encountered, reached via a rutted side road through Katódhio hamlet; there's a surprising number of villas, rooms and tavernas in the ravine behind the 150m of fine gravel and sheltered, turquoise water. **Apélla** is the best of the beaches you can – just about – reach by road, but has no amenities other than a spring. The end of this route is **SPÓA**, high above the shore on the island's spine, with a snack bar at the edge of the village; there's also a good traditional kafenío a short way down. **Áyios Nikólaos**, 5km below, is a beach and port with tavernas and a large, if overgrown, early Christian town to explore.

Northern Kárpathos

Although connected by dirt road with Spóa, much the easiest way to get to northern Kárpathos is by boat – inter-island ferries call at Dhiafáni once a week, or there are smaller tour boats from Pigádhia daily. These take a couple of hours, and are met at Dhiafáni by buses for the eight-kilometre transfer up to Ólymbos, the traditional village that is the main attraction of this part of the island.

Ólymbos and around

Originally founded as a pirate-safe refuge in Byzantine times, windswept **ÓLYMBOS** straddles a long ridge below slopes studded by mostly ruined windmills. Two restored ones, beyond the main church, grind wheat and barley during late summer, and the basement of one houses a small ethnographic museum (odd hours; free). Indeed the village has long attracted foreign and Greek ethnologists, who treat it as a living museum of peasant dress, crafts, dialect and music long since gone elsewhere in Greece. It's still a very picturesque place, yet traditions are vanishing by the year; nowadays it's only the older women and those working in the several tourist shops who wear the striking and magnificently colourful traditional dress.

After a while you'll notice the prominent role that the women play in daily life: tending gardens, carrying goods on their shoulders, or herding goats. Nearly all Ólymbos men emigrate or work outside the village, sending money home and returning only on holidays. The long-isolated villagers also speak a unique dialect, said to maintain traces of its Doric and Phrygian origins – thus "Ólymbos" is pronounced "Élymbos" locally. Traditional music is still heard regularly and draws crowds of visitors at festival times, in particular Easter and August 15, when you've little hope of finding a bed.

At other times, the daytime commercialization of Ólymbos makes a good reason to **stay** overnight in one of an increasing number of **rooms** places. The *Ólymbos* (☎0245/51 252; ②), near the village entrance, is a good bare-bones option, while *Hotel Aphrodite* (☎0245/51 307; ③) offers both en-suite facilities and a southerly ocean view. There are also plenty of places to **eat** – *Parthenonas*, on the square by the church, is excellent; try their *makaroúnes*, a local dish of homemade pasta with onions and cheese.

From the village, the west coast and tiny port and beach at **Frísses** are a dizzy drop below, or there are various signposted **hikes** up into the mountains. It's also possible to walk between Ólymbos and Spóa or Messokhóri in the south, a six-to-seven hour trek made less scenic by the aftermath of fires. Perhaps the most attractive option, and certainly the easiest, is to walk back down to Dhiafáni, beginning just below the two working windmills. The route is well marked, eventually dropping to a ravine amidst extensive forest. The hike takes around ninety minutes downhill – too long to accomplish in the standard three or four hours allowed on day trips if you want to explore Ólymbos as well. By staying overnight in the village, you could also tackle the trail north to the Byzantine ruins at **Vrykoúnda**, via the seasonally inhabited hamlet of Avlóna.

Dhiafáni

Although its popularity is growing – especially since the completion of a new dock – rooms in **DHIAFÁNI** are still inexpensive, and the pace of life slow outside of August. There are plenty of places at which to stay and eat, shops that will change money and even a small travel agency. The obvious non-en-suite hotels opposite the quay are noisy; try instead the garrulously friendly *Pansion Delfini* (☎0245/51 391; ②) or *Pansion Glaros* (☎0245/51 259; ②; high season only), up on the southern hillside. On the front, the favourite taverna is *Anatoli*, easily recognizable by the folk reliefs that sprout from its roof.

There are boat trips to various nearby **beaches** – as well as to Byzantine ruins on the uninhabited islet of **Sariá** or through the narrow strait to Trístomo anchorage and the ruins of Vrykoúnda (see above) – or there are several coves within walking distance. Closest is **Vanánda**, a stony beach with an eccentric campsite-snack bar in the oasis behind. To get there, follow the pleasant signposted path north through the pines, but don't believe the signs that say ten minutes – it's over thirty minutes away, shortcutting the more recent road.

Rhodes (Ródhos)

It's no accident that **Rhodes** is among the most-visited Greek islands. Not only is its east coast lined with numerous sandy beaches, but the capital's nucleus is a beautiful and remarkably preserved medieval city, the legacy of the crusading Knights of Saint John who used the island as their main base from 1309 until 1522. Unfortunately this showpiece is jammed to capacity with up to 100,000 tourists a day, nine months of the year. Of transient visitors, Germans, Brits, Swedes, Italians and Danes predominate in

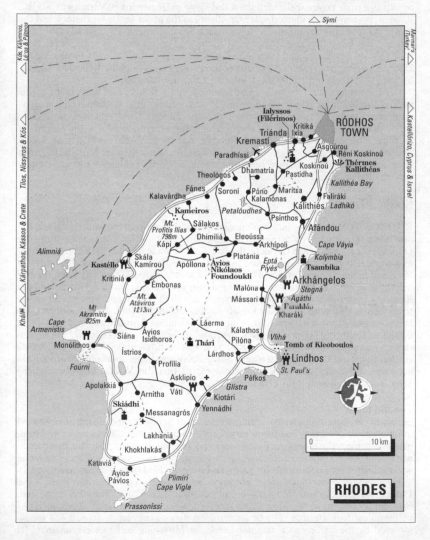

that order; accordingly fish fingers, smörgåsbord and pizza jostle alongside moussaká on menus at tourist tavernas.

Blessed with an equable climate and strategic position, Rhodes was important from earliest times despite a lack of many good harbours. The best natural port spawned the ancient town of Lindos which, together with the other city states, Kameiros and Ialyssos, united in 408 BC to found the new capital of Rhodes at the northern tip of the island. At various moments the cities allied themselves with Alexander, the Persians, Athenians or Spartans as prevailing conditions suited them, generally escaping retribution for backing the wrong side by a combination of seafaring audacity, sycophancy and burgeoning wealth as a trade centre. Following the failed siege of Demetrios Polyorkites in 305 BC, Rhodes prospered even more, displacing Athens as the major venue for rhetoric and the arts in the east Mediterranean. The town, which lies underneath virtually all of the modern city, was laid out by one Hippodamus in the grid layout much in vogue at the time, with planned residential and commercial quarters. Its perimeter walls totalled nearly 15km, enclosing nearly double the area of the present town, and the Hellenistic population was said to exceed 100,000, a staggering figure for late antiquity.

Decline set in when Rhodes became involved in the Roman civil wars, and Cassius sacked the town; by late imperial times, it was a backwater, a status confirmed by numerous Barbarian raids during the Byzantine period. The Byzantines were compelled to cede the island to the Genoese, who in turn surrendered it to the Knights of St John. The second great siege of Rhodes, during 1522–23, saw Ottoman sultan Süleyman the Magnificent oust the stubborn knights, who retreated to Malta; the town once again lapsed into relative obscurity, though heavily colonized and garrisoned, until the Italian seizure of 1912.

Ródhos Town

RÓDHOS TOWN divides into two unequal parts: the compact old walled city, and the new town which sprawls around it in three directions. The latter dates from the Ottoman occupation, when Greek Orthodox – forbidden to dwell in the old city – founded several suburb villages or *marásia* in the environs. In the walled town, the tourist is king, and in the modern district of Neokhóri west of Mandhráki yacht harbour, the few buildings which aren't hotels are souvenir shops, car rental or travel agencies and bars – easily a hundred in every category. Around this to the north and west stretches the **town beach** (standing room only for latecomers), complete with deckchairs, parasols and showers. At the northernmost point of the island an **Aquarium** (daily 9am–9pm; 600dr), officially the "Hydrobiological Institute", offers some diversion with its subterranean maze of seawater tanks. Upstairs is a less enthralling collection of half-rotten stuffed sharks, seals and even a whale. Some 200m southeast stands the **Murad Reis mosque**, a Muslim cemetery, and just west of this the **Villa Cleobolus**, where Lawrence Durrell lived from 1945 to 1947.

The old town

Simply to catalogue the principal monuments and attractions cannot do full justice to the infinitely more rewarding **medieval city**. There's ample gratification to be derived from slipping through the eleven surviving gates and strolling the streets, under flying archways built for earthquake resistance, past the warm-toned sandstone and limestone walls splashed with ochre and blue paint, and over the *khokhláki* (pebble) pavement.

Dominating the northeast sector of the city's fourteenth-century fortifications, is the **Palace of the Grand Masters** (summer Mon 12.30–7pm, Tues–Fri 8am–7pm, Sat–Sun 8am–3pm; winter Mon 12.30–3pm, Tues–Sun 8.30am–3pm; 1200dr, includes medieval exhibit). Destroyed by an ammunition depot explosion in 1856, it was reconstructed by the Italians as a summer home for Mussolini and Victor Emmanuel III

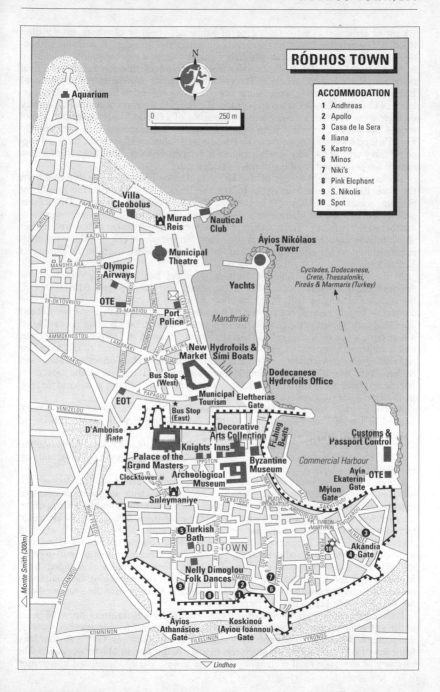

RÓDHOS TOWN

ACCOMMODATION
1 Andhreas
2 Apollo
3 Casa de la Sera
4 Iliana
5 Kastro
6 Minos
7 Niki's
8 Pink Elephant
9 S. Nikolis
10 Spot

Aquarium

Villa Cleobolus

Murad Reis

Nautical Club

Áyios Nikólaos Tower

Municipal Theatre

Olympic Airways

Yachts

Cyclades, Dodecanese, Crete, Thessaloníki, Pireás & Marmaris (Turkey)

OTE

Port Police

Mandhráki

New Market

Hydrofoils & Sími Boats

Bus Stop (West)

Dodecanese Hydrofoils Office

EOT

Municipal Tourism

Eleftherías Gate

D'Amboise Gate

Bus Stop (East)

Decorative Arts Collection

Customs & Passport Control

Knights' Inns

Palace of the Grand Masters

Byzantine Museum

Commercial Harbour

Clocktower

Archeological Museum

Ayía Ekateríni Gate

OTE

Süleymaniye

Mýlon Gate

PL. EVREON +MARTYRON

Turkish Bath

OLD TOWN

Akándia Gate

Nelly Dimoglou Folk Dances

Monte Smith (300m)

Áyios Athanásios Gate

Koskinoú (Ayíou Ioánnou) Gate

Líndhos

("King of Italy and Albania, Emperor of Ethiopia"), neither of whom ever visited Rhodes. The exterior, based on medieval engravings and accounts, is passably authentic, but inside matters are on an altogether grander scale: a marble staircase leads up to rooms paved with Hellenistic mosaics from Kós, and the movable furnishings rival many a northern European palace. The ground floor is home to the splendid **Medieval Exhibit** (Tues–Sat 8am–2.30pm; same ticket), whose collection highlights the importance of Christian Rhodes as a trade centre. The Knights are represented with a display on their sugar-refining industry and a gravestone of a Grand Master; precious manuscripts and books precede a wing of post-Byzantine icons, moved here permanently from Panayía Kástrou (see below). On Tuesday and Saturday afternoons, there's a supplementary tour of the **city walls** (one hour, 2.45pm; 1200dr), beginning from a gate next to the palace and finishing at the Koskinoú gate.

The heavily restored **Street of the Knights** (Odhós Ippotón) leads due east from the Platía Kleovoúlou in front of the Palace; the "Inns" lining it housed the Knights of St John, according to linguistic and ethnic affiliation, until the Ottoman Turks compelled them to leave for Malta after a six-month siege in which the defenders were outnumbered thirty to one. Today the Inns house various government offices and cultural institutions vaguely appropriate to their past, but the whole effect of the renovation is predictably sterile and stagy (indeed, nearby streets were used in the filming of *Pascali's Island*).

At the bottom of the hill, the Knights' Hospital has been refurbished as the **Archeological Museum** (Tues–Sat 8.30am–6pm, Sun 8.30am–3pm; 600dr), though the arches and echoing halls of the building somewhat overshadow the badly labelled contents – largely painted pottery dating from the sixth and seventh centuries. Behind the second-storey sculpture garden, the Hellenistic statue gallery is more accessible: in a rear corner stands the so-called "Marine Venus", beloved of Lawrence Durrell, but lent a rather sinister aspect by her sea-dissolved face – in contrast to the friendlier *Aphrodite Bathing*. Virtually next door is the **Decorative Arts Collection** (Tues–Sun 8.30am–3pm; 4600dr), gleaned from old houses across the Dodecanese; the most compelling artefacts are carved cupboard doors and chest lids painted in naïve style with mythological or historical episodes.

Across the way stands the **Byzantine Museum** (Tues–Sun 8.30am–3pm; 600dr), housed in the old cathedral of the Knights, who adapted the Byzantine shrine of Panayía Kástrou for their own needs. Medieval icons and frescoes lifted from crumbling chapels on Rhodes and Khálki, as well as photos of art still in situ, constitute the exhibits; it's worth a visit since most of the Byzantine churches in the old town and outlying villages are locked.

If instead you head south from the Palace of the Grand Masters, it's hard to miss the most conspicuous Turkish monument in Rhodes, the candy-striped **Süleymaniye mosque**. Rebuilt in the nineteenth century on foundations three hundred years older, it's currently under scaffolding like most local Ottoman monuments. The old town is in fact well sown with mosques and *mescids* (the Islamic equivalent of a chapel), many of them converted from Byzantine shrines after the 1522 conquest, when the Christians were expelled from the medieval precinct. A couple of these mosques are still used by the sizeable **Turkish-speaking minority** here, some of them descended from Muslims who fled Crete between 1898 and 1913. Their most enduring civic contribution is the imposing **hamam** or Turkish bath on Platía Ariónos up in the southwest corner of the medieval city (Wed & Sat pm; 500dr).

Heading downhill from the Süleymaniye mosque, **Odhós Sokrátous**, once the heart of the Ottoman bazaar, is now the "Via Turista", packed with fur and jewellery stores, and tourists. Beyond the tiled central fountain in Platía Ippokrátous, Odhós Aristotélous leads into the Platía tón Evréon Martyrón (Square of the Jewish Martyrs), renamed in memory of the large local community that was almost totally annihilated in summer

1944. You can sometimes visit the ornate **synagogue** on Odhós Simíou just to the south, maintained essentially as a memorial to the 2000 Jews of Rhodes and Kós sent from here to the death camps; plaques in French – the language of educated Ottoman Jews across the east Aegean – commemorate the dead.

About a kilometre west of the old town, overlooking the west-coast road, the sparse remains of **Hellenistic Rhodes** – a restored theatre and stadium, plus a few columns of an Apollo temple – perch atop Monte Smith, the hill of Áyios Stéfanos renamed after a British admiral who used it as a watchpoint during the Napoleonic wars. The wooded site is popular with joggers and strollers, but for summer shade and greenery the best spot is probably the **Rodini park**, nearly 2km south of town on the road to Líndhos. On August evenings a wine tasting festival (8pm–midnight) is held here by the municipal authorities.

Practicalities

All international and inter-island **ferries** dock at the middle of Rhodes' three ports, the commercial harbour; the only exceptions are local **boats** to and from Sými, and the **hydrofoils**, which use the yacht harbour of Mandhráki. Its entrance was supposedly once straddled by the Colossus, an ancient statue of Apollo built to celebrate the end of the 305 BC siege; today two columns surmounted by bronze deer are less overpowering replacements.

The **airport** is 13km southwest of town, near the village of Paradhíssi; public urban buses bound for Paradhíssi, Kalavárdha, Theológos or Sálakos pass the gate on the main road fairly frequently between 6.30am and 9pm. A taxi fare into town is 2000–2500dr. Orange-and-white KTEL **buses** for both the west and east coasts of Rhodes leave from two almost adjacent terminals on Papágou and Avérof, just outside the Italian-built New Market (a tourist trap). Between the lower eastern station and the **taxi** rank at Platía Rimínis there's a helpful **tourist office** (May–Oct daily 9am–9pm), while some way up Papágou on the corner of Makaríou is the **EOT office** (Mon–Fri 8am–2pm); both dispense bus and ferry schedules.

ACCOMMODATION

Inexpensive pensions abound in the old town, contained almost entirely in the quad bounded by Omírou to the south, Sokrátous to the north, Perikléous to the east and Ippodhámou to the west. In addition, there are a few more possibilities in the former Jewish quarter, east of Perikléous. At crowded seasons, or late at night, it's prudent to accept the offers of proprietors meeting the ferries and change base next day if necessary.

Andreas, Omírou 28d (☎0241/34 156, fax 74 285). Perennially popular, this hotel is the most imaginative of the local old-house restorations. All rooms have sinks. There is a terrace bar with a view, and French and English is spoken. ④.

Apollo, Omírou 28c (☎0241/35 064). Basic but clean and friendly rooms place; the self-catering kitchen makes it good for longer stays. ③.

Casa de la Sera, Thisséos 38 (☎0241/75 154). A Jewish-quarter renovation, with wonderful floor tiles in the en-suite rooms, and a breakfast bar. ④.

Kastro, Platía Ariónos (☎0241/20 446). The proprietor is a famous eccentric artist renowned for his royalist leanings, but the hotel is fine for budget rooms; garden rooms are quieter than those overlooking nearby restaurants. ③.

Iliana, Gavála 1 (☎0241/30 251). This former Jewish mansion exudes a Victorian boarding-house atmosphere, but is clean and quiet enough with private facilities. ③.

Minos, Omírou 5 (☎0241/31 813). Modern and hence a bit sterile, but with great views, this neat pension is managed by an English-speaking family. ③.

Niki's, Sofokléous 39 (☎0241/25 115). Rooms can be on the small side, but ground-floor units are en suite, and upper-storey ones have fine views. ③.

Pink Elephant, Irodhótou 42 (☎0241/22 469). A recent entry on the scene, managed by *Cleo's Restaurant*, with Scots reception; a variety of rooms, en suite and not. ③.

S. Nikolis, Ippodhámou 61 (☎0241/34 561, fax 32 034). A variety of establishments in the west of the old town. Hotel rates ⑥ include a huge breakfast, and there's the option of self-catering apartments (⑤) or a simple pension (③). Booking essential for hotel and apartments, but accepted only with credit-card number.

Spot, Perikléous 21 (☎0241/34 737). Not the most inspired renovation, but this hotel is spotless, and you won't find en-suite rooms elsewhere for this price, except at *Niki's*. ③.

EATING AND DRINKING

Eating well for a reasonable price in and around Ródhos Town is a challenge, but not an insurmountable one. As a general rule, the further back from Sokrátous you go, the better value you'll find.

Aigaion, Eskhílou 47, cnr Aristofánous. Run by a welcoming Kalymniot family, this ouzerí features brown bread and curiosities such as *foúski* (soft-shell oyster).

Alatopipero/Salt and Pepper, Mihkaïl Petrídhi 76 (☎0241/65 494), southwest edge of new town, northwest of Rodíni Park. Upmarket ouzerí serving such vegetarian oddities as stuffed cyclamen leaves and *khortópittes* (wild green pies) plus more conventional delicacies, accompanied by limited bottlings from Greece's microwineries. It'll cost 3000dr if you stick to mezédhes, 4500 if you do a main course. Supper only, closed Mon.

Cleo's, Ayíou Fanouríou 17 (☎0241/28 415). Rather overpriced but tasty nouvelle Italian, strong on appetizers and pasta dishes. Count on 4500dr a head; reservations recommended. Closed Sun.

Le Bistrot, Omírou 22–24. Open for lunch and supper daily except Sunday, this is a genuine French-run bistro with excellent if pricey food. Always full, with a loyal expatriate clientele.

O Meraklis, Aristotélous 32. This *pátsas* (tripe-and-trotter soup) kitchen is only open 3–7am for a motley clientele of post-club lads, Turkish stallholders, night-club singers and travellers just stumbled off an overnight ferry. Great free entertainment, and the soup's good, too.

Metaxi Mas, Claude Pepper, Ámmos district. An excellent, tiny ouzerí overlooking Zéfyros beach, with unusual vegetarian and seafood dishes.

Mikis, alley behind Sokrátous 17. Very inexpensive hole-in-the-wall place, serving only fish, salads and wine.

Nireas, Platía Sofkléous 22 (☎0241/21 703). A good, family-run Greek ouzerí; reservations advised in the evenings.

Palia Istoria, Mitropóleos 108 (☎0241/32 421), cnr Dhendhrínou, in south extension of new town, Álmoss district. Reckoned to be the best ouzerí on Rhodes, but very expensive for such dishes as celery hearts in egg-lemon sauce and scallops with artichokes. Supper only; reservations essential.

Yiannis, Apéllou 41, below *Hotel Sydney*. Fair portions of *mayireftá*, dished out by a family long resident in New York.

NIGHTLIFE

The old town formerly had a well-deserved reputation for being tomb-silent at night, though this has changed as establishments have cropped up catering to those bored with the estimated two hundred bars and clubs in Neokhóri, where theme nights and various other gimmicks predominate. Dance clubs and bars are mostly along the streets and alleys bounded by Alexándhrou Dhiákou, Orfanídhou (aka "Skandi Street", after the latter-day Vikings), Fanouráki and Nikifórou Mandhilará.

Sedate by comparison, Ministry-of-Culture-approved folk dances (April–Oct Mon–Fri 9.20pm; 2500dr) are presented by the Nelly Dimoglou Company, performed in the landscaped "Old Town Theatre" off Andhroníkou, near Platía Ariónos. More of a techno extravaganza is the **Sound and Light** show, spotlighting sections of the city walls, playing in a garden just off Platía Rimínis. There's English-language narration nightly except Sunday, its screening time varying from 8.15pm to 10.15pm (2000dr).

Thanks to a large contingent from the local university, there are several cool-season (indoor) **cinemas** in the new town showing first-run fare. Choose from among the Rodon Municipal Theatre, next to the Town Hall in Neokhóri; the Metropol, southeast of the old town opposite the stadium; the nearby Pallas on Dhimokratías; and the Titania on Kolokotróni, off Kanadhá, open most of the year.

Araliki, Aristofánous 45, Old Town. The bohemian set hangs out at this old-style kafenío on the ground floor of a medieval house; simple *mezédhes* provided by Italian proprietress Miriam accompany drinks, which even include Nissirot *soumádha*. Open all year.

Arkhaia Agora, Omírou 70, Old Town. Very elegant, upscale bar with good taped music, food service and a garden at the rear, shared with the affiliated *Sotiris Nikolis* hotel.

Blue Lagoon Pool Bar, 25-Martíou 2, Neokhóri. One of the better theme bars, in this case a "desert island" with palm trees, waterfalls, a shipwrecked galleon – and taped music.

Café Chantant, Aristotélous 22, Old Town. Respected as a long-established music café (Greek popular and *rembétika*), but steel yourself for the drink prices and often ear-shattering noise.

Christos' Garden, Dhilberáki 59, Neokhóri. This combination art-gallery/bar/café, run by Christos Voulgaris, occupies a carefully restored old house and courtyard with pebble-mosaic floors throughout. Incongruously classy for the area.

Hard Rock Café, Orfanídhou 29, Neokhóri. Yes there's one here too, whether a genuine affiliate or a trademark ripoff is hard to say. "Hard rock, soft lights, driving music" promised.

Mango Bar, Platía Dhoriéos 3, Old Town. Piped music and a variety of drinks at this durable bar on an otherwise quiet plaza; also a good source of breakfast after 8am, served under a plane tree.

Nyn kai Aei, cul-de-sac off Sofokléous 4t, Old Town. An elegant, live-music bar in a vaulted, thirteenth-century building, attracting a thirty-something clientele; the name means "now and forever" in ancient Greek.

Popeye's, Sofokléous 38, Old Town. Serves cheap beer and house wine to a collegiate crowd; favourite haunt of yacht hostesses between assignments.

Presley's, Íonos Dhragoúmi 27, Neokhóri. A small and thus often crowded bar, featuring a wide range of 50s and 60s music (the cocktails are named after Elvis's hits).

Rolóï, Orféos 1, Old Town. The baroque clocktower erected by Ahmet Fetih Pasha in 1857 is now the focus of possibly the most exclusive café/bar in the old town. Admission charge to climb the tower, and steeply priced drinks, but you are paying for the terrific view.

Shooters, Apolloníou Rodhíou 61, Neokhóri. The haunt of divers, as it's run by the Waterhoppers scuba outfitters; live acoustic music Tuesday and Thursday.

Sticky Fingers, Anthoúla Zérvou 6, Neokhóri. Long lived music bar with reasonable drinks; the place for rock, often live, nightly from 10pm onwards.

Listings

Airlines British Airways, Platía Kýprou 1 (☎0241/27 756); KLM, Ammokhóstou 3 (☎0241/21 010); Air Greece, c/o Triton Holidays Plastíra 9 (☎0241/21 690); Olympic, Iérou Lókhou 9 (☎0241/24 571). Scheduled flights are exorbitant; there's a very faint chance of picking up an unclaimed return charter seat to northern Europe – ask at the various group tour offices.

Car rental Prices at non-international chains are fairly standard at £33/US$50 per day, but can be bargained down to about £27/US$43 a day, all-inclusive, out of peak season. More flexible local outfits, all in the new town, include Alexander, Afstralías 58 (☎0241/27 547); Alamo, Mandihlará 64 (☎0241/38 400); Just, Orfanídhou 45 (☎0241/31 811); Kosmos, Papaloúka 31 (☎0241/74 374); MBC, 25-Martíou 29 (☎0241/28 617); Orion, Yeoryíou Leóndos 36 (☎0241/22 137); and Payless, Íonos Dhragoúmi 29 (☎0241/26 586).

Exchange Most bank branches are near Platía Lýprou in Neokhóri, keeping weekday evening and Saturday morning hours; at other times use the cash dispensers of the Commercial Bank, Credit Bank, Ionian Bank (with a useful branch in the old town), or National Bank.

Ferries Tourist office handouts list the bewildering array of representatives for the numerous boat and hydrofoil companies which operate here; authoritative schedule information is available at the *limenarkhío*, on Mandhráki esplanade near the post office.

Laundries Express Service, Dhilberáki 97, cnr Orfanídhou and Neokhóri; Lavomatic, 28-Oktovríou 32, Neokhóri; Hobby, Plátonos 32, old town.

Motorbike rental Mopeds will make little impact on Rhodes; sturdier Yamaha 125s, suitable for two people, go for as little as 3500dr a day. There are plenty of outlets in Neokhóri, especially around Odhós Dhiákou.

Phones At the corner of Amerikís and 25-Martíou in the new town, and at the foot of the jetty in the commercial harbour; the latter also has several booths dedicated to ATT Direct and MCI service to North America.

Post office Main branch with outgoing mail, poste restante and exchange windows on Mandhráki harbour, open Mon–Fri 7.30am–8pm; less reliable mobile office on Órfeos in the old town, open shorter hours.

Travel agencies Recommended in the old town is Castellania, Evripídhou 1–3, corner Platía Ippokrátous; GEM Travel at Papaloúka 31 (☎0241/76 206) is good for cheap flights back to the UK, in particular unclaimed return seats or one-way tickets. Visa at Grigóri Lambráki 54 (☎0241/33 282) and Contours at Ammokhóstou 9 (☎0241/36 001) are also worth contacting.

The east coast

Heading down the coast from the capital you have to go some way before you escape the crowds from local beach hotels, their numbers swelled by visitors using the regular buses from town or on boat tours out of Mandhráki. You might look in at the decayed, abandoned spa of **Thérmes Kallithéas**, dating from the Italian period. Located 3km south of Kallithéa resort proper, down an unsigned road through pines, the spa is set in a palm grove and is illuminated at night to create a hugely enjoyable spectacle of mock-orientalia. The former fishing village of **FALIRÁKI**, which draws a youngish package clientele, is all too much in the mode of a Spanish *costa* resort, while the scenery just inland – arid, scrubby sand-hills at the best of times – has been made that much more dreary by fire damage that stretches way beyond Líndhos.

The enormous mass of **Tsambíka**, 26km south of town, is the first place at which most will seriously consider stopping. Actually the very eroded flank of a much larger extinct volcano, the hill has a monastery at the summit offering unrivalled views along some 50km of coastline. From the main highway, a steep, 1500-metre cement drive leads to a small car park and a snack bar, from which steps lead to the summit. The monastery here is unremarkable except for its September 8 festival: childless women climb up – sometimes on their knees – to be relieved of their barrenness, and any children born afterwards are dedicated to the Virgin with the names Tsambikos or Tsambika, which are particular to the Dodecanese. From the top you can survey **Kolýmbia** just to the north, a beach stretching south from a tiny cove ringed with volcanic rocks, backed by a dozen, low-rise hotels. Shallow **Tsambíka bay** on the south side of the headland warms up early in the spring, and the excellent beach, though protected by the forest service from development other than a taverna and a few cantina caravans, teems with people all summer.

The next beach south, gravelly **Stégna**, can only be reached by a steep road east from **ARKHÁNGELOS**, a large village just inland overlooked by a crumbling castle and home to a dwindling leather crafts industry. Though you can disappear into the warren of alleys between the main road and the citadel, the place is now firmly caught up in package tourism, with a full complement of banks, tavernas, mini-marts and jewellery stores.

A more peaceful overnight base on this stretch of coast would be **KHARÁKI**, a pleasant if undistinguished two-street fishing port with mostly self-catering accommodation (generally ③) overlooked by the stubby ruins of **Feraklós castle**, the last stronghold of the Knights to fall to the Turks. You can swim off the town beach if you don't mind an audience from the handful of waterfront cafés and tavernas, but most people head west out of town, then north 800m to the secluded **Agáthi beach**. Best tavernas at Kharáki are *Tommy's*, run by a professional fisherman, and *Efterpi* 200m south at so-called Massári beach.

Líndhos

LÍNDHOS, the island's number-two tourist attraction, erupts from barren surround-ings 12km south of Kharáki. Like Ródhos Town itself, its charm is heavily undermined by commercialism and crowds – up to half a million visitors in a typical year. At midday dozens of coaches park nose-to-tail on the narrow access road, with even more on the drive down to the beach. Back in the village itself, those few vernacular houses not snapped up by package operators have, since the 1960s, been bought up and refur-bished by wealthy British and Italians. The old *agorá* or serpentine high street presents a mass of fairly indistinguishable bars, creperies, mediocre restaurants and travel agents. Although high-rise hotels have been prohibited inside the municipal bound-aries, the result is a relentlessly commercialized theme park, hot and airless in August, but quite ghostly in winter.

Nonetheless, if you arrive before or after peak season, when the pebble-paved streets between the immaculately whitewashed houses are relatively empty of both people and droppings from the donkeys shuttling up to the acropolis (see below), you can still appreciate the beautiful, atmospheric setting of Líndhos. The most imposing fifteenth-to-eighteenth-century **captains' residences** are built around *khokhláki* courtyards, their monumental doorways often fringed by intricate stonework, with the number of braids or cables supposedly corresponding to the number of ships owned. Several are open to the public, most notably the **Papkonstandis Mansion**, the most elaborate and now home to an unofficial museum; entrance to the "open" mansions is free but some pressure will probably be exerted on you to buy something, especially the lace and embroidery for which the place is noted.

On the bluff above the town, the ancient acropolis with its scaffolding-swaddled Doric **Temple of Athena** is found inside the Knights' **castle** (summer Mon–Fri 8.30am–6.40pm, Sat–Sun 8.30am–2.40pm; rest of year Tues–Sun 8.30am–3pm; 1200dr) – a surprisingly felicitous blend of two cultures. Though the ancient city of Lindos and its original temple date from at least 1100 BC, the present structure was begun by the tyrant Kleovoulos in the sixth century BC and replaced by the present structure after a fourth-century fire.

Líndhos' north beach, once the main ancient harbour, is overcrowded and polluted: if you do base yourself here, cleaner, quieter **beaches** are to be found one cove beyond at Pállas beach (with a nudist annexe around the headland), or 5km north at **Vlikhá** bay. South of the acropolis huddles the small, perfectly sheltered **St Paul's harbour**, where the apostle is said to have landed in 58 AD on a mission to evangelize the island.

PRACTICALITIES

There are almost no places to **stay** that are not booked semi-permanently by overseas tour companies. The oft-cited exceptions of *Pension Electra* (☎0244/31 226; ④) and *Pension Katholiki*, next door to each other on the way to the north beaches, are both of a relatively low standard and vastly overpriced. It could be more productive to throw yourself on the mercy of *Pallas Travel* (☎0244/31 494, fax 31 595) for any stray vacan-cies. Another useful contact is the Independent Association of Lindian Property Owners (☎0244/31 221, fax 31 571).

Local **restaurants** tend to be bland, although *Agostino's* by the southerly car park, possesses the important virtues of bulk Émbonas wine and real country sausages (not imported hot dogs). The apotheosis of **nightlife** is the *Epos Club*, a disco with a capac-ity of a thousand, a swimming pool and rooftop bar; the bar *Jody's Flat* can also be rec-ommended for its video-cinema matinees. A unique combination laundry/lending library behind Pallas Travel, open during normal shop hours, is run by an American expat; she both sells and lends second-hand books. Local **car rental** rates tend to be cheaper than in Ródhos Town, though the cars less roadworthy. There are two proper **banks**, working normal hours and giving normal exchange rates.

The west coast

Rhodes' west coast is the windward flank of the island, so it's damper, more fertile and more forested; most beaches, however, are exposed and decidedly rocky. None of this has deterred development, and as in the east the first few kilometres of the busy shore road down from the capital have been surrendered entirely to tourism. From the aquarium down to the airport the asphalt is fringed by an uninterrupted line of Miami-beach-style hotels, though such places as Triánda, Kremastí and Paradhíssi are still nominally villages. This was the first part of the island to be favoured by the package operators, and tends to be frequented by a decidedly middle-aged, sedate clientele.

There's not much inducement to stop, till you reach the important archeological site of **KAMEIROS**, which with Líndhos and Ialyssos was one of the three Dorian powers that united in the fifth century BC to found the powerful city-state of Rhodes. Soon eclipsed by the new capital, Kameiros was abandoned and only rediscovered in the last century. As a result it is a particularly well-preserved Doric townscape, doubly worth visiting for its beautiful hillside site (Tues–Sun 8.30am–3pm; 800dr). While none of the individual remains are spectacular, you can make out the foundations of a few small temples, the restored pillars of a Hellenistic house, and the *stoa* of the *agora*, complete with a water catchment basin. Because of the gentle slope of the site, there were no fortifications, nor was there an acropolis. On the beach below Kameiros there are several tavernas, ideal while waiting for one of the two daily buses back to town (if you're willing to walk 4km back to Kalavárda you'll have a better choice of service).

There are more restaurants clustered at **SKÁLA KAMÍROU** 15km south, a tiny anchorage which somewhat inexplicably is the target of coach tours. Less heralded is the daily pair of competing kaïkia which leave for the island of **Khálki** at 2.30pm, weather permitting, returning early the next morning; on Wednesdays and Sundays there are day trips departing at 9am and returning at 4pm.

A couple of kilometres south of Skála, the "Kastello", signposted as **Kástro Kritinías**, is from afar the most impressive of the Knights' rural strongholds, and the access road is too rough for tour buses to pass. Close up it proves to be no more than a shell, but a glorious shell, with fine views west to assorted islets and Khálki. You make a "donation" to the formidable little old lady at the car park in exchange for fizzy drinks, seasonal fruit or flowers.

Beyond Kritiniá itself, a quiet hillside village with a few rooms and tavernas, the main road winds south through the forests of Mount Akramítis to **SIÁNA**, the most attractive mountain settlement on the island, famous for its aromatic pine-sage honey and *soúma*, a grape-residue distillation identical to Italian *grappa*. Bus tours also stop at the church on the square, with heavily restored eighteenth-century frescoes. The tiered, flat-roofed farmhouses of **MONÓLITHOS**, 4km southwest at the end of the public bus line, are scant justification for the long trip out here, and food at the two **tavernas** is indifferent owing to the tour-group trade, but the view over the bay is striking and you could use the village as a base by staying in rooms or at the pricier *Hotel Thomas* (☎0246/22 741 or 61 291; ③), self-catering and open most of the year. Diversions in the area include yet another **Knights' castle** 2km west of town, photogenically perched on its own pinnacle (the "monolith" of the name) and enclosing a couple of chapels, and the fine gravel beach of **Foúrni**, five bumpy, curvy kilometres below the castle, its 800-metre extent unsullied except for a seasonal drinks stand. Beyond the headland, to the left as you face the water, are some caves that were hollowed out by early Christians fleeing persecution.

The interior

Inland Rhodes is hilly, and still mostly wooded, despite the depredations of arsonists. You'll need a vehicle to see its highlights, especially as the main enjoyment is in getting away from it all; no single site justifies the tremendous expense of a taxi or the inconvenience of trying to make the best of the sparse bus schedules.

Ialyssos and the Valley of the Butterflies

Starting from the west coast, turn inland at the central junction in Tríanda for the five-kilometre uphill ride to the scanty acropolis of ancient **Ialyssos** (Tues–Fri 8.30am–6pm, Sat–Mon 8.30am–3pm; 800dr) on flat-topped Filérimos hill; from its Byzantine castle Süleyman the Magnificent directed the 1522 siege of Rhodes. Filérimos means "lover of solitude", after the tenth-century settlement here by Byzantine hermits. The existing **Filérimos monastery**, restored successively by Italians and British, is the most substantial structure here. As a concession to the Rhodian faithful, the church alone is usually open to pilgrims after the stated hours. Directly in front of the church sprawl the foundations of third-century **temples to Zeus and Athena**, built atop a far older Phoenician shrine. Below this, further towards the car park, lies the partly subterranean church of **Áyios Yeóryios**, a simple, barrel-vaulted structure with fourteenth- and fifteenth-century frescoes, not as vivid or well-preserved as those at Thári or Asklipío. A bit southeast of the parking area, a hillside **Doric fountain** with a columned facade was only revealed by subsidence in 1926. Southwest of the monastery and archeological zone, a "Way of the Cross", with the fourteen stations marked out in copper plaques during the Italian era, leads to an enormous concrete crucifix, a recent replacement of an Italian-era one; you're allowed to climb out onto the cross-arms for a supplement to the already amazing view. Illuminated at night, the crucifix is clearly visible from the island of Sými and – perhaps more pertinently – infidel Turkey across the way.

The only highly publicized tourist "attraction" in the island's interior, **Petaloúdhes** or the **"Butterfly Valley"** (April–Sept daily 9am–5pm; 300dr) reached by a seven-kilometre paved side road bearing inland from the west coast road between Paradhíssi and Theológos, is actually a rest stop for Jersey tiger moths (*Panaxia quadripunctaria*). Only in summer do these creatures congregate here, attracted for unknown reasons by the abundant *Liquidambar orientalis* trees. In season, the moths roost in droves on the tree trunks; they cannot eat during this final phase of their life cycle, must rest to conserve energy, and die of starvation soon after mating. When sitting in the trees, the moths are a well-camouflaged black and yellow, but flash cherry-red overwings in flight.

Eptá Piyés to Profítis Ilías

Heading inland from Kolýmbia junction on the main highway, it's a four-kilometre walk or drive to **Eptá Piyés**, a superb oasis with a tiny dam created by the Italians for irrigation. A shaded streamside **taverna**, immensely popular at weekend with islanders and visitors alike, serves no-nonsense, hearty fare. A trail, or a rather claustrophobic Italian aqueduct-tunnel, both lead from the vicinity of the springs to the reservoir.

Continuing inland, you reach **ELEOÚSSA** after another 9km, in the shade of the dense forest at the east end of Profítis Ilías ridge. Two other undisturbed villages, Platánia and Apóllona, nestle on the south slopes of the mountain overlooking the start of the burned area, but most people keep straight on 3km further from Eleoússa to the late Byzantine church of **Áyios Nikólaos Foundoúkli** (St Nicholas of the Hazelnuts). The partly shaded site has a fine view north over cultivated valleys, and locals descend in force for picnics on weekends; the frescoes inside, dating from the thirteenth to the fifteenth centuries, could do with a good cleaning but various scenes from the life of Christ are recognizable.

Negotiating an unsignposted but fairly obvious welter of dirt tracks gets you finally to **Profítis Ilías**, where the Italian-vintage chalet-hotel *Elafos/Elafina* (shut down) hides in deep woods just north of the 798-metre marker, Rhodes' third-highest point. There's good, gentle strolling around the summit and the namesake monastery, and a nearby snack bar is generally open in season.

Atáviros villages

All tracks and roads west across Profítis Ilías converge upon the main road from Kalavárda bound for **ÉMBONAS**, a large and architecturally nondescript village backed up against the north slope of 1215-metre **Mount Atáviros**. Émbonas, with its two pensions and meat-oriented tavernas, is more geared to handling tourists than you might expect, since it's the venue for summer "folk-dance tours" from Ródhos Town. The village also lies at the heart of the island's most important wine-producing districts, and CAÏR – the Italian-founded vintners' cooperative – produce a range of acceptable mid-range varieties. However, products of the smaller, family-run Emery winery (✆0246/41 208; Mon–Fri 9am–3pm for tasting tours) at the village outskirts are even more esteemed. To see what Émbonas would be like without tourists, carry on clockwise around the peak past the Artámiti monastery, to less-celebrated **ÁYIOS ISÍDHOROS**, with as many vines and tavernas (try *Snag* (sic) *Bar Ataviros*), a more open feel, and the **trailhead** for the five-hour return ascent of Atáviros. This path, beginning at the northeast edge of the village, is the safest and easiest way up the mountain, which has extensive foundations of a Zeus temple on top.

Thári Monastery

The road from Áyios Isídhoros to Siána is paved; not so the appalling one that curves for 12km east to Láerma, but it's worth enduring if you've any interest in Byzantine monuments. The **Monastery of Thári**, lost in pine forests five kilometres south, is the oldest religious foundation on the island, re-established as a living community of half a dozen monks in 1990 by a charismatic abbot from Pátmos. The striking kathólikon (open all day) consists of a long nave and short transept surmounted by barrel vaulting. Despite two recent cleanings, the damp of centuries has smudged the frescoes, dating from 1300 to 1450, but they are still exquisite: the most distinct, in the transept, depict the Evangelist Mark and the Archangel Gabriel, while the nave boasts various acts of Christ, including such rarely illustrated scenes as the *Storm on the Sea of Galilee*, *Meeting Mary Magdalene* and *Healing the Cripple*.

The far south

South of a line connecting Monólithos and Lárdhos, you could easily begin to think you had strayed onto another island. Gone are the five-star hotels and roads to match, and with them most of the crowds. Gone too are most tourist facilities and public transport. Only three weekly buses serve the depopulated villages here, approaching along the east coast; tavernas grace the more popular stretches of sand, and there are a few places to stay outside the package enclaves of Lárdhos and Péfkos.

A new auxiliary airport is planned for the area, however, so this state of affairs won't persist indefinitely. Already massive construction is beginning behind the sandier patches south of **LÁRDHOS**, solidly on the tourist circuit despite an inland position between Láerma and the peninsula culminating in Líndhos. The beach 2km south is gravelly and the water can be dirty, so it's best to continue 3km to Glístra cove, a small but delightful crescent which sets the tone for the coast from here on. Four kilometres east, **PÉFKOS** (Péfki on some maps) is a low-key package resort on the beach road to Líndhos; the sea is cleaner than at Lárdhos, and the beaches are small and well hidden.

Asklipío

Nine kilometres beyond Lárdhos, a paved side road heads 4km inland to **ASKLIPÍO**, a sleepy village guarded by a crumbling castle and graced by the Byzantine church of **Kímisis Theotókou**. To gain admission, call at the priest's house behind the apse, or if that doesn't work, haul on the belfry rope. The building dates from 1060, with a ground plan nearly identical to that of Thári, except that two subsidiary apses were added during the eighteenth century, supposedly to conceal a secret school in a subterranean crypt. The frescoes within are in far better condition than Thári's owing to the drier local climate; the priest claims that the final work at Thári and the earliest here were executed by the same hand, a master from Khíos.

The format and subject matter of the frescoes is rare in Greece: didactic "cartoon strips" which extend completely around the church in some cases, and extensive Old Testament stories in addition to the more usual lives of Christ and the Virgin. There's a complete sequence from Genesis, from the Creation to the Expulsion from Eden; note the comically menacing octopus among the fishes in the panel of the Fifth Day. A seldom-encountered *Revelation of John the Divine* takes up most of the east transept, and pebble mosaic flooring decorates both the interior and the vast courtyard.

To the southern tip

Back on the coast road, the beachfront hamlet of **KIOTÁRI** gets few visitors, partly because it's omitted from most maps, and also because the Orthodox Church, major landowner hereabouts, isn't selling to developers. The gravel beach has a line of tavernas behind and a few self-catering units.

There are far more ample facilities at **YENÁDHI**, including **car rental**, a **post office**, some rooms and a few **tavernas** behind the seemingly endless sand-and-gravel beach. South of Yennádhi, just 2km inland, **LAKHANIÁ** village with its eponymous **hotel** (☎0244/43 089; ③) and smattering of private rooms makes another possible base. On the main platía at the lower, eastern end of the village, the *Platanos* taverna has seating between the church and two wonderful fountains, one with an Ottoman inscription.

You can go directly from Lakhaniá to Khokhlakás, which straddles the paved side road south to **Plimíri**, an exceptionally well-protected sandy bay backed by dunes; so far the only facility is a good-value rustic **taverna**. Beyond Plimíri the road curves inland to **KATAVIÁ**, over 100km from the capital, marooned amidst grain fields. There are several tavernas at the junction that doubles as the platía, a few rooms to rent, and a filling station; the village, like so many in the south, is three-quarters deserted, the owners of the closed-up houses off working in Australia or North America.

From Kataviá a wide dirt track leads on to **Prassoníssi**, Rhodes' southernmost extremity. From May to October you can stroll across the wide sands to visit, but winter storms swamp this tenuous link and render Prassoníssi a true island. Even in summer the prevailing northwesterly winds drive swimmers to the lee side of the spit, leaving the exposed shore to the world-class windsurfers who come here to train. In season the scrubby junipers rustle with tents and caravans; water comes from two tavernas flanking the access road. The outfit next to the old windmill is more characterful, but beware of their fish grills – tasty but among the most expensive in Greece.

The far southwest

From Lakhaniá it's also possible to head 9km northwest along a narrow paved road to the picturesque hilltop village of **MESSANAGRÓS**. This already existed in some form by the fifth century AD, if foundations of a ruined basilica at the village outskirts are anything to go by. A smaller, but equally venerable thirteenth-century chapel squats amidst mosaic-floor patches of the larger, earlier church, with a *khokhláki* floor and stone barrel arches (key from the nearby kafenío).

The onward road to Skiádhi monastery, 6km distant, is shown incorrectly on most maps. Take the Kataviá-bound road initially, then bear right onto an unsigned dirt track after about 2km; the last 4km are quite badly surfaced. Known formally as Panayía Skiadhení, **Skiádhi monastery** – despite its undistinguished modern buildings – was founded in the thirteenth century to house a miraculous icon of the Virgin; in the fifteenth century a heretic stabbed the painting, and blood flowed from the wound in the Mother of God's cheek. The offending hand was, needless to say, instantly paralysed; the fissure, and intriguing brown stains around it, are still visible. The immediate surroundings of the monastery are rather dreary since a fire in 1992, but the views west are stunning. Khténia islet is said to be a petrified pirate ship, so rendered by the Virgin in answer to prayers from desperate locals. Except on September 7/8, the festival of the icon, you can stay the night on arrangement with the caretaker priest Ioannis Kermaïtzis and his wife (☎0244/46 006; donation).

West of Kataviá, the island loop road – now completely paved – emerges onto the deserted, sandy southwest coast; Skiádhi can easily be reached from this side too, the road up from here better signposted than from Messanagrós. If freelance camping and nudism are your thing, this is the place to indulge, though you'll need to be completely self-sufficient. Only strong swimmers should venture far offshore here.

The nearest inland village is nondescript, agricultural **APOLAKIÁ**, 7km north of the Skiádhi turning and equipped with a couple of pensions and shops. Northwest the road leads to Monólithos, due south back to Kataviá, and the northeasterly road cuts quickly back to Yennádhi via Váti.

Khálki

Khálki, a tiny (20 square kilometres), waterless, limestone speck west of Rhodes, is a fully fledged member of the Dodecanese, though all but three hundred of the former population of three thousand have decamped (mostly to Rhodes or to Florida) in the wake of a devastating sponge blight early in this century. Despite a renaissance through tourism in recent years, the island is tranquil compared with its big neighbour, with a slightly weird, hushed atmosphere. The big event of the day is the arrival of the regular afternoon kaïkia from Skála Kámiros on Rhodes.

Emborió

EMBORIÓ's houses are pretty much block-booked from April to October by the tour companies and occupied by a rather staid, upper-middle-class clientele; independent travellers will be lucky to find anything at all, even early or late in the season. Non-package **accommodation**, all requiring advance reservations, includes the delightful, en-suite *Captain's House* (☎0241/45 201; ④), where the English manager can point you in likely directions if she's full; *Pension Cleanthe* (☎0241/45 334) near the school; the hillside studios of *Pension Argyrenia* (☎0241/45 205; ④) below the municipal cistern; and *Hotel Manos* (☎0241/45 295; ③), in a converted sponge factory. Of the half-dozen **tavernas** along the field-stoned, pedestrianized waterfront, *O Khouvardas*, *Arapakis* and *Omonia* are good for reasonable standard fare, while *Mavri Thalassa* is worth the extra expense for its good mezédhes and crab salad. **Bars** and **cafés** cluster at mid-quay: *Areti* for cake and coffee, *Kostas* dispensing foreign beer on tap, and *To Steki* with a central bar and music. There's a **post office** (the best place to change money), three stores, two bakeries, and two **travel agencies** which sell boat tickets.

The rest of the island

Three kilometres west lies the old pirate-safe village of **KHORIÓ**, abandoned in the 1950s but still crowned by the Knights' castle. Except during the major August 14–15 festival, the church here is kept securely locked to protect its frescoes. Across the valley, the little monastery of **Stavrós** is the venue for the other big island bash on September 14. There's little else to see or do inland, though you can spend three hours **walking** across the island on the recently opened road, the extension of the cement "Tarpon Springs Boulevard" donated by the expatriate community in Florida. At the end of the road you'll come to the monastery of **Ayíou Ioánnou Prodhrómou**; the caretaking family there can put you up in a cell (except around August 29, the other big festival date), but you'll need to bring supplies. The terrain en route is monotonous, but compensated by views over half the Dodecanese and Turkey. Occasionally the island's lone, twenty-seater **bus** runs excursions out here, with an hour to look around.

Longish but narrow **Póndamos**, fifteen minutes' walk west of Emborió, is the only sandy beach on Khálki. The sole facility is the somewhat pricey *Nick's Pondamos Taverna*, serving lunch only. Small and pebbly **Yialí**, west of and considerably below Khorió via a jeep track, lies an hour's hike away from Póndamos. A thirty-minute walk north of Emborió lies **Kánia**, with a rocky foreshore and a rather industrial ambience from both power lines and the island's only petrol pump, adjacent.

Since these three coves are no great shakes, it's worth signing on at Emborió quay for **boat excursions** to more remote beaches. More or less at the centre of Khálki's southern shore, directly below Khorió's castle, **Trakhía** consists of two coves to either side of an isthmus. North-coast beaches figuring as excursion-boat destinations include the pretty **Arétta**, **Áyios Yeóryios** just beyond, and the remote double bay of **Dhýo Yialí**.

Alimniá (Alimiá) islet

The most interesting boat excursion is to **Alimniá (Alimiá) islet**, roughly halfway between Khálki and Rhodes, a favourite swimming and barbecuing venue for both islanders and tour clients. Despite a reliable spring, the deserted village here, overlooked by a few palm trees and yet another Knights' castle, was never re-inhabited after World War II. It is claimed the locals were deported after they admitted to assisting British commandos sent to sabotage the Italian submarines who used the deep harbour here. The commandos themselves were captured here by the Nazis, bundled off to Rhodes and summarily executed as spies rather than regular prisoners of war; Kurt Waldheim allegedly countersigned their death sentences. If you go snorkelling, you can glimpse outlines of the submarine pens to one side of the deep bay. Most of the houses are now boarded up; some bear sombre lines of bullet-holes, while inside others you can glimpse crude paintings of ships and submarines sketched by bored soldiers. Today just one is inhabited on a seasonal basis, when Alimniá is used by shepherds grazing livestock.

Kastellórizo (Meyísti)

Kastellórizo's official name, Méyisti (biggest), seems more an act of defiance than a statement of fact. While the largest of a tiny group of islands, it is actually the smallest of the Dodecanese, over seventy nautical miles from its nearest Greek neighbour (Rhodes) but barely more than a nautical mile off the Turkish coast at the narrowest straits. At night its lights are quite outnumbered by those of the Turkish town of Kaş, across the bay, with whom Kastellórizo generally has excellent relations.

Less than a century ago there were 14,000 people here, supported by a fleet of schooners that transported goods, mostly timber, from the Greek towns of Kalamaki (now Kalkan) and Andifelos (Kaş) on the Anatolian mainland opposite. But the advent of steam power, the withdrawal of privileges after the 1908 "Young Turk" revolution and the Italian seizure of the Dodecanese in 1912 sent the island into decline. A French occupation of 1914–21 prompted destructive shelling from the Ottoman-held mainland, a harbinger of worse to come (see below). Shipowners failed to modernize their fleets, preferring to sell ships to the British for the Dardanelles campaign, and the new frontier between the island and republican Turkey, combined with the expulsion of all Anatolian Greeks in 1923, deprived any remaining vessels of their trade. During the 1930s the island enjoyed a brief renaissance when it became a major stopover point for French and Italian seaplanes, but events at the close of World War II put an end to any hopes of the island's continued viability.

When Italy capitulated to the Allies in the autumn of 1943, a few hundred Commonwealth commandos occupied Kastellórizo, leaving in response to German dive-bombing late in the spring of 1944. In early July, a harbour fuel dump caught fire and an adjacent arsenal exploded, taking with it more than half of the two thousand houses on Kastellórizo. Even before these events most of the population had left for Rhodes, Athens, Australia (especially Perth) and North America. Today there are fewer than 200 people living permanently on Kastellórizo, largely maintained by remittances from over 30,000 emigrants and by subsidies from the Greek government, which fears that the island will revert to Turkey should their numbers diminish any further.

Notwithstanding its apparently terminal plight, Kastellórizo may have a future of sorts. Expatriated "Kassies" have recently begun renovating their crumbling ancestral homes as a retirement or holiday home. Each summer, the population is swelled by returnees of Kassie ancestry, some of whom celebrate traditional weddings in the **Áyios Konstandínos** cathedral at Khoráfia, which incorporates ancient columns from Patara in Asia Minor.

Perhaps the biggest recent boost for Kastellórizo was its role as location for the 1991 film *Mediterraneo*, which has resulted in a tidal wave of Italian visitors. You will either love it and stay a week, or crave escape after a day; detractors dismiss Kastellórizo as a human zoo maintained by the government for the edification of nationalists, while partisans celebrate an atmospheric, barely commercialized outpost of Hellenism.

Kastellórizo Town

The current population is concentrated in the northern town of **KASTELLÓRIZO** – the finest harbour, so it is claimed, between Beirut and Pireás – and its little "suburb" of **Mandhráki**, just over the fire-blasted hill with its half-ruined castle of the Knights. Its keep now houses the local **museum** (Tues–Sun 7.30am–2.30pm; free), with displays including plates from a Byzantine shipwreck, frescoes rescued from decaying churches, and a reconstruction of an ancient basilica underneath a contemporary, gaudy church at Khoráfia. Just below and beyond the museum, in the cliff-face opposite Psorádhia islet, is Greece's only **Lycian house-tomb**; it's unmarked, but you can find it easily enough by following the shoreline walkway, then climbing some steps opposite the first wooden lamp standard.

Most of the town's surviving mansions are ranged along the waterfront, their tiled roofs, wooden balconies and long, narrow windows having obvious counterparts in the originally Greek-built houses of Kalkan and Kaş just across the water. One street behind the port, however, many properties are derelict – abandonment having succeeded where World War I shelling, a 1926 earthquake and the 1944 explosions failed – sepia-toned posters and postcards on sale show the town in its prime.

Practicalities
Pensions in the old houses tend to be fairly basic, with long climbs up and down stairs to a single bathroom. If you're not met off the boat, the best budget option is the restored mansion-pension of the Mavrothalassitis family (☎0241/49 202; ②), one of the very few with en-suite baths. Otherwise, try *Paradhisos* (☎0241/49 074; ②) at the west

end of the seafront, *Barbara* (☎0241/49 295; ②), at the opposite end of things, or the more modern *Kristallo* (☎0241/41 209; ②). More luxury is available at the *Hotel Meyisti* (☎0241/49 272, fax 49 221; ⑤), on the opposite side of the bay from the ferry jetty.

Apart from fish, and whatever can be smuggled over from Kaş, Kastellórizo has to bring foodstuffs and often drinking water from Rhodes; prices for **eating** out are consequently higher than usual, bumped up further by the island's recent celebrity status. Apart from *Mikro Parisi/Little Paris* on the waterfront, the better restaurants are to be found inland. Especially recommended are *Iy Orea Meyisti*, run by the Mavrothalassitis family (they of the pension), and the *O Meyisteas* ouzerí, behind the disused municipal market building, which specializes in goat chops. The simple *Ta Platania*, opposite Áyios Konstandínos in Khoráfia district, is good for *mayireftá* and homemade desserts.

The **post office** is behind *Hotel Meyisti*; there's no OTE or bank. Most ferry companies are represented by one of several grocery stores, while the only travel agency, DiZi Travel, has a monopoly on **flights** back to Rhodes (you cannot book a return flight in Ródhos Town) and will also change money.

It is usually possible to arrange a ride over **to Turkey** on the supply boat Varvara, run by the *Taverna Apolavsi*; you'll have to pay a "special visa fee" to customs, and an additional 5000dr per person for the boat.

The rest of the island

Kastellórizo's austere hinterland is predominantly bare rock, flecked with stunted vegetation; incredibly, two generations ago much of the countryside was carefully tended, producing wine of some quality. A rudimentary road system links points between Mandhráki and the airport, but there aren't many specific places to go and no scooters for rent. Karstic cliffs drop sheer to the sea, offering no anchorage for boats except at the main town.

The shoreline and Rhó

Swimming is complicated by a total absence of beaches and an abundance of sea urchins and razor-sharp limestone reefs; the safest entry near town lies beyond the graveyard at Mandhráki, or at the tiny inlet of **Áyios Stéfanos**, a forty-minute walk north of town along the obvious trail beginning behind the post office. Once clear of the shore, you're rewarded by clear waters with a rich variety of marine life. Over on the southeast coast, accessible only by a 45-minute boat ride from town, the grotto of **Perastá** deserves a look for its stalactites and strange blue light effects; the low entrance, negotiable only by inflatable raft, gives little hint of the enormous chamber within. Two-hour raft trips (2000dr per person) visit only the cave, or for 5000dr on a larger kaïki, you can take it in as part of a five-hour tour that includes Rhó islet.

Should you make the trip out to **Rhó**, the tomb of *Iy Kyrá tis Rhó* (**The Lady of Rhó**), aka Dhespina Akhladhiotis (1893–1982) – who resolutely hoisted the Greek flag each day on that islet in defiance of the Turks on the mainland – is the first thing you see when you dock at the sandy, northwestern harbour. From here a path heads southeast for 25 minutes to the islet's southerly port, past the side trail up to the intact Hellenistic fortress on the very summit. The islet has no facilities – just one caretaker, several dogs and hundreds of goats – so bring your own food and water.

Rural monasteries and ruins

Heat permitting, you can hike up the obvious, zigzag stair-path, then south through desolate, recently fire-charred vineyards for forty minutes, to the rural **monastery of Áyios Yeóryios toú Vounioú**. The sixteenth- to eighteenth-century church boasts fine rib vaulting and a carved *témblon*, but its highlight is a **crypt**, with the frescoed, **sub-**

terranean chapel of Áyios Kharálambos off to one side; access is via a steep, narrow passage descending from the church floor – bring a torch. The only way to gain access is to go early in the morning with the key-keeper, who lives behind *Little Paris* taverna. Alternatively, a fifteen-minute, walk west of the port leads to the peaceful monastery of **Ayías Triádhas**, perched on the saddle marked by the OTE tower.

The onward path arrives after 25 minutes at the ancient citadel of **Paleókastro**, where you'll find masonry from Classical to medieval times, a warren of vaulted chambers, tunnels, cisterns plus another, ruined monastery with a *khokhláki* courtyard. From any of the heights above town there are tremendous views north over sixty kilometres of Anatolian coast.

Sými

Sými's most pressing problem, lack of water, is in many ways also its saving grace. As with so many dry rocky Dodecanese, if the rain cisterns don't fill during the winter, water must be imported at great expense from Rhodes. As a result the island can't hope to support more than a handful of large hotels; instead hundreds of people are shipped in daily during the season from Rhodes, relieved of their money and sent back. This arrangement suits both the islanders and those visitors lucky enough to stay longer, or even to own houses here.

Sými Town

The island's capital – and only proper town – consists of **Yialós**, the port, and **Khorió**, on the hillside above, collectively known as **SÝMI**. Incredibly, less than a hundred years ago the town was richer and more populous (30,000) than Rhodes, its wealth generated by shipbuilding and sponge-diving, skills nurtured since pre-Classical times. Under the Ottomans, Sými, like most of the smaller Dodecanese, enjoyed considerable autonomy in exchange for a yearly tribute in sponges to the sultan; but the Italian-imposed frontier, the 1919–22 war, the advent of synthetic sponges, and the gradual replacement of the crews by Kalymniotes spelled doom for the local economy. Vestiges of past nautical glories remain at still-active boatyards at Pédhi and Kharáni, but today the souvenir-shop sponges come mostly from overseas, and many of the magnificent nineteenth-century mansions stand roofless and deserted, their windows gaping blankly across the excellent natural harbour.

The 2500 remaining Symiotes are scattered fairly evenly throughout the mixture of Neoclassical and more typical island dwellings; despite the surplus of properties many outsiders have preferred to build anew, rather than restore derelict shells accessible only by donkey or on foot. As on Kastellórizo, a wartime ammunition blast – this time set off by the retreating Germans – levelled hundreds of houses up in Khorió. Shortly afterwards, the official surrender of the Dodecanese to the Allies was signed here on May 8, 1945: a plaque marks the spot at the present-day *Restaurant Les Katerinettes*, and each year on that date there's a fine festival with music and dance.

At the lively **port**, an architecturally protected area since the early 1970s, spice-and-sponge stalls are thronged with Rhodes-based day-trippers. But one street back from the water the more peaceful pace of village life takes over. Two massive stair-paths, the Kalí Stráta and Katarráktes, effectively deter many of the day-trippers and appear most dramatic if climbed towards sunset; massive ruins along the lower reaches of the Kalí Stráta are lonely and sinister after dark.

A series of blue arrows through Khorió leads to the excellent local **museum** (Tues–Sun 10am–2pm; 500dr). Housed in a fine old mansion at the back of the village,

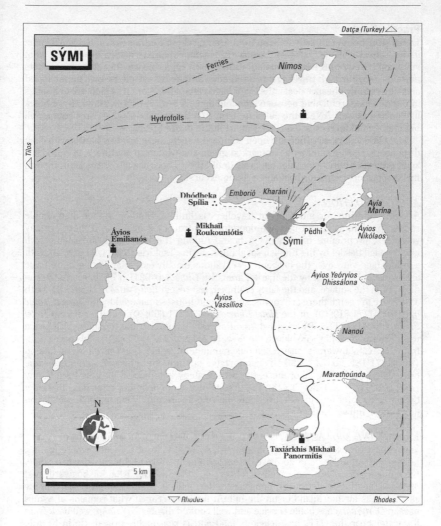

the collection concentrates on Byzantine and medieval Sými, with exhibits on frescoes in isolated, locked churches and a gallery of medieval icons. On the way back to central Khorió, the nineteenth-century pharmacy, with its apothecary jars and wooden drawers labelled for exotic herbal remedies, is worth a look.

At the very pinnacle of things, a **castle of the Knights** occupies the site of Sými's ancient acropolis, and you can glimpse a stretch of Cyclopean wall on one side. A dozen churches grace Khorió; that of the Ascension, inside the fortifications, is a replacement of the one blown to bits when the Germans torched the munitions cached there. One of the bells in the new belfry is the nose-cone of a thousand-pound bomb, hung as a memorial.

Practicalities

Excursion boats run daily to Sými from Mandhráki in Ródhos Town, but you'll come under considerable pressure at the quay to buy an expensive return ticket – not what you want if you're off island-hopping. Either insist on a one-way ticket, or buy tickets more cheaply through travel agents on Rhodes or take the islanders' own unpublicized and significantly cheaper boats, the Symi I and catamaran Symi II, which sail to Rhodes in the morning, returning between 2pm and 6pm. A few times a week there are main-line ferries as well. ANES, the outlet for Symi I/II tickets, and Psyhas, the agent for all big inter-island **ferries**, are one alley apart in the market place.

The **OTE** and **post office** are open standard hours; there are two **banks** with cash dispensers. During summer an unmarked green-and-white van shuttles between Yialós and Pédhi via Khorió at regular intervals until 11pm. There are also three taxis, though this is a perfect island for boat and walking excursions.

ACCOMMODATION

Accommodation for independent travellers is limited. Studios, rather than simple rooms, predominate, and package operators control most of these; if there are any vacancies, proprietors meet arriving boats. Among the best value are rooms with kitchen facilities let by the English-speaking Katerina Tsakiris (☎0241/71 813; ③), with a grandstand view over the harbour; reservations usually essential. Rather more basic are two standbys down by the market area, the *Glafkos* (☎0241/71 358; rooms ②, studios ③) on the square, and the fairly cramped, last-resort *Egli* (☎0241/71 392; ②). With a bit more to spend, there are rooms, studios and houses managed by the *Jean & Tonic* bar (☎0241/71 819; ③), or the *Hotel Khorio* (☎0241/71 800; ④) and the adjacent *Hotel Fiona* (☎0241/72 088; ④) are good, traditional-style outfits at the top of the Kalí Stráta up in Khorió. If money's no object, the *Alyki* (☎ & fax 0241/71 665; ⑤), a few paces right from the clocktower, is also a famous monument, while the *Dorian* right behind (☎0241/71 181, fax 72 292; ⑤) is comfortable enough, and cheaper within the same price category. Failing all of these, the best strategy is to appeal for help from Sunny Land (☎0241/71 320, fax 71 413), the first agency you encounter after disembarking: their weekly rates for villas, houses and apartments are highly competitive even if you don't stay a full seven days.

EATING AND DRINKING

You're best off avoiding entirely the north and west side of the port, where menus, prices and attitudes tend to have been terminally warped by the day-trip trade. Exceptions are *Tholos*, an excellent ouzerí out beyond the Kharáni boatyard, and *Mythos*, a nearby, pricier ouzerí opposite the ferry dock. Matters improve perceptibly as you press further inland or up the hill. At the very rear of what remains of Sými's bazaar, *O Meraklis* has polite service and well-cooked dishes; *Neraidha*, well back from the water near the OTE, has delicious food and is reasonably priced. Up in Khorió, *Georgios* is a decades-old institution, serving large portions of Greek *nouvelle cuisine* in a pebble-mosaic courtyard – excellent value, but open for dinner only.

With a large ex-pat community, a few **bars** are run by foreigners: in Khorió, *Jean & Tonic* caters to a mixed clientele; down at Yialós, *Vapori* is the oldest bar on the island, welcoming customers with desserts, breakfast and free newspapers.

Around the island

Sými has no big sandy beaches, but there are plenty of pebbly stretches at the heads of the deep narrow bays which indent the coastline. **PÉDHI**, a 45-minute walk from Yialós, retains some of its former identity as a fishing hamlet, with enough water in the plain behind – the island's largest – to support a few vegetable gardens. The beach is average-to-poor, though, and the giant *Pedhi Beach* hotel (packages only) has considerably humped up prices at the three local tavernas, of which the most reasonable and authentic is *Iy Kamares*. Many will opt for another thirty minutes of walking via a rough but obvious path along the south shore of the almost landlocked bay to **Áyios Nikólaos**. The only all-sand beach on Sými, this offers sheltered swimming, tamarisks for shade and a mediocre taverna. Alternatively, a marked path on the north side of the inlet leads within an hour to **Ayía Marína**, where there's another, better taverna and a monastery-capped islet which you can easily swim to.

Around Yialós, you'll find tiny **Nós** "beach" ten minutes past the boat yards at Kharáni, but there's sun here only until lunchtime and it's packed with daytrippers. You can continue along the coastal track here past tiny gravel coves and rock slabs where nudists disport themselves, or cut inland from the Yialós platía past the abandoned desalination plant, to the appealing **Emborió** bay, with a taverna at one end and an artificially sand-strewn beach at the other. Inland from this are Byzantine mosaic fragments under a protective shelter, and, nearby, a catacomb complex known locally as **Dhódheka Spília**.

Plenty of other, more secluded coves are accessible by energetic walkers with sturdy footwear, or those prepared to pay a modest sum for the taxi-boats (daily in season 10am–1pm, returning 4–5pm; return fares only). These are the best way to reach the southern bays of **Marathoúnda** and **Nanoú**, and the only method of getting to the spectacular, fjord of **Áyios Yeóryios Dhissálona**. Dhissálona lies in shade after 1pm, and Marathoúnda lacks a taverna, making Nanoú the most popular destination for day trips. The 200-metre beach there consists of gravel, sand and pebbles, with a scenic backdrop and a reasonable taverna behind.

On foot, you can cross the island – which has retained patches of its natural juniper forest – in two hours to **Áyios Vassílios**, the most scenic of the gulfs, or in a little more time to **Áyios Emilianós** at the island's extreme west end, where you can stay the night (bring supplies) in a cloister. On the way to the latter you might look in at the monastery of **Mikhaïl Roukouniótis**, Sými's oldest, with lurid eighteenth-century frescoes and a peculiar ground plan: the current kathólikon is actually superimposed on an earlier, lower structure abandoned to the damp. The less intrepid can explore on guided walks to several beaches led by Hugo Tyler (☎0241/71 670), which are generally met by a boat for the ride home.

The Archangel is also honoured at the huge monastery of **Taxiárkhis Mikhaïl Panormítis**, Sými's biggest rural attraction and generally the first port of call for the excursion boats from Rhodes. These allow only a quick thirty-minute tour; if you want more time, you'll have to come on a "jeep safari" from Yialós, or arrange to stay the night (for a donation), in the *xenónas* set aside for pilgrims. There are numbers of these in summer, as Mikhaïl has been adopted as the patron of sailors in the Dodecanese.

Like many of Sými's monasteries, it was thoroughly pillaged during the last war, so don't expect too much of the building or its treasures. An appealing pebble-mosaic court surrounds the central kathólikon, tended by the single remaining monk, lit by an improbable number of oil lamps and graced by a fine *témblon*, though the frescoes are recent and mediocre. The small museum (nominal fee) contains a strange mix of precious antiques, junk (stuffed crocodiles and koalas), votive offerings, models of ships, and a chair piled with messages-in-bottles brought here by Aegean currents – the idea being that if the bottle or toy boat arrived, the sender got their wish. There's a tiny beach, a shop/kafenío and a taverna; near the taverna stands a memorial commemorating three Greeks, including the monastery's abbot, executed in February 1944 by the Germans for aiding British commandos.

Tílos

The small, blissfully quiet island of **Tílos** has a population of only 350 (shrinking to 80 in winter), and is one of the least frequented of the Dodecanese, although it can be visited on a day trip by hydrofoil once or twice a week. Why anyone should want to come for just a few hours is unclear: while it's a great place to rest on the beach or go walking, there is nothing very striking at first glance. After a few days, however, you may have stumbled on several of the seven small castles of the Knights of St John which stud the crags, or gained access to several inconspicuous medieval chapels, some with frescoes or with *khokhláki* (pebble-mosaic) courtyards, clinging to hillsides.

Tílos shares the characteristics of its closest neighbours: limestone mountains resembling those on Khálki, plus volcanic lowlands, pumice beds and red-lava sand as on Níssyros. Though rugged and scrubby on the heights, the island has ample water – mostly pumped up from the agricultural plains – and groves of oak and terebinth near the cultivated areas. The volcano on neighbouring Níssyros has contributed pumice beds and red-lava-sand beaches to the landscape as well. From many points on the island you've fine views across to Sými, Turkey and Níssyros. Tílos's main cement-paved road runs 7km from Livádhia, also the port village, to Megálo Khorió, the capital and only other significant habitation. When boats arrive, a fleet of three **buses** – including a large one for high season – links the two. At other times at least one bus adheres to a schedule of sorts; there's also a single **taxi**, or you can rent a **motorbike** from two outlets in Livádhia, or charter one of the minibuses.

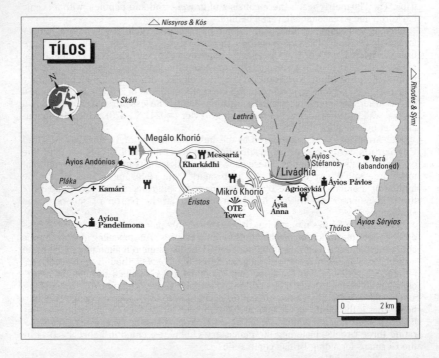

Livádhia

Of the two settlements, **LIVÁDHIA** remains better equipped to deal with tourists, and is clos-er to good walking opportunities. If there are vacancies, **room** and **hotel** owners meet the ferries, but in peak season it's well worth phoning ahead. Budget options include *Paradise* (aka *Stamatia's*; ☎0241/44 334; ②) on the waterfront, or the recently refurbished and good-value *Hotel Livadhia* (☎0241/44 266; ②) inland, which also runs *Studios Sofia* (③) just behind. Nearby, on the east side of the tiny platía here, stands the *Pension Periyali* (☎0241/44 398; ②), while 400m east down the beach, then inland, is *Kastello* (☎0241/44 292; ②). At the top end of things is the *Irini*, 200m from mid-beach (☎0241/44 293, fax 44 238; ④).

Of the seafront **tavernas**, *Sofia's* is a convivial meeting place for ex-pats, in particu-lar Laskarina clients, but you'll probably get a better, more authentically Greek meal at *Irina* or *Stelios*, at the far east end of the beach. The best place for fish grills is *Blue Sky*, an unmissable place perched above the ferry dock. For **breakfast** or pre-dinner drinks, *Omonia* – under the trees strung with fairy lights, near the post office – is enduringly popular, though lately rivalled by the *Vayos* breakfast bar and creperie, next to the *Periyali*. Organized **nightlife** in or near Livádhia is limited to two bars: *La Luna* at the ferry pier (scheduled to move shortly out next to *Stelios*) and a durable music pub in Mikró Khorió (see below).

The **post office** is the only place to change money; the two **card-phones** are usual-ly out of order, in which case you'll have to patronize the metered one at Stefanakis Travel, one of two agencies at the jetty dividing the **ferry-ticket** trade between them. There's also a **bakery** and three **supermarkets**.

Around the island

From Livádhia you can trail-walk an hour north to the pebble bay of **Lethrá**, or for slight-ly longer south to the sandy cove of **Tholoú**. The track to the latter begins by the ceme-tery and the chapel of **Áyios Pandelímon** with its Byzantine *khokhláki* court, then curls around under the seemingly impregnable castle of **Agriosykiá**; from the saddle over-looking the descent to Tholoú, a route marked with cairns leads northwest to the citadel in twenty minutes. It's less than an hour's walk west by trail, cutting across the road curves, up to the ghost village of **Mikró Khorió**, whose 1200 inhabitants left for Livádhia during the 1950s. The only intact structures are the church (locked except for the August 15 festival) and an old house which has been restored as a long-hours **music pub**.

Megálo Khorió and Éristos

The rest of Tílos's inhabitants live in or near **MEGÁLO KHORIÓ**, with an enviable perspective over the vast agricultural *kámbos* stretching down to Éristos (see overleaf), and are overlooked in turn by the vast Knights' castle which encloses a sixteenth-cen-tury chapel. The castle was built on the site of ancient Tílos – from which recycled masonry is evident – and is reached by a stiff, thirty-minute climb that begins on the lane behind the Ikonomou **supermarket** before threading its way through a vast jum-ble of cisterns, house foundations and derelict chapels, the remains of the much large medieval Megálo Khorió. Two more flanking fortresses stare out across the plain: the easterly one of **Messariá** helpfully marks the location of the **Kharkádhi** cave where Pleiocene midget-elephant bones were discovered in 1971. A 500-metre track goes there from the road, ending just beyond the spring-fed cypress below the cave-mouth, which was hidden for centuries until a World War II artillery barrage exposed it. The bones themselves have been transferred to a small **museum** in Megálo Khorió, which opens only on application to the town hall.

Your choices for **accommodation** in the village are the *Pension Sevasti* (☎0241/44 237; ②), the central *Miliou Apartments* (☎0241/44 204; ③), or *Studios Ta Elefandakia* (☎0241/44 213; ③) by the car park. Among a handful of **tavernas**, the *Kali Kardhia*, next to the *Pension Sevasti*, is under energetic young management and has the best view – in addition to good food. Megálo Khorió now also has a few **nightspots**, one of them at the start of the track north for remote **Skáfi** beach (sandy but often windy).

South of and below Megálo Khorió, a sign directs you along the six-kilometre paved side road to the long, pink-sand **Éristos** beach, the island's best, where nudism will goes unremarked. About halfway down the road on the right amongst the orchards is *Taverna-Rooms Tropikana* (☎0241/44 242; ②), nothing special in either category but the only reliable year-round eating place near the beach; at peak season a simple snack bar may operate behind the sand.

The far northwest

The main road beyond Megálo Khorió hits the coast again at **Áyios Andónios**, with a single **hotel/taverna**, the *Australia* (☎0241/44 296; ③), and an exposed, average beach. At low tide you can find more lava-trapped skeletons strung out in a row – human this time, presumably tide-washed victims of a Nissirian eruption in 600 BC, and discovered by the same archeologists who found the miniature pachyderms.

There's better swimming at isolated **Pláka** beach, 2km west of Áyios Andónios, where people camp rough despite a total lack of facilities. The road finally ends 8km west of Megálo Khório at the fortified monastery of **Ayíou Pandelímonas**, founded in the fifteenth century for the sake of its miraculous spring. Now the place is usually deserted except from July 25 to 27, when it hosts the island's major festival. A tower-gate and oasis setting more than two hundred forbidding metres above the west coast seem its most memorable features, though the eminently photogenic inner courtyard boasts yet another *khokhláki* floor, and the church a fine tessellated marble floor. On the interior walls, an early eighteenth-century fresco, recently restored, shows the founder-builder holding a model of the monastery, while behind the ornate altar screen hides another fresco of the Holy Trinity.

To guarantee access, you need to visit with the regular Sunday-morning minibus tour from Megálo Khorió (fare 1000dr; 1hr to look around), or contact Pandelis Yiannourakis, the key-keeper, in Megálo Khorió. To vary the return, you can walk back on a signposted path; it's shown correctly on the FOTA-sponsored map, and ends at the minor monastery of Kamári near Áyios Andónios.

Níssyros

Volcanic **Níssyros** is noticeably greener than its southern neighbours Tílos, Khálki, and Sými, and has proved attractive and wealthy enough to retain more of its population, staying lively even in winter. While remittances from abroad (particularly Astoria, New York) are necessarily important, much of the island's income is derived from quarrying gypsum and pumice.

The main island's peculiar geology is potentially a source of other benefits: DEI, the Greek power company, spent much of the years between 1988 and 1992 sinking exploratory **geothermal wells** and attempting to convince the islanders of the benefits of cheap electricity.

In 1993, a local referendum went massively against the project, and DEI, together with its Italian contractor, took the hint and packed up. The desalination plant, reliant on expensive power from the fuel-oil generator, scarcely provides enough fresh water to spur a massive growth in package tourism. The relatively few tourists who stay the night, as opposed to the daytrippers from Kós, still find peaceful villages with a minimum of concrete eyesores, and a friendly tight-knit population. Níssyros also offers

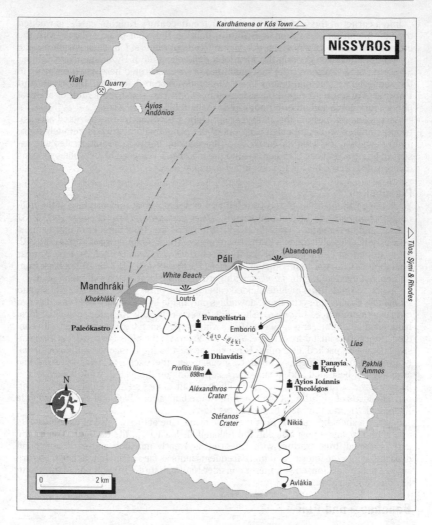

good walking opportunities, and wherever you stroll you'll hear the contented grunting of pigs as they gorge themselves on acorns from the many oak trees. Autumn is a wonderful time, especially when the landscape has perked up after the first rains, and the late-January almond-blossoming is one of the island's glories.

Mandhráki

MANDHRÁKI is the deceptively large port and island capital, where the wooden balconies and windows of its tightly packed white houses provide splashes of bright colour. Except for the drearier fringes near the ferry dock, the bulk of the place looks cheerful, arrayed around the community orchard or *kámbos* and overlooked by two ancient fortresses.

Into a corner of the first of these, the fourteenth-century Knights' castle, is wedged the little monastery of **Panayía Spilianí**, built on this spot in accordance with the instructions of the Virgin, given in a vision to one of the first Christian islanders. The monastery's prestige grew in the form of a rich collection of Byzantine icons; raiding Saracens failed to discover the vast quantities of silver secreted here. On the way up to the monastery, you might stop in at the house restored for the **Historical and Popular Museum** (erratic hours; free admission), two small rooms full of archival photos, heirlooms and other ethnographic memorabilia.

As a defensive bastion, the 2600-year-old Doric **Paleókastro** (unrestricted access), twenty minutes' well-signposted walk out of the Langadháki district, is infinitely more impressive than the Knights' castle, and ranks as one of the more underrated ancient sites in Greece. You can clamber up onto the massive, Cyclopean-block walls by means of a broad staircase beside the still-intact main gateway.

Practicalities

You'll see a handful of **hotels** on your left as you disembark at the port; best of the mid-range options are the helpful and friendly *Hotel/Restaurant Three Brothers* (☎0242/31 344; ③) and the *Romantzo* (☎0242/31 340; ③). There are also a number of more atmospheric, quieter establishments in the town proper. The *Pension Níssyros* (☎0241/31 052; ③) is at the foot of the castle, or try the small *Hotel Ipapandi* (☎0241/31 485; ③) near Mandhráki's luxury accommodation, the *Hotel Porfyris* (☎0242/31 376; ④), set back from the sea, but overlooking the *kámbos*, with gardens and a large, deep swimming pool.

Culinary **specialities** include pickled caper greens, *pittiá* (chickpea croquettes), and *soumádha*, an almond-syrup drink nowadays only made by one family and served at two tavernas (*Romantzo* and *Karava*). Shoreline **tavernas** include *Kleanthis*, a popular local hangout at lunchtime, and adjacent *Mike's* which offers such treats as yoghurt with candied grapes. Just inland from these, *Taverna Nissiros* – the oldest in town – is inexpensive and always packed after dark. However the best eating is inland: on the nocturnally lively Platía Ilikioméni, shaded by ficus trees, the excellent *Taverna Irini* has arguably the best food and most generous portions on the island, while *Panorama*, a bit east towards the Porfyris, has more idiosyncratic dishes such as snails and suckling pig. The focus of **nightlife** is again not the shore but various bars and cafés near Platía Ilikioméni, the most durable being *Cactus Bar*.

There's a short-hours **OTE** near the same platía. One of the two **travel agencies** acts as a bank rep, and a post office in the Italian-built "palace" at the harbour. Also by the jetty is a small **bus station**, with (theoretically) early morning and early afternoon departures into the interior and more frequent jaunts as far as Páli. In practice these are subject to cancellation, so you might consider renting a **motorbike** at one of three outlets on the main street.

Beaches – and Páli

Beaches on Níssyros are in even shorter supply than water, so much so that the tour agency here can successfully market excursions to a sandy cove on **Áyios Andónios** islet, just next to the mining apparatus on Yialí. Closer at hand, the black-rock beach of **Khokhláki**, behind the Knights' castle, is impossible if the wind is up, and the town beach of **Miramáre** at the east edge of the harbour would be a last resort in any weather. It's better to head east along the main road, passing the refurbished spa of **Loutrá** (hot mineral-water soaks June–Oct; 550dr per day) and the smallish **"White Beach"** (properly Yialiskári), 2km along and dwarfed by an ugly eponymous hotel (☎0242/31 498, fax 31 389; ④), generally booked by tour groups.

A kilometre or so further, the fishing village of **PÁLI** makes a more attractive base. Here you'll find the *Hotel Ellenis* (☎0242/31 453; ③), two **rooms** places (fanciest at the west end of the quay) and a good taverna, *Afroditi*, featuring white Cretan wine and homemade desserts. Another dark-sand beach extends east of Páli to an apparently abandoned new spa, but to reach Níssyros' best beaches, continue in that direction for an hour on foot (or twenty minutes by moped along the road), past an initially discouraging seaweed- and cowpat-littered shoreline, to the delightful cove of **Líes**, where the track ends. Walking a further ten or fifteen minutes along a trail over the headland brings you to the idyllic, 300-metre expanse of **Pakhiá Ámmos**.

The interior

It is the central, dormant **volcano** which gives Níssyros its special character and fosters the growth of the abundant vegetation – and no stay would be complete without a visit. When excursion boats arrive from Kós, the Polyvotis Tours coach and usually one of the public buses are pressed into service to take customers into the interior. Tours tend to set off at about 10.30am and 2.30pm, so time yourself accordingly for relative solitude, and ideally make the trip on foot or by moped.

The road up from Páli winds first past the virtually abandoned village of **EMBORIÓ**, where pigs and cows far outnumber people, though the place is slowly being bought up and restored by Athenians and foreigners. New owners are often surprised to discover natural saunas, heated by volcano steam, in the basements of the crumbling houses; at the outskirts of the village there's a public **steam bath** in a grotto, whose entrance is outlined in white paint. If you're descending to Páli from here, an old cobbled way offers an attractive short cut of the four-kilometre road.

NIKIÁ, the large village on the east side of the volcano's caldera, is more of a going concern, and its spectacular situation 14km from Mandhráki offers views out to Tílos as well as across the volcanic crater. Of the three **kafenía** here, the one on the engaging, round platía is rarely open, while the one in the middle of town usually has food. There are also a few **rooms**, but these tend to be substandard and overpriced. By the bus turnaround area, signs point to the 45-minute **trail** descending to the crater floor; a few minutes downhill, you can detour briefly to the eyrie-like **Monastery of Áyios Ioánnis Theológos**. The picnic benches and utility buildings come to life at the annual festival, the evening of September 25. To **drive** directly to the volcanic area you have to take the unsignposted road which veers off just past Emborió

However you approach the **volcano**, a sulphurous stench drifts out to meet you as fields and scrub gradually give way to lifeless, caked powder. The sunken **main crater** of Stéfanos is extraordinary, a moonscape of grey, brown and sickly yellow; there is another, less visited double crater (dubbed Aléxandhros) to the west, equally dramatic, with a clear trail leading up to it from the access road. The perimeters of both are pocked with tiny blowholes from which jets of steam puff constantly and around which little pincushions of pure sulphur crystals form. The whole floor of the larger crater seems to hiss, and standing in the middle you can hear something akin to a huge cauldron bubbling away below you. According to legend this is the groaning of Polyvotis, a titan crushed here by Poseidon under a huge rock torn from Kós. When there are tourists around, a small, overpriced café functions in the centre of the wasteland.

Since the destruction of the old trail between the volcano and Mandhráki, pleasant options for walking back to town are limited. If you want to try, backtrack along the main crater access road for about 1km to find the start of a clear but unmarked path which passes the volcanic gulch of **Káto Lákki** and the monastery of **Evangelistrías** on its two-hour course back to the port. You can lengthen the trip by detouring from Evangelistrías south to Profítis Elías, the island's summit – a two-hour detour roundtrip, the route well marked with cairns and white paint.

Kós

After Rhodes, **Kós** is the second largest and most popular island in the Dodecanese, and there are superficial similarities between the two. Here also the harbour is guarded by an imposing castle of the Knights of St John; the streets are lined with grandiose Italian public buildings, and minarets and palm trees punctuate extensive Hellenistic and Roman remains.

Though sandy and fertile, the hinterland of Kós lacks the wild beauty of Rhodes' interior, and it must also be said that the main town has little charm aside from its antiquities. Rhodes-scale tourist development imposed on an essentially sleepy, small-scale island economy, and a population of only 22,000, has resulted most obviously in even higher food and accommodation prices than on Rhodes. Except for the main town and perhaps Mastikhári resort, this is not an island that attracts many independent travellers, and from early July to early September you'll be lucky to find any sort of room at all without reservations far in advance, or a pre-booked package. All this acknowledged, Kós is still definitely worth a few days' time while island-hopping; its handful of mountain villages are appealing, the tourist infrastructure excellent (even extending to such amenities as cycle paths) and swimming opportunities are limitless – virtually the entire coast is fringed by beaches of various sizes, colours and consistencies.

Kós Town

The town of **KÓS**, home to most of the island's population, spreads in all directions from the harbour; apart from the Knights' castle, the first thing you see on arrival, its most compelling attraction lies in the wealth of Hellenistic and Roman remains, many of which were only revealed by an earthquake in 1933, and excavated afterwards by the Italians. It was they also who planned and laid out the "garden suburb" that extends east of the central grid. Elsewhere, vast areas of open space alternate with a hotchpotch of Ottoman monuments and later mock-medieval or Art-Deco buildings.

The **castle** (Tues–Sun 8.30am–3pm; 800dr) is reached via a causeway over its former moat, now filled in and planted with palms (hence the avenue's Greek name, Finíkon). The existing double citadel, built in stages between 1450 and 1514, replaced an original fourteenth-century fort deemed not capable of withstanding advances in medieval artillery. A fair proportion of ancient Koan masonry has been recycled into the walls, where the escutcheons of several Grand Masters of the Knights of St John can also be seen.

Immediately opposite the castle entrance stands the riven trunk of Hippocrates' plane tree, its branches now propped up by scaffolding instead of the ancient columns of yore; at seven hundred years, it's not really old enough to have seen the great healer, though it has a fair claim to being one of the oldest trees in Europe. Adjacent are a hexagonal Ottoman fountain and the eighteenth-century mosque of Hassan Pasha, also known as the Loggia Mosque after the portico on one side; its ground floor – like that of the **Defterdar mosque** on Platía Eleftherías – is taken up by rows of shops.

Opposite the latter stands the Italian-built **Archeological Museum** (Tues–Sun 8.30am–3pm; 800dr), with a predictable Latin bias in the choice of exhibits. Four rooms of statuary are arrayed around an atrium with a mosaic of Hippocrates welcoming Asklepios to Kós; the most famous item, purportedly a statue of Hippocrates, is indeed Hellenistic, but most of the other highly regarded works (such as Hermes seated with a lamb) are Roman.

The largest single section of ancient Kós is the **agora**, a sunken, free-access zone containing a confusing jumble of ruins, owing to repeated earthquakes between the second and sixth centuries AD. More comprehensible are the so-called western excavations, lent definition by two intersecting marble-paved streets and the restored

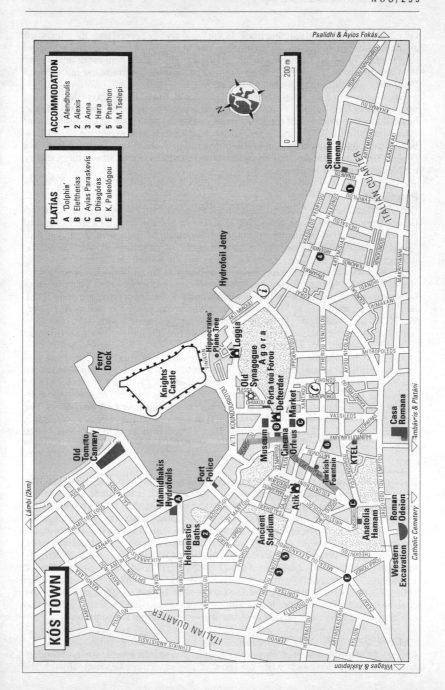

KÓS TOWN

Lámbi (2km) ▽

ITALIAN QUARTER

◁ Psalídhi & Áyios Fokás △

PLATÍAS

A 'Dolphin'
B Eleftherías
C Ayías Paraskevís
D Dhiagóras
E K. Paleológou

ACCOMMODATION

1 Afendhoulis
2 Alexis
3 Anna
4 Hara
5 Phaethon
6 M. Tselepi

200 m

Summer Cinema

ITALIAN QUARTER

Hydrofoil Jetty

Ferry Dock

Knights' Castle

Hippocrates' Plane Tree

Loggia

Old Synagogue

Porta tou Forou

Agora

Market

Detterdar

Old Tomato Cannery

Mamidhakis Hydrofoils

Port Police

Hellenistic Baths

Museum

Cinema Orfeus

Atik

Turkish Fountain

Ancient Stadium

Anatolia Hamam

Roman Odeion

Western Excavation

Casa Romana

KTEL

Catholic Cemetery ▷

◁ Ambávris & Platáni

Villages & Asklepíon ▽

ITALIAN QUARTER

colonnade of the covered running track. In the same area lie several floor mosaics, such as the famous one of Europa, though these tend to be hidden under protective gravel or off-limits. To the south, across Grigoríou toú Pémptou, are a Roman-era odeion and the **Casa Romana** (Tues–Sun 8.30am–3pm; 500dr), a third-century house built around three atria with suriviving patches of mosaic floors.

Kós also boasts a thoroughly commercialized **old town**, lining the pedestrianized street running from behind the market on Eleftherías as far as Platía Dhiagóras and the isolated minaret overlooking the western archeological zone. One of the few areas of town to survive the 1933 earthquake, today it's crammed with expensive tourist boutiques, cafés and snack bars. About the only genuinely old thing remaining here is a capped **Turkish fountain** with an calligraphic inscription, found where the walkway cobbles cross Odhós Venizélou.

Practicalities

Large **ferries** anchor just outside the harbour at a special jetty by one corner of the castle; **excursion boats** to neighbouring islands sail right in and dock all along Aktí Koundouriótou. **Hydrofoils** tie up south of the castle at their own berth, on Aktí Miaoúli. Virtually all ferry and excursion boat agents sit within 50m of each other at the intersection of pedestrianized Vassiléos Pávlou and the waterfront.

The **airport** is 26km west of Kós Town in the centre of the island; an Olympic Airways shuttle bus meets Olympic flights, but if you arrive on any other flight you'll have to either take a taxi or head towards the giant roundabout outside the airport gate and find a KTEL bus – they run from here to Mastikhári, Kardhámena and Kéfalos as well as Kós Town. The **KTEL terminal** in town is a series of stops around a triangular park 400m back from the water; the municipality also runs a **local bus** service through the beach suburbs and up to the Asclepion, with a ticket and information office at Aktí Koundouriótoun 7.

The municipal **tourist office** at Vassiléos Yeoryíou 3 (July–Aug daily 7am–9pm; winter Mon–Fri 8am–3pm; spring/autumn Mon–Fri 7.30am–8pm & Sat 8am–3pm), keep stocks of local maps, bus timetables and ferry schedules (the latter not to be trusted implicitly). The Trapeza Pisteos/Credit Bank on the waterfront has an automatic notechanger as well as a cash dispenser; several other banks also have cash dispensers. The **post office** is at Venizélou 14, while the **OTE** at Výronos on the corner of Xánthou is open until 11pm daily. **Laundries** include Happy Wash laundry at Mitropóleos 14 and Laundromat Centre at Alikarnassoú 124.

ACCOMMODATION

If you're just in transit, you're virtually obliged to **stay** in Kós Town, and even if you plan a few days on the island, it still makes a sensible base, as it is the public transport hub and has the greatest concentration of transport hire and nightlife. Good budget choices in the centre include the deservedly popular *Pension Alexis* (☎0242/28 798; ③), Irodhótou 9 at the corner of Omírou, across from the Roman *agora*; the same welcoming family has the *Hotel Afendoulis* (☎0242/25 321; ④), about 600m south at Evripílou 1. If they're full, try the well-maintained *Hotel Phaethon* at Venizélou 75 (☎0242/28 901; ④), the simpler, adjacent *Pension Anna* at no. 77 (☎024/223 030; ③), or the popular *Hara* at Khálkonos 6 (☎0242/22 500; ③). For longer stays, the rooms let by Moustafa Tselepi (☎0242/28 896; ④) at Venizélou 29, on the corner of Metsóvou, are good, and some have cooking facilities. The well-appointed **campsite** is 2500m out towards Cape Psalídhi, and can be reached by the city bus service, but is open only during the summer.

EATING, DRINKING AND NIGHTLIFE

It's easy to **eat** well, and even cheaply as long as you search inland, north of the harbour. You can pretty much write off most of the waterfront tavernas, though the

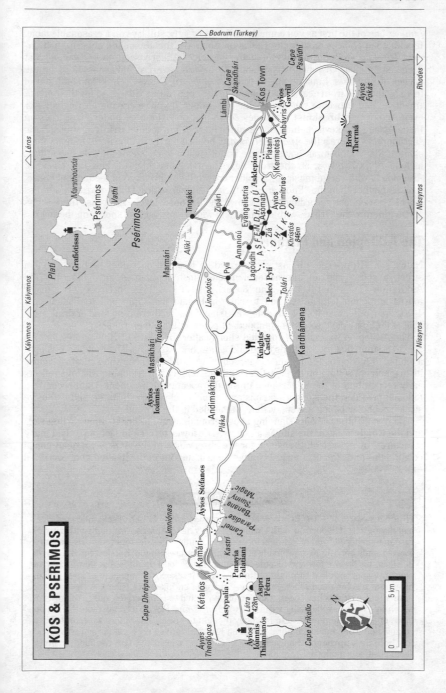

KÓS & PSÉRIMOS

△ Bodrum (Turkey)

△ Léros

△ Kálymnos ▽ Kálymnos

▽ Rhodes

▽ Níssyros

▽ Níssyros

Marathoúnda

Vathi

Psérimos

Psérimos

Platí

Grafiótissa

Cape Dhréparo

Límniónas

Áyios Theológos

Áyios Ioánnis Thiamianós

Kéfalos

Astypalía

Látra 428m

Panayía Palatianí

Kastrí

Kamári

Áyios Stéfanos

"Camel"

"Paradise"

"Banana"

"Sunny" "Magic"

Aspri Pétra

Cape Kríkello

Cape Skandhári

Lámbi

Kós Town

Cape Psalídhi

Ambávris Áyios Gavriíl

Áyios Fokás

Brós Thermá

Platáni (Kermetés)

Tingáki

Zipári

Evangelístria

Asómati

Áyios Dhimítrios

ASFENDHIOÚ Asklepion

Ziá

D H Í K E O S

Khristós 846m

Alikí

Amanioú

Lagoúdhi

Marmári

Pylí

Linopótis

Paleó Pylí

Tolári

Kardhámena

Troúlos

Mastikhári

Áyios Ioánnis

Andimákhia

Pláka

Knights' Castle

N

0 _____ 5 km

Limnos, one of the first as you come from the ferry jetty, still lays on a reasonable table. Inland, good choices include the Hellas on Amerikís, the cheap and cheerful fish taverna *Nikolaos O Psaras* on Avérof at the corner of Alikarnassoú, the *Olympiadha* at Kleopátras 2 near Olympic Airways, and *To Kokhili* ouzerí at Alikarnassoú 64 on the corner of Amerikís. Equal to any of these is *Ambavris* (May–Oct), 800m south out of town by the road from near Casa Romana, in the eponymous village; go for their *pikilía* (medley), and expect to wait for a table in summer. If you're craving an English – or even American – **breakfast**, two cafés serve that or just coffee under giant trees on Platía Ayías Paraskevís, behind the produce market. For a quiet **drink** in atmospheric surroundings, there's the *Anatolia Hamam*, housed partly in a former Ottoman mansion off Platía Dhiagóras (eating there is not such a good idea); durable music bars include *Blues Brothers*, on the front near the "Dolphin Square", and *Jazz Opera* at Arseníou 5, with varied music for an older crowd. If you prefer loud techno and house, look no further than the "Pub Lanes", officially Nafklírou and Dhiákou; every address is a bar, just choose according to the crowd and the noise level. Otherwise there is one active **cinema**, the Orfeas, with summer and winter premises as shown on the map.

The Asklepion and Platáni

Native son **Hippocrates** is justly celebrated on Kós; not only does he have a tree, a street, a statue and an international medical institute named after him, but the **Asklepion** (Tues–Sun 8.30am–3pm; 800dr), one of just three in Greece, is a major tourist attraction (city buses run to site via Platáni 8am–2pm and to Platáni only 4–10.30pm; otherwise it's a 45-minute walk). Incidentally, there is no food or drink available at the Asklepion, so come equipped, or pause in Platáni en route.

The Asklepion was actually founded shortly after the death of Hippocrates, but it's safe to assume that the methods used and taught here were his. The building was both a temple to Asklepios (god of medicine, son of Apollo) and a renowned curative centre; its magnificent setting on three artificial hillside terraces overlooking Anatolia reflects early recognition of the importance of the therapeutic environment. Until recently, a fountain provided the site with a constant supply of clean, fresh water, and extensive stretches of clay piping are still visible, embedded in the ground.

Today very little remains standing above ground, owing to the chronic earthquakes and the Knights' use of the site as a quarry. The lower terrace in fact never had many structures, being instead the venue for the observance of the *Asklepieia*, quadrennial celebrations and athletic/musical competitions in honour of the healing god. Sacrifices

---

HIPPOCRATES

Hippocrates (c. 460–370 BC) is generally regarded as the father of scientific medicine, and through the Hippocratic oath – which probably has nothing to with him and is in any case much altered from its original form – he still influences doctors today. Hippocrates was certainly born on Kós, probably at Astypalia near present-day Kéfalos, but otherwise details of his life are few and disputed; what seems beyond doubt is that he was a great physician who travelled throughout the Classical Greek world but spent at least part of his career teaching and practising at the Asklepion on his native island. A vast number of **medical writings** have been traditionally attributed to Hippocrates, only a minority of which he could have actually written; *Airs, Waters and Places*, a treatise on the importance of environment on health, is widely thought to be his, but others were probably a compilation from a medical library kept on Kós. This stress on good air and water, and the **holistic approach** of ancient Greek medicine, can in the late twentieth century seem positively modern.

to Asklepios were conducted at an **altar**, the oldest structure on the site, whose foundations can still be seen near the middle of the second terrace. Just to its west, the Corinthian columns of a second-century AD **Roman temple** were partially re-erected by the nationalistic Italians. A monumental **staircase** mounts from the altar to the second-century BC Doric temple of Asklepios on the topmost terrace, the last and grandest of a succession of the deity's shrines at this site.

About halfway to the Asklepion, the village of **PLATÁNI** (also Kermetés, from the Turkish name *Germe*) is, along with the Kós Town, the remaining place of residence for the island's dwindling community of ethnic Turks. Until 1964 there were nearly three thousand of them, but successive Cyprus crises and the worsening of relations between Greece and Turkey prompted mass emigration to Anatolia, and a drop in the Muslim population to currently under a thousand. Near or at main crossroads junction, with a working Ottoman fountain, are several tavernas and kafenía, the better of them run by Turks: *Arap* (summer only) and *Gin's Palace* (all year), each offering Anatolian-style mezédhes and kebabs better than most places in Kós Town.

Just outside Plataní on the road back to the port, the island's **Jewish cemetery** lies in a dark conifer grove, 300m beyond the Muslim graveyard. Dates on the headstones stop after 1940, after which none of the local Jews were allowed the luxury of a natural death prior to their deportation in summer 1944. Their former synagogue, a wonderfully orientalized Art-Deco specimen at Alexándhrou Dhiákou 4, has recently been refurbished as a municipal hall.

Eastern Kós

If you're looking for anything resembling a deserted **beach** near the capital, you'll need to make use of the city bus line connecting the various resorts to either side of town, or else rent a vehicle; pedal bikes can take advantage of the cycle paths extending as far east as Cape Psalídhi. Closest is **Lámbi**, 3km north towards Cape Skandhári with its military watchpoint, the last vestige of a vast army camp which has deferred to the demands of tourism.

The far end of the city bus line beginning at Lámbi is Áyios Fokás, 8km southeast, with the unusual and remote **Brós Thermá** 5km further on, easiest reached by rented vehicle. Here **hot springs** pour out of a sluice into a shoreline pool protected by boulders, heating the seawater to an enjoyable temperature. Winter storms typically disperse the boulder wall, rebuilt every spring, so that the pool changes from year to year. There's a small taverna above the parking area but no other facilities.

Tingáki and Marmári

The two neighbouring beach resorts of Tingáki and Marmári are separated from each other by the salt marsh of **Alykí**, which retains water until June after a wet winter. Between January and April Alykí is host to hundreds of migratory birds, and most of the year you'll find tame terrapins to feed near the outlet to the warm, shallow sea. There's almost always a breeze along this coast, which means plenty of windsurfers for hire at either resort. The profiles of Kálymnos, Psérimos and Turkey's Bodrum peninsula all make for spectacular scenery. If you're aiming for either of these resorts from town, especially on a bike of any sort, it's safest and most pleasant to go by the obvious **minor road** which takes off from the southwest corner of town; the entire way to Tingáki is paved, and involves the same distance as using the main trunk road and marked turnoff. Similarly, a grid of paved rural lanes links the inland portions of Tingáki and Marmári.

TINGÁKI, a busy beachside resort with half-a-dozen medium-sized hotels, lies 12km west of the harbour. Oddly, there's very little accommodation near the beach; most of this is scattered inland through fields and cow pastures. One of the better choices is

Hotel Ilios (☎0242/29 411; ③), a well designed bungalow complex; closer to the seafront turnaround square, the *Meni Beach* (☎0242/29 217; ④) is perhaps more convenient if less peaceful. The best taverna here is *Ambelis* (supper only), way off at the east end of the developed area, south of the minor road noted above. The beach itself is white-sand, long and narrow – it improves, and veers further out of earshot from the frontage road, as you head southwest.

MARMÁRI, 15km from town, has a smaller built-up area than Tingáki, and the beach itself is broader, especially to the west where it forms little dunes. Most hotels here are monopolized by tour groups, but further inland, on the west side of the access road down from the island trunk road, *Exokhiki Psistaria Apostolis* is a real find for **eating**, offering fresh fish and meat-grills, an amazing wine list, engaging decor, and reasonable prices. You can also **horse-ride** locally at the Marmari Riding Centre (☎0242/41 783), on the east side of the usual access road.

The Asfendhioú villages

Inland, the main interest of eastern Kós resides in the villages of **Mount Dhíkeos**, a handful of settlements collectively referred to as **Asfendhioú**, on the slopes of the island's only natural forest. Together they give a good idea of what Kós looked like before tourism and ready-mix concrete, and all are now severely depopulated by the mad rush to the coast. They are accessible via the curvy side-road from Zipári, a badly marked but paved minor road to Lagoúdhi, or by the shorter access road for Pylí.

The first Asfendhioú village you reach up the Zipári road is Evangelístria, where a major crossroads by the parish church and the *Asfendhiou* taverna leads to Lagoúdhi and Amanioú (west), Asómati (east) and Ziá (uphill). **ZIÁ**'s spectacular sunsets make it the target of evening tour buses, though the village has barely ten families still resident. Best of the **tavernas** here is the *Olympiada*, at the start of the pedestrian walkway up to the church; runner up, by the same church, is *Iliovasilema/Sunset*, with an unbeatable, car-free situation. Ziá is also the trailhead for the ascent of 846-metre Dhíkeos peak, a two-and-a-half-hour round-trip, initially on track but mostly by path. The route is fairly obvious, and the views from the pillbox-like summit chapel of Metamórfosis are ample reward for the effort.

Heading east from Ziá or Evangelístria, roads converge at **ASÓMATI**, home to about thirty villagers and numbers of outsiders restoring abandoned houses; the evening view from the church of Arkhángelos with its pebble mosaic rivals that of Zía, though there are no facilities as yet. **ÁYIOS DHIMÍTRIOS**, 2km beyond on a steadily worsening track, is marked by its old name of Khaïkhoúdhes on some maps, and is today completely abandoned except for a shepherd living next to the attractive church; you can continue from here on 3.5km of more rough road to the junction with the paved road linking Platáni with the municipal rubbish tip.

Pylí

PYLÍ can be reached via the paved road through Lagoúdhi and Amanioú, or from the Linopótis pond on the main island trunk road. In the upper of its two neighbourhoods, 100m west of the pedestrianized square and church, the simple *Piyi* taverna serves inexpensive fare in a superb setting beside the giant cistern-fountain (*piyí*), decorated with carved lion-head spouts. Pyli's other attraction is the so-called **Kharmýlio** (Tomb of Kharmylos), vaguely signposted near the top of the village. This consists of a subterranean, niched vault, probably a Hellenistic family tomb; immediately above, traces of an ancient temple have been incorporated into the medieval chapel of Stavrós.

Paleó (medieval) **Pylí**, roughly 3km southeast of its modern descendant, was the Byzantine capital of Kós. Head there via Amanioú, keeping straight at the junction where painted lettering on a house corner points left to Ziá and Lagoúdhi. In any case, the castle should be obvious on its rock, straight ahead; the deteriorating road ends next to a spring, opposite which a stair-path leads within fifteen minutes to the roof of the fort. En route you pass the remains of the abandoned town tumbling southward down the slope, as well as three chapels often locked to protected fresco fragments within.

Western Kós

Near the arid, desolate centre of the island, well sown with military installations, a pair of giant roundabouts by the airport funnels traffic northwest towards the Mastikhári, northeast back towards town, southwest towards Kéfalos, and southeast to Kardhámena.

Mastikhári and Andimákhia

The least developed, least "packaged" and least expensive of the northern shore resorts, **MASTIKHÁRI** has a shortish, broad beach extending west, and a less attractive one at **Troúllos**, 1.5km east. At the end of the west beach, inside a partly fenced enclosure, lie remains of the fifth-century basilica of **Áyios Ioánnis**, one of several on the island. If you want to stay, quieter digs near the west beach include the well run *Studios Irini* (☎0242/51 269; ②) or the nearby *Filio* (☎0242/51 518; ③). *O Makis*, one street inland from the quay, is the place to eat. Mastikhári is also the port for the least expensive small **ferries** to Kálymnos; there are three well spaced departures in each direction most of the year, timed more or less to coincide with Olympic Airways flight schedules.

The workaday village of **ANDIMÁKHIA**, 5km southeast of Mastikhári, straggles over several ridges; the only concession to tourism is a much-photographed windmill on the main street, preserved as a working museum with its unfurled sails. For a token fee you can climb up to the mast loft and observe its workings. East of Andimákhia, reached via a marked, three-kilometre side road, an enormous, triangular **Knights' castle** overlooks the straits to Níssyros. Once through the imposing north gateway (unrestricted access), you can follow the well-preserved west parapet, and visit two interior chapels: one with patches of fresco, the other with fine rib vaulting.

Kardhámena

KARDHÁMENA, on the southeast coast 31km from Kós Town, is the island's largest package resort after the capital itself, with visitors (mostly Brits) outnumbering locals by twenty to one in peak season. Runaway local development has banished whatever redeeming qualities the place may once have had; the logos of Carling Black Label or Foster's, and bar names like the *Bubble and Squeak Bistro*, pretty much set the tone of the place. A hefty sand beach stretches to either side of the town, hemmed in to the east with ill-concealed military bunkers and a road as far as Tolári, home to the massive *Norida Beach* all-inclusive complex.

Kardhámena is most worth knowing about as a place to catch a **boat to Níssyros**. There are supposedly two daily sailings in season: the morning tourist excursion kaïki at approximately 9.30am, and another, less expensive one – the Chyrssoula – at 2.30pm, but in practice the afternoon departure is only reliable on Mondays and Thursdays, at some time between 1.30pm and 6.30pm, depending on when the Nissyrians have finished their shopping.

Outside high season, there are generally a few **rooms** not taken by tour companies, and prices are not outrageous. For more comfort, the *Hotel Rio* (☎0242/91 627, fax 91 895; ③) gets good reviews, and like most accommodation here is underpriced for its class. **Tavernas** are predictably poor, though the longest-lived and most reasonable one is *Andreas*, right on the harbour; inland, a **bakery** (signed with red arrows) does homemade ice cream, yoghurt and sticky cakes.

South coast beaches

The thinly populated portion of Kós southwest of the airport and Andimákhia boasts the most scenic and secluded beaches on the island, plus a number of minor ancient sites. Though given fanciful names and shown as separate extents on tourist maps, and the south-facing **beaches** form essentially one long stretch at the base of a cliff. **Magic**, officially Poléni, is the longest, broadest and wildest. **Sunny**, easily walkable from Magic, has sunbeds and a taverna. **Banana** (Langádha) is the cleanest and most picturesque, with junipers tumbling off its dunes. **Paradise**, often dubbed Bubble Beach (because of volcanic gas vents in the tidal zone) is small and oversubscribed.

Uninterrupted beach resumes at **Áyios Stéfanos**, overshadowed by a huge Club Med complex, and extends 5km west to Kamári (see below). A badly marked public access road leads down to the beach just west of a small peninsula, crowned with the exquisite remains of two triple-aisled, sixth-century basilicas. Though the best preserved on the island, several columns have been toppled since the 1980s, and wonderful bird mosaics languish under a permanent layer of "protective" gravel. The basilicas overlook tiny but striking Kastrí islet with its little chapel; in theory it's an easy swim (sometimes wading) across from the westerly beach, with some of the best snorkelling on Kós around the rock formations, but you must run the gauntlet of boats from the local water-ski school.

The far west

Essentially the shore annexe of Kéfalos (see below), **KAMÁRI** is a growing package resort pitched a few notches above Kardhámena; it's a major water-sports centre, and an alternative departure point for Níssyros, up to five days weekly in season. Independent hotels or pensions that can be recommended include *Sydney* (☎0242/71 286; ④) and the adjacent *Maria* (☎0242/71 308; ③), on the seafront west of the main road up to **KÉFALOS**, 43km from Kós Town. Squatting on a bluff looking down the length of the island, this is the end of the line for buses: dull but worth knowing about for its post office and as a staging point for expeditions into the rugged peninsula terminating dramatically at Cape Kríkello.

Main highlights of a half-day tour here are a Byzantine church incorporating an ancient temple, 1km south of the village; the late Classical amphitheatre (May–Oct), with two rows of seats remaining, of **ancient Astypalia**, 500m further at the side-path signposted "Palatia"; and the cave of **Asprí Pétra** (inhabited in the Neolithic period), marked rather vaguely off the paved ridge road. A rough dirt track west from after Astypalia leads to an often windy beach, taverna and small chapel at **Áyios Theológos**, 7km from Kéfalos; keeping to the main paved road until the end of the line brings you to the appealing (but mostly locked) monastery of **Áyios Ioánnis Thymianós**, also 7km from the village.

About 1.5km north of Kéfalos on the road tracing the island's summit ridge, an obvious dirt track veers north again for 3.5km to **Limniónas**, the only north-facing beach and fishing anchorage on this part of Kós. Of the two fish tavernas, *Limionas* – nearer the jetty – is preferable. Two compact sandy beaches sit either side of the peninsula.

Psérimos

PSÉRIMOS could be an idyllic little island if it weren't so close to Kós and Kálymnos, a factor which results in day-trippers by the boatload every day of the season. Numerous excursion boats compete to dock at the undersized harbour, and not surprisingly the islanders are apt to respond in a surly fashion to visitors. There are a couple of other, less attractive beaches to hide away on during the day: Vathý (sand), a thirty-minute walk east, or Marathoúnda (pebble), a forty-five-minute walk north.

Nowhere on Psérimos, including the monastery of Grafiótissa (its festival is on August 15), is much more than an hour's walk away.

Even during the season there won't be too many other overnighters, since there's a limited number of **rooms** available. Pick of the several small pensions are *Pension Tripolitis* (☎0243/23 196; ③) over the *Saroukos* taverna, and rooms managed by the postmistress, Katerina Xyloura (☎0243/23 497; ③) above her taverna on the eastern side of the harbour. There's just one small **store**, and most of the island's supplies are brought in daily from Kálymnos. **Eating out** however, won't break the bank, and there's often fresh fish in the handful of **tavernas**.

Virtually all boats based at Kós harbour operate triangle tours, which involve departure between 9.30am and 10am, followed by a stop for swimming on either Platí islet or adjacent Psérimos, lunch in Póthia, the port of Kálymnos, and another swimming stop at whichever islet wasn't visited in the morning. If you want to spend the entire day on Psérimos, you must ride one-way on a boat taking it as the first stop, and then cadge a lift back on another boat having Psérimos as its afternoon call, around 4pm. You should pay no more than forty percent of the full excursion price (currently about 5000dr) for each leg of the journey, and it would probably be a good idea to pack basic overnight gear in case the afternoon boat refuses to take you back to Kós.

The islanders themselves don't bother with the excursion boats, but use their own small craft, the Grammatiki, to visit Kálymnos for shopping on Monday, Wednesday and Friday (returning early afternoon); if you've been staying a few days, you might ask for a ride on this, or on your host's own boat.

Astypálea

Geographically, historically and architecturally, **Astypálea** would be more at home among the Cyclades – on a clear day you can see Anáfi or Amorgós in the west far more easily than any of the other Dodecanese (except the western tip of Kós), and it looks and feels more like these than its neighbours to the east. Astypálea is not the most beautiful of islands. The heights, which offer modest walking opportunities, are bleak and covered in thornbush. Yet the herb *alisfakiá*, brewed as a tea, flourishes too, and somehow hundreds of sheep survive – as opposed to snakes, which are (uniquely in the Aegean) entirely absent. Lush citrus groves and vegetable patches in the valleys signal a relatively ample water supply, hoarded in a reservoir. The few beaches along the generally featureless coastline are often stony or strewn with seaweed.

In antiquity the island's most famous citizen was **Kleomedes**, a boxer disqualified from an early Olympic Games for causing the death of his opponent. He came home so enraged that he demolished the local school, killing all its pupils. Things have calmed down a bit in the intervening 2500 years, and today Astypálea is renowned mainly for its honey and fish. However, the abundant local catch has only been shipped to Athens since the late 1980s, a reflection of the traditionally poor ferry links in every direction. These have improved recently with the introduction of new services to Piréas and Kós, but you still risk being marooned here for an extra day or three; indeed Laskarina Holidays deleted the island from their list in 1995, frustrated by chronically unreliable connections to the nearest airport.

Despite the relative isolation, plenty of people find their way to Astypálea during the short, intense summer, when the 1200 permanent inhabitants are all but overrun by upwards of seven thousand guests a day, and the noise and commotion at the densely built port is incredible. Most arrivals are Athenians, supplemented by large numbers of Italians and foreign owners of holiday homes in the understandably popular Khóra. At such times you won't find a bed without reserving well in advance, and camping rough is expressly frowned upon.

Skála and Khóra

The main harbour of **SKÁLA** or Péra Yialós dates from the Italian era (Astipálea was the first island the Italians occupied in the Dodecanese) and most of the settlement between the quay and the line of nine windmills is even more recent. As you climb up beyond the port towards **KHÓRA** though, the neighbourhoods get progressively older and more attractive, their steep streets enlivened by the *poúndia* or colourful wooden balconies of the whitewashed houses. The whole culminates in the thirteenth-century **kástro**, one of the finest in the Aegean, erected by the Venetian Quirini clan and subsequently modified by the Ottomans. Until well into this century over three hundred people lived inside the kástro, but depopulation, World War II damage and a 1956 earthquake have combined to leave only a desolate shell today. The fine rib vaulting over the entrance supports the church of Evangelístria Kastrianí, one of two intact here, the other being Áyios Yeóryios (both usually locked).

Skála, and to a lesser extent Khóra, have **accommodation** ranging from spartan rooms to new luxury studios; proprietors meet ferries if there are vacancies. Owing to high-season noise – particularly the sound of ferries dropping anchor at 3am – you might prefer the remoter, restored self-catering units up in Khóra. Obvious, inexpensive **hotels** down in the port include the *Astynea* (☎0243/61 209; ④) and the elderly *Paradisos* (☎0243/61 224; ③), both en suite. *Vangelis* (☎0243/61 281; ③) and *Karlos* (☎0246/61 330; ③) are well appointed studio units on the east shore of the bay, the former above a good restaurant. A high-season **campsite** operates about 4km along the road to Análipsi, though it's water-logged in winter and thus mosquito-plagued in summer.

At peak season, something like 45 **tavernas** set up shop across the island, few of which are memorable. Among the more reliable year-round options, *To Akroyiali* behind Skála's tiny beach has good food offsetting haphazard service; its nearby inland rival, *Australia*, has less tasty food but friendly management. *Iy Monaxia* (aka *Viki's*), one block inland from the ferry jetty by the old power plant, has excellent home-style cooking. For carnivorous meals, *Psitopolio* Galini behind the *Hotel Astynea* is fine, while *Dhimitris*, just above the downhill road from Khóra does fish dishes.

Most **nightlife** happens up in more atmospheric Khóra, where two traditional kafenía on the main square are joined in season by music bars such as *Kastro* and *La Luna*. The **post office** and most shops are here, though **OTE** and the island's only **bank** (Emboriki), complete with cash dispenser, are down at Skála quay.

A single **bus** runs along the paved road between Khóra, Skala, Livádhia and Analípsi in July and August, and less frequently out of season – posted timetables are unreliable. There are only two official **taxis**, far too few to cope with passenger numbers in season; several places rent out **scooters**, the most reliable being Lakis and Manolis, with branches at Khóra and Skála. The island **map** sold locally is grossly inaccurate, even by flexible Greek standards.

Around the island

A thirty-minute walk (or a short, frequent bus journey) from the capital lies **LIVÁDHIA**, a fertile green valley with a popular, good beach but a rather motley collection of restaurants behind. You can **rent a room** or bungalow in the beach hamlet – for example from the Kondaratos family (☎0243/61 269; ②), or for more comfort, at *Studios Electra* (☎0243/61 270; ③), with castle views. Among the **tavernas**, *Thomas* and *Kalamia* are decent enough.

If the busy beach here doesn't suit, continue southwest fifteen minutes on a footpath to three small single coves at **Tzanáki**, packed out with naturists in mid-summer. The third bay beyond, easier reached by motorbike, is **Áyios Konstandínos**, a partly shaded, sand and-gravel cove with a good seasonal taverna. Around the headland, the lonely beaches of **Vátses** and **Kaminákia** are more usually visited by excursion boat from Skála.

A favourite outing in the west of the island is the two-hour walk or 45-minute motor bike trip from Khórato the oasis of **Áyios Ioánnis**, 10km distant. Proceed northwest along the dirt track beginning from the fifth or sixth windmill, veering left away from the side track to Panavía Flevariotíssas monastery. Beyond this point the main track, briefly dampened by a spring-seep, curls north towards farming cottages at Messariá before reaching a junction with gates across each option. Take the left-hand one, and soon the walled orchards of the uninhabited farm-monastery of Áyios Ioánnis come into view. From the balcony of the church, a steep, faint path leads down to the base of a ten-metre waterfall with bathing pools.

Northeast of the harbour, are three coves, known as **Marmári A, B** and **C**. The first is home to the power plant, the next hosts the campsite (see above), while the third, reasonably attractive, also marks the start of the path east to the coves of **Mamoúni** ("bug" or "critter" in Greek). Beyond Marmari C, the middle beach at **Stenó** ("narrow", after the isthmus here) with clean sand and a seasonal taverna, is the best.

ANÁLIPSI, widely known as Maltezána after medieval Maltese pirates, is about a ten-kilometre bus-trip or taxi-ride from town. Although it's the second-largest settlement on Astipálea, there's little for outsiders save a narrow, sea-urchin-speckled beach (there are better ones east of the main bay) and a nice view south to some islets. Despite this, blocks of **rooms** are sprouting like mushrooms, spurred by the proximity of the airport, 700m away. At the edge of the surrounding olive groves are the well-preserved remains of **Roman baths**, with floor mosaics representing zodiacal signs and the seasons. Facilities are limited to a pair of small **tavernas** (*Obelix* is the better one) and a high-season disco, one of just two on the island.

The motorable road ends at Mésa Vathý, from where an appalling track continues to ÉXO VATHÝ, a sleepy fishing village with a single reasonable taverna and a superb small-craft harbour. Following several accidents, this is no longer the **backup ferry port** in winter, when Skála is buffeted by the prevailing southerlies; foot passengers (but no vehicles) are transferred ashore to the unlit quay at Áyios Andhréas, just west of Marmári C.

Kálymnos

Most of the population of **Kálymnos** lives in or around the large port of Póthia, a wealthy but not conventionally beautiful town famed for its sponge divers. Unfortunately almost all the Mediterranean's sponges, with the exception of a few deep-water beds off Italy, have been devastated by disease, and only three or four of the fleet of thirty-odd boats can now be usefully occupied. In response to this disaster, the island has recently established a tourist industry – so far confined to one string of beach resorts – and has also customized its sponge boats for deep-sea fishing. Warehouses behind the harbour still process and sell sponges all year round, though most of these are imported from Asia and America. There are also still numbers of elderly gentlemen about who rely on two sticks or zimmer frames, stark evidence of the havoc wrought in their youth by nitrogen embolism (the "bends"), long before divers understood its crippling effects. The departure of the remaining sponge fleet, usually just after Easter, is preceded by a festive week known as *Iprogrós*, with food, drink and music; the fleet's return, approximately six months later, has historically also been the occasion for more uproarious, male-orientated celebration in the port's bars.

Kálymnos essentially consists of two cultivated and inhabited valleys sandwiched between three limestone ridges, harsh in the full glare of noon but magically tinted towards dusk. The climate, especially in winter, is alleged to be drier and healthier than that of neighbouring Kós or Léros, since the quick-draining limestone strata, riddled with many caves, doesn't retain as much moisture. The rock does, however, admit sea-water, which has invaded Póthia's wells; drinking water must be brought in by tanker truck from Vathý. In the cultivated valley bottoms, mosquitoes can be a problem; chemical or electrical remedies are sold locally.

Since Kálymnos is the home port of the very useful local namesake ferry (see p.280), and moreover where the long-distance ferry lines from the Cyclades and Astypálea join up with the main Dodecanesian routes, many travellers arrive unintentionally, and are initially most concerned with how to move on quickly. Yet Kálymnos has sufficient attractions to justify a stay of several days while island-hopping – or even longer, as the package industry at the western beaches suggests.

Póthia

PÓTHIA, without being particularly picturesque, is colourful and authentically Greek, its houses arrayed in tiers up the sides of a natural rock amphitheatre. Your first, and likely overwhelming impression will be of the phenomenal amount of noise engendered by motorbike traffic and the cranked-up sound systems of the dozen waterfront cafés. This is not entirely surprising, since with about 11,000 inhabitants, Póthia ranks as the third largest city in the Dodecanese after the main towns of Rhodes and Kós.

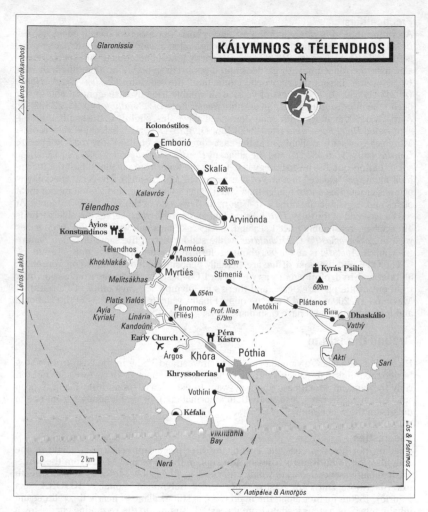

KÁLYMNOS & TÉLENDHOS

Léros (Xirókambos)

Glaroníssia

Léros (Lakkí)

Kolonóstilos

Emborió

Skalía

▲ 589m

Kalavrós

Télendhos

Aryinónda

Áyios Konstandínos

Télendhos

Arméos

Khokhlakás

Massoúri

▲ 533m

Melitsákhas

Myrtiés

Stimeniá

Kyrás Psilís

Platís Yialós

▲ 654m

▲ 609m

Ayia Kyriakí

Pánormos (Fliés)

Prof. Ilías 679m

Metókhi

Plátanos

Linária

Rína

Dhaskálio

Kandoúni

Vathý

Early Church

Péra Kástro

Árgos

Khóra

Póthia

Aktí

Khryssoherías

Sarí

Vothíni

Kéfala

Vlikhádhia Bay

los & Psérimos

0   2 km

Nerá

▽ Astipálea & Amorgós

Perhaps the most rewarding way to acquaint yourself with Póthia is by wandering the backstreets, where elegant Neoclassical houses are surrounded by surprisingly large gardens, and craftsmen ply their trade in a genuine workaday bazaar. During the Italian occupation, local houses were painted blue and white to irritate the colonial overlords, and though the custom is beginning to die out, the Greek national colours are still evident, interspersed amongst pink and ochre buildings – even some of the churches, such as the eighteenth-century **Khristós**, are painted blue.

The local **museum** (Tues–Sun 10am–2pm; 500dr; guided tours only), is lodged in a grand former residence of the Vouvallis family, local sponge magnates. A rather eclectic collection, including a kitsch-furnished Belle Epoque parlour and small troves from the island's several caves, it's not exactly required viewing.

Practicalities

Accommodation is rarely a problem, since pension proprietors usually meet the ferries. The town's best, and quietest **hotel**, though often monopolized by package groups, is the *Villa Themelina* (☎0243/22 682; ④), partly housed in a nineteenth-century mansion near the museum, with gardens and a pool. Three places in Amoudhára district (west of the harbour) are worth contacting: the en-suite *Pension Greek House* (☎0243/29 559; ②; open most of year) with volubly friendly management and kitsch decor; the more subdued but non-en-suite *Rooms Katerina Smalliou* (☎0243/22 186; ②; April–Oct), 100m above, with good views; and above this, slightly to the south, the well-signposted *Hotel Panorama* (☎0243/23 138; ④; April–Oct), with balconied view rooms. More sea views are available, near the east edge of town on the Vathý road, at *Pension Gourlas* (☎0243/29 087; ②) and the adjacent *Pension Panorama* (☎0243/29 249; ②).

For **eating out**, the best strategy is to follow the waterfront northeast past the Italian-built municipal "palace" to a line of fish **tavernas** and **ouzerís**. The local speciality is octopus croquettes, more tender than you'd expect. Get these, and a good mix of meat plates and vegetable mezédhes, at *Minore tis Avyis*, one of the first establishments. At the far east end of the quay, *Barba Petros* (aka *Adherfi Martha*), serves sizeable portions of excellent, reasonably priced seafood. Sticky-cake fans will want to take three paces west to *Zakharoplastiki O Mikhalaras*, while still further in the same direction, before the church, *Apothiki* is an old warehouse refurbished as a bar and live music venue.

The **OTE** and the **post office** are virtually opposite each other inland on Venizélou; all **boat** and **hydrofoil** agents, as well as an **EOT** post, line the waterfront as you bear right out of the pier-area gate, and there's an Olympic Airways office at Patriárkhou Maxímou 17, 200m inland from the quay. Finally, waterfront branches of the National and Ionian **banks** both have cash dispensers.

Around the island

Buses run as far as Aryinóndas in the northwest and Vathý in the east, from a stop beside the municipal "palace", with schedules helpfully posted. Departures are not terribly frequent, in which case you may want to use shared **taxis** from Platía Kýprou (more than KTEL rates, less costly than a normal taxi), or rent a **scooter** from one of outlets on the waterfront.

The castles

Heading northwest across the island, the first place you reach is a castle of the Knights of St John, **Kástro Khryssokherías**, in the suburb of Mýli. From the white-washed battlements there are wonderful views southeast over town to Kós, and north towards Khóra and Péra Kástro. The former Kalymnian capital of **KHÓRA** (aka Khorió), 1500m further along the main road, is still a village of nearly three thousand inhabitants. Steep steps lead up from its easterly summit to the Byzantine citadel-town of **Péra Kástro**, appropriated by the Knights of St John and inhabited until late in the eighteenth century. Once inside the imposing gate, all is rubble now, except several well maintained, whitewashed chapels, some unlocked to permit a glimpse of late medieval fresco fragments.

West coast resorts

From the ridgetop pass at Khorió the road dips into a tree-shaded valley leading to the consecutive **beach resorts** of Kandoúni, Myrtiés and Massoúri. **KANDOÚNI**, some 200m of brown, hard-packed sand favoured by the locals, is the shore annexe of the rich agricultural valley-village of **Pánormos** (aka Eliés). At the north end of the same bay, **Linária**, has better sand and is set apart from Kandoúni proper by a rock outcrop. The next beach north, **Platýs Yialós**, though a bit shorter than Kandoúni, is arguably the best on the island: cleaner than its southern neighbours, more secluded, and placed scenically opposite Ayía Kyriakí islet. A lone taverna at the base of the cliff behind the sand will do for lunch; those after even more privacy can hunt out tiny coves in the direction of Linária, reachable only on foot.

The main road, descending in zigzags, finally meets the sea again 8km from Póthia at **MYRTIÉS**, which together with **MASSOÚRI** 1km to the north sees most of Kálymnos's tourism: lots of neon-lit music bars, souvenir shops and the like. The beach at Myrtiés is narrow, pebbly and cramped by development, though it does improve as you approach Massoúri. The closest really good beach to Myrtiés lies 500m south, at **Melitsakhás** cove. Possibly this coast's most appealing feature is its position opposite the evocatively shaped islet of Télendhos (see below), which frames some of the most dramatic sunsets in Greece. It's also possible to go from Myrtiés directly to Léros aboard the daily mid morning kaïki. *Atlantis Hotel*, on the landward side of the road in Myrtiés, represents fair value (☎0243/47 497; ③), while the smallish *Pension Hermes* (☎0243/47 693; ③) overlooks the sea. A bit more remote, but enjoying the best views of all, is *Niki's Pension* (☎0243/47 201; ③), up the hill between Myrtiés and Massoúri. For **eating out**, *To Iliovasilema* at Myrtiés is a fine carnivorous option despite its tacky decor; homely, standard-Greek *Barba Yiannis* at Massoúri is amongst the last tavernas to shut in autumn.

Some 5km beyond Massoúri, **ARYINÓNDA** has a pebble beach backed by a single taverna and some rooms; try *Akroyiali* (☎0243/47 521; ③). The end of the bus line, **EMBORIÓ**, 19km from the port, offers more **tavernas** and **accommodation** – *Harry's Taverna Paradise*, with attached garden apartments (☎0243/47 434, ④) and *Themis* (☎0243/47 277; ③) much further inland. If the irregular bus service fails you, there is sometimes a shuttle boat back to Myrtiés.

Télendhos

The trip across the strait to the striking, volcanic-plug islet of **TÉLENDHOS** is arguably the best reason to come to Myrtiés; little boats shuttle to and fro constantly throughout the day and into the night. According to local legend, Télendhos is a petrified princess, gazing out to sea after her errant lover; her rocky profile is most evident at dusk. The hardly less pedestrian geological explanation has the islet sundered from Kálymnos by a cataclysmic earthquake in 554 AD; traces of a submerged town are said to lie at the bottom of the straits.

Télendhos is car-free and blissfully tranquil. For diversion and sustenance you'll find the ruined thirteenth-century **monastery of Áyios Vasílios**, a castle at remote Áyios Konstandínos, a tiny beach, several tavernas and inexpensive pensions, all in or near the single village. If you want to book ahead (mandatory in summer), try *Pension Uncle George* (☎0243/47 502; ②), atop an excellent taverna; *Pension Rita* (☎0243/47 914; ②) next door, above its welcoming café; *Dhimitris Harinos* (☎0243/47 916; ②), at the north end of the waterfront; or *Foukena Galanomati* (☎0243/47 401; ②), with another taverna, off by itself beyond the ruined monastery. The recent *Hotel Port Potha* (☎0243/47 321, fax 48 108; ③) is comparatively luxurious. A well signed, ten-minute path leads over the ridge to **Khokhlakás** pebble beach, small but very scenic, with sunbeds for hire. Heart and soul of **nightlife**, at the very north end of things, is the Greek-Australian-run *On the Rocks Cafe*, in the grounds of Áyios Kharálambos chapel, which also incorporates a Byzantine baths complex.

Vathý

Heading east from Póthia, an initially unpromising, ten-kilometre ride ends dramatically at **VATHÝ** a long, fertile valley, carpeted with orange and tangerine groves, whose colour provides a startling contrast to the lifeless greys elsewhere on

Kálymnos. At the simple fjord port of **RÍNA**, little distinguishes the adjacent **tavernas** *Panormitis* and *Popy's*, both pricier than you'd expect owing to patronage from the numerous yachts which call here. Nevertheless, Rína doesn't make a bad base, especially for a walking holiday; you could **stay** at the *Hotel Galini* (☎0243/31 241; ③), overlooking the boatyard, or the *Pension Manolis* (☎0243/31 300; ②), on the slope to the south, with cooking facilities and a helpful proprietor. If necessary, the tavernas can also muster a few simple rooms.

The steep-sided inlet has no beach to speak of; the closest, about 3km back towards Póthia, is **Aktí**, a functional pebble beach with sunbeds and a single snack bar, reached by a steep cement driveway. Boat excursions sometimes visit the stalactite cave of **Dhaskálio**, inhabited in Neolithic times, out towards the fjord mouth on its north flank. For **walkers** the lush valley behind, criss-crossed with rough tractor-tracks and narrower lanes, may prove an irresistible lure, but be warned that it will take you the better part of three hours, most of it shadeless once you're out of the orchards, to reach either Póthia or Aryinóndas via the old paths. You'll need to carry food and water with you, and be wary of maps showing the Aryinónda-bound trail going via Stiménia – it doesn't.

The southwest

Some 6km southwest of Póthia, the small bay of **Vlyhádhia** is reached via a narrow ravine draining from the nondescript village of Vothíni. The sand-and-pebble beach here isn't really worth a special trip, unless you're headed for the local **scuba** operation, since Vlyhádhia is one of the limited number of legal diving areas in Greece.

Póthia-based kaïkia also make well publicized excursions to the cave of **Kéfala** just to the west, the most impressive of half-a-dozen caverns around the island. You have to walk thirty minutes from where the boats dock, but the vividly coloured formations repay the effort; the cave was inhabited before recorded history, and later served as a sanctuary of Zeus (who is fancifully identified with a particularly imposing stalagmite in the biggest of six chambers).

Léros

Léros is so indented with deep, sheltered anchorages that during World War II it harboured, in turn, the entire Italian, German, and British Mediterranean fleets. Unfortunately, many of these magnificent fjords and bays seem to absorb rather than reflect light, and the island's relative fertility can seem scraggy and unkempt when compared with the crisp lines of its more barren neighbours. These characteristics, plus the island's lack of spectacularly good beaches, meant that until the late 1980s just a few thousand foreigners (mostly Italians who grew up on the island), and not many more Greeks, came to visit each August. Such a pattern is now history, with German, Dutch and British package operators forming the vanguard of those "discovering" Léros and the company of islanders unjaded by mass tourism. But foreign tourism has stalled of late, with matters unlikely to change until and unless the tiny airport is expanded to accommodate jets.

Not that the island needs, nor particularly encourages, mass tourism; various prisons and sanatoriums have dominated the Lerian economy since the 1950s, directly or indirectly employing about a third of the population. Under the junta the island hosted an infamous detention centre at Parthéni, and today the **mental hospital** on Léros is still the repository for many of Greece's more intractable psychiatric cases; another asylum is home to hundreds of mentally handicapped children. The island's domestic image problem is compounded by its name, the butt of jokes by mainlanders who pounce on its similarity to the word *léra*, connoting rascality and unsavouriness.

In 1989 a major scandal emerged concerning the administration of the various asylums, with EU maintenance and development funds found to have been embezzled by administrators and staff, and the inmates kept in degrading and inhumane conditions. Since then, an influx of EU inspectors, foreign psychiatrists and extra funding have resulted in drastic improvements in patient treatment, including the establishment of halfway houses across the island.

More obvious is the legacy of the **Battle of Léros** of November 12–16, 1943, when overwhelming German forces displaced a British division which had landed on the island following the Italian capitulation. Bomb nose cones and shell casings turn up as gaily painted garden ornaments in the courtyards of churches and tavernas, or are pressed into service as gateposts. Each year for three days following September 26, memorial services and a naval festival commemorate the sinking of the Greek battleships *Queen Olga* and *Intrepid* during the German attack.

Unusually for a small island, Léros has abundant ground water, channelled into cisterns at several points. These, plus low-lying ground staked with the avenues of eucalyptus trees planted by the Italians, makes for an active mosquito contingent, so come prepared. The island is compact enough to walk around, but there is a bus service and several cycle-rental outfits, with enough hills to give mountain-bikers a good work-out.

Lakkí and Xirókambos

All large **ferries** arrive at the main port of **LAKKÍ**, once the headquarters of a bustling Italian naval base. Boulevards far too wide for today's paltry amount of traffic are lined with some marvellous Art-Deco edifices, including the cinema (closed since 1985), the primary school and the defunct *Leros Palace Hotel*.

Buses don't meet the ferries – instead there are taxis that charge set fares to standard destinations. Few people stay at any of the three moribund hotels in Lakkí, preferring to head straight for the resorts of Pandéli, Álinda or Vromólithos (see below). There's just one bona-fide **taverna**, *To Petrino*, next to the **post office** inland, and both of the island's cash dispensers are here, attached to the National and Commercial banks. Gribelos is the island's sole G&A ferry agent. The nearest approximation of a **beach** is at Kouloúki, 500m west, where there's a seasonal taverna and some pines for shade, though it's too close to the ferry jetty for most tastes. You can carry on to the pavement's end at Merikiá which is a slight improvement and also has a taverna.

XIRÓKAMBOS, nearly 5km from Lakkí in the extreme south of the island, is the point of arrival for kaïkia from Myrtiés on Kálymnos. Billed as a resort, it's essentially a fishing port – the beach here is poor to mediocre, improving as you head west. **Accommodation** is available at *Villa Maria* (☎0247/22 827; ③) on the beach or, a bit inland, at the well-maintained *Yianoukas Rooms* (☎0247/23 148; ②); the island's **campsite** is in an olive grove at the village of Lepídha, 750m back up the road to Lakkí. **Meals** can be had at *Taverna Tzitzifies*, just by the jujube trees at the east end of things, where the road hits the shore.

Pandéli and Vromólithos

Just less than 3km north of Lakkí, Pandéli and Vromólithos together form the fastest-growing resort on the island – and are certainly two of the more attractive and scenic places to stay.

PANDÉLI is still very much a working port, the cement jetty primarily for local fishermen rather than the yachts which call here. A negligible beach is compensated for by a relative abundance of non-package **accommodation**, such as *Pension Kavos* (☎0247/23 247; ③), with a pleasant breakfast terrace, or *Pension Happiness* (☎0247/23 498; ③), where the road down from Plátanos meets the sea. Up on the ridge dividing Pandéli from Vromólithos, the *Pension Fanari* (☎0247/23 152; ④) is a good choice for its calm setting below the road and views across to the castle, while the peace at the *Hotel Rodon* (☎0247/23 524; ③) is disturbed only by wafts of music from the *Beach Bar*, perched on a rock terrace below, facing Vromólithos. The other long-lived bar is the civilized *Savana*, at the opposite end of Pandéli, but the soul of the place is its waterfront **tavernas**, which come alive after dark. These get less expensive and less pretentious as you head east, culminating in *Maria's*, a local institution, decked out in coloured lights and whimsically painted gourds – but the grilled octopus is reliable. *Zorba's* is about the best of the other three pricier tavernas, usually offering fresh fish.

VROMÓLITHOS boasts the best easily accessible beach on the island, car-free and hemmed in by hills studded with massive oaks. The **beach** is gravel and coarse sand, and the water's fine, but as so often on Léros you have to cross a nasty, sharp reef at most points before reaching a dropoff to deeper water. Two tavernas behind the beach trade more on their location than their cuisine, but the standard of **accommodation** here is higher than at Pandéli, with the result that much of it tends to be monopolized by package companies; try *Studios Paradise* (☎0247/23 247; ④) or *Pension Margarita* (☎0247/22 889; ④), both slightly inland.

Plátanos and Ayía Marína

The Neoclassical and vernacular houses of **PLÁTANOS**, the island capital 1km west of Pandéli, are draped gracefully along a saddle between two hills, one of them crowned by the inevitable Knights' castle. Locally known as the **Kástro**, this is reached either by a paved but rutted road peeling off the Pandéli road, or via a more scenic stair-path from the central square; the battlements, and the views from them, are dramatic, especially near sunrise or sunset. The medieval church of Panayía tou Kástrou, inside the gate, houses a small museum (daily 8.30am–12.30pm, also Wed, Sat & Sun 4–8pm; token admission), though its carved *témblon* and naive oratory are more remarkable than the sparse exhibits, which incongruously include a chunk of the Berlin Wall.

Except for *Hotel Eleftheria* (π0247/23 550; ③), elevated and quiet enough to be desirable, Plátanos is not really a place to stay or eat, although it has plenty of **shops** and **services**. Olympic Airways (π0247/24 144) is south of the junction to Pandéli, while the **post office** and short-hours **OTE** are down the road towards Ayía Marína. **Buses** ply four to six times daily between Parthéni in the north and Xirókambos in the south.

Plátanos merges seamlessly with **AYÍA MARÍNA**, 1km north on the shore of a fine bay. If you're travelling to Léros on an excursion boat or hydrofoil, this will be your port of entry. Although there's no accommodation here, it's arguably the best place to **eat** on the island. On route to the quay, the *Ayia Marina* taverna is the oldest and best established place for mayireftá, open year-round with stylish indoor seating. Just west of the police station, on the water, *Mezedhopolio Kapaniri* is a good, reasonable ouzerí, at its best after dark, featuring plenty of fried vegetable first courses. Just inland opposite the *Agrotiki Trapeza* in a little alley, the *Kapetan Mikhalis* ouzerí claims to be open all day and proffers a range of inexpensive local specialities, including various fish marinated in salt (*pastós*). A semblance of **nightlife** is provided by various bars, such as *Garbo's* near Kapaniri, and *Kharami* on the quay. Among a cluster of tourist shops 300m up the road back towards Plátanos, the pottery studio of expatriate Richard Smith merits a mention for his engaging raku ware.

Álinda and the north

ALÍNDA, 3km northwest of Ayía Marína, ranks as the longest-established resort on Léros, with development just across the road from a long narrow strip of beach. It's also the first area for accommodation to open in spring, and the last to shut in autumn. Many of the first dozen **hotels** and **pensions** here are block-booked by tour companies, but you may have better luck at *Hotel Gianna* (π247/23 153; ④) or *Studios Diamantis* (π247/23 213; ③) just inland, both overlooking the war cemetery (see below), or at *Rooms Papafotis* (π0247/22 247; ③) at the north end of the strip. At Krithóni, 1.5km south, there's also the en-suite *Hotel Konstantinos*, overlooking the sea (π0247/22 337; ④). **Restaurant** options aren't brilliant, except for *To Steki* next to the war cemetery, open year round with good grills and mezédhes plates attracting a local clientele.

An **Allied War Graves Cemetery**, mostly containing casualties of the November 1943 battle, occupies a walled enclosure at the south end of the beach; immaculately maintained, it serves as a moving counterpoint to the holiday hubbub outside. The other principal sight at Álinda is the privately run **Historical and Ethnographic Museum** (summer daily 9am–noon & 6–9pm), housed in the castle-like Bellini mansion; along with the usual rural artefacts, you'll find extensive exhibits on the printing trade including rare documents and clippings.

Alternative beaches near Álinda include **Panayiés**, a series of gravel coves (one naturist) at the far northeast of the bay, and **Goúrna**, the turning for which lies 1km or so off the trans-island road. The latter, Léros's longest sandy beach, is hard-packed and gently shelving; it's also wind-buffeted, bereft of any nearby facilities, and fringed at the back with an impromptu car park and construction rubble. A separate road beyond the Goúrna turning leads to **Kokálli**, no great improvement beach-wise, but flanked to one side by the scenic islet of **Áyios Isídhoros** which is tethered to the mainland by a causeway, its eponymous chapel perched on top.

Seven kilometres from Álinda along the main route north is the marked side track for the **Temple of Artemis**, on a slight rise just west of the airport. In ancient times, Léros was sacred to the goddess, and the temple here was supposedly inhabited by guinea fowl – the grief-stricken sisters of Meleager, metamorphosed thus by Artemis following their brother's death. All that remains now are some jumbled, knee-high walls, but the view is superb. The onward road skims the shores of sumpy, reed-fringed Parthéni Bay, with its dreary army base, until the paved road ends 11km along at **Blefoútis**, a rather more inspiring sight with its huge, virtually landlocked bay. The beach has tamarisks to shelter under and a decent taverna, *Iy Thea Artemi*, for lunch.

Pátmos

Arguably the most beautiful, certainly the best known of the smaller islands in the Dodecanese, **Pátmos** has a distinctive, immediately palpable atmosphere. It was in a cave here that St John the Divine (in Greek, *O Theologos*), received the New Testament's Revelations and unwittingly shaped the island's destiny. The monastery which commemorates him, founded here in 1088 by the Blessed Khristodhoulos (1021–1093), dominates Pátmos both physically – its fortified bulk towering high above everything else – and, to a considerable extent, politically. While the monks inside no longer run the island as they did for more than six centuries, their influence has nevertheless stopped Pátmos going the way of Rhodes or Kós.

Despite vast numbers of visitors, and the island's firm presence on the cruise, hydrofoil and yacht circuits, tourism has not been allowed to completely take Pátmos over. Although there are a number of clubs and even one disco around Skála, drunken rowdiness is virtually unknown, and this is one island where you do risk arrest for nude bathing. Package clients have only recently begun to outnumber independent visitors, and are pretty much confined to Gríkou and a few newish mega-hotels on the west side of Skála. There are still more daytrippers than overnighters, and Pátmos seems an altogether different place once the last cruiser has gone at sunset. Away from Skála, development is appealingly subdued if not deliberately retarded, thanks to the absence of an airport.

Skála and around

SKÁLA seems initially to contradict any solemn, otherworldly image of Pátmos, the waterside lined with ritzy-looking cafés. During peak season, the quay and commercial district heave by day with hydrofoil and cruise-ship passengers souvenir-hunting or being shepherded onto coaches for the ride up to the monastery; after dark there's still a considerable traffic in well-dressed cliques of visitors. In winter, the town seems moribund as most shops and restaurants close, their owners and staff back in Rhodes or Athens.

Melöï Beach is 1500m to the north (see p.278), and one of the most convenient and popular coves on the island; Khóra, a bus or taxi-ride up the mountain, is a more attractive base but has few rooms. Yet given time – especially in spring or autumn – Skála reveals some more enticing corners in the residential fringes to the east and west, where vernacular mansions hem in pedestrian lanes creeping up the hillsides. The

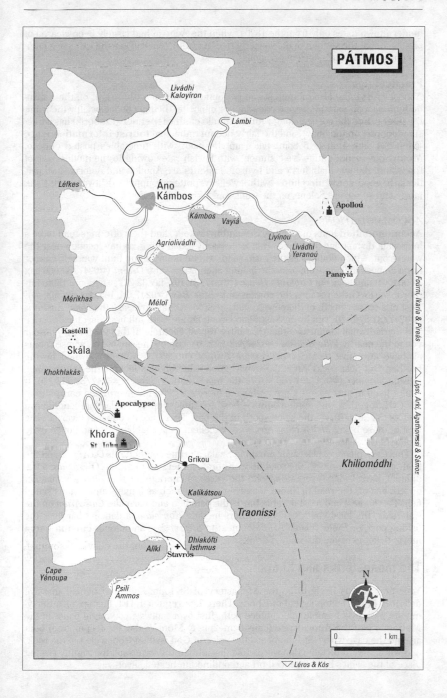

PÁTMOS

Livádhi
Kaloyíron

Lámbi

Léfkes

Áno
Kámbos

Apolloú

Kámbos   Vayiá

Agriolivádhi

Liyínou

Livádhi
Yeranoú

Panayiá

Mérikhas

Méloï

Kastélli

Skála

Khokhlakás

Apocalypse

Khóra
St. John

Gríkou

Khiliomódhi

Kalikátsou

Traoníssi

Dhiakófti
Isthmus

Alíkí   Stavrós

Cape
Yénoupa

Psilí
Ámmos

N

0   1 km

△ Foúrni, Ikaría & Pireás

△ Lípsi, Arkí, Agathoníssi & Sámos

▽ Léros & Kós

modern town dates only from the 1820s, when the Aegean had largely been cleared of pirates, but at the summit of the westerly rise, **Kastélli**, you can see the extensive foundations of the island's ancient acropolis.

Practicalities

Almost everything else of interest can be found within, or within sight of, the Italian-built municipal "palace": large ferries anchor opposite, the port police occupy the front, the **post office** the corner, along with an Ethniki **cash dispenser** (Emboriki has a free-standing one on the quay), and the fairly helpful municipal **tourist information** office (Mon–Sat 9am–1pm & 5–8pm) takes up the back, with timetables posted outside. **Motorbike rental** outfits are common, with lowish rates owing to the modest size of the island; the two main ferry and hydrofoil **agents** are Apollon and Astoria. Two particularly good **souvenir shops**, with jewellery, pottery, puppets, driftwood art, batik fabric and so on, are Selene, on the front, and Ekfrasis inland.

ACCOMMODATION

Accommodation touts meet all ferries and hydrofoils, and their offerings tend to be a long walk distant and/or inland – not necessarily a bad thing, as any location near the waterfront, which doubles as the main road, will be noisy. If you hunt yourself, calmer hotel choices include – opposite the fishing anchorage – the *Delfini* (☎0247/32 060, fax 32 061; ④) and adjacent *Captain's House* (☎0247/31 793, fax 32 277; ⑤); some 150m further towards Gríkou stands the comfortable *Blue Bay* (☎0247/31 165, fax 32 303; ④). Best of a cluster north of the power plant, near Mérikhas cove, are the *Hotel Australis* (☎0247/31 576; ③), run by an Australian-Greek family, with full breakfast for the price and myriad small kindnesses that guarantee repeat clientele. If they're full they'll refer you to the nearby *Villa Knossos* (☎0247/32 189; ③), run by the son-in-law, whose rooms all have attractive terraces, or *Pension Sydney* (☎0247/31 139; ③), owned by the brother. Out near rocky Khokhlakás bay, good-value options include the comfortable, hillside *Summer* (☎0247/31 769; ④) or the more modest *Sunset* (☎0247/31 411; ③). If you're keen to stay nearer a proper beach, there's a good but overpriced **campsite** at **MELÓÏ**, together with some **rooms** – best are those run by Loula Koumendhourou (☎0247/32 281; ③), on the slope south of the bay. There are a couple of tavernas, the best of these being *Melloi* (alias *Stefanos*): excellent, reasonably priced and open early or late in the season.

There are plenty of places for **meals** in Skála: a prime contender is *O Grigoris*, on the front at the junction with the road up to Khóra; runners-up might be *O Vrakhos*, a traditional, barrel-wine taverna opposite the yacht anchorage, or the good *Khiliomodhi* ouzerí, just off the road to Khóra, featuring seafood such as limpets and various salted fish. The biggest and most durable **bar** is the panelled and barn-like *Café Arion* on the waterside, the local youth hangout; others include *Konsolato*, a dancing bar near the fishing port, or *Byblos* inland. At Melóï, next to *Stefanos'*, is an outdoor **cinema-bar**: a movie ticket gets you discounted drinks.

The monasteries and Khóra

Your first stop is likely to be the Monastery of St John, sheltered behind massive defences in the hilltop capital of Khóra. There is a regular KTEL bus up, or a thirty-minute walk by a beautiful old cobbled path. Just over halfway, you might pause at the **Monastery of the Apocalypse** (daily 8am–2pm & Mon, Wed & Fri 4–6pm; free) built around the cave where St John heard the voice of God issuing from a cleft in the rock, and where he sat dictating his words to a disciple. In the cave wall, the nightly resting place of the saint's head is fenced off and outlined in beaten silver.

This is merely a foretaste of the **Monastery of St John** (daily 8am–2pm & Mon, Tues, Thurs & Sun 4–6pm). In 1088, the soldier-cleric Ioannis "The Blessed" Khristodhoulos was granted title to Pátmos by Byzantine Emperor Alexios Komnenos; within three years he and his followers had completed the essentials of the existing monastery, the threats of piracy and the Selçuk Turks dictating a heavily fortified style. A warren of interconnecting courtyards, chapels, stairways, arcades, galleries and roof terraces, it offers a rare glimpse of a Patmian interior; hidden in the walls are fragments of an ancient Artemis temple which stood here before being destroyed by Khristodhoulos. Off to one side, the **treasury** (same hours; 500dr) merits a leisurely visit for its magnificent array of religious treasure, mostly medieval icons of the Cretan school, but pride of place goes to the eleventh-century parchment chrysobull (edict) of Emperor Alexios Komnenos, granting the island to Khristodhoulos.

Khóra

The promise of security afforded by St John's stout walls spurred the growth of **KHÓRA** immediately outside the fortifications. It remains architecturally homogeneous, with cobbled lanes sheltering dozens of shipowners' mansions from the island's seventeenth-to eighteenth-century heyday. High, windowless walls and imposing wooden doors betray nothing of the opulence within: painted ceilings, pebble-mosaic terraces, flag-stoned kitchens, and carved furniture. Away from the principal thoroughfares are lanes that rarely see traffic, and by night, when the monastery ramparts are floodlit to startling effect, it's hard to think of a more beautiful Dodecanesian village. Neither should you miss the **view** from Platía Lódza (named after the remnant of an adjacent Venetian *loggia*), particularly at dawn or dusk. Landmasses to the north, going clockwise, include Ikaría, Thýmena, Foúrni, Sámos with the brooding mass of Mount Kérkis, Arkí, and the double-humped Samsun Dağ (ancient Mount Mykale) in Turkey.

You can **eat** well at *Vangelis* on the inner square, which has a wonderful old jukebox in addition to a varied, reasonable menu. There are, however, very few places to **stay**; foreigners here are mostly long-term occupants, who have bought up and restored almost a third of the crumbling mansions since the 1960s. Getting a short-term room can be a pretty thankless task, even in spring or autumn; the best strategy is to contact *Vangelis* taverna early in the day, or phone ahead for reservations to Yeoryia Triandafyllou (☎0247/31 963; ④) or Marouso Kouva (☎0247/31 026; ④).

The rest of the island

Pátmos, as a locally published guide once memorably proclaimed, "is immense for those who know how to wander in space and time". Lesser mortals may find it easier to get around on foot, or by bus. There's still scope for **walking** despite a dwindling network of paths; otherwise a single **bus** offers surprisingly reliable service between Skála, Khóra, Kámbos and Gríkou – the main stop, with a posted timetable, is right in front of the main ferry dock.

After its extraordinary atmosphere and magnificent scenery, **beaches** are Patmos's principal attraction. From Khóra, a paved road (partly shortcut by the path) winds east to the sandiest part of rather overdeveloped and cheerless **GRÍKOU**, the main venue for Patmian package tourism. The beach itself, far from the island's best, forms a narrow strip of hard-packed sand giving way to large pebbles towards the south. En route you pass the hillside *Flisvos* taverna, oldest and most reliable here, with a few simple rooms (☎0247/31 380; ③). From either Gríkou or Khóra, you can ride a moped over dirt roads as far as Stavrós chapel on the Dhiakoftí isthmus, beyond which a thirty-minute walk southwest leads to **Psilí Ámmos** beach. This is the only pure-sand cove on the island with shade lent by tamarisks, and there's a good lunchtime **taverna**. There's also a summer kaíki service here from Skála, departing by 10am and returning at 3.30pm.

More good beaches are to be found in the north of the island, tucked into the startling eastern shoreline; most are accessible from side roads off the main route north from Skála. **Melóï** is handy and quite appealing, with tamarisks behind the slender belt of sand, and good snorkelling offshore. The first beach beyond Méloï, **Agriolivádhi**, has a patch of sand at its broad centre, kayak rental and a high-season taverna. The next beach, **Kámbos**, is popular with Greeks, and the most developed remote resort on the island, with seasonal watersports facilities and tavernas, though its appeal is diminished by the road just inland and a rock shelf in the shallows. East of Kámbos are several less frequented coves, including pebble **Vayiá** and sand-and-gravel **Livádhi Yeranoú**, the latter with more tamarisks, a seasonal drinks cantina and an islet to swim out to. From Kámbos you can also journey north to the bay of **Lámbi**, best for swimming when the prevailing wind is from the south, and renowned for an abundance of multicoloured volcanic stones. Of the two adjacent **tavernas**, the first encountered, *Lambi*, is better for food, while the second, *To Dhelfini tis Lambis*, rents simple **rooms** (☎0247/34 074; ②). Weather permitting, this is also the most northerly port of call for the daily excursion kaïkia that ply the east coast in season.

Lipsí

Of the various islets to the north and east of Pátmos, **LIPSÍ** is the largest, most interesting and most populated, and the one that is beginning to get a significant summer tourist trade.

During quieter months, however, Lipsí still makes an idyllic halt, its sleepy pace making plausible a purported link between the island's name and that of **Calypso**, the nymph who held Odysseus in thrall. Deep wells water many small farms, but there is only one spring in the west, and pastoral appearances are deceptive – four times the relatively impoverished full-time population of 450 is overseas (many in Tasmania, for some reason). Most of those who stayed cluster around the fine harbour, as does most of the food and lodging.

A prime **accommodation** choice in all senses is the welcoming *Apartments Galini* (☎0247/41 212, fax 41 012; ③), the first building you see above the ferry jetty; the proprietor is a fishermen and takes kaïki tours on request. Other good options include *Rena's Rooms* (☎0247/41 363; ③), overlooking Liendoú, the *Flisvos Pension* at the east end of the port (☎0247/41 261; ②) and *Studios Barbarosa* (☎0247/41 312; ④), just up the stairway into the town centre. Top of the heap is the new *Aphrodite Hotel* (☎0247/41 000; ④), a studio-bungalow complex designed to accommodate package clients, though they're not adverse to walk-ins at slow times.

The half-dozen **tavernas** are comparable in quality, though they specialize: *Barbarosa*, on the slope near *Rena's Rooms*, does good vegetable-based *mayireftá*; *Fish Restaurant* on the quay only opens when the owner has caught something, and *To Dhelfini*, next to the police station, falls somewhere in between. On the waterfront to either side of the *Kalypso* (the grill is recommended but the hotel isn't), idiosyncratic kafenía and ouzerís with minimal decor offer mezédhes outdoors: an atmospheric pre-supper ritual. On or near the square up by the cathedral, you'll find the **post office** and **OTE** (but no bank), and a hilariously indiscriminate **Ecclesiastical Museum** featuring such "relics" as oil from the sanctuary on Mount Tabor and water from the Jordan River.

The island's **beaches** are rather scattered: closest to town is **Liendoú**, immediately west, but the most attractive is **Katsadhiá**, a collection of small, sandy coves south of the port, with a good, simple taverna, *Andonis* (May–Sept only), just inland from a music bar, *Dilaila*, which dominates the main cove here and runs an informal campsite (free but you must buy a meal daily). **Khokhlakoúra**, on the east coast, by contrast consists of rather grubby shingle with no facilities. An hour's walk along the paved road leading west from town brings you to **Platýs Yialós**, a small, sheltered, sandy bay with a single taverna (June–Sept). In high season enterprising individuals run pick-up trucks, with bench seats, along a route between town and all three of the above bays; a schedule of sorts is posted on a kafenío window. **Monodhéndhri**, on the northeast coast, is accessible on foot or by **moped** only; there are now a few rental outlets for the latter.

A bare handful of surviving paths and narrow tracks provide opportunities for **walks** through the undulating countryside, dotted with blue-domed churches. One of the better treks heads west from Liendoú to the bay of **Kímisi** (3hr round trip), where an octogenarian religious hermit dwells in a tiny monastery above the shore, next to the single island spring. An ugly track has been bulldozed in from the north to disturb his solitude – it's only suitable for jeeps, not bikes.

Arkí, Maráthi and Agathónissi

About two-thirds the size of Lipsí, **Arkí** is considerably more primitive, lacking drinking water, mains electricity (there are solar panels), a ferry dock, or any discernible village centre. Just 39 permanent inhabitants cling to life here, most engaged in fishing, though complete depopulation is conceivable within the next decade. It's an elective, once-weekly stop on the *Nissos Kalymnos* and Miniotis Lines routes: if you want to disembark here, you must warn the captain well in advance, so he can radio for the shuttle service from the island. Of the two taverna rooms (☎0247/32 371 and ☎0247/32 230; both ②), the remoter one doubles as a music pub, courtesy of the owner's enormous collection of jazz tapes. There's no proper beach on Arkí; the nearest one is just offshore on the islet of **Maráthi**, where another pair of tavernas cater to the daytrippers who come several times a week from Pátmos or Lipsí – links with Arkí are unreliable. Both tavernas let some fairly comfortable **rooms**, (no phones; ②), making Maráthi perhaps a better option than Arkí for acting out Robinson Crusoe fantasies.

The small, sheer-sided, waterless islet of **Agathoníssi (Gaïdharo)** is too remote – much closer to Turkey than Pátmos, in fact – to be included in day excursions, so that only intrepid backpackers include it in their itineraries. Even though hydrofoil connections dovetail well with appearances of the *Nissos Kalymnos*, you should count on staying three days, especially if the wind's up. Despite the lack of springs (cisterns are ubiquitous), the island is greener and more fertile than apparent from the sea; scrub on the heights overlooks two arable plains in the west. Just 140 people live here, down from several hundred before the last war, but those who've opted to stay seem determined to make a go of raising goats or fishing, and there are virtually no abandoned or neglected dwellings. Most of the population lives in the hamlet of **MEGÁLO KHORIÓ**, just visible on the ridge above the harbour of **Áyios Yeóryios**, and level with tiny **Mikró Khorió**. Except for two café restaurants (*Dhekatria Adherfia* is best for lunch) and the *Katsoulieri Pension* (☎0247/24 385; ②) in Megálo Khorió, all amenities are in the port. Here the choice is between rooms operated by Theoloyia Yiameou (☎0247/23 692; ②), Maria Kamitsi (☎0247/23 690; ②) and those inland at *George's Pension* (☎0247/24 385; ②). **Eating** options in Áyios Yeóryios are limited to *Seagull/Glaros*, at mid-quay, and *George's* at the base of the jetty.

As on Lipsí, **walking** consists of following the cement or dirt road network, or striking out cross-country over rough terrain. If you don't swim at the port, which has the only beach, you can walk twenty minutes southwest along a track to shingle-gravel **Spiliás**, or an hour-plus to **Thóli** in the far southeast of the island. Here there's a passable beach, one of a few small fish farms around the coastline, and (just inland) an arcaded Byzantine structure, probably a combination granary and trading post. Along with snorkelling over the tiny reef here, it's by far the most interesting sight on Agathoníssi.

travel details

To simplify the lists below, the *Nissos Kalymnos* has been left out. This small car ferry is the most regular lifeline of the smaller islands (aside from Kárpathos and Kássos) – it visits them all twice a week between March and December. Its schedule is currently as follows: Monday and Friday 7am, leaves Kálymnos for Kós, Níssyros, Tílos, Sými, Rhodes; out to Kastellórizo late afternoon, turns around at midnight. Tuesday and Saturday 9am, departs Rhodes for Sými, Tílos, Níssyros, Kós, Kálymnos, with an evening return trip to Astypálea; Wednesday and Sunday departs Kálymnos 7am for Léros, Lipsí, Pátmos, Arkí (Wed only), Agathónissi, Pythagório (Sámos), returning from Sámos at 2.30pm bound for Kálymnos via the same islands; Thursday morning 7am from Kálymnos to Astypálea and back, some years with a return trip to Kós done in the afternoon. This ship can be poorly publicized on islands other than its home port; if you encounter difficulties, you should phone the central agency on Kálymnos (☎0243/29 612).

Ferries

Be aware that the following frequencies are only valid for the period mid-June to mid-September; in spring or autumn some of the more esoteric links, such as Astypálea to Tílos or Sými to Lipsí, will not be operating.

Agathóníssi 1 weekly to Arkí, Lipsí, Pátmos, Sámos.

Astypálea 2–3 weekly to Amórgos, Náxos, Páros, Sýros, Pireás; 1–2 weekly to Kós, Kálymnos, Léros, Rhodes, Níssyros, Tílos.

Kálymnos Similar ferry service to Kós, plus 1 weekly to Astypálea, Amorgós (both ports), Náxos, Páros, Sýros, and no departure to Thessaloníki. Morning kaïki, afternoon speedboat to Kós Town; 3 daily kaïkia to Mastikhári. Daily kaïki (1pm) from Myrtiés to Xirókambos on Léros.

Kárpathos (Pigádhia) and Kássos 2 weekly with each other and Rhodes Town; 1 weekly to Khálki, Crete (Áyios Nikólaos and/or Sitía), Mýlos, Santoríni, Íos, Páros, and Pireás. NB Dhiafáni is served by only one weekly mainline ferry to Rhodes, Khálki, Kássos, Crete, and select western Cyclades.

Kastellórizo (Méyisti) 1–2 weekly to Rhodes; 1–2 weekly to Pireás indirectly, via select Dodecanese and Cyclades.

Khálki 1–2 weekly to Rhodes Town, Kárpathos (both ports), Kássos, Crete and select Cyclades, all subject to cancellation in bad weather. Once-daily kaïki (5.30am) to Rhodes (Skála Kámiros).

Kós 7–10 weekly to Rhodes and Pireás; 6 weekly to Kálymnos, Léros and Pátmos; 1 weekly to Tílos and Níssyros; 1 weekly to Sámos and Thessaloníki; 1 weekly to Astipálea, Sými, Lipsí, Náxos, Páros, Sýros. Excursion boats 3 daily year-round from Mastikhári to Kálymnos; 1–2 daily from Kós Town to Kálymnos; 1 daily (9.30am) to Psérimos; 1 daily from Kardhámena to Níssyros; 4–6 weekly from Kós Town and Kéfalos to Níssyros.

Léros daily to Pireás, Pátmos, Kálymnos, Kós and Rhodes; 1 weekly to Lipsí, Náxos, Páros, Sýros; seasonal daily excursion boats from Ayía Marína to Lipsí and Pátmos (2pm), and from Xirókambos to Myrtiés on Kálimnos (7.30am).

Lipsí 1–2 weekly to Sýros, Páros, Náxos, Pireás, Pátmos, Sými, Tílos, Níssyros, Kós, Kálymnos, Léros.

Níssyros and Tílos Same as for Sými, plus additional 1 weekly between each other, Rhodes, Kós, Kálymnos, Léros, Lipsí, Pátmos and Pireás. Excursion boats between Níssyros and Kós as follows: to Kardhámena daily at 3.30pm; to Kéfalos 4 weekly at 4pm; and the islanders' cheaper "shopping special", 4 weekly at 7.30–8am; 4–6 weekly to Kós town (seasonal and expensive).

Pátmos Similar ferry service to Léros, with the addition of 1 weekly to Foúrni, Arkí, Lipsí, Ikaría, Sámos; seasonal tourist boats to Sámos (Pythagório), Lipsí, and Maráthi on a daily basis; less often to Arkí.

Rhodes 10–12 weekly to Kós and Pireás; 7–10 weekly to Kálymnos; daily to Léros and Pátmos; 2 weekly to Crete (Sitía or Iráklion); 1–2 weekly to Sými, Lipsí, Tílos, Níssyros, Astypálea, Kárpathos, Kássos, Khálki; 1 weekly to Santoríni, Náxos, Páros, Sýros, Sámos, Thessaloníki. Excursion boats twice daily to Sými.

Sými 1 weekly to Rhodes, Tílos, Níssyros, Kós, Kálymnos, Léros, Lipsí, Pátmos, Náxos, Páros and Pireás. Excursion boats twice daily to Rhodes.

Hydrofoils

Two hydrofoil companies, Samos Hydrofoils and Nearkhos Mamidhakis (aka Dodecanese Hydrofoils) serve the Dodecanese between late

May and mid-October, operating out of Rhodes, Kós, Kálymnos and Sámos. Typically, the single craft of Sámos Hydrofoils leaves that island at 7am, reaching Kós along a varying itinerary by 11am or noon, returning via the same islands at 1 or 2pm. Dodecanese Hydrofoils have three craft, and schedules are accordingly more complicated; in peak season, one leaves Rhodes at 8am for Kós, returning in the evening; another leaves Kálymnos or Kós at 7 or 8am for Sámos (Pythagório) via select islands, returning at 2.30pm; while the third craft tends to serve a changing cast among the small Dodecanese between Kálymnos and Rhodes, including (occasionally) Astypálea. For current routes and schedules, phone ☎0241/24 000 or 0242/25 920 for Nearkhos Mamidhakis, ☎0273/27 337 for Sámos Hydrofoils.

Flights

Kárpathos 2–3 daily to Rhodes; 2–4 weekly to Kássos; 2–4 weekly to Athens; 1 weekly to Crete (Sitía).

Kássos 2–4 weekly to Kárpathos; 4–7 weekly to Rhodes; 1 weekly to Crete (Sitía).

Kastellórizo (Meyísti) 1 daily to Rhodes.

Kós 2–3 daily to Athens; 2–3 weekly to Rhodes.

Léros 1 daily to Athens.

Rhodes 4–5 daily to Athens; 4 weekly to Iráklion; 3–4 weekly to Santoríni; 2 weekly to Thessaloníki.

International ferries

Kós 3–14 weekly to Bodrum, Turkey (45min). Greek boat leaves 9am, returns 4pm; £19/$30 return Greek tax inclusive, £18/$28 one-way; no cheap day return, no Turkish tax. Turkish boat, departing 4.30pm, is dearer at £33/$52 return, £22/$35 one way, but provides the only service in winter.

Rhodes Daily to Marmaris, Turkey (1–2hr) by Greek hydrofoil or more expensive Turkish car ferry; 2–3 weekly to Limassol, Cyprus (18hr) and Haifa, Israel (39hr).

CHAPTER FIVE

THE EAST AND NORTH AEGEAN

T he seven substantial islands and four minor islets scattered off the north Aegean coast of Asia Minor and northeast Greece form a rather arbitrary archipelago. Although there is a passing similarity in architecture and landscape, virtually the only common denominator is the strong individual character of each island. Despite their proximity to modern Turkey, members of the group bear few signs of an Ottoman heritage, especially when compared with Rhodes and Kós. There's the occasional mosque, often shorn of its minaret, but by and large the enduring Greekness of these islands is testimony to the 4000-year Hellenic presence in Asia Minor, which ended only in 1923. This heritage is regularly referred to by the Greek government in its propaganda war with Turkey over the sovereignty of these far-flung outposts. Tensions here are, if anything, worse than in the Dodecanese, aggravated by potential undersea oil deposits in the straits between the islands and the Anatolian mainland. The Turks have also persistently demanded that Límnos, astride the sea lanes to and from the Dardenelles, be demilitarized, but so far Greece has shown no signs of agreeing.

The heavy military presence can be disconcerting, especially for lone woman travellers, and large tracts of land are off-limits as military reserves. But as in the Dodecanese, local tour operators do a thriving business shuttling passengers for inflated tariffs (thanks to punitively high docking fees at both ends) between the easternmost islands and the Turkish coast with its amazing archeological sites and busy resorts. Most of these islands' main ports and towns are not quaint, picturesque spots, but rather urbanized bureaucratic, military and commercial centres. In most cases you should suppress an initial impulse to take the next boat out, and press on into the interiors.

ACCOMMODATION PRICE CODES

Throughout the book we've used the following **price codes** to dènote the cheapest available room in high season; all are prices for a double room, except for category ①, which represents per person rates. Out of season, rates can drop by up to fifty percent, especially if you are staying for three or more nights. Single rooms, where available, cost around seventy percent of the price of a double.

Rented private rooms on the islands usually fall into the ② or ③ categories, depending on their location and facilities, and the season; a few in the ④ category are more like plush self-catering apartments. They are not generally available from late October through to the beginning of April, when only hotels tend to remain open.

① 1400–2000dr	④ 8000–12,000dr
② 4000–6000dr	⑤ 12,000–16,000dr
③ 6000–8000dr	⑥ 16,000dr and upwards

For more accommodation details, see pp.39–41.

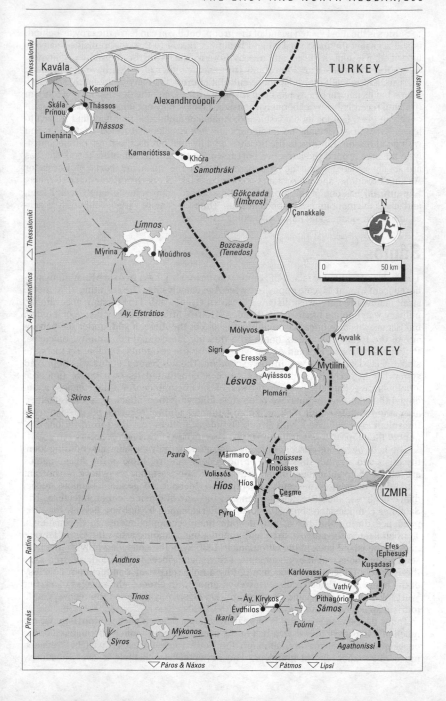

Sámos is the most visited island of the group, but if you can leave the crowds behind, is still arguably the most verdant and beautiful. **Ikaría** to the west remains relatively unspoiled, if a minority taste, and nearby **Foúrni** is a haven for determined solitaries, as are the Khíos satellites **Psará** and **Inoússes**, neither of which have any package tourism. **Khíos** itself offers far more cultural interest than any of its southern neighbours, but its natural beauty has been ravaged by fires, and the development of tourism has until recently been deliberately retarded. **Lésvos** may not impress initially, though once you get a feel for its old-fashioned, Anatolian ambience, you may find it hard to leave. By contrast virtually no foreigners and few Greeks visit **Áyios Efstrátios**, and with good reason. **Límnos** to the north is a bit livelier, but its appeal is confined mostly to the area around the attractive port town. To the north, Samothráki and Thássos are totally isolated from the others, except via the mainland ports of Kavála or Alexandhroúpoli, and it remains easier to visit them from northern Greece. **Samothráki** has one of the most dramatic seaward approaches of any Greek island, and one of the more important ancient sites. **Thássos** is more varied, with sandy beaches, mountain villages and minor archeological sites.

Sámos

The lush and seductive island of Sámos was formerly joined to Asia Minor, until sundered from Mount Mycale opposite by Ice Age cataclysms. The resulting 2500-metre strait is now the narrowest distance between Greece and Turkey, and, accordingly, military watchpoints bristle on both sides. There's little tangible evidence of it today, but Sámos was also once the wealthiest island in the Aegean and, under the patronage of the tyrant Polycrates, home to a thriving intellectual community: Epicurus, Pythagoras, Aristarchus and Aesop were among the residents. Decline set in as the star of Classical Athens was in the ascendant, though Sámos' status was improved somewhat in early Byzantine times when it constituted its own *theme* (imperial administrative district). Towards the end of the fifteenth century, the Genoese abandoned the island to the mercies of pirates; following their attacks, Sámos remained almost uninhabited until 1562, when an Ottoman admiral received permission from the sultan to repopulate it with Greek Orthodox settlers recruited from various corners of the empire.

The heterogeneous descent of today's islanders largely explains an enduring identity crisis and a rather thin topsoil of indigenous culture. Most of the village names are either clan surnames, or adjectives indicating origins elsewhere – constant reminders of refugee descent. Consequently there is no genuine Samiote music, dance or dress, and little that's original in the way of cuisine and architecture. The Samiotes compensated somewhat for their deracination by fighting fiercely for independence during the 1820s, but, despite their accomplishments in decimating a Turkish fleet in the narrow strait and annihilating a landing army, the Great Powers handed the island back to the Ottomans in 1830, with the consoling proviso that it be semi-autonomous, ruled by an appointed Christian prince. This period, referred to as the *Iyimonía* (Hegemony), was marked by a mild renaissance in fortunes, courtesy of the hemp and tobacco trades. However, union with Greece, the ravages of a bitter World War II occupation and mass emigration effectively reversed the recovery until tourism appeared on the horizon during the 1980s.

Today the Samian economy is increasingly dependent on package **tourism**, far too much of it in places; the eastern half of the island has pretty much surrendered to the onslaught of holidaymakers, although the more rugged western part has retained much of its undeveloped grandeur. The rather sedate clientele is overwhelmingly

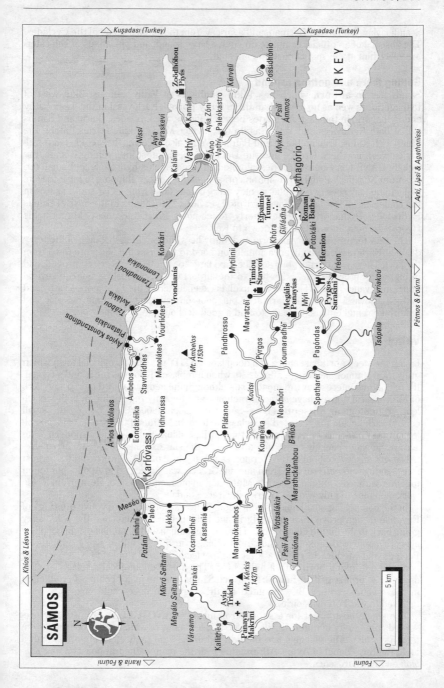

△ Kuşadası (Turkey)   △ Kuşadası (Turkey)

TURKEY

Zoödhóhou Piyis
Kamára
Ayia Zóni
Paleókastro
Kérveli
Possidhónio
Psilí Ammos
Mykáli
Pythagório
Nissí
Ayia Paraskeví
Kalámi
Ano Vathý
Vathý
Efpalínio Tunnel
Khóra
Glifádha
Roman Baths
Potokáki Baths
Heraíon
Iréon
Kokkári
Lemonákia
Tzamadhou
Vrondianís
Mytilinii
Timíou Stavroú
Megális Panayías
Mýli
Pýrgos Saráki
Kyriakoú
Tzabou
Aviákia
Platanákia
Ávios Konstandínos
Vourliótes
Manolátes
Stavrinídhes
Ambelos
Mt. Ambelos 1153m
Mavratzéi
Koumaradhéi
Pándhrosso
Pýrgos
Pagóndas
Tsopéla
Kondakéika
Idhroússa
A¹ios Nikólaos
Koútsi
Spatharéi
Karlóvassi
Plátanos
Neokhóri
Koumeíka
Bállos
Mesao
Paleó
Paleó
Lékka
Kosmadhéi
Kastaniá
Marathókambos
Koumeíka
Ormos Marathókámbou
Votsaláakia
Limáni
Potámi
Mikró Seitáni
Megálo Seitáni
Dhrakéi
Psilí Ammos
Limniónas
Várisamo
Ayia Triádha
Mt. Kérkis 1437m
Evangelístrias
Kallithéa
Panayía Makríni

SÁMOS

N

0   5 km

Scandinavian, Dutch and German, and a far cry from the singles scene of the Cyclades. The absence of an official campsite on such a large island, and phalanxes of self-catering villas, hint at the sort of custom expected.

Getting there and getting around

Sámos has an **airport**, which lies 14km southwest of Vathý and just 3km west of Pythagório, as well as no fewer than three **ferry ports** – Karlóvassi in the west, Vathý and Pythagório in the east. All ferries between Pireás, the Cyclades, Ikaría and Sámos call at both Karlóvassi and Vathý, as do the smaller Miniotis Line ferries linking the island with Khíos, Foúrni, Ikaría and Pátmos. Vathý also receives the weekly G&A sailing between northern Greece and the Dodecanese, via most intervening islands, the weekly DANE ferry between Thessaloníki and Rhodes, plus hydrofoils and small ferries from Kuşadasi. Pythagório siphons off a bit of the Turkey shipping in high season, and additionally sees two regular weekly ferry connections from as far south as Kós in the Dodecanese. Both ports have hydrofoil services: Vathý is the home base of Samos Hydrofoils, Pythagório the northerly touch-point for Dodecanese/Mamidhakis Hydrofoils, both lines extending down to Kós.

The **bus terminals** in Pythagório and Vathý lie within walking distance of the ferry dock; at Karlóvassi, a bus is occasionally on hand to take you the 3km into town from the port. There is no airport bus service; **taxi** fares to various points are controlled, and in high season taxis (☎0273/28 404) to the airport or docks must be booked several hours in advance. The KTEL service itself is excellent along the Pythagório–Vathý and Vathý–Karlóvassi via Kokkári routes, but poor otherwise; with numerous car and motorbike rental outlets, it's easy to find a good deal outside August.

Vathý

Lining the steep northeast shore of a deep bay, **VATHÝ** is a busy provincial town which grew from a minor anchorage after 1830, when it replaced Khóra as the island's capital. It's of minimal interest for the most part – although the pedestrianized bazaar and tiers of Neoclassical houses have some attraction – and the only real highlight is the excellent **Archeological Museum** (Tues–Sun 9am–2.30pm; 800dr), set behind the small central park beside the restored Neoclassical town hall. One of the best provincial collections in Greece is housed in both the old Paskallion building and a modern wing across the way, specially constructed to house the star exhibit: a majestic, five-metre-tall *kouros*, discovered out at the Heraion sanctuary (see p.291). The *kouros*, the largest free-standing effigy to survive from ancient Greece, was dedicated to Apollo, but found together with a devotional mirror to Mut (the Egyptian equivalent of Hera) from a Nile workshop, one of only two discovered in Greece to date.

In the compelling small-objects collection of the Paskallion, more votive offerings of Egyptian design prove trade and pilgrimage links between Sámos and the Nile valley going back to the eighth century BC. The Mesopotamian and Anatolian origins of other artwork confirm the exotic trend, most tellingly in a case full of ivory miniatures: Perseus and Medusa in relief, a kneeling, perfectly formed mini-*kouros*, a pouncing lion, and a drinking horn with a bull's head. The most famous local artefacts are the dozen or so bronze **griffin-heads**, for which Sámos was the major centre of production in the seventh century BC; mounted on the edge of bronze cauldrons, they were believed to ward off evil spirits.

The single best target for a short stroll inland is **ÁNO VATHÝ**, an officially preserved community of tottering, tile-roofed houses, a few of which date from the seventeenth century. The village's late medieval churches are neglected, but still worth a look: the tiny chapel of **Áyios Athanásios** near the main cathedral boasts a fine *témblon* and naive frescoes.

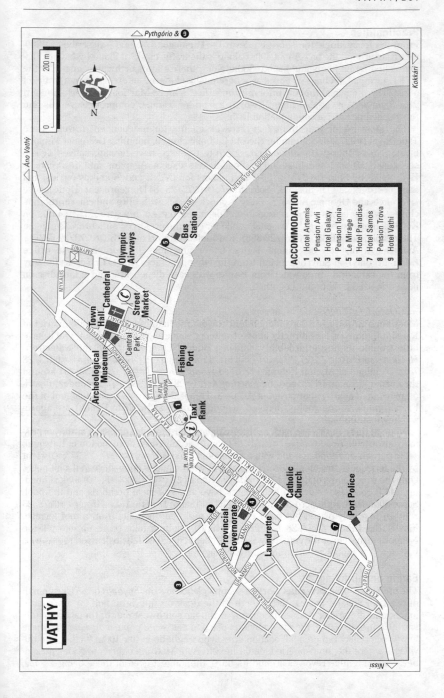

VATHÝ

△ Pythgório & **9**

200 m

N

△ Áno Vathý

Kokkári ▷

Nissí ▽

ACCOMMODATION

1	Hotel Artemis
2	Pension Avli
3	Hotel Galaxy
4	Pension Ionia
5	Le Mirage
6	Hotel Paradise
7	Hotel Samos
8	Pension Trova
9	Hotel Vathi

Bus Station

Olympic Airways

Town Hall

Cathedral

Street Market

Central Park

Archeological Museum

Fishing Port

Taxi Rank

Provincial Governorate

Laundrette

Catholic Church

Port Police

KANARI

THEMISTOKLI SOFOULI

SINHAVS

MYKALIS

ALEX PASHALI

MATVAEL KETEVAL

KAPETAN STAMATI

PL. ATIA PYTHAGORA

PL. AYIOU NIKOLAOU

GOSNIE

SOFOULI

THEMISTOKLI

ARLOU

MANOLI

KALOMIRI

YKRIDOU

GRAMMOU

ENGLIANOU

KELA LIPOULOU

Practicalities

From the **ferry dock** the shore boulevard – Themistoklí Sofoúli – describes a 1300-metre arc around the bay. About 400m along is the traffic circle of Platía Pythagóra, distinguished by its lion statue; some 800m along there's a major turning inland to the **KTEL** terminal, a chaos of buses at a perennially cluttered intersection by the ticket office. The municipal **tourist information** office is on 25-Martíou (summer Mon–Fri 9am–3pm; winter variable hours), worth a stop for leaflets, comprehensive bus and ferry schedules and accommodation listings.

The most useful waterfront **ferry/travel agents** for independent travellers are Tzoutzakis (☎0273/27 337) under the old Catholic church, handling G&A and Miniotis boats; Samos Tours (Horiatopoulos), opposite the jetty, have helpful, native-English-speaking staff and sell most other boat tickets except Agapitos and Dodecanese Hydrofoils; By Ship (☎0273/27 337) sell tickets for DANE and Nomikos ferries; and Samina Tours at Themistoklí Sofoúli 67 (☎0273/28 841), represent Dodecanese Hydrofoils and Olympic Airways. Vathý is chock-a-block with **bike** and **car rental** franchises, which keeps rates reasonable. For bikes try Louie's (☎0273/24 438), on Kefalopoúlou just before the hospital, while for cars the preferred outlets are Budget at Themistoklí Sofoúli 31 (☎0273/28 856), Eurodollar/Aramis at no. 5 (☎0273/22 682) or Autoplan, a division of Samina Tours. Other amenities include the **post office** (Mon–Fri only) on Smýrnis, inland from the Olympic offices, the **OTE** across the way from the cathedral, three waterfront **banks** with cash dispensers, and a **laundry** on pedestrianized Lykoúrgou Logothéti.

ACCOMMODATION

Most **accommodation** for independent travellers clusters in the hillside district of Katsoúni, more or less directly above the ferry dock; except in August, you'll have little trouble finding affordable vacancies. Budget choices include the waterfront *Hotel Artemis* (☎0273/27 792; ③) just off "Lion Square"; *Pension Ionia* (☎0273/28 782; ②) inland at Manoli Kalomíri 5; the *Pension Trova* (☎0273/27 759; ②) around the corner at Kalomíri 26; and the *Pension Avli* (☎0273/22 939; ②), a wonderful period piece up a nearby stair-street at Aréos 2. This is the former convent school of the French nuns, so the rooms, arrayed around a courtyard(*avlí* in Greek) are appropriately institutional.

None of these outfits are palaces by any means; for more luxury start at the surprisingly affordable *Hotel Galaxy* (☎0273/22 665; ③) at Angéou 1 near the top of Katsoúni, set in garden surroundings and with a small pool. *Samos Hotel* (☎0273/28 377; ④) right by the ferry dock, frequently drops its rates in winter, and is open all year, if a bit noisy. Only the front rooms of the *Hotel Paradise* at Kanári 21 (☎0273/23 911; ④) look at lined-up KTEL coaches – side and rear rooms have views of local orchards and the pool. Some 50m north right across from the KTEL at Ioánni Lekáti 11, *Le Mirage* (☎0273/23 868; ③) is grimly placed but quiet enough at night and benefits from a roof terrace. Finally, the *Vathi* (☎0273/28 124, fax 24 045; ③), quite a hike south up into hillside Neapolis district near the cemetery, is an excellent choice with its balconied rooms with bay view, small pool and friendly family management.

Eating and drinking

The only waterfront **tavernas** worth a second glance are the *Stefanos* ouzerí, just north of the Lion Square; *Stelios*, 150m north of the dock on the right, fine for a pre-ferry lunch; and the pricier *Apanemia* ouzerí, at the far southwest end of the shore boulevard. Up in Áno Vathý, the most obvious place to eat is the popular *Agrambeli*, where low prices reflect rather small portion sizes; you might do better 100m further into the village, where the atmospheric kafenío next to Ayía Matróna church provides mezédhes. Vathý nightlife revolves around its **bars**, the longest lived of these being *Escape*,

Platía Ippokrátous, Rhodes

Mosaics in a cloister, Filérimos, Rhodes

Ruined windmill, Váti, Rhodes

Taverna terrace

Flagstone colours, Sými

View of Kástro and Khóra, Astypálea

Kaïki-building, Pátmos, Dodecanese

Mermaid Madonna Chapel, Lésvos

Tomatoes drying, Khíos

Monastery steps, Níssyros

A ferry at Foúrni

Wild flowers, Thássos

Orthodox priest

MARC S. DUBIN

Monastery roofs, Evangelístria, Skiáthos

CHARLES BOWMAN

MARC S. DUBIN

Shipwreck Bay, Zákynthos

Bright walls, Gáïos, Paxí

on a sea-view terrace at Kefalopoúlou 9 (north of the jetty). *Eternity*, on the ground floor of the closed-down Catholic church (sic), is the newest entry. *Metropolis*, in the orchards behind the *Hotel Paradise*, is Vathý's bona fide disco.

Around Vathý

The immediate environs of Vathý offer some modest beaches and small hamlets, ideal targets for day trips. Two kilometres east of (and above) Vathý spreads the vast inland plateau of Vlamarí, devoted to vineyards and supporting the hamlets of **AYÍA ZÓNI** and **KAMÁRA**, each with simple tavernas. From Kamára you can climb up a partly cobbled path to the cliff-top **monastery of Zoödhókhou Piyís**, for views across the end of the island to Turkey.

Heading north out of Vathý, the narrow road ends after 7km at the pebble bay and fishing port of **AYÍA PARASKEVÍ** (or Nissí), with good swimming. Of two tavernas here, *Nissi* is by far the best, with grilled meats and seafoods, a well-selected *dhískos* (tray) of proffered mezédhes and cheerful terrace service offsetting the slightly bumped-up prices.

As you head southeast from Vathý along the main island loop road, the triple chapel at **Treis Ekklisíes** marks an important junction, with another fork 100m along the left-hand turning. Bearing left twice takes you through the hilltop village of **Paleókastro**, 3km beyond which is another junction. Forking left yet again, after another 3km you reach the quiet, striking bay of **Kérveli**, with a small beach, a pair of tavernas (*Iy Kharavyi* is better) by the water and another characterful favourite, *Iy Kryfi Folia*, about 500m uphill along the access road. It's not worth continuing along the right fork to the road's end at **Possidhónio**, whose single taverna is mediocre and beach negligible. Turning right at the junction before Paleókastro leads to the beaches of Mykáli and Psilí Ámmos, the only spots in this section with a bus service. **Mykáli**, a kilometre of windswept sand and gravel, has recently been encumbered with three package-only hotels; the sole place to try on spec here is *Villa Barbara* (☎0273/25 192; ④), apartments behind the Sirenes Beach hotel. **Psilí Ámmos**, further east around the headland, is a crowded, sandy cove, whose best and longest-established taverna is on the right as you arrive. If you swim to the islet beware of strong currents which sweep through the narrow straits.

Pythagório and around

Most traffic south of Vathý heads for **PYTHAGÓRIO**, the island's premier resort, renamed in 1955 to honour native son Pythagoras, ancient mathematician, philosopher and mystic. Until then it was known as Tigáni (Frying Pan) – in mid-summer you'll learn why. The sixth-century BC tyrant Polycrates had his capital here, and excavations of the site have forced modern Pythagório to expand northeast and uphill. The village core of cobbled lanes and thick-walled mansions abuts a small **harbour**, fitting almost perfectly into the confines of Polycrates' ancient port, but today devoted almost entirely to pleasure craft and overpriced cocktail bars.

Sámos's **castle**, the nineteenth-century *pýrgos* of local chieftain Lykourgos Logothetis, overlooks both the town and the shoreline. Logothetis, together with "Kapetan Stamatis" and Admiral Kanaris, chalked up decisive victories over the Turks in the summer of 1824. The final battle was won on Transfiguration Day (6 August), and accordingly the church beside the tower bears a huge sign in Greek announcing that "Christ Saved Sámos 6 August 1824". More ancient antiquities include the fairly dull **Roman baths** 400m west of town (Tues–Sun 8.30am–3pm; free) and a minuscule **archeological collection** in the town hall (Tues–Thur & Sun 9am–2pm, Fri–Sat 10am–2pm; free). Considerably more interesting is the **Efpalinio tunnel** (Tues–Sun 9am–2.30pm; 500dr), a 1040-metre aqueduct bored through the mountain just north of

Pythagório at the behest of Polycrates. To get there, take the signposted path from the shore boulevard at the west end of town, which meets the vehicle access road towards the end of a twenty-minute walk.

You can also climb to the five remaining chunks of the Polycratian **perimeter wall** enclosing his hilltop citadel. There's a choice of routes: one leading up from the Glyfádha lagoon west of Pythagório past an **ancient watchtower** now isolated from any other fortifications, and the other – which is easier – leading from the monastery of **Panayía Spilianí**. Though most of this has been insensitively restored and touristified, beyond the courtyard lies a grotto, at one end of which is a subterranean shrine to the Virgin (open daylight hours; free). This was the presumed residence of the ancient oracular priestess Fyto, and a pirate-safe hideout in medieval times.

Practicalities

If there are any **accommodation** vacancies – and it's best not to assume this in mid-season – proprietors meet incoming ferries. The **tourist information booth** (☎0273/61 389), on the main thoroughfare Lykoúrgou Logothéti, can help in finding rooms, and also dispenses town plans and transport schedules. Quietly located at the seaward end of Odhós Pythagóra, south of Lykoúrgou Logothéti, the modest *Tsambika* (☎0273/61 642; ③) and *Sydney* (③) pensions are worth considering; 50m inland from the north side of the harbour past the customs house, *Lambis Rooms* on Odhós Íras (☎0273/61 396; ③) also comes recommended. Another peaceful area is the hillside north of Platía Irínis, where *Pension Despina* (☎0273/61 472; ③) sits just north of the square, while *Hotel Galini* is one of the better small outfits (☎0273/61 167; winter ☎01/98 42 248; ④). Further uphill, on the road to Vathý, the rear units of *Studios Anthea* (☎0273/62 086; ④) are fairly noise-free and allow you to self-cater.

Eating out can be frustrating in Pythagório, with value for money often a completely alien concept. Away from the water, the *Platania* taverna, under two eucalyptus trees opposite the town hall, is a good choice for a relatively simple meal; for waterside dining, you're best off at the extreme east end of the quay, where the *Remataki* ouzerí features plenty of vegetarian dishes such as *angináres ala políta* (artichokes cooked with carrots, potatoes, vinegar and oil). Night-owls gather at either *Disco Labito* in town, or *Edem* (aka *San Lorenzo*) 1km out on the Vathý road.

If none of this appeals, the outbound **bus stop** lies just west of the intersection of Lykoúrgou Logothéti and the road to Vathý. Two **banks** (both with cash dispensers) and the **post office** are also on Lykoúrgou Logothéti; there is currently no OTE. The flattish country to the west is ideal for cycling, a popular activity, and if you want to rent a **moped**, there are several outfits on the main street.

Around Pythagório

The main local beach stretches for several kilometres west of the Logothetis "castle", punctuated about halfway along by the end of the airport runway, and the cluster of nondescript hotels known as **POTOKÁKI**. Just before the turnoff to the heart of the beach sprawls the ultra-luxurious *Doryssa Bay* complex, which includes a meticulously concocted fake village, guaranteed to confound archeologists of future eras. No two of the units, joined by named lanes, are alike, and there's even a platía with an expensive café. If you actually intend to stay in the area, however, the *Fito Bungalows Hotel* (☎0273/61 582; ⑤) is more affordable. If you don't mind the hotel crowds and low-flying jets, the sand-and-pebble **beach** here is well groomed and the water clean; you'll have to head out to the end of the road for more seclusion.

The Potokáki access road is a dead end, with the main island loop road pressing on past the turnoff for the airport and Iréon hamlet. Under layers of alluvial mud, plus today's runway, lies the processional Sacred Way joining the ancient city with the **Heraion**, the massive shrine of the Mother Goddess (Tues–Sun 8.30am–3pm; 800dr). Much touted in tourist literature, this assumes humbler dimensions – one surviving column and assorted foundations – upon approach. Yet once inside the precinct you sense the former grandeur of the temple, never completed owing to Polycrates' untimely death at the hands of the Persians. The site chosen, near the mouth of the still-active Imvrassós stream, was Hera's legendary birthplace and site of her trysts with Zeus; in the far corner of the fenced-in zone you glimpse a large, exposed patch of the paved Sacred Way.

The modern resort of **IRÉON** nearby is a nondescript grid of dusty streets behind a coarse-shingle beach, attracting a slightly younger and more active clientele than Pythagório. Here you'll find more non-package rooms and two small hotels: *Venetia* (☎0273/61 195; ③) and *Heraion* (☎0273/61 180; ③), both within sight of the water. The oldest and most authentic **taverna** is the *Ireon*, at the far west end by the fishing harbour.

Southern Sámos

Since the circum-island bus only passes through or near the places below once or twice daily, you really need your own vehicle to explore them. Some 4km west of Khóra, an inconspicuous turning leads uphill to the still-active monastery of **Timíou Stavroú**, whose annual September 14 festival is more an excuse for a tatty bazaar in the courtyards than for any music or feasting. Another 1km on, another detour bears off to **MAVRATZÉÏ**, one of two Samian "pottery villages"; this one specializes in the *Koúpa tou Pythagóra* or "Pythagorean cup", supposedly designed by the sage to leak over the user's lap if he over-indulged. More practical wares can be found in **KOUMARADHÉÏ**, back on the main road, another 2km along.

From here you can descend a paved road through burned forest to the sixteenth-century monastery of **Megális Panayías** (in theory daily mornings & 4.30–6.30pm, ring keeper on ☎61 449 to check), containing the finest frescoes on the island. This route continues to **MÝLI**, submerged in lemon groves and also accessible from Iréon. Four kilometres above Mýli sprawls **PAGÓNDAS**, a large hillside community with a splendid main square and an unusual communal fountain house on the south hillside. From here, a scenic paved road curls 9km around the hill to **SPATHARÉÏ** – its surroundings devastated by fire in 1993 – but set on a natural balcony offering the best sea views this side of the island. From Spatharéï, the road loops back 6km to **PÝRGOS**, lost in pine forests at the head of a ravine, and the centre of Samian honey production.

The rugged and beautiful coast south of the Pagóndas–Pýrgos route is largely inaccessible, glimpsed by most visitors for the first and last time from the descending plane bringing them to Sámos. **Tsópela**, a highly scenic sand-and-gravel cove at a gorge mouth, is the only beach here with marked track access and a good seasonal taverna; you'll need a sturdy motorcycle (not a scooter) or jeep to get down there. The western reaches of this shoreline, which suffered comprehensive fire damage in 1994, are approached via the small village of **KOUMÉÏKA**, with a massive inscribed marble fountain and a pair of kafenía on its square. Below extends the long, pebble bay at **Bállos**, with sand, a cave and naturists at the far east end. Bállos itself is merely a sleepy collection of summer houses, several **rooms** to rent and a few **tavernas**, the best of which is the *Cypriot*, tucked away inland. Returning to Kouméïka, the dubious-looking side road just before the village marked "Velanidhiá" is in fact usable by any vehicle, and a very useful short cut if you're travelling towards the beaches beyond Órmos Marathokámbou (see p.294).

Kokkári and around

Leaving Vathý on the north coastal section of the island loop road, there's little to stop for until you reach **KOKKÁRI**, the third major Samian tourist centre after Pythagório and the capital. Sadly, while lower Vathý and Pythagório had little beauty to sacrifice, much has been irrevocably lost here. The town's profile, covering two knolls behind twin headlands, remains unaltered, and several families still doggedly untangle their fishnets on the quay, but in general its identity has been altered beyond recognition, with constant inland expansion over vineyards and the abandoned fields of baby onions that gave the place its name. With exposed, rocky beaches buffeted by near-constant winds, developers have made a virtue of necessity by developing the place as a highly successful windsurfing resort.

Practicalities

As in Vathý and Pythagório, a fair proportion of Kokkári's **accommodation** is block-booked by tour companies; one establishment not completely devoted to such trade is the pleasant *Hotel Olympia Beach* (☎0273/92 353; ④), on the western beach road, co-managed with the *Olympia Village* apartments (☎0273/92 420; ⑤). Another amenable pension is that of Ioannis Perris (☎0273/92 040; ③), also on the west beach. Otherwise Yiorgos Mikhelios has a wide range of rooms and apartments to rent (☎0273/92 456; ③), including the *Pension Green Hill*. If you get stuck, seek assistance from the seasonal **EOT post** (☎0273/92 217), housed in a portacabin near the main church.

Most **tavernas** line the north waterfront, and charge above the norm, though they're steadily losing ground to breakfast or cocktail bars. At the eastern end of things, *Ta Adhelfia* is as close as you'll get to a simple, unpretentious psistariá, while on the less commercialized western beach, *To Koutouki* does standard taverna fare without too many airs and graces. Inland, *Farmer's* – on the village through-road, a few steps east of the summer **cinema** – is highly regarded for its locally grown food, and in autumn may offer *moustalevriá* (grape-must dessert). The *Cabana Disco-Club* is the hot new entry on the nightlife scene.

Other amenities include a short-hours **bank** on the through road, a **post office** in a portacabin on a seaward lane, and a **laundry** next to that.

West of Kokkári: the coast

The closest sheltered beaches are thirty to forty minutes' walk away to the west, all with permanently anchored umbrellas. The first, **Lemonákia**, is a bit too close to the road, with an obtrusive café; 1km beyond, the graceful crescent of **Tzamadhoú** figures in virtually every EOT poster of the island. With path-only access, it's a bit less spoiled, and each end of the saucer-shaped pebble beach is by tacit consent a nudist zone. There's one more pebble bay west of Avlákia called **Tzábou**, but it's not worth a special detour when the prevailing northwest wind is up.

The next spot of any interest along the coast road is **Platanákia**, essentially a handful of tavernas and rooms for rent at a bridge by the turn off for Manolátes (see over page); best in each category are *Taverna Apolafsi* and *Rooms Kalypso* (☎0273/94 124; ③), both on the shore side of the road. Platanákia is actually the eastern suburb of **ÁYIOS KONSTANDÍNOS**, whose surf-pounded esplanade has been "improved". However, there are no usable beaches within walking distance, so the collection of warm-toned stone buildings constitutes a peaceful alternative to Kokkári. In addition to modest **hotels** such as the *Four Seasons* (③) or the *Atlantis* (☎0273/94 329; ③) just above the highway, there's a new generation of more modern rooms below the road, such as *Maria's* (☎0273/94 460). For food, look no further than the excellent *To Kyma* at the east end of the quay.

Once past "Áyios", as bus conductors habitually bellow it out, the mountains hem the road in against the sea, and the terrain doesn't relent until **Kondakéïka**, whose diminutive shore annexe of **Áyios Nikólaos** is an excellent venue for fish meals, particularly at *Iy Psaradhes*, its terrace lapped by the waves. There's also a reasonable beach here ten minutes walk east past the last studio units.

Hill villages

Inland between Kokkári and Kondakéïka, an idyllic landscape of pine, cypress and orchards is overawed by dramatic mountains, so far little burned. Despite destructive nibblings by bulldozers, some of the trail system linking the various **hill villages** is still intact, and walkers can return to the main highway to catch a bus home. Failing that, most of the communities can provide a bed at short notice.

The monastery of **Vrondianís** (Vrónda), directly above Kokkári, is a popular destination, although since the army now uses it as a barracks, the place only really comes alive during its annual festival (7–8 September). **VOURLIÓTES**, 2km west of the monastery, has beaked chimneys and brightly painted shutters sprouting from its typical tile-roofed houses. On the photogenic central square, the oldest and arguably best of several tavernas is *The Blue Chairs*, serving two local specialities: *revithokeftédhes* (chickpea patties), and the homemade *moskháto* dessert wine.

MANOLÁTES, further uphill and an hour-plus walk away via a deep river canyon, also has several simple tavernas (the best of these being *Loukas* at the top of the village), and is the most popular trailhead for the five-hour round-trip up **Mount Ámbelos** (Karvoúnis), the island's second highest summit. From Manolátes you can no longer easily continue on foot to Stavrinídhes, the next village, but should plunge straight down, partly on a cobbled path, through the shady valley known as **Aïdhónia** (Nightingales), to Platanákia.

Karlóvassi

KARLÓVASSI, 35km west of Vathý and the second town of Sámos, is decidedly sleepier and more old-fashioned than the capital, despite having roughly the same population. Though lacking in distinction, it's popular as a base from which to explore western Sámos's excellent beaches and walking. The name, despite a vehement denial of Ottoman legacy elsewhere on Sámos, appears to be a corruption of the Turkish for "snowy plain" – the plain in question being the conspicuous saddle of Mount Kérkis overhead. The town divides into four straggly neighbourhoods: Néo, well inland, whose untidy growth was spurred by the influx of post-1923 refugees; Meséo, across the usually dry river bed, tilting appealingly off a knoll towards the shore; and postcard-worthy Paleó (or Áno), above Limáni, the small harbour district.

Most tourists stay at or near **LIMÁNI**, which has a handful of rooms and several expensive hotels. The **rooms**, all in the inland pedestrian lane behind the through road, are quieter – try those of Vangelis Feloukatzis (☎0273/33 293; ③) or Yiorgos Moskhoyiannis (☎0273/32 812; ③). The port itself is an appealing place with a working boatyard at the west end and all the **ferry-ticket agencies** grouped at the middle; often a shuttle bus service operates from Néo Karlóvassi, timed to boat arrivals and departures. Tavernas and bars are abundant, but none are worth singling out.

Immediately overhead is the partly hidden hamlet of **PALEÓ**, its hundred or so houses draped on either side of a leafy ravine. The only facilities are the sporadically functioning café *To Mikro Parisi*, and a seasonal taverna on the path down towards **MESÉO**. The latter is a conceivable alternative base to Limáni, with **rooms** along the 500m between the playground and the sea, and the *Aspasia* (☎0273/32 363; ④) well-sited 100m west of the wood-fired bakery. Following the street linking the central square to the waterfront, you pass one of the improbably huge, turn-of-the-century churches, topped with twin belfries and a blue-and-white dome, which dot the coastal plain here. Just at the intersection with the shore road you'll find the friendly, good-value *To Kyma* ouzerí (April–Oct), the best place in town to watch the sunset over a selection of mezédhes.

NÉO has little to recommend it besides a wilderness of derelict stone-built warehouses and mansions down near the river mouth, reminders of the long-vanished leather industry which flourished here during the first half of this century. However, if you're staying at Limáni, you'll almost certainly visit one of the three **banks** (cash dispensers), the **post office**, the OTE or the **bus stop** on the main lower square.

Western Sámos

Visitors tolerate dull Karlóvassi for the sake of western Sámos' excellent **beaches**. Closest of these is **Potámi**, forty minutes' walk away via the coast road from Limáni or an hour by a more scenic, high trail from Paleó. This broad arc of sand and pebbles gets crowded at summer weekends, when virtually the entire population of Karlóvassi descends on the place. Near the end of the trail from Paleó stands *To Iliovasilema*, a friendly fish taverna; there are also a very few **rooms** signposted locally, and you can camp along the lower reaches of the river which gives the beach its name.

A streamside path leads twenty minutes inland, past the eleventh-century church of **Metamórfosis** – the oldest on Sámos – to an apparent dead end. Beyond here you must swim and wade 100m in heart-stoppingly cold water through a sequence of fern-tufted rock pools before reaching a low but vigorous waterfall; bring shoes with good tread and perhaps even rope if you want to explore above the first cascade. You probably won't be alone until you dive in, since the canyon is well known to locals and tour agencies. Just above the Metamórfosis church, a clear if precipitous path leads up to a small, contemporaneous **Byzantine fortress**. There's little to see inside other than a subterranean cistern and badly crumbled lower curtain wall, but the views out to sea and up the canyon are terrific, while in October the place is carpeted with pink autumn crocuses.

The coast beyond Potámi ranks among the most beautiful and unspoiled on Sámos; since the early 1980s it has served as a protected refuge for the rare monk seal. The dirt track at the west end of Potámi bay ends after twenty minutes on foot, from which you backtrack a little to find the side trail running parallel to the water. After twenty minutes along this you'll arrive at **Mikró Seïtáni**, a small pebble cove guarded by sculpted rock walls. A full hour's walk from the trailhead, through partly fire-damaged olive terraces, brings you to **Megálo Seïtáni**, the island's finest beach, at the mouth of the intimidating Kakopérato gorge. You'll have to bring food and water, though not necessarily a swimsuit – there's no dress code at either of the Seïtáni bays.

Southwestern beach resorts
Heading south out of Karlóvassi on the island loop road, the first place you'd be tempt-ed to stop off is **MARATHÓKAMBOS**, a pretty, amphitheatrical village overlooking the eponymous gulf; there's a taverna or two, but no short-term accommodation. Its port, **ÓRMOS MARATHOKÁMBOU**, 18km from Karlóvassi, has recently emerged as a tourist resort, though some character still peeks through in its backstreets. The port has been improved, with kaïkia offering day trips to Foúrni and the nearby islet of Samiopoúla, while the pedestrianized quay has become the focus of attention, home to several indistinguishable tavernas.

The beach immediately east from Órmos is hardly the best; for better ones continue 2km west to **VOTSALÁKIA** (officially signposted as "Kámbos"), Sámos' fastest-growing resort, straggling a further 2km behind the island's longest (if not its most beautiful) beach. But for most Votsalákia is still a vast improvement on the Pythagório area, and the mass of 1437-metre Mount Kérkis overhead rarely fails to impress (see below). As for **accommodation**, Emmanuil Dhespotakis (☎0273/31 258; ③) has premises towards the quieter, more scenic western end of things. Also in this vicinity is *Akroyialia*, the most traditional **taverna**, with courtyard seating and fish and meat grills. Other facilities include branches of nearly all the main Vathý travel agencies, offering **vehicle rental** (necessary, as only two daily buses call here) and money exchange.

If Votsalákia doesn't suit, you can continue 3km past to the 600-metre beach of **Psilí Ámmos**, more aesthetic and not to be confused with its namesake beach in the southeast corner of Sámos. The sea shelves very gently here, and cliffs shelter clusters of naturists at the east end. Surprisingly there is still little development: one fair-sized apartment complex in the pines at mid-beach, and two tavernas back up on the road as you approach, both of these fine for a simple lunch. Access to **Limniónas**, a smaller cove 2km further west, snakes past a villa complex rather grandiosely dubbed "Samos Yacht Club". Yachts do occasionally call at the protected bay, which offers decent swimming away from a rock shelf at mid-strand, especially at the east end where there's a simple **taverna**; inland are a very few accommodation facilities.

Mount Kérkis and around

Gazing up from a supine seaside position, you may be inspired to climb **Mount Kérkis**. The classic route begins at the west end of the Votsalákia strip, along the bumpy jeep track leading inland towards Evangelistrías convent. After thirty minutes on the track system, through fire-damaged olive groves and past charcoal pits (a major local industry), the path begins, more or less following power lines up to the convent. A friendly nun may proffer an oúzo in welcome and point you up the paint-marked trail, continuing even more steeply up to the peak. The views are tremendous, though the climb itself is humdrum once you're out of the trees. About an hour before the top there's a chapel with an attached cottage for sheltering in emergencies. All told, it's a seven-hour outing from Votsalákia and back, not counting rest stops.

Less ambitious walkers might want to circle the flanks of the mountain, first by vehicle and then by foot. The road beyond Limniónas to Kallithéa and Dhrakéï, truly back-of-beyond villages with views across to Ikaría, is paved as far as Kallithéa, making it possible to venture out here on an ordinary motorbike. The bus service is better during the school year, when a vehicle leaves Karlóvassi (12.30pm, Mon–Fri) bound for these remote spots; during summer it only operates two days a week (currently Mon & Fri).

From **DHRAKÉÏ**, the end of the line with just a pair of very simple kafenía to its credit, a ninety-minute trail descends through partly burned forest to Megálo Seïtáni, from where it's easy enough to continue on to Karlóvassi within another two-and-a-half hours. People attempting to reverse this itinerary often discover to their cost that the bus (if any) returns from Dhrakéï early in the day, at 2.30pm, compelling them to stay at one of two rather expensive **rooms** establishments (summer only) in **KALLITHÉA**, and dine there at either the simple psistariá on the square or a newer, more varied taverna on the western edge of the village. From Kallithéa, a newer track (from beside the cemetery) and an older trail both lead up within 45 minutes to a spring, rural chapel and plane tree on the west flank of Kérkis, with path-only continuation for another thirty minutes to a pair of cave-churches. **Panayía Makriní** stands detached at the mouth of a high, wide but shallow grotto, whose balcony affords terrific views of Sámos' west tip. By contrast **Ayía Triádha**, a ten-minute scramble overhead, has most of its structure made up of cave wall; just adjacent, another long, narrow, volcanic cavern can be explored with a torch some hundred metres into the mountain.

After these subterranean exertions, the closest spot for a swim is **Vársamo** (Válsamo) cove, 4km below Kallithéa and reached via a well-signposted dirt road. The beach here consists of multicoloured volcanic pebbles, with two caves to shelter in and a single taverna just inland.

Ikaría

Ikaría, a narrow, windswept landmass between Sámos and Mýkonos, is little visited and invariably underestimated; the name supposedly derives from the legendary Icarus, who fell into the sea just offshore after the wax bindings on his wings melted. For years the only substantial tourism was generated by a few **hot springs** on the south coast, some reputed to cure rheumatism and arthritis, some to make women fertile, though others are so highly radioactive that they've been closed for some time.

Ikaría, along with Thessaly on the mainland, western Sámos and Lésvos, has traditionally been one of the Greek Left's strongholds. This tendency dates from the long decades of right-wing domination in Greece, when (as in past ages) the island was used as a place of **exile** for political dissidents. Apparently the strategy backfired, with the transportees outnumbering and even proselytizing their hosts; at the same time, many Ikarians emigrated to North America, and ironically their regular capitalist remittances help keep the island going. It can be a bizarre experience to be treated to a monologue on the evils of US imperialism, delivered by a retiree in perfect Alabaman English.

These are not the only Ikarian quirks, and for many the place is an acquired taste. Except for forested portions in the west, it's not a strikingly beautiful island, with most of the terrain consisting of scrub-covered schist used as building material. The mostly desolate south coast is fringed by steep cliffs, while the north face is less sheer but nonetheless furrowed by deep canyons creating hairpin bends which are extreme even by Greek standards. Neither are there many picturesque villages, since the rural schist-roofed houses are generally scattered so as to be next to their famous apricot orchards, vineyards and fields.

The Ikarians have resisted most attempts to develop their island for conventional tourism: no charter flights land here, since the northeastern airport can't accommodate jets. Long periods of seemingly punitive neglect by Athens have made the locals profoundly self-sufficient and idiosyncratic, and tolerant of the same characteristics in others.

Áyios Kírykos

About two-thirds of ferries call at the south-coast port and capital of **ÁYIOS KÍRYKOS**, about 1km southeast of the island's main thermal resort. Because of the spa trade, beds are at a premium in town; arriving in the evening from Sámos, accept any reasonable offers of rooms at the jetty, or – if in a group – proposals of a taxi ride to the north coast, which shouldn't be more than 7500dr per vehicle to the end of the line. A cream-and-green **bus** sets out across the island from the main square (daily, in theory 10am & 1.30pm on Mon, Wed & Fri to Armenistís; Mon–Fri noon to Évdhilos only).

The baths (daily 8am–1pm) in **Thérma** are rather old-fashioned, with preference given to those under medical care. A better bet for a less formal soak are the more natural, shoreline hot springs at **Thérma Lefkádhos**, 3km southwest of Áyios Kírykos, below a cluster of villas. Here the seaside spa is derelict, leaving the water to boil up right in the shallows, mixing with the sea between giant volcanic boulders to a pleasant temperature.

Practicalities

Hydrofoils and the kaïki for Foúrni use the small east jetty; large ferries dock at the main west pier. There are several **hotels**, such as the *Isabella* (☎0275/22 839; ④), or the friendly, basic but spotless *Akti* (☎0275/22 694; ②), on a knoll east of the hydrofoil and kaïki quay, with views of Foúrni from the garden. Otherwise, **pensions** and **rooms** are not especially cheap: directly behind the base of the ferry jetty and a little to the west

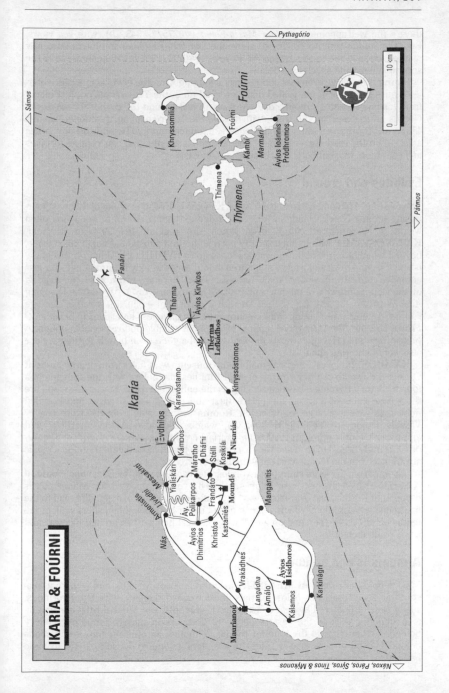

IKARÍA & FOÚRNI

△ Pythagório

△ Sámos

▽ Pátmos

▽ Náxos, Páros, Sýros, Tínos & Mýkonos

Foúrni

Khryssomiliá

Foúrni

Kámbi

Marmári

Ávios Ioánnis
Pródhromos

Thímena

Thímena

Thýmena

Fanári

Thérma

Ávios Kírykos

Thérma
Lefkádhos

Khrysóstomos

Ikaría

Karavóstamo

Évdhilos

Kámbos

Máratho

Dháfni

Stélli

Nikariás

Kosikiá

Yialiskári

Mesakhti

Livádhi

Áy.
Polikarpos

Frandáto

Moundé

Mangarítis

Armenístis

Nás.

Ávios
Dhimítrios

Khristós

Kastaniés

Vrakádhes

Langádha
Amálo

Ávios
Isídhoros

Karkinágri

Maurianoú

Kálamos

0   10 km

there's the well-appointed *Pension Maria-Elena* (☎0275/22 543; ③), with sea views. Both the *Studios* (☎0275/22 276; ④) above the *Snack Bar Dedalos* and the prominently marked, clean *dhomátia* run by Ioannis Proestos (☎0275/23 496; ③), get noise from the several kafenía and snack bars below.

Eating out, you've even less choice than in lodging. Give the obvious quayside eateries a miss in favour of the grilled dishes served up at the *Tzivaeri* ouzerí, just inland from Ioannis Proestos's rooms, or *Iy Klimataria* just around the corner for *mayireftá*. Glitz is all the rage on the front, with *Casino* the last remaining traditional kafenío. There are two **banks** with cash dispensers, a limited-hours **OTE** and the post office adjacent on the road out, and three ferry/hydrofoil **agents**. You can **rent** motorbikes and cars here, too, but both are cheaper in Armenistís.

Évdhilos and around

The twisting, 41-kilometre road from Áyios Kírykos to Évdhilos is one of the most hair-raising on any Greek island, and the long ridge extending the length of Ikaría often wears a streamer of cloud, even when the rest of the Aegean is clear. **KARAVÓSTAMO**, with its tiny, scruffy port, is the first substantial north coast place, beyond which a series of three beaches leads up to **ÉVDHILOS**. Although this is the island's second town and a ferry stop three to four times weekly in summer, it's far less equipped to deal with visitors than Áyios Kírykos. There are two **hotels**, the *Evdoxia* on the slope southwest of the harbour (☎0275/31 502, fax 31 571; ④) and the low-lying *Atheras* (☎0275/31 434, fax 31 926; ④) with a small pool – plus a few rather average **rooms**. Among several waterfront **restaurants**, the nameless kafestiatorio between *O Flisvos* and the *Blue Nice* travel agency is the most reliable and reasonable option. A **post office** and **OTE** up towards the *Evdoxia*, and a good town **beach** to the east, are also worth knowing about.

KÁMBOS, 2km west, offers a small hilltop museum with finds from nearby **ancient Oinoe**; the twelfth-century church of Ayía Iríni lies just below, with the remains of a fourth-century Byzantine basilica serving as the entry courtyard. Lower down still are the sparse ruins of a Byzantine palace (just above the road) used to house exiled nobles, as well as a large sandy beach. **Rooms** are available from the store run by Vassilis Dhionysos (☎0275/31 300; ③), which also acts as the unofficial and enthusiastic tourist office for this part of Ikaría, keeping the keys for church and museum. For **nightlife**, *Petrino* above the east end of the beach has a diet of traditional music at variance with the techno currently the rage in Greece.

Starting from the large church in Évdhilos, you can also visit the Byzantine **castle of Nikariás** (Koskiná), just over 15km south. The road signposted for Manganítis is paved until Kosikiá, just over 9km away; thereafter you've 2km of steep dirt road to the marked side track, along which you can get a bike or jeep to within a short walk of the tenth-century castle, perched on a distinctive conical hill, with an arched gateway and a fine vaulted chapel.

Armenistís and around

Most people carry on to **ARMENISTÍS**, 57km from Áyios Kírykos, and with good reason: this little resort lies below Ikaría's finest wooded scenery, with two enormous, sandy beaches battered by near-constant surf – **Livádhi** and **Messakhtí** – five and fifteen minutes' walk to the east respectively. Campers in the river-mouth greenery behind each stretch set the tone for the place, though an official campsite functions behind Livádhi in peak season, and the islanders' tolerance doesn't extend to nude bathing, as signs advise you.

A dwindling number of older buildings, plus fishing boats hauled up in a sandy cove, lend Armenistís the air of a Cornish fishing village; it's a tiny place, reminiscent of similar youth-oriented spots in southern Crete, though gentrification has definitely set in. Several "music bars" operate seasonally behind the nearer beach – these often with live Greek sessions – and at the quay's north end, but for most visitors **nightlife** is mostly about extended sessions in the tavernas and cafés overlooking the anchorage. Along the shore lane, the adjacent *Paskhalia* and *Delfini* **tavernas** are the best, the former offering full breakfasts as well as good-value, en-suite **rooms** (☎0275/71 302; winter 01/24 71 411; ③). On the hill to the south the *Armena Inn* (☎0275/71 320; ③) is of a similar standard, plus there are several other "rooms" along the road west to Nás. For more luxury, there are two adjacent hotels about 700m east of the main junction here, both with pools and hosting the local package custom: the *Cavos Bay* (☎0275/71 381, fax 71 380; ④) and the *Daidalos* (☎0275/71 390, fax 71 393; ④). Better than either, just above Messakhtí, is the *Messakhti Village* complex (☎0275/71 331, fax 713 30; ④), with a large pool (necessary here, as the deep water off the beach is often unsafe due to undertow) and fine common areas and private terraces making up for the rather plain rooms. Just east of here is the fishing settlement of **YIALISKÁRI**, which has a handful of tavernas and half-a-dozen "rooms" looking out to a picturesque church on the jetty.

Among four travel agencies/car rental/money exchange outfits in Armenistís, Marabou is about the most helpful, offering mountain bikes as well as walking tours of western Ikaría; Glaros has reasonably maintained scooters. The sole drawback to staying in Armenistís is getting away, since both taxis and buses are elusive. Theoretically, **buses** head for Áyios Kírykos daily at 2 or 3pm, usually with a change or layover in Évdhilos, and out of school term only at 7am most days, but all these departures are unreliable even by Ikarian standards and should be double-checked. If you've a ferry to catch, it's far easier on the nerves to pre-book a taxi.

Rákhes

Armenistís is actually the shore annexe of four inland hamlets – Áyios Dhimítrios, Áyios Polýkarpos, Kastaniés and Khristós – collectively known as **RÁKHES**. Despite the modern, mostly paved access roads through the pines (trails shortcut them), the settlements retain a certain Shangri-La quality, with the older residents speaking a positively Homeric dialect. On an island not short of foibles, Khristós is particularly strange inasmuch as the locals sleep much of the day, but shop and eat from early afternoon to the small hours; in fact most of the villages west of Évdhilos adhere to this schedule, defying central-government efforts to bring them in line with the rest of Greece.

Near the small main square, paved in schist and studded with gateways fashioned from the same rock, there's a **post office** and a **hotel/restaurant** (☎0275/71 269; ③), but for lunch you'll have to scrounge something at one of two unmarked tavernas or the more prominent kafenía. The slightly spaced-out demeanour of those serving may be attributable to over-indulgence in the excellent home-brewed **wine** which everyone west of Évdhilos makes. The local festival is August 6, though better ones take place further southwest in the woods at Langádha valley (August 14–15) or at Áyios Isídhoros monastery (May 14).

Nás

By tacit consent, Greek or foreign hippies, naturists and dope-fiends have been allowed to shift 3km west of Armenistís to **Nás**, a tree-clogged river canyon ending in a small but sheltered sand-and-pebble beach. This little bay is almost completely enclosed by weirdly sculpted rock formations, and it's very unwise to swim outside the cove's natural limits. The crumbling foundations of the fifth-century temple of **Artemis**

Tavropoleio (Patroness of Bulls) overlook the permanent deep pool at the mouth of the river. If you continue inland along this past colonies of campers, you'll find secluded rock pools for freshwater dips. Back at the top of the stairs leading down to the beach from the road are several tavernas (the oldest and best is *O Nas*), most offering **rooms** – *Pension Artemis* (☎0275/71 255; ②) can be booked in advance.

Satellite islands: Thímena and Foúrni

The straits between Sámos and Ikaría are speckled with islets, though the only ones permanently inhabited are Thímena and Foúrni. More westerly **Thímena** has one tiny hillside settlement, at which a regular kaïki calls on its way between Ikaría and Foúrni, but there are no tourist facilities, and casual visits are explicitly discouraged. Foúrni is home to a huge fishing fleet and one of the more thriving boatyards in the Aegean. Thanks to these, and the improvement of the jetty to receive car ferries, Foúrni's population is stable, unlike so many small Greek islands. The islets were once the lair of Maltese pirates, and indeed many of the islanders have a distinctly North African appearance.

The above-cited **kaïki** leaves Ikaría at about 1pm (Mon, Wed & Fri), stays overnight at Foúrni and returns the next morning. Another twice-weekly kaïki from Karlóvassi, and the larger car ferries which appear every few days, are likewise not tourist excursion boats but exist for the benefit of the islanders. The only practical way to visit Foúrni on a day trip is by using one of the summer morning hydrofoils out of Sámos (Vathý or Pythagório).

Foúrni

Apart from the remote hamlet of Khryssomiliá in the north, where the island's main road goes, most of Foúrni's inhabitants are concentrated in the **port** and Kámbi hamlet just to the south. The harbour community is larger than it seems from the sea, with a generally friendly ambience. Among several **rooms** establishments, the most desirable are those run by Manolis and Patra Markakis (☎0275/51 268; ③), immediately to your left as you disembark. If they're full you can head inland to the modern blocks of *Evtykhia Amoryianou* (☎0275/51 364; ③) or *Maouni* (☎0275/51 367; ③).

Of three waterfront **tavernas**, the local favourite is *Rementzo*, better known as *Nikos'*; if you're lucky the local *astakós* or Aegean lobster, actually an oversized saltwater crayfish, may be on the menu. The central "high street", fieldstoned and mulberry-shaded, ends well inland at a little platía with traditional kafenía under each of two plane trees; between them stands a Hellenistic sarcophagus found in a nearby field, and overhead is a conical hill, site of the ancient acropolis. There's a **post office** (but no bank) where you can change money, plus several well-stocked shops.

A fifteen-minute walk south from the school, skirting the cemetery and then slipping over the windmill ridge, brings you to **KÁMBI**, a scattered community overlooking a pair of sandy, tamarisk-shaded coves which you'll share with chickens and hauled-up fishing boats. There are two cafés, the lower one with seven **rooms** that are admittedly spartan but have arguably the best views on the island. A path continues to the next bay south, which like Kámbi cove, is a preferred anchorage for wandering yachts.

Heading north from the harbour via steps, then a trail, you'll find more **beaches**: **Psilí Ámmos** in front of a derelict fish-processing plant, with shade at one end, plus two more secluded ones at **Kálamos**, reached by continuing along the path. At the extreme north of the island, idyllic **KHRYSSOMILIÁ** is still best approached by boat, despite the improved road. The village, split into a shore district and a hill settlement at the top of a canyon, has a decent beach flanked by better but less accessible ones. Near the dock are very rough-and-ready combination kafenía/tavernas; simple **rooms** can be arranged on the spot.

Khíos

"Craggy Khíos", as **Homer** aptly described his probable birthplace, has a turbulent
history and (unlike neighbouring Sámos) a strong identity. It has always been
relatively prosperous, in medieval times through the export of mastic resin – a trade
controlled by Genoese overlords between 1346 and 1566 – and later under the
Ottomans, who dubbed the place Sakız Adası (Resin Isle). Since 1912, several shipping dynasties have emerged here continuing the pattern of wealth. Participation in

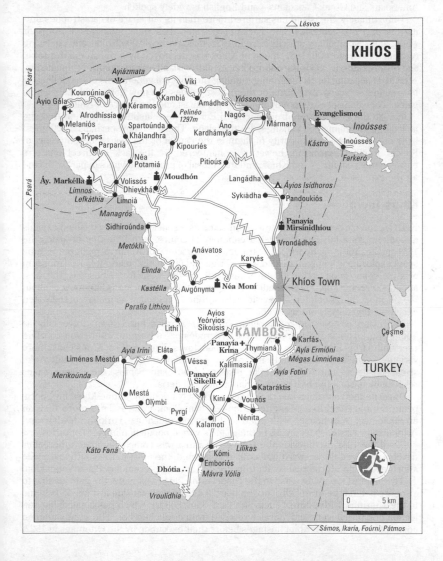

the maritime way of life is widespread, with many people serving as radio operators or officers in the merchant navy.

The more powerful shipowning families and the military authorities did not encourage tourism until the late 1980s, but with the worldwide shipping crisis, and the saturation of other, more obviously "marketable" islands, resistance has dwindled. Increasing numbers of foreigners are discovering Khíos beyond its rather daunting port capital: fascinating villages, important **Byzantine monuments** and a respectable complement of beaches. While unlikely ever to be dominated by tourism, the local scene has a distinctly modern flavour – courtesy of numerous returned Greek-Americans and Greek-Canadians – and English is widely spoken.

Unfortunately, the island has suffered more than its fair share of catastrophes during the past two centuries. The Turks perpetrated their most infamous, if not their worst, anti-revolutionary atrocity here in 1822, massacring 30,000 Khiots and enslaving or exiling even more. In 1881, much of Khíos was destroyed by a violent **earthquake**, and throughout the 1980s the natural beauty of the island was markedly diminished by several devastating forest fires, compounding the effect of generations of tree-felling by boat-builders. Nearly two-thirds of the majestic pines are now gone, with substantial patches of woods persisting only in the far northeast and the centre of Khíos.

In 1988 the first charters from northern Europe were instituted, an event that signalled equally momentous changes for the island. There are now perhaps 5,000 guest beds on Khíos, the vast majority of them in the capital or the nearby beach resort of Karfás. Further expansion, however, is hampered by the lack of direct charters between most countries and Khíos, and the refusal of property owners to part with land for the extension of the airport runway.

Khíos Town

KHÍOS, the harbour and main town, will come as a shock after modest island capitals elsewhere; it's a bustling, concreted commercial centre, with little that predates the 1881 quake. Yet in many ways it is the most satisfactory of North Aegean ports; time spent exploring is amply rewarded with a large and fascinating marketplace, a museum or two, some good, authentic tavernas and, on the waterfront, possibly the best attended evening volta (promenade) in Greece. Although it's a sprawling town of about 30,000, most things of interest to visitors lie within a hundred or so metres of the water, which is fringed by Leofóros Egéou.

South and east of the main platía, officially Plastíra but known universally as Vounakíou, extends the marvellously lively tradesmen's **bazaar**, where you can find everything from live monkeys to cast-iron woodstoves. The bakers of Khíos boast more varieties of bread than any other in Greece – including corn, wholewheat, multigrain, so-called "dark" and "village". Like nearby Lésvos and Sámos, the island makes respectable oúzo – the best commercial brand is Tetteris.

Opposite the Vounakíou taxi rank, the grandiosely titled "Byzantine Museum", occupying the old **Mecidiye Mosque** (Mon–Fri 9am–2pm; free), is little more than an archeological warehouse, with marble fragments such as Turkish, Jewish and Armenian gravestones testifying to the island's varied population in past centuries.

Until the 1881 earthquake, the Genoese **Kástro** was completely intact; thereafter developers razed the seaward walls, filled in much of the moat to the south and made a fortune selling off the real estate thus created around present-day Platía Vounakíou. Today the most satisfying entry to the citadel is via Porta Maggiora, the gate leading to a square behind the town hall. The top floor of a medieval mansion just inside is home to the **Justiniani Museum** (Tues–Sun 9am–3pm; 500dr), which has a satisfying collection of unusual icons and mosaics rescued from local churches. The small dungeon adjacent briefly held 75 Khiot hostages before their execution by the Ottomans in 1822.

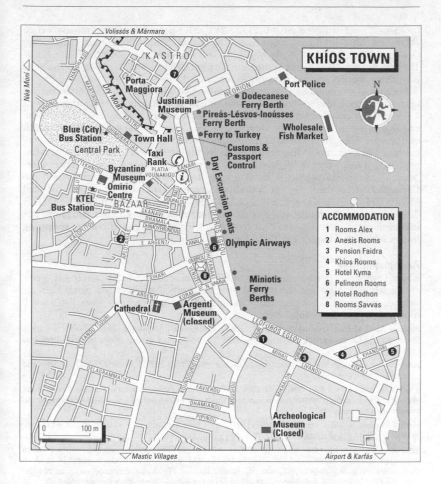

KHÍOS TOWN

ACCOMMODATION

1 Rooms Alex
2 Anesis Rooms
3 Pension Faidra
4 Khíos Rooms
5 Hotel Kyma
6 Pelineon Rooms
7 Hotel Rodhon
8 Rooms Savvas

The old residential quarter inside what remains of the castle walls, formerly the Muslim and Jewish neighbourhoods, is well worth a wander; among the wood-and-plaster houses you'll find assorted Ottoman monuments in various states of decay, including a cemetery, a small mosque, several inscribed fountains and a former dervish convent converted into a church after 1923.

Arrival, information and services

The **airport** lies 4km south along the coast at Kondári; any of the blue urban buses labelled "Kondári Karfás" departing from the station on the north side of the park pass the airport gate. **Ferry** agents cluster to either side of the customs building, towards the north end of the waterfront Egéou and its continuation Neoríon: NEL is a few paces south of customs (☎0271/23 971) and Miniotis Lines, at Neoríon 21–23 (☎0271/24 670), operates a regular morning service to Çeşme and small ferries to many neighbouring islands, and as well as representing G&A boats. The Turkish evening ferry to Çeşme, as well as the most regular boat to Inoússes (see p.312), are currently handled by Faros Travel at Egéou 26 (☎0271/27 240). The helpful municipal **tourist office** (May–Sept Mon–Fri 7am–2.30pm & 6–9.30pm, Sat 10am–1.30pm, Sun 10am–noon; Oct–April Mon–Fri 7am–2.30pm; ☎0271/44 389) is at Kanári 18, near the Ionian Bank. The conspicuous "Hadzelenis Tourist Information Office" (☎0271/26 743) on the quay is a private concern, geared primarily to accommodation.

Because of its central location on the island's east shore, and the preponderance of tourist facilities, Khíos is the obvious base for exploration, especially if you're without a vehicle. The green-and-cream **KTEL buses** leave from a parking area on the opposite side of the park, behind the Omirio Cultural Centre. While services to the south of Khíos are adequate, those to the centre and northwest of the island are almost non-existent. For explorations there it's well worth renting a powerful **motorbike** or a car, or sharing a **taxi** – they're bright red here, not grey as in most of Greece. Three independent **car rental** agencies sit in a row along Evyenías Khandhrí, behind the *Chandris Hotel*; of these, George Sotirakis/European Rent a Car (☎0271/29 754) and MG (☎0271/23 377), also with a branch at Karfás, can be recommended. The **OTE** is directly opposite the tourist office, while the **post office** is on Omírou, and numerous **banks** all have cash dispensers. A final Khiot idiosyncrasy is afternoon **shopping hours** limited to Monday and Thursday in summer.

Accommodation

Khíos Town has a relative abundance of affordable accommodation, rarely – if ever – completely full. Most line the water or the perpendicular alleys and parallel streets behind, and almost all are plagued by traffic noise to some degree – we've listed some of the more peaceful establishments.

Rooms Alex, Mikhaïl Livanoú 29 (☎0271/26 054). The friendly proprietor often meets ferries arriving at unsociable hours; otherwise ring the bell. There's a roof garden above the well-furnished rooms. ③.

Anesis, cnr Vasilikári and Aplotariás, in the bazaar (☎0271/44 801). Rooms with bath, fridges and air-conditioning; quiet after dark. ④.

Faidra, Mikhaíl Livanoú 13 (☎0271/41 130). Well-appointed pension, in an old mansion with stone arches in the downstairs winter bar; in summer the bar operates outside, so ask for a rear room to avoid nocturnal noise. ④.

Khios Rooms, Kokáli 1, cnr Egéou (☎0271/27 295). Clean, antique, second-floor rooms, which are relatively quiet for a seafront locale. ②.

Kyma, east end of Evyenías Khandhrí (☎0271/44 500). A Neoclassical mansion with a modern extension, splendid service and big breakfasts. The old wing saw a critical moment in modern Greek history in September 1922, when Colonel Nikolaos Plastiras commandeered it as his HQ after the Greek defeat in Asia Minor, and announced the deposition of King Constantine I. ⑤.

Pelineon Rooms, Omírou 9, cnr Egéou (☎0271/28 030). Many rooms have a sea view (though not the singles). ③.

Rodhon, Zakharíou 17 (☎0271/24 335). The owners can be crotchety, and the more basic rooms are a bit steeply priced, but it's just about the only place inside the kástro, and is very quiet. ③.

Rooms Savvas, Roïdhou 15 (☎0271/24 892). Fairly quiet pension tucked onto a tiny plaza just inland from the water; the rear rooms unfortunately overlook the public toilets. ④.

Eating

Eating out in Khíos Town can be more pleasurable than the fast-food joints and *barákia* on the waterfront would suggest; it is also usually a fair bit cheaper than on the neighbouring islands of Sámos and Lésvos.

Agrifoglio, Stávrou Livanoú 2 (start of road to Karfás). *The* place for an Italian blowout.

Ouzeri Aïvali, Egéou 80. Newest and (marginally) best of a handful of such outfits on the front.

Ta Dhyo Adherfia, Mikhaïl Livanoú 38. Standard taverna where students and soldiers go for a cheap feed.

Dhodhoni, Egéou 102. Local outlet of Greece's best (and priciest) ice-cream chain; also pastries.

Estia, cnr Roïdhou and Venizélou, near *Rooms Savvas*. Small milk bar serving sheep's milk yoghurt from Lésvos, *loukoumádhes* and occasionally rice pudding.

Ta Mylarakia, by three restored windmills at Tambakhika, road to Vrondádhos (☎0271/40 412). Good food and atmospheric outdoor seating make reservations advisable in summer.

Ouzeri Theodhosiou, junction Egéou and Neoríon. The genuine article, with a large, reasonable menu, though it's best to wait until the ferries which dock immediately opposite have departed. Dinner only.

Drinking, nightlife and entertainment

Iviskos. Tasteful café that's the most popular daylight hangout on the quay, with a range of juices, coffees and alcoholic drinks.

To Loukoumi, alley off Aplotariás 27/c. Old warehouse refitted as a café (8am–2pm), ouzerí (8pm–2am) and occasional events centre. Well executed and worth checking out.

Metropolis, Egéou 92. Currently the best bar in terms of music, decor and crowd.

Omírio, south side of the central park. Cultural centre and events hall well worth stopping at: there are frequently changing exhibitions, and foreign musicians often come here after Athens concerts to perform in the large auditorium.

Beaches around Khíos Town

Khíos Town itself has no beaches worth mentioning; the closest decent one is at **KARFÁS**, 7km south past the airport and served by frequent blue buses. Once there you can **rent bikes** at Rabbit, or **cars** at MG, both uphill from the bus stop. Most of the Khiot tourist industry is based here, to the considerable detriment of the 500-metre-long beach itself, sandy only at the south end. The main bright spot is a unique **pension**, *Markos' Place* (☎0271/31 990; April–Nov, other times by arrangement; ③), installed in the former pilgrims' cells at the **Monastery of Áyios Yeóryios and Áyios Pandelímon**, on the hillside south of the bay. Markos Kostalas, who leases the premises from Thymianá municipality, has created a unique environment much loved by special-activity groups. Guests are lodged in the former pilgrims' cells, with a kitchen available; individuals are more than welcome (there are several single "cells"), though advance reservations are strongly suggested. At the south end of the beach, *O Karfas* (locally known as *Yiamos* after the proprietor) is a fair bet for reasonable and abundant **food**, including vegetables from their own plot. The slightly more expensive *Karatzas* mid-beach is rated second, though the seaview **hotel** upstairs (☎0271/31 180; ③) is the only one here still geared to non-package-tour custom. However, the best food of all is to be had at *O Dholomas*, 3km back towards town at Kondári, on a side road between the municipal swimming pool and the *Morning Star Hotel*.

Some 2km further along the coast from Karfás, **AYÍA ERMIÓNI** is less a beach than a fishing anchorage surrounded by a handful of tavernas and apartments to rent. The actual beach is at **Mégas Limniónas**, a few hundred metres further, even smaller than Kárfas but more scenic, especially at its south end where low cliffs provide a backdrop. *Taverna Angyra* is about the best and most popular eating place hereabouts. Both Ayía Ermióni and Mégas Limniónas are served by extensions of the blue bus route to either Karfás or Thymianá, the nearest inland village.

The coast road loops up to Thymianá, from where you can (with your own transport only) continue 3km south towards Kalimassiá to the turning for **Ayía Fotiní**, a 700-metre pebble beach with exceptionally clean water. There's no shade, however, unless you count shadows from the numerous blocks of rooms under construction behind the main road; a few **tavernas** cluster around the parking area where the side road meets the sea. The last settlement on this coast, 5km beyond Kalimassiá and served by long-distance bus, is beachless **KATARÁKTIS**, remarkable mainly for its pleasant water-front of balconied houses. The choicest among the tavernas here is *O Tsambos*.

Southern Khíos

The olive-covered, gently rolling countryside in the south of the island is also home to the **mastic bush**, *Pistacia lentisca*, for centuries used as a base for paints, cosmetics and chewable jelly beans which became a somewhat addictive staple in the Ottoman harems. Indeed, the interruption of the flow of mastic from Khíos to Istanbul by the revolt of spring 1822 was one of the root causes of the brutal Ottoman reaction.

The wealth engendered by the mastic trade supported twenty *mastikhokhoriá* (mastic villages) from the time the Genoese set up a monopoly in the substance during the fourteenth and fifteenth centuries, but the end of imperial Turkey, and the industrial revolution with its petroleum-based products, knocked the bottom out of the mastic market. Now it's just a curiosity, to be chewed – try the sweetened *Elma* brand gum – or drunk as a liqueur called *mastíkha*, though it has had medicinal applications since ancient times. These days, the *mastikhokhoriá* live mainly off their tangerines, apricots and olives.

The towns themselves, the only settlements on Khíos spared by the Ottomans in 1822, are architecturally unique, laid out by the Genoese but retaining a distinct Middle-Eastern feel.

The mastic villages

ARMÓLIA, 20km from town, is the first, smallest and least imposing of the mastic villages. Its main virtue is its pottery industry – the best shops are the last two on the right, driving southwest. **PYRGÍ**, 5km further south, is perhaps the liveliest of the communities, its houses elaborately embossed with *xistá*, geometric patterns cut into the plaster and then outlined with paint. In autumn, strings of tomatoes hung to dry from balconies add a splash of colour. On the northeast corner of the central square the twelfth-century Byzantine church of **Áyii Apóstoli** (Tues–Thurs & Sat 10am–1pm), embellished with much later frescoes, is tucked under an arcade. The giant **Cathedral of the Assumption** on the square itself boasts a *témblon* in an odd folk style dating from 1642, and an equally bizarre carved figure peeking out from the base of the pulpit. Pyrgí has a handful of **rooms**, many of them bookable through the Women's Agricultural and Tourist Cooperative (☎0271/72 496; ③). In the medieval core you'll find a bank, a post office, a minuscule OTE stall on the platía and a few souvláki grills (but no real tavernas). **OLÝMBI**, 7km further west along the bus route serving Armólia and Pyrgí, is the least visited of the mastic villages, but not devoid of interest. The characteristic tower-keep, which at Pyrgí stands half-inhabited away from the modernized main square, here looms bang in the middle of the platía, its ground floor occupied by two kafenía.

MESTÁ, 11km west of Pyrgí, has a more sombre feel and is considered the finest example of the genre. From its main square, dominated by the **Church of Taxiárkhis** (the largest on the island), a bewildering maze of cool, shady lanes leads off in all directions. But most streets end in blind alleys, except the critical half-dozen leading to as many gates; the northeast one still has an iron grate. If you'd like to stay, there are half a dozen **rooms** in restored traditional dwellings managed by Dhimitris Pipidhis (☎0271/76 319; ③); those run by the Floradhi (☎0271/76 455; ③) and Yialouri (☎0271/76 234; ②) households are somewhat less costly. Of the two **tavernas** on the main platía, *O Morias sta Mesta* is renowned for its tasty rural specialities, including pickled *krítamo* (rock samphire) and the locally produced raisin wine: heavy, semisweet and sherry-like. However, *Mesaionas* – whose tables share the square here – has perhaps the more helpful proprietor. One or the other place will be open in spring or autumn; there's even a **bar** or two in season, but Mestá remains just the right side of twee as most people here still work the land.

The south coast

One drawback to staying in Mestá is the dearth of good beaches nearby; the closest candidate is at **Merikoúnda**, 4km west of Mestá. Reached by an improved seven-kilometre side road starting between Olými and Pyrgí, the little beach of **Káto Faná** is popular with Greek summer campers, who blithely disregard signs forbidding the practice; there are no facilities. A vaunted Apollo temple in the vicinity amounts to scattered masonry around a medieval chapel, located by the roadside some 400m above the shore.

Pyrgí is actually closest to the two major beach resorts in this corner of the island. The nearest, 6km distant, is **EMBORIÓS**, an almost landlocked harbour with three passable **tavernas** (*Porto Emborios* having the edge); there's a scanty, British-excavated acropolis on the hill to the northeast, vaguely signposted 1km along the road to Kómi. For swimming, follow the road to its end at an oversubscribed car park and the beach of **Mávra Vólia**, then continue by flagstoned walkway over the headland to two more dramatic pebble (part nudist) strands of red and black volcanic stones, twice the length and backed by impressive cliffs.

If you want golden sand you'll have to go to **KÓMI**, 3km northeast, also accessible from Armólia via Kalamotí; there are just a few tavernas (most reliable of these being the *Bella Mare*) and summer apartments behind the pedestrianized beachfront. The bus service, is fairly good in season, often following a loop route through Pyrgí and Emboriós. **Lílikas**, 2km east, has quieter pebble coves.

Central Khíos

The portion of Khíos extending west from Khíos Town, matches the south in terms of interesting **monuments**, and the road network makes touring under your own power an easy matter. There are also several **beaches** on the far shore of the island which, though not the best on Khíos, are fine for a dip at the end of the day.

The Kámbos

The **Kámbos**, a vast fertile plain carpeted with citrus groves, extends southwest from Khíos Town almost as far as the village of Khalkió. The district was originally settled by the Genoese during the fourteenth century, and remained a preserve of the local aristocracy until 1822. Exploring it by bicycle or motorbike is apt to be less frustrating than going by car, since the web of poorly marked lanes sandwiched between high walls guarantee disorientation and frequent backtracking; behind the walls you catch fleeting glimpses of ornate old mansions built from locally quarried sandstone. Courtyards are paved in pebbles or alternating light and dark tiles, and most still contain a *mánganos*, or water-wheel, once used to draw water up from wells up to 30m deep.

Many of the sumptuous three-storey dwellings, constructed in a hybrid Italo-Turco-Greek style, have languished in ruins since 1881, but a few have been converted for use as unique accommodation. Most famous of these is the *Villa Argenti*, ancestral home of the Italo-Greek counts Argenti de Scio; it was sold in 1996, however, and is currently shut. For now, stay at the well-marked and publicized *Hotel Perivoli* (☎0271/31 513, fax 32 042; ⑤), just 100m north of *Villa Argenti* (blue urban buses bound for Thymianá pass just 200m to the east). The rooms, no two alike, have fireplaces and (in most cases) en-suite baths and sofas. For **eating**, head for nearby Neokhóri where *O Kípos ton Oneíron* has a wide range of mezédhes and attractive marble decor.

Not strictly speaking in Kámbos, but most easily reached from it en route to the *mastikhokhoriá*, is an outstanding rural Byzantine monument. The thirteenth-century **church of Panayía K* Kína**, isolated amidst orchards and woods, is well worth the challenge of the maze of dirt tracks beyond Vavili village, 9km from town. It's usually closed for snail's-pace restoration, but a peek through the apse window will give you a fair idea of the finely frescoed interior, sufficiently lit by a twelve-windowed drum. The alternating brick and stonework of the exterior alone justifies the trip here, though architectural harmony is marred by the later addition of a clumsy lantern over the narthex.

Néa Moní

Almost exactly in the middle of the island, the **monastery of Néa Moní** was founded by the Byzantine Emperor Constantine Monomakhos (The Dueller) IX in 1042, on the spot where a wonder-working icon had been discovered. It ranks among the most beautiful and important monuments on any of the Greek islands; the mosaics, together with those of Dháfni and Óssios Loukás on the mainland, are among the finest surviving art of their age in Greece, and the setting – high in still partly forested mountains 15km west of the port – is no less memorable.

Once a powerful and independent community of six hundred monks, Néa Moní was pillaged in 1822 and most of its residents put to the sword; since then many of its outbuildings have languished in ruins. The 1881 tremor caused comprehensive damage (skilfully repaired), while exactly a century later a forest fire threatened to engulf the place until the resident icon was paraded along the perimeter wall, miraculously repelling the flames. Today the monastery, with its giant refectory and vaulted water cisterns, is inhabited by just two elderly, frail nuns and a couple of lay workers.

Bus excursions are provided by the KTEL on Tuesday and Friday mornings; otherwise come by motorbike, or **walk** from Karyés, 7km northeast, to which there is a regular blue-bus service. Taxis from town, however, are not prohibitive, at about 5000dr round-trip per carload, including a wait while you look around.

Just inside the **main gate** (daily 8am–1pm & 4–8pm) stands a chapel/charnel house containing the bones of those who met their death here in 1822; axe-clefts in children's skulls attest to the savagery of the attackers. The katholikón, with the cupola resting on an octagonal drum, is of a design seen elsewhere only in Cyprus; the frescoes in the exonarthex are badly damaged by holes allegedly left by Turkish bullets, but the **mosaics** are another matter. The narthex contains portrayals of the *Saints of Khios* sandwiched between *Christ Washing the Disciples' Feet* and *Judas' Betrayal*, missing the kiss, which has unfortunately been smudged out. In the dome of the sanctuary, which once contained a complete life-cycle of Christ, only the *Baptism*, part of the *Crucifixion*, the *Descent from the Cross*, the *Resurrection* and the *Evangelists Mark and John* survived the earthquake.

The west coast

With your own transport, you can proceed 5km west of Néa Moní to **AVGÓNYMA**, a cluster of dwellings on a knoll overlooking the coast; the name means "Clutch of Eggs", an apt description when it is viewed from the ridge above. Since the 1980s, the place has been almost totally restored as a summer haven by descendants of the original villagers, though the permanent population is just seven. A returned Greek-American family runs an excellent, reasonable **taverna**, *O Pyrgos*, in an arcaded mansion on the main square; they also rent a few rooms (☎0271/42 175; ③), though the classiest **accommodation** option here is *Spitakia*, a complex of small restored houses for up to five people (☎0271/20 513; fax 43 052; ⑤).

A paved side road continues another 4km north to **ANÁVATOS**, whose empty, dun-coloured dwellings, soaring above pistachio orchards, are almost indistinguishable from the 300-metre-high bluff on which they're built. During the 1822 insurrection, some four hundred inhabitants and refugees threw themselves over this cliff rather than surrender to the besieging Ottomans, and it's still a preferred suicide leap. Anávatos can now only muster five souls, and, given a lack of reliable facilities and the eerie atmosphere, it's no place to be stranded at dusk.

West of Avgónima, the main road descends 6km to the coast in well-graded loops, also giving access to the northwest of Khíos (see below). Turning right (north) at the junction leads first to the beach at **Elínda**, alluring from afar but rocky and murky up close; it's better to continue towards more secluded coves to either side of Metókhi, or below **SIDHIROÚNDA**, the only village hereabouts, which enjoys a spectacular hilltop setting overlooking the coast.

All along this coast, as far southwest as Liménas Mestón, are round **watchtowers** erected by the Genoese to look out for pirates – the first swimmable cove you reach by turning left from the junction has the name **Kastélla**. A sparse weekday-only bus service resumes 9km south of the junction at **LITHÍ**, a friendly village of whitewashed buildings perched on a wooded ledge overlooking the sea. There are tavernas and kafenía near the bus stop, but the only places to stay are at recently prettified **Paralía Lithíou** 2km below, a weekend target of Khiot townies for the sake of its large but windswept beach. You may stay at *Kyra Dhespina* (☎0271/73 373; ③), but **eat** next door at *Ta Tria Adhelfia*; both are open most of the year.

Some 5km south of Lithí, the valley-bottom village of **VÉSSA** is an unsung gem, more open and less casbah-like than Mestá or Pyrgí, but still homogeneous. Its honey-coloured buildings are arrayed in a vast grid punctuated by numerous belfries; there's a simple taverna (*Snack Bar Evanemos*) installed in a tower-mansion on the main road, and you can stay at an old inn, *To Petrino* (☎0271/25 016; ④). Your last chance for a swim near Véssa is provided by a series of secluded sandy bays along the 16-kilometre road west to Liménas Mestón; only that of **Ayía Iríni** has a taverna, and all suffer from exposure to northerly winds.

Northern Khíos

Northern Khíos never really recovered from the 1822 massacre, and the desolation left by fires in 1981 and 1987 will further dampen inquisitive spirits. Since early this century the villages have languished all but deserted much of the year, which means that bus services are correspondingly sparse. About one-third of the former population now lives in Khíos Town, venturing out here only on the dates of major festivals or to tend grapes and olives, for at most four months of the year. Others, based in Athens or the US, visit their ancestral homes for just a few intensive weeks at mid-summer, when marriages are arranged between local families.

The road to Kardhámyla

Blue city buses run north from Khíos Town up to **VRONDÁDHOS**, an elongated coastal suburb that's a favourite residence of the island's many seafarers. Homer is reputed to have lived and taught here, and in terraced parkland just above the little fishing port you can visit his purported lectern, more probably an ancient altar of Cybele. Accordingly many of the buses out here are labelled "Dhasalópetra". Some 15km out of town, just past the tiny bayside hamlet of Pandoukiós, a side road leads to stony **Áyios Isídhoros** cove, home to the rather inconveniently located island **campsite**, *Chios Camping* (☎0271/74 111), though the site itself is shaded and faces Inoússes islet across the water.

Travelling by bus, **LANGÁDHA** is probably the first point on the eastern coast road where you'd be tempted to alight. Set at the mouth of a deep valley, this attractive little harbour settlement looks across its bay to a pine grove, and beyond to Turkey. There are a couple of rooms outfits, but most night-time visitors come for the sake of the excellent **seafood** at *Tou Koupelou*, better known as *Stelios*'s, on the quay; the remainder of the esplanade has been taken over by patisseries, bars and cafés. There is no proper beach anywhere nearby; **Dhelfíni** bay just north is an off-limits naval base.

Just beyond Langádha an important side road leads 5km up and inland to **PITYOÚS**, an oasis in a mountain pass presided over by a tower-keep; continuing 4km more brings you to a junction allowing quick access to the west of the island and the Volissós area (see over page).

Kardhámyla and around

Most traffic proceeds to **ÁNO** and **KÁTO KARDHÁMYLA**, the latter 37km out of the main town. Positioned at opposite edges of a fertile plain rimmed by mountains, they initially come as welcome, green relief from Homer's crags. Káto, better known as **MÁRMARO**, is the larger, indeed the island's second town, with a bank, post office, OTE branch and filling station. However, there is little to attract a casual visitor: the port, mercilessly exposed to the *meltémi*, is strictly businesslike, and there are few tourist facilities. An exception is *Hotel Kardamyla* (☎0272/23 353; ⑤), co-managed with Khíos Town's *Hotel Kyma*. It has the bay's only pebble beach, and its **restaurant** is a reliable source of lunch if you're touring.

For better swimming head west 5km to **Nagós**, a gravel-shore bay at the foot of an oasis. The lush greenery is nourished by active springs up at a bend in the road, enclosed in a sort of grotto overayed by tall cliffs. The place name is a corruption of *naós*, after a large Poseidon temple that once stood near the springs, but centuries of orchard-tending, antiquities-pilfering and organized excavations after 1912 mean that nothing remains visible. Down at the shore the swimming is good, if a bit chilly, and there are two tavernas and one **rooms** place (☎0272/23 540; ③). Your only chance of relative solitude in July or August lies fifteen minutes' walk west at **Yióssonas**. This is a much longer beach, but less sheltered, rockier and with no facilities.

Northwestern villages

Few outsiders venture beyond Yióssonas; on rare occasions an afternoon bus covers the distance between Mármaro and Kambiá village, 20km west. Along the way, **AMÁDHES** and **VÍKI** are attractive enough villages at the base of 1297-metre **Pilinéo**, the island's summit, easiest climbed from Amádhes. **KAMBIÁ**, overlooking a ravine dotted with chapels, has very much an end-of-the-line feel, despite the recent paving of the onward road south through Spartoúnda and Kipouriés to its union with the trans-island road to Volissós.

From Spartoúnda, a dirt road leads 8km west to another paved circuit taking in the far northwest of the island. Turning north through Khálandhra, you have a choice at Afrodhíssa: straight and downhill to the spa of **AYIÁZMATA**, with its tumbledown pier, seaweed-strewn beach and ugly new spa; or, better, turn left onto what approximates a coastal road for this part of the island. **KOUROÚNIA**, 6km from Afrodhíssia, is beautifully arranged in two separate neighbourhoods, looking out from thick forest cover. After 10km more, you reach **ÁYIO GÁLA**, where a disproportionate number of old ladies in headscarves hobble about. The place's claim to fame is a **grotto-church** complex, built into a palisade at the bottom of the village. Except on the August 23 festival date, you'll need to find Petros the key-keeper, who lives beside a eucalyptus tree at the top of the stairs leading down to the grotto. The larger of two churches occupies the mouth of the cave system; it's originally fifteenth century but has had an unfortunate pink exterior paint job that makes it look like a recent villa. Inside, however, a fantastically intricate *témblon* vies for your attention with a tinier, older chapel, built entirely within the rear of the cavern. Its frescoes are badly smudged, except for a wonderfully mysterious and mournful Virgin holding a knowing Child.

Volissós and around

VOLISSÓS, 42km from Khíos Town by the most direct road (45km via the easier Avgónyma route), was once the most important of the northwestern villages, and its old stone houses still lie appealingly beneath the crumbling hilltop Byzantine fort. The Genoese improved the towers, and near the top of the village is an utterly spurious "House of Homer" signpost, also Genoese. Volissós can seem depressing at first, with the bulk of its 250 remaining, mostly elderly, permanent inhabitants living in newer constructions around the main square – opinions improve with longer acquaintance.

Grouped around the platía you'll find a **post office** (but no bank), two shops and three mediocre **tavernas**; far better ones are found up in Pýrgos district, where *Pyrgos* (aka *Vasilis*) and the vegetarian *Kafenio E*, run by Nikos Koungoulios, are your options; reservations (☎0274/21 480) are advised for *Kafenio E*. A filling station operates 2.5km out of town, the only one hereabouts; you should plan on overnighting since the **bus** only comes out here on Sundays on a day-trip basis, and on Monday, Wednesday and Friday in the afternoon. This should cause no dismay, since the area has the best beaches on Khíos, and some of the most interesting **accommodation** on the island. Some sixteen old houses, most in Pýrgos, have been meticulously restored by Stella Tsakiri and Argyris Angelou (☎0274/21 421, fax 21 521; ④) and usually accommodate two people – all have terraces, fully equipped kitchens and features such as tree trunks upholding sleeping lofts. Larger families or groups should try for the three equally impressive units managed by Elysian Holidays (☎0274/21 128, fax 21 013; ④), very high up near the castle.

LIMNIÁ, the port of Volissós, lies 2km south, with kaïki skippers coming and going from Psará (mid-June to mid-Sept, Mon, Wed & Fri mid-morning). The best **tavernas** here are the long-established *Ta Limnia* on the jetty for *mayireftá*, and summer only *To Limanaki* at the rear of the cove. At Limniá you're not far from the fabled beaches either. A 1500-metre walk southeast over the headland brings you to **Managrós**, a seemingly endless sand-and-pebble beach; nearest **lodgings** are the bungalows of *Marvina Alvertou* (☎0274/21 335; ③). More intimate, sandy **Lefkáthia** lies just a ten-minute stroll along the cement drive threading over the headland north of the harbour; amenities are limited to a seasonal snack bar on the sand, and Ioannis Zorbas' apartments (☎0274/21 436; ④), beautifully set in a garden where the concrete track joins an asphalt road down from Volissós. This heads towards **Límnos** (not to be confused with Limniá), the next protected cove 400m east of Lefkáthia, with a seasonal psistariá operating behind the sand, and the *Latini Apartments*, graced with multiple stone terraces (☎0274/21 401, ⑤).

Ayía Markélla, 5km further west of Límnos, stars in many local postcards; it's a long, stunning beach fronting the monastery of Khíos's patron saint, the latter not especially interesting or useful for outsiders. Its cells are reserved for Greek pilgrims, while in an interesting variation on the expulsion of the money-changers from the temple, only religious souvenirs are allowed to be sold in the holy precincts, while all manner of plastic junk is on offer just outside. There's a snack bar as well, and around July 22 – the island's biggest festival – local "No Camping" signs are not enforced. The dirt road past the monastery grounds is passable to any vehicle, emerging up on the paved road between Melaniós and Volissós.

Satellite islands: Psará and Inoússes

There's a single settlement, with beaches and an isolated rural monastery, on both of Khíos's satellite isles, but each is surprisingly different from the other, and of course from their large neighbour. **Inoússes**, the nearer and smaller islet, has a daily kaïkia service from Khíos Town in season; **Psará** has less regular services subject to weather conditions (in theory minimum 3 weekly), and is too remote to be done justice on a day trip.

Psará

The birthplace of revolutionary war hero Admiral Kanaris, **Psará** devoted its merchant fleets – the third largest in 1820s Greece after Ídhra and Spétses – to the cause of independence, and paid dearly for it. Vexed beyond endurance, the Turks landed overwhelming forces in 1824, to stamp out this nest of resistance. Perhaps 3000 of the 30,000 inhabitants escaped in small boats which were rescued by a French fleet, but the majority retreated to a hilltop powder magazine and blew it (and themselves) up rather than surrender. The nationalist poet Solomos immortalized the incident in famous stanzas:

> *On the Black Ridge of Psará,*
> *Glory walks alone.*
> *She meditates on her heroes*
> *And wears in her hair a wreath*
> *Made from a few dry weeds*
> *Left on the barren ground.*

Today the year-round population barely exceeds four hundred, and it's a sad, stark place, never having really recovered from the holocaust; the Turks burned whatever houses and vegetation the blast had missed. The only positive recent development was a decade-long revitalization project instigated by a French-Greek descendant of Kanaris and a Greek team. The port was improved, mains electricity and pure water provided, a secondary school opened, and cultural links between France and the island established, though so far this has not been reflected in increased tourist numbers.

Arrival can be something of an ordeal: the regular small ferry from Khíos Town takes up to four hours to cover the 57 nautical miles of habitually rough sea. Use the port of Limniá to cross in at least one direction if you can; this route takes half the time at just over half the price.

Since few buildings in the east-facing harbour community predate this century, it's a strange hotchpotch of ecclesiastical and secular architecture that greets the eye on disembarking. There's a distinctly southern feel, more like the Dodecanese or the Cyclades, and some peculiar churches, no two alike in style.

If you **stay overnight**, there's a choice between a handful of fairly basic rooms and three large outfits: *Khakhaoulis Studios* (☎0274/61 233; ④) and *Apartments Restalia* (☎0274/61 000; ④), both a bit stark but with balconies and kitchens, or the EOT *xenónas* (☎0274/61 293; ③) in a restored prison. For **eating**, the best and cheapest place by far is the EOT-run *Spitalia*, housed in a restored medieval hospital at the north edge of the port. A **post office**, bakery and shop complete the list of amenities; there is no bank.

Psará's **beaches** are decent, improving the further northeast you walk from the port. You quickly pass Káto Yialós, Katsoúni and Lazarétta with its off-putting power station, before reaching **Lákka** ("narrow ravine"), fifteen minutes along, apparently named after its grooved rock formations in which you may have to shelter; much of this coast is windswept, with a heavy swell offshore. **Límnos**, 25 minutes out along the coastal path, is big and pretty, but there's no reliable taverna here, or indeed at any of the other beaches. The only other thing to do on Psará is to walk north across the island to the **Monastery of the Kímisis**; uninhabited since the 1970s; this comes to life only during the first week of August when its revered icon is carried in ceremonial procession to town, and then back again on August 6.

Inoússes

Inoússes has a permanent population of about three hundred – less than half its prewar figure – and a very different history from Psará. For generations this medium-sized islet has provided the Aegean with many of her wealthiest shipping families: the richest Greek shipowner in the world, Kostas Lemos, was born here, and virtually every street or square on Inoússes is named for one member or other of the numerous Pateras clan. This helps explain the large villas and visiting summer yachts in an otherwise sleepy Greek backwater – as well as a sporadically open **Maritime Museum** near the quay, endowed by various shipping magnates. At the west end of the quay, the bigwigs have also funded a large nautical academy.

Only on Sundays can you make an inexpensive **day-trip** to Inoússes from Khíos with the locals' ferry *Inousses*; on other days of the week this arrives at 3pm, returning early the next morning. On weekdays during the tourist season you must participate in the pricey excursions offered from Khíos, with return tickets running up to three times the cost of the regular ferry.

Two church-tipped islets, each privately owned, guard the unusually well-protected harbour; the **town** of Inoússes is surprisingly large, draped over hillsides enclosing a ravine. Despite the wealthy reputation, its appearance is unpretentious, the houses displaying a mix of vernacular and modest Neoclassical style. There is just one, fairly comfortable **hotel**, the *Thalassoporos* (☎0272/51 475; ④), on the main easterly hillside lane. **Eating out** is similarly limited to a simple ouzerí just below the nautical academy. It's best to come equipped with picnic materials, or be prepared to patronize one of the three shops (one on the waterfront, two up the hill). Beside the museum is a **post office** and a **bank**, with the **OTE** a few paces further west.

The rest of this tranquil island, at least the southern slope, is surprisingly green and well tended; there are no springs, so water comes from a mix of fresh and brackish wells, with a reservoir in the offing. The sea is extremely clean and calm on the sheltered southerly shore; among its beaches, choose from **Zepága**, **Biláli** or **Kástro**, five, twenty and thirty minutes' walk west of the port respectively. More secluded **Farkeró** lies 25 minutes east: first along a cement drive ending at a seaside chapel, then by path past pine groves and over a ridge. As on Psará, there are no reliable facilities at any of the beaches.

At the end of the westerly road, beyond Kástro, stands the somewhat macabre convent of **Evangelizmoú**, endowed by the Pateras family. Inside reposes the mummified body of the lately canonized daughter, Irini, whose prayers to die of cancer in place of her terminally ill father Panagos were answered early in the 1960s on account of her virtue and piety; he's entombed here also, having outlived Irini by some years. The abbess, presides over some twenty nuns; only women are allowed admission, and even then casual visits are not encouraged.

Lésvos (Mytilíni)

Lésvos, the third largest Greek island after Crete and Évvia, is not only the birthplace of Sappho, but also of Aesop, Arion and – more recently – the Greek primitive artist Theophilos, the Nobel laureate poet Odysseus Elytis and the novelist Stratis Myrivilis. Despite these **artistic associations**, Lésvos may not at first strike the visitor as particularly interesting or beautiful; much of the landscape is rocky, volcanic terrain, dotted with thermal springs and alternating with vast grain fields, salt pans or even near-desert. But there are also oak and pine forests as well as vast olive groves, some of these over five hundred years old. With its balmy climate and suggestive contours, the island tends to grow on you with prolonged acquaintance.

Lovers of medieval and Ottoman **architecture** certainly won't be disappointed. Castles survive at the main town of Mytilíni, at Mólyvos, Eressós and near Ándissa; most of these date from the late fourteenth century, when Lésvos was given as a dowry to a Genoese prince of the Gateluzzi clan following his marriage to the niece of one of

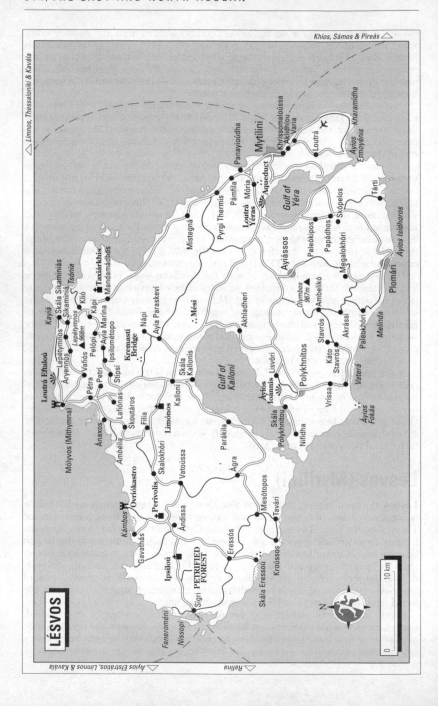

Khíos, Sámos & Pireás ◁

LÉSVOS

Kaviá
Skála Sikaminiás
Sikaminiá
Tsónia
Kló
Kápi
Taxiárkhis
Lepétymnos
968m
Mandamádhos
Ayía Marína
Pelópi
Ipsilométopo
Petrí
Kremastí
Bridge
Nápi
Vafiós
Ayía Paraskeví
Stípsi
Molyvos (Míthymna)
Loutrá Eftaloú
Petra
Anaxos
Lafiónas
Skoutáros
Ambélia
Fília
Ovriókastro
Límonos
Skalokhóri
Perivolís
Vatoússa
Gavatás
Andissa
Ipsiloú
PETRIFIED
FOREST
Sígri
Skála Eressoú
Eressós
Kroússos
Taváris
Mesótopos
Agra
Parákila

Mistegná
Mési
Akhládheri
Skála
Kallonís
Kallonís
Gulf of
Kallóni
Ayios
Ioánnis
Skála
Polykhnítou
Nifídha

Lepétymnos
Árvennos
Panayioúdha
Pámfila
Móría
Pyrgí Thermís
Pámfila
Loutrá
Yéras
Aqueduct
Gulf of
Yéra
Mytilíni
Khríssomaloússa
Aklidhíou
Variá
Loutrá
Áyios
Ermoyénis
Kharamídha
Panayioúdha
Ayiássos
Paleókipos
Papádhos
Skópelos
Megalokhóri
Ólymbos
967m
Ambelikó
Stavrós
Akrássi
Lisvóri
Káto
Stavrós
Polykhnítos
Vríssa
Vaterá
Paleokhóri
Melínda
Plomári
Áyios Isídhoros
Tárti
Áyios
Fokás

N

10 km
0

Faneroméni
Nissópi

the last Byzantine emperors. Apart from Crete and Évvia, Lésvos was the only Greek island where Turks settled significantly in rural villages (they usually stuck to the safety of towns), which explains the odd Ottoman bridge, shed-like mosque or crumbling minaret often found in the middle of nowhere. Again, unusually for the Aegean islands, Ottoman reforms of the eighteenth century encouraged the emergence of a Greek Orthodox land- and industry-owning aristocracy, who built rambling mansions and tower-houses, a few of which survive.

Social and economic idiosyncrasies persist: anyone who has attended one of the lengthy village *paniyíria*, with music for hours on end and tables in the streets groaning with food and drink, will not be surprised to learn that Lésvos has the highest alcoholism rate in Greece. Breeding livestock, especially horses, is disproportionately important, and traffic jams caused by mounts instead of parked cars are not unheard of – signs reading "Forbidden to Tether Animals Here" are still part of the picture.

Historically, the olive plantations, oúzo distilleries, animal husbandry and fishing industry supported those who chose not to emigrate, but with these enterprises relatively depressed, mass-market **tourism** has made considerable inroads. However, there are still few large hotels outside the capital or Mólyvos, rooms still just outnumber villa-type accommodation, and the first official campsites only opened in 1990. Tourist numbers have in fact dropped in recent years, the result of stalled plans to expand the airport, unrealistic hotel pricing, and the dropping of the island from several tour operators' programs.

Public **transport** tends to radiate out from the harbour for the benefit of working locals, not daytripping tourists. Carrying out bus excursions from Mytilíni is next to impossible anyway, owing to the size of the island – about 70km by 45km at its widest points – and the poor state of many roads. Furthermore, the topography is complicated by the two deeply indented gulfs of Kallóni and Yéra, with no bridges at their mouths, which means that going from A to B involves an obligatory change of bus at either the port capital, on the east shore, or the town of Kallóni, in the middle of the island. It's best to decide on a base and stay there for a few days, exploring its immediate surroundings on foot or by rented vehicle.

Mytilíni Town

MYTILÍNI, the port and capital, sprawls between and around two bays divided by a fortified promontory, and in Greek fashion sometimes doubles as the name of the island. On the promontory sits the Byzantine-Genoese-Ottoman **fortress** (Tues–Sun 8.30am–3pm; 600dr), comprising ruined structures from all these eras and an Ottoman inscription above a Byzantine double-headed eagle at the south gate. Further inland, the town skyline is dominated in turn by the Germanic spire of **Áyios Theodhóros** and the mammary dome of **Áyios Therápon**, together expressions of the post-Baroque taste of the nineteenth-century Ottoman Greek bourgeoisie. They stand more or less at opposite ends of the **bazaar**, whose main street, Ermoú, links the town centre with the little-used north harbour of Páno Skála. On its way there Ermoú passes half a dozen well-stocked but expensive antique shops near the roofless **Yeni Tzami**. Between Ermoú and the castle lies a maze of atmospheric lanes lined with grandiose Belle Epoque mansions and elderly vernacular houses.

The excellent **Archeological Museum** (Tues–Sun 8.30am–3pm; 600dr) is housed partly in the mansion of a large estate just behind the ferry dock. Among the well-labelled and well-lit exhibits are a complete set of mosaics from a Hellenistic dwelling, rather droll terracotta figurines, votive offerings from a sanctuary of Demeter and Kore excavated in the castle, and Neolithic finds from present-day Thermí. A specially built annexe at the rear contains stone-cut inscriptions of various edicts and treaties, and – more interesting than you'd think – *stelae* featuring *nekródhipna* or portrayals of funerary meals. Yet another annexe 150m up the hill is not yet operational.

There's also a **Byzantine Art Museum** just behind Áyios Therápon, containing various icons (Mon–Sat 10am–1pm; 200dr), including one by Theophilos (see below). The small **Folk Art Museum** (Mon–Fri 9am–1pm; 300dr) on the quay next to the blue city-bus stop, is not worth the admission and can be skipped without regret.

Practicalities

There's no bus link with the **airport**, and a shared taxi for the 7km into Mytilíni is the usual method; Olympic Airways is southwest of the main harbour at Kavétsou 44. As on Khíos, there are two **bus stations**: the *astykó* (blue bus) service departing from the middle of the quay, the *iperastikó* (standard KTEL) buses leaving from a small station near Platía Konstandinopóleos at the southern end of the harbour. If you're intent on getting over to Ayvalík in **Turkey**, book tickets through either Dimakis Tours at Koundouriótou 73 (☎0251/27 865) or Mytilana Travel at no. 69 (☎0251/41 318). NEL has its own agency at no. 47 (☎0251/28 480), while G&A ferries are handled by Andonis Pikoulos at no. 73a (☎0251/27 000).

Car rental is best arranged through reputable chain franchises like Payless (Koundouriótou 49; ☎0251/43 555); Budget, next door (☎0251/25 846); Thrifty at no. 69 (☎0251/41 464) or Just at no. 47 (☎0251/43 080) – though it's generally cheaper to rent at the resort of your choice. Other amenities include the **OTE** and **post office**, next to each other on Vournázon, behind the central park, and three **banks** with cash dispensers: the Ethniki (National), Alpha Pisteos (Credit) – both on Koundouriótou – and the Emboriki (Commercial) on Ermoú. Before leaving town, you might stop at the jointly housed **tourist police/EOT office** (daily 8.30am–8pm; ☎0251/22 776), behind the customs building, in order to get hold of their excellent town and island maps, plus other brochures. If they're shut; try the **EOT** regional headquarters 300m away at Aristárkhou 6 (Mon–Fri 8am–2.30pm).

ACCOMMODATION

Finding **accommodation** can be difficult: the waterfront hotels are noisy and exorbitant, with few single rooms to speak of. If you need to stay, it's best to hunt for rooms between the castle and Ermoú. Yeoryíou Tertséti street in particular has two possibilities: the friendly *Pelayia Koumniotou* at no. 6 (☎0251/20 643; ②), or the fancier *Vetsikas/Dhiethnes* at no. 1 (☎0251/24 968; ③), whose rooms are en suite.

Past the Yeni Tzami, two quieter establishments between the north harbour and fortress are advertised – *Salina's Garden Rooms*, behind the Yeni Tzami at Fokéas 7 (☎0251/42 073; ③), co-managed with the *Thalia Rooms* across the street (☎0251/24 640; ③). *Zoumbouli Rooms*, facing the water on Navmakhías Ellís (☎0251/29 081; ③), are en suite, and may get more noise from traffic and the bar below. The bougainvillea-clad Neoclassical *Hotel Rex* at Katsakoúli 3, behind the Archeological Museum (☎0251/28 523; ③), looks inviting from the outside, but the en-suite rooms (no singles) are gloomy and a bit overpriced. For Belle Epoque character you're better off in the far south of town, at the *Villa 1900*, a restored mansion with period furnishings and ceiling murals, at P Vostáni 24 (☎0251/43 437; ⑤), where you may be able to bargain the price down a little.

EATING, DRINKING AND NIGHTLIFE

Dining options in Mytilíni are somewhat limited. The obvious, if blatantly touristy, venue for a seafood blow-out is the line of four **fish tavernas** on the southerly quay known as Fanári; all are comparable in terms of price and food. Stumbling off a ferry at dawn, revive yourself with *patsás* at *Averof*, next to the Alpha Credit Bank on Koundouróti. Clockwise around the quay at Koundouriótou 56, the *Asteria* (no sign) is a safe option for meat-and-

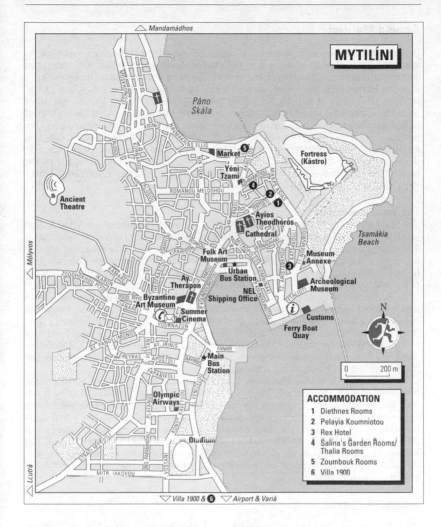

veg oven casseroles. A last surviving example of a dying breed is the *Krystal* ouzerí, on Koudouriótou between the Ionian Bank and the Bank of Greece, whose cavernous, wood-floored interior is lined with mirrors, bench seats and gaming tables.

If you're stuck here involuntarily, awaiting a dawn-departing ferry, some consolation can be derived from the town's decent **nightlife** and **entertainment**. *Hott Spott* is a fairly accurate self-description of the bar at Koundouriótou 63, near the NEL agency; *Cafe Iguana*, on the ground floor of the ex-*Hotel Bretannia* on the west quay is another popular watering hole. More formal live events form the heart of the Lesviakó Kalokéri, held in the castle from mid-July to mid-September, while the summer **cinema** Pallas is between the post office and the park on Vournázon.

Around Mytilíni

Beyond the airport and Krátigos village, the paved road becomes dirt up to **Kharamídha**, 14km from town and the closest decent beach (the fee-entry town "beach" at Tsamákia is mediocre); the eastern bay has a few tavernas. The double cove at **Áyios Ermoyénis**, 4km west, is more scenic but crowded at weekends, and has no facilities. The latter is directly accessible from Mytilíni via Loutrá village. For other pleasant immersions near Mytilíni, make for **Loutrá Yéras**, 8km along the main road to Kalloní. These public baths (daily: summer 8am–7pm; winter 10am–6pm; 200dr) are just the thing if you've spent a sleepless night on a ferry, with three ornate spouts that feed just-above-body-temperature water into a marble-lined pool in a vaulted chamber; there are separate facilities for each sex. A snack-bar/café operates seasonally on the roof of the bath house overlooking the gulf, and there is even an old **inn** nearby (☎0251/21 643; ②) for hydro-cure fanatics.

The Variá museums

The most rewarding single targets near Mytilíni are a pair of museums at **VARIÁ**, 3km south of town (half-hourly buses). The **Theophilos Museum** (Tues–Sun 9am–1pm & 4.30–8pm; 250dr) honours the painter, born here in 1873, with four rooms of wonderful, little-known compositions specifically commissioned by his patron Thériade (see below) in the several years leading up to his death in 1934; virtually the only familiar piece is likely to be *Erotokritos and Arethousa* in Room 3. A wealth of detail is evident in elegiac scenes of fishing, reaping, olive-picking and baking from the pastoral Lésvos which Theophilos obviously knew best; there are droll touches also, such as a cat slinking off with a fish in *The Fishmongers*. In classical scenes – *Sappho and Alkaeos*, a landscape series of Egypt, Asia Minor and the Holy Land, and historical episodes from wars historical and contemporary – Theophilos was clearly on shakier ground. *Abyssinians Hunting an Italian Horseman*, for instance, is clearly fantastic, being nothing more than Native Americans chasing down a Conquistador.

The adjacent **Thériade Museum** (Tues–Sun 9am–2pm & 5–8pm; 500dr) is the brainchild of another native son, Stratis Eleftheriades. Leaving the island at an early age for Paris, he gallicized his name to Thériade and went on to become a renowned avant-garde art publisher, convincing some of the leading artists of the twentieth century to participate in his ventures. The displays consist of lithographs, engravings, wood-block prints and watercolours by the likes of Miró, Chagall, Picasso, Léger, Rouault and Villon, either annotated by the painters themselves or commissioned as illustrations for the works of prominent poets and authors – an astonishing collection for a relatively remote Aegean island.

Southern Lésvos

The southernmost portion of the island is indented by two great inlets, the gulfs of **Kalloní** and **Yéra** – the first curving in a northeasterly direction, the other northwesterly, thus creating a fan-shaped peninsula at the heart of which looms 968-metre Mount Ólymbos. Both shallow gulfs are in turn almost landlocked by virtue of very narrow outlets to the open sea.

Plomári and around

Due south of Mount Ólymbos, at the edge of the "fan", **PLOMÁRI** is the only sizeable coastal settlement in the south, and indeed the second largest on Lésvos, whose famous oúzo is produced at several nearby distilleries. Despite a lack of good beaches within walking distance, it's besieged in summer by hordes of Scandinavian tourists, but you can usually find a **room** (they are prominently signposted) at the edge of the old, charmingly dilapidated town, or (better) 1km west in Ammoudhélli suburb, which has a small gravel beach. Two specific outfits above Platía Beniamín include *Pension Lida* (☎0252/32 620; ③) and *Pension Kamara* (☎0252/31 901; ③). Rustling up a decent meal may present more difficulties, with the dinner-only *Platanos* taverna at the central plane tree often unbearably busy, and nothing special at that. Best of a usually mediocre bunch on the waterfront is *To Margaritari*, within sight of the bus stop, about the only place open reliably for lunch. Ammoudhélli can offer *To Ammoudhélli*, a seafood ouzerí perched over the water, and *Mama Katerina* on the opposite side of the road.

You'll probably do no worse at **Áyios Isídhoros**, 3km east, which is where most tourists actually stay; try the adjacent *Iy Mouria* or *Mama Papas* (sic), where the road turns inland to cross the creek draining to the long, popular pebble beach. Another beach is 6km west of Plomári at **Melínda**, an idyllic strand guarded by monoliths, where *Maria's* (☎0252/93 239; ③) taverna/rooms can be heartily recommended: it's an endearingly ramshackle place with good food at very reasonable prices. Even more unspoiled (thanks partly to the dreadful 7km side road in), **Tárti**, some 22km in total from Plomári, is a 400-metre bay where Lésvos hoteliers and restaurant owners take their holidays. Of the three **tavernas**, the one closest to road's end is by far the best and cheapest; **rooms** also line the final stretch of road should you want to stay.

The bus into Plomári travels via the pretty villages of Paleókipos and Skópelos (as well as Áyios Isídhoros), but if you have your own two-wheeler you can take a slight short cut by using the daytime-only ferry (no cars carried) between Skála Loutrón and Pérama across the neck of the Yéra Gulf. The road north from Plomári to Ayiássos has paving and public transport only up to Megalokhóri.

Ayiássos

AYIÁSSOS, nestled in a remote, wooded valley under the crest of Mount Ólymbos, is the most beautiful hill town on Lésvos – the ranks of traditional houses lining the narrow, cobbled streets are all protected by law. On the usual, northerly approach, there's no clue of the enormous village until you see huge ranks of parked cars at the southern edge of town (where the bus also leaves you).

Don't be put off by the endless ranks of wooden and ceramic kitsch souvenirs, aimed mostly at Greeks, but continue past the central **Church of the Panayía Vrefokratoússa**, built in the twelfth century to house an icon supposedly painted by the Evangelist Luke, to the old bazaar, with its kafenía, yoghurt shops and butchers' stalls. In certain kafenía bands of *santoúri*, clarinet, lap-drum and violin play on weekend afternoons, accompanying inebriated dancers on the cobbles outside. With such a venerable icon as a focus, the local August 15 *paniyíri* is one of the liveliest in Greece, let alone Lésvos.

The best **restaurants** are *Dhouladhelli*, on your left as you enter the village from the extreme south (bus stop) end, or *Dhayielles*, further along. At either of these spots you can eat for a fraction of the prices asked at the coastal resorts. There are a very few **rooms** available; ask at the *Anatoli* grill, between the two aforementioned restaurants.

Vaterá – and spas en route

A different bus route from Mytilíni leads to Vaterá beach via the inland villages of Polykhnítos and more attractive Vríssa. If you're after a hot bath, the small, domed spahouse 1500m east of **Polykhnítos** has been well restored by an EU programme (Mon–Sat 7–11.30am & 4–7pm, Sun 7–11.30am; token admission); alternatively there are those at **Áyios Ioánnis** (token admission), fairly well signposted 2km below the village of Lisvóri. Flanking the chapel are two vaulted-chamber pools, though the water is odoriferous, iron-stained and best enjoyed on a cool evening.

VATERÁ itself is a huge, seven-kilometre-long sand beach, backed by vegetated hills; the swimming is delightfully calm and clean. The west end of this strip has several accommodation options, the nicest of the **hotels** clustered here being the Greek- and American-run *Vatera Beach* (☎0252/61 212, fax 61 164; ④). It also has a good attached restaurant with shoreline tables from where you can gaze on the cape of Áyios Fokás 3km to the west, where only foundations remain of a **temple of Dionysus** and a superimposed early Christian basilica. The **campsite** (*Dhionysos*) at Vaterá lies slightly inland from the portion of the beach east of the T-junction, where studio/villa units predominate. Here several more **tavernas** line the shore road, though none is especially brilliant and one (*Zouros*) is definitely to be avoided. If you intend to stay here you'll probably want your own transport, as the closest shops are 4km away at Vríssa, and the bus appears only a few times daily.

To the east, an intermittently paved road leads via Stavrós and hidden Ambelikó to either Ayiássos or Plomári within ninety minutes. When leaving the area going north towards Kalloní, the short cut via the coast guard base at **Akhladherí** is well worth using and is well paved despite tentative depiction on local maps.

Western Lésvos

The main road west of Loutrá Yéra is surprisingly devoid of settlement, with little to stop for before Kalloní other than the traces of an ancient **Aphrodite temple** at Mési (Messon), 1km north of the main road, and signposted just east of the Akhladherí turn-off. At the site (Tues–Sun 8.30am–3pm; free) just eleventh-century BC foundations and a few column stumps remain, plus the ruins of a fourteenth-century Genoese-built basilica; it was once virtually on the sea but a nearby stream has silted things up in the intervening millennia. All told, it's not worth a special trip, but certainly make the short detour if passing by – and brace yourself for the manically voluble caretaker.

KALLONÍ itself is an unembellished agricultural and market town more or less in the middle of the island, but you may spend some time here since it's the intersection of most bus routes. Some 3km south lies **SKÁLA KALLONÍS**, a principally Dutch and English package resort with a long, if coarse, beach on the lake-like gulf. Of the handful of restaurants, only the *Orange* merits a mention, though the bakery between the square and harbour does a good range of pies and croissants. **Cycle rental** – ideal for the flat terrain hereabouts – is the resort's main distinction; the other is its role as a **bird-watching** centre, attracting hundreds of twitchers for the spring nesting season in the adjacent salt marshes.

Inland monasteries and villages

West of Kalloní, the road winds 4km uphill to the **Monastery of Limónos**, founded in 1527 by the monk Ignatios. It is a huge complex, with just a handful of monks and lay workers to maintain three storeys of cells ringing the giant courtyard, adorned with strutting peacocks and huge urns with potted plants. Beside, behind and above are respectively an old-age home, a lunatic asylum and a hostel for pilgrims. The katholikón, with its carved-wood ceiling and archways, is built in Asia-Minor style and is traditionally off-limits to women; a sacred spring flows from below the west foundation wall. A former abbot established a **museum** (daily 9am–3pm, some evenings; 300dr) on two floors of the rear wing; the ground-floor ecclesiastical collection is good enough, but you should prevail upon the warden (easier done in large groups) to open the upper, ethnographic hall. The first room is a re-created Lesvian *salóni*, while the next is crammed with an indiscriminate mix of kitsch and priceless objects – Ottoman copper trays to badly stuffed egrets by way of brightly painted trunks – donated since 1980 by surrounding villages. An overflow of farm implements is stashed in a corner storeroom below, next to a chamber where giant *pithária* (urns) for grain and olive oil are embedded in the floor.

Beyond, the road west passes through Fília, where you can turn off for a time-saving short cut to Skoutáros and the north of Lésvos. Most traffic continues through to the tiered village of **SKALOKHÓRI**, its houses at the head of a valley facing the sea and the sunset, and **VATOÚSSA**, a landlocked and beautiful western settlement.

Some 8km beyond Vatoússa, a short track leads down to the sixteenth-century **Monastery of Perivolís** (daily 8am–7pm; pull on the bell rope for admission), built in the midst of a riverside orchard (*perivóli*). You should appear well before sunset, as only natural light is available to view the fine if faded frescoes in the narthex. In an apocalyptic panel worthy of Bosch, the *Earth and sea yield up their dead*, the whore of Babylon rides her chimaera and assorted sea-monsters disgorge their victims. On the north side you see a highly unusual iconography of *Abraham, the Virgin, and the penitent thief of calvary in paradise*. Further interest is lent by a humanized icon of Christ, under glass at the *témblon*.

ÁNDISSA, 3km further on, nestles under the west's only pine grove; at the edge of the village a sign implores you to "Come Visit Our Square", and that's not a bad idea, for the sake of its three enormous plane trees which shade several cafés and tavernas. Directly below Ándissa, a paved road leads 6km north to the fishing hamlet of **GAVATHÁS**, with a narrow, partly protected beach and a few places to eat and stay – such as the *Hotel Restaurant Paradise* (☎0253/56 376; ③). A dirt side track leads to the huge wave-battered beach of **Kámbos**, one headland east; you can keep going in the same direction, following signs pointing to "Ancient Andissa". They actually lead you to **Ovriókastro**, the most derelict of the island's Genoese castles, evocatively placed on a promontory within sight of Mólyvos.

Just beyond modern Ándissa there's an important junction. Keeping straight leads you past the still-functioning **Monastery of Ipsiloú**, founded in 1101 atop an extinct volcano and still home to four monks. The katholikón, tucked in one corner of a large, irregular courtyard, has a fine wood-lattice ceiling but had its frescoes repainted to detrimental effect in 1992; more intriguing are portions of Iznik tile stuck in the facade, and the handsome double gateway. Upstairs you can visit a fairly rich museum of ecclesiastical treasure (in theory 9am–3pm; small donation). Ipsiloú's patron saint is John the Theologian, a frequent dedication for monasteries overlooking apocalyptic landscapes like the surrounding parched, boulder-strewn hills.

Signposted just west is the turning for one of the main concentrations of specimens from Lésvos' rather overrated **petrified forest**, indicated by forest service placards which also warn of severe penalties for pilfering souvenir chunks. For once contemporary Greek arsonists cannot be blamed for the state of the trees, created by the combined action of volcanic ash and hot springs some fifteen to twenty million years ago. The other main cluster is south of Sígri (see below), but locals seem amazed that anyone would want to trudge though the barren countryside in search of them; upon arrival you may agree, since the mostly horizontal, two-to-three-metre-long sequoia chunks aren't exactly one of the world's wonders. If you're curious, there are a fair number of petrified logs strewn about the courtyard of Ipsiloú.

Sígri

SÍGRI, near the western tip of Lésvos, has an appropriately end-of-the-line feel accentuated by the recent local tourism slump. The bay here is guarded both by a Turkish **castle** and the long island of Nissopí, which protects the place somewhat from prevailing winds; accordingly it's an important NATO naval base, with the few weekly NEL ferries to Rafína, Áyios Efstrátios and Límnos obliged to dodge numbers of battleships anchored here. The eighteenth-century castle sports the sultan's monogram over the entrance, something rarely seen outside Istanbul, and a token of the high regard in which this productive island was held. A vaguely Turkish-looking church is in fact a converted **mosque**, while the town itself presents a drab mix of old and cement dwellings. The town **beach**, south of the castle headland, is narrow and hemmed in by the road; the far better beach of **Faneroméni** is 3.5km north by coastal dirt track from the northern outskirts of town, plus another 2km south, just below the fifteen-kilometre dirt track to Eressós; neither beach has any facilities.

If you want to **stay**, there's the *Hotel Nisiopi* (☎0253/54 316; ④), and a handful of **rooms**, including *Nelly's Rooms and Apartments* (☎0253/54 230; ③) looking right at the castle. Among very few **tavernas**, *Galazio Kyma* – the white building with blue trim, opposite the jetty – gets first pick of the fishermen's catch and can offer unbeatably fresh seafood.

Skála Eressoú

Most visitors to western Lésvos park themselves at the resort of **SKÁLA ERESSOÚ**, accessible via the southerly turning between Ándissa and Ipsiloú. The beach here, given additional character by an islet within easy swimming distance, runs a close second to Vaterá's, and consequently the place is beginning to rival Plomári and Mólyvos in visitor numbers – they form an odd mix of Brits, Scandinavians, Greek families, neo-hippies and lesbians (of whom, more below). Behind stretches the largest and most attractive agricultural plain on Lésvos, a welcome green contrast to the volcanic ridges above.

There's not much to Skála – just a roughly rectangular grid of perhaps five streets by eight, angling up to the oldest cottages on the slope of Vígla hill. The waterfront pedestrian zone (officially Papanikolí) is divided by a café-lined round platía mid-waterfront dominated by a bust of Theoprastus – the renowned botanist who hailed from **ancient Eressos**. This was not, as you might suppose, on the site of the modern inland village, but atop Vígla hill at the east end of the beach; some of the remaining citadel wall is still visible from a distance. Once on top the ruins prove even scantier, but it's worth the scramble up for the views – you can discern the ancient jetty submerged beyond the modern fishing anchorage.

Another famous reputed native of ancient Eressos was **Sappho**, and there are usually appreciable numbers of gay women here paying homage, particularly at the one hotel (*Antiopi*) devoted to their exclusive use, and in the clothing-optional zone of the beach west of the river mouth. In the river itself are about a hundred terrapins who have learned to come ashore for feeding and finger-nippings, so beware. Ancient Eressós endured into the Byzantine era, whose main legacy is the **Basilica of Áyios Andhréas** behind the modern church, merely foundations and an unhappily covered floor mosaic; the nearby museum of local odds and ends is even less compelling.

Skála has countless **rooms** and **apartments**, but ones near the sea fill early in the day or are block-booked by tour companies; in peak season often the best and quietest you can hope for is something inland overlooking a garden or fields. Late in the day it's wise to entrust the search to an agency, such as *Krenelos* (☎0253/53 246), just off the round "square"; you pay a small commission but it saves trudging about for vacancies. There are few bona fide **hotels**; longest established of these, well placed on the front if potentially noisy, is *Sappho the Eressia* (☎0253/53 233; ③).

Most **tavernas**, with elevated wooden dining platforms, crowd the beach; worthy ones, both on the eastern walkway, are *Iy Gorgona*, with friendly service and a large menu of Greek standards, and the British-run *Bennett's* at the far end of things opposite the islet. Inland, on the way to the museum, the *Aphrodite Home Cooking* taverna lives up to its name, with fair portions and comfortable garden seating. Back on the front, Canadian-run *Yamas* is the place for pancake breakfasts, veggie burgers, wholemeal bread and decadent chocolate desserts; they also function as an Anglophone bar at night. *Sympathy*, a few doors down, is coolly musical, with a mostly Greek-bohemian clientele. The gay women's contingent currently favours *Dhekati Mousa/Tenth Muse*, on the Theophrastos platía; a summer **cinema** further inland rounds up the nightlife.

Skála has an adjacent **post office** and **OTE**, a coin-op **laundry** near the church, and a cash dispenser booth on the seafront.

If you're returning to the main island crossroads at Kalloní, you can complete a loop from Eressós along the western shore of the Gulf of Kalloní via the hill villages of Mesótopos and Ágra; this route is currently all paved except for the first 11km out of Eressós, which should be asphalted by 1999.

Northern Lésvos

The main road north of Kalloní winds up a ridge and then down the other side into increasingly attractive country, stippled with poplars and blanketed by olive groves. Long before you can discern any other architectural detail, the silhouette of Mólyvos castle indicates your approach to the oldest established tourist spot on Lésvos.

Mólyvos (Míthymna)

MÓLYVOS (officially Míthymna), 61km from Mytilíni, is arguably the most beautiful village on Lésvos. Its tiers of sturdy, red-tiled houses, some standing defensively with their rear walls to the sea, mount the slopes between the picturesque harbour and the **Genoese castle** (Tues–Sun 8.30am–3pm; 500dr), which provides interesting rambles around its perimeter walls and views of Turkey across the straits. Closer examination reveals a score of weathered Turkish fountains along flower-fragrant, cobbled alleyways, a reflection of the fact that before 1923 Muslims constituted 35 percent of the local population and owned most of the finest mansions. You can try to gain admission to the Greek-built **Krallis** and **Yiannakos mansions**, or the municipal art gallery occupying the former residence of local author Argyris Eftaliotis, which hosts changing exhibits. The small **archeological museum** (Tues–Sun 8.30am–3pm; free) in the basement of the town hall, features finds from the ancient town, including blue Roman beads to ward off the evil eye (belief in this affliction is age-old and pan-Mediterranean). Archival photos depict the Greek conquest of the island in November 1912. Barely excavated **ancient Mithymna** to the northwest is of essentially specialist interest, though a necropolis has been unearthed next to the bus stop.

Modern dwellings and hotels have been sensibly banned from the preserved municipal core – the powerful Athenian watchdog group "Friends of Molyvos" has seen to that but this has inevitably sapped all the authentic life from the upper bazaar, just one lonely tailor still plies his trade amongst the redundant souvenir shops. Having been cast as an upmarket resort, there are few phallic postcards or other tacky accoutrements in Mólyvos, but still constant reminders that you are strolling through a stage-set, however tasteful, for mass tourism.

PRACTICALITIES
The **town beach** is mediocre – though it improves somewhat as you head towards the southern end and a clothing-optional zone. Advertised **boat excursions** to bays as remote as Ánaxos and Tsónia (see p.324 and p.325) seem a frank admission of this failing; there are also six to eight daily **minibus shuttles** in season, linking all points between Ánaxos and Eftaloú.

The main sea-level thoroughfare, straight past the tourist office, heads towards the harbour; along it stands a number of bona fide **hotels**. These include *Adonis* (☎0253/71 866, fax 71 636; ④), comfortable enough though used as a brothel in winter, and the durable *Sea Horse* (☎0253/71 320; ④) down at the fishing harbour, fine if you're not interested in making an early night of it in season. For rooms, good choices to seek out include *Villa Ioanna* (☎0253/71 234; ③), an older house with painted ceilings; the modern studio units of Khryssi Bourdhadonaki (☎0253/72 193; ③), towards Ayía Kyriakí;

those of Panayiotis Baxevanellis (☎0253/71 558; ③), with a preponderance of double beds and a common kitchen; and the quiet, simple rooms of Varvara Kelesi (☎0253/71 460; ②), way up by the castle. Otherwise, rooms can be reserved through the municipal **tourist office** by the bus stop (daily: summer 8am–3pm & 6.30–8.30pm; spring & autumn 8.30am–3pm). The official **campsite**, *Camping Methymna*, lies 2km northeast of town on the Eftaloú road.

The sea view **tavernas** along the lower market lane of 17-Noemvríou are all much of a muchness, where you pay primarily for the view; it's far better to head down to the fishing port, where *The Captain's Table* combines the virtues of fresh seafood, meat grills and vegetarian mezédhes. The Irish-run *Galley*, hidden away by the little church, offers more westernized fare such as tomato-herb soup. Many consider the five-kilometre trip east to Vafiós worth it to patronize either *Taverna Vafios* or *Taverna Ilias*, especially the latter with its wonderful bread and bulk wine – avoid all fried dishes at either place and you'll be happier. Also highly recommended is *Iy Eftalou*, 4km northeast near the eponymous spa (see below), where the food and tree-shaded setting are splendid. For dessert, try the pudding-and-cake shop *El Greko* on the lower market lane, where the proprietor is a wonderful raconteur (in several languages).

Midsummer sees a short **festival** of music and theatre up in the castle. Night-owls are well catered for with a selection of **music bars**: the lively *Music Bazaar* and more sedate, retro *Skala* near the harbour; disco-ish *Congas Bar* below the shore road, and *Gatelouzi Piano Bar* near the Olive Press Hotel, a more genteel branch of state-of-the-art outdoor disco *Gatelouzi*, 3km towards Pétra, the place to be seen on a Saturday night. There's also an excellent, first-run summer **cinema** next to the taxi rank. Around the tourist office you'll find an automatic money-changing machine beside the National Bank, and numerous **motorbike** and **car rental** places. The main **post office** is near the top of the upper commercial street, with a seasonal branch on the shore road Mikhaíl Goútou.

Pétra and Ánaxos

Since there are political and practical limits to the expansion of Mólyvos, many package companies are now shifting their emphasis towards **PÉTRA**, 5km due south and marginally less busy. The town is beginning to sprawl untidily behind its broad sand beach and seafront square, and diners on the square regularly get sprayed by the exhaust fumes from buses, but the core of old stone houses, many with Levantine-style balconies overhanging the street, remains. Pétra takes its name from the giant rock monolith located some distance inland and enhanced by the eighteenth-century church of the **Panayía Glykofiloússa**, reached up over a hundred steps. Other local attractions include the sixteenth-century church of **Áyios Nikólaos**, with three phases of well preserved frescoes, and the intricately decorated **Vareltzídhena** mansion (Tues–Sun 8.30am–3pm; free guided tour).

There are a few small **hotels**, and a Women's Agricultural Tourism Cooperative (☎0253/41 238 or 41 340, fax 41 309), formed by Pétra's women in 1984 to offer something more unusual for visitors. In addition to operating an excellent, inexpensive **restaurant** on the square (which also serves as a tourist office, crafts shop and general information centre), they arrange **rooms** (②) in one of about 25 affiliated premises where advance reservations are usually needed. Aside from the cooperative's eatery, **tavernas** (like those behind the north beach) lack distinction, and you're better off either at the *Pittakos* ouzerí (dinner only) 100m south of the square, the old-fashioned *O Rigas* hidden in the back streets, or the *Grill Bar* right on the platía, ideal for a quick *souvláki* or octopus tentacle. At **Avláki**, 1.5km southwest en route to Ánaxos, there's an excellent, signposted eponymous taverna behind a tiny beach – well worth the trip out.

ÁNAXOS, 3km south of Pétra, is a jerry-built resort fringing by far the cleanest beach in the area: a kilometre of sand cluttered with sunbeds, pedaloes and not especially memorable snack bars. The blocks of **rooms** behind are fairly well monopolized by tour companies, and anyway you'd be plagued by mosquitoes from the river mouth. From anywhere along here you enjoy beautiful sunsets between and beyond three offshore islets.

Around Mount Lepétymnos

East of Mólyvos, the villages of **Mount Lepétymnos**, marked by tufts of poplars, offer a day or two of rewarding exploration. The first stop, though not exactly up the hill, might be **Loutrá Eftaloú**, some rustic (and painfully hot) **thermal baths** 5km along the road passing the campsite. These are housed in an attractive, recently restored domed structure (always open; 200dr). Take a candle for nocturnal visits, and use it like a Swedish sauna – dashes out of the side door into the sea make subsequent immersion in the 44° water bearable. Nearby, there are a considerable number of luxury hotels and bungalow complexes, some surprisingly reasonable – the *Panselinos* (π0253/71 904; ⑤) gets good marks.

The main road around the mountain first heads 5km east to **VAFIÓS**, with its two aforementioned **tavernas**, before curling north around the base of the peaks. Paving of this stretch should be complete by mid-1998, but twice-daily bus service back towards Mytilíni does not resume until Áryennos, 6km before the exquisite hill village of **SYKAMINIÁ** (Sykamiá), birthplace of the novelist Stratis Myrivílis. Below the "Plaza of the Workers' First of May", with its two traditional kafenía and views north to Turkey, one of the imposing basalt-built houses is marked as his childhood home. A marked trail shortcuts the twisting road down to **SKÁLA SYKAMINIÁS**, easily the most picturesque fishing port on Lésvos. Myrivílis used it as the setting for his best-known book, *The Mermaid Madonna*, and the tiny rock-top chapel at the end of the jetty will be instantly recognizable to anyone who has read the novel.

On a practical level, Skála has a few **pensions**, such as the central *Gorgona* (π0253/55 301; ③), and four **tavernas**, the best and longest-lived of these being *Iy Skamnia* (aka *Iy Mouria*), with seating under the mulberry tree in which Myrivílis used to sleep on hot summer nights. In addition to good seafood, you can try the late-summer speciality of *kolokitholoúloudha yemistá* (stuffed squash blossoms). The only local beach, however, is the pebble strand of **Kayiá** 1.5km east, so Skála is perhaps better as a lunch stop rather than a base. A fairly rough, roller-coaster track follows the coast west back to Mólyvos.

Continuing east from upper Sykaminiá, you soon come to **KLIÓ**, whose single main street (marked "*kentrikí agorá*") leads down to a platía with a plane tree, fountain, kafenía and views across to Turkey. The village is set attractively on a slope, down which a six-kilometre dirt road, marked in English or Greek and better than maps suggest, descends to **Tsónia** beach. Here, 600m of beautiful pink volcanic sand has just a single taverna and another café at the fishing-anchorage end, and two new rooms places at the beach end.

South of Klió, the route forks at **KÁPI**, from where you can complete a loop of the mountain by bearing west along a mostly paved road. **PELÓPI** is the ancestral village of the unsuccessful 1988 US presidential candidate Michael Dukakis, and sports a former mosque now used as a warehouse on the main square. **IPSILOMÉTOPO**, the next village along, is punctuated by a minaret (but no mosque) and hosts revels on July 17, the feast of Ayía Marína. By the time you reach sprawling **STÍPSI**, you're almost back to the main Kalloní–Mólyvos road; there's a sporadic bus service out again, as well as a large **taverna** at the edge of town where busloads of tourists descend for "Greek Nights". There are also **rooms** to let, so Stípsi makes a good base for rambles along Lepétymnos' steadily dwindling network of trails; in recent years donkey-trekking has become more popular than walking, and you'll see outfitters advertising throughout the north of the island.

The main highway south from Klió and Kápi leads back to the capital through **MAN-DAMÁDHOS**. This attractive inland village is famous for its pottery, including the Ali-Baba style *pithária* (olive-oil urns) seen throughout Lésvos, but more so for the "black" icon of the Archangel Michael, whose enormous **monastery** (daily: summer 6am–10pm; winter 6.30am–7pm) in a valley just northeast, is the powerful focus of a thriving cult, and a popular venue for baptisms. The image – in legend made from a mixture of mud and the blood of monks slaughtered in a massacre – is really more idol than icon, both in its lumpy three-dimensionality and in the manner of veneration which seems a hangover from pagan times. First there was the custom of the coin wish, whereby you pressed a coin to the Archangel's forehead – if it stuck, your wish would be granted. Owing to wear and tear on the image, the practice is now forbidden, with supplicants referred to an alternative icon by the main entrance.

It is further believed that while carrying out his various errands on behalf of the faithful, the Archangel wears through more footwear than Imelda Marcos. Accordingly the icon was until recently surrounded not by the usual *támmata* (votive medallions) but by piles of miniature gold and silver shoes. The ecclesiastical authorities, embarrassed by these "primitive" practices, removed all the little shoes in 1986. Since then, a token substitute has re-appeared: several pairs of tin slippers which can be filled with money and left in front of the icon. Just why his devotees should want to encourage these perpetual peripatetics is unclear, since in Greek folklore the Archangel Michael is also the one who fetches the souls of the dying, and modern Greek attitudes towards death are as bleak as those of their pagan ancestors.

Límnos

Límnos is a prosperous agricultural island whose remoteness and peculiar ferry schedules have until now protected it from the worst excesses of the holiday trade. Most summer visitors are Greek, and as a foreign traveller, you're still likely to find yourself an object of curiosity and hospitality, though the islanders are becoming increasingly used to numbers of German and British visitors. Accommodation tends to be comfortable and pricey, with a strong bias towards self-catering units.

Among young Greek males, Límnos has a dire reputation, largely due to its unpopularity as an army posting; there is a conspicuous **military** presence, with the islanders making a good living off the soldiers and family members coming to visit. In recent years, the island has been the focus of disputes between the Greek and Turkish governments; Turkey has a long-standing demand that Límnos should be demilitarized and Turkish aircraft regularly overfly the island, serving to worsen already tense Greek–Turkish relations.

The bays of Bourniá and Moúdhros, the latter one of the largest natural harbours in the Aegean, almost divide Límnos in two. The west of the island is dramatically bare and hilly, with abundant volcanic rock put to good use as street cobbles and house masonry. Like most volcanic islands, Límnos produces excellent **wine** from westerly vineyards – a dry white of denomination quality – and some of the best retsina in Greece. The east is low-lying and speckled with marshes popular with duck-hunters, where it's not occupied by cattle, combine harvesters and vast cornfields.

Despite popular slander to that effect, Límnos is not flat, barren or treeless; much of the countryside consists of rolling hills, well vegetated except on their heights, and with substantial clumps of almond, myrtle, oak, poplar and mulberry trees. The island is, however, extremely dry, with irrigation water pumped from deep wells, and a limited number of potable springs. Yet various terrapin-haunted creeks bring sand to several long, sandy **beaches** around the coast, where it's easy to find a stretch to yourself – though there's no escaping the stingless jellyfish which periodically pour out of the

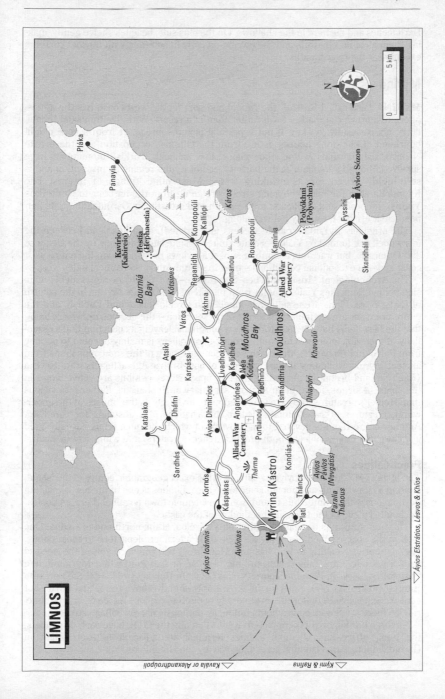

LÍMNOS

Dardanelles and die here in the shallows. On the plus side, beaches shelve gently, making them ideal for children, and they warm up early in summer, with no cool currents except near the river mouths.

Mýrina

MÝRINA (also called Kástro), the capital and port on the west coast, has the atmosphere of a provincial market town rather than of a resort. With five thousand inhabitants, it's pleasantly low-key, if not especially picturesque, apart from a core neighbourhood of old stone houses dating from the Ottoman occupation and the ornate Neoclassical mansions at Romeïkos Yialós. Few explicitly Turkish monuments have survived, though a fountain at the harbour end of Kýdha retains its inscription and is still highly prized for its drinking water. Most other things of interest line Kýdha/Karatzá, the main shopping street stretching from the harbour to **Romeïkós Yialós**, the beach and esplanade to the north of the castle, or Garoufalídhou, its perpendicular offshoot, roughly halfway along.

The originally Byzantine **castle** (access unrestricted), on a headland between the ferry dock and Romeïkós Yialós, is quite ruined despite later additions by the Genoese and Ottomans, but warrants a climb at sunset for views over the town, the entire west coast and – in exceptional conditions – over to Mount Áthos, 35 nautical miles west.

The **Archeological Museum** (Tues–Sun 8.30am–3pm; 600dr) occupies an old mansion behind Romeïkós Yialós, not far from the site of Bronze-Age Myrina in the suburb of Ríkha Nerá. Finds are assiduously labelled in Greek, Italian and English, and the entire premises are exemplary in terms of presentation – the obvious drawback being that the best items have been spirited away to Athens, leaving a collection that's essentially of specialist interest. The south ground-floor gallery is mainly devoted to pottery from Polyókhni (Polychni), the north wing contains more of the same plus items from ancient Myrina, while upstairs are galleries of post-Bronze-Age artefacts from Kavírio (Kabireio) and Ifestía (Hephaestia). The star upper-storey exhibits are votive lamps in the shape of **sirens**, found in an Archaic sanctuary at Hephaestia. Rather less vicious than Homer's creatures, they are identified more invitingly as the "muses of the underworld, creatures of superhuman wisdom, incarnations of a nostalgia for paradise". Another entire room is devoted to metalwork, of which the most impressive are gold jewellery and bronze objects, both practical (cheese graters) and whimsical (a snail).

Practicalities

The **airport** is 22km east of Mýrina, almost at the exact geographic centre of the island, sharing a runway with an enormous air-force base. Límnos is one of the few remaining destinations sharing a shuttle bus to and from the Olympic town terminal. **Ferries** dock at the southern end of the town, in the shadow of the castle.

The **bus station** is on Platía Eleftheríou Venizélou, at the north end of Kýdha. One look at the sparse schedules (only a single daily afternoon departure to most points, slightly more frequently to Kondiás and Moúdhros) will convince you of the need to **rent a vehicle**. Cars, motorbikes and bicycles can be had from either Myrina Rent a Car (☎0254/24 476), Petridou Tours (☎0254/22 039), Holiday (☎0254/24 357) or Auto Europe (☎0254/23 777); rates for bikes are only slightly above the island norm, but cars are expensive. A motorbike is generally enough to explore the coast and the interior, as there are few steep gradients but many perilously narrow village streets.

All three **banks**, two of them just off Kýdha flanking the **OTE**, have cash dispensers; the **post office** and Olympic airlines terminal are adjacent to each other on Garoufalídhou, with a laundry across the way by the Hotel Paris.

ACCOMMODATION

Despite Límnos' upmarket reputation, you may still be met off the boat with offers of a **room**. Otherwise, try the *Hotel Lemnos* (☎0254/22 153, fax 23 329; ④), by the harbour and available through Sunvil; the secluded *Apollo Pavillion* (☎ & fax 0254/23 712) on Frínis, a cul-de-sac about halfway along Garoufalídhou, with pricey hostel-type facilities in the basement (②) or large studios on the upper floors (③); or the quiet *Hotel Ifestos* in Andhróni district (☎0254/24 960, fax 23 623; ④) also available through Sunvil.

Romeïkós Yialós has several **pensions** housed in its restored houses, though all are affected by evening noise from the bars below; best value of the bunch is *Kosmos* at no. 21 (☎0254/22 050; ④). One block inland at Sakhtoúri 7, the *Pension Romeïkos Yialos* (☎0254; 23 787; ④) in a stone mansion is quieter. Just north of Romaïkós Yialós, the areas of Ríkha Nerá and Áyios Pandelímonas are likely bets for **self-catering units**; the best positioned are the hilltop *Afroditi Apartments* at Áyios Pandelímonas (☎0254/23 489; ⑤), again bookable through Sunvil. Finally, the *Akti Myrina* (☎0254/22 310, fax 22 352; winter ☎01/41 37 907) is a self-contained luxury complex of 110 wood-and-stone bungalows at the north end of Romeïkós Yialós, with all conceivable diversions and comforts. It's ferociously expensive – £180/$290 double half-board minimum in July – but costs considerably less if booked through a British tour operator.

There's no official campsite on Límnos, though Greek caravanners and campers tend to congregate at the north end of Platí beach (see below).

EATING AND DRINKING

About halfway along Kýdha, *O Platanos* serves traditional oven food on an atmospheric little square under two plane trees, while *Avra*, on the quay next to the port police, makes a good choice for a pre-ferry meal or an evening grill. **Seafood** is excellent on Límnos due to its proximity to the Dardanelles and seasonal fish migrations; accordingly there are no less than six tavernas arrayed around the little fishing port. There's little to distinguish their prices or menus, though *O Glaros* at the far end is considered the best – and works out slightly more expensive.

Not too surprisingly given the twee setting, the restaurants and bars along Romeïkós Yialós are pretty poor value except for a drink in sight of the castle – the northernmost bar often has live music. The tree-shaded tables of *Iy Tzitzifies* on the next bay north are a better option for beachfront dining.

Western Límnos

As town **beaches** go, Romeïkós Yialós is not at all bad, but if you're looking for more pristine conditions, head 3km north past *Akti Myrina* to **Avlónas**, unspoiled except for the *Porto Marina* luxury complex flanking it on the south. Some 6km from town you work your way through **KÁSPAKAS**, its north-facing houses in pretty, tiled tiers, before plunging down to **Áyios Ioánnis**. Here, the island's most unusual taverna features seating in the shade of a volcanic outcrop, with sandy coves beckoning beyond the fishing anchorage. If it's shut, *Taverna Iliovasilemata* to the south is good and friendly.

PLATÝ, 2km southeast of Mýrina, is a village of considerable architectural character, home also to three eating places. Best of these, 100m south of the pair on the main square, is the *Zimbabwe*, where the quality of the food (and the prices) belie its humble appearance. The long sandy **beach**, 700m below, is popular and usually jellyfish-free; except for the unsightly luxury compound at the south end, the area is still resolutely rural, with sheep wondering about at dawn and dusk. In the middle of the beach, the low-rise *Plati Beach Hotel* (☎0254/24 301, fax 23 583; ③) has an enviable position but is often full of package clients; there are basic rooms available at *Tzimis*

Taverna (☎0254/24 142; ③). More expensive, both for rooms and food, there's the poolside bar/restaurant attached to the tastefully landscaped *Villa Afroditi* (☎0254/23 141, fax 25 031; winter ☎01/96 41 910; ⑥), which has what could be the best buffet breakfast in Greece.

THÁNOS, roughly 2km to the southeast, seems a bigger version of Platý village, with a few tavernas and rooms in evidence; **Paralía Thánous**, a rough track ride below the village, is perhaps the most scenic of the southwestern beaches, with two tavernas, one (*O Nikos*) renting studio-apartments (☎0254/22 787; ③). Beyond Thános, the road curls over to the enormous beach at **Nevgátis** (Áyios Pávlos), flanked by weird volcanic crags òn the west and reckoned to be the island's best. Despite this, there's only a seasonal drinks stall on the sand, and a taverna across the road.

Some 3km further along (11km from Mýrina), **KONDIÁS** is the island's third largest settlement, cradled between two hills tufted with Limnos's only pine forest. Stone-built, red-tiled houses combine with the setting to make Kondiás the most attractive inland village, though facilities are limited to a few noisy **rooms** above one of two kafenía. **Eating** is better at the two simple tavernas of **Dhiapóri**, 2km east, the shore annexe of Kondiás; the beach is unappealing, with the main interest lent by the narrow isthmus dividing the bays of Kondiás and Moúdhros.

Eastern Límnos

The shores of **Moúdhros bay**, glimpsed south of the trans-island road, are muddy and best avoided. The bay itself enjoyed considerable importance during World War I, when it served as the staging area for the unsuccessful Gallipoli campaign, and later saw the Ottoman surrender aboard the British warship HMS Agamemnon on October 30, 1918. The port of **MOÚDHROS**, the second largest town on Límnos, is a dreary place, with only a wonderfully kitsch, two-belfried church to recommend it. The closest decent beach is at **Khavoúli**, 4km south by dirt track and still far from the open sea. Yet there are three **hotels** here, including *To Kyma* (☎0254/71 333; ⑤), whose moderately priced restaurant is well placed for a lunch break when if you're visiting the archeological sites and beaches of eastern Límnos.

About 300m along the Roussopoúli road, you unexpectedly pass an **Allied military cemetery** (unlocked) maintained by the Commonwealth War Graves Commission, its neat lawns and rows of white headstones incongruous in such parched surroundings. In 1915, Moúdhros Bay was the principal base for the disastrous Gallipoli campaign. Of the 36,000 Allied dead, 887 are buried here, with 348 more at another graveyard near Portianoú – mainly battle casualties who died after having been evacuated to the base hospital at Moúdhros.

Indications of the most advanced Neolithic civilization in the Aegean have been unearthed at **Polyókhni (Polyochni)**, 3km from the gully-hidden village of **KAMÍNIA** (7km east of Moúdhros; two simple grill-tavernas). Since the 1930s, Italian excavations have uncovered four layers of settlement, the oldest from late in the fourth millennium BC, pre-dating Troy on the Turkish coast opposite; the town met a sudden, violent end from war or earthquake in about 2100 BC. The actual **ruins** (daily 9.30am–5.30pm; free) are of essentially specialist interest, though a *bouleuterion* (assembly hall) with bench seating, a mansion and the landward fortifications are labelled. During August and September the Italian excavators are about, and may be free to show you around the place. The site occupies a bluff overlooking a long, narrow rock-and-sand beach flanked by stream valleys.

Ifestía and Kavírio, the other significant ancient sites on Límnos, are reached via the village of Kondopoúli, 7km northeast of Moúdhros. Both sites are rather remote, and only feasible to visit if you have your own transport. Ifestía (Hephaestia), 4km from Kondopoúli by rough, signposted track, has little to offer non-specialists. **Kavírio**

(**Kabireio**), on the opposite shore of Tigáni Bay and accessed by the same road serving a new luxury complex, is more evocative. The ruins (daily 9.30am–3.30pm; free) are those of a sanctuary connected with the cult of the Samothracian Kabiroi (see p.333), though the site here is probably older. Little survives other than the ground plan, but the setting is undeniably impressive. Eleven column stumps stake out a stoa, behind eight spots marked as column bases in the telestirio or shrine where the cult mysteries took place. More engaging, perhaps, is a nearby sea-grotto identified as the Homeric **Spiliá toú Filoktíti**, where the Trojan war hero Philoctetes was abandoned by his comrades-in-arms until his stinking, gangrenous leg had healed. Landward access to the cave is via steps leading down from the caretaker's shelter.

The beach at **Kéros**, 2.5km by dirt road below **KALLIÓPI** (two snack bar/tavernas), is the best in this part of the island. A 1500-metre stretch of sand with dunes and shallow water, it attracts a number of Greek tourists and Germans with camper vans and windsurfers; a small drinks/snack bar operates near the parking area.

On the other side of Kondopoúli, reached via Repanídhi village, the pleasant if somewhat hard-packed beach of **Kótsinas** is set in the protected western limb of Bourniá Bay. The nearby anchorage offers a pair of tavernas and, up on a hill overlooking the jetty, a corroded, sword-brandishing statue of Maroula, a Genoese-era heroine who delayed the Ottoman conquest by a few years, and a large church of **Zoödhókhou Piyís** (the lifegiving spring). This is nothing extraordinary, but beside it 62 steps lead down through an illuminated tunnel in the rock to the brackish spring in question, oozing into a cool, vaulted chamber.

Áyios Efstrátios (Aï Strátis)

Áyios Efstrátios is without doubt one of the quietest and most isolated islands in the Aegean. Historically, the only outsiders to stay here were compelled to do so – it served as a place of exile for political prisoners under both the Metaxas regime of the 1930s and the various right-wing governments that followed the Civil War. It's still unusual for travellers to show up on the island, and, if you do, you're sure to be asked why you've come.

You may initially ask yourself the same question, for **ÁYIOS EFSTRÁTIOS** village – the only habitation on the island – is one of the ugliest in Greece. Devastation caused by an earthquake in 1967 which killed half the population, was compounded by the reconstruction plan: the contract went to a company with junta connections, who prevented the survivors from returning to their old homes and used army bulldozers to raze even those that could have been repaired. From the hillside, some two dozen structures of the old village overlook its replacement, whose grim rows of prefabs constitute a sad monument to the corruption of the junta years. If you're curious, there's a photograph of the village taken before the earthquake in the kafenío by the port.

Architecture apart, Áyios Efstrátios still functions as a very traditional fishing and farming community, with the prefabs set at the mouth of a wooded stream valley draining to the harbour beach. Tourist amenities consist of just two very basic **tavernas** and a single **pension** in one of the surviving old houses, which is likely to be full in the summer, so call in advance (☎0254/93 202; ②). Nobody will object, however, if you **camp** at the far end of the town beach.

As you walk away from the village – there are few cars and no real roads – things improve rapidly. The landscape, dry hills and valleys scattered with a surprising number of oak trees, is deserted apart from wild rabbits, sheep, an occasional shepherd, and some good beaches where you can camp in isolation. **Alonítsi**, on the north coast – a ninety-minute walk from the village following a track up the north side of the valley – is a two-kilometre stretch of sand with rolling breakers and views across to Límnos.

South of the village, there's a series of greyish sand beaches, most with wells and drinkable water, although with few proper paths in this part of the island, getting to them can be something of a scramble. **Lidharío**, at the end of an attractive wooded valley, is the first worthwhile beach, but again it's a ninety-minute walk, unless you can persuade a fisherman to take you by boat. Some of the caves around the coast are home to the rare Mediterranean monk seal, but you're unlikely to see one.

Ferries between Límnos and Kavála to Rafína call at Áyios Efstrátios every two or three days throughout the year; in summer a small Límnos-based ferry, the Aiolis, calls twice a week. Despite recent harbour improvements, this is still a very exposed anchorage, and in bad weather you could end up stranded here far longer than you bargained for. If an indefinite stay does not appeal, it's best to visit from Límnos on the day-trip offered by the Aiolis (usually Sun).

Samothráki (Samothrace)

After Thíra, **Samothráki** has the most dramatic profile of all the Greek islands. Originally colonized by immigrants from Thrace, Anatolia and Lésvos, it rises abruptly from the sea in a dark mass of granite, culminating in 1611-metre Mount Fengári. Seafarers have always been guided by its imposing outline, and in legend its summit provided a vantage point for Poseidon to watch over the siege of Troy. The forbidding coastline provides no natural anchorage, and landing is still very much subject to the vagaries of the notoriously bad local weather. Yet despite these difficulties, for over a millennium pilgrims journeyed to the island to visit the **Sanctuary of the Great Gods** and to be initiated into its mysteries. The Sanctuary remains the outstanding attraction of the island, which, too remote for most tourists (except during July and August), combines earthy simplicity with natural grandeur.

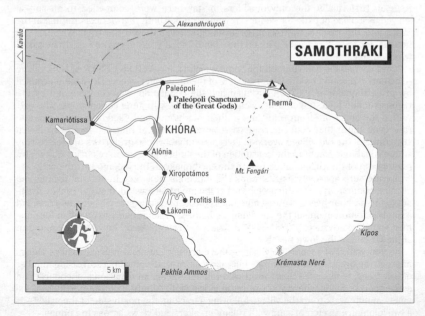

Kamariótissa and Khóra

Ferries and hydrofoils dock at the somewhat shabby and uninteresting port of **KAMARIÓTISSA**, where you're unlikely to want to stay long. There are nonetheless three hotels behind the tree-lined seafront and various rooms for rent in the maze of streets behind. As on most islands with a short season, accommodation is pricey for what you get, and bargaining is usually unproductive, especially in midsummer. Turning left as you step ashore, the first – and cheapest – hotel is the spartan *Kyma* (☎0551/41 263; ②); rooms overlooking the water can get noise from the *barákia* which constitute Samothráki's main **nightlife**. Calmer, but ridiculously pricey, is the *Niki Beach* (☎0551/41 545; ⑤) at the far north end of the quay. The seafront is also lined with **tavernas**, but the best one – *Orizontas*, with quick-served *mayireftá* and bulk wine – is slightly inland on the Khóra road.

Motorbikes and **cars** are in short supply, so it's worth grabbing one immediately on disembarkation – or reserving a bike in advance from Khanou Brothers (☎0551/41 511) or a car from Niki Tours (☎0551/41 465). The latter is also the Olympic Airways and main ferry/hydrofoil **agent**. As with lodging, rented transport is expensive by island standards, but if you've the means go for a car, as island roads are dangerously windswept for those on bikes. Note that there is only one **fuel pump** on the entire island, 1km above the port en route to Khóra. Kamariótissa also has a **bank** (no cash dispenser) but no post office.

Buses six times daily in season (but only twice weekly in winter) along the north coast to Thermá via Palaeópoli (the site of the Sanctuary) or Karyótes, or directly inland seven times daily to **KHÓRA**, the largest village and island capital. Far larger than implied by the portion visible from the sea, its attractive, whitewashed Thracian-style houses lie around a hollow in the western flanks of Mount Fengári, dominated by the Genoese Gateluzzi fort, of which little survives other than the gateway. Khóra has no reliable short-term **accommodation**, though asking for unadvertised rooms in the various kafenía along the winding commercial street may be productive. On the atmospheric, irregularly shaped platía, the *Iy Platia* ouzerí and the more down-to-earth *To Kastro* taverna between them provide the best (and not vastly overpriced) **suppers** on the island, with such delicacies as stuffed squid and *mýdhia saganáki*. Away from the square is the pleasant breakfast and evening **bar** *To Stenaki*, offering real coffee and a mix of good Greek and foreign music. There have been mutterings of moving the administrative capital down to Kamariótissa, but until further notice the island's **post office**, **OTE** branch and **tourist police** (☎0551/41 203) are found here.

The Sanctuary of the Great Gods

A wide but rough track leads north from Khóra to the hamlet of Paleópoli (see overleaf), and, in a stony ravine between it and the plunging northeastern ridge of Mount Fengári, lie the remains of the **Sanctuary of the Great Gods**. From the late Bronze Age to the early Byzantine era, the mysteries and sacrifices of the cult of the Great Gods were performed on Samothráki, indeed in ancient Thracian dialect until the second century BC. The island was the spiritual focus of the northern Aegean, and its importance in the ancient world was comparable (although certainly secondary) to that of the Mysteries of Eleusis.

The religion of the Great Gods revolved around a hierarchy of ancient Thracian fertility figures: the Great Mother Axieros, a subordinate male deity known as Kadmilos, and the potent and ominous twin demons the *Kabiroi*, originally the local heroes Dardanos and Aeton. When the Aeolian colonists arrived (traditionally c 700 BC) they simply syncretized the resident deities with their own – the Great Mother became

Cybele, her consort Hermes, and the *Kabiroi* were fused interchangeably with the *Dioskouroi* Castor and Pollux, patrons of seafarers. Around the nucleus of a sacred precinct the newcomers made the beginnings of what is now the Sanctuary.

Despite their long observance, the mysteries of the cult were never explicitly recorded, since ancient writers feared incurring the wrath of the *Kabiroi* (who could brew up sudden, deadly storms), but it has been established that two levels of initiation were involved. Both ceremonies, in direct opposition to the elitism of Eleusis, were open to all, including women and slaves. The lower level of initiation or *myesis* may, as is speculated at Eleusis, have involved a ritual simulation of the life, death and rebirth cycle; in any case, it's known that it ended with joyous feasting and it can be conjectured, since so many clay torches have been found, that it took place at night. The higher level of initiation or *epopteia* carried the unusual requirement of a moral standard (the connection of theology with morality so strong in the later Judeo-Christian tradition was rarely made by the early Greeks). This second level involved a full confession followed by absolution and baptism in bull's blood.

The site
The **site** (Tues–Sun 8.30am–3pm; 600dr) is well labelled, simple to grasp and strongly evokes its proud past. It's a good idea to visit the **museum** first (open same hours as site; 600dr), with exhibits spanning all eras of habitation, from the Archaic to the Byzantine. Highlights among these include a frieze of dancing girls from the propylon of the temenos, entablatures from different parts of the Sanctuary, and Roman votive offerings such as coloured glass vials from the necropolis of the ancient town east of the Sanctuary.

The **Anaktoron** or hall of initiation for the first level of the mysteries, dates in its present form from Roman times. Its inner sanctum was marked by a warning *stele* (now in the museum) and at the southeast corner you can make out the **Priestly Quarters**, an antechamber where candidates for initiation donned white gowns. Next to it is the **Arsinoeion**, the largest circular ancient building known in Greece, used for libations and sacrifices. Within its rotunda are the walls of a double precinct (fourth century BC) where a rock altar, the earliest preserved ruin on the site, has been uncovered. A little further south, on the same side of the path, you come to the **Temenos**, a rectangular area open to the sky where the feasting probably took place, and, edging its rear corner, the conspicuous **Hieron**. Five columns and an architrave of the facade of this large Doric edifice (which hosted the higher level of initiation) have been erected; dating in part from the fourth century BC, it was heavily restored in Roman times. The stone steps have been replaced by modern blocks, but Roman benches for spectators remain in situ, along with the sacred stones where confession was heard.

To the west of the path you can just discern the outline of the **theatre**, while just above it, tucked under the ridge is the **Nymphaeum (Fountain) of Nike**, famous for the exquisitely sculpted marble centrepiece – the *Winged Victory of Samothrace* – which once stood breasting the wind at the prow of a marble ship. It was discovered in 1863 by the French and carried off to the Louvre, with a copy belatedly forwarded to the local museum. Due west of the theatre, occupying a high terrace, are remains of the main **stoa**; immediately north of this is an elaborate medieval fortification made entirely of antique material.

The rest of the island

The only accommodation near the site itself is in the tiny hamlet of **PALEÓPOLI**, where the old and basic *Xenia Hotel* (☎0551/41 166; ③) tries hard to compete with the *Kastro Hotel* (☎0551/41 001; ⑥), which comes with pool and restaurant; there are also some basic but en-suite **rooms** (③) down on the seashore below the *Kastro*. Four kilometres east, near Karyótes, is the much smaller *Elektra* (☎0551/98 243; ④), though despite the family feel here, the lack of a restaurant means you may prefer to be nearer the action – such as it is – in Thermá (Loutrá), a further 2km east.

With its running streams, giant plane trees and namesake hot springs, **THERMÁ** is one of the better places to stay on Samothráki, although it's packed in late July and August, mainly with an odd mixture of German hippies and elderly Greeks here to take the waters. These are dispersed in three facilities: the sterile, junta-era main **baths** (daily 8am–1pm & 5–7pm; 400dr); the *psarováthres* or "fish ponds", a trio of pleasantly rustic open-air pools with a wooden sun-shade; and a small cottage with a very hot pool (keys from the warden of the main baths). The latter two facilities are reached by a dirt road starting above and to the right as you face the "improved" spa. The low waterfalls and rock pools of **Gría Váthra** are signposted 1500m up the paved side road leading east from the main Thermá access drive.

Thermá is a rather dispersed place, with a small jetty under construction to hopefully receive hydrofoils in calm weather. **Accommodation** includes the *Kaviros Hotel* (☎0551/98 277, fax 98 278; ⑤), just east of the "centre", and – further dowhill, 700m from the beach – the *Mariva Bungalows* (☎0551/98 258; ③). None of the four **tavernas** in "central" Thermá is very inspired, a possible result (or cause) of a predominance in self-catering rooms; *Paradhisos* has the best setting and charges accordingly. Near the *Mariva Bungalows*, *Iphestos* is lively and popular; try the roast goat or chicken. At the bus stop, *Kafenio Ta Therma* doubles as the nightspot for Greek and foreign hippies; about halfway along the track to Gría Váthra, *Shelter Pub* occupies the old schoolhouse.

Beyond Thérma, on the wooded coastline, are two municipal **campsites**: the first, 1500m from the village, although large, has no facilities except toilets, while the second, 3km from the village, is more expensive but has hot water, electricity, a small shop, restaurant and bar. The bus from Kamariótissa usually passes both sites.

Beaches on Samothráki's north shore are uniformly pebbly and exposed, but it's still worth continuing along the road east from Thermá. At **Cape Foniás** there's a Gateluzzi watchtower, and 45 minutes' walk inland along the stream, there are waterfalls and cold pools much more impressive than at Gría Váthra. The road surface ends at Foniás, but you can bump along the dirt road beyond to its end, 15km from Thermá at **Kípos** beach, a long strand facing the Turkish-held island of Ímvros. There's a rock overhang for shelter at one end, a spring, shower and summer drinks *kantína*, but no food available.

From the warmer south flank of the island, you've fine views out to sea, as well as looming Imvros, now officially Gökçeada. Up to three daily buses go as far as **PROFÍTIS ILÍAS**, an attractive hill village with good tavernas but no place to stay, via Lákoma. From the latter a wide, eight-kilometre dirt track, passable for cars, leads east to **Pakhiá Ámmos**, an 800-metre sandy beach with a taverna-rooms place (☎0551/94 235; ③) at the west end. The nearest (meagre) supplies are at Lákoma, but this doesn't deter big summer crowds who also arrive by excursion kaïkia. These also continue east to **Vátos**, a secluded (nudist) beach also accessible by land, the **Kremastá Nerá** coastal waterfalls, and finally Kípos beach (see above).

Thássos

Just 12km from the mainland, **Thássos** has long been a popular resort island for northern Greeks, and since the early 1990s has attracted a cosmopolitan variety of foreign tourists, drawn by the fame of French School excavations here. Accordingly, it's far from unspoiled, but there is only one mega-resort complex, so enclaves of bars and discos haven't completely swamped ordinary Greek rural life. Besides marble and olives, beekeeping, fruit and nuts are important products. Beehives often line the roadsides, and local honey or candied walnuts can be purchased everywhere. *Tsípouro* rather than

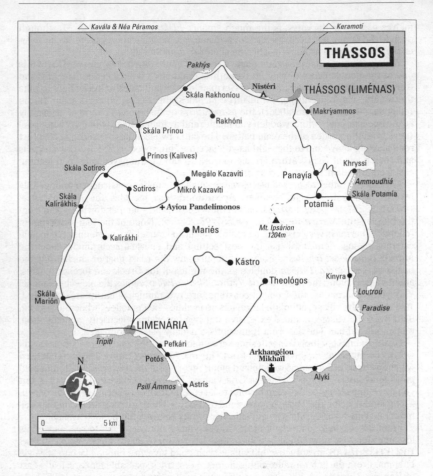

wine is the main local tipple; pear extract, onions or spices like cinnamon or anise are added to homemade batches.

Inhabited since the Stone Age, Thássos was settled by Parians in the seventh century BC, attracted by gold deposits between modern Liména and Kínyra. Buoyed by revenues from these, and from silver mines under Thassian control on the mainland opposite, the ancient city-state here became the seat of a medium-sized seafaring empire. Commercial acumen did not spell military invincibility however; the Persians under Darius swept the Thasian fleets from the seas in 492 BC, and in 462 Athens permanently deprived Thássos of its autonomy after a three-year siege. The main port continued to thrive into Roman times, but lapsed into Byzantine and medieval obscurity.

Thássos is just small enough to circumnavigate in one full day on a rented motorbike or car, which would give you an idea where you'd want to base yourself. The KTEL will do the driving for you – albeit with little chance for stopping – some six times daily. **Car rental** is dominated by Potos Care Rental (☎0593/23 969), with branches in all main resorts, or Rent-a-Car Thassos (☎0593/22 535), also widely represented.

Liménas

LIMÉNAS (also known as Limín or Thássos), is the island's capital, though not the only port. Kavála-based ferries stop down the coast at Skála Prínou, with a KTEL bus always on hand to meet arrivals. The town, though largely modern, is partly redeemed by its pretty fishing harbour and the substantial remains of the ancient city which appear above and below the streets.

With its mineral wealth and safe harbour, **ancient Thássos** prospered from Classical to Roman times. The largest excavated area is the **agora**, a little way back from the fishing harbour. The site (free) is fenced but not always locked, and is best seen towards dusk. Prominent are two Roman *stoas* but you can also make out shops, monuments, passageways and sanctuaries from the remodelled Classical city. At the far end of the site (away from the sea) a fifth-century BC passageway leads through to an elaborate sanctuary of Artemis, a good stretch of Roman road and a few seats of the *odeion*. The archeological museum is shut until 1999 for extensive expansion, the new wings designed to accommodate a huge backlog of finds.

From a temple of Dionysos behind the fishing port, a path curls up to a **Hellenistic theatre**, fabulously positioned above a broad sweep of sea. It's currently out of bounds for excavations, though summer drama performances will be re-instituted in the future. On the same corner of the headland as the theatre, you can still see the old-fashioned kaïkia being built, and gaze across to the uninhabited islet of Thassopoúla. It's possible to **rent boats** from the fishing harbour, self-skippered or not, to take you there and elsewhere.

From just before the theatre, the trail winds on to the acropolis, where a **Venetian-Byzantine-Genoese fort** arose between the thirteenth and fifteenth centuries constructed from recycled masonry of an Apollo temple which stood here. You can continue, following the remains of a massive circuit of fifth-century **walls** to a high terrace supporting the foundations of the **Athena Polyoukhos** (Athena Patroness of the City) temple, with Cyclopean walls. An artificial cavity in the rock outcrop just beyond was a **shrine of Pan**, shown in faint relief playing his pipes. From behind the summit, a rock-hewn **stairway** provided a discrete escape route to the Gate of Parmenon, the only gate to have retained its lintel; it's named from an ancient inscription ("Parmenon Made Me") on a nearby wall slab. From here a track, then a paved lane descend through the southerly neighbourhoods of the modern town, for a satisfying one-hour circuit.

Practicalities

Given the package-resort ethos, cuisine is not Liménas' strong point, and is generally overpriced. The picturesque **tavernas** at the old harbour are predictably touristy, and greasy fast food is all too abundant. A dependable favourite serving *mayireftá* is *Iy Piyi*, up at the south corner of the main square, next to the natural sunken spring of the name. Carnivores should head for *Vasilis's Grill*, on a pedestrian lane north of the square. A more recent entry on the scene is the eminently reasonable *Iy Stoa* ouzerí, on the waterfront near the Hotel Alkyon. Finally, *Orestis*, at the northwest corner of the square near *Iy Piyi*, serves the best ice cream on the island. By contrast, there's plenty of choice in local **bars**. *Full Moon* and the co-managed *Anonymous Cafe* near the *Hotel Amfipolis* are the Anglophile watering-holes; *Platia Cafe Bar* on yet another corner of the basilica square, has good music; while *Marina's Bar* near the *Hotel Alkyon* is the best waterfront nightspot, with a mainly Greek clientele.

Mountain- and motor-bikes can be had from Billy's Bikes (☎0593/22 490) or Thomai Tsipou (☎0593/22 815). The KTEL is on the front, virtually opposite the ferry mooring; the service is good, with regular daily buses to Panayía and Skála Potamiás,

Limenária via Potós, Theológos, Kínyra and Alykí. Thassos Tours (☎0593/23 250), at the east end of the waterfront, is the agent for Olympic Airways (closest airport at Khryssoúpoli on the mainland). The Ethniki/National and Emboriki/Commercial **banks** have cash dispensers.

ACCOMMODATION
At first glance Liménas – plagued with vehicle traffic and often noisy bars – seems an unlikely resort, with few **hotels** enjoying much in the way of calm or views. Despite this, there are some worthy finds; if none from the list below suits, there's also a zone in the southwest of town with a few relatively quiet rooms (②). The closest **campsite** to town is the good one at Nistéri cove, 2.5km west.

Akropolis (☎0593/22 488). Occupying a fine traditional house with flagstone floors, though it can get traffic noise; worth a try at slow times. ③.

Alkyon (☎0593/22 148, fax 25 662). Certainly the quietest of the harbour hotels; English tea and breakfast, plus friendly, voluble management make it a home from home for independent British travellers. Open most of the year; ask also about their cottage in Sotíros and beach villa at Astrís. ③.

Amfipolis (☎0593/23 101, fax 22 110). Housed in a folly, this is the town's most exclusive outfit – and you pay dearly for the privilege, though a package booking may yield some savings over rack rates. ⑥.

Athanasia (☎0593/23 247). Giant and eccentrically furnished rooms with balconies; take the lane inland from behind the *Xenia Hotel* to reach it. Run by a friendly fisherman, this place takes the overflow from the *Alkyon*. ③.

Dionysos (☎0593/22 198). Smallish, en-suite hotel just east of the central square, but quiet despite its location. ③.

Lena (☎0593/22 933). Good-value hotel near the post office, with English-speaking management; no packages. ③.

Mirioni (☎0593/23 256, fax 22 132). Excellent value, well run and allergic to package companies: enough said. It's co-managed with the more comfortable *Victoria* (④) next door, with which it shares a common breakfast room. ③.

Around the coast

Whether you plan to circumnavigate the island clockwise, or in the opposite direction, plan on a lunch stop at **Alykí**, roughly a third of the way along in the sequence described below.

Panayía, Potamiá and Mount Ipsárion
The first beach east of Liménas, **Makrýammos**, is an expensive playground for package tourists, so it's best to carry on to **PANAYÍA**, the attractive hillside village overlooking Potamiá Bay. It's a large, thriving place where life revolves around the central square with its large plane trees, fountain and slate-roofed houses. Top **accommodation** choice is the *Hotel Thassos Inn* (☎0593/61 612, fax 61 027; ④), up in the Tris Piyés district near the Kímisis church, with fine views over the rooftops. Second choice, slightly lower down, is the vine-shrouded *Hotel Theo* (☎0593/61 284; ④), more old fashioned but with a nice ground-floor bar. Down on the main road, beside the municipal car park, the newish, clean *Pension Stathmos* (☎0593/61 666; ④) is the quietest of several nearby, with stunning views out the back. There's reasonable **food** at *Iy Thea*, a view-terrace psistari-iá at the southeast edge of town en route to Potamiá.

POTAMIÁ, much lower down in the river valley, is far less prepossessing and thus little visited, though it has a lively winter carnival. It also offers the **Polygnotos Vayis Museum** (Tues–Sat 9am–1pm, summer also 6–9pm, Sun 10am–2pm; free), devoted to the locally born sculptor; though Vayis emigrated to America when young, he bequeathed most of his works to the Greek state. Potamiá also marks the start of the commonest route up to the 1204-metre summit of **Mount Ipsárion**. Follow the bulldozer track to the big spring near the head of the valley extending west of the village (last water here), where you'll see the first red-painted arrows on trees. Beyond this point, cairns mark the correct turnings in a modern track system; forty minutes above the spring, take an older, wide track, which ends ten minutes later at a gulch and the current trailhead. The path is steep, strenuous and unmaintained, and you'll be dependent on cairns and painted arrows. Go early in the day or season, and allow for three-and-a-half hours up from Potamiá, and nearly as much for the descent.

Skála Potamiás and Khryssí Ammoudhiá

The onward road from Potamiá is lined with *dhomátia* and apartment-type accommodation. Just before reaching the coast at **SKÁLA POTAMIÁS** at the southern end of the bay, the road splits: the right fork leads to Skála itself and some fairly uninspired tavernas; the left-hand option brings you to sand dunes extending all the way to the far end. An honourable exception amongst the **tavernas** is *Flor International* (no sign), at the corner where the bus turns around; the best places to **stay** would be either above the square amongst the vegetation – try *Hera* (☎0593/61 467; ③) – or north along the shore towards the sandy beach, in rooms to either side of the *Arion* (☎0593/61 486; ④) and *Anna* (☎0593/61 070; ④) hotels, themselves often booked by tours. The *Hotel Delfini*, quietly placed 100m back from the road (☎0593/61 462; ③), is also recommended. The north end of this beach is called **KHRYSSÍ AMMOUDHIÁ**, merely another cluster of tavernas, hotels and a campsite; a separate road (no bus service) descends the 5km from Panayía. Once there, you can choose between the self-catering *Villa Khrysafis* (☎0593/61 979; ⑤), or the elderly, twin premises of the *Phedra* (☎0593/61 471; ③) or *Golden Sand* hotels (☎0593/61 474; ③). The *Golden Beach* **campsite** (☎0593/61 472) is the only official one on this side of the island.

Kínyra and Alykí

The tiny hamlet of **KÍNYRA**, some 24km south of Liménas, is overlooked by depressing burned zone and endowed with a poor beach, a couple of grocery stores and several small **hotels**. Those not block-booked include *Villa Athina* (☎0593/41 214; ②), whose top floor rooms see the water over the olive trees, and the welcoming *Pension Marina* (☎0593/31 384; ②). There are few independent tavernas – try asking for half board from your hosts. Kínyra is convenient for the superior beaches of **Loutroú** (1km south) and **Paradise** (3km along), officially Makrýammos Kinýron. The latter ranks as most scenic of all Thassian beaches, with still-forested cliffs inland and a namesake islet offshore beyond the extensive shallows, with much cleaner water than at Khyrssí Ammoudhiá.

The south-facing coast of Thássos has the balance of the island's best beaches. **ALYKÍ** hamlet, 35km from Liménas, faces a perfect double bay which almost pinches off a headland. Alone of Thassian seaside settlements, it retains its original architecture as the presence of extensive antiquities here has led to a ban on local development. The ruins include an ancient temple to an unknown deity, and two exquisite early Christian basilicas out on the headland, with a few columns re-erected. The sand-and-pebble west bay, with its four tavernas, gets oversubscribed in peak season, though you can always get away to the less crowded east cove, or snorkel off the marble formations on the headland's far side. Among the **tavernas**, *O Glaros* up on the north hillside is the oldest and considered the best by island regulars. The *Koala Café* down on the sand provides a semblance of **nightlife**, and there are a half-a-dozen **rooms** establishments, beginning beside *O Glaros* and trailing out along the main highway.

Arkhangélou Mikhaïl to Potós

Some 5km west of Alykí, the **convent of Arkhangélou Mikhaïl** (open reasonable daylight hours) clings spectacularly to a cliff on the seaward side of the road. Though founded in the twelfth century above the spot where a spring had gushed forth, it has been hideously renovated by the nuns resident here since 1974. A dependency of Filothéou on Mount Áthos, its prize relic is a purported nail from the Crucifixion.

At the extreme south tip of Thássos, 9km further west, **ASTRÍS** (Astrídha) can muster two medium-sized hotels, a few rooms and a good beach. Just 1km west is another beach, **Psilí Ámmos**, with watersports on offer. After Liménas, **POTÓS** is the island's prime package venue, and is very densely built up. However, the kilometre-long beach to the south is still unspoiled, and on the semi-pedestrianized seafront, the original taverna *Iy Mouria* remains one of the cheaper and better places; next door, *Michael's Place* has great ice cream. There are plenty of rental outlets for cars, scooters and mountain bikes, including the headquarters of Potos Rent a Car; Potós is also the southernmost port for the summer hydrofoils which call at all west-coast resorts. **Pefkári** with its manicured beach, 1km west, is essentially an annexe of Potós, with high-rent resort complexes, but there are also more modest **accommodation** options such as *Prasino Veloudho* (☎0593/52 001, fax 51 232; ③).

Limenária and the west coast

LIMENÁRIA, the island's second town, was built to house German mining executives brought in by the Ottomans at the turn of the century. Their remaining mansions, scattered on the slopes above the harbour, lend some character, and the municipality has made a stab at prettifying the waterfront, but it remains one of the least attractive spots on Thássos, handy mainly for its **banks** and **post office**. At the east end of the quay, in some 1960s blocks, are a cluster of very basic **hotels** such as the *Menel* (☎0593/51 396; ③), with mostly Greek clientele. There are also plenty of **rooms** on offer, and a **campsite** between Limenária and Pefkári: the *Pefkari* (☎0593/51 190; June–Sept). For **eating** out, the *Pelikanos* restaurant (supper only) is noted for its soups among other dishes. The closest good beach is unsignposted **Trypití**, a couple of kilometres west – turn left into the pines at the start of a curve right. All development is well inland from the broad, 800-metre long strand, though there are umbrellas and chaise longues for rent.

Continuing clockwise from Limenária to Thássos town, there's progressively less to stop off for. The various *skáles* such as Skála Kalirákhis and Skála Sotíros are bleak, straggly and windy. **SKÁLA MARIÓN**, 13km from Limenária, is the exception that proves the rule: an attractive little bay, with fishing boats hauled up on the sandy foreshore, and the admittedly modern low-rise village arrayed in a U-shape all around. There are **rooms** available, a few tavernas, and most importantly two fine beaches to either side. **SKÁLA PRÍNOU** has little to recommend it, other than ferry connections to Kavála. Buses are usually timed to coincide with the ferries, but if you want to stay, there are several **hotels**, numerous **rooms**, quayside **tavernas** and an EOT **campsite** (☎0593/71 171; June–Sept) 1km south of the ferry dock. **SKÁLA RAKHONÍOU**, between here and Liménas, has more accommodation (including the *Perseus* campsite) and fish restaurants, as well as proximity to **Pakhýs** beach, 9km short of Liménas, and by far the best strand on the northwest coast. Narrow dirt tracks lead past various tavernas through surviving pines to the sand, partly shaded in the morning.

The interior

Few people get around to exploring inland Thássos – with the post-fire scrub barely waist-high, it's not always rewarding – but there are several worthwhile excursions to or around the hill villages besides the aforementioned trek up Mount Ipsárion from Potamiá.

From Potós you can head 10km up a good road to **THEOLÓGOS**, founded in the sixteenth century by refugees from Constantinople, which was the island's capital under the Ottomans (the last Muslims only departed after 1923). Its houses, most with oversized chimneys and slate roofs, straggle in long tiers to either side of the main street, surrounded by generous kitchen gardens or walled courtyards. Several **tavernas** advertise themselves on the approach road; of these, *Psistaria Lambiris* is longest established, and about the only one open for lunch. Most, such as *Kleoniki/Tou Iatrou* near the bus stop, are at their best in the evening when the *souvles* loaded with goat and suckling pig start turning. A few basic **rooms** are available (though none are signposted) – the baker on the square has rooms near the *Psistaria Lambiris*.

Despite apparent proximity on the map, there's no straightforward way from Theológos to **KÁSTRO**, the most naturally protected of the anti-pirate redoubts; especially with a car, it's best to descend to Potós and head up a rough, 17-kilometre dirt track from Limenária. Thirty ancient houses and a church surround a rocky pinnacle, fortified by the Byzantines and the Genoese, which has a sheer drop on three sides. Summer occupation by shepherds is becoming the rule after total abandonment in the last century, when mining jobs at Limenária proved irresistible, but there's only one kafenío on the ground floor of the former school, one telephone therein, far more sheep than people, and no mains electricity.

From Skála Marión an unmarked but paved road (slipping under the main highway bridge to the north) proceeds 11km inland to attractive **MARIÉS** at the top of a wooded stream valley; of two **tavernas** here, the well-signed one to the right is more of a going concern. From Skála Sotíros, a steep road heads 3.5km up to **SOTÍROS**, the only interior village with an unobstructed view of sunset over the Aegean and thus popular with foreigners who've bought up about half of the houses for restoration. On the ridge opposite are exploratory shafts left by the miners, whose ruined lodge looms above the church. On the plane-shaded square below the old fountain, *O Platanos* **taverna** is congenially run and there's good bulk wine.

From Prínos (Kalíves) on the coast road, you've a six-kilometre journey inland to the Kazavíti villages, shrouded in greenery that escaped the fires; they're signposted and mapped officially as Megálo and Mikró Prínos but still universally known by their Ottoman name. **MIKRÓ KAZAVÍTI** offers the simple grill-taverna *Paradhisos*, and the start of the track south for the **convent of Ayíou Pandelímona**. **MEGÁLO KAZAVÍTI**, 1km beyond, is the architectural showcase of the island, a fact not lost on the numerous outsiders who have summer homes here; on the magnificent platía are two fairly pricey **tavernas**. Some 4km up from its *skala*, **RAKHÓNI** is well set at the head of its denuded valley, paired with the small village of Áyios Yeóryios across the way. The road up to the square has plenty of simple **tavernas**.

travel details

To simplify the lists that follow we've excluded a regular sailing of the G&A company, which once a week runs a ferry in each direction (exact day changes according to season), linking Alexandhroúpoli with Límnos, Lésvos, Khíos, Sámos, Pátmos, Kálymnos, Kós and Rhodes; in peak season Ikaría, Léros and Sitía (Crete) are also included. Each one-way trip takes 26–36hr depending on the number of stops. We've also omitted the weekly DANE sailing of the *Patmos* between Rhodes, Kós, Sámos and Thessaloníki (22hr for the full run, usually at the weekend).

Sámos (Vathý) 4–7 weekly to Ikaría, Náxos, Páros, Sýros Pireás (14hr); 2–3 weekly to Khíos and Foúrni; 1–2 weekly to, Mýkonos and Tínos.

Sámos (Karlóvassi) As for Vathý, plus 2 weekly kaïki departures, usually early Mon and Thurs afternoon, to Foúrni.

Sámos (Pythagório) 1–2 weekly to Foúrni, Ikaría, Pátmos; 1–2 weekly (usually Wed and Sun afternoon) to Agathónissi, Lipsí, Pátmos, Léros, Kálymnos, with onward connections to all other Dodecanese (see p.280). Also expensive excursion kaïkia daily in season to Pátmos.

Ikaría 3–7 weekly to Sámos (both northern ports), Páros and Pireás (at least 3 weekly services via Évdhilos year-round); 3–4 weekly to Náxos and Sýros; 3 kaïkia weekly, from Áyios Kírykos, to Foúrni; 2–3 weekly to Khíos, Foúrni, Pátmos; 1–2 weekly to Mýkonos and Tínos.

Foúrni 4–5 weekly ferries, to Sámos (northern ports), Páros and Pireás; smaller ferries twice weekly to Sámos (Pythagório or Vathý), Ikaría, Pátmos, Khíos; morning kaïki to Ikaría, Mon, Wed, Fri, on weekends only by demand; twice weekly (usually Mon and Thur) morning kaïki to Karlóvassi (Sámos).

Khíos 5–9 weekly to Pireás (10hr) and Lésvos (3hr 30min); 1–2 weekly to Límnos (10hr); 2–3 weekly small ferries to Sámos (5hr); 1–2 weekly to Foúrni and Pátmos. Daily afternoon kaïki to Inoússes except Sunday morning; 3 weekly small ferries from Khíos Town to Psará (4hr), 2 weekly kaïkia on different days, mid-June to early September only, from Limní to Psará (2hr).

Psará 1 weekly direct to Pireás (8hr) and Lésvos (Mytilíni).

Lésvos 5–16 weekly from Mytilíni to Pireás (12hr direct, 13hr 30min via Khíos or Psará); 5–10 weekly to Khíos (3hr 30min); 4–8 weekly to Límnos (6hr from Mytilíni, 5hr from Sígri); 2 weekly to Thessaloníki (14hr); 1–2 weekly to Áyios Efstrátios (4hr) from Sígri only; 1–3 weekly to Kavála (12hr from Mytilíni, 10hr from Sígri); 1 weekly to Rafína (8hr from Sígri); 1 weekly to Psará (4hr); 1 weekly to Vólos, Sýros, Ándhros (July–Aug only).

Límnos 3–5 weekly to Kavála and Lésvos (Mytilíni or Sígri); 2–4 weekly to Áyios Efstrátios and Rafína; 1–3 weekly to Thessaloníki, Pireás, Khíos. Also a small local ferry to Áyios Efstrátios 3 times weekly.

Áyios Efstrátios 3–4 weekly to Límnos; 2–3 weekly to Rafína and Kavála; 1–2 weekly to Lésvos (Sígri).

Samothráki 2–3 daily ferries to/from Alexandhroúpoli (2hr 15min) in season, dropping to 5–6 weekly out of season. Also 2 weekly spring or autumn, up to 5 weekly in peak season, to Kavála (and thence other North Aegean islands).

Thássos 8–10 ferries daily, depending on season, between Kavála and Skála Prínou (1hr 15min; 7.30am–9.30pm, 6am–8pm to Kavála from the island); 10 daily between Keramotí and Liménas (45min; 7am–10pm, 6am–8.30pm from

Thássos). Except for extremely unreliable excursion kaïkia to Samothráki, no direct connections with any other island, you must travel via Kavála.

Hydrofoils

Just one company, Sámos Hydrofoils, operates in the **east Aegean**. Based on Sámos itself, this offers nearly daily early morning service from Vathý and Pythagório to Pátmos, Léros, Kálymnos and Kós (in the Dodecanese), returning in the late afternoon; 3–5 times weekly Lipsí is included; Ikaría is called at 2 times weekly, with Foúrni and Agathónissi served once weekly. Complementary service is provided by Dodecanese Hydrofoils (see p.280), based in Kálymnos and Rhodes, which go northbound in the morning and head south in the afternoon.

Thássos is served by hydrofoils from Kavála, which depart for Liménas 8–15 times daily from 7am–9pm (6am–8pm from Thássos); in summer there are also 2–4 daily departures from Kavála to the west-coast resorts of Skála Kalirákhon, Skála Marión, Limenária and Potós.

Samothráki is served by hydrofoil from Alexandhroúpoli from mid-May to mid-June and in September, once daily in the morning (1hr 30min); from mid-June through August another company kicks in with two more departures, usually afternoon, three days a week. One of these may continue on to Límnos, replacing a defunct ferry link from Samothráki.

International Hydrofoils

Service once daily (in theory), mid-June to mid-Sept, between Vathý (Sámos) and Kuşadası (Turkey). Fares are currently much the same as for a conventional ferry (see section below) if you bargain.

International ferries

Vathý (Sámos)–Kuşadası (Turkey) At least 1 daily, late April to late October; otherwise a Turkish boat only by demand in winter, usually Fri or Sat. Morning Greek boat (passengers only), afternoon Turkish boats (usually 2 in season taking 2 cars apiece). Rates are £29/US$43 one way including taxes on both the Greek and Turkish sides, £33/$55 return; no day return rate. Small cars £30/$45 one way. Journey time 1hr 30min.

Also regular (2–3 weekly) services in season from **Pythagório**.

Khíos–Çeşme (Turkey) 2–12 boats weekly, depending on season. Thursday night and Saturday morning services tend to run year-round. Rates are £31/$49 one-way, £40/$64 return (no day return fare), including Greek taxes; no Turkish taxes. Small cars £42/$67 each way. Journey time 45min.

Mytilíni (Lésvos)–Ayvalik (Turkey) 5–9 weekly in season; winter link unreliable. Rates are similar to Khíos. Journey time 1hr 30min.

Flights

Khíos–Athens (4–5 daily; 50min)

Lésvos–Athens (3–5 daily; 45min)

Lésvos–Khíos (2 weekly; 25 min)

Lésvos–Thessaloníki (9 weekly; 1hr 10min–2hr)

Límnos–Athens (2–3 daily; 1hr)

Límnos–Lésvos (1 daily; 40min)

Límnos–Thessaloníki (1 daily; 50min)

Sámos–Athens (3–4 daily; 1hr)

Sámos–Thessaloníki (2 weekly; 1hr 40min)

CHAPTER SIX

THE SPORADES AND ÉVVIA

The three northern **Sporades**, Skiáthos, Skópelos and Alónissos, are scattered (as their Greek name suggests) just off the mainland, their mountainous terrain betraying their origin as extensions of Mount Pelion in Thessaly. They are archetypal holiday islands, with a wide selection of good beaches, transparent waters and thick, pine forests. They're all very busy in season, with Skiáthos attracting by far the most package tours.

Skiáthos has the best beaches, and is still the busiest island in the group, though these days **Skópelos** gets very crowded, too. **Alónissos** is the quietest of the three, and has the wildest scenery, so it's really more for nature lovers than night owls. **Skýros**, further southeast, retains more of its traditional culture than the other three islands, though development is now well under way. The main town doesn't yet feel like a resort, but its main street is not without its fast food and souvenir shops. Unlike the other three islands, the best beaches are those close to the main town. To the south, the huge island of **Évvia** (or Euboea) runs for 150km alongside the mainland. It is one of the most attractive Greek islands, with a forested mountain spine and long stretches of rugged, largely undeveloped coast. Perhaps because it lacks any impressive ruins or real island feel due to its proximity to the mainland, Évvia is explored by few foreign tourists, though Athenians visit the island in force and have erected holiday homes around half a dozen of its major resorts.

The Sporades are well connected by bus and ferry both with Athens (via Áyios Konstandínos or Kými), Thessaloniki and Vólos, and it's easy to island-hop in the northern group. The only ferry connection to Skýros is from Kými, plus a Flying Dolphin

---

ACCOMMODATION PRICE CODES

Throughout the book we've used the following **price codes** to denote the cheapest available room in high season; all are prices for a double room, except for category ①, which represents per person rates. Out of season, rates can drop by up to fifty percent, especially if you are staying for three or more nights. Single rooms, where available, cost around seventy percent of the price of a double.

Rented private rooms on the islands usually fall into the ② or ③ categories, depending on their location and facilities, and the season; a few in the ④ category are more like plush self-catering apartments. They are not generally available from late October through to the beginning of April, when only hotels tend to remain open.

① 1400–2000dr	④ 8000–12,000dr
② 4000–6000dr	⑤ 12,000–16,000dr
③ 6000–8000dr	⑥ 16,000dr and upwards

For more accommodation details, see pp.39–41.

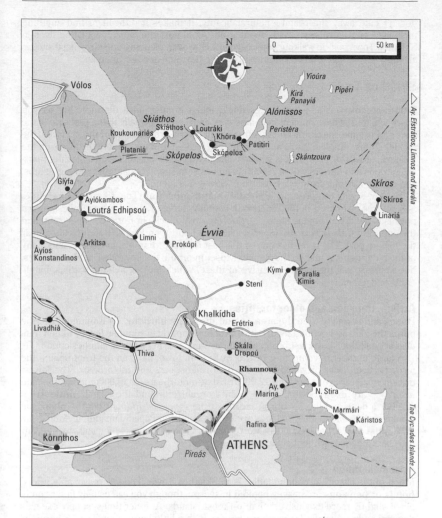

hydrofoil service in summer from Vólos via the other Sporades. Évvia is linked to the mainland by a bridge at its capital Khalkídha, and by a series of shuttle-ferries. Both Skiáthos and Skýros have airports.

Skiáthos

The commercialization of **Skiáthos** is legendary among foreigners and Greeks: it's a close fourth to that of Corfu, Mýkonos and Rhodes. But if you've some time to spare, or a gregarious nature, you might still break your journey here to sample the best, if most overcrowded, **beaches** in the Sporades. Along the south and southeast coasts, the road serves an almost unbroken line of villas, hotels and restaurants, and although this doesn't take away the island's natural beauty, it makes it difficult to find anything unspoiled or particularly Greek about it all. As almost the entire population lives in Skiáthos Town, a little walking soon pays off. However, camping outside official sites is strongly discouraged, since summer turns the dry pine-needles to tinder.

Skiáthos Town

Skiáthos Town, where the ferries dock, looks great from a distance, but as you approach, tourist development becomes very apparent, especially to the east side of the port and around Alexándhrou Papadhiamándi Street, where most of the services, the tackier shops, "English" pubs and eateries are located. But tucked into the alleys on the western, older side of town, it is still possible to find some pockets of charm: older houses, gardens and flowers galore. Skiáthos boasts some good restaurants and nightclubs, and can be fun, in a crowded, boisterous way.

The few sights comprise the **Papadhiamánti museum** (Tues–Sun 9.30am–1pm & 5–8pm; free) – housed in the nineteenth-century home of one of Greece's best-known novelists – and two antique shops, *Archipelago* two blocks in from the waterfront, and the enduring *Galerie Varsakis* (open usual shop hours), on Platía Trión Ierarkhón near the fishing port. The latter has one of the best **folklore displays** in Greece, and many of the older items would do the Benaki Museum proud; the proprietor neither expects, nor wants, to sell the more expensive of these, which include antique textiles, handicrafts and jewellery.

Arrival, transport and other facilities

Buses and **taxis** ply from the area around the **ferry harbour**. To Koukounariés, the bus is the cheapest option (280dr); it runs at least hourly in summer (every fifteen minutes at peak times), the last bus returning at 3am. Sharing a taxi is another option.

A large number of competing **rental outlets** in town, most on the front behind the ferry harbour, offer bicycles, mopeds, motorbikes, cars and motorboats. The lowest priced, small cars go for around 12,000dr a day, motorboats for 15,000dr a day; fuel and insurance are extra. Several travel agents organize "round the island" **mule trips** (5200dr a day), and there's **horse riding** at the *Pinewood Riding Club* (no phone) at Koukounariés. Most other facilities are on Alexándhrou Papadhiamándi, including the **OTE**, **post office**, **banks** and the Mare Nostrum travel agency, which will change your travellers' cheques without a commission.

Accommodation

Much of the island's accommodation is in Skiáthos Town. The few reasonably priced **hotels** or **pensions** are heavily booked in season, though you can usually find a room, albeit slightly more expensively than on most islands. At other times, supply exceeds demand and you can find very cheap **rooms** with a little bargaining. Try for locations in the older quarters to the west. There is no official accommodation bureau but there are several tourist agencies; lodgings in the flatlands to the north as they tend to be noisy. For an honest and helpful approach, try the *Mare Nostrum* at Papadhiamándi 21 (☎0427/21 463/4). Another option is Adonis Stamelos's rooms just outside town at Megáli Ammos (☎0427/22 962; ④). Good, small hotels include the *Bourtzi* (☎0427/22 694; ⑤) and *Pothos* (☎0427/21 304; ⑥), both immaculate with delightful gardens, and the *Orza Pension* (☎0427/22 430; ⑤), a remodelled house overlooking the sea on the west side of the port. Other fine options are the *Alkyon Hotel*, on the seafront at the commercial port end (☎0427/22 981; ⑤), or the *Meltemi Hotel*, on the front near the taxi rank (☎0427/22 493; ⑥).

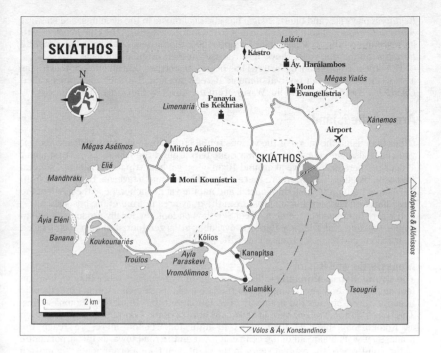

▽ *Vólos & Áy. Konstandínos*

The island has four official **campsites** – at Koliós, Koukounariés, Asélinos and Xanémos beach. Koliós is by far the best, but Koukounariés and Asélinos are fairly decent too. Xanémos beach is 3km northeast of Skiáthos Town, right next to the airport runway, and, apart from being within walking distance of the town, has little to recommend it.

Eating, drinking and nightlife

You're spoiled for choice for **eating places**, but nothing is particularly cheap apart from the few burger/*gyros* joints. One of the best of the cheaper tavernas is *Zorba's*, opposite the taxi rank, while *Mesogeia*, above and to the west of Plátia Trión Ierarkhón, has excellent moussaka and home-cooked dishes. The English-run *Lemon Tree Restaurant* behind the National Bank, with its vegetarian food and *tapas*, now has a nearby rival, the *Daskalio Cafe Bar*, to the right of the police station, whose laid-back British owners serve excellent curries. For more elegant dining, head for *Agnantio*, at the start of the road to Evangelístria, for superlative Greek cuisine and views; *The Windmill* at the top of the hill above Áyios Nikólaos, for nouvelle cuisine and views; and *Desperado*, on the east waterfront, for great Mexican food. Back on the west side, above the flat rocks where people sunbathe, *Tarsanas* is a converted boatbuilders' yard with a picturesque veranda – the best place in town for an evening drink as the harbour lights come on.

Nightlife centres on the clubs on or near Polytekhníou. The best places are *Borzoi*, the oldest club on the island, *Stones* and the *Apothiki Music Hall* for Greek music and a good atmosphere, while on the seafront *BBC* pulses till dawn. In the bars in the back streets around Polytekniou you can hear a wider range of music; places like the *Banana* are pop-oriented and popular among British beer drinkers, the old and much loved

Kentavros plays jazz and blues, *Adagio* has classical music in the evenings, and stalwart *Admiral Benbow* belts out vintage Sixties soul. On the east shore, the chic *Remezzo* with its maritime motifs, is a perennial favourite. Skiáthos's new outdoor cinema *Refresh Paradiso*, on the ring road, shows new releases in their original language.

The little offshore Boúrtzi fortress has been transformed into an outdoor theatre for a six-week-long summer **festival** of music (Greek pop and classical) and drama, called *Óneiro tou Kyma* (Dream on the Wave), from the novel by Papadhiamándis.

Around the island

Other than using the buses or the various rental outlets in town (for which see above), you could also get your bearings on a **boat trip** around the island. These cost about 4000dr per person and leave at around 10am. Or try a boat trip to the islet of Tsougriá (opposite Skiáthos Town), where there's a good beach and a taverna. Boats leave from the fishing harbour beyond the Boúrtzi, and not the yacht anchorage to the north of the ferry harbour; east-coast boats leave from the quay area in front of the bus station.

If you're interested in seeing more of Skiáthos on foot, the locally produced guide to **walks** (by Rita and Dietrich Harkort; available in larger tourist shops) has detailed instructions and maps for trails all over the island.

Monasteries and Kástro

The **Evangelístria Monastery** (daily 8am–noon & 4–8pm) is more than an hour on foot out of Skiáthos Town. Founded in the late eighteenth century, it is exceptionally beautiful, even beyond the grandeur of isolation you find in all Greek monasteries. The Greek flag was raised here in 1807, and heroes of the War of Independence such as Kolokotronis pledged their oaths to fight for freedom here. To reach the monastery, walk 500m out of the centre of town on the road towards the airport until, at the point where the asphalt veers to the right, you take a prominently signposted tarmac track that veers left; be careful to stick to the tarmac and not to wander off onto the dirt roads.

Beyond Evangelístria, a mule track continues to the abandoned **Áyios Kharálambos monastery**, from where it's possible to walk across the island to the ruined capital of Kástro (see below) along another dirt road; this takes about two hours. To reach Kástro from Skiáthos Town, it's quicker to take the direct road, though in all it's still a hard five- to six-kilometre uphill slog; the turning is signposted on the road behind town, some distance beyond the turning for Evangelístria. You'll find it much easier if you do the walk in reverse. Just take a round the island kaïki ride and get off at the beach below Kástro. Another option is to ride a motorbike up the hill and then explore on foot.

Just over halfway between Evangelístria and Kástro, a well-used dirt track (signposted) turns left and heads towards the abandoned fifteenth-century monastery of **Panayía tís Kekhriás**, three hours' walk from town. It's said to be the oldest on the island and has a colony of bats inside. It's a beautiful walk (or organized donkey-ride), and there are two pebbly beaches below, one with a welcoming stream that provides a cool shower. Ignoring this excursion, the paved road continues to within a thirty-minute walk of **Kástro** – a spectacular spot, built on a windswept headland. In the past, the entrance was only accessible by a drawbridge, which has been replaced by a flight of steps. The village was built in the sixteenth century, when the people of the island moved here for security from pirate raids. It was abandoned three hundred years later in 1830, following independence from Turkey, when the population moved back to build the modern town on the site of ancient Skiáthos. The ruins are largely overgrown, and only three churches survive intact, the largest still retaining some original frescoes. From outside the gates, a path leads down the rocks to a good pebble **beach**; with a stream running down from the hills and a daytime café (with slightly overpriced food and drinks), it makes a good place to camp. For an apparently inaccessible spot though, it does attract a surprising number of people. All the island excursion boats call here, and even when they've gone, there's little chance of having the ruins or beach to yourself.

Finally, the seventeenth-century **Kounístra monastery**, can be reached by turning right off the paved road that runs up the island from Tróulos, the last beach before Koukounariés, to the beach at Asélinos. It's a very pretty spot, with a beautiful carved icon screen, splendid icons, a grape arbour and a taverna.

The beaches

The real business of Skiáthos is **beaches**. There are reputed to be more than sixty of them, but that's hardly enough to soak up the numbers of summer visitors: at the height of the season, the local population of five thousand can be swamped by up to fifty thousand visitors. The beaches on the northeast coast aren't easily accessible unless you pay for an excursion kaïki: reaching them on foot requires treks more arduous than those described above. The bus, though, runs along the entire south coast, and from strategic points along the way you can easily reach a good number of beaches. The prevailing summer *meltémi* wind blows from the north, so the beaches on the south coast are usually better protected. Most of the popular beaches have at least a drinks/snacks stall; those at Vromólimnos, Asélinos and Troúlos have proper tavernas.

The beaches before the **Kalamáki peninsula** (where English and rich Greeks have their villas) are unexciting, but on the promontory itself are the highly-rated **Ayía Paraskeví** and **Vromólimnos beaches**, flanked by the campsite and Kanapítsa hamlet; Vromólimnos offers windsurfing and waterskiing. For scuba enthusiasts, there is the *Dolphin Diving Centre* (☎0427/22 520) at the *Nostos* hotel, on the eastern side of the Kalamáki peninsula.

Just before Troúlos you can turn right up a paved road, which runs 4km north to **Mégas Asélinos**, a very good beach with a campsite and a reasonable taverna. A daily bus and excursion boats stop here, so it's crowded in season. A fork in the paved road leads to Kounístra monastery (see above) and continues to **Mikrós Asélinos**, just east of its larger neighbour and somewhat quieter.

The bus only goes as far as **KOUKOUNARIÉS**, a busy resort, though the three beaches are excellent if you don't mind the crowds. There's a majestic sandy bay of clear, gradually deepening water, backed by acres of pines, which despite its popularity it merits at least one visit if only to assess the claim that it's the best beach in Greece. The road runs behind a small lake at the back of the pine trees, and features a string of **hotels, rooms** and **restaurants**, as well as a good campsite. Here, the *Strofilia* apartments which sleep four (☎0427/49 251; ⑥) are particularly nicely furnished. Jet-skis, motorboats, windsurfing and waterskiing are all available off the beach.

Banana Beach (also known as Krassá), the third cove on the far side of Poúnda headland, is the trendiest of the island's nudist beaches. For the less adventurous, the turning for **Ayía Eléni**, 1km from the road, is a pleasant beach with a drinks kiosk. Further north, **Mandhráki** and **Eliá** beaches have similar facilities, and are accessible by bus.

The famed **Lalária beach**, on the northern stretch of coast, can be reached by "taxi-boats" from the town. Covered with smooth white stones, it's beautiful, with steep cliffs rising behind it; the swimming is excellent, but beware of the undertow. The island's three natural grottos – Skotiní, Glazía and Khalkiní – are nearby, and are included in many of the "round-the-island" trips. Southwest of Kástro are the greyish sands of **Mégas Yialós**, one of the less crowded beaches, and **Xánemos**, another nudist beach; both suffer from airport noise.

The only real way to get away from the crowds is to persuade a boat owner to take you out to one of Skiáthos' **islets**. Tsougriá, in particular, has three beaches, with a taverna on the main one.

Skópelos

Bigger, more rugged and better cultivated than Skiáthos, **Skópelos** is almost as busy, but its concessions to tourism are lower key and in better taste than in Skiáthos. Most of the larger beaches have sunbeds, umbrellas and some watersports, but smaller, secluded coves do exist. Inland, it is a well-watered place, growing olives, plums, pears and almonds. **Glóssa** and **Skópelos**, its two main towns, are also among the prettiest in the Sporades, clambering uphill along paved steps, their houses distinguished by attractive wooden balconies and grey slate roofs. A number of **nationalities** have occupied the island at various stages of its history, among them the Romans, Persians, Venetians, French and, of course, the Turks. The Turkish admiral, Barbarossa (Redbeard), had the entire population of the island slaughtered in the sixteenth century.

Loutráki, Glóssa and the west

Most boats call at both ends of Skópelos, stopping first at the small port of **LOUTRÁKI** with its narrow pebble beach, small hotels and rooms for rent. The village has been spoiled a little by development at either end, but it's not a bad place to stay if you're after peace and quiet; try *O Stelios* (④), a simple pension next to the *Flisvos* taverna, the *Pension Valentina* (☎0424/33 694; ④), or the *Avra* (☎0424/33 550; ⑤). Though most of the quayside tavernas don't offer value for money, there are exceptions: the café/shop in the platía by the harbour is shaded by beautiful chestnut trees and sells a highly recommended, home-made retsina; the *Flisvos* is a friendly place with decent pasta dishes, and the small ouzeri is good.

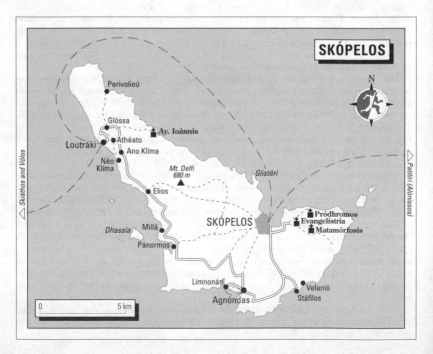

High above Loutráki, **GLÓSSA** would be perhaps a preferable base if it had more places to stay. It is a sizeable and quite beautiful, totally Greek town, with several kafenía, a taverna and a few rooms to let, some of which are hot and musty, with erratic water pressure. *Kostas and Nina's* place (☎0424/33 686; ②) has simple, clean rooms, some with a view; they also rent out studios longer term, or you could stay at the *Selinounda apartments* (☎0424/33 570; ④) on the road between Loutráki and Glóssa. There's one taverna, *To Agnandi*, which is a lively and authentic place to eat, and full most evenings. Incidentally, it's a good idea to accept offers of a taxi ride up to Glóssa from Loutráki; it's a stiff walk up even if you know the path short cuts, and taxi drivers will know if there are any vacancies. If it's really high season, though, and even Glóssa is packed, two nearby villages, Athéato and Paleó Klíma have rooms, while Élios on the coast below has two big hotels, bungalows and rooms.

Ninety minutes' walk from Glóssa, up to the north coast, will bring you to a **beach** the locals call **Perivolioú**. The walk itself is worthwhile, passing a **monastery** next to a stone cairn containing masses of human bones and skulls. There's also a huge hollow oak tree here, in the heart of which is a small tank of drinking water. The beach, when you get there, is nothing out of the ordinary, but there's spring water for drinking and a cave for shade.

East of Glóssa, a dirt road leads to the splendidly sited monastery of **Áyios Ioánnis Kastrí**, perched on the top of a rock high above a small sandy cove where you can swim. A new unsightly house nearby has spoiled the isolation somewhat, but the walk from Glóssa (again, about ninety minutes) is beautiful and peaceful, with hawks and nightingales for company.

Skópelos Town

If you stay on the ferry beyond Loutráki – probably the best plan – you reach **SKÓPELOS TOWN**, sloping down one corner of a huge, almost circular bay. The best way to arrive is by sea, with the town revealed slowly as the boat rounds the final headland. Though more and more people seem to have discovered Skópelos Town, the locals are making a tremendous effort to keep it from going the way of Skiáthos. The harbour area is practically wall-to-wall tavernas and cafés, but the shops and eateries in the back alleys tend to be imaginative and tasteful, with wooden, hand-painted name signs; the two real eyesores date from the junta years. Spread below the oddly whitewashed ruins of a Venetian **Kástro**, are an enormous number of churches – 123 reputedly – though some are small enough to be mistaken for houses and most are locked except for their annual festival day. Other sights include a **folklore museum** and photography exhibitions in summer.

Outside town, perched on the slopes opposite the quay, are two convents: **Evangelístria** (daily 8am–1pm & 4–7pm), which is within view of the town, and **Pródhromos** (daily 8am–1pm & 5–8pm). The monastery of **Metamórfosis**, also on this promontory, was abandoned in 1980 but is now being restored by the monks and is open to visitors. Access is simplest by following an old road behind the line of hotels along the bay to Evangelístria (an hour's walk). From there it's an extra half hour's scramble over mule tracks to Pródhromos, the remotest and most beautiful of the three. Ignore the new road that goes part way – it's longer, and misses most of the beauty of the walk.

Practicalities

The **ferry quay** is at the western end of a long promenade, lined with an array of boutiques, bars, stores and restaurants. To get to the **bus station**, turn left where the quay meets the main road, and follow the sea until you pass the children's swings and the second períptero; at the point where the road divides around a car park. Opposite the bus station entrance, a short road leads into a maze of lanes and signposts to the **post office**. There are banks about 50m from the quay.

In the main body of the town there are dozens of **rooms** for rent. Alternatively, there are three pleasant small hotels: *Andromache* (inquire at Madro Travel ☎0424/22 145; ④), in a quiet old house near the post office; relaxed and casual *Kyr Sotos* (☎0424/22 549; ④) also near the post office; and the clean, if basic *Lina Guest House* on the front (☎0424/22 637; ④). For larger, more **expensive hotels** higher up from the port, you're unlikely to find a space without having booked through a tour operator, but if you fancy the likes of the cosy *Elli* (☎0424/22 943; ⑤) on the east side of town, the modern *Aperitton* (☎0424/22 256; ⑥) on the ring road above the town, or the neo-rustic *Dionysos* (☎0424/23 210; ⑥), also on the ring road – each with a pool – ask about vacancies at Madro Travel (see above) on the quay; they're also the local Flying Dolphin agents.

There's a wide variety of **places to eat**, ranging from the acceptable to the truly excellent. Those at the near end of the harbour, like *Angelos-Ta Kymata*, *Molos* and *Klimataria*, all offer decent meals, while *Spyros* in the middle has been a reliable favourite for years. *To Aktaion* is also a good bet, with exceptionally pleasant staff and large, delicious and reasonably priced portions. Two *souvláki* places, both named *O Platanos*, compete for the distinction of having the best *yíros*. It's also worth heading a couple of kilometres towards Stáfilos to the *Terpsis* taverna for their stuffed-chicken speciality. And for a gourmet treat, the *Perivoli* is the place; you must make a reservation. It is located near "Souvlaki Square" – above the waterfront to the east of town.

Nightlife in Skópelos is on the increase, but is more of the late-night bar than the nightclub variety. That said, *Labikos*, *Kirki*, *Ano Kato* and *Kounos* on the back streets behind the waterfront, are popular in season, The *bouzouki* joint *Meintani* is housed in an old olive press near Souvlaki Square, while the *Skopelitissa* and *Anatoli* on top of the Kástro play Greek music till the early hours. Among the bars, look out for *Vengera*, in a restored house that compares favourably with the town's folk art museum.

Around the rest of the island

Buses cover the island's one paved road between Skópelos Town and Loutráki via Glóssa (around 6 times daily 7am–10.30pm), stopping at the paths to all the main beaches and villages. **Stáfylos**, 4km south of town, is the closest beach, though rather small and rocky. It's getting increasingly crowded, but the *Terpsis* taverna, which rents **rooms**, is a very pleasant spot shaded by a vast pine tree.

There's a very prominent "No Camping" sign at Stáfilos, but if you walk five minutes around the coast north to **Velanió**, there's spring water and a campsite near the beach. Here the pines and surf always draw a small, summer (often nudist) community.

Further around the coast to the west, the tiny horseshoe-shaped harbour of **AGNÓNDAS** (with its fish tavernas and rooms) is the start of a fifteen-minute path (2km by road) or half-hourly kaïkia trip to **LIMONÁRI**, 100m of fine sand set in a closed, rocky bay.

PÁNORMOS is very much a full-blown, commercial resort, with rooms, tavernas, a campsite, yacht anchorage and watersports. The beach here is gravelly and steeply shelving, but there are small secluded bays close by. The thirty-room *Panormos Beach Hotel* (☎0424/22 711; ⑤) has a beautiful garden, fine views, and is lovingly looked after; beyond it the *Adrina Beach* (☎0424/23 373; ⑤) is one of the most attractive and most expensive hotels, in the Sporades. Slightly further on at **MILIÁ**, there is a tremendous, 1500m sweep of tiny pebbles beneath a bank of pines, facing the islet of Dhassiá. There's one taverna and the *Kefalonitis Studios* (☎0424/23 998; ④) in this languid setting; nudist swimming is possible at a lovely five-hundred-metre-long beach a little way north. The shore beyond is indented with many tiny coves, ranging from individual- to family-size.

Further north, **ÉLIOS**, 9km short of Glóssa, is a medium-sized, fairly new resort settled by residents of the earthquake-damaged villages above it, with nothing special to offer besides a pleasant beach. Beyond here, the refurbished village of Paleó Klíma marks the start of a beautiful forty-minute **trail** to Glóssa, via the empty hamlet of Áyii Anáryiri and the oldest village on the island, **Athéato**.

West of Skópelos Town, various jeep tracks and old paths wind through olive and plum groves toward **Mount Dhélfi** and the Vathiá forest, or skirt the base of the mountain northeast to Revíthi hill with its fountains and churches, and the site of **Karyá**, with its *sendoúkia*: ancient rock-cut tombs which may be early Christian. To the northwest of Skópelos Town, **Glystéri** is a small pebble beach with no shade, whose taverna is much frequented by locals on Sundays. A fork off the Glýstéri and Mount Dhélfi tracks can – in theory – be followed across the island to Pánormos within ninety minutes; it's a pleasant walk though the route isn't always obvious.

Alónissos and some minor islets

The most remote of the Sporades, **Alónissos** is also, at first sight, the least attractive. It has an unfortunate recent history. The vineyards were wiped out by disease in 1950 and the Khóra was damaged by an earthquake in 1965. Although its houses were mostly repairable, lack of water combined with corruption and the social control policies of

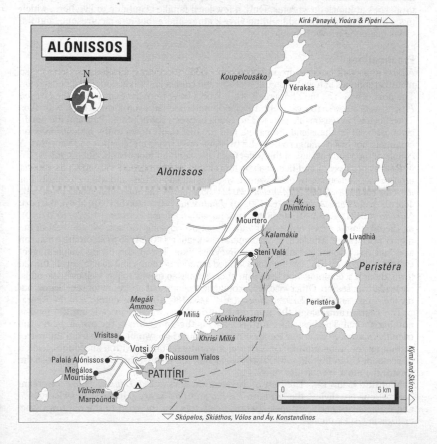

the new junta were instrumental in the transfer of virtually the entire population down to the previously unimportant anchorage of Patitíri. The result is a little soulless, but what charm may be lacking in the built environment on the coast is made up for by the hospitality of the islanders.

Patitíri and the old town

PATITÍRI is not a good introduction to the island, but it's trying hard to rectify that. The port, a pretty cove flanked by pine trees, is marred by the rows of flat-roofed concrete buildings rising up behind it. Nevertheless, the line of near-identical bars and restaurants that run along the waterfront is not unappealling. Alónissos attracts fewer visitors than Skíathos or Skópelos; most of those who do come stay in Patitíri, and from mid-July to the end of August it can get very crowded. It's easy, though, to pick up connections here for beaches and the old town, and there are several good hotels to choose from.

PALEÁ ALÓNISSOS is a fine but steep fifty-minute walk via a donkey track – signposted on the left just outside Patitíri. Alternatively, there's a frequent bus service in the mornings and afternoons. Although some houses are still derelict, much of the village has been painstakingly restored, mainly by the English and Germans who bought the properties at knock-down rates. Only a few local families continue to live here, which gives the village a rather odd and un-Greek atmosphere, but it is picturesque, and the views make the trip worthwhile.

Practicalities

All the important facilities are in Patitíri; the **OTE** (becoming obsolete as there are so many cardphones in town) is on the seafront and **buses** and **taxis** congregate next door. The **post office** is on the Khóra road, while kaïkia leave from the quay beside the *Pension Flisvos* (see below). You can rent a moped, motorbike an even a car (check with Ikos Travel below) at reasonable prices. The roads between Patitíri, Stení Vála and the northernmost point on the island are paved, and the dirt roads down to the beaches in good condition: not half as dangerous as the twisting, busy roads on Skíathos and Skópelos. A couple of the rental places on the waterfront also rent out motorboats and dinghies.

Rooms are easy to find here, as you'll probably be approached with offers as you get off the ferry, sometimes by older women wearing traditional blue and white costumes. For low-cost rooms try *Eleni Athanasiou* (☎0424/65 240; ③), the *Ioulieta* pension (☎0424/65 463; ④), and *Pantheon* (☎0424/65 139; ④). *Liadromia* (☎0424/65 521; ④), above the port; *Niirides* (☎0424/65 643; ⑤), studio apartments with pool; and *Paradise* (☎0424/65 160; ④), on the promontory east of the port with a pool overlooking the sea, are the best in the higher price range. The local room-owners' association (☎0424/65 577), on the front, can also find you a room in Patitíri or nearby Vótsi. Ikos Travel, the Flying Dolphin agent (☎0424/65 320), can do bookings for a limited number of rooms and apartments in the old town, though accommodation here is in short supply so expect to pay well over the odds, particularly in season. Otherwise, ask around; few people put up "room for rent" signs, but try the simple and clean *Fadasia House* (☎0424/65 186; ④), at the entrance to the Khóra.

The **restaurants** along the front of Patitíri are reasonably priced, but the food is nothing special. The best place for breakfast is the *To Korali*; in the evenings, try the friendly *Pension Flisvos*. For the best meal in Patitíri go two blocks up from the petrol station on the waterfront to *To Kamaki*, a wonderful ouzerí with a amazing selection of seafood. Up in the old town, *Astrofengia* has the tastiest food, and *Paraport* at the Kástro the most spectacular views.

Nightlife is low key. The best of the seafront bars is *Pub Dennis*, whose ice-cream concoctions are divine, though both *En Plo* and *La Vie* are popular. Club-wise, *Borio* and *Enigma* are fairly European, while *Rembetika*, on the road to the old town, specializes in Greek music.

The island's beaches

Alónissos has some of the cleanest water in the Aegean, but it's lacking in sand beaches. There's only one really sandy beach on the island (Výthizma), the rest varying from rough to fine pebbles. There's no bus, but kaïkia run half-hourly from Patitíri north to Khrissí Miliá, Kokkinókastro, Steni Vála, Kalamákia and Áyios Dhimítrios, and south around the coast to Marpoúnda, Výthizma and Megálos Mourtiás. Kaïkia also sail occasionally to Livádhia and Peristéra islet.

At Patitíri there's decent swimming from the rocks around the promontory to the north; pick your way along a hewn-out path past the hotels and you're there (ladder provided). To the north, above the headlands, Patitíri merges into two adjoining settlements, **Roussoúm Yialós** and **Vótsi**. For better beaches, you'll have to get in a boat or on a bike.

Khryssí Miliá, the first good beach, has pine trees down to the sand and a taverna; there are a couple of new hotels on the hillside above, and it can get crowded in summer. At **Kokkinókastro**, over the hill to the north, excavations have revealed the site of ancient Íkos and evidence of the oldest known prehistoric habitation in the Aegean. There's nothing much to see, but it's a beautiful spot with a good red pebble beach, and, in July and August, a daytime bar.

THE MEDITERRANEAN MONK SEAL

The **Mediterranean monk seal** has the dubious distinction of being the European mammal most in danger of extinction. Fewer than eight hundred survive worldwide, the majority around the Portuguese Atlantic island of Madeira. A large colony off the coast of the West African state of Mauritania was decimated early in 1997: an estimated two hundred seals died, possibly poisoned by algae. Small numbers survive in the Ionian and Aegean seas; the largest population here, of around thirty seals, lives around the deserted islands north of Alónissos.

Monk seals can travel up to 200km a day in search of food, but they usually return to the same places to rear their **pups**. They have one pup every two years, and the small population is very vulnerable to disturbance. Originally, the pups would have been reared on sandy beaches, but with increasing disturbance by man, they have retreated to isolated sea caves, particularly around the coast of the remote islet of Pipéri.

Unfortunately, the seals compete with fishermen for limited stocks of fish, and, in the overfished Aegean, often destroy nets full of fish. Until recently it was common for seals to be killed by fishermen. This occasionally still happens, but in an attempt to protect the seals, the seas around the northern Sporades have been declared a **marine wildlife reserve**: fishing is restricted in the area north of Alónissos and prohibited within 5km of Pipéri. On Alónissos, the conservation effort and reserve have won a great deal of local support, mainly through the efforts of the Hellenic Society for the Protection of the Monk Seal (HSPMS), based at Steni Vála. The measures have won particular support from local fishermen, as tighter restrictions on larger, industrial-scale fishing boats from other parts of Greece should help preserve fish stocks, and benefit the fishermen financially.

Despite this, the government has made no serious efforts to enforce the restrictions, and boats from outside the area continue to fish around Pipéri. There are also government plans to reduce the prohibited area around Pipéri to 500m. On a more positive note, the HSPMS, in collaboration with the Pieterburen Seal Creche in Holland, has reared several abandoned seal pups, all of which have been successfully released in the seas north of Alónissos.

For the moment, your chances of actually seeing a seal are remote, unless you plan to spend a few weeks on a boat in the area. It's recommended that you shouldn't visit Pipéri or approach sea caves on other islands which might be used by seals, or try to persuade boat owners to do so.

STENÍ VÁLA, opposite the island of Peristéra, a haven for the yachts and flotillas that comb the Sporades, has almost become a proper village, with two shops, several houses, a bar, rooms and four tavernas, one of which stays open more or less throughout the year. There's a campsite (☎0424/65 258) in an olive grove by the harbour, a long pebble beach — Glýfa, where boats are repaired — and some stony beaches within reasonable walking distance in either direction. KALAMÁKIA, to the north, also has a couple of tavernas, and a few rooms.

If you want real solitude, Áyios Dhimítrios, Megaliámmos, and Yérakas (an old shepherds' village at the northernmost point) are possibilities. However, before committing yourself to a Robinson Crusoe existence, take one of the round-the-island trips available, and return the next day with enough food for your stay: there are no stores outside the port and Stení Vála. In the opposite direction from Patitíri, Marpoúnda features a large hotel and bungalow complex and a rather small beach. It's better to turn left after the campsite towards Megálos Mourtiás, a pebble beach with several tavernas linked by dirt track with Palaiá Alónissos, 200m above. Výthizma, the lovely beach just before Megálos Mourtiás, can only be reached by boat, the path here having been washed out. Further north, visible from Palaiá Alónissos, Vrisítsa is tucked into its own finger-like inlet. There's sand and a taverna, but little else.

Beyond Alónissos: some minor islets

Northeast of Alónissos, half-a-dozen tiny islets speckle the Aegean. Virtually none of these has any permanent population, or a ferry service, and the only way you can reach them – at least Peristéra, Kyrá Panayiá and Yioúra – is by excursion kaïki (ask at Ikos Travel), weather permitting. No boats are allowed to take you to the other, more remote islets, as they are protected areas within the Sporades National Marine Park. But though it is possible to be left for a night or more on any of the closer islands, when acting out your desert-island fantasies, be sure to bring more supplies than you need: if the weather worsens you'll be marooned until such time as small craft can reach you.

Peristéra is the closest islet to Alónissos, to which it was once actually joined, but subsidence (a common phenomenon in the area) created the narrow straits between the two. It is graced with some sandy beaches and there is rarely anyone around, though some Alónissans do come over for short periods to tend the olive groves, and in season there are regular evening "barbecue boats" from the main island. As on Alónissos, a few unofficial campers are tolerated, but there is only one spot, known locally as "Barbecue Bay", where campfires are allowed.

Kyrá Panayiá (also known as Pelagós) is the next islet out and is equally fertile. It's owned by the Meyístis Láuras monastery of Mount Áthos and there are two monasteries here, one still inhabited. Boats call at a beach on the south shore, one of many such sandy stretches and coves around the island. There's no permanent population other than the wild goats.

Nearby Yioúra boasts a stalactite cave reputed to be that of Polyphemus, the Cyclops who imprisoned Odysseus, but you won't be able to check its credentials. No one is allowed within 500m of the island, since, like Pipéri, it lies inside the restricted zone of the Marine Park.

Pipéri, near Yioúra, is a sea-bird and monk-seal refuge, and permission from a ministry of the environment representative (in Alónissos) is required for visits by specialists; non-scientists are not allowed. Tiny, northernmost Psathoúra is dominated by its powerful modern lighthouse, although here, as around many of these islands, there's a submerged ancient town, brought low by the endemic subsidence. Roughly halfway between Alónissos and Skýros, green Skántzoura, with a single empty monastery and a few seasonal shepherds, is a smaller version of Kyrá Panayiá.

Skýros

Despite its proximity to Athens, **Skýros** remained a very traditional and idiosyncratic island until recently. Any impetus for change had been neutralized by the lack of economic opportunity (and even secondary schooling), forcing the younger Skyrians to live in Athens and leaving behind a conservative gerontocracy. A high school has at last been provided, and the island has been somewhat "discovered" in the past decade. It's now the haunt of continental Europeans, chic Athenians and British, many of whom check into the "New Age" Skýros Centre, to "rethink the form and direction of their lives".

Meanwhile, Skýros still ranks as one of the most interesting places in the Aegean. It has a long tradition of painted **pottery** and ornate **woodcarving**, and a *salonáki skyriani* (handmade set of chairs) is still considered an appropriate partial dowry for any young Greek woman. A very few old men still wear the vaguely Cretan traditional costume of

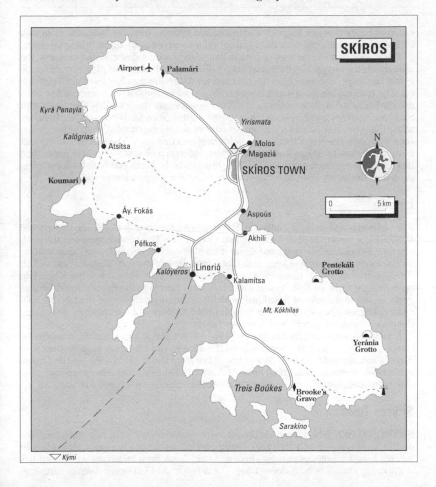

GOAT DANCES AND WILD PONIES

Skýros has some particularly lively, even outrageous festivals. The *Apokriatiká* (pre-Lenten) carnival here is structured around the famous **goat dance**, performed by masked revellers in the village streets. The foremost character in this is the Yéros, a menacing figure concealed by a goatskin mask and weighed down by garlands of sheep bells. Accompanying him are Korélles and Kyriés (who are transvestites, as only the men participate) and Frangi (maskers in "Western" garb). For further details, read Joy Koulentianou's *The Goat Dance of Skyros*, available in Athens and occasionally on the island.

The other big annual event takes place near Magaziá beach on August 15, when children race domesticated members of the **wild pony** herd, native to Skýros and said to be related to the Shetland pony (if so, it must be very distantly). They are thought, perhaps, to be the diminutive horses depicted in the Parthenon frieze, and at any time of the year you might find some of the tame individuals tethered and grazing near Skýros Town.

---

cap, vest, baggy trousers, leggings and *trokhádhia* (Skýrian sandals), but this is dying out. Likewise, old women still wear the favoured yellow scarves and long embroidered skirts.

The theory that Skýros was originally two islands seems doubtful, but certainly the character of the two parts of the island is very different. The north has a greener and more gentle landscape, and away from the port and town it retains much of its original pine forest. The sparsely inhabited south is mountainous, rocky and barren; there are few trees and the landscape is more reminiscent of the Cyclades than the Sporades. Compared with Skiáthos, Skópelos and Alónissos, Skýros isn't a great place for beaches. Most **beaches** along the west coast attract a certain amount of sea-borne rubbish, and, although the scenery is sometimes spectacular, the swimming isn't that good. The beaches on the east coast are all close to Skýros Town, and the best option is probably to stay here rather than heading for somewhere more isolated. The beaches at the north end have been commandeered by the big air force base there, which otherwise keeps a low profile.

Linariá

After crossing a seemingly endless expanse of sea, the boat docks at the tiny port of **LINARIÁ**, a functional place on the island's west coast. Most buildings are in the modern Greek-concrete-box style, and while it's a pleasant place to wile away time waiting for the ferry, there's little to keep you. Once here, try out the *mezedhopolío* next to *Kalí Kardhia* taverna, which has a wide selection of delectable dishes, and the *Kavos* bar, open day and night. In high season, kaïkia ply from Linariá to the Pentekáli and Yeránia **grottos**, and to the islet of **Sarakino**, which has a cave and some of the Skyrian wild ponies. There's a reasonable sandy **beach** called Kalóyeros a few minutes' walk along the main road from Linariá, where you can camp.

A tarmac road connects Linariá to Skýros town, 10km away, and then continues round past the airport to Atsítsa, where the Skyros Centre has a branch; **buses** to **Skýros** and **Magaziá**, on the coast below, leave from the quay. Midway up the Linariá to Skýros-town route, a side road links Ahíli with Kalamítsa. Most other roads are passable by moped, apart from the direct track between Skýros town and Atsítsa.

Skýros Town

SKÝROS TOWN (also known as *Khorió*), with its decidedly Cycladic architecture, sits on the landward side of a high rock rising precipitously from the coast. According to legend, King Lycomedes pushed Theseus to his death from its summit. The town has a workaday atmosphere; it doesn't feel like a resort and isn't especially picturesque.

The older and more intriguing parts of town are higher up, climbing towards the **Kástro**, a mainly Byzantine building, built on the site of the ancient **acropolis**. There are few traces of the acropolis, although remains of the classical city walls survive below on the seaward side of the rock. The kástro is open to visitors; to reach its upper parts you pass through a rather private-looking gateway into the monastery, then through an attractive shaded courtyard and up a whitewashed tunnel. There's little to see at the top, apart from a few churches in various states of ruin, but there are great views over the town and the island, and the climb up takes you through the quieter and more picturesque part of town, with glimpses into traditionally decorated houses. With their gleaming copper pots, porcelain plates and antique embroideries decorating the hearth, these dwellings are a matter of intense pride among the islanders, who are often found seated in their doorways on tiny carved chairs.

At the northern end of town is the striking and splendidly incongruous **Memorial to Rupert Brooke**. It takes the form of a bronze statue of "Immortal Poetry" and its nakedness caused a scandal among the townspeople when it was first erected. Brooke, who visited the south of the island very briefly in April 1915, died shortly after of blood poisoning on a French hospital ship anchored offshore and was buried in an olive grove above the bay of Trís Boúkes. (The site can be reached on foot from Kalamítsa, by kaïki, or, less romantically, by taxi.) Brooke, who became something of a local hero, despite his limited acquaintance with Skýros, was adopted by Kitchener and later Churchill as the paragon of patriotic youth, in the face of his forthright socialist and internationalist views.

Just below the Brooke statue are two museums. The **Archeological Museum** (Tues–Sat 9am–3.30pm, Sun 9.30am–2.30pm; 500dr) has a modest collection of pottery and statues from excavations on the island, and a reconstruction of a traditional Skýros house interior. The privately-run **Faltaits Museum** (daily 10am–1pm & 5.30pm–8pm; free), in a nineteenth-century house built over one of the bastions of the ancient walls, is more interesting, with a collection of domestic items, costumes, embroideries, porcelain and rare books.

Practicalities

The **bus** from Linariá leaves you by the school; just below the main platía; the **OTE**, **post office** and **bank** are all nearby. Skyros Travel (☎0222/91 123 or 91 600), on the main street above the platía, can provide **information** and advice and can find a room or hotel; in high season it's a good idea to telephone them in advance. There are a few **moped** and **motorbike** rental places in the area around the platía.

You'll probably be met off the bus with offers of **rooms**, which it's as well to accept. If you'd like to stay in a traditional Skyrian house, those of *Anna Stergiou* (☎0222/91 657; ③) and *Maria Mavroyiorgi* (☎0222/91 440; ③) are both clean and cosy. Or you could try the pleasant *Nefeli* hotel (☎0222/91 964; ⑥) on the main road before the platía. There's a picturesque **campsite** nearer the beach, at the bottom of the steps below the archeological museum, with basic amenities but a good bar and a friendly management.

The platía and the main street running by it are the centre of village life, with a couple of noisy pubs and a wide choice of kafenía, tavernas and fast-food places. There are few outstanding **places to eat**; most are overpriced, or serve undistinguished food. *O Glaros*, just below the platía, is an exception: many of the local people eat here. It's a very basic taverna with a limited menu, but the owners are friendly and the food is good and reasonably priced. *Maryetis* has the best grilled fish and meat, *Sisyphos* has vegetarian specialities, and the *Sweets Workshop* does some wonderful cakes. For a special occasion, try *Kristina's* restaurant below the taxi rank (signposted); its Australian owner has an imaginative menu which has great desserts.

The town's **nightlife** is mostly bar-based until very late, when the few clubs get going. The most popular **bars** are *Renaissance*, *Kalypso* which plays jazz and blues, and

Rodon, also known for its good music. Later on, *Iy Stasis* is one of the most popular places. The best clubs include the *Skyropoula* and *Mylos*. Some bars also serve good breakfasts; here the favourite is *Anemos*, followed by *Kalypso* which has genuine Danish pastries.

Magaziá and Mólos and nearby beaches

A path leads down past the archeological museum towards the small coastal village of **MAGAZIÁ**, coming out by the official campsite. From Magaziá, an 800-metre-long sandy beach stretches to the adjacent village of **MÓLOS**. In recent years, a sprawl of new development between the road and the beach has more or less joined the two villages together. Despite this, the beach is good, and there are lots of **rooms** down here for the young crowd that uses the beach's watersports and volleyball facilities. The Skyrian style *Katsarelia* at Magaziá (☎0222/91 446; ③), *Stamatis Marmaris* (☎0222/91 672; ③) beyond Mólos, and *Manolis Balotis* (☎0222/91 386; ③) near the campsite, are all excellent choices. A more up-market option is the *Paliopyrgos* hotel (☎0222/91 014; ⑤), 200m from the beach with a wonderful view. The beachfront **tavernas** compare favourably with those in town: the *Green Corner* opposite the campsite has delicious, cheap food to make up for its slow service, while the *Koufari* ouzeri near the *Xenia Hotel*, has excellent food for higher prices. At Mólos try the *Maryetis* garden restaurant and the ouzerí at *Balabani's Mill*, both at the end of the beach. It's worth sampling lobster in Skýros: it's a local speciality.

For quieter beaches, take the road past Mólos, or better, try the excellent and undeveloped (unofficial nudist) beach, *Papa tou Houma*, directly below the kástro. The path down to the beach is 150m beyond the *Skyropoula* disco, and isn't obvious from above. However, following the road south of here, the beaches are disappointing until **Aspoús**, which has a couple of tavernas and rooms to rent. Further south, **Akhíli**, had one of the best beaches on the island until the construction of its new marina. Southeast of Akhíli, the coast is rocky and inaccessible, although you can take a kaïki trip down to the bay of **Trís Boúkes**, passing some picturesque sea caves on the way.

Around the rest of the island

In summer, the whimsical bus service visits the more popular beaches. But if you want to branch out on your own, hire a moped. Roads, tracks and footpaths diverge from the main circle road, leading inward and seaward. Among the most interesting places to head for is **Palamári**, the neglected site of an early Bronze-Age settlement and a spectacular beach. Turn right after the road has begun to descend to the airport plain.

For a taste of the wooded interior, a hike on the dirt track from Skýros Town to **ATSÍTSA** is well worth the effort; it takes three to four hours, and is too rough for a moped. Atsítsa is an attractive bay with pine trees down to the sea (tapped by the Skyrian retsina industry), and an increasing number of rooms, in addition to the Skyros Centre buildings. The beach here is rocky and isn't great for swimming, but there are small sandy beaches fifteen and twenty minutes' walk to the north at **Kalógrias** and **Kyrá Panayiá**, though they are nothing out of the ordinary.

Elsewhere in the coniferous north, **Áyios Fokás** and **Péfkos** bays are easiest reached by a turning from the paved road near Linariá, while access from Atsítsa is via a reasonable dirt road. Both are in the process of being discovered by villa companies, but they have few rooms. Though quite primitive, Áyios Fokás has a very basic, excellent taverna; Péfkos has one too (both are only open in high season, as are all the other tavernas away from Lshould Linariá, Skýros Town, Magaziá and Mólos). The bay is beautiful, and the beach reasonable but not that clean – the beaches around Skýros Town are much better for swimming.

As for exploring the great southern mountain of **Kókhylas**, this is best attempted only if you have a four-wheel drive vehicle, as the road is poor. A good road runs south of Kalamítsa to the naval base at Trís Boúkes (where Rupert Brooke is buried), which makes getting to the southern beaches easier. Kalamítsa, just south of Linariá, lacks character, but the *Mouries* taverna between it and Linariá is worth a stop, as is the remote beach half way to Trís Boúkes, which has no facilities.

Évvia (Euboea)

Évvia is the second-largest Greek island (after Crete), and seems more like an extension of the mainland to which it was in fact once joined. At **Khalkídha**, the gateway to the island, the curious old drawbridge has only a forty-metre channel to span, the island reputedly having been split from Attica and Thessaly by a blow from Poseidon's trident (earthquakes and subsidence being the more pedestrian explanations). Besides the new suspension bridge bypassing Khalkídha and linking Évvia to the mainland, there are ferry crossings at no fewer than seven points along its length, and the south of the island is closer to Athens than it is to northern Évvia.

Nevertheless, Évvia *is* an island, in places a very beautiful one. But it has an idiosyncratic history and demography, and an enduringly strange feel that has kept it out of the mainstream of tourism. A marked **Albanian influence** in the south, and scattered Lombard and Venetian watchtowers give it a distinctive flavour. Indeed, the island was the longest-surviving southerly outpost of the Ottoman Turks, who had a keen appreciation of the island's wealth, as did the Venetians and Lombards before them. The last **Ottoman garrison** was not evicted until 1833, hanging on in defiance of the peace settlement that awarded Évvia to the new Greek state. Substantial Turkish communities, renowned for their alleged brutality, remained until 1923.

Economically, Évvia has always been prized. By Greek standards, it's exceptionally **fertile**, producing everything from grain, corn and cotton to kitchen vegetables and livestock. The classical name "Euboea" means "rich in cattle," but nowadays cows are few and far between; its kid and lamb, however, are highly rated, as is the local retsina. Because of the collapse of much of its mining industry, parts of the island are actively seeking foreign tourism. For the moment, however, Greeks predominate, especially in the north around the spa of **Loutrá Edhipsoú**. In July and August, Évvia can seem merely a beach annexe for much of Thessaly and Athens.

In the rolling countryside of the **north**, grain-combines whirl on the sloping haymeadows between olive groves and pine forest. This is the most conventionally scenic part of the island, echoing the beauty of the smaller Sporades. The **northeast coast** is rugged and largely inaccessible, its few sandy beaches surf-pounded and often plagued by flotsam and jetsam; the **southwest** is gentler and more sheltered, though much disfigured by industrial operations. The **centre** of the island, between Khalkídha and the easterly port of Kými, is mountainous and dramatic, while the far **southeast** is mostly dry and very isolated.

Public **transport** consists of seasonal hydrofoils along the protected southwest coast from Khalkídha upwards, and passable bus services along the main roads to Káristos in the southeast, and Loutrá Edhipsoú in the northwest. Otherwise, explorations are best conducted by rented car; any two-wheeler will make little impact on the enormous distances involved.

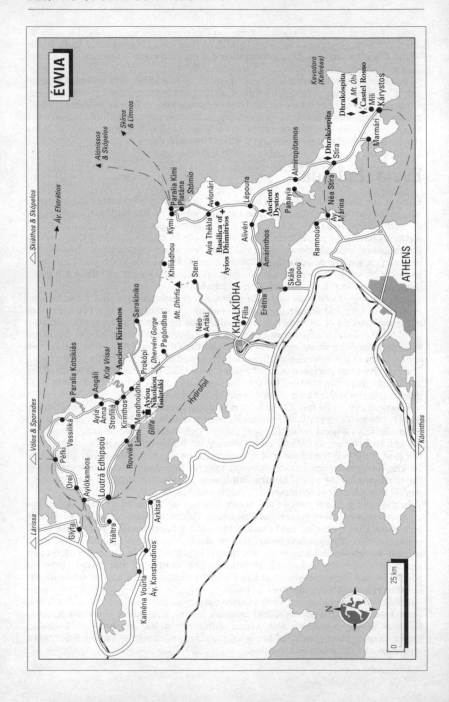

ÉVVIA

Khalkídha

The heavily industrialized island-capital of **KHALKÍDHA** (the ancient *Chalkis*, an appellation still used) is the largest town on Évvia, with a population of 50,000. A shipyard, rail sidings and cement works make it a dire place, apart from the old Ottoman quarter, **Kástro**, south of Venizélou Street, and the area around the Turkish fortress on the mainland. Hardly a trace remains of Khalkídha's once-thriving Jewish community, whose presence here dates back around 2500 years.

The entrance to the kástro – on the right as you head inland from the old Euripos bridge – is marked by the handsome fifteenth-century **mosque**, nominally a museum of Byzantine artefacts, but permanently locked. Beyond lie the remains of Karababa, the seventeenth-century Ottoman fortress, an arcaded Turkish aqueduct and the unique basilican **church of Ayía Paraskeví** (shut except during services). The church is an odd structure, converted by the Crusaders during the fourteenth century into a Gothic cathedral. In the opposite direction, in the new town, an **archeological museum**, Venizélou 13 (daily except Mon 8.30am–3pm; 500dr), has a good display of prehistoric, Hellenic and Roman finds from all over the island. The waterside overlooks the **Évripos**, the narrow channel dividing Évvia from the mainland, whose strange currents have baffled scientists for centuries. You can stand on the bridge that spans the narrowest point and watch the water swirling by like a river. Every few hours the current changes and the "tide" reverses. Aristotle is said to have thrown himself into the waters in despair at his inability to understand what was happening, so if you're puzzled you're in good company; there is still no entirely satisfactory explanation.

Practicalities

For most visitors, though, such activities are strictly time-fillers, with much the best view of the place to be had from the bus, train or hydrofoil on the way out. **Trains** arrive on the mainland-side of the channel, beneath the old fortress; given numerous, quick rail links with Athens, there's no conceivable reason to stay overnight. Most other services of interest lie within sight of the old Évripos bridge. The **hydrofoil** terminal sits just northeast, on the mainland side of the channel. The **bus station** is 400m from the bridge along Kótsou, then 50m right; no schedules are posted, but you should get a connection for any corner of the island as long as you show up by 2pm. The OTE is on Venizélou, near the museum, and cardphones are ubiquitous.

Options for **eating out** range from the restaurants lining the waterfront, where Athenians flock on Sundays to feast on Khalkídha's superior seafood, to a handful of acceptable grills serving adequate lunches in the immediate vicinity of the bus station.

Khalkídha to Kými

The coast road heading east out of Khalkídha is an exceptionally misleading introduction to the interior of Évvia. The industrial zone gives way to nondescript hamlets, which are succeeded between Erétria and Amárinthos by sequestered colonies of Athenian second homes and rather bleak beaches and large hotels frequented by British and German package-tour companies. There are some intriguing **Frankish towers** at Fýlla, worth a detour inland from Vasilikó if you have a car, and some easy connections to Athens, but little else.

Modern **ERÉTRIA** is a rather dreary resort laid out on a grid plan; for non-package travellers its main asset is a well-advertised ferry service across to Skála Oropoú in Attica. The site of **ancient Erétria** is more distinguished, though much of it lies under the town. A few scanty remains are dotted around the town centre, most conspicuously an **agora** and a **Temple of Apollo**, but more interesting are the excavations in the northwest corner, behind the excellent small museum (Tues– Sun 8.30am–3.15pm; 500dr), opened in 1991 in collaboration with the Swiss School of Archeology. Here a **theatre** has been uncovered; steps from the orchestra descend to an underground vault used for sudden entrances and exits. Beyond the theatre are the ruins of a **gymnasium** and a **sanctuary**. The museum guard will be happy to unlock the fourth-century BC **House of Mosaics**, five minutes' walk from the museum.

Just before Alivéri, an enormous modern power plant and a virtually intact medieval castle seem incongruously juxtaposed, and more Fýlla-type towers look down from nearby hills; thereafter, the route heads inland. Beyond Lépoura, where the road branches north and south, the scenery improves drastically. Take the north fork towards Kými, and cross some of the most peaceful countryside in Greece.

Twelve kilometres north of Lépoura, at Kháni Avlonaríou, stands the Romanesque thirteenth- or fourteenth-century **Basilica of Áyios Dhimítrios**, Évvia's largest and finest (ask for the key at the café next door). **AVLONÁRI** proper, 2km east, is dominated by a hill that commands most of the island's centre. At its crown is a huge Lombard or Venetian tower, rearing above the Neoclassical and vernacular houses that tier the lower slopes. This is the first place you'd probably choose to break a journey from Khalkídha, if you have your own vehicle; there's a single taverna below the platía, though no accommodation.

This part of Évvia is particularly well endowed with Byzantine chapels, since Avlonári was an archiepiscopal see from the sixth century onwards. Back on the road to Kými, a left fork just north of Kháni Avlonaríou (the bus goes this way) leads past the hamlet of Ayía Thékla, where a small, shed-like **chapel** of that saint, probably slightly later than Áyios Dhimítrios, hides in a lush vale below the modern church. Inside, enough fresco fragments remain with their large-eyed faces to suggest what has been lost over time. The right fork leads towards the coast and takes you past Oxílithos, with its somewhat more elaborate chapels of **Áyios Nikólaos** and **Ayía Ánna**, both at least a hundred years older than Áyios Dhimítrios.

The road hits the coast at the fine beach of **Stómio** (known also as just Paralía, or "Beach"), some 1500m of sand closing off the mouth of a river, which is deep, swimmable and often cleaner than the sea. To the north and east you glimpse the capes enclosing the broad bay of Kými. Up on the road, there are a couple of cafés and a small pension; most facilities, however, are further round the coast at **PLATÁNA**, where another river is flanked by a line of older houses, many with rooms or flats to rent.

Despite its name, the extremely functional port of **PARALÍA KÝMIS** has no real beach, and is not a particularly congenial place to be stuck overnight waiting for a ferry or hydrofoil to the Sporades or Límnos. The most substantial and traditional **taverna** is *Spanos/To Egeo*, at the south end of the front; there are just two **hotels**, *Coralli* (☎0222/22 212; ④) and *Beis* (☎0222/22 604; ④).

Most travellers get to **KÝMI** (the main ferry port to Skýros) by bus, which takes the inland route via Ayía Thékla. The upper part of town is built on a green ridge overlooking both the sea and Paralía Kými, 4km below. At the bottom of town, on the harbour-bound road, you can visit the **Folklore Museum**, which has an improbably large collection of costumes, household and agricultural implements, and old photos recording the doings of Kýmians both locally and in the USA, where there's a huge community. Among the emigrants was Dr George Papanikolaou, deviser of the "Pap" cervical smear test, and there's a statue honouring him up in the upper-town platía, where you might ask about **rooms**. There are some good **tavernas** like *To Balkoni*, on the main road towards the shore, with its superb view, where you can sample the products of the local vineyards.

To get up into the rugged country west of Kými, you must negotiate jeep tracks through the forest, or return to Khalkídha for the bus service up to **STENÍ**, a large and beautiful village at the foot of Mount Dhírfys. The village has a few cheap psistariés and two **hotels**, the *Dirfys* (☎0228/51 217; ③) and the *Steni* (☎0228/51 221; ③). It's a good area for hiking, most notably up the peaks of Dhírfys and Xirovoúni, and beyond to the isolated beach hamlets of Khiliádhou and Ayía Iríni, though you'll need a specialist hiking guide to do this (see "Books", p.458).

Southeast Évvia

The extension of Évvia southeast of Lépoura, so narrow that you can sometimes glimpse the sea on both sides, has a flavour very distinct from the rest of the island. Often bleak and windswept, it forms a geological unit with neighbouring Ándhros, with shared slates and marble. Ethnically, the south has much in common with that northernmost Cyclade: both were heavily settled by Albanian immigrants from the early fifteenth century onwards, and Arvanítika – a **medieval dialect** of Albanian – was until recently the first language of the remoter villages here. Even non-Arvanítika speakers often betray their ancestry by their startlingly fair colouring and aquiline features. For a place so close to Athens, the south is often surprisingly untouched by modernity; some of the houses have yet to lose their original slate roofs. Many lack electricity, and the few fields on the steep slopes are far more often worked by donkeys and horses than by farm machinery.

Immediately southeast of Lépoura, most maps persist in showing the lake of Dhístos in bright blue. In fact, the lake area has been almost totally drained and reclaimed as rich farmland, much to the detriment of the migratory birds who used to stop off here, and to the annoyance of Greek and foreign environmentalists who would prefer that they still did so. Atop the almost perfectly conical hill in the centre of the flat basin are the sparse fifth-century BC ruins of **ancient Dystos**, and a subsequent medieval citadel, hard to explore because the surroundings are so swampy.

Beyond the Dhístos plain, the main road continues along the mountainous spine of the island to Káristos at the southern end of the paved road system and bus line. If you have your own transport, it's worth stopping off at **STYRA**, above which are a cluster of **Dhrakóspita** (Dragon Houses), signposted at the north edge of the village and reached by track, then trail. They are so named because only mythological beings were thought capable of shifting into place their enormous masonry blocks. Their origins and uses have yet to be definitively established. The most convincing theory suggests that they are sixth-century BC temples built by immigrants or slaves from Asia Minor working in the nearby marble and slate quarries.

The shore annexe of **NÉA STYRA**, 5km downhill from the hill village, is a fairly standard package resort, worth knowing about only for its handy ferry connection to Ayía Marína (which gives access to ancient Rhamnous) on the Attic peninsula. Much the same can be said for **MARMÁRI**, 19km south, except in this case the ferry link is with Rafína. The road between Marmári and Káristos has been messed up considerably in the lengthy process of constructing a superhighway through the island, a project whose end is not in sight.

Kárystos and around

At first sight **KÁRYSTOS** is a rather boring grid (courtesy of nineteenth-century Bavarian town-planners), which ends abruptly to east and west and is studded with modern buildings. King Otho liked the site so much that he contemplated transferring the Greek capital here, and there are still some graceful Neoclassical buildings dating from that period. Kárystos improves with prolonged acquaintance, though you're unlikely to stay for more than a few days. What it can offer is the superb (if often windy) beach of **Psilí Ámmos** to the west, and a lively, genuine working-port atmosphere. Only one plot of fenced-in foundations, in the central bazaar, bears out the town's ancient provenance, and the oldest obvious structure is the fourteenth-century Venetian **Bourtzi** (permanently locked) on the waterfront. This small tower is all that remains of once-extensive fortifications. Every evening the shore road is blocked with a gate at this point to allow an undisturbed promenade by the locals.

PRACTICALITIES

Rafína-based **ferries** and **hydrofoils** also serve Kárystos; **buses** arrive inland, above the central platía and below the National Bank, near a tiny combination grill/ticket office labelled KTEL. This has information on the extremely infrequent (once daily at best) departures to the remote villages of the Kavodóro (Kafiréas) cape to the east. Additional information on the August wine festival and sightseeing in the region is provided by the friendly office in the restored Town Hall.

Finding affordable **accommodation** can be a problem. The best bet in the middle range is the *Karystion* (☎0224/22 391; ④), in the park beyond the Bourtzi on the shore road, followed by the big *Galaxy* (☎0224/22 600; ④) on the west side of the waterfront, and the *Als*, just inland at mid-esplanade (☎0224/22 202; ③), which can be pretty noisy. Another strategy is to follow up signs in restaurant windows advertising **rooms** inland.

By contrast, you're spoilt for choice when **eating out**, as Kárystos must have more restaurants than the rest of Évvia put together. Among the best choices are the *Kavo Doros*, a friendly and reasonable taverna on Párodos Sakhtoúri just behind the front, which serves oven food; *Ta Kalamia*, at the west end of the esplanade by the start of Psilí Ámmos beach is a cheap, filling and popular lunchtime option; while the English-speaking *Ta Ovreika*, in the old Jewish quarter, Sakhtoúri 114, has both Greek and imaginative international cuisine.

AROUND KÁRYSTOS

The obvious excursion from Kárystos is inland towards **Mount Ókhi** (1399m) Évvia's highest peak after Dhírfys and Xirovoúni. **MÝLI**, a fair-sized village around a spring-fed oasis, 3km straight inland, makes a good first stop, with its few tavernas. Otherwise, the medieval castle of **Castel Rosso** beckons above, a twenty-minute climb up from the main church (longer in the frequent, howling gales). Inside the castle is a total ruin, except for an Orthodox **Chapel of Profítis Ilías** built over the Venetians' water cistern, but the sweeping views over the sea and the town make the trip worthwhile.

Behind, the ridges of Ókhi are as lunar and inhospitable as the broad plain around Káristos is fertile. From Míli, it's a three-hour-plus hike up the largely bare slopes, mostly by a path cutting across the new road, strewn with unfinished granite columns, abandoned almost two thousand years ago. The path passes a little-used alpine-club shelter (fed by spring water) and yet another *dhrakóspito*, even more impressive than the three smaller ones at Stýra. Built of enormous schist slabs, seemingly sprouting from the mountain, this one is popularly supposed to be haunted.

From Khalkídha to Límni

The main road due north from Khalkídha crosses a few kilometres of flat farmland and salt marsh on either side of the refugee settlement of Néa Artáki, after which it climbs steeply through forested hills and the **Dhervéni gorge**, gateway to the north of Évvia.

The village of **PROKÓPI** lies beyond the narrows, in a valley defined by the rich and beautiful woods that make it famous. A counterpoint, in the village itself, is the ugly 1960s pilgrimage church of **St John the Russian**, which holds the saint's relics. The "Russian" was actually a Ukrainian soldier, captured by the Turks in the early eighteenth century and taken to Turkey where he died. According to locals, his mummified body began to sponsor miracles, and the saint's relics were brought here by Orthodox Greeks from Cappadocian Prokópi (today Ürgüp) in the 1923 population exchange –

Évvian Prokópi is still referred to by the locals as Ahmétaga, the name of the old Turkish fiefdom here that was bought by an English nobleman, Edward Noel, a cousin of Lord Byron's, right after the War of Independence. His descendants now run summer courses in various crafts, based in the manor house.

Following a shady, stream-fed glen for the 8km north of Prokópi, you suddenly emerge at Mandoúdhi, much the biggest village in the north of the island, though now squarely in the doldrums following the collapse of the local magnesite industry; ignore signs or depictions on certain maps of a beach at Paralía Mandoúdhi, which is nothing more than abandoned quarries and crushing plants. The closest serviceable beach is at **Paralía Kírinthos**, better known as **Krýa Výssi** (take a right-hand turning off the main road, 3km beyond Mandoúdhi). At the coast, a river and an inlet bracket a small beach, with the headland south of the river supporting the extremely sparse remains of **ancient Kirinthos**. The hamlet of Kirinthos, just past Mandoúdhi, has some visitors, owing to the craft school there.

Back on the main road, a fork at Strofiliá, 8km north of Mandoúdhi, offers a choice of routes: continue north to the coastal resorts that curl round the end of the island (see below), east to Pýli and then south to some unspoiled beaches on the way to Cape Sarakíniko, or head west for Límni.

Límni

If you're hunting for a place to stay, **LÍMNI**, on the west coast 19km from Strofiliá, is by far the most practical and attractive base north of Khalkídha. The largely Neoclassical, tile-roofed town, built from the wealth engendered by nineteenth-century shipping prowess, is the most appealing on the island, with serviceable beaches and a famous convent nearby. A small **folk art museum** features pottery, coins and sculpture fragments, as well as local costumes, fabrics and furniture.

There is a regular **hydrofoil** service to Khalkídha and the Sporades, and buses from Khalkídha stop at the north side of the quay. Límni has an **OTE**, a **post office** and **two banks**, all inland just off the main through-road inito town from Strofiliá.

As yet, Límni gets few package tours, and accommodation is usually available in its rooms or hotels, except during August. At the extreme south, quieter, end of the waterfront, the *Límni* (☎0227/31 316; ③) is good value, with singles and doubles; the *Plaza* beside the bus stop, (☎0227/31 235; ②), is a bit more reasonable, but has no singles and gets some noise from nocturnal revels outside. The *Pyrofanis* (☎0227/31 640), an ouzerí beyond the *Plaza*, rents some **rooms** upstairs (⑤) and apartments (④) north of town. The best **place to eat** in terms of setting, menu and popularity is *O Platanos* (under the enormous quayside plane tree). Other local favourites are *Kallitsis* inland from the waterfront, and *Lambros* and *O David* on the way to Katounia beach to the south of town.

Around Límni

There are no recommendable beaches in Límni itself, though if you continue 2.5km northwest from the town you reach the gravel strand of **Kokhýli**, with a basic but leafy **campsite** out on the cape, 500m beyond mid-beach. Here there are some congenial places to stay, most notably *Denis House* (☎0227/31 787; ④) and the more luxurious *Ostria* (☎0227/32 247; ⑥) which has a pool.

ROVVIÉS, some 14km west of Límni, doesn't stand out, but with its medieval tower, rooms, hotels, grid of weekenders' apartments and services, it's the last place of any sort along the scenic coast road to Loutrá Edhipsoú.

The outstanding excursion from Límni is 7km south (under your own steam) to the **Convent of Ayíou Nikoláou Galatáki**, superbly set on the wooded slopes of Mount Kandhíli, overlooking the north Evvian Gulf. To get there, veer up and left at the unsigned fork off the coast road; there's no formal scheme for visiting, but don't show up in the early afternoon or around sunset as the gates will be shut. Though much rebuilt since its original Byzantine foundation atop a Poseidon temple, the convent retains a thirteenth-century tower built to guard against pirates, and a crypt. One of a dozen or so nuns will show you frescoes in the katholikón dating from the principal sixteenth-century renovation. Especially vivid, on the right of the narthex, is the *Entry of the Righteous into Paradise*; the righteous ascend a perilous ladder, being crowned by angels and received by Christ while the wicked miss the rungs and fall into the maw of Leviathian.

Below Ayíou Nikoláou Galatáki, and easily combined with it to make a full half-day outing, are the pebble-and-sand beaches of **Glyfá**, arguably the best on Évvia's south-west-facing coast. There are several in succession, leading up to the very base of Mount Kandhíli, some reachable by paths, the last few only by boat. The shore is remarkably clean, considering the number of summer campers who pitch tents here for weeks on end; a single roadside spring, 2km before the coast, is the only facility in the whole zone.

Northern coastal resorts

Returning to the junction at Strofiliá, take the main road north for 8km to **AYÍA ÁNNA** (locally and universally elided to *Ayiánna*), which has long enjoyed the unofficial status of Évvia's most **folkloric village**, by virtue of traditional costumes worn by the older women, and an assiduous local ethnographer, Dimitris Settas, who died in 1989. The place itself is nothing extraordinary, and most passers-by are interested in the prominently marked turnoff for **Angáli beach**, 5km east. This is billed as the area's best, and it's sandy enough, but like this entire coast it's exposed and can get garbage-strewn, the low hills behind lending little drama. A frontage road, set back 200m or so, is lined by a few kilometres of anonymous villas and apartments, with the "village" at the north end.

Ten kilometres north of Ayía Ánna, a side road heads downhill for 6km, past the village of Kotsikiá, to **Paralía Kotsikiás**. The small cove with its taverna and rooms serves primarily as a fishing-boat anchorage, and its tiny, seaweed-strewn beach is of little interest. **Psaropoúli beach**, 2km below Vassiliká village (13km north of the Kotsikiá turnoff), is more useable in its three-kilometre length, but like Ayía Ánna it is scruffy and shadeless, with a smattering of rooms, self-catering units and tavernas not imparting much sense of community. **Elliniká**, the next signposted beach, lies only 800m below its namesake village inland; it's far smaller than Angáli or Psaropoúli, but cleaner and certainly the most picturesque spot on this coast, with a church-capped islet offshore as a target to swim to. The approach driveway has a very limited number of facilities: a minimarket, one taverna and a few studios.

Beyond Elliniká, the road (and bus line) skirts the northern tip of Évvia to curl southwest towards **PÉFKI**, a seaside resort mobbed with Greeks in summer, which straggles for some two kilometres along a mediocre beach. The best **restaurants**, near the north end of this strip, include *Ouzeri Ta Thalassina* and *Psitopolio O Thomas*, while *Zakharoplastio O Peristeras* proffers decadent desserts. **Accommodation** is the usual Évvian mix of self-catering units and a few seaside hotels such as *Galini* (☎0226/41 208; ④) and *Myrtia* (☎0226/41 202; ④), all resolutely pitched at mainlanders; the **campsite**, *Camping Pefki*, is 2km north of town behind the beach, rather pricey and geared to people with caravans.

The next resort (14km southwest), **OREÍ**, is a low-key fishing village, whose cafés are favoured by those in the know as the best places to watch the sun set. It has a fine statue of a Hellenistic bull, hauled up from the sea in 1965, and is also the last **hydrofoil stop** en route to Vólos and the Sporades. Some 7km further along the coast, **AYIÓKAMBOS** has a frequent ferry connection to Glyfá on the mainland opposite, from where there are buses to Vólos. Ayiókambos is surprisingly pleasant considering its port function, with a patch of beach, two or three tavernas and a few rooms for rent.

The trans-island bus route ends 14km south of Ayiókambos at **LOUTRÁ EDHIP-SOÚ**, which attracts older Greeks (filling more than a hundred creaky hotels and pensions) who come to bathe at the **spas** renowned since antiquity for curing everything from gallstones to depression. There are less regimented **hot springs** at **Yiáltra**, 15km west around the head of Edhipsós bay, where the water boils up on the rocky beach, warming the shallows to comfortable bath temperature. From Loutrá Edhipsoú, the coast road heads southeast to Límni.

travel details

Alkyon Tours (in cooperation with Nomicos ferry lines), and the competing Goutos Lines, provide expensive **conventional ferry** services out of Vólos, Áyios Konstandínos and Kými, with fares almost double those on Cyclades or Dodecanese lines. On the plus side, Alkyon maintain an Athens office (Akadhimías 97; ☎01/38 43 220) for purchase of ferry, Flying Icarus and combined bus-and-ferry tickets. Between April and October, Flying Dolphin and Flying Icarus **hydrofoils** operate between various mainland ports and the Sporades. These are pricier than the ferries but cut journey times virtually in half.

SKIÁTHOS, SKÓPELOS AND ALÓNISSOS

Ferries

Áyios Konstandínos to: Skiáthos (14 weekly; 3hr); Skópelos (10 weekly; 5hr 6 continuing to Alónissos, 6hr).

Kými to: Alónissos (1 weekly; 3hr) and Skópelos (4 weekly; 3hr 30min).

Vólos to: Skiáthos (3–4 daily; 3hr) and Skópelos (3–4 daily; 4hr); Alónissos (at least daily; 5hr; this is the most consistent service out of season, and is always the cheapest).

Flying Dolphins (April–Oct only)

Áyios Konstandínos to: Skiáthos, Glóssa, Skópelos and Alónissos (April, May and early Oct 1–3 daily; June–Sept 3–5 daily).

Néos Marmarás (Khalkidhikí): to: Skiáthos, Skópelos, Alónissos (June–Aug 3 weekly).

Plataniás (Pílion) to: Skiáthos, Skópelos and Alónissos (June–Aug 1 daily).

Thessaloníki to: Skiáthos, Glóssa, Skópelos and Alónissos (June–Aug daily).

Tríkeri (Pílion) to: Vólos (June–mid-Oct daily); Skiáthos (June–mid-Sept 1 daily); Skiáthos, Skópelos and Alónissos (April–Oct daily).

Vólos to: Skiáthos, Glóssa and Skópelos (April, May and Oct 2 daily; June–Sept 4 daily); at least 2 daily (April–Oct) continue from Skópelos to Alónissos.

Flights

Athens to Skiáthos (3 daily; 40min).

SKÝROS

Ferries

Skýros is served by conventional ferry, the *Lykomides*, from Kými (2hr). Services are at least twice daily mid-June to mid-Sept (usually at around noon and 5pm), once daily (5pm) the rest of the year, ☎0222/22 020 for current information. There is a connecting bus service for the afternoon boat, from the Liossíon 260 terminal in Athens (departs 12.30pm).

Flying Dolphins

A weekly **hydrofoil** (June–Aug; Wed) links Skýros with Skiáthos, Skópelos and Alónissos.

Flights

Athens to: Skýros (mid June–Oct; 5 weekly; Nov–June 2 weekly).

ÉVVIA

Buses

Athens (Liossíon 260 terminal) to: Khalkídha (every 30min 7.45am–9pm; 1hr 40min); Kými (4–5 daily; 3hr 40min).

Khalkídha to: Kárystos (1–2 daily; 3hr); Límni (4 daily; 1hr 30min); Loutrá Edhipsoú (4 daily; 3hr); Kými (4 daily; 1 hr 45 min).

Trains

Athens (Laríssis station) to: Khalkídha (18 daily; 1hr 25min).

Ferries

Arkítsa to: Loutrá Edhipsoú (12 daily 6.45am–11pm; 50min).

Ayía Marína: to: Néa Stýra (summer 12–20 daily; 50min); Panayía (summer 3–4 daily; 50min).

Glýfa to: Ayiókambos (8 daily; 30min).

Rafína: to Kárystos (Mon–Thurs 4 daily, Tues–Thurs 2 daily, Fri, Sat & Sun 5 daily; 1hr); Marmári (4 daily; 1hr).

Skála Oropoú to: Erétria (hourly 5am–10pm; 25min).

Flying Dolphins

Khalkídha to: Límni, Loutrá Edhipsoú, Oreí, Skiáthos and Skópelos (May to mid-Oct 5 weekly; usually late afternoon).

Oreí to: Vólos, Skópelos and Alónissos (June to mid-Sept daily); Skiáthos (June to mid-Oct 2 daily).

Ilio Line Hydrofoils

Rafína to: Kárystos (mid-June to late Sept 4 weekly).

Tínos/Mýkonos (Cyclades) to: Kárystos (mid-June to late Sept 3 weekly).

Connecting buses from Athens run to Rafína (every 30min; 1hr 30min), Ayía Marína (5 daily; 1hr 15min) and Skála Oropoú (hourly; duration) all from the Mavromatéon terminal, and to Arkítsa and Glýfa from the Liossíon 260 terminal.

CHAPTER SEVEN

THE IONIAN ISLANDS

T he six **Ionian** islands, shepherding their satellites down the west coast of the mainland, float on the haze of the Adriatic, their green, even lush, silhouettes coming as a shock to those more used to the stark outlines of the Aegean. The fertility is a direct result of the heavy rains which sweep over the archipelago – and especially Corfu – from October to March, so if you visit in the off-season, come prepared.

The islands were the Homeric realm of Odysseus, centred on Ithaca (modern Itháki) and here alone of all modern Greek territory the Ottomans never held sway. After the fall of Byzantium, possession passed to the **Venetians** and the islands became a keystone in that city state's maritime empire from 1386 until its collapse in 1797. Most of the population must have remained immune to the establishment of Italian as the official language and the arrival of Roman Catholicism, but Venetian influence remains evident in the architecture of the island capitals, despite damage from a series of earthquakes.

On Corfu, the Venetian legacy is mixed with that of the **British**, who imposed a military "protectorate" over the Ionian islands at the close of the Napoleonic Wars, before ceding the archipelago to Greece in 1864. There is, however, no question of the islanders' essential Greekness: the poet Dioníssios Solómou, author of the National Anthem, hailed from the Ionians, as did Nikos Mantzelos, who provided the music, and the first Greek president, Ioannis Kapodistrias.

Today, **tourism** is the dominating influence, especially on **Corfu** (Kérkyra), which was one of the first Greek islands established on the package-holiday circuit. Its east coast is one of the few stretches in Greece with development to match the Spanish *costas*, and in summer even its distinguished old capital, Kérkyra Town, wilts beneath the onslaught. However, the island is large enough to retain some of its charms and is perhaps the most scenically beautiful of the group. Parts of **Zákynthos** (Zante) –

ACCOMMODATION PRICE CODES

Throughout the book we've used the following **price codes** to denote the cheapest available room in high season; all are prices for a double room, except for category ①, which represents per person rates. Out of season, rates can drop by up to fifty percent, especially if you are staying for three or more nights. Single rooms, where available, cost around seventy percent of the price of a double.

Rented private rooms on the islands usually fall into the ② or ③ categories, depending on their location and facilities, and the season; a few in the ④ category are more like plush self-catering apartments. They are not generally available from late October through to the beginning of April, when only hotels tend to remain open.

① 1400–2000dr	④ 8000–12,000dr
② 4000–6000dr	⑤ 12,000–16,000dr
③ 6000–8000dr	⑥ 16000dr and upwards

For more accommodation details, see pp.39–41.

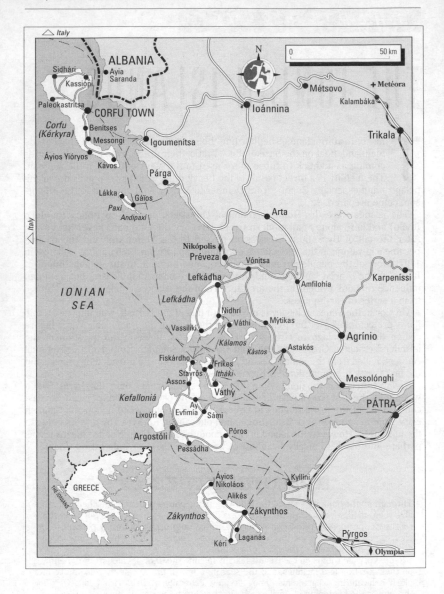

which with Corfu has the Ionians' best beaches – seem to be going along the same tourist path, following the introduction of charter flights from northern Europe, but elsewhere the pace and scale of development is a lot less intense. Little **Páxi** is a bit too tricky to reach and lacks the water to support a large-scale hotel, while **Lefkádha** – which is connected to the mainland by a causeway and "boat bridge" – has, so far at least, quite a low-key straggle of ports and only two major resorts. Perhaps the most

> The islands of **Kýthira** and **Andikýthira**, isolated at the foot of the Peloponnese, are historically part of the Ionian islands. However, at some 200km from the nearest other Ionians, and with no ferry connections to the northerly Ionians, they are most easily reached from **Yíthio** or **Neápoli** and are thus covered in Chapter Two.
> Similarly, the islet of **Kálamos**, Lefkádha's most distant satellite, is inaccessible from the islands and covered therefore in Chapter Four.

rewarding duo for island-hopping are **Kefalloniá** and **Itháki**, the former with a series of "real towns" and a life in large part independent of tourism, the latter, Odysseus's rugged capital, protected by an absence of sand. The Ionian islands' claims to Homeric significance are manifested in the countless bars, restaurants and streets named after characters in the Odyssey including the "nimble-witted" hero himself, Penelope, Nausica, Calypso and Cyclops.

Corfu (Kérkyra)

Between the heel of Italy and the west coast of mainland Greece, green, mountainous **Corfu (Kérkyra)** was one of the first Greek islands to attract mass tourism in the 1960s. Indiscriminate exploitation turned parts into eyesores, but much is still uninhabited olive groves, mountain or woodland. The majority of package holidays are based in the most developed resorts, but unspoiled terrain is often only a few minutes' walk away.

Corfu is thought to have been the model for Prospero and Miranda's place of exile in Shakespeare's *The Tempest*, and was certainly known to writers like Spenser, Milton and, – more recently – Lear, Miller, and Gerald and Lawrence Durrell. Lawrence Durrell's *Prospero's Cell* evokes the island's "delectable landscape", still evident in some of the best beaches in the whole archipelago.

Kérkyra Town

The capital, **Kérkyra Town** (or Corfu Town), was renovated for an EU summit in 1994, and is now one of the most elegant island capitals in the whole of Greece. Although many of its finest buildings were destroyed by Nazi bombers in the World War II, its two massive forts, the sixteenth century church of Áyios Spirídonhas, and buildings dating from French and British administrations remain intact. As the island's sole port of entry by ferry or plane, Corfu is packed in summer.

Arrivals, information and services

Ferries from Italy dock at the New Port (Néo Limáni) west of the Néo Froúrio (New Fort); those connecting to the mainland (Igoumenítsa, Párga and Pátra) dock further west on the seafront. The Old Port (Paléo Limáni), east of the New Port, is used for day excursions and ferries to Paxí. There are ferry offices at both ports; ferries to Italy or south towards Pátra become very busy in summer and booking is advisable. The port police (☎0661/32 655) can advise on services.

The **airport** is 2km south of the city centre. There are no airport buses, although local **blue buses** #5 and #6 can be flagged at the junction where the airport approach meets the main road (500m). It's a forty minute walk on flat terrain into town (right at the junction then follow the sea road). **Taxis** charge around 2000dr (but agree the fare in advance) or phone (☎0661/33 811) for a radio cab.

The **tourist office** (Mon–Fri 8am–2pm; ☎0661/37 520) on the corner of Vouleftón and Mantzárou has accommodation and transport details. The **OTE** at is Mantzárou 3

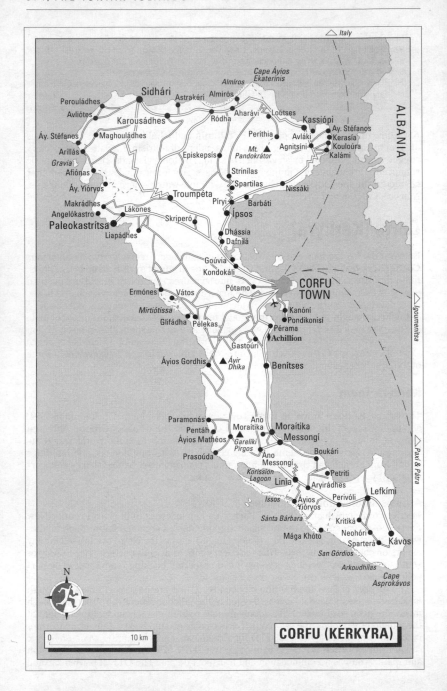

△ *Italy*

ALBANIA

Cape Áyios
Ekaterínis

Almíros

Sidhári

Astrakéri   Almirós

Perouládhes

Avliótes

Karousádhes   Ródha   Aharávi   Loútses

Áy. Stéfanos   Kassiópi
                                                                            Ay. Stéfanos
       Maghouládhes   Períthia   Avláki   Kerasía
Arillás   Agnitsíni   Kouloúra
Gravia   Episkepsís   Mt.   Kalámi
Afiónas   Pandokrátor

Áy. Yióryos   Strinílas

Makrádhes   Spartílas
                        Troumpéta   Nissáki
Angelókastro   Lákones   Píryi
                                                     Barbáti
Paleokastrítsa   Skriperó   **Ípsos**
          Liapádhes
                                      Dhássia
                                      Dafnílá

                           Goúvia
                           Kondokáli

                  Vátos   Pótamo   **CORFU
Ermónes   TOWN**

Mirtiótissa   Kanóni
Glifádha   Pélekas   Pondikonísi
                                         Pérama
                     Gastoúri   **Achíllion**

Áyios Gordhis   ▲ *Áyir
                     Dhíka*   Benítses

Paramonás   Áno
      Pentáti   Moraítika   **Moraítika**
Áyios Mathéos   ▲   **Messongí**
                       *Garelíki
Prasoúda   Pírgos*   Boukári
                              Áno
                            Messongí   Petríti
                   *Korission
                    Lagoon*   Liniá   Aryirádhes   Lefkími
                                             Perivóli
                 Issos   Áyios
                          Yióryos   Kritiká
                   Sánta Bárbara   Neohóri
                         Mága Khóto   Spárterá   **Kávos**
                                 San Górdios
                                   Arkoudhílas
                                            Cape
                                         Asprokávos

△ *Igoumenítsa*

△ *Paxí & Pátra*

N

0   10 km

CORFU (KÉRKYRA)

(daily 6am–midnight; ☎0661/45 699) and the **post office** is on the corner of Alexándhras and Zafiropoúlou (Mon–Fri 7.30am–8pm).

Transport

Corfu's **bus** service radiates from the capital. There are **two** terminals; the island-wide service is based on Avramíou, and the suburban system, which also serves nearby resorts such as Benítses and Ípsos, is based in Platía San Rocco (Platía G. Theotóki). Services stop around 6pm, and are scant on Sundays. Avramíou also serves Athens and Thessaloníki, and sells combined bus/ferry tickets. Major **ferry** lines have franchises on Ethníkis Antistásseos opposite the New Port: Minoan/Strintzis (☎0661/25 000 or 25 332), Anek (☎0661/32 664) and Adriatica (☎0661/38 089).

Cars can also be rented from international agencies at the airport; try Avis, Ethníkis Antistásseos 42 (☎0661/24 404), Budget, Venízelou 22 (☎0661/49 100; airport ☎0661/44 017) or Hertz (☎0661/33 547). Among local companies, Sunrise, Ethníkis Antistásseos 14, in the New Port (☎0661/44 325) rents out cars and **bikes**.

Accommodation

Accommodation in Corfu is busy all year round, and expensive. Room owners meet mainland and international ferries, and taxi drivers will often know of decent rooms. Budget travellers might best head straight for the **campsite** (☎0661/91 202) 2km north at Kondokáli – or, even further out, the superior campsite with cheap bungalows at **Dhássia** (see p.379). Most hotels are in the old town, or on the seafront.

Arcadian, Kapodhistríou 44 (☎0661/37 670). Mid-range hotel in a central setting. Street noise can be a problem. ③.

Astron, Dónzelot 15 (☎0661/39 505). A basic but reliable travellers' favourite for decades. Open year round. ④.

Atlantis, Xenofóndos Stratígou 48 (☎0661/35 560). Large and spacious air-conditioned hotel. Open year round. ③.

Bella Venezia, Zambéli 4 (☎0661/46 500). Smart and very good value: just behind the *Cavalieri*, with all the *Cavalieri*'s comforts, but cheaper. Open year round. ⑤.

Cavalieri, Kapodhistríou 4 (☎0661/39 041 or 39 336). Smart and friendly, with great views and a roof bar open to the public. Open year round. ⑥.

Europa, Yitsiáli 10 (☎0661/39 304). Small family hotel one block back from the Igoumenítsa ferry quay. ④.

Hermes, Markóra 14 (☎0661/39 268). A favourite with budget travellers. Overlooks the noisy market. Open year round. ②.

Kypros, Ayíon Patéron 13 (☎0661/40 675). Basic, but one of the best bets in the town; it's very central, so be prepared for noise. ③.

Olympic, Ioníou Voulís 4 (☎0661/30 532). Big international-style hotel with large and comfortable en-suite rooms. Open year round. ④.

The Town

Corfu Town comprises a number of distinct areas. The **Campiello**, the oldest, sits on the hill above the old port, while the streets running between the Campiello and Velisáriou are what remains of the town's **Jewish Quarter**. These districts form the core of the old town, and their tall, narrow alleys conceal some of Corfu's most beautiful architecture. **Mandoúki**, beyond the Old Port, is the commercial and dormitory area for the port, and is worth exploring as a living quarter of the city, away from the tourism racket. The town's **commercial area** lies inland from the **Spianádha** (Esplanade), roughly between G (Georgíou) Theotóki, Alexandhrás and Kapodhistríou streets, with shops and boutiques around Voulgaréous and G Theotóki and off Platía Theotóki. Tucked behind Platía San Rocco and Odhós Theotóki is the old **morning market** which sells fish and farm produce.

CORFU TOWN (KÉRKYRA)

ACCOMMODATION

1 Arcadian
2 Astron
3 Atlantis
4 Bella Venezia
5 Cavalieri
6 Europa
7 Hermes
8 Kypros
9 Olympic

0   200 m

The most obvious sights are the forts, the **Paleó Froúrio** and **Néo Froúrio**, whose designations (*paleó* – "old", *néo* – "new") are a little misleading, since what you see of the older structure was begun by the Byzantines in the mid-twelfth century, just a hundred years before the Venetians began work on the newer citadel. They have both been modified and damaged by various occupiers and besiegers since, the last contribution being the Neoclassical shrine of **St George**, built by the British in the middle of Paleó Froúrio during the 1840s. Looming above the old port, the Néo Froúrio (daily 9am–9pm; 400dr), is the more interesting of the two. The entrance, at the back of the fort, gives onto cellars, dungeons, and battlements, with excellent views over town and bay; there's a small gallery and café at the summit. The Paleó

Froúrio (daily 9am–9pm; 800dr) is rather dull in comparison but hosts daily son et lumière shows.

Just west of the Paleó Froúrio, the **Listón**, an arcaded street built during the French occupation by the architect of the Rue de Rivoli in Paris, and the green **Spianádha** (Esplanade) it overlooks, are the focus of town life. At the south end of the Spianádha, the **Maitland Rotunda** was built to honour the first British High Commissioner of Corfu and the Ionian islands. The neighbouring statue of Ioannis Kapodistrias celebrates the local hero and statesman (1776–1831) who led the diplomatic efforts for independence and was made Greece's first president in 1827. At the far northern end of the Listón, the nineteenth-century **Palace of SS Michael and George**, a solidly British edifice built as the residence of their High Commissioner (one of the last of whom was the future British Prime Minister William Gladstone), and later used as a palace by the Greek monarchy. The former state rooms house the **Sino-Japanese Museum** (Tues–Sat 8.30am–3pm, Sun 9.30am–2.30pm; 500dr) is a must for aficionados of Oriental culture. Amassed by Corfiot diplomat Gregorios Manos (1850–1929), it includes Noh theatre masks, woodcuts, wood and brass statuettes, samurai weapons, and art works from Thailand, Korea and Tibet. Opened in 1996, the adjoining **Modern Art Museum** (same hours and price) holds a small collection of contemporary Greek art. It's an interesting diversion, as are the gardens and café-bar •secreted behind the palace.

In a nearby back street off Arseníou, five minutes' from the palace, is the **museum** (Mon–Fri 5–8pm; 200dr) dedicated to modern Greece's most famous poet, **Dionissios Solómous**. Born on Zákynthos, Solomos was author of the poem *Hýmnos yiá Élefthería* (*Hymn to Liberty*), which was to become the Greek national anthem. He studied at Corfu's Ionian Academy, and lived in a house on this site for much of his life.

Up a short flight of steps on Arseníou, the **Byzantine Museum** (Tues–Sun 9am–3pm; 200dr) is housed in the restored church of the Panayía Andivouniótissa. It houses sculptures and sections of mosaic floors from Paleópolis and church frescoes. There are also some pre-Christian artefacts, and a collection of icons dating from the fifteenth to nineteenth centuries. Just to the southwest is Corfu's **Cathedral**, packed with icons, including a fine sixteenth-century painting of *St George slaying the dragon* by the Cretan artist Michael Damaskinos.

A block behind the Listón, down Odhós Spirídhonas, is the **church of Áyios Spirídhon**, whose maroon domed campanile dominates the town. Here you will find the silver-encrusted coffin of the island's patron saint, **Spirídhon** – Spiros in the diminutive – after whom about half the male population is named. Four times a year (Palm Sunday and the following Saturday, August 11, and the first Sunday in November), to the accompaniment of much celebration and feasting, the relics are paraded through the streets of Kérkyra. Each of the days commemorates a miraculous deliverance of the island credited to the saint – twice from plague during the seventeenth century, from a famine of the sixteenth century and (a more blessed release than either of those for any Greek) from the Turks in the eighteenth century.

Corfu Town's **Archeological Museum** (Tues–Sun 9am–3pm; 800dr, free on Sun), just south round the coast, is the best in the archipelago. The most impressive exhibit is a massive (17m) gorgon pediment excavated from the Doric temple of Artemis at Paleópolis; this dominates an entire room, the gorgon flanked by panthers and mythical battle scenes. The museum also has fragments of Neolithic weapons and cookware, and coins and pots from the Corinthian era.

Just south of Platía San Rocco and signposted on the corner of Methodíou and Kolokotróni, the **British Cemetery** features some elaborate civic and military memorials. It's a quiet green space away from the madness of San Rocco, and in spring and early summer is alive with dozens of species of orchids and other exotic blooms.

The outskirts

Each of the following sights on the outskirts of the city is easily seen in a morning or afternoon, and best visited from the town rather than outlying resorts.

Around the bay from the Rotunda and Archeological Museum, tucked behind Mon Repos beach, the **Mon Repos** estate (8am–8pm; free) contains the most accessible archeological remains on the island. Thick woodland conceals two **Doric temples**, dedicated to Hera and Artemis. The Neoclassical Mon Repos **villa**, built by British High Commissioner Frederic Adam in 1824 and handed over to Greece in 1864, was the birthplace of Prince Philip and is due to be opened to the public in the near future.

The most famous excursion from Corfu Town is to the islets of **Vlakhérna** and **Pondikoníssi**, 2km south of town. A dedicated bus (#2) leaves San Rocco square every half hour, or it is a pleasant walk of under an hour. Reached by a short causeway, the tiny white convent of Vlakhérna is one of the most photographed images on Corfu. Pondikoníssi ("Mouse Island") can be reached by a short boat trip from the dock (500dr). Tufted with greenery and a small chapel, Vlakhérna is identified in legend with a ship from Odysseus's fleet, petrified by Poseidon in revenge for the blinding of his son Polyphemus, the Homeric echoes somewhat marred by the thronging masses and low flying aircraft from the nearby runway. A quieter destination is **Vido**, the wooded island visible from the old port, reached from there by hourly shuttle kaïki.

Four kilometres further to the south, past the resort sprawl of Peramá, is a rather more bizarre attraction: the **Achillion** (daily 9am–3pm; 700dr), a palace built in a (fortunately) unique blend of Teutonic and Neoclassical styles in 1890 by Elizabeth, Empress of Austria. Henry Miller considered it "the worst piece of gimcrackery" that he'd ever laid eyes on and thought it "would make an excellent museum for surrealistic art". The house and collection are small and, like the gardens, mostly roped off from visitors.

Eating and drinking

Most **restaurants** are around the old town, with some hard-to-find places favoured by locals concealed in the Campiello. Restaurants on main thoroughfares tend to be indifferent, though the *Averof*, in the old port behind Zavitsiánou, is a Corfu institution, offering above-par taverna cuisine. Below the Palace of SS Michael and George, the *Faliráki* is reasonably priced for its setting and has an imaginative menu. The *Orestes*, on Xenophóntos Stratígou in Mandoúki, is probably the best seafood restaurant in town. The *Pizzeria*, on Guildford Street, has a wide range of pizzas with a pleasing choice for vegetarians, as does *Quattro Stagione*, off the north side of N Theotóki. One of the smartest joints in town is the *Rex*, on Zavitsiánou behind the Listón, and no one staying in Corfu Town should miss the *Venetian Well Bistro*, on Platía Kremásti, a tiny square a few alleys to the south of the cathedral.

Nightlife

Corfu Town has plenty to offer in the way of **bars** and nightlife. On the Listón, avoid the mark-ups at the *Magnet* and follow the locals to *Koklia*, *Aegli* or *Olympia*, or drink in one of the hotels: the *Cavalieri* rooftop bar can be heaven at night. For local atmosphere, try *Dirty Dick's*, on the corner of Arseníou and Zavitsiánou, or the expat hangout *Mermaid*, on Agíon Pantón off the Listón, which will give you a different spin on island culture.

Corfu's self-proclaimed **disco** strip lies a few kilometres north of town, en route to Kondokáli. Here, at the (unofficial) *Hard Rock Café*, the *Hippodrome* disco complex (the town's biggest, with its own pool), and the bizarrely decorated *Apokalypsis* and *Coco Flash*, party animals dress up for wild and fairly expensive nights out. In some clubs, women travelling without male partners should beware *kamákia* – slang for

Greek males "spearfishing" for foreign women. Corfu Town's two **cinemas** – the Pallas on G Theotóki and the Orfeus on the corner of Akadimiás and Aspióti – tend to wind business down in high summer, but both often show English-language films.

The northeast and the north coast

The northeast, at least beyond the immediate suburbs, is the most typically Greek part of Corfu – it's mountainous, with a rocky coastline chopped into pebbly bays and coves, above wonderfully clear seas. Green **buses** between Corfu Town and Kassiópi serve all resorts, along with some blue suburban buses to Dhássia and Ípsos.

Corfu Town to Ípsos

The landscape between Corfu Town and Kondokáli is an industrial wasteland, and things don't improve much at **KONDOKÁLI** itself, a small village overrun by holiday developments. The old town consists of a short street with a number of bars and traditional psistariés, the best of which are *Gerekos* and *Takis*, and an international restaurant, *Flags*.

Neighbouring **GOÚVIA** is also Corfu's largest yachting marina. The village boasts a couple of small **hotels**, notably the *Hotel Aspa* (☎0661/91 303; ④), and some **rooms** – try Maria Lignou (☎0661/91 348; ④) or Yorgos Mavronas (☎0661/91 297 or 90 297; ④). There are a number of decent **restaurants**, including *The Captain's Table* and *Aries Taverna*, and a couple of pizzerias, *Bonito* and *Palladium*. The very narrow shingle **beach**, barely five metres wide in parts, shelves into sand; given the sea traffic the water quality is doubtful. Goúvia is the turn-off point for the **Danília Village** "Corfu Experience" (10am–3pm & 6pm–midnight), about 2km inland. It's an earnest attempt to encapsulate Greek village architecture and culture – a slick operation supposed to look like nineteenth-century Corfu, with workshops and a museum, and evening entertainment set around a reproduction village.

Two kilometres beyond Goúvia the coastline begins to improve at **DHÁSSIA** and **DHAFNILÁ**, set in two small wooded bays with pebbly beaches. Two large and expensive **hotels**, the *Dasía Chandris* (☎0661/33 871; ⑤) and *Corfu Chandris* (☎0661/97 100; ⑥), dominate Dhássia, with extensive grounds, pools and beach facilities. The more reasonable *Hotel Amalia* (☎0661/93 523; ⑤) has pleasant en-suite rooms and its own pool and garden. Rooms are scarce, although 3phros Rengls's minimarket has a few (☎0661/90 282; ③). Dhássia does, however, have the best **campsite** on the island, *Dionysus Camping Village* (☎0661/91 417, fax 91 760); tents are pitched under terraced olive trees. *Dionysus* also has simple bungalow huts, a pool, shop, bar and restaurant, and the friendly, multilingual owners offer a ten percent discount to Rough Guide readers.

ÍPSOS, 2km north of Dhássia, can't really be recommended to anyone but hardened bar-hoppers. There isn't room to swing a cat on the thin pebble beach, right beside the busy coast road, and the resort is pretty tacky. Most **accommodation** is pre-booked by package companies, although Ípsos Travel (☎0661/93 661) can offer rooms. *Corfu Camping Ípsos* (☎0661/93 579) has a bar and restaurant, and offers standing tents. Ípsos is also the base for the island's major **diving centre**, *Waterhoppers* (☎0661/93 876). **Eating** on the main drag is dominated by fast food, though a more traditional meal and a quieter setting can be found in the *Akrogiali* and *Asteria* tavernas, by the marina to the south of the strip.

North to Áyios Stéfanos

Ípsos has now engulfed the neighbouring hamlet of Pýryi, which is the main point of access for the villages and routes leading up to **Mount Pandokrátor**; the road, signposted Spartílas, is 200km beyond the junction in Pýryi. A popular base for walkers is the village of **STRINÍLAS**, 16km from Pýryi. Accommodation is basic but easy to come by: the *Elm Tree Taverna*, a long-time favourite with walkers, can direct you to rooms. In summer the main routes are busy, but there are quieter walks taking in the handsome Venetian village of Episkepsís, 5km northwest of Strinílas – anyone interested in walking the Pandokrátor paths is advised to get the **map** of the mountain by island-based cartographer Stephan Jaskulowski.

The coast road beyond Ípsos mounts the slopes of Pandokrátor towards **BARBÁTI**, 4km further on. Here you'll find the best beach on this coast and ample facilities; it's a favourite with families, and much **accommodation** is pre-booked in advance. There are some rooms – *Paradise* (☎0663/91 320; ③) and *Roula Geranou* (☎0663/92 397; ③).

The mountainside becomes steeper and the road higher beyond Barbáti, and the population thins drastically. **NISSÁKI** is a rather spread-out village with a number of coves, the first and last accessible by road, the rest only by track – one dominated by the gigantic, expensive and rather soulless *Nissaki Beach Hotel* (☎0663/91 232; ⑥). There are a couple of shops and a bakery, and a few travel and **accommodation agencies**. The British-owned Falcon Holidays (☎0663/91 318) rents out apartments above the first beach, a tiny, white-pebble cove with a trio of fine tavernas.

The two places no one visiting this coast should miss are Kalámi and neighbouring Kouloúra: the first for its Durrell connection, the latter for its exquisite bay (though neither has a beach worth mentioning). **KALÁMI** is on the way to being spoiled, but the village is still small; you can imagine how it would have been in the year Lawrence Durrell spent here on the eve of World War II. The **White House**, where Durrell wrote *Prospero's Cell*, is now split in two: the ground floor is an excellent taverna; the upper floor is let through CV Travel (see p.5). The owner of the *White House*, Tassos Athineos (☎0663/91 251), has rooms, and Yannis Vlachos (☎ and fax 0663/91 077) has rooms, apartments and studios in the bay, as do Sunshine Travel (☎0663/91 170) and Kalámi Tourism Services (☎0663/91 062, fax 91 369). The **restaurant** at the White House is recommended, as is *Matella's*, the *Kalami Beach Taverna* and *Pepe's*, which is on the beach.

The tiny harbour of **KOULOÚRA** has managed to keep its charm intact, set at the edge of an unspoiled bay with nothing to distract from the pine trees and kaïkia. The fine **taverna** here has to be the most idyllic setting for a meal in the whole of Corfu.

Around the coast to Akharávi

Two kilometres beyond Kouloúra down a shady lane, the large pebble cove of **Kerasiá** shelters the family-run *Kerasia Beach Taverna*. The most attractive resort on this stretch of coast, 3km down a lane from Agnitsíni on the main road, is **ÁYIOS STÉFANOS**. Most **accommodation** here is upmarket, and the village has yet to succumb to any serious development; so far only the *Kokhyli* pizzeria has rooms and apartments (☎0663/81 522). Recommended are the *Garini* and *Kaporelli* **tavernas**, and the *Eucalyptus* over by the village's small beach.

A thirty-minute walk from the coastguard station above Áyios Stéfanos, along a rough track, is the beach of **Avláki**, a pebble bay that provides lively conditions for the **windsurfers** who visit the beach's windsurf club. There are two **tavernas**, the *Barbaro* and *Avlaki*, and some **rooms** a few hundred yards back from the beach – *Mortzoukos* (☎0663/81 196; ④), and *Tsirimiagos*, ☎0663/81 522; ④).

Further round the coast is **KASSIÓPI**, a fishing village that's been transformed into a major party resort. Emperor Tiberius had a villa here, and the village's sixteenth-century church is believed to be on the site of a temple of Zeus, once visited by Nero. Little evidence of Kassiópi's past survives, apart from an abandoned Angevin kástro on the headland – most visitors come for the nightlife and the five pebbly beaches. Most **accommodation** in Kassiópi is through village agencies; the largest, Travel Corner (☎0663/81 220, fax 81 108), is a good place to start. An independent alternative, the smart *Kastro* café-pension, overlooks the beach behind the castle (☎0663/81 045; ④), and *Theofilos* (☎0663/81 261; ②) offers bargain rooms on Kalamíonas beach. Anglicized cuisine and fast food dominate **eating** in Kassiópi, but for something more traditional, head for the *Three Brothers* taverna on the harbour, or the neighbouring *Porto* fish restaurant. At night, Kassiópi rocks to the cacophony of its music and video bars: flashest is the gleaming hi-tech *Eclipse*, closely followed by the *Baron*, *Angelos* and *Jasmine*, all within falling-over distance of the small town square. The *Axis Club* boasts imported British DJs, and frolics sometimes extend onto the beach until dawn.

The coastline beyond Kassiópi is overgrown and marshy, until little-used **Almyrós Beach**, one of the longest on the island. It is also the least developed beach, with only a few apartment buildings under construction at the hamlet of **Almyrós**. Cape Áyios Ekaterínis, to the east, is backed by the **Antinióti lagoon**, smaller than Korissíon but still a haven for birds and twitchers. With its wide main road, **AKHARÁVI**, the next stop west on the main coast road, resembles an American Midwest truck stop, but the village proper is tucked behind this in a quiet crescent of old tavernas, bars and shops. Akharávi makes a quieter beach alternative to the southerly strands, and should also be considered by those seeking alternative routes up onto **Mount Pandokrátor**. Roads to small hamlets such as Áyios Martínos and Lafkí continue onto the mountain, and even a stroll up from the back of Akharávi will find you on the upper slopes in under an hour. **Accommodation** isn't easy to find, but a good place to start is Castaway Travel (☎0663/63 541, fax 63 376). There are a number of **restaurants** on Akharávi's main drag; go for the *Pump House* steak and pasta joint, the traditional tavernas *Chris's* and *George's*, or the *Young Tree*, which specializes in Corfiot dishes such as *sofríto* and *pastitsáda*. The bar-restaurants tend to get quite rowdy at night, although the light and airy *Captain's Bar* is a pleasant watering hole. For a quieter drink, head for the leafy awning of the friendly *Vevaiotis* kafenío in the old village.

Ródha, Sidhári and Avliótes

Just to the west, **RÓDHA** has tipped over into overdevelopment, and can't be recommended. Its central crossroads have all the charm of a service station, and the beach is rocky in parts and swampy to the west. "Old Ródha" is a small warren of alleys between the main road and the seafront, where you'll find the best **restaurants** and **bars**: the *Taverna Agra* is the oldest in Ródha and is the best place for fish, and the *Rodha Star Taverna* and *New Harbour* are also good. For bars, try *Nikos* near the *Agra* and the upmarket bar-club *Skouna*. For **accommodation**, the large *Hotel Afroditi* (☎0663/63 147, fax 63 125; ④) has decently priced en-suite rooms with sea views. Both the Anglo-Greek NSK UK Travel (☎0663/63 471, fax 63 274) and Yuko Travel on the main drag (☎0663/63 810; ③) rent rooms and handle car rental.

The next notable resort, **SIDHÁRI**, is expanding rapidly; it has a small but pretty town square, with a bandstand set in a small garden, but this is lost in a welter of bars, boutiques and snack joints. The beach is sandy but not terribly clean, and many people tend to head just west to the curious coves, walled by wind-carved sandstone cliffs. However, the main reason to visit Sidhári is to reach the **Dhiapóndia islands**; day trips to Mathráki, Othoní and Eríkoussa (see p.387) leave weekday mornings around 9am; unless you catch the 5.30am Sidhári bus from Corfu Town, your only option is to stay the night. The boats are run by Nearchos Seacruises (☎0663/95 248) and cost around 3000dr return per person. The best sources of **rooms** are Kostas Fakiolas at the *Scorpion* café-bar at the west of town (☎0663/95 046; ②) and Nikolaos Korakianitis's minimarket on the main road (☎0663/95 058; ③). The biggest accommodation agency is run by young tycoon Philip Vlasseros, whose Vlasseros Travel (☎0663/95 695) also handles car rental, excursions and horse riding. Sidhári's **campsite**, *Dolphin Camping* (☎0663/31 846), is some way inland from the junction at the western end of town. Most **restaurants** are pitched at those looking for a great night out rather than a quiet meal in a taverna. The *Olympic* is the oldest taverna here; also recommended are the

Diamond and *Sea Breeze* tavernas. There are no quiet bars in Sidhári, and two **nightclubs** vie for your custom, the *Remezzo* and its younger rival, *Ecstasy*.

The Sidhári bus usually continues to **AVLIÓTES**, a handsome hill town with bars and tavernas but few concessions to tourism. Avliótes is noteworthy for two reasons, however: its accessibility to the quiet beaches below the quiet village of Perouládhes, just over a kilometre away, and the fact that **Áyios Stéfanos** (opposite) is under thirty minute's walk from here, downhill through lovely olive groves.

Paleokastrítsa and the northwest coast

The northwest conceals some of the island's most dramatic coastal scenery; the interior, violent mountainscapes jutting out of the verdant countryside. The area's honeypot attraction, **Paleokastrítsa**, is the single most picturesque resort on Corfu, but is suffering from its popularity. Further down the west coast, the terrain opens out to reveal long sandy beaches, such as delightful **Myrtiótissa** and the backpackers' haven of **Áyios Górdhis**. Public transport to the west coast is difficult: virtually all buses ply routes from Corfu Town to single destinations, and rarely link resorts.

Paleokastrítsa

PALEOKASTRÍTSA, a small village surrounded by dramatic hills and cliffs, has been identified as the Homeric city of Scheria, where Odysseus was washed ashore and escorted by Nausica to the palace of her father Alcinous, King of the Phaeacians. It's a stunning site though, as you would expect, one that's long been engulfed by tourism. The focal point of the village is the car park on the seafront, which backs onto the largest and least attractive of three **beaches**, home to sea taxis and kaïkia. The second beach, to the right and signed by flags for Mike's Ski Club, is stony with clear water, and the best of the three is a small unspoiled strand reached along the path by the *Astakos Taverna*. Protected by cliffs, it's undeveloped apart from the German-run Korfu-Diving Centre (☎0663/41 604) at the end of the cove. From the beach in front of the main car park, **boat trips** (around 2000dr) leave for the blue grottoes, a trip worth taking for the spectacular coastal views. Boats also serve as a taxi service to three neighbouring beaches, Áyia Triánda, Platakía and Alípa, which all have snack bars.

On the rocky bluff above the village, the **Theotókos Monastery** (7am–1pm & 3–8pm; free, although donations invited) is believed to have been established in the thirteenth century. There's also a museum, resplendent with icons, jewelled bibles and other impedimenta of Greek Orthodox ritual, though the highlight is the gardens, with spectacular coastal views. Paleokastrítsa's ruined castle, the **Angelokástro**, is around 6km up the coast; only approachable by path from the hamlet of Kriní, it has stunning, almost circular views of the surrounding sea and land.

Unfortunately, perhaps due to the pressure of commerce in such a small space, there's a rather aggressive air about tourism here. **Accommodation** is at a premium, and you may be expected to commit yourself for three to seven days in some places. A good **hotel** is the small, family-run *Odysseus* (☎0663/41 209, fax 41 342; ⑤) on the road into town, and the modern *Akrotiri Beach* (☎0663/41 237, fax 41 277; ⑥) is friendly and unpretentious for such a large and expensive hotel, and accessible on foot. There are good-value **rooms** for rent above Alípa Beach on the road down into Paleokastrítsa: try Andreas Loulis at the *Dolphin Snackbar* (☎0663/41 035; ③), Spiros and Theodora Michalas (☎0663/41 485; ③), or George Bakiras at the *Green House* (☎0663/41 311; ③). Above the village, past Nikos' Bikes, the friendly Korina family also have rooms (☎0663/44 0641; ④). *Paleokastritsa Camping* (☎0663/41 204, fax 41 104), is just off the main road into town, a ten-minute walk from the centre.

There isn't a huge choice of **restaurants** in the centre of Paleokastrítsa. The *Astakos Taverna* and *Corner Grill* are two traditional places, while *Il Pirata* offers a variety of

Italian and Greek dishes, including local fish and seafood, and the seafront *Smurfs* has good seafood menu. Also recommended are the very smart *St Georges on the Rock*, and the restaurant of the *Odysseus Hotel*. **Nightlife** hangouts include the restaurant-bars in the centre, and those straggling up the hill towards Lákones. By the Lákones turning is Paleokastrítsa's one nightclub, *The Paleo Club*, a small disco-bar with a garden.

Áyios Yéoryios and Áyios Stéfanos

Like many of the west coast resorts, **ÁYIOS YÉORYIOS**, 6km north of Paleokastrítsa, isn't actually based around a village. The resort has developed in response to the popularity of its large sandy bay, and it's a major **windsurfing** centre, busy even in low season. There are a couple of good **hotels** – the *Alkyon Beach* (0663/96 222; ④) and the *Chrisi Akti* (0663/96 207; ⑤) – and some rooms.

The most northerly of the west coast's resorts, **ÁYIOS STÉFANOS** is a low-key family resort, a quiet base from which to explore the northwest and the Diapóntia islands, visible on the horizon. Day trips to Mathráki, Othoní and Eríkoussa (see p.387) run every Thursday in season, and cost around 3000dr per person. Áyios Stéfanos's oldest **hotel**, the *Nafsika* (☎0663/51 051, fax 51 112; ②) has a large restaurant, a favourite with villagers, and gardens with a pool and bar, and in recent years, has been joined by the upmarket *Thomas Bay* (☎0663/51 787, fax 51 553; ③) and *Romanza* hotels (☎0661/22 873, fax 41 878; ⑤). For those on a budget, Peli's and Maria's gift shop offers bargain **rooms** (☎0663/51 424; ②), and the *Restaurant Evnios* (☎0663/51 766; ③) and *Hotel Olga* (☎0663/71 252; ②) have apartments above the village. A number of travel agencies handle accommodation, among them San Stefano (☎0663/51 157) and Mouzakitis Travel in the centre. Besides the *Nafsika*, good options for **eating** include the *Golden Beach Taverna*, and the *Waves Taverna*, on the beach. The *O Manthos* taverna serves Corfiot specialities like *sofríto* and *pastitsáda*. For **nightlife**, there's a couple of lively music bars, the *Condor* and the *Athens*, plus the small *Enigma* nightclub.

Central and southern Corfu

Two natural features divide the centre and south of Corfu. The first is the **Plain of Rópa**, whose fertile landscape backs on to some of the best beaches on this coast. Settlements and development stop a little to the south of Paleokastrítsa and only resume around **Ermónes** and Pelekas – a quick bus ride across the island from Corfu Town. Down to the south, a second dividing point is the **Korissíon lagoon**, the sandy plains and dunes that skirt this natural feature being great places for botanists and ornithologists. Beyond, a single road trails the interior, with sporadic side roads to resorts on either coast. The landscape here is flat, an undistinguished backdrop for a series of relatively undefiled beaches and, in the far south, **Kávos**, Corfu's big youth resort.

Ermónes to the Korísson Lagoon: the west coast

ERMÓNES, south of Paleokastrítsa, is one of the busiest resorts on the island, its lush green bay backed by the mountains above the Rópa River. The resort is dominated by the upmarket *Ermones Beach* **hotel** (☎0661/94 241; ⑥), which provides guests with a funicular railway down to the beach. More reasonable accommodation can be found at the *Pension Katerina* (③) and *Georgio's Villas* (③). Head for *George's* **taverna** above the beach for some of the best Greek food here: the mezédhes are often a meal in themselves. Just inland is the Corfu Golf and Country Club (☎0661/94 220), the only golf club in the archipelago, and said to be the finest in the Mediterranean.

The nearby small village of **VÁTOS** has a couple of tavernas, a disco and rooms, and is on the Glyfádha bus route from Corfu Town. Spiros Kousounis, owner of the *Olympic Restaurant and Grill* (☎0661/94 318; ④) has rooms and apartments, as does

Prokopios Himarios (☎0661/94 503; ④), next to the Doukakis café-minimarket. The Mirtiótissa **path** is signposted just beyond the extremely handy, if basic, *Vatos Camping* (☎0661/94 393).

Far preferable to the gravely sand of Ermónes are the sandy beaches just south of the resort, at Myrtiótissa and Glyfádha. In *Prospero's Cell*, Lawrence Durrell described **Myrtiótissa** as "perhaps the loveliest beach in the world"; until recently a well-guarded secret, the place hasn't been entirely swamped, but it's best visited at either end of the day or out of high season. Above the beach is the tiny whitewashed **Myrtiótissa Monastery**, dedicated to Our Lady of the Myrtles.

The sandy bay of **GLYFÁDHA**, walled in by cliffs, is dominated by the *Louis Grand* (☎0661/94 140, fax 94 146; ⑥), a large and expensive **hotel** in spacious grounds. There's another hotel at the far north end of the beach, the *Glifada Beach* (☎0661/94 258; ④) whose owners, the Megas family, also have a fine taverna. Most of the other accommodation is block-booked – it's a very popular family beach – but the *Gorgona* pool bar and *Restaurant Michaelis* might have rooms. Nightlife centres on two music bars, the *Kikiriko* and *Aloha*.

PÉLEKAS, inland and 2km south of Glyfádha, has long been popular for its views – the **Kaiser's Throne** viewing tower, along the road to Glyfádha, was Wilhelm II's favourite spot on the island. New developments are beginning to swamp the town, but there are still some good **hotels** here, including the elegant, upmarket *Pelekas* (☎0661/94 230; ⑥) and the friendlier, budget *Nicos* (☎0661/94 486; ④), as well as rooms at the *Alexandros* taverna (☎0661/94 215; ③). Among the **tavernas**, the *Alexandros* and *Roula's Grill House* are highly recommended. Pélekas's sandy **beach** is reached down a short path, where *Maria's Place* is an excellent family-run **taverna/rooms** place (☎0661/94 601; ③) with fish caught daily by the owner's husband.

Around 7km south of Pélekas, **ÁYIOS GÓRDHIS** is one of the key play beaches on the island, largely because of the activities organized by the startling **Pink Palace** complex (☎0661/53 101) which dominates the resort. It has pools, games courts, restaurants, a shop and a disco. Backpackers cram into communal rooms for up to ten (smaller rooms and singles are also available) for 5000dr a night, including breakfast and evening meal. Other accommodation is available on the beach, notably at the quieter *Michael's Place* taverna (☎0661/53 041; ③); the neighbouring *Alex-in-the-Garden* **restaurant** is also a favourite.

Inland from the resort is the south's largest prominence, the humpback of **Áyii Dhéka** (576m), reached by path from the hamlet of Áno Garoúna – it is the island's second largest mountain after Pandokrátor. The lower slopes are wooded, and it's possible to glimpse buzzards wheeling on thermals over the higher slopes.

Around 5km south by road from Áyios Górdhis, the fishing hamlet of **PENDÁTI** is still untouched by tourism. There is no accommodation here, but *Angela's* café and minimarket and the *Strofi* grill cater to villagers and the few tourists who stray by. Another 4km on, **PARAMONÁS** affords excellent views over the coastline, and has only a few businesses geared to tourism: the *Paramonás Bridge* restaurant (☎0663/75 761; ③) has **rooms** and **apartments** to rent, as does the *Areti Studios* (☎0661/75 838; ④) on the road in from Pentáti.

The town of **ÁYIOS MATHÉOS**, 3km inland, is still chiefly an agricultural centre, although a number of kafenía and tavernas offer a warm if bemused welcome to passers-by: head for the *Mouria* snack bar-grill, or the modern *Steki*, which maintains the tradition of spiriting tasty mezédhes onto your table unasked. On the other side of Mount Áyios Mathéos, 2km by road, is the **Gardhíki Pýrgos**, the ruins of a thirteenth-century castle built in this unlikely lowland setting by the Despots of Epirus. The road continues on to the northernmost tip of the beach on the sea edge of the **Korissíon lagoon**, which is most easily reached by walking from the village of Linía (on the Kávos bus route) via Íssos Beach; other, longer routes trail around the north end of the lagoon from Ano Messóngi and Hlomotianá. Over 5km long and 1km wide at its centre, Korissíon is home to turtles, tortoises, lizards, and numerous indigenous and migratory birds.

Benítses to Petríti: the east coast

South of Corfu Town, there's nothing to recommend before **BENÍTSES**, whose old town at the north end is reverting to a quiet bougainvillaea-splashed Greek village. There's really little to see here, beyond the ruins of a Roman bathhouse at the back of the village, and the tiny **Shell Museum**, part-exhibit, part-shop. **Rooms** are plentiful: try Bargain Travel (☎0661/72 137, fax 72 031; ②) and All Tourist (☎0661/72 223; ②). With the decline in visitors, however, some **hotels** are almost as cheap. The *Corfu Maris* (☎0661/72 035; ③), on the beach at the southern end of town, has modern en-suite rooms with balconies and views, while the friendly *Hotel Benitsa* and neighbouring *Agis* in the centre (both ☎0661/39 269; ③) offer quiet rooms set back from the main road. Benítses has its fair share of decent if not particularly cheap **tavernas**, notably *La Mer de Corfu* and the Corfiot specialist *Spiros*, as well as the plush *Marabou*. The **bars** at the southern end of town are fairly lively, despite new rules controlling all-night partying, and the *Stadium* **nightclub** still opens occasionally. If you're looking for a quiet drink head for the north end of the village, away from the traffic.

MORAÍTIKA's main street is an ugly strip of bars, restaurants and shops, but its beach is the best between Corfu Town and Kávos. Reasonable beach-side **hotels** include the *Margarita Beach* (☎0661/76 267; ④) and the *Three Stars* (☎0661/92 457; ④). There are **rooms** between the main road and beach, and up above the main road: try Alekos Bostis (☎0661/75 637; ③) or Kostas Vlachos (☎0661/55 350; ③). Much of the main drag is dominated by souvenir shops and minimarkets, as well as a range of **bars**, including the village's oldest, *Charlie's*, which opened in 1939. *Islands* **restaurant** is recommended for its mix of vegetarian, Greek and international food, as is the unfortunately named beach restaurant *Crabs*, where the seafood and special salads are excellent. The village proper, **ÁNO MORAÍTIKA**, is signposted a few minutes' hike up the steep lanes inland, and is virtually unspoiled. Its tiny houses and alleys are practically drowning in bougainvillea, among which you'll find two **tavernas**: the *Village Taverna* and the *Bella Vista*, which has a basic menu but justifies its name with a lovely garden, sea views and breezes.

Barely a hundred metres on from the Moraítika seafront, **MESSÓNGI** is disappointing; parts of the resort are sadly moribund. The sandy beach is dominated by the vast *Messonghi Beach* **hotel** complex (☎0661/76 684, fax 75 334; ⑥), one of the plushest on the island. Both the cheaper *Hotel Gemini* (☎0661/75 221, fax 75 213; ⑤) and *Pantheon Hall* (☎0661/75 802, fax 75 801; ③) have pools and gardens, and en-suite rooms with balconies. Half a kilometre inland from Messóngi, the *Sea Horse* **campsite** (☎0661/75 364) is a trek from the beach, but is one of the best on the island, with a pool, restaurant and shops, pitches shaded by olive trees and modern cabins (①). Despite several closures, Messóngi still has a number of good **restaurants**: notably the *Memories* taverna, which specializes in Corfiot dishes and serves its own barrel wine, and the upmarket *Castello*. An alternative is to head for the beach-side *Almond Tree* and *Sparos* tavernas a short walk south on the road to Boukári.

The quiet road from Messóngi to **BOUKÁRI** follows the seashore for about 3km, often only a few feet above it. Boukári itself comprises little more than a handful of tavernas, a shop and a few small, family-run hotels; the *Boukari Beach* is the best of the **tavernas**. The very friendly Vlachopoulos family who run the taverna also manage two small hotels nearby, the *Boukari Beach* and *Penelopi* (☎0661/51 269; ④), as well as good rooms attached to the taverna (②). Boukári is out of the way, but an idyllic little strip of unspoiled coast for anyone fleeing the crowds elsewhere on the island, and inland from here is the unspoiled wooded region around **Aryirádhes**, rarely visited by tourists and a perfect place for quiet walks.

Back on the coastline, the village of **PETRÍTI** fronts onto a small but busy dirt-track harbour, but is mercifully free of noise and commerce; its beach is rock, mud and sand, set among low olive-covered hills. The *Pension Egrypos* (☎0661/51 949; ④) has **rooms** and a **taverna**. At the harbour, three tavernas serve the trickle of sea traffic: the smart *Limnopoula* guarded by caged parrots, and the more basic but friendly *Dimitris* and *Stamatis*. Some way back from the village, near the hamlet of Vassilátika, is the elegant *Regina* **hotel**, with gardens and pool (☎0661/52 132, fax 52 135; ②).

Southern Corfu

Across the island on the west coast, the beach at **ÁYIOS YÉORYIOS** spreads as far south as Mága Khóro Point, and north to encircle the edge of the Korission lagoon, around 12km of uninterrupted sand. The village itself, however, is an unprepossessing sprawl. British package operators have arrived in force, with bars competing to present bingo, quizzes and video nights. The *Golden Sands* (☎0661/51 225; ⑤) has a pool, open-air restaurant and gardens, but the best **hotel** bargain is the smaller *Blue Sea* (☎0661/51 624, fax 51 172; ③). The most likely place to head for good **rooms** is at the southern end of the strip: the *Barbayiannis* taverna-bar (☎0661/52 110; ③). Besides the *Barbayiannis*, Áyios Yióryios has a number of good **restaurants**: *La Perla's* which serves Greek and north European food in a walled garden; the *Napoleon* pistariá; and the *Florida Cove*, with its beachcomber theme. **Nightlife** centres around music and pool bars like the *Gold Hart* and *Traxx*, although the best bar in Áyios Yióryios is the sea-edge *Panorama*, which has views as far south as Paxí.

A few minutes' walk north of Áyios Yéoryios, **Íssos** is by far the best and quietest beach in the area; the dunes north of Íssos are an unofficial nude bathing area. Facilities around Íssos are sparse: one **taverna**, the *Rousellis Grill* (which sometimes has rooms) a few hundred metres from the beach on the lane leading to Linía on the main road, and the *Friends* snack bar in Linía itself. An English-run **windsurfing school** operates on the beach.

Anyone interested in how a Greek town works away from the bustle of tourism shouldn't miss **LEFKÍMI**, on the island's east coast. The second largest town after Corfu, it's the administrative centre of the south of the island, and has some fine architecture, including two striking churches: **Áyios Theodóros**, on a mound above a small square, and **Áyios Arsénios**, with a vast orange dome that can be seen for miles. There are some **rooms** at the *Cheeky Face* taverna (☎0661/22 627; ②) and the *Maria Madalena* apartments (☎0661/22 386; ②), both by the bridge over the canal that carries the Chimáros River through town. A few **bars** and **restaurants** sit on the edge of the canal – try the *River* psistariá. Away from the centre, the *Hermes* bar has a leafy garden, and there are a number of other good local places where tourists are rare enough to guarantee you a friendly welcome, including the *Mersedes* and *Pacific* bars, and, notably, the *Kavouras* and *Fontana* tavernas.

There are no ambiguities in **KÁVOS**, directly south of Lefkími: either you like 24-hour drinking, clubbing, bungee-jumping, go-karts, video bars named after British sit-coms and chips with almost everything, or you should avoid the resort altogether. Kávos stretches over 2km of decent sandy beach, with watersports galore. This is very much package-tour territory; if you want independent **accommodation**, try Britannia Travel (☎0661/61 400) and Island Holidays (☎0661/23 439), and the nearest to genuine Greek **food** you'll find is at the *Two Brothers* psistariá, at the south end of town. *Future* is still the biggest **club**, with imported north European DJs, followed by *Whispers*. Favourite **bars** include *JCs*, *Jungle*, *The Face* and *Net*.

Beyond the limits of Kávos, where few visitors stray, a path leaving the road south to the hamlet of Sparterá heads through unspoiled countryside; after around thirty minutes of walking it reaches the cliffs of **Cape Asprokávos** and the crumbling **monastery of Arkoudhílas**. The cape looks out over the straits to Paxí, and down over deserted **Arkoudhílas beach**, which can be reached from Sparterá, 5km by road but only 3km by the signed path from Kávos. Even wilder is **San Górdhios beach**, 3km further on from Spartéra, one of the least visited on the island.

Corfu's satellite islands

Corfu's three inhabited satellite islands, **Eríkoussa**, **Othoní** and **Mathráki**, in the quintet of **Dhiapondía islands**, are 20km off the northwest coast. Some travel agencies in the northern resorts offer **day trips** to Eríkoussa only, often with a barbecue thrown in – fine if you're happy to spend the day on the beach. A trip taking in all three islands from Sidhári or Áyios Stéfanos is excellent value: the islands are between thirty and sixty minutes apart by boat, and most trips allow you an hour on each (longer on sandy Eríkoussa).

Locals use daytrip boats between the islands, so it's possible to pay your way between them. There is also a twice-weekly **ferry** from Corfu Town, the *Alexandros II*, which brings cars and goods to the islands, but given that it has to sail halfway round Corfu first, it's the slowest way to proceed.

Mathráki

Hilly, densely forested and with a long empty beach, beautiful **Mathráki** is the least inhabited of the three islands. The beach begins at the edge of the tiny harbour, and extends south for 3km of fine, dark-red sand, a nesting site for the endangered **loggerhead turtle** (see p.401). It's important therefore not to camp anywhere near the beach – and not to make any noise there at night.

A single road rises from the harbour into the interior and the scattered village of **KÁTO MATHRÁKI**, where just one friendly taverna-kafenío-shop overlooks the beach and Corfu. The views are magnificent, as is the sense of isolation. However, construction work above the beach suggests Mathráki is expecting visitors, and islander Tassos Kassimis (☎0663/71 700; ②) already rents **rooms**. The road continues to the village of **Áno Mathráki**, with its single, old-fashioned kafenío next to the church, but this is beyond walking distance on a day visit.

Othoní

Six kilometres north, **Othoní** is the largest, and at first sight the least inviting of Corfu's satellite islands. The island has a handful of good tavernas and rooms for rent in its port, **ÁMMOS**, but the reception from islanders who aren't in the tourism trade is rather cool. Ámmos has two beaches, both pebbly, one in its harbour. The village kafenío serves as a very basic shop, and there's one smart **restaurant**, *La Locanda dei Sogni*, which also has **rooms** (☎0663/71 640; ④) – though these tend to be pre-booked by Italian visitors. Three tavernas, *New York*, *Mikros*, and tiny *Rainbow*, offer decent but fairly limited menus; the owner of the *New York* also offers rooms for rent (☎0663/71 581; ③). The island's interior is dramatic, and a path up out of the village leads through rocky, tree-covered hills to the central hamlet, **Khorió**, after a thirty-minute walk. Khório, like other inland villages, is heavily depopulated – only about sixty people still live on the island through the winter – but it's very attractive, and the architecture is completely traditional.

Eríkoussa

East of Othoní, **Eríkoussa** is the most popular destination for daytrippers. It's invariably hyped as a "desert island" trip, although this is a desert island with a medium-sized hotel, rooms, tavernas and a year-round community. In high season, it gets very busy: Eríkoussa has a large diaspora living in America and elsewhere who return to family homes in their droves in summer, so you may find your *yia sou* or *kaliméra* returned in a Brooklyn accent.

Eríkoussa has an excellent golden sandy beach right by the harbour, with great swimming, and another, quieter, beach reached by a path across the wooded island interior. The island's cult following keeps its one **hotel**, the *Erikoussa* (☎0663/71 555; ③), busy through the season; rooms are en suite with balconies and views. Simpler rooms are available from the *Anemomilos* **taverna** (☎0663/71 647; ③). If you're hoping to stay, phoning ahead is essential, as is taking anything you might not be able to buy – the only shop is a snack bar selling basic groceries.

Paxí (Paxos) and Andípaxi

Verdant, hilly and still largely unspoiled, **Paxí (Paxos)** is the smallest of the main Ionian islands. Barely 12km by 4km, it has no sandy beaches, no historical sites, only two hotels and a serious water shortage, yet is so popular it is best avoided in high season. Despite haphazard ferry connections with Corfu, Igoumenítsa and Párga, it still draws vast crowds, who can make its three harbour villages rather cliquey. It's also popular with yachting flotillas, whose spending habits have brought the island an upmarket reputation, and made it the most expensive place to visit in the Ionian islands (with the possible exception of Fiskárdho on Kefallonía). There is only one – rather remote – official camp-site (there are pockets of unauthorized camping) and most accommodation is block-booked by travel companies, though there are local tour operators whose holiday deals are often a fraction of the price. The capital, **Gáïos**, is quite cosmopolitan, with delis and boutiques, but northerly **Lákka** and tiny **Longós** are where hardcore Paxophiles head.

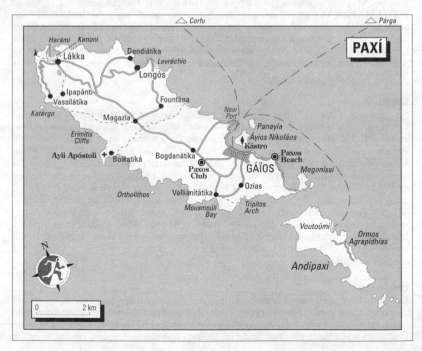

Gáïos

Most visitors arrive at **GÁÏOS**, or at the new port, 1km to the north. Gáïos is a pleasant town built around a small square on the seafront overlooking two islands, Áyios Nikoláos and Panayía. Room owners usually meet ferries, although it's advisable to phone ahead: try Gáïos Travel (☎0661/32 033), run by the friendly, English-speaking Ioannis Arvanatakis, and Paxos Tourist Enterprises (☎0661/31 675), both situated on the seafront. Paxí's two seasonal **hotels** are both near Gáïos: the *Paxos Beach Hotel* (☎0661/31 211; ⑤) which has smart en-suite bungalows on a hillside above a pebbly beach 2km south of town, and the fairly luxurious *Paxos Club Hotel* (☎0661/32 450, fax 32 097; ⑤), 2km inland from Gáïos.

Gáïos boasts a number of decent **tavernas**, the best of them being *Carcoleggio's*, 1.5km out of town towards Bogdanátika. The menu and wine list are limited, and opening hours unpredictable, but it fills up with islanders who flock for its *souvláki*. Also recommended are the *Blue Grotto*, *Spiro's*, *Dodo's*, and the *Gaïos Grill*, just off the west side of the town square. Of the pricey joints running down one side of the square, the *Volcano* is the best; the kafenía by the ferry ramp and at the bottom of the square is a much better bargain. The *Phenix* (sic) disco out by the New Port opens sporadically and has a terrace for sub-lunar fun. The island's one (basic) **campsite** is at Mogoníssi, 45 minutes' walk south (there's no bus), with a taverna above an imported sand beach.

Inland are some of the island's oldest settlements, such as Oziás and Vellianitátika, in prime walking country, but with few if any facilities. Noel Rochford's book, *Landscapes of Paxos* (Sunflower), lists dozens of walks, and cartographers Elizabeth and Ian Bleasdale's *Paxos Walking Map* is on sale in most travel agencies.

The rest of the island

Paxí's one main road runs along the spine of the island, with a turning at the former capital Magazía, leading down to the tiny port of Longós. The main road continues to Lákka, the island's funkiest resort, set in a breathtaking horseshoe bay. Two buses ply the road between Gáïos and Lákka six times a day, diverting on alternate trips to swing through Longós. The Gáïos–Lákka bus (45min) affords panoramic views, and the route is an excellent walk of under three hours (one way). A taxi between the two costs around 2000dr.

Approached from the south, **LÁKKA** is an unprepossessing jumble of buildings, but once in its maze of alleys and neo-Venetian buildings, or on the quay with views of distant Corfu, you do get a sense of its charm. Lákka's two **beaches**, Harámi and Kanóni, are the best on the island, although there have been complaints in high season of pollution from the yachts that cram the bay. Kanóni is a favourite with campers, but has no facilities. **Accommodation** is plentiful (except in high season) from the island's two biggest agencies: Planos Holidays (☎0661/31 744, fax 31 010) or Routsis (☎0661/31 807, fax 31 161), both on the seafront. The latter runs two bargain rooming houses, *Ilios* and *Lefcothea*. There's an embarrassment of good tavernas: the long running family taverna *Souris*, the friendly *Butterfly*, the *Nautilus*, which has the best view of any Paxiot restaurant, the hip *Ubu*, or the exotic *Rosa di Paxos* for a splurge. There's a similar wealth of bars: the lively *Harbour Lights*, the seafront *Romantica* cocktail bar, *Serano's* in the square, or Spiro Petrou's friendly kafenío – the hub of village life. Lákka is also best-sited for **walking**: up onto either promontory, to the lighthouse or Vassilátika, or to Longós and beyond. One of the finest walks – if combined with a bus or taxi back – is an early evening visit to the **Erimítis cliffs**, near the hamlet of Boikátika: on clear afternoons, the cliffs change colour at twilight like a seagoing Ayers Rock.

LONGÓS is the prettiest village on the island, and perfectly sited for morning sun and idyllic alfresco breakfasts. The village is dominated by the upmarket villa crowd, but the Planos office here (☎0661/31 530) is the best place to look for accommodation.

It has some of the island's best restaurants: the *Nassos*, with a wide variety of fish and seafood, the seafront *Vassilis*, where you have to squeeze in for the island bus when it rumbles by, and *Kakarantzas*. The hip jazz dive *Piano Bar* on the front, which drew crowds from all over the island, closed in 1996, but is rumoured to be reopening elsewhere in the village.

Longós has a small, scruffy beach, with sulphur springs favoured by local grannies, but most people swim off Levrékhio beach in the next bay south, which gets the occasional camper. (Islanders are touchy about camping for fear of fires; it's politic to ask at the beach taverna if it's acceptable to camp.) Longós is at the bottom of a steep winding hill, making **walking** a chore, but the short circle around neighbouring **Dendiátika** provides excellent views, and the walk to **Fontána** and **Magazía** can be done to coincide with a bus back to Longós.

Andípaxi

A mile south of Paxí, its tiny sibling **Andípaxi** has no accommodation and no facilities beyond a couple of beach tavernas open during the day in season. The sandy, bluewater coves have been compared with the Caribbean, but you'll have to share them with kaïkia and sea taxis from all three villages, plus larger craft from Corfu (boats from Paxí will also take you to its sea stacks and caves, the most dramatic in the Ionian islands). The trick is to head south away from the pleasure-craft moorings, although path widening has made even the quieter bays more accessible. Paths lead inland to connect the handful of homes and the southerly lighthouse, but there are no beaches of any size on Andípaxi's western coastline. In low season, there's also the risk of bad weather keeping pleasure craft in port and stranding you here.

Lefkádha (Lefkas)

Lefkádha is an oddity. Connected to the mainland by a long causeway through lagoons, it barely feels like an island – and historically in fact it isn't. It is separated from the mainland by a canal cut by Corinthian colonists in the seventh century BC, which has been redredged (after silting up) on various occasions since, and today is spanned by a thirty-metre boat-drawbridge built in 1986. Lefkádha was long an important strategic base, and approaching the causeway you pass a series of fortresses, climaxing in the fourteenth-century castle of **Santa Maura** – the Venetian name for the island. These defences were too close to the mainland to avoid an Ottoman tenure, which began in 1479, but the Venetians wrested back control a couple of centuries later. They were in turn overthrown by Napoleon in 1797 and then the British took over as Ionian protectors in 1810. It wasn't until 1864 that Lefkádha, like the rest of the Ionian archipelago, was reunited with Greece.

At first glance Lefkádha is not overwhelmingly attractive, although it is a substantial improvement on the mainland just opposite. The whiteness of its rock strata – *lefkás* means "white" – is often brutally exposed by road cuts and quarries, and the highest ridge is bare except for ugly military and telecom installations. With the marshes and sumpy inlets on the east coast, mosquitoes can be a midsummer problem. On the other hand, the island is a fertile place, supporting cypresses, olive groves and vineyards, particularly on the western slopes, and life in the mountain villages remains relatively untouched, with the older women still wearing traditional local dress – two skirts (one forming a bustle), a dark headscarf and a rigid bodice.

Lefkádha has been the home of various literati, including two prominent Greek poets, Angelos Sikelianos and Aristotelis Valaoritis, and the short-story writer Lefcadio Hearn, son of American missionaries. Support for the arts continues in the form of a

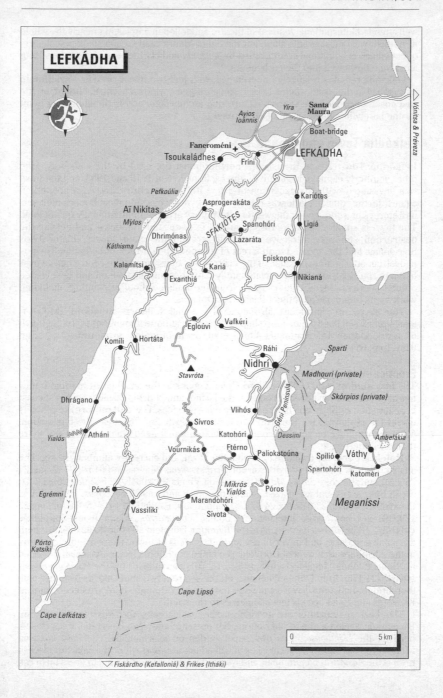

LEFKÁDHA

N

Áyios Ioánnis

Yíra

Santa Maura

Boat-bridge

Faneroméni +

Tsoukaládhes

Fríni

LEFKÁDHA

Pefkoúlia

Kariótes

Aï Nikítas

Asprogerakáta

Mýlos

Spánohóri

Ligiá

Dhrimónas

SFAKIÓTES

Lazaráta

Káthisma

Kalamítsi

Kariá

Epískopos

Exanthiá

Nikianá

Egloúvi

Vafkéri

Komíli

Hortáta

Ráhi

Spartí

Nidhrí

Madhoúri (private)

Dhrágano

Skórpios (private)

Stavróta

Vlihós

Sívros

Katohóri

Dessími

Ambelákia

Yialós

Atháni

Vournikás

Ftérno

Paliokatoúna

Spilió

Váthy

Spartohóri

Katoméri

Egrémni

Póndi

Mikrós Yialós

Póros

Marandohóri

Meganíssi

Vassilikí

Sívota

Pórto Katsíki

Cape Lipsó

Cape Lefkátas

0   5 km

▽ *Fiskárdho (Kefalloniá) & Frikes (Itháki)*

△ *Vónitsa & Préveza*

Gáia Peninsula

well-attended international **festival** of theatre and folk-dancing lasting nearly the whole of August, with most events staged in the Santa Maura castle. On a smaller scale, frequent village celebrations accompanied by *bouzouki* and clarinet ensure that the strong local wine flows well into the early hours.

Lefkádha remains relatively undeveloped, with just two major resorts: **Vassilikí**, in its vast bay in the south, claims to be Europe's biggest windsurf centre; **Nidrhí**, on the east coast, overlooks the island's picturesque archipelago, and is the launching point for the barely inhabited island of **Meganíssi**.

Lefkádha Town and around

Lefkádha Town sits at the island's northernmost tip, hard by the causeway. Like other southerly capitals, it was hit by the earthquakes of 1948 and 1953, and the town was devastated, with the exception of a few **Italianate churches**. As a precaution against further quakes, little was rebuilt above two storeys, and most houses built second storeys of wood, giving the western dormitory area an unintentionally quaint look. The town is small – you can cross it on foot in under ten minutes – and despite the destruction still very attractive, especially around the main square, Platía Áyios Spiridónas, and the arcaded high street of Ioánnou Melá. Much of Lefkádha Town is pedestrian-only, mainly because of the narrowness of its lanes. The centre boasts over half a dozen richly-decorated private family churches, usually locked and best visited around services. Many contain gems from the Ionian School of painting, including work by its founder, Zakynthian Panayiotis Doxaras.

The alleys off Spiridónas also conceal a small **folklore museum** (Mon–Fri 9am–9pm; 200dr) and a museum/shop dedicated to antique phonographs. To the north of town, Odhós Pfaneroménis houses an **archeological museum** (Tues–Sun 9am–1pm; free).

Practicalities

The **bus station** is on Odhós Dimítri Golémi opposite the small yacht marina. It now has services to almost every village on the island, and Nidrhí, Vassilikí and west coast beaches such as Kathísma have extensive daily services. **Car** and **motorbike** rental is useful for exploring; try EuroHire, Golémi 5 (☎0645/267 76), near the bus station. Most resorts have bicycle hire outlets, although you'll need stamina to do any more than local touring.

Hotels are actually dwindling in Lefkádha Town, and currently number just six. The smarter hotels, like the stylish seafront *Nirikos*, Ayías Mávras (☎0645/24 132, fax 23 756; ④) and the cosy *Santa Maura*, Spirídhon Viánta 2 (☎0645/22 342, fax 26 253; ⑤) are in busy areas, but are glazed against the noise and heat. The *Lefkas*, Pétrou Filípa Panáyou 2 (☎0645/23 916, fax 24 579; ⑥) and *Xenia*, Panagoú 2 (☎0645/24 762, fax 25 129; ⑤) are both large international hotels. The *Patron*, Platía Áyios Spiridónas (☎0645/22 359; ③) is a bargain, as is the *Byzantio*, Dörpfeld 40 (☎0645/22 629; ③): both are small and basic, and in very busy and noisy areas of town. There are basic **rooms** in the dormitory area west of Dörpfeld: the Lefkádha Room Owners Association, based in Nidrhí (Odhós Megálo Vlachí 8; ☎0645/92 701) can help, or try the *Pinepolis Rooms* (☎0645/24 175; ③) in Odhós Pinépolis, off the seafront two short blocks from the pontoon bridge. Lefkádha Town's campsite has closed, although there are decent sites at Karyótes and Epískopos, a few kilometres to the south.

The best **restaurants** are hidden in the backstreets: the *Reganto* taverna, on Dhimarkoú Venióti is the local favourite, but opening hours can be erratic. If it's closed, head for the *Lighthouse*, in its own small garden on Filarmoníkis. The *Romantika* on Mitropóleos has nightly performances of Lefkadhan *kantáthes*, while the smartest place in town is the *Adriatica*, Faneroménis and Merarkhías, where people tend to dress up to eat.

Of the **bars** in the main square, the *Thalassina* ouzerí is the cheapest, with occasional evening entertainment from buskers, jugglers and even fire-eaters. Further from the action the best is the *Cafe Karfakis*, on Ioánnou Melás, an old-style kafenío with splendid mezédhes. The most stylish bar is the hard-to-find *Vengera*, on Odhós Maxáïra, signposted a block down from the bus station, set in a shady garden and with a hip music policy. The town's **cinema**, *Eleni*, beyond the Archeological Museum on Pfaneroménis, is the only outdoor cinema in the archipelago; programmes change daily.

Around Lefkádha Town

The town has a decent and fairly large pebble beach across the lagoon at **Yíra**, a forty-minute walk from the top of Dörpfeld, either across the bridge or along Sikeliánou. In season there's also a bus (hourly 9am–4pm) from the bus station. Roughly 4km long, the beach is often virtually deserted even in high season; there's a **taverna** at either end, and at the western end a couple of **bars** in the renovated windmills, as well as the trendy *Club Milos*.

The uninhabited **Faneroméni monastery** (daily 8am–2pm & 4–8pm; free) is reached by any of the west-coast buses, or on foot from town (30min) through the hamlet of Fríni. There's a small museum, a chapel, and an ox's yoke and hammer, used when Nazi occupiers forbade the use of bells. There are wonderful views over the town and lagoon from the Fríni road.

The island's **interior**, best reached by bus or car from Lefkádha Town, offers mountainscapes of Alpine prospect and excellent walking between villages only a few kilometres apart. **KARYÁ** is its centre, with a hotel, the *Karia Village Hotel* (☎0645/51 030; ④), tucked away above the village, and some rooms: try Haritini Vlachou (☎0645/41 634; ③), the Kakiousis family (☎0645/61 136; ③), Olga Lazari (☎0645/61 547; ③) or Michael Chalikias (☎0645/61 026; ③). The leafy town square has a popular taverna, *La Platania*, and off it the smarter *O Rousos*. Kariá is the centre of the island's lace and weaving industry, with a fascinating small **museum** set in a lacemaker's home. The historic villages of **Vakféri** and **Engloúvi** are within striking distance, with the west coast hamlets of **Dhrimónas** and **Exanthía** a hike over the hills.

The east coast to Vassilikí

Lefkádha's east coast is the most accessible and the most developed part of the island. Apart from the campsites at Kariótes (*La Pissina* ☎0645/71 103) and Epískopos (*Episcopos Beach*, ☎0645/71 388), there's little point stopping before the small fishing ports of **LIYIÁ** which has some rooms and the hotel *Konaki* (☎0645 711 267; ④), or **NIKIANÁ**, where you'll find the hotels *Pegasos* (☎0645/71 766, fax 25 290; ⑤), and the smarter but considerably cheaper *Ionion* (☎0645/71 720; ④). Nikianá also has a trio of fine tavernas, notably the *Pantazis*, which also has rooms to let. Beaches here tend to be pebbly and small.

Most package travellers will find themselves in **NIDHRÍ**, the coast's biggest resort with ferry connections to Meganíssi and myriad **boat trips** around the nearby satellite islands. The German archeologist Wilhelm Dörpfeld believed Nidhrí, rather than Itháki, to be the site of Odysseus's capital, and did indeed find Bronze-Age tombs on the plain nearby. His theory identifying ancient Ithaca with Lefkádha fell into disfavour after his death in 1940, although his obsessive attempts to give the island some status over its neighbour are honoured by a statue on Nidhrí's quay. Dörpfeld's tomb is tucked away at Ayía Kiriakí on the opposite side of the bay, near the house in which he once lived, visible just above the chapel and lighthouse on the far side of the water.

Nidhrí is the prettiest resort on this coast, with some good pebble beaches and a lovely setting, but the centre is an ugly strip with heavy traffic. The best place to stay is the

Hotel Gorgona (☎0645/92 268, fax 92 558; ③), set in a lush garden away from the traffic a minute along the Ráhi road, which leads to Nidhrí's very own **waterfall**, a forty-five minute walk inland. There are also rooms in the centre – try Emilios Gazis (☎0645/92 703; ③) and Athanasios Konidaris (☎0645/92 749; ④). The town's focus is the Ákti Aristotéli Onássi quay, where most of the rather ritzy **restaurants** and **bars** are found. The *Barrel* and *Il Sappore* restaurants are recommended, as is the *Agra* on the beach. Nightlife centres around bars like *No Name* and *Byblos*, and the late-night *Sail Inn Club*.

Nidrhí sits at the mouth of a deep inlet stretching to the next village, somnolent **VLIKHÓS**, with a few good tavernas and mooring for yachts. Over the Géni peninsula across the inlet is the large **Dhessími Bay**, home to two adjacent campsites: *Santa Maura Camping* (☎0645/95 007, fax 26 087), and *Dessimi Beach Camping* (☎0645/95 374), right on the beach but often packed with outsized mobile homes.

The coast road beyond Vlikhós turns inland and climbs the foothills of Mount Stavróta, through the hamlets of Katohóri and Paliokatoúna to **Póros**, a quiet village with few facilities. Just south of here is the increasingly busy beach resort of **MAKRÝS YIALÓS**. It boasts a handful of **tavernas**, a few rooms at *Oceanis Studios* (☎and fax 0654/95 095; ④), plus the upmarket *Poros Beach Camping* (☎0654/23 203) which has bungalows (⑥), shops and a pool. Try the *Mermaid* taverna back from the beach.

Along the main road, walkers and drivers are recommended to take the panoramic detour to quiet **Voúrnika** and **Sývros** (the Lefkádha–Vassilíki bus also visits), which both have tavernas and some private rooms. It's around 14km to the next resort, the fjord-like inlet of **SÝVOTA**, 2km down a steep hill (bus twice daily). There's no beach except for a remote cove, but some fine fish tavernas: the *Ionion* is the most popular, but the *Delfinia* and *Kavos* are also good. Thomas Skliros (☎0645/31 151; ③) at the furthest supermarket, has a few **rooms**, and there's a basic unofficial campsite by the bus stop at the edge of the village.

Beyond the Syvóta turn, the mountain road dips down towards Kontaraína, almost a suburb of **VASSILIKÍ**, the island's premiere watersports resort. Winds in the huge bay draw vast numbers of windsurfers, with light morning breezes for learners and tough afternoon blasts for advanced surfers. Booking your **accommodation** ahead is mandatory in high season. The *Paradise* (☎0645/32 156; ②), a basic but friendly hotel overlooking the small rocky beach beyond the ferry dock, is the best bargain. Also good-value for its class is the neighbouring upmarket *Hotel Apollo* (☎0645/31 122, fax 31 142; ⑤). In the centre of town, the two main hotels are the smart and reasonably-priced *Vassiliki Bay Hotel* (☎0645/23 567, fax 22 131; ④), and the *Hotel Lefkátas* (☎0645/31 801, fax 31 804, ④), a large, modern building overlooking the busiest road in town. Rooms and apartments are available along the beach road to Póndi: *Billy's House* (☎0645/31 418), *Christina Politi's Rooms* (☎0645/31 440) and the *Samba Pension* (☎0645/31 555) are smart and purpose-built, though not particularly cheap. The largest of the three beach windsurf centres, Club Vassiliki, offers all-in **windsurf tuition** and accommodation deals. Vassilikí's only **campsite**, the large *Camping Vassiliki Beach* (☎0645/31 308, fax 31 458), is about 500m along the beach road; it has its own restaurant, bar and shop.

Vassilikí's pretty quayside is lined with tavernas and bars, notably the *Dolphin Psistaria*, the glitzier *Restaurant Miramare*, and the *Penguin*. One of the cheapest places to drink on the entire island is the no-name kafenío next to the bakery. Fliers sometimes advertise **raves** on the beach at Pórto Katsíki.

The beach at Vassilikí is stony and poor, but improves 1km on at tiny **PÓNDI**; most non-windsurfers however, use the daily kaïki trips to nearby Agiofíli or around Cape Lefkátas to the superior beaches at Pórto Katsíki and Egrémni on the sandy west coast. There's little accommodation at Póndi, but great views of the bay and plain behind, particularly from the terrace of the *Ponti Beach Hotel* (☎0645/31 572, fax 31 576; ④), which is very popular with holidaying Greeks, and has a restaurant and bar open to non-residents.

The west coast

Tsoukaládhes, just 6km from Lefkádha, is developing a roadside tourism business, but better beaches lie a short distance to the south, so there's very little reason to stay here. Four kilometres on, the road plunges down to the sand-and-pebble **Pefkoúlia beach**, one of the longest on the island, with a taverna, *Oinilos*, that has rooms at the north end, and unofficial camping down at the other end, about 3km away.

Jammed into a gorge between Pefkoúlia and the next beach, Mylos, is **AÏ NIKÍTAS**, the prettiest resort on Lefkádha, a jumble of lanes and small wooden buildings. The back of the village is a dust-blown car park, which detracts from the appeal of the pleasant, if basic, *O Aï Nikitas* **campsite** (☎0645/97 301), set in terraced olive groves. The most attractive **accommodation** is in the *Pension Ostria* (☎0645/97 483; ⑤), a beautiful blue and white building above the village decorated in a mix of beachcomber and ecclesiastical styles. Other options are in the alleys that run off the main drag; the best bets are the *Pansion Aphrodite* (☎0645/97 372; ④), the small *Hotel Selene* (☎0645/97 369; ④), and quieter *Olive Tree* (☎0645/97 453; ④). Best tavernas include the *Sapfo* and the *Agnantia*.

Sea taxis (1000dr one way) ply between Aï Nikítas and **Mýlos** beach, or it's a 45-minute walk (or bus ride) to the most popular beach on the coast, **Káthizma**, a shadeless kilometre of fine sand. There are two tavernas: the barn-like *Kathisma Beach*, and the *Sunset*, which has **rooms** (☎0645/24 142; ④). Beyond Káthisma, hairpin bends climb the flank of Stavróta towards the tiny village of **KALAMÍTSI**, where Spiro Karelis (☎0645/99 214; ②) and Spiro Verginis (☎0645/99 411; ②) have rooms. *Hermes* (☎0645/99 417; ③), the *Blue and White House* (☎0645/99 269; ③) and *Deili Rooms and Studios* (☎0645/99 456; ④) have larger rooms and apartments. There are also three good tavernas: the *Paradeisos* in its own garden with fountain, the more basic *Ionio* and, just north of the village, the aptly titled *Panorama View*. Three kilometres down a rough track is the village's quiet sandy beach.

South of Kalamítsi, past the hamlets of Khortáta and Komíli, the landscape becomes almost primeval. At 38km from Lefkádha Town, **ATHÁNI** is Lefkádha's most remote resort, with a couple of good tavernas which both have rooms: the *Panorama* (☎0645/33 291; ②) and *O Alekos* (☎0656/33 484; ③).

The road continues 14km to barren **Cape Lefkátas**, which drops abruptly 75 metres into the sea. Byron's *Childe Harold* sailed past this point, and "saw the evening star above, Leucadia's far projecting rock of woe: And hail'd the last resort of fruitless love". The fruitless love is a reference to Sappho, who in accordance with the ancient legend that you could cure yourself of unrequited love by leaping into these waters, leaped – and died. In her honour the locals termed the place *Kávos tis Kyrás* ("lady's cape"), and her act was imitated by the lovelorn youths of Lefkádha for centuries afterwards. And not just by the lovelorn, for the act (known as *katapontismós*) was performed annually by scapegoats – always a criminal or a lunatic – selected by priests from the Apollo temple whose sparse ruins lie close by. Feathers and even live birds were attached to the victims to slow their descent and boats waiting below took the chosen one, dead or alive, away to some place where the evil banished with them could do no further harm. The rite continued into the Roman era, when it degenerated into little more than a fashionable stunt by decadent youth. These days, Greek hang-gliders hold a tournament from the cliffs every July.

Lefkádha's satellites

Lefkádha has four satellite islands clustered off its east coast, although only one, **Meganíssi**, the largest and most interesting, is accessible. **Skórpios**, owned by the Onassis family, fields armed guards to deter visitors, **Madhourí**, owned by the family of poet Nanos Valaoritis, is private and similarly off-limits, while tiny **Spartí** is a large scrub-covered rock. Day trips from Nidhrí skirt all three islands, and some stop to allow swimming in coves.

Meganíssi

MEGANÍSSI, twenty minutes by frequent daily ferries from Nidrhí, is a large island with few facilities but a magical, if bleak landscape, a situation that's made it a favourite with island aficionados. Ferries stop first below **SPARTOKHÓRI**, an immaculate village with whitewashed buildings and an abundance of bougainvillea. The locals – many returned émigrés from Australia – live from farming and fishing and are genuinely welcoming. You arrive at a jetty on a pebble beach with a few tavernas and a primitive but free (for a night or two only) campsite provided by the *Star Taverna* (☎0645/51 107, fax 51 186). The village proper boasts three restaurants: a pizza place called the *Tropicana*, which can direct you to **rooms** (☎0645/51 425; ③), the *Rooftop Cafe*, and the traditional taverna *Lafkis*.

The attractive inland village of **KATOMÉRI** is an hour's walk through magnificent country. It has the island's one **hotel**, the *Meganisi*, a comfortable place with a restaurant (☎0645/51 240, fax 51 639; ③), and a few bars. Ten minutes' walk downhill is the main port of **VATHÝ**, with some accommodation (*Different Studios*: ☎0645/22 170; ③) and the island's best restaurants, notably the waterside taverna, *Porto Vathi*, which Lefkádhans flock to on ferries for Sunday lunch. After the high-season madness of Nidrhí, Meganíssi's unspoiled landscape is a tonic, and it's easy to organize a **day trip** from Nidrhí, getting off at Spartokhóri, walking to Katoméri for lunch at the *Meganisi*, and catching a ferry back from Váthy. Paths lead from Katoméri to remote beaches, including popular **Ambelákia**, but these aren't accessible on a day trip.

Kefalloniá

Kefalloniá is the largest of the Ionian islands – a place that has real towns as well as resorts. Like its neighbours, Kefalloniá was overrun by Italians and Germans in World War II; the "handover" after Italy's capitulation in 1943 led to the massacre of 5000 Italian troops on the island by invading German forces. These events form a key passage in Louis de Bernière's novel, *Captain Corelli's Mandolin*, a tragi-comic epic of life on the island from before the war to the present day.

Until the late 1980s, the island paid scant regard to tourism; perhaps this was in part a feeling that it could not easily be marketed. Virtually all of its towns and villages were levelled in the 1953 earthquake, and these masterpieces of Venetian architecture had been the one touch of elegance in a severe, mountainous landscape. A more likely explanation, however, for the island's late emergence on the Greek tourist scene is the Kefallonians' legendary reputation for insular pride and stubbornness.

Having decided on the advantages of an easily exploitable industry, however, Kefalloniá is at present in the midst of a tourism boom. Long favoured by Italians, it has begun attracting British package companies, for whom a new airport terminal has been constructed, while virtually every decent beach has been endowed with restaurants. There are definite attractions here, with some beaches as good as any in the Ionian islands, and a fine (if pricey) local wine, the dry white *Rombola*. Moreover, the island seems able to soak up a lot of people without feeling at all crowded, and the magnificent scenery can speak for itself, the escarpments culminating in the 1632-metre bulk of **Mount Énos**, declared a national park to protect the fir trees (*Abies cephalonica*) named after the island.

Kefalloniá airport is 11km south of town; there are no airport buses, so you'll have to resort to a taxi. The **bus** system is basic but expanding, and with a little legwork it can be used to get you almost anywhere on the island. Key routes connect Argostóli with Sámi, Fiskárdho, Skála and Póros. There's a useful connection from Sámi to the tiny resort of **Ayía Evfimía**, which attracts many package travellers. Using a moped, take care as the terrain is very rough in places – almost half the roads are unsurfaced – and the gradients can sometimes be a bit challenging for underpowered machines. The island has a plethora of **ferry** connections, principally from Fiskárdho to Lefkádha and Itháki, and from Sámi to Lefkádha, Itháki and the mainland, as well as links to Zákynthos, Kýllíni and Pátra.

Sámi and around

Most boats dock at the large, and not very characterful, port and town of **SÁMI**, built and later rebuilt near the south end of the Ithaki straits, more or less on the site of ancient Sámi. This was the capital of the island in Homeric times, when Kefalloniá was part of Ithaca's maritime kingdom: today the administrative hierarchy is reversed, Itháki being considered the backwater. With ferries to most points of the Ionian islands, and several companies introducing direct links to Italy – and one even to Pireas, Sámos and Turkey – the town is clearly preparing itself for a burgeoning future. Two kilometres beyond ancient Sámi, is a fine pebble beach, **Andisámi**.

The town has two smart **hotels**: the beachside *Sami Beach* (☎0674/22 802, fax 22 846; ⑥), and the quieter *Pericles* (☎0674/22 780, fax 22 787; ⑤) 500m back from the quay, which has extensive grounds, two pools and sports facilities. The best mid-range bet is the *Melissani* (☎0674/22 064; ④), behind the seafront; others in the category include the seafront *Ionion* (☎0674/22 035; ④) and *Athina* (☎0674/23 066; ④). The *Kyma* (☎0674/22 064; ③) on Platía Kyproú is very basic and old-fashioned. Both *periptera* on the quay offer rooms, as do a variety of private homes a few blocks back from the front. Sámi's one **campsite**, *Camping Karavomilos Beach* (☎0674/22 480, fax 22 932), has over 300 spaces, a taverna, shop and bar, and opens onto the beach.

Sámi doesn't have a great many **tavernas** beyond those on the seafront; visitors tend to go to the smart *Adonis Restaurant*, but the best bet is to follow the Greeks themselves to *Delfinia*, which produces succulent fresh fish and meat dishes, as well as a variety of vegetarian options. The *Riviera* is the favourite **bar** in the evenings, while the best place for a snack breakfast is *Captain Jimmy's*.

The Drogharáti and Melissáni caves

The one good reason to stay in Sámi is its proximity to the Drogharáti and Melissáni caves; the former 5km out of town towards Argostóli, the latter 3km north towards Ayía Evfimía. A very impressive stalagmite-bedecked chamber, **Drogharáti** (April–Oct daily 8am–6pm; 800dr) was previously used for concerts thanks to its marvellous acoustics – Maria Callas once sang here. **Melissáni** (same hours and price) is partly submerged in brackish water which, amazingly, emerges from an underground fault which leads the whole way under the island to a point near Argostóli. At this point, known as Katovóthres, the sea gushes endlessly into a subterranean channel – and, until the 1953 earthquake disrupted it – the current was used to drive seamills. That the water, now as then, still ends up in the cave has been shown with fluorescent tracer dye.

Ayía Evfimía

AYÍA EVFIMÍA, 9km north of Sámi, is a friendly little fishing harbour popular with package operators, yet with no major developments. Its two drawbacks are its beaches – the largest, Paradise Beach, is around 20m of shingle, although there are other coves to the south – and its poor connections (daily buses to Sámi and Fiskárdho, weekly to Ássos, a ferry to Itháki). **Accommodation** here is good at two small, smart **hotels**: *Pilaros* (☎0674/61 210; ④) and *Moustakis* (☎0674/61 030; ④). The *Dendrinos* **taverna**

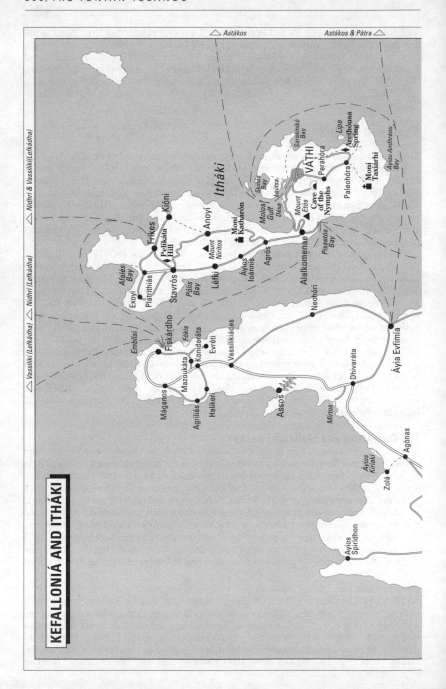

KEFALLONIÁ AND ITHÁKI

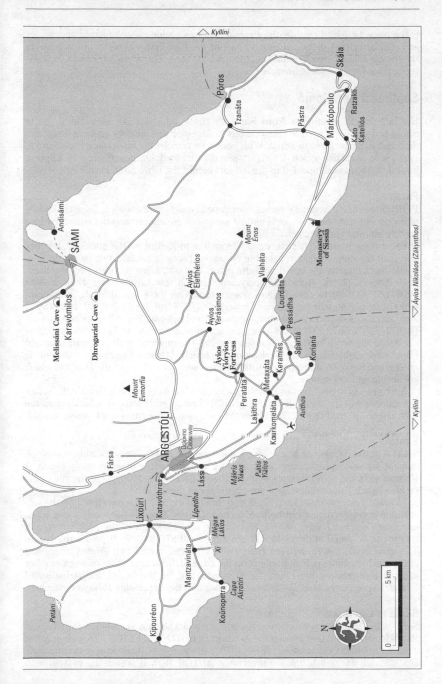

is the place for island cuisine; the *Pergola* also has a wide range of island specialities and standard Greek dishes. Hipsters head for the *Cafe Triton* at night, philhellenes to the *Asteria* kafenío, which doubles as the town barber's. The *Strawberry* zakharoplastío is the place for a decadent breakfast.

Southeast Kefalloniá

Heading directly **southeast from Sámi** by public transport is impossible; to get to **Skála** or **Póros** you need to take one bus to Argostóli and another on from there; five daily run to Skála, three to Póros. With your own vehicle, the back route from Sámi to Póros is an attractive option. It's eighty percent dirt track but negotiable with a decent moped; the road is signposted to the left just before the Dhrogaráti cave.

Póros

PÓROS was one the island's earliest developed resorts, and shows it. Its small huddle of hotels and apartment blocks is almost unique on Kefalloniá, and not enhanced by a scruffy seafront and thin, pebbly beach.

Póros does, however, have a regular ferry link to **Kyllíni** on the mainland, a better link than the only alternative, remote **Astakós**. Póros is actually two bays: the first, where most tourists are based, and the actual harbour, a few minutes over the headland. There's plenty of rooms, apartments and a few **hotels**. The *Pension Astir* (☎0674/72 443; ③) has good-value en-suite rooms on the seafront, while the elegant new *Odysseus Palace* in the centre of town (☎0674/72 036, fax 72 148; ⑥), has offered good discounts in recent summers. Among **travel agents**, Poros Travel on the front (☎0674/72 476 or 72 284) offers a range of accommodation, as well as services such as car rental and ferry bookings. The seafront has the majority of the **restaurants**, and Póros's one nightclub, *J&A's*, overlooking the beach. At night, however, the old port is quieter and has more atmosphere, with tavernas such as *Tzivas* and the *Dionysus* which are strong on local seafood.

A rough road twists 12km around the rocky coastline from Póros to Skála at the southern extremity of the island. It's a lovely, isolated route, with scarcely a building on the way, save for a small chapel, 3km short of Skála, next to the ruins of a **Roman temple**.

Skála

SKÁLA is also developing as a resort, but in total contrast to Póros it's a low-rise development set among handsome pines above a few kilometres of good sandy beach. A **Roman villa** and some mosaics were excavated here in the 1950s, near the site of the Golden Beach Palace rooms, and are open daily to the public.

Its faithful return crowd keep Skála busy until well after Póros has closed for the season, and accommodation can be hard to find. Dennis Zapantis has studios and apartments at *Dionysus Rooms* (☎0671/83 283; ③), a block south of the high street, and rooms can be found at the *Golden Beach Palace* (☎0671/83 327; ③) above the beach. The more upmarket *Tara Beach Hotel* (☎0671/83 250, fax 83 344; ⑤) has rooms and individual bungalows in lush gardens on the edge of the beach. Skála boasts a number of good **restaurants**: the *Pines*, the *Flamingo*, and, on the beach, the *Paspalis* and *Sunset*. Drinkers head for *The Loft* cocktail **bar** and the beach-side *Pikiona* music bar.

Skála to Lourdháta

Some of the finest sandy beaches on the island are just beyond Skála below the village of Ratzákli; and around the growing micro-resort of **KÁTO KATELIÓS** which already has a hotel, the smart *Odyssia* (☎0671/81 614; ⑤), and some self-contained **apartments** available through the stylish *Arbouro* **taverna** (☎0671/81 192). However, the coast around

LOGGERHEAD TURTLES

The Ionian islands harbour the Mediterranean's main concentration of **loggerhead sea turtles** (*Caretta caretta*). These creatures, which lay their eggs at night on sandy coves, are under direct threat from the tourist industry in Greece. Each year, many turtles are injured by motorboats, their nests are destroyed by bikes ridden on the beaches, and the newly hatched young die entangled in deckchairs and umbrellas left out at night on the sand. The turtles are easily frightened by noise and lights, too, which makes them uneasy cohabitants with freelance campers and late-night discos.

The Greek government has passed **laws** designed to protect the loggerheads, including restrictions on camping at some beaches, but local economic interests tend to prefer a beach full of bodies to a sea full of turtles.

On Kefalloniá, the turtles' principal nesting ground is just west of Skála. Other important locations include Zákynthos, although numbers have dwindled to half their former strength in recent years, and now only about 800 remain. **Nesting grounds** are concentrated around the fourteen-kilometre bay of Laganás, but Greek marine zoologists striving to protect and study the turtles are in angry dispute with locals and the burgeoning tourist industry. Ultimately, the turtles' main hope of survival may rest in their being appreciated as a unique tourist attraction in their own right.

While capitalists and environmentalists are still at, well, loggerheads, the **World Wildlife Fund** has issued guidelines for visitors:

1. Don't use the beaches of Laganás and Yérakas between sunset and sunrise.
2. Don't stick umbrellas in the sand in the marked nesting zones.
3. Take your rubbish away with you – it can obstruct the turtles.
4. Don't use lights near the beach at night – they can disturb the turtles, sometimes with fatal consequences.
5. Don't take any vehicle onto the protected beaches.
6. Don't dig up turtle nests – it's illegal.
7. Don't pick up the hatchlings or carry them to the water, as it's vital to their development that they reach the sea on their own.
8. Don't use speedboats in Laganás Bay – a 9kph speed limit is in force for vessels in the bay.

Káto Kateliós is also Kefalloniá's key breeding ground for the **loggerhead turtle** (see above). Camping is discouraged and would, anyway, strand you miles from any facilities.

At the inland village of **MARKÓPOULO**, claimed by some to be the birthplace of homophonous explorer Marco Polo, the **Assumption of the Virgin festival** (August 15) is celebrated in unique style at the local church with small, harmless snakes with cross-like markings on their heads. Each year, so everyone hopes, they converge on the site to be grasped to the bosoms of the faithful; a few, in fact, are kept by the priests for those years when they don't naturally arrive. The celebrants are an interesting mix of locals and gypsies – some of whom come over from the mainland for the occasion. It's quite a spectacle.

The coastline is largely inaccessible until the village of **VLAKHÁTA**, which has some rooms – *Maria Studios* (☎0671/31 055) – and a good taverna, the *Dionysus*, but you're better off continuing to **LOURDHÁTA**, 2km to the south. It has a fine 1km shingle beach and a couple of **tavernas** on a tiny plane-shaded village square – the *New World* and the *Diamond* – as well as the smarter *Spiros* steak and grill house above. *Adonis* (☎0671/31 206; ②) and *Ramona* (☎0671/31 032; ③) have **rooms** just outside the village on the approach road, while the one **hotel**, the *Lara* (☎0671/31 157, fax 31 156; ⑤), by the beach, has en-suite rooms with sea views.

Argostóli and around

ARGOSTÓLI, Kefalloniá's capital, is a large and thriving town, virtually a city, with a marvellous site on a bay within a bay. The stone bridge, connecting the two sides of the bay, was initially constructed by the British in 1813. A small obelisk remains, but the plaque commemorating "the glory of the British Empire" has disappeared. The town was totally rebuilt after the earthquake but has an enjoyable street life that remains defiantly Greek, especially during the evening volta around Platía Metaxá – the nerve centre of town.

The **Korgialenío History and Folklore Museum** (Tues–Sun 8.30am–2pm; 500dr), on Ilía Zervoú behind the Municipal Theatre, has a rich collection of local cultural artefacts, including photographs taken before and after the 1953 quakes. The **Archeological Museum** (Tues–Sun 8.30am–2pm; 500dr), on nearby R. Vergóti, has two large rooms of pottery, jewellery, funerary relics and statuary, as well as a small Pan figure, once priapic but now bluntly detumescent, from a shrine found at the Melissáni lake.

Practicalities

Argostóli's shiny new **Kefallonía airport** lies 11km south of town. There are no airport buses, and suburban bus services are so infrequent that a taxi (around 3500dr) is the only dependable connection. Those arriving in Argostóli by bus from Sámi or elsewhere will wind up at the brand-new KTEL **bus station**, a minute from the Drapano causeway and close to the main square, **Platía Metaxá**. Argostóli's friendly **tourist office** (Mon–Fri 8am–2pm; open till 10pm in August; ☎0671/22 248 or 24 466) is on Metaxá at the north end of the seafront, next to the port authority and has information about rooms, and can advise on transport and other resorts around the island.

Hotels around Platía Metaxá stay open year round, but tend to be pricey: the best bet here is the *Mirabel* (☎0671/25 381, fax 25 384; ④). A good mid-range option away from the square is the *Mouikis*, Výronos 3 (☎0671/23 454; ④); and a decent budget hotel is the friendly *Parthenon*, Zakýnthou 4 (☎0671/22 246; ②), tucked behind the Mouikis. In a working town with a large permanent population, **private rooms** aren't too plentiful. Some of the best bargains can be found through waterfront tavernas, such as the *Kalafatis* (☎0671/22 627; ②), nearest to the Dhrápano bridge on the Metaxá waterfront, the *Tzivras* (☎0671/22 628; ②) on Vandorou, just off the centre of the waterfront, or Spiro Rouhotas' taverna (☎0671/23 941; ②), opposite the Lixoúri ferry ramp. A number of travel agencies also offer rooms, apartments and villas: try Ionian Options (☎0671/22 054) on 21-1 Máiou, by the Lixoúri ferry, or Filoxenos Travel (☎0671/23 055) on R Vergóti. The town's one **campsite**, *Argostoli Camping* (☎0671/23 487), lies 2km north of the centre, just beyond the Katovóthres sea mills; there's only an infrequent bus service in high season, so you'll probably have to walk.

The waterfront *Tzivras* or *Kalafatis* **tavernas** are the place to try Kefallonián cuisine; the *Captain's Table* just off the platía is worth a splurge and to hear Kefallonián *kantathes*. Local posers hang out at the *Da Cappo* café-bar, the *Flonitiko* café and the *Koukos* club-bar, on Vassiléos Yeoryíou off the square. The quay bars, particularly the kafenío by the Dhrápano bridge, are quiet, cheap and have the best views.

South of Argostóli: beaches and Áyios Yeóryos

Many package travellers will find themselves staying in **LÁSSI**, a short bus ride or twenty-minute walk from town. Lássi sprawls unattractively along a busy four-lane highway, but it does have good sandy beaches, particularly at **Makrýs Yiálos** and **Platýs Yiálos**, although they're right under the airport flight path. **Beaches** such as **Ávythos** are well worth seeking out, although if you're walking beyond

Kourkomeláta there is a real if occasional risk of being attacked by farm dogs, particularly during the hunting season (Sept 25–Feb 28). There is very little accommodation in the region, and precious few shops or bars. **Pessádha** has a regular ferry link with Zákynthos in summer, but little else.

With a moped, the best inland excursion is to **ÁYIOS YEÓRYOS**, the medieval Venetian capital of the island. The old town here supported a population of 15,000 until its destruction by an earthquake in the seventeenth century: substantial ruins of its **castle** (Tues–Sun 8.30am–3pm), churches and houses can be visited on the hill above the modern village of Peratata. Byron lived for a few months in the nearby village of Metaxáta and was impressed by the view from the summit in 1823; sadly, as at Messolóngi, the house where he stayed no longer exists. Two kilometres south of Áyios Yeóryos is a fine collection of religious icons and frescoes kept in a restored church that was part of the nunnery of Áyios Andréas.

Mount Énos

At 15km from a point halfway along the Argostóli–Sámi road, **Mount Énos** isn't really a walking option, but roads nearly reach the official 1632-metre summit. The mountain has been declared a national park, to protect the *Abies cephallonica* firs (named after the island) which clad the slopes. There are absolutely no facilities on or up to the mountain, but the views from the highest point in the Ionian islands out over its neighbours and the mainland are wonderful. In low season, watch the weather, which can deteriorate with terrifying speed.

Lixoúri

Hourly ferries (every two hours at weekends) ply between the capital and **LIXOÚRI** throughout the day. The town was flattened by earthquakes, and hasn't risen much above two storeys since. It's a little drab, but has good restaurants, quiet hotels, and is favoured by those who want to explore the eerie quakescapes left in the south and the barren north of the peninsula. The bargain **hotel** is the *Giardino* (☎0671/92 505, fax 92 525; ②), four blocks back from the front. There are also two decent beach hotels just south of town: the *Poseidon* (☎0671/92 518; ④) and *Summery* (☎0671/91 771, fax 91 062; ⑤). Two agencies offer accommodation in town: A. D. Travel (☎0671/93 142) a few blocks from the quay, and Perdikis Travel (☎0671/91 097, fax 92 503) on the quay. Among the tavernas, *Akrogiali* on the seafront draws admirers from all over the island. Nearby *Antoni's* mixes traditional dishes with steaks and European food, while *Maria's* is a good basic family taverna.

Lixoúri's nearest beach is **Lípedha**, a 2km walk south. Like the **Xí** and **Mégas Lákkos** beaches (served by bus from Lixoúri) it has rich red sand and is backed by low cliffs. Those with transport can also strike out for the monastery at **Kipouréon**, and north to the spectacular beach at **Petáni**.

The west coast and the road north

The journey between Argostóli and Fiskárdho, by regular bus or hire vehicle, is the most spectacular ride in the archipelago. Leaving town, the road rises into the Evmorfía foothills and, beyond Agónas, clings to nearly sheer cliffs as it heads for Dhiváráta, the stop for **Mýrtos beach**. It's a 4km hike down on foot (you can also drive down), with just one taverna on the beach, but from above or below, this is the most dramatic beach in the Ionian islands – a splendid strip of pure white sand and pebbles.

Six kilometres on is the turning for the atmospheric village of **ÁSSOS**, clinging to a small isthmus between the island and a huge hill crowned by a ruined fort.

Accommodation is scarce – villagers invariably send you to Andreas Roukis's rooms (☎0674/51 523; ③). Ássos has a small pebble beach, and a couple of tavernas, notably the *Nefeli Garden* and the *Platanis Grill*, on a plane-shaded village square backed by the shells of mansions ruined in the quake. It can get a little claustrophobic, but there's nowhere else like it in the Ionian islands.

Fiskárdho

FISKÁRDHO, on the northernmost tip of the island, sits on a bed of limestone that buffered it against the worst of the quakes. Two **lighthouses**, Venetian and Victorian, guard the bay, and the ruins on the headland are believed to be from a twelfth-century chapel begun by Norman invader Robert Guiscard, who gave the place his name. The nineteenth-century harbour frontage is intact, nowadays occupied by smart restaurants and chic boutiques.

The island's premier resort, Fiskárdho is very busy through to the end of October, with accommodation at a premium. Bargain rooms are *Regina's* (no phone; ②) at the back of the village. *Theodora's Café Bar* has rooms in whitewashed houses along the quay (☎0674/41 297 or 41 310; ③), and the Koria handicraft shop has rooms on the seafront (☎0674/41 270; ④). A quieter option is the *Nitsa Rooms* (☎0674/41 327; ④) in the alley to the side of Nikos's bike rental on the quay, set in an exquisite garden. At the top of the price range, *Fiskardhona* (☎0674/41 436; ⑤), opposite the post office, and *Philoxenia* (☎0674/41 319; ⑤), next to Nikos's bike rental, offer rooms in renovated traditional island homes in the village. There's a wealth of good restaurants: the *Tassia* has a vast range of seafood, and the *Captain's Table* serves succulent Greek and Kefallonián fare. *Sirenes* is the favoured bar, although the seafront kafenía's mezédhes are the finest to be had anywhere. There are two good pebble beaches – **Émblisi** 1km back out of town, **Fókis** just to the south – and a nature trail on the northern headland. Daily **ferries** connect Fiskárdho to Itháki and Lefkádha in season.

Itháki

Rugged **Itháki**, Odysseus's legendary homeland, has had no substantial archeological discoveries but it fits Homer's description to perfection: "There are no tracks, nor grasslands . . . it is a rocky severe island, unsuited for horses, but not so wretched, despite its small size. It is good for goats." In C Cavafy's splendid poem *Ithaca*, the island is symbolized as a journey to life:

> *When you set out on the voyage to Ithaca*
> *Pray that your journey may be long*
> *full of adventures, full of knowledge.*

Despite the romance of its name, and its proximity to Corfu, very little tourist development has arrived to spoil the place. This is doubtless accounted for in part by a dearth of beaches, though the island is good walking country, with a handful of small fishing villages and various pebbly coves to swim from. In the north, apart from the ubiquitous drone of mopeds, the most common sounds are sheep bells jangling and cocks (a symbol of Odysseus) crowing.

Its beaches are minor, mainly pebble with sandy seabeds, but relatively clean and safe; the real attractions are the interior and sites from the **Odyssey**. Some package travellers will find themselves flying into Kefalloniá and being bussed to Fiskárdho (sit on the left for the bus ride of your life), for a short ferry crossing to **Fríkes** or the premier resort **Kióni**. Most visitors will arrive at **Váthy**, the capital.

Váthy

Ferries from Pátra, Kefalloniá, Astakós, Corfu and Italy land at the main port and capital of **VÁTHY** (Itháki Town), a bay within a bay so deep that few realize the mountains out "at sea" are actually the north of the island. This snug town has only a few streets and little traffic, and boasts the most idyllic seafront setting of all the Ionian capitals. Like its southerly neighbours, it was damaged by the 1953 earthquake, but some fine examples of pre-quake architecture remain here and in the northern port of **Kióni**. Váthy has a small **archeological museum** on Odhos Kalliníko (Tues–Sun 8.30am–2pm; free) a short block back from the quay. There are banks, a post office, police and a medical centre in town.

Váthy's two basic but decent **hotels** bookend the seafront: the *Odysseus* (☎0674/32 381; ④) is to the right of the ferry dock, the *Mentor* (☎0674/32 433, fax 32 293; ④) to its left. Room owners meet ferries until the last knockings of the season, but you can also call ahead to Vassili Vlassopoulou (☎0674/32 119; ②), whose rooms are in pleasant gardens by the church above the quay. Also within easy access are those owned by Sotiris Maroulis at Odhós Odysseus 29, near the Perakhóra road (☎0674/28 300; ③). The town's two travel agents, Polyctor Tours (☎0674/33 120, fax 33 130) and Delas Tours (☎0674/321 104, fax 33 031) on the quay have accommodation throughout the island.

Even though it's tiny, Váthy has a wealth of **tavernas** and **bars**. Many locals head off south around the bay with a torch towards *Gregory's*, popular for its lamb and fish, and the more traditional *Tziribis* and *Vlachos*. In town, *O Nikos* is an excellent taverna that fills early. The *Sirenes Ithaki Yacht Club* is upmarket with a nautical theme, while the no-relation *Ithaki Yacht Club* on the front looks private but is actually a bar open to all. Otherwise, head for the town's ancient kafenío one street back from the front.

There are two reasonable pebble **beaches** within fifteen minutes' walk of Váthy: **Dhéxa**, over the hill above the ferry quay, and tiny **Loútsa**, opposite it around the bay. Better beaches at Sarakinikó and Skinós to the south are an hour's trek by rough track leaving the opposite side of the bay. In season, daily kaïkia ply between the quay and remote coves.

Odysseus sites

Three of the main **Odysseus** sights are just within walking distance of Váthy: the Arethoúsa Spring, the Cave of the Nymphs and ancient Alalkomenae, although the last is best approached by **bus** or **taxi** (no more than 5000dr).

The Arethóusa Spring

The walk to the **Arethóusa Spring** – allegedly the place where Eumaeus, Odysseus's faithful swineherd, brought his pigs to drink – is a three-hour round trip along a track signposted next to the seafront OTE. The unspoiled landscape and sea views are magnificent, but the walk crosses slippery inclines and might best be avoided if you're nervous of heights. The route is shadeless, so take a hat and plenty of water.

Near the top of the lane leading to the spring path, a signpost points up to what is said to have been the **Cave of Eumaeus**. The route to the spring continues for a few hundred metres, and then branches off onto a narrow footpath through gorse-covered steep cliffs. Parts of the final downhill track involve scrambling across rock fields (follow the splashes of green paint), and care should be taken around the small but vertiginous ravine that houses the **spring**. The spring is sited at the head of a small ravine below a crag known as **Korax** (the raven), which matches Homer's description of the meeting between Odysseus and Eumaeus. In summer it's just a dribble of water.

The spring is a dead end – the only way out is back the way you came. If weather and time allow, there is a small cove for swimming a short scramble down from the spring. If you're uneasy about the gradients involved, it's still worth continuing along the track that runs above it, which loops round and heads back into the village of **Perakhóra** above Váthy, which has views as far as Lefkádha to the north. On the way, you'll pass **Paleokhóra**, the ruined medieval capital abandoned centuries ago, but with vestiges of houses fortified against pirate attacks and some churches still with Byzantine frescoes.

The Cave of the Nymphs
The **Cave of the Nymphs** (Marmarospíli), is about 2.5km up a rough but navigable road signposted on the brow of the hill above Déxa beach. The cave is atmospheric, but it's underwhelming compared to the caverns of neighbouring Kefalloniá, and these days is illuminated by coloured lights. The claim that this is the *Odyssey*'s Cave of the Nymphs, where the returning Odysseus concealed the gifts given to him by King Alcinous, is enhanced by the proximity of Déxa beach, although there is some evidence that the "true" cave was above the beach, and was unwittingly demolished during quarrying many years ago.

Alalkomenae and Pisaetós
Alalkomenae, Heinrich Schliemann's much-vaunted "Castle of Odysseus", is signposted on the Váthy–Pisaetos road, on the saddle between Dhéxa and Pisaetós, with views over both sides of the island. The actual site, however, some 300m up hill, is little more than foundations spread about in the gorse. Schliemann's excavations unearthed a Mycenean burial chamber and domestic items such as vases, figurines and utensils (displayed in the archeological museum), but the ruins actually date from three centuries after Homer. In fact, the most likely contender for the site of Odysseus' castle is above the village of Stavrós (see below).

The road (though not buses) continues to the harbour of **Pisaetós**, about 2km below, with a large pebble beach that's good for swimming and popular with local rod-and-line fishermen. A couple of tavernas here largely serve the ferries from Fiskárdho, Sámi and Áyia Evfimía on Kefalloniá.

Northern Itháki

The main road out of Váthy continues across the isthmus and takes a spectacular route to the northern half of Itháki, serving the villages of **Léfki**, **Stavrós**, **Fríkes** and **Kióni**. There are three evenly spaced daily **buses**, though the north of Itháki is excellent moped country; the close proximity of the settlements, small coves and Homeric interest also make it good rambling country. Once a day a kaïki also visits the last two of those communities – a cheap and scenic ride used by locals and tourists alike to meet the mainline ferries in Váthy. As with the rest of Itháki there is only a limited amount of accommodation.

Stavrós and around
STAVRÓS, the second largest town on the island, is a steep 2km above the nearest beach (Pólis Bay). It's a pleasant enough town nonetheless, with kafenía edging a small square that's dominated by a rather fierce statue of Odysseus and a tiny **museum** (Tues–Sun 9am–3pm) displaying local archeological finds. Stavrós's Homeric site is on the side of **Pelikáta Hill**, where remains of roads, walls and other structures have been suggested as the possible site of Odysseus's castle. Stavrós is useful as a base if both Fríkes and Kióni are full up, and is an obvious stopping-off point for exploring the

northern hamlets and the road up to the medieval village of Anóyi (see below). Both Polyctor and Delas handle **accommodation** in Stavrós, and a number of the town's traditional tavernas, including the *Petra* (☎0674/31 596), offer rooms.

A scenic mountain road leads 5km southeast from Stavrós to **ANOYÍ**, whose name translates roughly as "upper land". Once the second most important settlement on the island, it is almost deserted today. The centre of the village is dominated by a freestanding Venetian campanile, built to serve the (usually locked) church of the **Panayía**; inquire at the kafenío about access to the church, whose Byzantine frescoes have been heavily restored following centuries of earthquake damage. On the outskirts of the village are the foundations of a ruined **medieval prison**, and in the surrounding countryside are some extremely strange rock formations, the biggest being the eight-metre-high Arakles (Heracles) rock, just east of the village. The **monastery of Katharón**, 3km further south along the road, has stunning views down over Váthy and the south of the island, and houses an icon of the *Panayía* – Virgin Mary – discovered by peasants clearing scrubland in the area. Byron is said to have stayed here in 1823, during his final voyage to Messolóngi. The monastery celebrates its festival on September 8 with services, processions and music.

Three roads leave Stavrós heading north: one, to the right, heads 2km down to Fríkes, while the main road, to the left, loops around the hill village of **Exoyí**, and on to **Platríthias**. On the outskirts of Platríthias, Mycenean remains establish that the area was inhabited at the time of Homer. A track leads down to **Afáles**, the largest bay on the entire island, with an unspoiled and little-visited pebble beach. The landscape around here, thickly forested in parts and dotted with vineyards, is excellent walking terrain.

Fríkes

At first sight, tiny **FRÍKES** doesn't appear to have much going for it. Wedged in a valley between two steep hills, it was only settled in the sixteenth century, and emigration in the nineteenth century almost emptied the place – as few as two hundred people live here today – but the protected harbour is a natural year-round port. Consequently, Fríkes stays open for tourism far later in the season than neighbouring Kióni, and has a better range of tavernas. There are no beaches in the village, but plenty of good, if small, pebble strands a short walk away towards Kióni. When the ferries and their cargoes have departed, Fríkes falls quiet and this is its real charm: a downbeat but cool place to lie low.

Fríkes' one **hotel** is the smart but pricey *Nostos* (☎0674/31 644, fax 31 716; ⑤). Kiki Travel (☎0674/31 726) has **rooms** and other accommodation, and the Polyctor Travel office (☎0674/31 771) offers accommodation in and around the village, as well as handling ferry tickets. Phoning ahead is advisable, but if you turn up here without a reservation, both the *Ulysses* taverna-kafenío on the front and the neighbouring souvenir shop have rooms as well. Fríkes has a wealth of good seafront **tavernas**, notably the *Symposium*, the *Kirki Grill* and the nearby *Penelope*.

Kióni

KIÓNI sits at a dead end 5km southeast of Fríkes. On the same geological base as the northern tip of Kefalloniá, it avoided the very worst of the 1953 earthquakes, and so retains some fine examples of pre-twentieth-century architecture. It's an extremely pretty village, wrapped around a tiny harbour, and tourism here is dominated by British blue-chip travel companies and visiting yachts.

The bay has a small **beach**, 1km along its south side, a sand and pebble strand below a summer-only snack bar. Better pebble beaches can be found within walking distance towards Fríkes. While the best **accommodation** has been snaffled by the Brits, some local businesses have rooms and apartments to let, among them *Apostolis* (☎0674/31 072),

Dellaportas (☎0674/31 481, fax 31 090) and *Kioni Vacations* (☎0674/31 668). A quieter option, a short walk uphill on the main road in the hamlet of Rákhi, are the rooms and studios run by Captain Theofilos Karatzis and his family (☎0674/31 679; ④), which have panoramic views. Alternatively, seek out the very helpful Yioryos Moraitis (☎0674/31 464, fax 31 702), whose boat rental company has access to accommodation in Kióni.

Kióni is poorly served for **restaurants**, with just two waterfront tavernas – the traditional *Avra* and the *Kioni* pizzeria – and the upmarket *Calypso* restaurant back in the village. Village facilities stretch to two well-stocked shops, a post office, and a couple of bars and cafes. Back up the hill towards the hamlet of Rákhi there's also the small, bunker-like *Kioni* cocktail bar and nightclub.

Zákynthos (Zante)

Zákynthos, most southerly of the six core Ionian islands, currently teeters between underdevelopment and indiscriminate commercialization. Much of the island is still green and unspoiled, but the sheer intensity of business in some resorts is threatening to spill over into the quieter parts.

The island has three distinct zones: the barren, mountainous north-west; the fertile central plain; and the eastern and southern coasts which house the resorts. The big resort – the biggest in the whole Ionian – is **Laganás**, on Laganás Bay in the south, a 24-hour party venue that doesn't give up from Easter until the last flight home in October. There are smaller, quieter resorts north and south of the capital, and the southerly Vassilikós peninsula has the best countryside and beaches, including exquisite **Yérakas**.

Although half-built apartment blocks are spreading through the central plain, this is where the quieter island begins: farms and vineyards, ancient villages, and the ruins of Venetian buildings levelled in the earthquakes. The island still produces fine wines, such as the white *Popolaro*, as well as sugar-shock inducing *mandoláto* nougat, whose honey-sweetened form is best. Zákynthos is also the birthplace of *kantádhes*, the hybrid of Cretan folk song and Italian opera ballad that can be heard in tavernas in Zákynthos Town and elsewhere. It is also one of the key breeding sites of the endangered **loggerhead sea turtle**, which breeds in Laganás Bay. The loggerhead (see p.401) is the subject of a continuing dispute between tourism businesses and environmentalists, has caused an international political scandal and even provoked a bomb attack against the environmentalists.

Zákynthos Town

The town, like the island, is known as both **ZÁKYNTHOS** and Zante. This former "Venice of the East" (*Zante, Fior di Levante*, "Flower of the Levant", in an Italian jingle), rebuilt on the old plan, has bravely tried to recreate some of its style, though reinforced concrete can only do so much.

The town stretches the length of a wide and busy harbour, bookended by the grand **Platía Solómou** square at the north, and the church of **Áyios Dhionýsios**, patron saint of the island, at the south. The square is named after the island's most famous son, the poet Dioníssios Solomoú, the father of modernism in Greek literature, who was responsible for establishing demotic Greek (as opposed to the elitist *katharevoúsa* dialect) as a literary idiom. He is also the author of the national anthem. There's a small **museum** devoted to his life and work in nearby Platía Ayíou Márkou (Mon–Sat 9am–noon; free) which shares its collection with the museum on Corfu (see p.377), where Solomoú spent most of his life. Platía Solomoú is also home to the town's **library**, which has a small collection of pre- and post-quake photography, and the

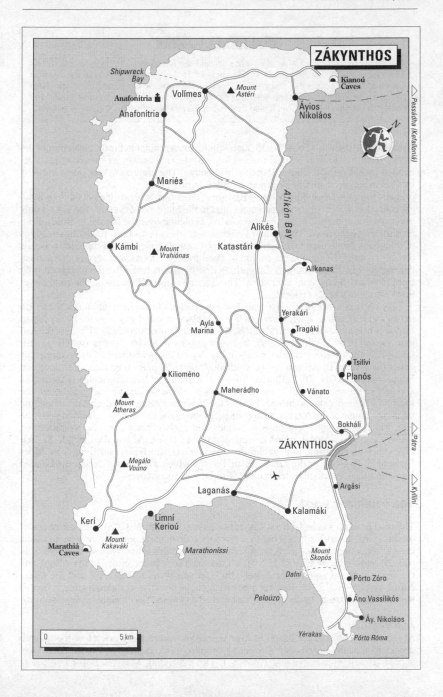

ZÁKYNTHOS

Shipwreck Bay

Anafonítria ✚
Anafonítria ●

Volímes ●

▲ Mount Astéri

Kianoú Caves ●

Áyios Níkoláos ●

△ Pessádha (Kefaloniá)

Mariés ●

Alikés ●
Katastári ●

Alíkón Bay

Kámbi ●
▲ Mount Vrahiónas

Alíkanas ●

Yerakári ●
Tragáki ●

Ayía Marína ●

Tsilívi ●
Planós ●

Kilioméno ●

Maherádho ●

Vánato ●

▲ Mount Átheras

Bokháli ●

ZÁKYNTHOS

△ Pátra
△ Kyllíni

▲ Megálo Voúno

✈

Argási ●

Laganás ●

Kalamáki ●

Kerí ●

Limní Kerioú ●

Marathiá Caves ■
▲ Mount Kakaváki

Marathoníssi

▲ Mount Skopós

Dafní

Pórto Zóro ●

Ano Vassilikós ●

Áy. Nikoláos ●

Peloúzo

Yérakas

Pórto Róma

0 ———— 5 km

BOAT TRIPS

At least six pleasure craft offer **day trips** around the island from the quay in Zákynthos Town for 2000–3000dr. All take in sights such as the blue-water grottoes of the **Kianoú Caves** at Cape Skinári, and moor in To Naváyio, **Shipwreck Cove**, and the **Cape Kéri** caves. Shop around for the trip with the most stops, as eight hours bobbing round the coast can become a bore. Check also that the operators actually take you into the caves.

Byzantine Museum (Tues–Sun 8.30am–3pm; 400dr), notable for its collection of art works from the Ionian School, the region's post-Renaissance art movement, spearheaded by Zakynthian painter Panayiotis Doxaras. The movement was given impetus by Cretan refugees, unable to practise under Turkish rule.

Apart from the small **Zákynthos Museum** (Tues–Sun 8.30am–3pm; 400dr) – a modest collection of local historical artefacts next to the Solomoú Museum – the town's only other notable attraction is its massive **kástro**, brooding over the hamlet of **Bokháli** on its bluff above the town. The ruined Venetian fort (daily 8am–4pm; 400dr) has vestiges of dungeons, armouries and fortifications, and stunning views in all directions. Below the kástro walls, Bokháli has a couple of good though expensive tavernas, some hosting nightly *kantáthes*, although Zakynthian driving habits make the thirty-minute walk from town a definite no-no after dark. The ugly new **amphitheatre** on the road out of town sometimes hosts concerts.

Zákynthos is a working town with few concessions to tourism, although there are hotels and restaurants aplenty, and it's the only place to stay if you want to see the island by public transport. Of the central hotels, the *Egli*, on Loútzi (☎0695/28 317; ③) is the bargain, tucked in beside the top-range and very expensive *Strada Marina* (☎0695/42 761, fax 28 733; ⑥). There are quieter hotels in the Repara district beyond Platía Solomoú: try either the *Reparo*, Dioníssiou Róma/Voultsou (☎0695/23 578; ④) or *Bitzaro*, Dhionysíou Róma (☎0695/23 644; ④), both near the scruffy municipal lido. The smart **restaurants** and bars of the seafront and Platía Ayíou Márkou are bedevilled by traffic, although the seafront *Village Inn* should be checked out for its bizarre gothic-Polynesian decor and the miniature jungle at the rear. First stop though, should be the friendly *Arekia* beyond the lido, which offers succulent taverna staples and nightly *kantádhes*. The neighbouring *Alivizos* also specializes in island cuisine and music. When the bored teens get off their bikes, they go **clubbing**, to bars like *Base* on Márkou, which plays anything from Miles Davis to Philip Glass, or the *Jazz Café*, on Tertséti which, despite plundering the London jazz club's logo, is actually a techno bar with DJ and 200dr cover.

The south and west

The road heading southeast from Zákynthos passes through **ARGÁSI**, the busiest resort on this coast, but with a beach barely a few feet wide in parts. It might, however, make a base for exploring the Vassilikós peninsula; there are rooms at the *Pension Vaso* (☎0695/44 599; ③) and *Andro* (☎0695/22 190; ③) on the main road in the centre of the village, and the seafront boasts some smart hotels: the *Locanda* (☎0695/45 386; ④) and the *Iliessa Beach* (☎0695/45 345; ④). Beyond a few indigenous tavernas, restaurant culture here is summed up, surreally, by an English caff that advertises a "Greek night" every Saturday.

Áno Vassilikó

At the southern tip of the island is **Áno Vassilikó**, where there are a few rooms with access to a sandy beach, and a great taverna/rooms hideaway at **Pórto Zóro** (also signed "Beach with Rocks and Flowers"). The expanding *Vasilikos Beach* (☎0695/24

114; ⑤) hotel/beach complex at **Áyios Nikólaos** has a good beach, with an embryonic hamlet and some rooms in the moon-like landscape behind it. Isolated Áyios Nikólaos lures day trippers from Argási, Kalamáki and Laganás with a **free bus** service in season.

Bulldozers are inventing new beaches, such as **Banana**, as quickly as their drivers can hack through the woods between the main road and the sea. The island's star is **Yérakas**, a sublime crescent of golden sand which is also a key loggerhead turtle breeding ground, and which is therefore off-limits between dusk and dawn. There's little here beyond two tavernas back from the beach and some pleasant, if remote, cabin accommodation at *Liuba Apartments* (☎0695/35 372; ⑤). The beach does draw crowds, but the 6am bus out of Zákynthos Town should secure you a few hours of Yérakas to yourself. Compared with Yérakas, **Pórto Róma**, on the east coast, is a disappointment, a small sand and pebble bay with a taverna and bar, some rooms on the approach road, and occasional hardy campers.

Laganás and Kalamáki

The vast majority of the 350,000 people or so who visit Zákynthos each year find themselves in **LAGANÁS**. The 9km beach in the bay is good, if trampled, and there are entertainments from watersports to ballooning, and even an occasional funfair. Beachfront bars and restaurants stretch for over a kilometre; the bars and restaurants on the main drag another kilometre inland. Some stay open around the clock; others just play music at deafening volume until dawn. The competing video and music bars can make Laganás at night resemble the set of *Bladerunner*, but that's how its predominantly English visitors like it. If this is your bag, there's no place better; if it isn't, flee. **Accommodation** is mostly block-booked by package companies. There's a basic campsite on the southern edge of town, where there are also quietish private rooms, and some bargain hotels – try the *Alexandros* (☎0695/51 580; ④) or *Galaxy* (☎0695/51 175; ④).

Neighbouring **KALAMÁKI** has a better beach than Laganás, and is altogether quieter, although both resorts suffer from airport noise. There are a number of good hotels, notably the *Crystal Beach* (☎0695/42 788, fax 42 917; ⑤), and the friendly Zakyta travel agency (☎0695/27 080) can also arrange accommodation. The two *Stanis* tavernas have extensive menus of Greek and international dishes, although the beachside version is geared more to lunches and its sibling more to evening meals. Alternatives include *Jools' Diner* and the *Merlis*. **Nightlife** centres around bars like *All Sutros*, and the *Byzantio Club* on the hillside above the village, which has a garden with breathtaking views.

Kerí

The village of **KERÍ** is hidden in a fold above the cliffs at the island's southernmost tip. The village retains a number of pre-quake, Venetian buildings, including the church of the **Panayía Kerioú** – the Virgin is said to have saved the island from marauding pirates by hiding it in a sea mist. Kerí is also famous for a geological quirk, a series of small tar pools mentioned by both Pliny and Herodotus, but these have mysteriously dried up in recent years. A rough path leaving the southern end of the village leads 1km on to the lighthouse, with spectacular views of the sea, sea arches and stacks.

Makherádho, Kilioméno and Kámbi

The bus system does not reach the wild western side of the island, but a hire car or sturdy motorbike will get you there. **MAKHERÁDHO** boasts impressive pre-earthquake architecture set in beautiful arable uplands, surrounded by olive and fruit groves. The church of **Ayía Mávra** has an impressive free-standing campanile, and inside a splendid carved iconostasis and icons by Zákynthian painter Nikolaos Latsis. The town's major festival – one of the biggest on the island – is the saint's day, which falls on the first Sunday in June. The other notable church in town, that of the Panayía, commands breathtaking views over the central plain.

KILIOMÉNO is the best place to see surviving pre-earthquake domestic architecture, in the form of the island's traditional two-storey houses. The town was originally named after its church **Áyios Nikólaos**, whose impressive campanile, begun over a hundred years ago, still lacks a capped roof.

The road from Kilioméno climbs to the tiny clifftop hamlet of **KÁMBI**, destination for numerous coach trips to catch the sunset over the sea. The village contains a small **folk museum**, with a collection of domestic and agricultural artefacts, and local crafts such as embroidery. Its cliff-top **taverna** has extraordinary views over the 300-metre-high cliffs and western horizon. On an incline above the village there's an imposing concrete cross, constructed in memory of islanders killed here in the war, either by Nationalist soldiers or Nazis. The tiny village of **Mariés**, 5km to the north and set in a wooded green valley, has the only coastal access on this side of Zákynthos, a 7km track leading down to the rocky inlet of **Stenítis Bay** where there's a taverna and yacht dock.

The north

North and west from Zákynthos Town, the roads thread their way through luxuriantly fertile farmland, punctuated with tumulus-like hills. **Tsilívi**, 5km north of the capital, is the first beach resort here, just below the hamlet of **PLANÓS**. Unfortunately, this part of the coastline suffers from occasional oil pollution, with nothing but the winter storms to clear it. There's a good, basic **campsite**, *Zante Camping* (☎0695/24 754), beyond Planós, and some rooms – try *Gregory's* (☎0695/61 853; ③) or *Dolphin* (☎0695/27 425; ③) – but most visitors here are on package deals.

Alykón bay

Ormós Alikón, 12km north of Tsilívi, is a large sandy bay with lively surf and two of the area's largest resorts. **ALÍKANAS** is a small but expanding village, much of its accommodation being overseas villa rentals and **ALYKÉS**, named after the spooky salt pans behind the village, has the best beach north of the capital. There are **rooms** on the beach (try the *Golden Dolphin* taverna), and a couple of **hotels** set back from the village but with sea views – the *Ionian Star* (☎0695/83 416; ④) and the *Montreal* (☎0695/83 241; ⑤). Alykés is the last true resort on this coast, and the one where the bus service gives out. **Koróni**, 4km north, has sulphur springs flowing into the sea – follow the smell – which provide the odd sensation of swimming in a mix of cool and warm water.

Áyios Nikólaos, 6km, is a small working port serving daily ferries to and from Pessádha on Kefaloniá. From here another good trip is a ride by **kaïki** (1000dr) to the extreme northern tip of the island, where the **Kianoú (Blue) Caves** are some of the more realistically named of the many contenders in Greece. They're terrific for snorkelling, and when you go for a dip here your skin will appear bright blue. The road snakes onwards through a landscape of gorse bushes and dry-stone walls until it ends at the lighthouse of **Cape Skináni**. With one cafeteria, and a view of the mountainous expanse of Kefalloniá, it's a good spot for unofficial camping.

Volímes, Katastári and Ayía Marina

The northern towns and villages are accessible only to those with cars or sturdy motorbikes, although there are guided coach tours from the resorts, and none are really geared to tourism. **VOLÍMES** is the centre of the island's embroidery industry – with your own transport, you could make it to the **Anafonítria monastery**, 3km south, thought to have been the cell of the island's patron saint, Dhionysios, whose festivals are celebrated on August 24 and December 17. A track leads on to the cliffs overlooking **Shipwreck Bay** (To Navágio), with hair-raising views down to the shipwreck below. In the other direction from Volímes, the road leads 10km to Cape Skinari, where a lighthouse and kafenío overlook the rocky northern headland and the Kiánou blue sea caves. Two kilometres inland from Alíkes, **KATASTÁRI** is the largest settlement after the capital. Although it's unprepared for tourism, it's the place to see Zákynthian life as it's lived away from the tourism racket.

AYÍA MARÍNA, a few kilometres south of Katastári, has a church with an impressive Baroque altar screen, and a belfry that's being rebuilt from the remnants left after the 1953 earthquake. Like most Zákynthos churches, the belltower is detached, in Venetian fashion. Just above Ayía Marína is the *Parthenonas* taverna rightly boasting one of the best views on the island. From here you can see the whole of the central plain from beyond Alykés in the north to Laganás Bay in the south.

travel details

Corfu (Kérkyra)

There are three daily **flights** between Corfu and Athens (45min), and one to Thessaloníki (1hr). Roughly hourly (5am–10pm) **ferries** run between Corfu and Igoumenítsa (1–2hr). Additionally, most ferries between Italy (Brindisi, Bari, Otranto) and Greece stop at Corfu; stopover is free if specified in advance. The high-speed catamaran service between Brindisi, Corfu, Paxí and Lefkádha has been suspended.

Erikoussa, Mathráki and Othoní

A **car ferry**, the *Aloxandroo II*, runs from Corfu Town to all the islands twice weekly (Tues & Sat, 6.30am). The ferry leaves from near the BP station on the seafront, midway between the Old and New Ports. Star Travel (☎0661/36 355) on the seafront has tickets and information, and also runs a seasonal excursion to the islands, although the Corfu connection involves sailing halfway round the island. Quicker access, favoured by islanders without vehicles, is via daily excursions from **Sidhári** run by Nearchos Seacruises (☎0663/95 248).

Paxí

Ferry connections to Paxí are haphazard: there is a weekly Monday morning **ferry** from Corfu through the year, and in season a ferry service (daily except Sun) from the Old Port of Corfu Town, leaving the quay below the Astron Hotel. At least one of the following should be sailing at either 2pm or 5pm: the *Pegasus*, *Dolphin*, *Paxos Star*, or the *Anna Maria*. Check with Corfu's port police (☎0661/32 655) or a Paxíot travel company, as services change every year.

Lefkádha

5 **buses** daily to and from Athens (7hr), and 4 buses daily (3 on Sun) to and from Préveza (30min), passing Áktio airport (30min). At least 5 **ferries** daily in season from Nidrhí to Meganíssi; daily seasonal connections from Nidrhí to Kefalloniá (Fiskárdho and Sámi) and Itháki (Fríkes) The **hydrofoil** service linking Lefkádha with Paxí and Corfu has been suspended.

Kefalloniá

1 daily **flight** to and from Athens (45min).

Daily **ferries** from **Sámi** to Pátra (5hr); Astakós (2hr); Váthy (Itháki; 30min); Vassilikí (Lefkádha; 3hr). Also ferries from **Póros** to Kyllíni (2 daily; 1hr 30min); Zákynthos Town (1 daily; 2hr 30min); **Fiskárdho** to: Fríkes (Itháki; 1 daily; 1hr); Nidrhí (Lefkádha; 1 daily; 1hr 30min); Pisaetós (Itháki; 1 daily; 1hr); Vassilikí (Lefkádha; 4 daily; 2hr); **Argostóli** to: Kyllíni (2 daily; 2hr 30min); Lixoúri (12 daily, 8 on Sun; 30min); **Ayía Evfimía** to: Pisaetós (Itháki; 1 daily; 30min); Váthy (Itháki 1 daily; 1hr); **Pessádha** to: Áyios Nikoláos (Zákynthos; 2 daily; 1hr 30min).

Itháki (Ithaca)

Seasonal ferries from: **Fríkes** to: Fiskárdho (Kefalloniá; 1 daily; 1hr); Nidhrí (Lefkádha; 1 daily; 2hr); Vassilikí (Lefkádha; 1 daily; 1hr).

Pisaetós to: Fiskárdho (Kefalloniá; 1 daily; 1hr); Sámi (Kefalloniá; 3 daily; 1hr 30min); Ayía Evfimía (Kefalloniá; 1 daily; 30min).

Váthy to: Sámi (Kefalloniá; 4 daily; 1hr); Astakós (2 daily; 1hr 30min); Pátra (2 daily; 5hr). **Off sea-** **son**, there is one daily service on each route, weather permitting.

Zákynthos

Seasonal ferries from: **Zákynthos Town** to: Kyllíni (5 daily; 1hr 30min); Pátra (daily; 3hr).

Áyios Nikoláos to: Pessádha (Kefalloniá; 2 daily May–Sept; 1hr 30min).

PART THREE

THE

CONTEXTS

THE HISTORICAL FRAMEWORK

This section is intended just to lend some perspective to travels around the Greek islands, and is heavily weighted towards the era of the modern, post-independent nation – especially the twentieth century. More detailed accounts of particular periods are to be found in the relevant sections of the guide.

NEOLITHIC, MINOAN AND MYCENAEAN AGES

Other than the solitary discovery of a fossilized Neanderthal skull near Thessaloníki, the earliest evidence of **human settlement** in Greece is to be found at Néa Nikomedhía, near Véria. Here, traces of large, rectangular houses dated to around 6000 BC have been excavated.

It seems that people originally came to this land in the eastern Mediterranean in fits and starts, predominantly from Anatolia. These **proto-Greeks** settled in essentially peaceful farming communities, made pottery and worshipped Earth/Fertility goddesses – clay statuettes of which are still found on the sites of old settlements. This simple way of life eventually disappeared, as people started to tap the land's resources for profit and to compete and trade.

MINOANS AND MYCENAEANS

The years between around **2000** and **1100 BC** were a period of fluctuating regional dominance, based at first upon sea power, with vast **royal palaces** serving as centres of administration. Particularly important were those at **Knossos** in Crete, and **Mycenae**, **Tiryns** and **Argos** in the Peloponnese.

Crete monopolized the eastern Mediterranean trade routes for an era subsequently called the **Minoan Age**, with the palace at Knossos surviving two earthquakes and a massive volcanic eruption on the island of Thíra (Santoríni), at some undefinable point between 1500 and 1450 BC. The most obvious examples of Minoan culture can be seen in frescoes, in jewellery and in pottery, the distinctive red-and-white design on a dark background marking the peak period of Minoan achievement. When Knossos finally succumbed to disaster, natural or otherwise, around 1400 BC, it was the flourishing centre of **Mycenae** that assumed the leading role (and gave its name to the civilization of this period), until it in turn collapsed around 1200 BC.

This is a period whose history and remains are bound up with its **legends**, recounted most famously by Homer. Knossos was the home of King Minos, while the palaces of Mycenae and Pylos were the respective bases of Agamemnon and Nestor; Menelaus and Odysseus hailed from Sparta and Ithaca. The Homeric and other legends relating to them almost certainly reflect the prevalence of violence, revenge and **war** as increasing facts of life, instigated and aggravated by trade rivalry. The increasing scale of conflict and militarization is exemplified in the massive fortifications – dubbed Cyclopean by later ages – that were built around many of the palaces.

The Greece of these years was by no means a united nation – as the Homeric legend reflects – and its people were divided into what were in effect a series of splinter groups, defined in large part by sea and mountain barriers and by access to **pasture**. Settlements flourished according to their proximity to and prowess on the sea and the fertility of their land; most were self-sufficient, specializing in the production of particular items for **trade**. Olives, for example, were associated with the region of Attica, and minerals with the island of Mílos.

THE DORIAN AND CLASSICAL ERAS

The Mycenaean-era Greek states had also to cope with and assimilate periodic influxes of new peoples and trade. The traditional view of the collapse of the Mycenaean civilization has it that a northern "barbarian" people, the **Dorians**, "invaded" from the north, devastating the existing palace culture and opening a "dark age" era. These days, archeologists see the influx more in terms of shifting trade patterns, though undoubtedly there was major disruption of the palace cultures and their sea powers during the eleventh century.

Two other trends are salient to the period: the almost total supplanting of the mother goddesses by **male deities** (a process begun under the Mycenaeans), and the appearance of an **alphabet** still recognizable by modern Greeks, which replaced the so-called "Linear A" and "Linear B" Minoan/Mycenaean scripts.

CITY-STATES: SPARTA AND ATHENS

The ninth century BC ushered in the beginnings of the Greek **city-state** (polis). Citizens – rather than just kings or aristocrats – became involved in government and took part in community activities and organized industry and leisure. Colonial ventures increased, as did commercial dealings, and a consequent rise in the import trade was gradually to create a new class of manufacturers.

The city-state was the life of the people who dwelled within it, and each state retained both its independence and a distinctive style, with the result that the sporadic attempts to unite in a league against an enemy without were always pragmatic and temporary. The two most powerful states to emerge were Athens and Sparta, who were to exercise a rivalry over the next five centuries.

Sparta was associated with the Dorians, who had settled in large numbers on the fertile Eurotas (Évrotas) river plain. The society of Sparta and its environs was based on a highly militaristic ethos, accentuated by the need to defend the exposed and fertile land on which it stood. Rather than build intricate fortifications, the people of Sparta relied upon military prowess and a system of laws decreed by the (semi-legendary) **Lycurgus**. Males were subjected to military instruction between the ages of seven and thirty. Weak babies were known periodically to "disappear". Girls too had to perform athletic feats of sprinting and wrestling, and even dwellings were more like barracks than houses.

Athens, the fulcrum of the state of Attica, was dynamic and exciting by contrast. Home to the administrations of **Solon** and **Pericles**, the dramatic talents of Sophocles and Aristophanes, the oratory of Thucydides and Demosthenes, and the philosophical power of Socrates and Plato, it made up in cultural achievement what it lacked in Spartan virtue. Yet Sparta did not deserve all the military glory. The Athens of the sixth and fifth centuries BC, the so-called **Classical period** in Greek history, played the major part in repelling the armies of the Persian king Xerxes at Marathon (490 BC) and Salamis (480 BC), campaigns later described by Aeschylus in *The Persians*.

Athens also gave rise to a tradition of **democracy** (*demokratia*), literally "control by the people" – although at this stage "the people" did not include either women or slaves. In Athens there were three organs of government. The Areopagus, composed of the city elders, had a steadily decreasing authority and ended up dealing solely with murder cases. Then there was the Council of Five Hundred (men), elected annually by ballot to prepare the business of the Assembly and to attend to matters of urgency. The Assembly gave every free man a political voice; it had sole responsibility for law-making and provided an arena for the discussion of important issues. It was a genuinely enfranchised council of citizens.

This was a period of intense creativity, particularly in Athens, whose actions and pretensions were fast becoming imperial in all but name. Each city-state had its **acropolis**, or high town, where religious activity was focused. In Athens, Pericles endowed the acropolis with a complex of buildings, whose climax was the temple of the Parthenon. Meanwhile, the era saw the tragedies of Sophocles performed, and the philosophies of Socrates and Plato expounded.

Religion at this stage was polytheistic, ordering all under the aegis of Zeus. In the countryside the proliferation of names and of sanctuary finds suggests a preference for the slightly more mundane Demeter and Dionysus.

THE PELOPONNESIAN WARS

The power struggles between Athens and Sparta, allied with various networks of city-states scattered across the islands and mainland, eventually culminated in the **Peloponnesian Wars** of 431–404 BC. After these conflicts, superbly recorded by Thucydides and nominally won by Sparta, the city-state ceased to function so effectively.

This was in part due to drained resources and political apathy, but to a greater degree a consequence of the increasingly commercial and complex pressures on everyday life. Trade, originally spurred by the invention of **coinage** in the sixth century BC, continued to expand; a revitalized Athens, for example, was exporting wine, oil and manufactured goods, getting corn in return from the Black Sea and Egypt.

The amount of time each man had to devote to the affairs of government decreased, and a position in political life became a professional job rather than a natural assumption. Democracy had changed, while in philosophy there was a shift from the idealists and mystics of the sixth and fifth centuries BC to the Cynics, Stoics and Epicureans – followers, respectively, of Diogenes, Zeno and Epicurus.

HELLENISTIC AND ROMAN GREECE

The most important factor in the decline of the city-states was meanwhile developing outside their sphere, in the kingdom of Macedonia.

THE MACEDONIAN EMPIRE

Based at the Macedonian capital of Pella, **Philip II** (359–336 BC) was forging a strong military and unitary force, extending his territories into Thrace and finally establishing control over Athens and southern Greece. His son, **Alexander the Great**, in a brief but glorious thirteen-year reign, extended these gains into Persia and Egypt and parts of modern India and Afghanistan.

This unwieldy empire splintered almost immediately upon Alexander's death in 323 BC, to be divided into the three Macedonian dynasties of **Hellenistic Greece**: the Antigonids based in Macedonia, the Seleucids in Syria and Persia and the Ptolemies in Egypt. Each were in turn conquered and absorbed by the new Roman Empire, the Ptolemies – under their queen Cleopatra – last of all.

ROMAN GREECE

Mainland Greece was subdued by the Romans over some seventy years of campaigns, from 215 to 146 BC. Once in control, however, **Rome** allowed considerable autonomy to the old territories of the city-states. Greek remained the official language of the eastern Mediterranean and its traditions and culture coexisted fairly peacefully with that of the overlords during the next three centuries.

In mainland Greece both **Athens** and **Corinth** remained important cities but the emphasis was shifting north – particularly to towns, such as **Salonica** (Thessaloníki), along the new Via Egnatia, a military and civil road engineered between Rome and Byzantium via the port of Brundisium (modern Brindisi). Out on the islands, Rhodes had declined since Hellenistic times but Kós, Lésvos, Thássos and Gortys on Crete remained important centres.

THE BYZANTINE EMPIRE AND MEDIEVAL GREECE

The shift of emphasis to the north was given even greater impetus by the decline of the Roman Empire and its apportioning into eastern and western empires. In the year 330 AD the Emperor Constantine moved his capital to the Greek city of Byzantium and here emerged Constantinople (modern Istanbul), the "new Rome" and spiritual and political capital of the **Byzantine Empire**.

While the last western Roman emperor was deposed by barbarian Goths in 476, this oriental portion was to be the dominant Mediterranean power for some 700 years; only in 1453 did it collapse completely.

CHRISTIANITY

Christianity had been introduced under Constantine, and by the end of the fourth century was the official state religion, its liturgies (still in use in the Greek Orthodox church), creed and New Testament all written in Greek. A distinction must be drawn, though, between perceptions of Greek as a language and culture, and as a concept. The Byzantine Empire styled itself Roman, or *Romios*, rather than Hellenic, and moved to eradicate all remaining symbols of pagan Greece. The Delphic Oracle was forcibly closed, and the Olympic Games discontinued, by the emperor Theodosius at the end of the fourth century.

The seventh century saw **Constantinople** besieged by Persians, and later Arabs, but the Byzantine Empire survived, losing only Egypt, the least "Greek" of its territories. From the ninth to the early eleventh centuries it enjoyed an archetypal "golden age", in culture, confidence and security. Tied up in the Orthodox Byzantine faith was a sense of spiritual superiority, and the emperors saw Constantinople as a "new Jerusalem" for their "chosen people". It was the beginning of a diplomatic and ecclesiastical conflict with the Catholic west that was to have disastrous consequences over the next five centuries. In the meantime the eastern and western patriarchs mutually excommunicated each other.

From the seventh through to the eleventh centuries **Byzantine Greece**, certainly in the islands, became something of a provincial backwater, with islands such as Lésvos, Kálymnos and Ikaría used (as they had been during Roman times) as places of exile for troublesome notables. Administration was absurdly top-heavy and imperial taxation led to semi-autonomous provinces ruled by military generals, whose lands were usually acquired from bankrupted peasants. This alienation of the poor provided a force for change, with a floating populace ready to turn towards or co-operate with the empire's enemies if terms were an improvement.

Waves of **Slavic raiders** needed no encouragement to sweep down from the north Balkans throughout this period. At the same time other tribal groups moved down more peaceably from **central Europe** and were absorbed with little difficulty. According to one theory, the nomadic **Vlachs** from Romania eventually settled in the Píndhos Mountains, and later, from the thirteenth century onwards, immigrants from **Albania** repopulated the islands of Spétses, Ídhra, Ándhros and Évvia, as well as parts of Attica and the Peloponnese.

THE CRUSADES: FRANKISH AND VENETIAN RULE

From the early years of the eleventh century, less welcome and less assimilable Western forces began to appear. The **Normans** landed first at Corfu in 1085, and returned again to the mainland with papal sanction a decade later on their way to liberate Jerusalem.

These were only a precursor, though, for the forces that were to descend en route for the **Fourth Crusade** of 1204, when Venetians,

Franks and Germans turned their armies directly on Byzantium and sacked and occupied Constantinople. These Latin princes and their followers, intent on new lands and kingdoms, settled in to divide up the best part of the Empire. All that remained of Byzantium were four small peripheral kingdoms or **despotates**: the most powerful in Nicaea in Asia Minor, less significant ones at Trebizond on the Black Sea, and (in present-day Greece) in Epirus and around Mystra in the Peloponnese (known in these times as the Morea).

There followed two extraordinarily involved centuries of manipulation and struggle between Franks, Venetians, Genoese, Catalans and Turks. The Paleologos dynasty at Nicaea recovered the city of Constantinople in 1261, but little of its former territory and power. Instead, the focus of Byzantium shifted to the Peloponnese, where the autonomous **Despotate of Mystra**, ruled by members of the imperial family, eventually succeeded in wresting most of the peninsula from Frankish hands. At the same time this despotate underwent an intense cultural renaissance, strongly evoked in the churches and shells of cities seen today at Mystra and Monemvassía.

TURKISH OCCUPATION

Within a generation of driving out the Franks, the Byzantine Greeks faced a much stronger threat in the expanding empire of the **Ottoman Turks**. Torn apart by internal struggles between their own ruling dynasties, the **Palaeologi** and **Cantacuzenes**, and unaided by the Catholic west, they were to prove no match for the Turks. On Tuesday, May 29, 1453, a date still solemnly commemorated by the Orthodox church, Constantinople fell to besieging Muslim Ottomans.

Mystra was to follow within seven years, and Trebizond within nine, by which time virtually all of the old Byzantine Empire lay under Ottoman domination. Only the **Ionian islands** (excluding Lefkádha) and the **Cyclades**, which remained Venetian, and a few scattered and remote enclaves – like the Máni in the Peloponnese, Sfakiá in Crete and Soúli in Epirus – were able to resist the Turkish advance.

OTTOMAN RULE

Under what Greeks refer to as the "Dark Ages" of **Ottoman rule**, the lands of present-day

Greece passed into rural provincialism, taking refuge in a self-protective mode of village life that has only recently been disrupted. Taxes and discipline, sporadically backed up by the geno- cide of dissenting communities, were inflicted by the Turkish Porte, but estates passed into the hands of local chieftains who often had con- siderable independence. On the larger, more fertile islands such as Crete, Lésvos and Évvia, rule was inevitably stricter with larger garrisons and more onerous taxes; small islands too impoverished to be exploited were left pretty much to their own devices.

Greek identity, meanwhile, was preserved through the offices of the **Orthodox church** which, despite instances of enforced conver- sion, the sultans allowed to continue. The **monasteries**, sometimes secretly, organized schools and became the trustees of Byzantine culture, though this had gone into stagnation after the fall of Constantinople and Mystra, whose scholars and artists emigrated west, adding impetus to the Renaissance.

As Ottoman administration became more and more decentralized and inefficient, individ- ual Greeks rose to local positions of consider- able influence, and a number of communities achieved a degree of autonomy. Sými was granted an empire-wide monopoly on sponge- diving in return for a yearly tribute to the sultan; Sámos was declared a "Muslim-free" zone and enjoyed special tax exemptions for two cen- turies. And on the Albanian repopulated islands of Ídhra and Spétses, as well as Kássos and Psára, a **Greek merchant fleet** came into being in the eighteenth century, permitted to trade throughout the Mediterranean. Greeks, too, were becoming organized overseas in the sizeable expatriate colonies of central Europe, which often had affiliations with the semi- autonomous village clusters of Zagória (in Epirus), Ambelákia (Thessaly) and Mount Pílion.

THE STRUGGLE FOR INDEPENDENCE

Despite these privileges, by the eighteenth cen- tury opposition to Turkish rule was becoming widespread on the mainland, exemplified most obviously by the **Klephts** (brigands) of the mountains. It was not until the nineteenth cen- tury, however, that a resistance movement could muster sufficient support and firepower to prove a real challenge to the Turks. In 1770 a

Russian-backed uprising had been easily and brutally suppressed, but fifty years later the position was different.

In Epirus the Turks were over-extended, sub- duing the expansionist campaigns of local ruler **Ali Pasha**. The French Revolution had given impetus to the confidence of "freedom move- ments", and the Greek fighters were given financial and ideological underpinning by the Filikí Etería, or "Friendly Society", a secret group recruited among the exiled merchants and intellectuals of central Europe.

This somewhat motley coalition of Klephts and theorists launched their insurrection at the monastery of **Ayia Lávra** near Kalávryta in the Peloponnese, where on March 25, 1821, the Greek banner was openly raised by the local bishop, Yermanos.

THE WAR OF INDEPENDENCE

To describe in detail the course of the **War of Independence** is to provoke unnecessary con- fusion, since much of the rebellion consisted of local and fragmentary guerrila campaigns. What is important to understand is that Greeks, though fighting for liberation from the Ottomans, were not fighting as and for a nation. Motives differed enormously: landowners assumed their role was to lead and sought to retain and reinforce their traditional privileges, while the peasantry saw the struggle as a means towards land redistribution.

Outside Greece, prestige and publicity for the insurrection was promoted by the arrival of a thousand or so European **Philhellenes**, almost half of them German, though the most impor- tant was the English poet, **Lord Byron**, who died while training Greek forces at Messolóngi in April 1824.

Though it was the Greek guerilla leaders, above all **Theodhoros Kolokotronis**, "the old man of the Morea", who brought about the most significant military victories of the war, the death of Byron had an immensely important effect on public opinion in the West. Aid for the Greek struggle had come neither from Orthodox Russia, nor from the Western powers of France and Britain, ravaged by the Napoleonic Wars. But by 1827, when Messolóngi fell again to the Turks, these three powers finally agreed to seek autonomy for certain parts of Greece and sent a combined fleet to put pressure on the sultan's Egyptian army, then ransacking and massacring in the Peloponnese. Events took over, and an accidental naval battle in **Navarino Bay** resulted in the destruction of almost the entire Turkish-Egyptian fleet. The following spring Russia itself declared war on the Turks and the sultan was forced to accept the existence of an autonomous Greece.

At a series of conferences from 1830 to 1832, Greek independence was confirmed by the Western powers and **borders** were drawn. These included just 800,000 of the 6 million Greeks living within the Ottoman empire, and the Greek territories which were for the most part the poorest of the Classical and Byzantine lands, comprising Attica, the Peloponnese and the islands of the Argo-Saronic, the Sporades and the Cyclades. The rich agricultural belt of Thessaly, Epirus in the west, and Macedonia in the north, remained in Turkish hands. Meanwhile, the Ionian islands were controlled by a British Protectorate and the Dodecanese by the Ottomans (and after 1913 by newly unified Italy).

THE EMERGING STATE

Modern Greece began as a republic and **Ioannis Capodistrias**, its first president, concentrated his efforts on building a viable central authority and government in the face of diverse protagonists from the independence struggle. Almost inevitably he was assassinated – in 1831, by two chieftains from the ever-disruptive Máni – and perhaps equally inevitably the great Western powers stepped in. They created a monarchy, gave limited aid and set on the throne a Bavarian prince, **Otho**.

The new king proved an autocratic and insensitive ruler, bringing in fellow Germans to fill official posts and ignoring all claims by the landless peasantry for redistribution of the old estates. In 1862 he was eventually forced from the country by a popular revolt, and the Europeans produced a new prince, this time from Denmark, with Britain ceding the Ionian islands to bolster support. **George I**, in fact, proved more capable: he built the first railways and roads, introduced limited land reforms in the Peloponnese, and oversaw the first expansion of the Greek borders.

THE MEGÁLI IDHÉA AND WAR

From the very beginning, the unquestioned motive force of Greek foreign policy was the **Megáli Idhéa** (Great Idea) of liberating Greek populations outside the country and incorporating the old territories of Byzantium into the kingdom. In 1878 **Thessaly**, along with southern Epirus, was ceded to Greece by the Turks.

Less illustriously, the Greeks failed in 1897 to achieve *énosis* (union) with **Crete** by attacking Turkish forces on the mainland, and in the process virtually bankrupted the state. The island was, however, placed under a High Commissioner, appointed by France, England and Russia, and in 1913 became a part of Greece.

It was from Crete, also, that the most distinguished Greek statesman emerged. **Eleftherios Venizelos**, having led a civilian campaign for his island's liberation, was elected as Greek Prime Minister in 1910. Two years later he organized an alliance of Balkan powers to fight the **Balkan Wars** (1912–13), campaigns that saw the Turks virtually driven from Europe. With Greek borders extended to include the northeast Aegean islands, northern Thessaly, central Epirus and parts of Macedonia, the Megáli Idhéa was approaching reality. At the same time Venizelos proved himself a shrewd manipulator of domestic public opinion by revising the constitution and introducing a series of liberal social reforms.

Division, however, was to appear with the outbreak of **World War I**. Venizelos urged Greek entry on the Allied side, seeing in the conflict possibilities for the "liberation" of Greeks in Thrace and Asia Minor, but the new king, Constantine I, who was married to a sister of the German Kaiser, imposed a policy of neutrality. Eventually Venizelos set up a revolutionary government in Thessaloníki, and in 1917 Greek troops entered the war to join the French, British and Serbians in the **Macedonian campaign**. On the capitulation of Bulgaria and Ottoman Turkey, the Greeks occupied **Thrace**, and Venizelos presented demands at Versailles for the predominantly Greek region of Smyrna on the Asia Minor coast.

This was the beginning of one of the most disastrous episodes in modern Greek history. Venizelos was authorized to move forces into Smyrna in 1919, but by then Allied support had evaporated and in Turkey itself a new nationalist movement was taking power under Mustafa Kemal, or **Atatürk** as he came to be known. In 1920 Venizelos lost the elections and monarchist factions took over, their aspirations unmitigated by the Cretan's skill in foreign diplomacy. Greek forces were ordered to advance upon Ankara in an attempt to bring Atatürk to terms.

This so-called **Anatolian campaign** ignominiously collapsed in the summer of 1922 when Turkish troops forced the Greeks back to the coast and into a hurried evacuation from **Smyrna**. As they left Smyrna, the Turks moved in and systematically massacred whatever remained of the Armenian and Greek populations before burning most of the city to the ground.

THE EXCHANGE OF POPULATIONS

There was now no alternative for Greece but to accept Atatürk's own terms, formalized by the Treaty of Lausanne in 1923, which ordered the **exchange of religious minorities** in each country. Turkey was to accept 390,000 Muslims resident on Greek soil. Greece, mobilized almost continuously for the last decade and with a population of under five million, was faced with the resettlement of over 1,300,000 Christian refugees. Many of these had already read the writing on the wall after 1918 and arrived of their own accord; significant numbers were settled on Lésvos, Khíos, Sámos, Évvia and Crete. The Megáli Idhéa had ceased to be a viable blueprint.

Changes were inevitably intense and far-reaching. The great agricultural estates of Crete, Évvia and Thessaly were finally redistributed, both to Greek tenants and refugee farmers, and huge shanty towns grew into new quarters around Athens, Pireás and other cities, a spur to the country's then almost nonexistent industry.

Politically, too, reaction was swift. A group of army officers assembled after the retreat from Smyrna, "invited" King Constantine to abdicate, and executed six of his ministers held most responsible for the debacle. Democracy was nominally restored with the proclamation of a republic, but for much of the next decade changes in government were brought about by factions within the armed forces. Meanwhile, among the urban refugee population, unions were being formed and the Greek Communist Party (KKE) was established.

By 1936 the Communist Party had enough democratic support to hold the balance of power in parliament, and would have done so

had not the army and the by-then restored king decided otherwise. King George II had been returned by a plebiscite held – and almost certainly manipulated – the previous year, and so presided over an increasingly factionalized parliament.

THE METAXAS DICTATORSHIP

In April 1936 George II appointed **General John Metaxas** as prime minister, despite the latter's support from only six parliamentary deputies. Immediately a series of KKE-organized strikes broke out and the king, ignoring attempts to form a broad liberal coalition, dissolved parliament without setting a date for new elections. It was a blatantly unconstitutional move and opened the way for five years of ruthless and at times absurd dictatorship.

Metaxas averted a general strike with military force and proceeded to set up a state based on **fascist** models of the age. Left-wing and trade union opponents were imprisoned or forced into exile, a state youth movement and secret police was set up, and rigid censorship, extending even to passages of Thucydides, imposed. It was, however, at least a Greek dictatorship, and though Metaxas was sympathetic to Nazi organization he completely opposed German or Italian domination.

WORLD WAR II AND THE GREEK CIVIL WAR

Using a submarine based on Léros, the Italians tried to provoke the Greeks into **World War II** by surreptitiously torpedoing the Greek cruiser Elli in Tínos harbour on August 15, 1940, but they met with no response. However, when Mussolini occupied Albania and sent an ultimatum on October 28, 1940, demanding passage for his troops through Greece, Metaxas responded to the Italian foreign minister with the apocryphal one-word answer **"ókhi"** (no). (In fact, his response, in the mutually understood French, was "C'est la guerre"). The date marked the entry of Greece into the war, and the gesture is still celebrated as a national holiday.

OCCUPATION AND RESISTANCE

Fighting as a nation in a sudden unity of crisis, the Greeks drove Italian forces from the country and took control of the long-coveted and predominantly Greek-populated northern Epirus (the south of Albania). However, the Greek army frittered away their strength in the snowy mountains of northern Epirus rather than consolidate their gains or defend the Macedonian frontier, and co-ordination with the British never materialized.

In April of the following year Nazi mechanized columns swept through Yugoslavia and across the Greek mainland, effectively reversing the only Axis defeat to date, and by the end of May 1941, airborne and seaborne **German invasion** forces had completed the occupation of Crete and the other islands. Metaxas had died before their arrival, while King George and his new self-appointed ministers fled into exile in Cairo; few Greeks, of any political persuasion, were sad to see them go.

The joint Italian–German–Bulgarian Axis **occupation** of Greece was among the bitterest experiences of the European war. Nearly half a million Greek civilians starved to death over the winter of 1941–42 as all available food was requisitioned to feed occupying armies, and entire villages throughout the mainland and especially on Crete were burned at the least hint of resistance activity. In the north, including on Thássos and Samothráki, the Bulgarians desecrated ancient sites and churches in a bid to annex "Slavic" eastern Macedonia and Thrace.

After the Italians capitulated in autumn 1943, the Jewish communities on Rhodes, Kós, Crete, Corfu, Évvia, and Zákynthos in particular were exposed to the full force of Nazi racial doctrine; on the latter two islands, co-operation between courageous church and municipal authorities and the budding resistance (see below) ensured that local Jews survived almost to a man, but elsewhere the communities were virtually wiped out.

With a quisling government in Athens – and an unpopular, discredited Royalist group in Cairo – the focus of Greek political and military action between 1942 and 1945 passed largely to the **EAM**, or National Liberation Front. By 1943 it was in virtual control of most areas of the country, including Sámos and Lésvos (but not Crete), working with the British on tactical operations, with its own army (**ELAS**), navy, and both civil and secret police forces. Initially it commanded widespread popular support, and appeared to offer an obvious framework for the resumption of postwar government.

However, most of its membership was communist, and the British Prime Minister, **Churchill**, was determined to reinstate the monarchy. Even with two years of the war to run, it became obvious that there could be no peaceable post-liberation regime other than a republic. Accordingly, in August 1943, representatives from each of the main resistance movements (including two non-communist groups) flew clandestinely to Cairo to request that the king not return unless a plebiscite had first voted in his favour. Both Greek and British authorities refused to consider the proposal, and the best possibility of averting civil war was lost.

The EAM contingent returned divided, as perhaps the British had intended, and a conflict broke out between those who favoured taking peaceful control of any government imposed after liberation, and the hardline Stalinist ideologues, who forbade participation in any "bourgeois" regime.

In October 1943, with fears of an imminent British landing force and takeover, ELAS launched a full-scale attack upon its Greek rivals; by the following February, when a ceasefire was arranged, they had wiped out all but the EDES, a right-wing grouping suspected of collaboration with the Germans. At the same time other forces were at work, with both the British and Americans infiltrating units into Greece in order to prevent the establishment of a communist government when the Germans began withdrawing their forces.

CIVIL WAR

In fact, as the Germans began to leave in October 1944, most of the EAM leadership agreed to join a British-sponsored "official" **interim government**. It quickly proved a tactical error, however. With ninety percent of the countryside under their control, the communists were given only one-third representation, the king showed no sign of renouncing his claims, and, in November, Allied forces ordered ELAS to disarm. On December 3 all pretences of civility or neutrality were dropped. Civilian demonstrators were shot dead, either by policemen or a provacateur; within days fighting broke out between ELAS and **British troops**, in the so-called **Dhekemvrianá** battle of Athens.

A truce of sorts was negotiated at Várkiza the following spring, but the agreement was never implemented. The army, police and civil service remained in right-wing hands, and while collaborationists were often allowed to retain their positions, left-wing sympathizers, many of whom were not communists, were systematically excluded. The elections of 1946 were won by the right-wing parties, followed by a plebiscite in favour of the king's return. By 1947 guerilla activity had again reached the scale of a full **civil war**.

In the interim, King George had died and been succeeded by his brother Paul (with his consort Frederika), while the **Americans** had taken over the British role, and begun putting into action the cold war **Truman doctrine**. In 1947 they took virtual control of Greece, their first significant postwar experiment in anticommunist intervention. Massive economic and military aid was given to a client Greek government, with a prime minister whose documents had to be countersigned by the American Mission in order to become valid.

In the mountains US "military advisers" supervised **campaigns against ELAS**, and there were mass arrests, court martials, and imprisonments – a kind of "White Terror" – lasting until 1951. Over three thousand executions were recorded, including a number of Jehovah's Witnesses, "a sect proved to be under communist domination", according to US Ambassador Grady.

In the autumn of 1949, with the Yugoslav–Greek border closed after Tito's rift with Stalin, the last ELAS guerillas finally admitted defeat, retreating into Albania from their strongholds on Mount Grámmos. Atrocities had been committed on both sides, including – from the Left – widescale destruction of monasteries, show trials followed by summary executions, and the dubious evacuation of children from "combat areas" (as told in Nicholas Gage's virulently anti-communist book *Eleni*). Such errors, as well as the hopelessness of fighting an American-backed army, undoubtedly lost ELAS much support.

RECONSTRUCTION AMERICAN-STYLE 1950–67

It was a demoralized, shattered Greece that emerged into the Western political orbit of the 1950s. It was also perforce American-dominated, enlisted into the Korean War in 1950 and NATO the following year. In domestic politics, the US Embassy – still giving the orders – foist-

ed a winner-takes-all electoral system, which was to ensure victory for the Right over the next twelve years. All leftist activity was banned; those individuals who were not herded into political "re-education" camps or dispatched by firing squads, legal or vigilante, went into exile throughout Eastern Europe, to return only after 1974.

The American-backed, highly conservative **"Greek Rally"** party, led by General Papagos, won the first decisive post-Civil War elections in 1952. After the general's death, the party's leadership was taken over – and to an extent liberalized – by **Constantine Karamanlis**. Under his rule, stability of a kind was established and some economic advances registered, particularly after the revival of Greece's traditional German markets. However, the 1950s was also a decade that saw wholesale **depopulation** of villages as migrants sought work in Australia, North America and Western Europe, or the larger Greek cities. This was most pronounced in the remoter islands of Kýthira, Kefalloniá, the northeast Aegean and the Dodecanese, where the longed-for union with Greece in 1948 ironically conferred the right to emigrate, mostly denied under the Ottomans and Italians.

The main crisis in foreign policy throughout this period was **Cyprus**, where a long terrorist campaign was waged by Greeks opposing British rule, and there was sporadic threat of a new Greek-Turkish war. A temporary and unworkable solution was forced on the island by Britain in 1960, granting independence without the possibility of self-determination or union with Greece. Much of the traditional Greek–British goodwill was destroyed by the issue, with Britain seen to be acting with regard only for its two military bases (over which, incidentally, it still retains sovereignty).

By 1961, unemployment, the Cyprus issue and the imposition of US nuclear bases on Greek soil were changing the political climate, and when Karamanlis was again elected there was strong suspicion of a fraud arranged by the king and army. Strikes became frequent in industry and even agriculture, and King Paul and autocratic, fascist-inclined Queen Frederika were openly attacked in parliament and at protest demonstrations. The far right grew uneasy about **"communist resurgence"** and, losing confidence in their own electoral influence, arranged the assassination of left-wing deputy **Grigoris Lambrakis** in Thessaloníki in May 1963. (The assassination, and its subsequent cover-up, is the subject of Vassilis Vassilikos's thriller *Z*, filmed by Costa-Gavras.) It was against this volatile background that Karamanlis resigned, lost the subsequent elections and left the country.

The new government – the first controlled from outside the Greek right since 1935 – was formed by **George Papandreou's** Centre Union Party, and had a decisive majority of nearly fifty seats. It was to last, however, for less than two years as conservative forces rallied to thwart its progress. In this the chief protagonists were the army officers and their constitutional Commander-in-Chief, the new king, 23-year-old **Constantine II**.

Since power in Greece depended on a pliant military as well as a network of political appointees, Papandreou's most urgent task in order to govern securely and effectively was to reform the armed forces. His first Minister of Defence proved incapable of the task and, while he was investigating the right-wing plot that was thought to have rigged the 1961 election, "evidence" was produced of a leftist conspiracy connected with Papandreou's son Andreas (himself a minister in the government). The allegations grew to a crisis and Yiorgos Papandreou decided to assume the defence portfolio himself, a move for which the king refused to give the necessary sanction. He then resigned in order to gain approval at the polls but the king would not order fresh elections, instead persuading members of the Centre Union – chief among them **Constantine Mitsotakis**, later premier – to defect and organize a coalition government. Punctuated by strikes, resignations and mass demonstrations, this lasted for a year and a half until new elections were eventually set for May 28, 1967. They failed to take place.

THE COLONELS' JUNTA 1967–74

It was a foregone conclusion that Papandreou's party would win popular support in the polls against the discredited coalition partners. And it was equally certain that there would be some sort of anti-democratic action to try and prevent them from reassuming power. Disturbed by the party's leftward shift, King Constantine was said to have briefed senior generals for a coup d'état, to take place ten days before the elec-

tions. However, he was caught by surprise, as was nearly everyone else, by the **coup** of April 21, 1967, staged by a group of "unknown" colonels. It was, in the words of Andreas Papandreou, "the first successful CIA military putsch on the European continent".

The **Colonels' junta**, having appropriated all means of power, was sworn in by the king and survived the half-hearted counter-coup which he subsequently attempted to organize. It was an ostensibly **fascist regime**, absurdly styling itself as the true "Revival of Greek Orthodoxy" against Western "corrupting influences", though in reality its ideology was nothing more than warmed-up dogma from the Metaxas era mixed with ultra-nationalism.

All political activity was banned, trade unions were forbidden to recruit or meet, the press was so heavily censored that many papers stopped printing or published blank pages in protest, and thousands of "communists" were arrested, imprisoned, and often tortured. Among the persecuted were both Papandreous, the composer Mikis Theodorakis (deemed "unfit to stand trial" after three months in custody) and Amalia Fleming (widow of Alexander Fleming). While relatively few people were killed outright, thousands were permanently maimed physically and psychologically in the junta's torture chambers. The best-known Greek actress, Melina Mercouri, was stripped of her citizenship in absentia, and thousands of prominent Greeks joined her in exile.

Culturally, the colonels put an end to most popular live music (banning, for example, bagpipes on Mýkonos lest visitors think Greece too "primitive"), and inflicted ludicrous censorship on literature and the theatre, including (as under Metaxas) a ban on production of the Classical tragedies. By contrast, chief colonel Papadopoulos' rambling, illiterate speeches became a byword for bad grammar, obfuscation and newspeak, a trend unfortunately imitated by most elected leaders in subsequent decades.

The colonels lasted for seven years, opposed (especially after the first two years) by the majority of the Greek people, excluded from the European community, but propped up and given massive aid by US presidents **Lyndon Johnson** and **Richard Nixon**. To them and the CIA the junta's Greece was not an unsuitable client state; human rights considerations were considered unimportant; orders were placed for sophisticated military technology and foreign investment on terms highly unfavourable to Greece was open to multinational corporations. It was a fairly routine scenario for the exploitation of an underdeveloped nation.

Opposition was from the beginning voiced by exiled Greeks in London, the United States and Western Europe, but only in 1973 did demonstrations break out openly in Greece – the colonels' secret police had done too thorough a job of infiltrating domestic resistance groups and terrifying everyone else into docility. On November 17 the students of Athens **Polytechnic** began an occupation of their buildings. The ruling clique lost its nerve; armoured vehicles stormed the Polytechnic gates and a still-undetermined number of students, perhaps as many as four hundred, were killed and buried in unmarked graves. (Today they are commemorated across the islands by streets named for the Iróōn Polytelkhníou – "Heroes of the Polytechnic".) Martial law was tightened and junta chief **Colonel Papadopoulos** was replaced by the even more noxious and reactionary **General Ioannides**, head of the secret police.

THE RETURN TO CIVILIAN RULE 1975–81

The end of the ordeal, however, came within a year as the dictatorship embarked on a disastrous political adventure in **Cyprus**, essentially a last playing of the Megáli Idhéa card. By attempting to topple the Makarios government and impose *énosis* (union) on the island, they provoked a Turkish invasion and occupation of forty percent of the Cypriot territory. The army finally mutinied and **Karamanlis** was invited to return from Paris to again take office. He swiftly negotiated a ceasefire (but no solution) in Cyprus, withdrew temporarily from NATO, and warned that US bases would have to be removed except where they specifically served Greek interest.

In November 1974 Karamanlis and his Néa Dhimokratía (New Democracy) party were rewarded by a sizeable majority in **elections**, with a centrist and socialist opposition. The latter was constituted by the **Panhellenic Socialist Movement (PASOK)**, a new party led by Andreas Papandreou.

The election of Néa Dhimokratía was in every sense a safe conservative option but to

Karamanlis's enduring credit it oversaw an effective and firm return to democratic stability, even legalizing the KKE (Communist Party) for the first time in its history. Karamanlis also held a **referendum on the monarchy** – in which 59 percent of Greeks rejected the return of Constantine – and instituted in its place a French-style presidency, a post which he himself occupied from 1980 to 1985 (and again from 1990 to 1995). Economically there were limited advances although these were more than offset by inflationary defence spending (the result of renewed tension with Turkey), hastily negotiated entrance into the EC, and the decision to let the drachma float after decades of its being artificially fixed at thirty to the US dollar.

Crucially though, Karamanlis failed to deliver on vital reforms in bureaucracy, social welfare and education, and though the worst figures of the junta were brought to trial and jailed for life, the face of Greek political life and administration was little changed. By 1981 inflation was hovering around 25 percent, and it was estimated that tax evasion was depriving the state of one-third of its annual budget. In foreign policy the US bases remained and it was felt that Greece, back in NATO, was still acting as little more than an American satellite. The traditional right was demonstrably inadequate to the task at hand.

PASOK: 1981–89

"Change" (Allayí) and "Out with the Right" (*Na fíyi iy dhoxiá*) were the watchwords of the election campaign which swept PASOK and Andreas Papandreou to power on October 18, 1981.

This victory meant a chance for Papandreou to form the first socialist government in Greek history and break a half-century monopoly of authoritarian right-wing rule. With so much at stake the campaign had been passionate even by Greek standards, and PASOK's victory was greeted with euphoria both by the generation whose political voice had been silenced by defeat in the Civil War, and by a large proportion of the young. Their hopes perhaps ran naively and dangerously high.

The electoral margin, at least, was conclusive. PASOK won 174 of the 300 parliamentary seats and the Communist KKE returned another thirteen deputies, one of them composer Mikis Theodorakis. Néa Dhimokratía moved into unaccustomed opposition. There appeared to be no obstacle to the implementation of a **radical socialist programme**: devolution of power to local authorities, the socialization of industry (though it was never clear how this was to be different from nationalization), improvement of the woefully skeletal social services, a purge of bureaucratic inefficiency and malpractice, the end of bribery and corruption as a way of life, an independent and dignified foreign policy following expulsion of US bases, and withdrawal from NATO and the European Community.

A change of style was promised, too, replacing the country's long traditions of authoritarianism and bureaucracy with openness and dialogue. Even more radically, where Greek political parties had long been composed of the personal followers of charismatic leaders, PASOK was to be a party of ideology and principle, dominated by no single individual member. Or so, at least, some of the youthful PASOK political enthusiasts thought.

The new era started with a bang. The wartime resistance was officially recognized; hitherto they hadn't been allowed to take part in any celebrations, wreath-layings or other ceremonies. Peasant women were granted pensions for the first time – 3000 drachmas a month (about US$55 in 1982), the same as their outraged husbands – and wages were indexed to the cost of living. In addition, civil marriage was introduced, family law reformed in favour of wives and mothers, and equal rights legislation was put on the statute book.

These quick, no-cost, popular **reformist moves** seemed to mark a break with the past, and the atmosphere had indeed changed. Greeks no longer lowered their voices to discuss politics in public places or wrapped their leftist newspaper in the respectably conservative *Kathimerini*. At first there were real fears that the climate would be too much for the military and they would once again intervene to choke a dangerous experiment in democracy, especially when Andreas Papandreou assumed the defence portfolio himself in a move strongly reminiscent of his father's attempt to remove the king's appointee in 1965. But he went out of his way to soothe **military susceptibilities**, increasing their salaries, buying new weaponry, and being super-fastidious in his attendance at military functions. But in reality, the resistance of the Polytechnic students to the junta was

mythologized, and PASOK activists could be relied upon to form cordons around party headquarters at the least sign of unrest in the armed forces.

THE END OF THE HONEYMOON

Nothing if not a populist, **Papandreou** promised a bonanza he must have known, as a trained and experienced academic economist, he could not deliver. As a result he pleased nobody on the **economic** front.

He could not fairly be blamed for the inherited lack of investment, low productivity, deficiency in managerial and labour skills and other chronic problems besetting the Greek economy. On the other hand, he certainly aggravated the situation in the early days of his first term in office by allowing his supporters to indulge in violently anti-capitalist rhetoric, and by the prosecution and humiliation of the Tsatsos family, owners of one of Greece's few profitable businesses (Hercules Cement) for the illegal export of capital, something of which every Greek with any savings is guilty. These were cheap victories and were not backed by any programme of public investment, while the only "socializations" were of hopelessly lame-duck companies.

Faced with this sluggish economy, and burdened with the additional charges of (marginally) improved social benefits and wage indexing, Papandreou's government had also to cope with the effects of **world recession**, which always hit Greece with a delayed effect compared with its more advanced European partners. **Shipping**, the country's main foreign-currency earner, was devastated. Remittances from emigré workers fell off as they joined the lines of the unemployed in their host countries, and tourism receipts diminished under the dual impact of recession and US President Ronald Reagan's warning to Americans to stay away from allegedly insecure and terrorist-prone Athens airport.

With huge quantities of imported goods continuing to be sucked into the country in the absence of domestic production, the **foreign debt** topped £10 billion in 1986, with inflation still at 25 percent and the balance of payments deficit approaching £1 billion. Greece also began to experience the social strains of **unemployment** for the first time. Not that it didn't exist before, but it had always been concealed as under-employment because of the family and the rural structure of the economy – as well as by the absence of statistics.

THE SECOND TERM

A modest spending spree transparently intended to buy votes, continued satisfaction with the discomfiture of the right, the popularity of his Greece-for-the-Greeks foreign policy and some much needed reforms saw Papandreou through into a **second term**, with an electoral victory in June 1985 scarcely less triumphant than the first. But his complacent and, frankly, dishonest slogan was "Vote PASOK for Even Better Days". By October they had imposed a two-year wage freeze and import restrictions, abolished the wage-indexing scheme and devalued the drachma by fifteen percent. Papandreou's fat was pulled out of the fire by none other than that former bogeyman, the **European Community**, which offered a huge two-part loan on condition that an IMF-style **austerity programme** was maintained.

The political fallout of such classic right-wing strategies, accompanied by shameless soliciting for foreign investment, was the alienation of the communists and most of PASOK's own political constituency. Increasingly autocratic (ironic given earlier pledges of openness), Papandreou's response to **dissent** was to fire recalcitrant trade union leaders and expel some three hundred members of his own party. Assailed by strikes, the government lost direction completely, and in the municipal October 1986 elections lost the mayoralties of the three major cities, Athens, Thessaloníki and Pátra, to Néa Dhimokratía.

Papandreou assured the nation that he had taken the message to heart, but all that followed was a minor government reshuffle and a panicky attempt to undo the ill-feeling caused by an incredible freeing of **rent controls** at a time when all wage-earners were feeling the pinch badly. Early in 1987 he went further and sacked all the remaining PASOK veterans in his cabinet, including his son, though it is said, probably correctly, that this was a palliative to public opinion. The new cabinet was so un-socialist that even the right-wing press called it **"centrist"**.

Similar about-faces took place in **foreign policy**. PASOK's initial anti-US, anti-NATO and anti-EC rhetoric was immensely popular, and

understandable for a people shamelessly bullied by bigger powers since 1830. There was some high-profile nose-thumbing, like refusing to join EC partners in condemning Jaruzelski's Polish regime, or the Soviet downing of a Korean airliner, or Syrian involvement in terrorist bomb-planting. There were some forgettable embarrassments, too, like suggesting Gaddafi's Libya provided a suitable model for alternative socialist development, and the Mitterrand-Gaddafi-Papandreou "summit" in Crete, which an infuriated Mitterrand felt he had been inveigled into on false pretences.

Much was made of a strategic opening to the Arab world. Yasser Arafat, for example, was the first "head of state" to be received in Athens under the PASOK government. Given Greece's geographical position and historical ties, it was an at least understandable policy. But if Gulf-Arab-state investment was hoped for, it never materialized.

In stark contrast to his early promises and rhetoric, the "realistic" policies that Papandreou pursued were far more conciliatory towards his big Western brothers. This was best exemplified by the fact that **US bases** remained in Greece, largely due to the fear that snubbing NATO would lead to Greece being exposed to Turkish aggression, still the only issue that unites the main parties to any degree. As for the once-reviled **European Community**, Greece had become an established beneficiary and its leader was hardly about to bite the hand that feeds.

SCANDAL

Even as late as mid-1988, despite the many betrayals and failures of Papandreou, and despite a level of popular displeasure that brought a million striking, demonstrating workers into the streets (February 1987), it seemed unlikely that PASOK would be toppled in the following year's **elections**.

This was due mainly to the lack of a credible alternative. Constantine Mitsotakis, a bitter personal enemy of Papandreou since 1965, when his defection had brought down his father's government and set in train the events that culminated in the junta, was an unconvincing and unlikeable character at the helm of Néa Dhimokratía. Meanwhile, the liberal centre had disappeared and the main communist party, KKE, appeared trapped in a Stalinist timewarp

WOMEN'S RIGHTS IN GREECE

Women's right to vote wasn't universally achieved in Greece until 1956 and, until the mid 1970s, adultery was still a punishable offence, with cases regularly brought to court. The socialist party, PASOK, was elected for terms of government in 1981 and 1985 with a strong theoretical programme for **women's rights**, and their women's council review committees, set up in the early, heady days, effected a landmark reform with the 1983 **Family Law**. This prohibited dowry and stipulated equal legal status and shared property rights between husband and wife.

Subsequently however, the PASOK governments did little to follow through on **practical issues**, like improved child care, health and family planning. Contraception is not available as part of the skeletal Greek public health service, leaving many women to fall back on abortion as the preferred method of birth control – still running (as for many years past) to an estimated 70–80,000 a year.

By far the largest womens'-rights organization is the **Union of Greek Women**. Founded in 1976, this espouses an independent feminist line and is responsible for numerous consciousness-raising activities across the country, though it remains too closely linked to PASOK for the comfort of many. Indeed, Margaret Papandreou felt compelled to resign from the Union following her well-publicized divorce from Andreas, leaving it without her effective and vocal leadership. Other, more autonomous groups have been responsible for setting up advice and support networks, highlighting women's issues within trade unions, and campaigning for changes in media representation.

None of this is easy in a country as polarized as Greece. In many rural areas women rely heavily on traditional extended families for security, and are unlikely to be much affected by legislative reforms or city politics. Yet Greek men of all classes and backgrounds are slowly becoming used to the notion of women in positions of power and responsibility, and taking a substantial share in child-rearing – both postures utterly unthinkable two decades ago, and arguably one of the few positive legacies with which PASOK can at least in part be credited.

---

under the leadership of Kharilaos Florakis. Only the Ellenikí Aristerá (Greek Left), formerly the Euro-wing of the KKE, seemed to offer any sensible alternative programme, and they had a precariously small following.

However a combination of spectacular **own goals**, plus perhaps a general shift to the Right influenced by the cataclysmic events in Eastern Europe, conspired against PASOK.

First came the extraordinary cavortings of the Prime Minister himself. Towards the end of 1988, the seventy-year-old Papandreou was flown to Britain for open-heart surgery. He took the occasion, with fear of death presumably rocking his judgement, to make public a year-long liaison with a 34-year-old Olympic Airways hostess, **Dimitra "Mimi" Liani**. Widespread media images of an old man shuffling about after a young blonde, to the public humiliation of Margaret, his American-born wife, and his family, were not popular. Papandreou subsequently divorced Margaret and married Mimi. His integrity was further questioned when he missed several important public engagements – including a ceremony commemorating the victims of the 1987 Kalamáta earthquake – preferring to hit the town with Mimi, reliving his youth in flashy nightspots.

The real damage, however, was done by **economic scandals**. It became known that a PASOK minister had passed off Yugoslav corn as Greek in a sale to the EC. Then, far more seriously, it emerged that a self-made, Greek-American con-man, **Yiorgos Koskotas**, director of the **Bank of Crete**, had embezzled £120m (US$190m) of deposits and, worse still, slipped though the authorities' fingers on a private jet and sought asylum in the US, where he'd begun his career as a housepainter. Certain PASOK ministers and even Papandreou himself were implicated in the scandal. Further damage was done by allegations of illegal **arms dealings** by still more government ministers.

United in disgust at this corruption, the other left-wing parties – KKE and Ellinikí Aristerá – formed a coalition, the **Synaspismós**, siphoning off still more support from PASOK.

THREE BITES AT THE CHERRY

In this climate of disaffection, an inconclusive result to the **June 1989 election** was no real surprise. What was less predictable, however, was the formation of a bizarre **"kathársis" (purgative) coalition** of conservatives and communists, united in the avowed intent of cleansing PASOK's increasingly Augean stables.

The Synaspismós would have formed a government with PASOK but set one condition for doing so – that Papandreou step down as Prime Minister – and the old man would have none of it. In the deal finally cobbled together between the left and Néa Dhimokratía, Mitsotakis was denied the premiership, too, having to make way for compromise choice **Tzannis Tzanetakis**, a popular former naval officer who had led a mutiny against the junta.

During the three months that the coalition lasted, *kathársis* turned out to be largely a question of burying the knife as deeply as possible into the ailing body of PASOK. Andreas Papandreou and three other ministers were officially accused of involvement in the Koskotas affair – though there was no time to set up their **trial** before the Greek people returned once again to the polls. In any case, the chief witness and protagonist in the affair, Koskotas himself, was still imprisoned in America, awaiting extradition proceedings.

Contrary to the Right's hope that publicly accusing Papandreou and his cohorts of criminal behaviour would pave the way for a Néa Dhimokratía victory, PASOK actually made a slight recovery in **November 1989 elections**, though the result was still inconclusive. This time the Left resolutely refused to do deals with anyone, and the result was a consensus caretaker government under the neutral aegis of an academic called Zolotas, who was dragged into the Prime Minister's office – somewhat unwillingly it seemed – from Athens University. His only mandate was to see that the country didn't go off the rails completely while preparations were made for yet more elections.

These took place in **April 1990** with the same captains at the command of their ships and with the Synaspismós having completed its about-face to the extent that in the five single-seat constituencies (the other 295 seats are drawn from multiple-seat constituencies in a complicated system of reinforced proportional representation), they supported independent candidates jointly with PASOK. Greek communists are good at about-turns, though; after all, composer Mikis Theodorakis, musical torchbearer of the Left during the dark years of the junta, and formerly a KKE MP, was by now standing for Néa Dhimokratía, prior to his resignation from politics altogether.

On the night, Néa Dhimokratía scraped home with a majority of one, later doubled with the defection of a centrist, and **Mitsotakis** finally realized his long-cherished dream of becoming prime minister. The only other memorable feature of the election was the first parliamentary representation for an independent member of the Turkish minority in Thrace, and for the Greens in Attica – a focus for many disaffected PASOK voters.

A RETURN TO THE RIGHT: MITSOTAKIS

On assuming power, Mitsotakis prescribed a course of **austerity measures** to try and revive the chronically ill economy. Little headway was made, though given the world recession, it was hardly surprising. Greek inflation was still approaching twenty percent annually, and at nearly ten percent, **unemployment** remained chronic.

The latter has been exacerbated since 1990, by the arrival of hundreds of thousands of impoverished **Albanians** who now form something of an underclass, especially those who aren't ethnically Greek, and are prey to vilification for all manner of ills. They have also led to the first real immigration measures in a country whose population is more used to being on the other side of such laws.

Other conservative measures introduced by Mitsotakis included laws to combat strikes and **terrorism**. This had been a perennial source of worry for Greeks since the appearance in the mid-1970s of a group called **Dhekaeftá Novemvríou** ("November 17", the date of the Colonels' attack on the Polytechnic in 1973). Since 1974 they (and more recent, copycat groups) have killed over twenty industrialists, politicians, foreign diplomats and NATO military personnel, and attacked foreign property in Athens; the lack of any significant arrests to date fuels continued speculation that they are a rogue faction from within PASOK itself. It hardly seemed likely that Mitsotakis's laws, however, were the solution. They stipulated that the typically long, ideological statements of the group could no longer be published, and led to one or two newspaper editors being jailed for a few days for defiance – much to everyone's embarrassment.

The **anti-strike laws** threatened severe penalties but were equally ineffectual, as breakdowns in public transport, electricity and rubbish collection all too frequently illustrated.

As for the **Koskotas scandal**, the man himself was eventually extradited and gave evidence for the prosecution against Papandreou and various of his ministers. The trial was televised and proved as popular as any soap opera, as indeed it should have done, given the twists of high drama – which included one of the defendants, Agamemnon Koutsoyiorgas, dying of a heart attack in court in front of the cameras. The case against Papandreou gradually petered out and he was officially acquitted (by a margin of one vote on the tribunal panel) in early 1992. The two other surviving ministers, Tsovolas and Petsos, were convicted, given jail sentences (bought off with a fine) and barred from public office for a time.

The great showcase trial thus went out with a whimper rather than a bang, and did nothing to enhance Mitsotakis's position. If anything, it served to increase sympathy for Papandreou, who was felt to have been unfairly victimized. The indisputable villain of the piece, Koskotas, was eventually convicted of major **fraud** and is now serving a lengthy sentence.

THE MACEDONIAN QUESTION

Increasingly unpopular because of the desperate austerity measures, and perceived as ineffective and out of his depth on the international scene, the last thing Mitsotakis needed was a major **foreign policy** headache. That is exactly what he got when, in 1991, one of the breakaway republics of the former Yugoslavia named itself Macedonia, thereby injuring Greek national pride and sparking off vehement protests at home and abroad. Diplomatically, the Greeks fought tooth and nail against anyone's recognizing the breakaway state, let alone its use of the name "Macedonia", but their position became increasingly isolated, and by 1993 the new country had gained official recognition from both the EU and the UN – albeit under the provisional title of the Former Yugoslav Republic of Macedonia (FYROM).

Salt was rubbed into Greek wounds when the FYROM started using the Star of Veryína as a national symbol on their new flag. Greece still refuses to call its neighbour Macedonia, instead referring to it as *Ta Skópia* after the capital –

and you can't go anywhere in Greece these days without encountering officially placed stickers proclaiming that "Macedonia was, is, and always will be Greek and only Greek!" Strong words.

THE PENDULUM SWINGS BACK

In effect, the Macedonian problem more or less directly led to Mitsotakis's **political demise**. In the early summer of 1993 his ambitious young foreign minister, **Andonis Samaras**, disaffected with his leader, jumped on the bandwagon of resurgent Greek nationalism to set up his own party, **Politikí Ánixi** (Political Spring). His platform, still right-wing, was largely based on firmer action over Macedonia, and during the summer of 1993 more ND MPs broke ranks, making Politikí Ánixi a force to be reckoned with. When parliament reconvened in September to approve severe new budget proposals, it became clear that the government lacked support, and early elections were called for October 1993. Mitsotakis had also been plagued for nearly a year by accusations of phone-tapping, theft of antiquities to stock his large private collection in Crete, and links with a nasty and complicated contracts scandal centred around the national cement company.

Many of ND's disillusioned supporters reverted directly to PASOK, and **Papandreou** romped to election victory.

THE MORNING AFTER

And so a frail-looking Papandreou, now well into his Seventies, became Prime Minister for the third time. He soon realized that the honeymoon was going to be neither as sweet nor as long as it had been in the Eighties.

PASOK immediately fulfilled two of its pre-election promises by removing restrictions on the reporting of statements by terrorist groups and renationalizing the Athens city bus company. The new government also set about improving the health system, and began to set the wheels in motion for Mitsotakis to be tried for his alleged misdemeanours, although all charges were mysteriously dropped in early 1995, prompting allegations of under-the-table dealings between Papandreou and his old nemesis.

The root of popular dissatisfaction was still **the economy**, which remained in dire straits despite ongoing austerity measures. There was increasing tension with Albania as refugees poured across the border in ever greater numbers, and several ethnic Greek activists went on trial in Tirana for subversive activities. PASOK could hardly claim any diplomatic victories on the Macedonian question, despite tough posturing; the only concrete move was a trade embargo imposed on the FYROM in late 1993, which merely landed Greece in trouble with the European Court of Justice – and succeeded in virtually shutting down the port of Thessaloníki. By contrast, alone among NATO members, Greece was conspicuous for its support of Serbia in the wars wracking ex-Yugoslavia, ostentatiously breaking that particular embargo with supply trucks to Belgrade via Bulgaria.

In autumn 1994, for the first time ever in a PASOK-sponsored reform, provincial governors were directly elected, rather than appointed from Athens. The following spring, presidential elections were held in parliament to designate a successor to the 88-year-old Karamanlís. The winner, agreed on by PASOK and Politikí Ánixi, was Kostis Stefanopoulos, former head of the defunct DIANA (Democratic Renewal – another ND offshoot), something of a nonentity but untainted by scandal and unlikely to cause an early end to PASOK's four-year term of office.

The prime recurring scandal for 1995 had to do with the high-security **Korýdhallos prison**, home to the surviving junta figures and Koskotas – and Colombian-style rackets. Two mass breakout attempts bracketed the discovery of an extensive drug-dealing ring controlled from inside; a call girl was detected in Koskotas' cell, as were large quantities of drugs, guns and ammunition in the office of the head warden (subsequently arrested). Meanwhile former junta boss Ioannides married a visiting sympathizer, though presumably without Koskotas's conjugal rights.

In November, Greece lifted its embargo on "Macedonia", opening the borders for tourism and trade in return for FYROM suitably editing its constitution and removing the offending emblem from its flag. Relations, in fact, were almost instantly normalized, though the name issue remains outstanding; current favourite solutions include "New Macedonia" or "Upper Macedonia".

THE END OF AN ERA

However, the dominant critical issue was the 76-year-old Papandreou's obstinate clinging to power despite obvious signs of dotage. Numerous senior PASOK figures became increasingly bold and vocal in their criticism, no longer fearing the sack or expulsion as in the past. By late 1995, Papandreou was desperately ill in intensive care at the Onassis hospital, stricken with severe lung and kidney infections, and dependent on life-support machinery. As there was no constitutional provision for replacing an infirm (but alive) prime minister, the country was essentially rudderless for two months, until the old demagogue finally faced up to his own mortality, and signed a letter **resigning** as Prime Minister in mid-January 1996. The palace clique of Mimi Liani and cohorts was beaten off in the parliamentary replacement vote in favour of the allegedly colourless but widely respected technocrat **Kostas Simitis**, who seemed to be just what the country needed after years of incompetent flamboyance. Upon assuming office, Simitis indicated that he wouldn't necessarily play to the gallery as Papandreou had with (for a Greek politician) a remarkable statement:

> *"Greece's intransigent nationalism is an expression of the wretchedness that exists in our society. It is the root cause of the problems we have had with our Balkan neighbours and our difficult relations with Europe."*

These principles were immediately put to the test by a tense armed face-off with Turkey over the uninhabited Dodecanese islet of **Ímia**, which very nearly degenerated into a shooting war. Simitis eventually bowed to US and UN pressure and ordered a withdrawal of Greek naval forces, conceding "disputed" status to the tiny goat-grazing outcrop – in hindsight a wise decision, but one for which at the time he was roundly criticised in parliament by fire-eating ND MPs and the media.

Papandreou finally succumbed to his illness on June 22, 1996, prompting a moving display of national mourning. This was promptly followed by PASOK's summer conference, where Simitis ensured his survival as party leader by co-opting his main internal foe, Papandreou's former head of staff, **Akis Tsokhatzopoulos**, with promises of future high office. Following the summer congress, Simitis cleverly rode the wave of pro-PASOK sympathy caused by Papandreou's death, and called general elections a year early in September 1996. The results were as hoped for: 162 seats for PASOK versus 108 for Néa Dhimokratía despite a margin of only three percentage points, the winner's strength artificially inflated by a convoluted electoral law. Given that the two main parties' agenda were broadly similar, the core issues boiled down to which was better poised to deliver results – and whether voters would be swayed by ND chief Evert's strident Slav- and Turk-baiting nationalism (they weren't). The biggest surprise was the collapse of Samaras' Politikí Ánixi, which failed to clear the three-percent nationwide hurdle for parliamentary representation, but three **leftist splinter parties** did well: eleven seats and just over five percent for Papariga's KKE, ten seats (including one Thracian Muslim deputy) with about the same tally for the Synaspismós under new chief Nikos Konstantopoulos, and nine seats at just under five percent for the Democratic Social Movement (DIKKI), founded early in the year by rehabilitated ex-minister Tsovolas to push for 1980s-vintage leftist policies. Evert resigned as ND leader, being succeeded by Karamanlis's nephew Kostas, who is now attempting to regain the centre ground. Néa Dhimokratía is down but by no means out, with Dhimitris Avramopoulos serving as its popular mayor of Athens and the party having actually increased its strength on the mainland in the last poll.

THE CURRENT SITUATION

For the time being, Simitis's position seems secure, although his first term of office in his own right has not been without its problems,

mainly arising from the economic squeeze caused by continuing **austerity measures**. In December 1996, the farmers staged dramatic protests, closing off the country's main road and rail arteries for several weeks, before dismantling the blockades in time for people to travel for the Christmas holidays. Much of 1997 saw the teachers or students (or both) on strike over proposed educational reforms – essentially about imposing some discipline on the notoriously lax school regimens.

Simitis, by nature far more pro-European than his maverick predecessor, shows no signs of being deflected from the unenviable task of getting the Greek economy in sufficiently good shape to meet the criteria for **monetary union**. Indeed, he has met with some success with his "hard drachma" policy (often propping it up by dumping hard currency reserves); the fact that inflation is well down into single figures for the first time in decades is testament to his ability as an accountant, for which he has received credit from friends and enemies alike. Increasingly amicable relations with its Balkan neighbours – Greece is the principal foreign investor in Bulgaria, for example – promise to generate jobs and trim unemployment, currently just over nine percent.

In September 1997, Greece received a timely boost to national morale and economic prospects with the awarding of the 2004 **Olympic games** to Athens. Simitis sensibly warned against people treating it as an excuse merely for unbridled money-making projects, and it is to be hoped that more substantial and long-lasting benefits will arise. One can at least confidently predict, if nothing else, that both the Athens metro and the new airport at Spáta will be completed on time.

MYTHOLOGY, AN A TO Z

While all ancient cultures had their myths, it is those from ancient Greece that have had the greatest influence on Western civilization. The Trojan War, the wanderings of Odysseus, the adventures of Heracles – these stories and many more have inspired some of the finest literature, music and art.

Homer and **Hesiod** were the first poets to write down the stories in around 800 BC, but they had existed for many years, perpetuated by word of mouth. With the enactment of the myths in the rituals of their religious festivals and ceremonies, along with their representation in the designs on their pots and the performances of the stories at the theatre and drama competitions, Greek myth and culture became inextricably blended.

Many versions of the myths exist, some of which are contradictory and confusing. Below is a summary of the principal **Gods** and **heroes**. For further reading Robert Graves' *The Greek Myths* is a good handbook although perhaps a bit dry and academic; Pierre Grimal's *Dictionary of Classical Mythology* is a very good reference, but perhaps the best starting point and a way into feeling how the myths might have been told is to read Homer's epics *The Iliad* and *The Odyssey*.

Agamemnon see Atreus; Trojan War

Aphrodite When Cronos castrated Uranus (see p.441) and threw his testicles into the sea, the water spumed and foamed and produced Aphrodite, which means "born from sea foam". Her girdle made people fall in love with the wearer, but her famed adultery with Ares ended in tears when she found herself ensnared in the nets that Hephaestus (see p.437), her husband, had made to expose her infidelity. She restored her virginity, but later had an affair with Hermes which produced the double-sexed offspring – Hermaphroditus. She particularly favoured the mortal Paris.

Apollo was the illegitimate son of Zeus and the nymph Leto. His twin sister Artemis was goddess of the moon and he was the god of the sun. His first noteworthy deed was to kill the Python snake that terrorized the land around Delphi, a city with which he had a great affinity. He established his shrine there, and through the priestess and the oracle, gave prophesies to those who wished to know the future. A god of outstanding beauty, he represents the arts of music and poetry and was often depicted with a lyre, which was a gift to him from Hermes. He was not unlucky in love, but was famously spurned by Daphne (see p.436).

Ares, the god of war and the son of Zeus and Hera, was usually attended by his demon henchmen Deimos (Fear) and Phobos (Terror). His violence, however, did not necessarily render him all-victorious – he was more than once outwitted by Athena and Heracles. As adulterous as the other gods, he was exposed in flagrante delicto with Aphrodite by her husband Hephaestus. The animals associated with Ares – the dog and the vulture – illuminate his character.

Argonauts, see Jason and the Argonauts

Ariadne, see Theseus, Ariadne and the Minotaur

Artemis, Apollo's twin, was the goddess of hunting and of the moon. She was the protecting deity for the Amazons – the tribe of warrior women who were independent of men – and was always described as a virgin with perpetual youth. She killed the huntsman Orion who tried to rape her, and instigated the death of Actaeon who had seen her bathe naked by changing him into a stag and setting his own hounds upon him.

Athena did not have a conventional birth – she sprang out of the head of Zeus ready for battle with armour, helmet and spear. Athena stayed a virgin and so her son Ericthonius was born in an equally unlikely way – he grew from her cast-off garments that had been soaked with Hephaestus' semen. She was the protectress of Athens, and was regarded as the goddess of reason and wisdom. She discovered olive oil, helped to build the Argo and looked after her favourite mortals, particularly Odysseus.

Atlas, see Heracles

Atreus (house of) A dynasty of revenge, murder, incest and tragedy. Atreus hated his younger brother Thyestes, and when their separate claims for kingship of Mycenae were voiced, the gods marked out Atreus for the task. Atreus banished Thyestes, but when he learned that his wife had had an affair with him, Atreus feigned forgiveness and recalled him from exile. He then had Thyestes's sons murdered, cut up, cooked and fed to Thyestes. When Thyestes had finished eating, Atreus showed him the heads of his children, making clear to him the true nature of the meal. He again banished Thyestes, who took refuge at Sicyon and, sanctioned by the gods, fathered Aegisthus by his daughter, Pelopia. Pelopia then married Atreus, her uncle, and Aegisthus (who did not know who his real father was) was brought up and cared for by Atreus. When Aegisthus came of age, Atreus instructed him to kill Thyestes, but Aegisthus found out the truth, returned to Mycenae and killed Atreus. Atreus's two sons were Agamemnon and Menelaus. Agamemnon paid for his father's crimes by dying at the hands of his wife Clytemnestra (who had committed adultery with Aegisthus while he Agamemnon was fighting at Troy). She ensnared him in a net while he took a bath and stabbed him to death. She in turn was killed by her son Orestes, who was absolved of matricide by Athena.

Bacchus, see Dionysos

Centaurs and Lapiths The Centaurs were monstrous beings with the heads and torsos of men and the lower bodies of horses. They lived a debauched life feeding on raw flesh and enjoying the pleasures of wine. There are many tales of Centaurs battling with Heracles on his journey to complete the twelve labours, but the most famous story is of the fight that broke out between them and the Lapiths, a race of heroes and warriors who were the descendants of the river god Pineus (the Piniós flows near Olympus). Pirithous, a Lapith who shared the same father as the Centaurs, invited them all to his wedding. At the feast the Centaurs tried to abduct the women, including the bride. A bloody brawl followed, of which the Lapiths were the victors.

Cronos The Titan Cronos was the youngest son of Gaia and Uranus, who seized power of the heavens by castrating his father. Once on the throne, Cronos lived in fear of the prediction that one of his offspring would one day overthrow him, and so swallowed all of his children except Zeus (see below) – Zeus's mother Rhea had substituted a stone for the bundle that Cronos thought was his baby. Cronos and his

Titan brothers were defeated in a vicious battle by Zeus and his Olympian supporters.

Daphne The nymph Daphne was one of the daughters of the river god Pineus. Apollo took a fancy to her and chased her through the woods to have his way, but just as he caught up with her, she prayed to her father to save her. He took pity and turned her into a laurel tree, and she became rooted to the spot. Apollo loved her even as a tree and made the laurel sacred, dedicating wreaths of its leaves as a sign of honour. Her name, to this day, is the Greek word for the laurel tree.

Demeter was the goddess of agriculture and corn, and she exercised her power when she made the whole Earth sterile, in protest against her daughter Persephone's abduction by Hades. She was greatly revered all over Greece, particularly where wheat was grown. She invented the mill and was highly respected at religious festivals associated with fertility and growth.

Dionysos, also known as Bacchus, was the god of wine and mystic ecstasy. He was the son of Zeus and because he was ripped from his mother's womb at six months, Zeus sewed him up in his thigh for the remaining three. As a young boy he was disguised as girl to hide him from Hera, and his feminine demeanour – long hair and dresses – stayed with him. He rode in a chariot drawn by panthers and draped in ivy and vines and was followed by a coterie of minor gods. He instituted the Bacchanalia where the people, but mostly the women (see Maenads), were inspired into frenzy and ecstasy. He rescued Ariadne from Naxos, and became associated with theatre, revelry and celebration.

Eurydice, see Orpheus and Eurydice

Golden Fleece, see Jason and the Argonauts

Hades' name means "the invisible", because in the battle with Cronos and the Titans he concealed himself by wearing the magic helmet given to him by the Cyclopes. (The helmet makes other appearances in Greek mythology; see Perseus below.) He drew by lot the realm of the Underworld. To refer to him as Hades was thought to bring about his awesome anger, so the Greeks called him by his surname Pluto, which means "the rich" and alludes to the wealth that lies hidden underground. His wife was Demeter's daughter, Persephone (see p.439).

Helen was the daughter of Zeus, who came as a swan to her mother Leda. She was believed to be the most beautiful woman in the world. Her husband Menelaus, king of Sparta, entertained the Trojans Paris and Aeneas and was foolish enough to leave them in her hospitality; Paris abducted her. Some say she went willingly, impressed by his beauty and wealth, others say she was raped. In either event her departure from Sparta was the cause for the Trojan War (see p.441).

Hera was Zeus's sister and wife and the most powerful of the goddesses – she wreaked her vengeance and jealousy on any who Zeus seduced and the offspring of most of his encounters (see Io). Zeus punished her heavily for her anger against Heracles by suspending her from her wrists from Mount Olympus, and weighing her ankles down with anvils. Despite her portrayal as jealous, vindictive and irascible, she was the protecting deity of wives.

Heracles was the superhero of the ancient world. His mother was the mortal Alcmene, and his father Zeus. Jealous Hera sent two snakes to kill Heracles while he was still in his cradle, which he duly strangled, all good preparation for his twelve labours.

The labours were commanded by King Eurystheus, although it's not clear why Heracles was compelled to perform them. Nevertheless, the tasks took him to the fringes of the known world, even involving his supporting it on his shoulders while Atlas took a break to lend him a hand in his final task. The tasks were: to kill the Nemean lion; to kill the many-headed Hydra monster; to bring back the wild boar Erymanthus alive; to hunt the Keryneian hind that was sacred to Artemis; to kill the man-eating birds at the lake of Stymphaleia; to clean the stables of King Augias; to bring back alive the untameable Cretan bull; to capture the flesh-eating horses of Diomedes; to fetch the girdle of the Amazon warrior queen; to fetch the herds of Geryon from beyond the edge of the ocean; to fetch Cerberus the guard dog of hell from the underworld; and finally to fetch the golden apples from the garden of the Hesperides.

The twelve labours proved that Heracles had the right stuff to be a god, and his death was as dramatic as his life. Deianeira his wife gave him a garment that she thought had magic powers and would protect him from being unfaithful to

her. When he put it on, it burned into his flesh and slowly and painfully killed him. The cloth had been drenched in the poisonous blood of the Centaur Nessus whom Heracles had killed when he had tried to rape Deianeira.

Hephaestus was the god of fire and a master craftsman. In his forges and workshops on volcanic Límnos (where the Cyclopes worked for him) he fashioned everything from jewellery to armour. He was made lame from the injuries he sustained when Zeus threw him from Olympus (a fall that lasted a full day) because he had defended Hera in a quarrel. He was very ugly, but was married to Aphrodite (see p.435), the most beautiful of the goddesses.

Hermes was the son of Zeus and Maia, the daughter of Atlas. He showed his mettle by stealing Apollo's cattle while still a baby, and then set to inventing the lyre (by stretching cowgut over a tortoise shell) and producing a flute from hollow reeds. He exchanged them both with Apollo (see p.435) for his cattle, the golden staff which Apollo had used to control the herd, and the secrets of the art of prophecy. He was the god of commerce and travel, often depicted wearing winged shoes, a wide-brimmed hat and carrying the staff which showed his position as the divine messenger.

Hippolytus and Phaedra Hippolytus, son of the hero Theseus and the Amazon Hippolyta was an accomplished hunter who revered Artemis and scorned Aphrodite. Aphrodite sought to teach him a lesson and conspired for Phaedra, the new wife of Theseus, to fall in love with the young man. When spurned by Hippolytus she feared he might reveal her advances and so accused him of rape. When Theseus heard this, he called upon Poseidon to kill his son and Hippolytus was flung from his chariot and torn apart by his horses. Phaedra in shame and remorse hanged herself.

Io was only one of the many mortals Zeus singled out for carnal satisfaction. Having had his way he chose to conceal his misdemeanour by turning her into a cow, denying to Hera (see opposite) that he had ever touched the beast. Hera demanded her as a present, and placed her under the watchful eyes (he had a hundred of them) of Argos the guard. She then proceeded to torment the poor cow by sending a stinging gadfly to goad her on her travels and drive her insane. She made for the sea, first to the

Ionian gulf, which was named after her, and then crossed the straits into Asia at the Bosphorus – literally the Cow Crossing. Before settling in Egypt, she wandered all over Asia, even bumping into Prometheus, who was chained for a few centuries to the Caucasus mountain range.

Jason and the Argonauts Jason, a great Greek hero, was set an almost impossible task by his step uncle Pelias to win the power that was his by birthright. He had to sail to the ends of the earth and bring back the Golden Fleece. He assembled his crew, which reads like a who's who of heroes of the Ancient Greek world, and commissioned a ship, called the Argo after its maker Argos, which was built with the help of Athena – its prow had the remarkable power of speech and prophecy. A long journey full of stories and surprises followed. Some of the crew didn't complete the voyage, including Heracles who missed the boat when it set sail because he was searching for his favourite, Hylas – the beautiful boy who had been abducted by the Nymphs. The prophet Phineus gave Jason directions and advice in return for him killing the Harpies that were plaguing him – he told Jason how to deal with the moving rocks and reefs that might smash his ship. Armed with this knowledge, Jason and the Argonauts reached their destination. On arrival in Colchis, however, the King Aeetes would not hand over the Golden Fleece until Jason had completed various labours. The king's daughter, the witch Medea (see opposite), fell in love with Jason and helped him with her magic powers. They stole the fleece and fled, pursued by Aeetes. Medea stalled her father by tearing up her brother Apsyrtus and casting his body parts into the sea; Aeetes had to slow down to collect the pieces. Zeus was greatly angered by this heinous crime and the Argo spoke to the crew telling them that they would have to purify themselves at Circe's island. After many more adventures and wanderings through treacherous seas, the crew arrived at Corinth where Jason dedicated the Golden Fleece to Poseidon.

Judgement of Paris The goddess Eris (Strife) began a quarrel between Athena, Hera and Aphrodite, by throwing a golden apple between them and saying that it belonged to whoever was the most beautiful. All the gods were too frightened to judge the contest, so Hermes took

them to the top of Mount Ida for Paris, the son of Priam of Troy to decide. Each used bribery to win his favour: Athena offered him wisdom and victory in combat, Hera the kingdom of Asia, but Aphrodite, the winner of the contest, offered him the love of Helen of Sparta.

Lapiths, see Centaurs and Lapiths

Maenads The Maenads were the possessed female followers of Dionysos (see p.436). They wore scanty clothes, had wreaths of ivy around their heads and played upon tambourines or flutes in their procession. They had power over wild animals, and their hysteria led their imagination to dizzy heights so that they believed they drank milk or honey from freshwater springs. In their orgiastic ecstasies and frenzies they tore limb from limb those who offended them, did not believe or who spied upon their rites – including Orpheus (see p.439).

Medea exacted gruesome revenge on any who stood against her. She persuaded the daughters of Pelias (see Jason opposite) to cut their father up and put him in a boiling cauldron having convinced them that if they did so she could rejuvenate him. His body parts, to their extreme disappointment, did not come back together. Acastus, Pelias' son, banished her and Jason as a punishment. She went with Jason to Corinth, where he abandoned her to marry Creusa the daughter of Creon, who banished her. In revenge, Medea orchestrated a gruesome death for Creusa, with her young sons instrumental in the deed, and then murdered them.

Minotaur, see Theseus, Ariadne and the Minotaur

Mount Olympus, see Zeus

Muses The muses were the result of nine nights of love making between Mnemosyne (Memory) and Zeus. They were primarily singers and were the inspiration for music (to which they gave their name), but also had power over thought in all its forms: persuasion, eloquence, knowledge, history, mathematics and astronomy. Apollo conducted their singing around the Hippocrene fountain on Mount Helicon.

Nymphs There were various subspecies of nymph: Meliads were the nymphs of the ash trees; Naiads lived in the springs and streams; Dryads were tree nymphs; Oreads were the mountain nymphs; and the Alseids lived in the groves. They were thought to be the daughters of Zeus and attended the great goddesses, particularly Artemis. Like the fairies of folk stories, they often occur in tales of love (see Daphne).

Odysseus Our word odyssey derives from Odysseus' ten-year journey home, which was no less fraught with danger, adventure and grief than the ten-year war against the Trojans which preceded it. Shipwrecked, tried and tested by the gods, held against his will by bewitching women, almost drawn to death by the hypnotic Sirens, witnessing his comrades devoured by the giant one-eyed Cyclops and all the time missing and desiring his faithful wife Penelope, Odysseus proved himself to be a great and scheming hero. At the end of his long and arduous journey he arrived at his palace on Ithaca to find suitors surrounding his wife. He contrived a cunning trap and killed them all with his bow. Penelope hardly recognized him; so long had he been away, that she had to test his identity by questioning him about their marriage bed. Odysseus answered correctly having made the bed himself from the olive tree that grew on the site of the palace and around which he had built his home.

Oedipus was a man cursed. The oracle said that Laius should not father any children, for if he did, one would kill him. When Oedipus was born Laius abandoned the baby, piercing his ankles with a nail and tying them together: this is how Oedipus got his name which means "swollen foot". But the baby was discovered and brought up at the court of the neighbouring king, Polybus, at Corinth. The Delphic Oracle revealed to the adult Oedipus that he would kill his father and marry his mother. When he heard this news he resolved not to return home to Corinth, but while making his journey he met with Laius, who was himself on the road to consult the oracle as to how to rid Thebes of the Sphinx. Because the road was narrow, Laius ordered Oedipus to get out of the way, and when one of the guards pushed him, Oedipus drew his sword in anger and, not knowing that Laius was his father, killed him and his entourage. He then made his way to the Thebes, where Laius had been king, and solved the riddle of the Sphinx, thus putting a stop to the plague. As a reward and in thanks, he was crowned king and offered Laius' widow Jocasta (his mother) in marriage. Plague then fell upon Thebes, because of the crimes of patricide and incest at the heart of the city. The Delphic Oracle instructed Oedipus to expel the murderer of Laius, and in his ignorance he cursed the murderer and banished him. The seer and prophet Teiresias then revealed the full nature of the crime to Jocasta and Oedipus; she hanged herself and he put out his own eyes. He left the city as a vagabond accompanied by his daughter Antigone, and only at his death was granted peace. Attica, the country that received his dead body, was blessed.

Orpheus and Eurydice Orpheus was the greatest musician and was given his lyre by Apollo himself. He sang so beautifully that the animals would stop what they were doing and the trees would uproot themselves to come closer to him to listen. Even the rocks and stones were moved by his songs. He enlisted in the crew of Argonauts and sang for them to row their oars in time. On his return from the Argo's voyage he married the nymph Eurydice. She was bitten by a snake on the banks of the river Pineus and died, and Orpheus was so distraught that he went to the Underworld to bring her back. His wish to restore her to life was granted by Hades on the condition that during the return journey to the Earth, he would not look back at her. As he approached daylight his mind became plagued with doubts and, turning around to see if she was behind him, he lost her forever. He preached that Apollo was the greatest god, much to the anger of Dionysos, who set the Maenads on him. They tore him apart and cast his head, still singing, into the river Hebrus. It was finally washed up on the shores of the island of Lesbos.

Pan The god of shepherds and flocks, Pan was the son of Hermes and a Nymph and, with his beard, horns, hairy body and cloven hooves, was said to be so ugly that his own mother ran from him in fear. He had an insatiable libido, energetically pursuing both sexes. Apollo learned the art of prophecy from Pan and hunters looked to him for guidance. He enjoyed the cool woodland shade and streams of Arcadia and relished his afternoon naps so much that he wreaked havoc if disturbed.

Pandora, see Prometheus

Pegasus, see Poseidon

Penelope, see Odysseus

Persephone was out picking flowers one day when the Earth opened up and swallowed her;

she had been abducted by Hades (see p.436). Her mother Demeter was distraught and when she found out the truth, she left Olympus in protest and made the Earth sterile so that it grew no crops. Zeus ordered Hades to return Persephone, but because she had eaten a magic pomegranate she was bound to him. The compromise was that she should be allowed to return to Earth for two thirds of the year and to reside with Hades for the remaining third. So Demeter divided the year into seasons and saw to it that while Persephone was with Hades the Earth would be sterile and in winter, but that while Demeter was on Earth the ground would be fertile for spring, summer and autumn.

Perseus A son of Zeus, and believed to be a direct ancestor of Heracles, Perseus was cast out to sea in a trunk with his mother Danae, because his grandfather feared that he would one day kill him. Danae and Perseus were washed up on an island, where they were discovered by a fisherman who looked after them. When Perseus came of age, the king of the island demanded that he bring back the head of Medusa the Gorgon, whose gaze could turn people to stone. Perseus acquired some special aids to perform the task —Hades' helmet, which made him invisible, and winged sandals to fly through the air – and had the divine assistance of Athena and Hermes. He cut off Medusa's head by looking at its reflection in Athena's polished shield. On his return flight he saw and fell in love with Andromeda, who was being offered as a sacrifice. He rescued her and returned home to find his mother had been raped by the King. He held up the gorgon's head, turned the king to stone and then presented the head as a gift to Athena, who placed it in the middle of her shield. Perseus went on to participate in the king of Larissa's celebratory games; he competed in the discus throwing competition but his throw went off course and killed his grandfather, who was a spectator.

Phaedra, see Hippolytus and Phaedra

Poseidon In the battle with Cronos and the Titans, Poseidon, the brother of Zeus, was given the trident by the Cyclopes which he used to shake both sea and land. He was awarded, by lot, the realm of the sea and lived in the salty deep. He produced some strange offspring, including the Cyclops Polyphemus who had it in for Odysseus (see p.439), and even had union with the gorgon Medusa – which resulted in the winged horse Pegasus. He quarrelled frequently with the other gods, competing with them for power over some of the major cities including Athens, Corinth and Argos, but his great hatred was for the Trojans who had double-crossed him by not paying him for helping them to build their city.

Prometheus For someone whose name means "forethought", Prometheus showed a distinct lack of it. In his desire to help mankind, he stole fire from the heavens and was immediately punished by Zeus who bound him in chains, tied him to the mountains and then sent an eagle to perpetually peck at his liver. Zeus then dealt with mankind by sending Pandora to Prometheus' brother Epimetheus, whose name means "afterthought". Her curiosity about the contents of his box got the better of her and, peeping inside, she unleashed all the evils and one good (hope) on the world. Prometheus gave some useful advice to Heracles when he passed by on one of his labours and Heracles repaid him by setting him free.

Theseus, Ariadne and the Minotaur
Theseus' father, Aegeus of Athens, sent him as a child away from Athens for his own safety. At sixteen the hero returned, in full strength and with the weapons that his father had set aside for him. Theseus was destined for a life of action, comparable to Heracles, and his greatest adventure was to kill the Minotaur on Crete. As a tribute from Athens, King Minos was owed six men and six women every nine years for sacrifice to the Minotaur – a gruesome beast, half-man half-bull, born from the bestial copulation of the queen Pasiphae with the huge bull sent by Poseidon. The Minotaur was kept in the labyrinth at Crete. Ariadne, Minos's daughter, contrived to help Theseus kill the Minotaur, having fallen in love with him. She gave him a ball of thread so that he would not lose his way in the labyrinth and then accompanied him in his flight from the island, only to be abandoned later on the island of Naxos. Dionysos saw her there weeping on the shore and took pity on her; he married her and took her to the land of the gods. Theseus, meanwhile, on his return to Athens forgot to hoist the white sails as a signal to his father that he was alive and Aegeus thinking that his son had been killed by the Minotaur threw himself into the sea which took his name: the Aegean.

Titans The Titans were the six male children of Uranus and Gaia. Their six sisters, who helped them father numerous gods, were called the Titanides. Cronos was the youngest Titan, and after he had overthrown his father he helped his brothers to power. The Titans lost their grip when they were toppled by the upstart Olympians, led by Zeus, in the giant battle called the Titanomachia.

Trojan War When Menelaus of Sparta realized that the Trojan Paris has made off with his wife, he called on his brother Agamemnon of Mycenae. Together they roused the might of Greece to get her back. With just about every Greek hero (Ajax, Achilles, Troilus, Hector, Paris, Odysseus, Priam, Diomedes, Aeneas) making an appearance in this epic, the story of the Trojan war is arguably the greatest tale from the ancient world. Homer's *Iliad* dealt with only one aspect of it, the wrath of Achilles. The ten-year war, fought over a woman and which sent many heroic souls down to Hades, was finally won by the trickery of the Greeks, who used a huge wooden horse left ostensibly as a gift to the Trojans to smuggle an armed platoon inside the city walls. The cunning plan was thought to be the work of Odysseus (see p.439), who, like many of the surviving heroes, had a less than easy journey home.

Sirens, see Odysseus

Uranus was the personification of the sky and by his conjugation with Gaia (Earth) fathered many children including Cronos and the Titans (see opposite). Gaia became so exhausted by her husband's continuing advances that she sought protection from her sons. Her youngest son Cronos was the only one to assist – he cut off Uranus's testicles with a sickle and threw them into the sea.

Zeus was the supreme deity, king of gods and men, but he did not get to this position without a struggle. His father, the Titan Cronos, seized power of the heavens by castrating Uranus the sky god, and lived in fear that one of his offspring would one day overthrow him, and so swallowed all of his children except Zeus, whose mother, Rhea, came to the rescue and hid him in a cave on the island of Crete. When he came of age, Zeus poisoned Cronos so that he vomited up all Zeus's siblings and with their help, and the assistance of the Cyclopes, cast Cronos and the Titans from Mount Olympus, the home of the gods. The Cyclopes gave Zeus the thunderbolt as a weapon to use in the battle and it became his symbol of power. He used his position to make laws, control the gods and men and to get his way with whomever he fancied. The myths are littered with the tales of his infidelities, libidinous desires and the deeds of his children who include Heracles, Perseus and Helen (see p.437).

Mark Espiner

MUSIC

Music is central to Greek island culture; even the most indifferent visitor will be aware of its presence in vehicles, tavernas, ferryboats and other public spaces. Like most aspects of Greece, it's an amalgamation of native and Oriental styles, with occasional contributions from the West. In fact, western music made little impression until recent decades, when aesthetic disputes arose between adherents of folk-derived styles, and the proponents of jazz/cabaret, symphonic and rock idioms.

Many older songs, invariably in Eastern-flavoured minor scales, have direct precedents in the forms and styles of both **Byzantine religious chant** and that of the **Ottoman Empire**, though some nationalists claim their partial descent from now-lost melodies of ancient Greece. Almost all native Greek instruments are near-duplicates of ones used throughout the Islamic world, though it's an open question as to whether the Byzantines, Arabs or Persians first constructed particular instruments. To this broadly Middle Eastern base, Slavs, Albanians and Italians have added their share, resulting in an extraordinarily varied repertoire of traditional and modern pieces.

The most promising times to hear regional island music are at the numerous **summer festivals**, when musicians (often based in Athens or other city clubs in winter) tour the island villages. However, it's as well to know that during the 1967–74 junta there was a marked decline in live performance, with the result that traditional instrumentation is now often replaced with something more appropriate to rock concerts. The musicians, who are deprived of – or actively scorn – the teachings of older master players, are also not what they could be.

Many island pieces are danceable, divided by rhythm into such categories as *kalamatianó* (a line dance), *khasaposérviko* or *syrtó*, the quintessential circle dance found across Greece. The quick-tempoed couples' dance of Crete, the *soústa*, is found with essentially the same rhythm in the east Aegean as *bállos*. Pieces for recitation at table or other assemblies include the slow, stately *rizítiko* of Crete, which relate, baldly or in metaphor, incidents or attitudes from the years of Ottoman rule.

CRETE, KÁSSOS, KHÁLKI AND KÁRPATHOS

This arc of southern islands is one of the most promising areas in Greece for hearing live music. The dominant instrument here is the **lýra**, a three-stringed fiddle directly related to the Turkish *kemençe*. This is played not on the shoulder but balanced on the thigh, often with tiny bells attached to the bow, which the musician can jiggle for rhythmical accent. The strings are metal, and since the centre string is just a drone, the player improvises only on the outer two. Usually the *lýra* is backed up by one or more **laoúta**, more elongated than the Turkish/Arab *oud* and not unlike the medieval lute. These are rarely used to their full potential – a *laoúto* solo is an uncommon treat – but a good player will find the harmonics and overtones of a virtuoso *lýra* piece, at the same time coaxing a pleasing, chime-like tone from his instrument.

In several places in the southern Aegean (notably northern Kárpathos) a primitive bagpipe, the **askómandra** or **tsamboúna**, joins the *lýra* and *laoúto*; during the colonels' dictatorship the playing of the bagpipe in the Cyclades was banned lest tourists think the Greeks "too primitive". In Kazantzakis's classic novel (and in the movie), Zorba himself played a **sandoúri**, or hammer dulcimer, for recreation, but it was actually little known until after 1923 on other islands, being introduced by Asia

The * symbol denotes a disc **available on CD**. Serial numbers are given when known, with "LP" preceding the number meaning it's only available on vinyl; all are Greek labels unless UK or US is stated,. Cassette pressing has mostly been discontinued in Greece.

If you're stopping over in Athens en route to the islands, the best **record stores** – Musiki Gonia, Xylouris and Metropolis – are within a few hundred metres of each other on Odhós Panepistimíou, between the university and Omónia. In the UK the best source is Trehantiri, 367 Green Lanes, London N4 (☎0181/802 6530), which also operates a worldwide mail-order service. In the USA, try Down Home Music on San Pablo Avenue in El Cerrito, CA.

DISCOGRAPHY

*Songs of ... (Society for the Dissemination of National Music, Greece). A thirty-plus-strong series of field recordings from the 1950s through 1970s, each covering traditional music of one region or type. All LPs contain lyrics in English and are easily available in Athens in LP, cassette or CD form, especially at the Musicological Museum on Dhioyénous 1–3 in the Pláka. Best island discs to date are *Mytilene & Chios* (SDNM 110); *Mytilene & Asia Minor* (SDNM 125); *Rhodes, Chalki & Symi* (SDNM 104); and *Kassos & Karpathos* (SDNM 103).

*Kassos: Skopi tis Lyras/Lyra Tunes (Lyra 0113). A recent collection from the bleakest of the Dodecanese, whose music however tends to be more digestible than that of neighbouring Kárpathos.

*Kritikí Musikí Parádhosi: Iy Protomastóri/ Cretan Musical Traditions: The First Masters (Aerakis). Boxed set of ten discs dedicated to the best composers and earliest recording artists of Cretan folk music; very good, vastly expensive (£120 for the lot) and fortunately partly available individually.

*Avthentika Nisiotika tou Peninda (Lyra CD 0168). Good Cretan and Pontic material from the 1950s, with the Dodecanese also represented, from the collection of the late Ted Petrides, musician and dance master.

*Kastellorizo (Syrtos 561) and ***Tradyoudhia keh Skopi tis Kalymnou** (Syrtos 564). Studio productions of Kalymniote musician Manolis Karpathios; the Kalymnos disc, with just three contemporary musicians, is harsh but compelling, the Kastellorizan more of the collected-and-remastered variety.

*Emilia Hatzidhaki *Thalassina Tragoudhia* (Panvox 16311). The only easily available collec-

tion dedicated to this artist, who otherwise appears only on *nisiotiká* anthologies.

*Irini Konitopoulou-Legaki *Athanata Nisiotika 1* (Tzina-Astir 1020). A 1978 warhorse, beloved of bus drivers across the islands, though the Konitopoulos family hails from Náxos.

Angeliki & Stella Konitopoulou *Mnimes tou Egeou* (LP, DPI 2028). Well regarded 1989 effort by Irini's sister and niece.

*Yiorgos Konitopoulos & Clan *Thalassa keh Paradhosi* (EMI 14C 064 71253). Standard taverna or party fare throughout the islands; slicker than *Athanata Nisiotika* but no worse for that.

*Lesvos Aiolis (Crete University Press 9/10). Some marvellous festival tunes and dances, mostly instrumental, demonstrating the ample Balkan/Jewish/Constantinopolitan influences present on this east Aegean island; worth the stiff price tag (over £20 equivalent for the double boxed set).

*Nikos Xylouris *O Arkhangelos tis Kritis, 1958–1968* (MBI 10376). The best anthology of the sweet-voiced Cretan, covering the first ten years of his career.

*Yannis Parios *Ta Nisiotika Vol 1* (Minos 430/431) & *Vol 2* (Minos 1017/1018). Parios sparked a renewal of interest in *nisiotikó* – traditional island music – with the first of these two discs made a decade apart, each accompanied by members of the Konitopoulos clan. Maybe not the most "authentic" versions, but easy on the ear, and both went platinum – Volume 1 with sales of nearly a million.

*Seryiani sta Nisia Mas (MBI 10371/10372). Excellent compilation of various pre-1960s *nisiótika* hits and artists. Highlight of Volume 1 is Emilia Khatzidhaki's rendition of *Bratsera*.

Minor refugees. Today, accomplished players are few and in *Kritikí* (Cretan music) and *nisiotiká* (island songs), the instrument, has been relegated to a supporting role. On older Cretan recordings you may hear solos on the *voúlgari*, a stringed instrument, essentially a small *saz* (Turkish long-necked, fretted lute), which has now all but died out. Modern Cretan artists to look out for on recordings include **Kostas Moundakis**, the late acknowledged *lýra* master, the late **Nikos Xylouris**, justifiably dubbed "The Nightingale of Crete" for his fine voice, and his brother Andonis who performs under the name **Psarandonis**.

NORTHERN DODECANESE AND CYCLADES

On the northern Dodecanese islands and the Cyclades, you'll find the *lýra* replaced by a more familiar-looking **violí**, essentially a western violin. Backing was provided until recently by *laóuto* or *sandoúri*, though these days you're more likely to be confronted (or affronted) by a bass-guitar-and-drum rhythm section. Hilltop shepherds used to pass the time fashioning a reed-wailer known as the *karamoúza*, made from two goat horns, though this too has all but disappeared.

Unlike Crete, where you can often catch the best music in special clubs or *kéndra*, Aegean island performances tend to be spontaneous and less specialized; festivals and saints' days in village squares offer the most promising opportunities. The melodies, like much folk music the world over, rely heavily on the pentatonic scale. Lyrics, especially on the smaller islands, touch on the perils of the sea, exile and – in a society where long periods of separation and arranged marriage were the norm – thwarted love. Although in the past three decades the **Konitopoulos** clan from Náxos, especially Irini Konitopoulou-Legaki, has become synonymous with this music, both live and recorded, older stars like the Dodecanesian sisters **Anna** and **Emilia Khatzidhaki** and **Effi Sarri** offer a warmer, more innocent delivery.

NORTHEAST AEGEAN ISLANDS

There's more obvious Anatolian and Constantinopolitan influence in both the music and instrumentation of these islands. Largely because of the refugee background of its population, there is no longer an indigenous musical tradition on Sámos. Matters are better on neighbouring Ikaría, where skilled musicians still perform at the spring and summer monastery-festivals in the west of the island. On Lésvos, which has perhaps the most vital festival tradition in all the islands, the *violí*, clarinet, lapdrum (*toumberléki*) or shoulder drum (*daoúli*) and frequently brass instruments are still encountered at festivals, groupings identical to those used in northwestern Anatolia both before and after 1923. They traditionally accompanied wedding marches or tunes marking the start of horse-racing or bull-sacrificing festivals. The keyed clarinet (*klaríno*) – as opposed to simple, single-reed, oboe-like instruments – was unknown in Greece before 1830 and (depending on whom you believe) was introduced either by the gypsies or Bavarians attached to the royal court.

IONIAN ISLANDS

Alone of all modern Greek territory, the Ionian islands – except for Lefkádha – never saw Turkish occupation and have a predominantly western musical tradition. The indigenous songform is Italian both in name, **kantádhes**, and instrumentation (guitar and mandolin); it's most often heard these days on **Lefkádha** and **Zákynthos**.

Marc Dubin,
with contributions from George Pissalides

WILDLIFE

For anyone who has first seen the smaller Greek islands at the height of summer with their brown parched hillsides and desert-like ambience, the richness of the wildlife – in particular the flora – may come as a surprise. As winter changes to spring, the countryside (and urban waste ground) transforms itself from green to a mosaic of coloured flowers, which attract a plethora of insect life, followed by birds. Isolated areas have had many thousands of years to develop their own individual species. Overall, Greece has around six thousand species of native flowering plants, nearly four times that of Britain but in the same land area. Many are unique to Greece, and make up about one third of Europe's endemic plants.

SOME BACKGROUND

In early antiquity Greece, including the islands, was thickly forested: Aleppo and Calabrian pines grew in coastal regions, giving way to fir or lack pine up in the hills and low mountains. But this **native woodland** contracted rapidly as human activities expanded. By Classical times, a pattern had been set of forest clearance, followed by agriculture, abandonment to scrub and then a resumption of cultivation or grazing. Huge quantities of timber were consumed in the production of charcoal, pottery and metal smelting, and for ships and construction work. Small patches of virgin woodland

have remained on the largest islands, but even these are under threat from the loggers and arsonists.

Modern Greek **farming** often lacks the rigid efficiency of northern European agriculture. Many peasant farmers still cultivate little patches of land, and even town dwellers travel at weekends to collect food plants from the countryside. Wild greens under the generic term *khórta* are gathered to be cooked like spinach; grape hyacinth bulbs are boiled as a vegetable. The buds and young shoots of capers, and the fruit of wild figs, carobs, plums, strawberry trees, cherries and sweet chestnuts are harvested. Emergent snails are collected after wet weather. The more resilient forms of wildlife can coexist with these land-uses, but for many Greeks only those species that have practical uses are regarded as having any value.

Despite an often negative attitude to wildlife, Greece was probably the first place in the world where it was an object of study. Theophrastus of Lésvos (372–287 BC) was the first recorded **botanist** and a systematic collector of general information on plants, while his contemporary, Aristotle, studied the animal world. During the first century AD the distinguished physician Dioscorides compiled a herbal that remained a standard work for over a thousand years.

Since the 1970s, tourist developments have ribboned out along coastlines, sweeping away both agriculture and wildlife havens as they do so. These expanding resorts increase local employment, often attracting inland workers to the coast; the generation that would have been shepherds and graziers on remote hillsides now work in bars and tavernas for the tourist. Consequently, the pressure of domestic animal grazing, particularly in the larger islands, has been significantly reduced and allows the regeneration of tree seedlings. Crete, for example, now has more woodland than at any time in the last five centuries.

FLOWERS AND PLANTS

Whereas in temperate northern Europe, plants flower from spring through into the autumn, the arid summers of Greece confine the main **flowering period** to the springtime, a climatic window when the days are bright, the temperatures are not too high and the ground water supply still adequate. **Spring** starts in the southeast, in Rhodes in early March, and then travels progressively westwards and northwards. Rhodes, Kárpathos and eastern Crete are at their best in March, western Crete in early April, the eastern Aegean from mid April to late April, and the Ionian islands in early May, though cold dry winters can cause several weeks' delay. In the higher island mountains the floral spring is held back until the chronological summer, with the alpine zones of central and western Crete in full flower in June.

The delicate flowers of early spring – orchids, fritillaries, anemones, cyclamen, tulips and small bulbs, are replaced as the season progresses by more robust shrubs, tall perennials and abundant annuals, but many of these close down completely for the fierce **summer**. A few tough plants, like shrubby thyme and savory, continue to flower through the heat and act as magnets for butterflies.

Once the worst heat is over, and the first showers of **autumn** arrive, so does a second "spring", on a much smaller scale but no less welcome after the brown drabness of summer. Squills, autumn cyclamen, crocus in varying shades, pink or lilac colchicum, yellow sternbergia and other small bulbs all come into bloom, while the seeds start to germinate for the following year's crop of annuals. By the new year early spring bulbs and orchids are flowering in the south.

SEASHORE

Plants on the **beach** tend to be hardy species growing in a difficult environment where fresh water is scarce. Feathery tamarisk trees are adept at surviving this habitat, and consequently are often planted to provide shade. On hot nights you may see or feel them dribbling away surplus saltwater from their branches.

Sand dunes in the southern and eastern islands may have the low gnarled trees of the prickly **juniper**. These provide shelter for a variety of colourful small plants like pink campions, yellow restharrow, white stocks, blue alkanet and violet sea-lavender. The flat sandy areas or slacks behind the dunes can be home to a variety of plants, where they have not been illegally ploughed for cultivation. Open stretches of beach sand usually have fewer plants, particularly nowadays in resort areas where the bulldozed "spring cleaning" of the beach removes the local flora along with the winter's rubbish.

FRESHWATER

Large areas of **freshwater** are scarce, particularly on the smaller islands. Many watercourses dry up completely in the hot season, and what seem to be summer dry river-courses are often simply flood-beds, which fill irregularly at times of torrential rain. Consequently, there are few true aquatic plants compared with much of Europe. However, species that survive periodic drying-out can flourish, such as the giant reed or **calamus**, a bamboo-like grass reaching up to 6m in height and often cut for use as canes. It often grows in company with the shrubby, pink-flowered and very poisonous oleander.

CULTIVATED LAND

Arable fields can be rich with colourful weeds: scarlet poppies, blue bugloss, yellow or white daisies, wild peas, gladioli, tulips and grape hyacinths. Small **meadows** can be equally colourful, with slower growing plants such as orchids in extraordinary quantities. The rather dull violet flowers of the mandrake conceal its celebrated history as a narcotic and surgical anaesthetic. In the absence of herbicides, olive groves can have an extensive underflora. In the presence of herbicides there is usually a yellow carpet of the introduced, weedkiller-resistant *Oxalis pes-caprae*, which now occurs in sufficient quantity to show up in satellite photographs.

LOWER HILLSIDES

The rocky earth makes cultivation on some hillsides difficult and impractical. Agriculture is often abandoned and areas regenerate to a rich mixture of shrubs and perennials – the **garigue** biome. With time, a few good wet winters, and in the absence of grazing, some shrubs develop into small trees, intermixed with tough climbers – the much denser **maquis** vegetation. The colour yellow often predominates in early spring, with brooms, gorse, Jerusalem sage and the three-metre-tall giant fennel, followed by the pink and white of large rockroses – *Cistus* spp. An abundance of the latter is often indicative of an earlier fire, since they flourish in the cleared areas. Strawberry trees are also resistant to fire; they flower in winter or early spring, producing an orange-red edible (though disappointingly insipid) fruit in the autumn. The Judas tree flowers on bare wood in spring, making a blaze of pink against the green hillsides.

A third vegetation type is **phrygana** – smaller, frequently aromatic or spiny shrubs, often with a narrow strip of bare ground between each hedgehog-like bush. Many **aromatic herbs** such as lavender, rosemary, savory, sage and thyme are natives to these areas, intermixed with other less tasty plants such as the toxic euphorbias and the spiny burnet or wirenetting bush.

Nearly 160 species of **orchid** are believed to occur in Greece; their complexity blurs species' boundaries and keeps botanists in a state of taxonomic flux. In particular, the *Ophrys* bee and spider orchids have adapted, through their subtleties of lip colour and false scents, to seduce small male wasps. These insects mistake the flowers for a potential mate, and unintentionally assist the plant's pollination. Other orchids mimic the colours and scents of honey-producing plants, to lure bees. Though all species are officially protected, many are still picked for decoration – in particular the giant *Barlia* orchid – and fill vases in homes, cafés, tavernas and even on graves.

Irises have a particular elegance and charm. The blue to violet winter iris, as its name suggests, is the first to appear, followed by the small blue *Iris gynandriris*. The flowers of the latter open after midday and into the night, to wither by the following morning. The widow iris is sombre-coloured in funereal shades of black and green, while the taller, white *Iris albicans*, the holy flower of Islam, is a relic of Turkish occupation. In the limestone peaks of Sámos, *Iris suavolens* has short stems, but huge yellow and brown flowers.

MOUNTAINS AND GORGES

The higher **mountains** of the Greek islands have winter snow cover varying with altitude, and cooler weather for much of the year, so the flowering is consequently later than at lower altitudes. The **limestone peaks** of islands such as Corfu, Kefalloniá, Crete, Rhodes, Sámos and Thássos hold rich collections of attractive flowering rock plants whose nearest relatives may be from the Balkan Alps or from the Turkish mountains. Gorges are another spectacular habitat, particularly rich in Crete. Their inaccessible cliffs act as refuges for plants that cannot survive the grazing, competition, or more extreme climates of open areas. Many of Greece's endemic plants – bellflowers, knap-

weeds and *Dianthus* spp. in particular – are confined to cliffs, gorges or mountains.

Much of the surviving **island forest** is in the mountainous areas of Kefalloniá, Évvia, Lésvos and Crete. Depending on the island, the woodland can comprise cypress (widespread at low altitudes), Greek fir (especially on Kefalloniá), oak (on Lésvos, Kéa and Crete) and a few species of pine: Calabrian or Aleppo at lower altitudes, black pine at the summits of Crete and Sámos. The cypress is native to the south and east Aegean, but in its columnar form it has been planted everywhere with a Mediterranean climate. It is sometimes said that the slim trees are the male and the broader, spreading form are female, but female cones on the thin trees prove this wrong. On Kárpathos, Sými and Crete there are extensive stands of juniper, while shady stream canyons of the largest islands shelter plane, Oriental sweetgum, chestnut and poplar. The cooler shade of woodland provides a haven for plants which cannot survive full exposure to the Greek summer. Such species are the wonderful red, pink or white peonies found on Sámos, along with helleborine and birdsnest orchids, and numerous ferns.

With altitude, the forest thins out to scattered individual hardy conifers and kermes oak, before finally reaching a limit ranging from 1000–1200m (Samothráki, Sámos) to 1400m (Kefalloniá), ending at about 1800m (Crete). Above this treeline are limited summer meadows, and then bare rock. If not severely grazed, these habitats are home to many low-growing, gnarled, but often splendidly floriferous plants.

BIRDS

Migratory species which have wintered in East Africa move north in spring through the eastern Mediterranean, from mid-March to mid May, or later, depending on the season and the weather. Some stop to breed in Greece, others move on into the rest of Europe. The southern islands can be the first landfall after a long sea-crossing, and smaller birds recuperate for a few days before moving on north. Larger birds such as storks and ibis often fly very high, and binoculars are needed to spot them as they pass over. In autumn the birds return, but usually in more scattered numbers. Although some species such as quail and turtle dove are shot, there is nothing like the wholesale slaughter that takes place in some other Mediterranean countries.

Swallows, and their relatives the martins, are constantly hawking through the air to catch insects, as are the larger and noisier swifts. Warblers are numerous, with the Sardinian warbler often conspicuous because of its black head, bright red eye, and bold habits; the Rüppell's warbler is considerably rarer, and confined to thicker woodland. Other small insect eaters include stonechats, flycatchers and woodchat shrikes.

At **night**, the tiny Scops owl has a very distinct, repeated single note call, very like the sonar beep of a submarine; the equally diminutive little owl by contrast is also visible by day, particularly on ruined houses, and has a strange repertoire of cries, chortles and a throaty hiss. Certainly the most evocative nocturnal bird is the nightingale, which requires wooded stream valleys and is most audible around midnight in May, its mating season.

Larger **raptors** are rare on the islands but can occur in remoter areas, particularly around mountain gorges and cliffs. Certain Dodecanese and Lésvos support populations of Eleonora's falcons, while peregrines visit the Ionian islands. Buzzards are perhaps the most abundant, and mistaken by optimistic birdwatchers for the much rarer, shyer eagles; vultures are also seen in passing on the largest islands. Lesser kestrels are brighter, noisier versions of the common kestrel, and often appear undisturbed by the presence of humans. Also to be seen in the mountains are ravens, and smaller, colourful birds such as black and white wheatears, wallcreepers and the blue rock thrush.

In lowland areas, hoopoes are a startling combination of pink, black and white, particularly obvious when they fly; they're about the only natural predator of the processionary caterpillar, a major pest in pine forests. The much shyer golden oriole has an attractive song but is rarely seen for more than a few moments before hiding its brilliant colours among the olive trees. Rollers are bright blue and chestnut, while multicoloured flocks of slim and elegant bee-eaters fill the air with their soft calls as they hunt insects. Brightest of all is the kingfisher, more commonly seen sea-fishing than in northern Europe.

In those areas of **wetland** that remain undrained and undisturbed, birds flourish. In salt marshes, coastal lagoons, estuaries and freshwater, herons and egrets, ducks, osprey, glossy ibis and spoonbills, black storks, white storks, pelicans, cormorants and many waders can be seen feeding. Greater flamingos sometimes occur, as lone individuals or small flocks, particularly in salt pans of the eastern Aegean.

MAMMALS

The island **mammal** population ranges from small rodents and shrews to hedgehogs, rabbits, hares and (on forested isles) the fast-moving, ferret-like, stone (or beech) marten, named for its habit of decorating stones with its droppings to mark territory. Rats are particularly common on Corfu and Sámos. Medium-sized island mammals include jackals and foxes, but there are no badgers, or larger predators such as bears or wolves. In the White Mountains of Crete an endemic **ibex**, known to Cretan hunters as *agrími* or *kri-kri*, is occasionally seen running wild or, more rarely, as a steak. Once in danger of extinction, a colony of them was established on the offshore island of Dhía, where they exterminated the rare local flora.

The extremely rare Mediterranean **monk seal** also breeds on some stretches of remote coast in the east Aegean and Sporades; the small world population is now highly endangered since losing many individuals – and most of its main breeding ground – to a toxic algal bloom off Morocco. If spotted, these seals should be treated with deference; they cannot tolerate human disturbance, and on present trends are unlikely to survive much beyond the millennium.

REPTILES AND AMPHIBIANS

Reptiles flourish in the hot dry summers of Greece and there are many species, the commonest being **lizards**. Most of these are small, slim, agile and wary, rarely staying around for closer inspection. They're usually brown to grey, with subtle patterns of spots, streaks and stripes though in adult males the undersides are sometimes brilliant orange, green or blue. The more robust green lizards, with long whip tails, are up to 50cm or more in length, but equally shy and fast-moving unless distracted by territorial disputes with each other.

On some islands, mainly in the central and eastern Aegean, lives the angular, iguana-like agama, sometimes called the Rhodes dragon.

Occasionally reaching a robust 30cm in length, their skin is rough and grey to brown with indistinct patterning. Unlike other lizards, they will often stop to study you, before finally disappearing into a wall or under a rock.

Geckoes are large-eyed nocturnal lizards, up to 15cm long, with short tails and often rough skins. Their spreading toes have claws and ingenious adhesive pads, allowing them to walk up house walls and on to ceilings in their search for insects. Groups of them lie in wait near bright lights that attract their prey, and small ones living indoors can have very pale, almost transparent skins. Not always popular locally – the Greek name means "defiler" after their outsized faeces – they should be left alone to eat mosquitoes and other bugs. The **chameleon** is a rare, slow-moving and swivel-eyed inhabitant of eastern Crete and some eastern Aegean islands such as Sámos. Although essentially green, it has the ability to adjust its coloration to match the surroundings.

Once collected for the pet trade, **tortoises** can be found on much of the mainland, and some islands, though not on Crete. Usually it is their noisy progress through vegetation on sunny or wooded hills that first signals their presence. They spend their often long lives grazing the vegetation and can reach lengths of 30cm. **Terrapins** are more streamlined, freshwater tortoises which love to bask on waterside mud by streams or ponds, including on many islands. They are usually shy and nervous, and are often only seen as they disappear underwater. They are scavengers and will eat anything, including fingers if handled.

Sea turtles occur, mostly in the Ionian, but also in the Aegean. The least rare are the loggerhead turtles (*Caretta caretta*), which nest on Zákynthos and Kefaloniá and occasionally in Crete. Their nesting grounds are disappearing under tourist resorts, and they are a protected endangered species (see p.401).

Snakes are abundant on many islands (though Astypálea has none); most are shy and non-venomous. Several species, including the Ottoman and nose-horned **vipers**, do have a poisonous bite, though they are not usually aggressive. They are adder-like and often have a very distinct, dark zigzag stripe down the back. They are only likely to bite if a hand is put in the crevice of a wall or a rock-face where one of them is resting, or if they are attacked.

Unfortunately, the locals in some areas attempt to kill any snake they see, and thus greatly increase the probability of their being bitten. Most snakes are not only completely harmless to humans, but beneficial in that they keep down populations of pests such as rats and mice. There are also three species of legless lizards – slow-worm, glass lizard and legless skink – all equally harmless, which suffer because they are mistaken for snakes. The general principle should be to leave them alone, and they will do the same for you.

Snakebites cause very few deaths in Europe. Many snakes will bite under stress, whether they are venomous or not. If a bite injects venom, then swelling will normally occur within 1–30 minutes. If it does, get medical attention. Keep the bitten part still, and keep all body movements as gentle as possible. Do not cut or suck the wound, but if medical attention is not nearby then bind the limb firmly to slow the blood circulation but not so tightly as to stop the blood flow. Many reptiles can harbour *Salmonella* bacteria, so should be handled cautiously and preferably not at all. This applies particularly to tortoises.

Frogs and **toads** are the commonest amphibians in most of Greece, particularly in the spring breeding season. The green toad has green marbling over a pinkish or mud-coloured background, and a cricket-like trill. Frogs prefer the wettest places, and the robust marsh frog particularly revels in artificial water storage ponds, where the concrete sides magnify their croaking impressively. **Tree frogs** are tiny jewels, usually emerald green, with huge and strident voices at night. They rest by day in trees and shrubs, and can sometimes be found in quantity plastered onto the leaves of waterside oleanders.

INSECTS

Greece teems with **insects**. Some pester, like flies and mosquitoes, but most are harmless to humans. The huge, slow-flying, glossy black carpenter bee may cause alarm by its size and noise, but is rarely a problem.

Grasshoppers and **crickets** swarm through open areas of vegetation in summer, with several larger species that are carnivorous on the smaller and can bite strongly if handled. Larger still is the grey-brown locust, which flies noisily before crash-landing into trees and shrubs. The high-pitched and endlessly repeated chirp of

FLORA AND FAUNA FIELD GUIDES

FLOWERS

Hellmut Baumann *Greek Wild Flowers and Plant Lore in Ancient Greece* (Herbert Press, UK). Crammed with fascinating ethnobotany, plus good colour photographs.

Marjorie Blamey and Christopher Grey-Wilson *Mediterranean Wild Flowers* (HarperCollins, UK). Comprehensive field guide, with coloured drawings.

Lance Chilton, *Plant check-lists* (Marengo Publications, UK). Plant and wildlife lists for a number of Greek islands and resorts.

Pierre Delforge *Orchids of Britain and Europe* (HarperCollins, UK). A comprehensive guide, with recent taxonomy, though beware small inaccuracies in translation.

Anthony Huxley and William Taylor *Flowers of Greece and the Aegean* (Hogarth Press, UK; o/p). The only volume dedicated to the islands (and mainland), with colour photographs, but now slightly dated for taxonomy.

Oleg Polunin *Flowers of Greece and the Balkans* (Oxford University Press, UK). Another older field guide, also with colour photographs, useful if Huxley and Taylor proves unfindable.

BIRDS

Richard Brooks *Birding in Lesbos* (Brookside Publishing, UK). Superb, if pricey little guide with colour photos, a list of birdwatching sites, and detailed maps, plus an annotated species-by-species bird list with much useful information.

George Khandrinos and T. Akriotis *Birds of Greece* (A&C Black, UK). A comprehensive guide that includes island birdlife.

Heinzel, Fitter and Parslow *Collins Guide to the Birds of Britain and Europe* (Collins, UK/Stephen Green Press, US).

Petersen, Mountfort and Hollom *Field Guide to the Birds of Britain and Europe* (Collins, UK/Stephen Green Press, US).

Though covering most of Europe, these two field guides have the best coverage of Greek birds outside of Lésvos.

MAMMALS

Corbet and Ovenden *Collins Guide to the Mammals of Europe* (Collins, UK/Stephen Green Press, US). The best field guide on its subject.

REPTILES AND AMPHIBIANS

Arnold, Burton and Ovenden *Collins Guide to the Reptiles and Amphibians of Britain and Europe* (Collins, UK/Stephen Green Press, US). A useful guide though excluding the Dodecanese and east Aegean islands.

Jiri Cihar *Amphibians and Reptiles* (Conran Octopus, UK). Selective coverage, but includes most endemic species of the Dodecanese and east Aegean isles.

INSECTS

Michael Chinery *Collins Guide to the Insects of Britain and Western Europe* (Collins, UK/Stephen Green Press, US). Although Greece is outside the geographical scope of the guide, it will provide general identifications for most insects seen.

Lionel Higgins and Norman Riley *A Field Guide to the Butterflies of Britain and Europe* (Collins, UK/Stephen Green Press, US). A thorough and detailed field guide that illustrates nearly all species seen in Greece.

house crickets can drive to distraction, as can the summer whirring of cicadas on the trunks of trees. The latter insects are giant relatives of the aphids that cluster on roses.

From spring through to autumn Greece is full of **butterflies**, particularly in late spring and early summer. There are three swallowtail species, named for the drawn-out corners of the hind wings, in shades of cream and yellow, with black and blue markings. Their smaller relatives, the festoons, lack the tails, but add red spots to the palette. The rarer, robust brown and orange pasha is unrelated but is Europe's largest butterfly. In autumn the black and orange plain tiger or African monarch may appear, sometimes in large quantities. In areas of deciduous woodland, look high up and you may see fast-flying large tortoiseshells, while lower down, southern white admirals skim and glide through clearings between the trees. Some of the smallest but most beautiful butterflies are the blues. Their subtle, camouflaging grey and black undersides make them vanish from view when they land and fold their wings.

Some of the Greek **hawkmoths** are equally spectacular, particularly the green and pink oleander hawkmoth. Their large caterpillars can be recognized by their tail horn. The hummingbird hawkmoth, like its namesake, hovers at flowers to feed, supported by a blur of fast-moving wings. Tiger moths, with their black and white forewings and startling bright orange hindwings, are the "butterflies" that occur in huge quantity in sheltered sites of islands such as Rhodes and Páros. The giant peacock moth is Europe's largest, up to 15cm across. A mixture of grey, black and brown, with big eye-spots, it is usually only seen during the day while resting on tree trunks.

Other insects include the camouflaged praying mantids, holding their powerful forelegs in a position of supplication until another insect comes within reach. The females are voracious, and notorious for eating the males during mating. Ant-lion adults resemble a fluttery dragonfly, but their young are huge-jawed and build pits in the sand to trap ants. Hemispherical carob beetles collect balls of dung and push them around with their back legs, while the huge longhorn beetles of the southern Ionian islands munch their way through tree trunks. Longhorns are named for their absurdly extended, whip-like antennae. Cockroaches of varying species live in buildings, particularly hotels, restaurants and bakeries, attracted by warmth and food scraps.

Corfu is famous for its extraordinary **fireflies**, which flutter in quantities across meadows and marshes on May nights, speckling the darkness with bursts of cold light to attract partners. Look carefully in nearby hedges, and you may spot the less flashy, more sedentary glow-worm.

Centipedes are not often seen, but the fast-moving, 20cm *Scolipendra* should be treated with respect since they can give very painful bites. Other non-vertebrates of interest include the land crabs, which are found on most islands with running streams. They need fresh water to breed, but can cause surprise when found walking on remote hillsides. There are plenty of genuine marine creatures to be seen, particularly in shallow seawater sheltered by rocks – sea cucumbers, sea butterflies, octopus, starfish and sea urchins.

Lance Chilton, with Marc Dubin

BOOKS

Where separate editions exist in the UK and USA, publishers are detailed below in the form "UK publisher; US publisher", unless the publisher is the same in both countries. Where books are published in one country – or Athens – only, this follows the publisher's name.

O/p signifies an out-of-print but still highly recommended book; the recommended Greek-specialist book dealers often have stocks of these. "University Press" is abbreviated as UP.

TRAVEL AND GENERAL ACCOUNTS

MODERN ACCOUNTS

Kevin Andrews *The Flight of Ikaros* (Penguin o/p). Intense and compelling account of an educated, sensitive archeologist loose in the backcountry during the aftermath of the Civil War.

Gerald Durrell *My Family and Other Animals* (Penguin). Sparkling, very funny anecdotes of Durrell's childhood on Corfu – and his passion for the island's fauna: toads, tortoises, bats, scorpions, the lot.

Lawrence Durrell *Prospero's Cell* (Faber & Faber; Penguin o/p); *Reflections on a Marine Venus* (Faber & Faber/Penguin); *The Greek Islands* (Faber & Faber/Penguin, the former o/p). The elder Durrell lived before World War II with Gerald and the family on Corfu, the subject of *Prospero's Cell*. *Marine Venus* recounts Lawrence's 1945–47 experiences as a press officer on Rhodes and other Dodecanese islands. *Greek Islands* is a lyrical but rather dated and occasionally bilious guide to the archipelagos.

John Gill *Stars over Paxos* (Pavilion, UK). The author of the *Rough Guide to Corfu* muses on life in the Ionian.

Elias Kulukundis *Journey to a Greek Island* (Cassell, o/p). More accurately, a journey back through time and genealogy by a diaspora Greek two generations removed from Kássos, the poorest of the Dodecanese. Worth the effort to track down.

Henry Miller *The Colossus of Maroussi* (Minerva, o/p; New Directions). Corfu and the soul of Greece in 1939, with Miller, completely in his element, at his most inspired.

James Pettifer *The Greeks: the Land and People since the War* (Penguin; Viking). A useful, if spottily edited introduction to contemporary Greece – and its recent past. Pettifer charts the state of the nation's politics, food, family life, religion, tourism, and other topics.

Patricia Storace *Dinner with Persephone* (Granta; Pantheon). A New York poet, resident for a year in Greece, puts the country's psyche on the couch (while avoiding the same position with various predatory males). Storace has a sly sense of humour, and in showing how permeated – and imprisoned – Greece is by its imagined past, gets it right 95 percent of the time.

William Travis *Bus Stop Symi* (Rapp & Whiting, o/p). Chronicles three years' residence there in the mid-Sixties; insightful, though Travis erroneously prophesied that the place would never see tourism.

Sarah Wheeler *An Island Apart* (Abacus, UK). Entertaining chronicle of a five-month ramble through Évvia, one of the least-visited islands. Wheeler has a sure touch with Greek culture and an open approach to nuns, goatherds or academics; the sole quibble is her success in making Évvia seem more interesting than it really is.

OLDER ACCOUNTS

James Theodore Bent *Aegean Islands: The Cyclades, or Life Among Insular Greeks* (o/p). Originally published in 1881, this remains the best account of island customs and folklore; it's also a highly readable, droll account of a year's Aegean travel, including a particularly violent Cycladic winter.

Edward Lear *The Corfu Years* (Denise Harvey, Athens). Superbly illustrated journals by the nonsense versifier and noted landscape painter, whose paintings and sketches of Corfu, Paxí and elsewhere offer a rare glimpse of the Ionian island landscape in the nineteenth century. His *The Cretan Journal* (Denise Harvey) will also be of interest.

Richard Stoneman, ed *A Literary Companion to Travel in Greece* (Getty Centre for the History of Art & the Humanities, US). Ancient and medieval authors, plus Grand Tourists – good for dipping into.

Terence Spencer *Fair Greece, Sad Relic: Literary Philhellenism from Shakespeare to Byron* (Denise Harvey, Athens, available in UK; Scholarly Press). Greece – and incipient philhellenism – from the fall of Constantinople to the War of Independence, as conveyed by English poets, essayists and travellers.

THE CLASSICS

Many of the classics make excellent companion reading for a trip around Greece – especially the historians **Thucydides** and **Herodotus**. Reading **Homer**'s *Odyssey* when you're battling with or resigning yourself to the vagaries of island ferries puts your own plight into perspective.

Most of the standard undergraduate staples are part of the **Penguin Classic** paperback series. **Routledge** also has a huge, steadily expanding backlist of Classical Studies, though many titles are expensive and quite specialized; paperback editions are indicated.

Homer *The Iliad, The Odyssey*. The first concerns itself, semi-factually, with the late Bronze Age siege of the Achaeans against Troy in Asia Minor; the second recounts the delayed return home, via seemingly every corner of the Mediterranean, of the hero Odysseus. For a verse rendition, Richard Lattimore's translation (University of Chicago, *Iliad*; HarperCollins, *Odyssey*) has yet to be bettered; for prose, the best choices are by the father-and-son team of E.V. Rieu (*Iliad*, Penguin) and D.C.H. Rieu (*Odyssey*, Penguin).

Herodotus *The Histories* (Penguin), or A. D. Godley, tr (Cambridge UP). Revered as the father of systematic history and anthropology, this fifth-century BC Anatolian writer chronicled both the causes and campaigns of the Persian Wars, as well as the contemporary, assorted tribes and nations inhabiting Asia Minor.

Ovid *Metamorphoses*, A. D. Melville, tr (Oxford UP). Though collected by a first-century AD Roman writer, this remains one of the most accessible renditions of the more piquant Greek myths, involving transformations as divine blessing or curse.

ANCIENT HISTORY AND INTERPRETATION OF THE CLASSICS

A.R. Burn *History of Greece* (Penguin). Probably the best general introduction to ancient Greece, though for a fuller and more interesting analysis you'll do better with one or other of the following more specialized titles.

M.I. Finley *The World of Odysseus* (Penguin). Good on the interrelation of Mycenaean myth and fact.

Simon Hornblower *The Greek World 479–323 BC* (Routledge). An erudite survey of ancient Greece at its zenith, from the end of the Persian Wars to the death of Alexander, which has become a standard university paperback text.

Robin Lane Fox *Alexander the Great* (Penguin). An absorbing study, which mixes historical scholarship with imaginative psychological detail.

Michael Grant and John Hazel *Who's Who in Classical Mythology* (Routledge). Gazetteer of over 1200 mythological personalities, together with historical and geographical background.

Pierre Grimal, ed *Dictionary of Classical Mythology* (Penguin). Though translated from the French, considered to still have the edge on the more recent Grant/Hazel title.

John Kenyon Davies *Democracy and Classical Greece* (Fontana; Harvard UP). Established and accessible account of the Classical period and its political developments.

Oswyn Murray *Early Greece* (Fontana; Harvard UP). The Greek story from the Mycenaeans and Minoans through to the beginning of the Classical period.

Robin Osborne *Greece in the Making 1200–479 BC* (Routledge). Well-illustrated paperback on the rise of the city-state.

F.W. Walbank *The Hellenistic World* (Fontana; Harvard UP). Greece under the sway of the Macedonian and Roman empires.

ANCIENT RELIGION

Walter Burkert *Greek Religion* (Blackwell; Harvard UP, o/p). Ancient religion, that is; a thorough discussion of rites, cults and deities in this translated German landmark text.

Matthew Dillon *Pilgrims and Pilgrimage in Ancient Greece* (Routledge). Pricey hardback exploring not only the main sanctuaries such as Delphi, but also minor oracles, the role of women and children, and secular festivities attending the rites.

Nano Marinatos and Robin Hagg *Greek Sanctuaries: New Approaches* (Routledge). Form and function of the temples, in the light of recent scholarship.

FOOD AND WINE

Andrew Dalby *Siren Feasts* (Routledge). Subtitled "A history of food and gastronomy in Greece", this analysis of Classical and Byzantine texts demonstrates just how little Greek cuisine has changed in three millennia; also excellent on the introduction and etymology of common vegetables and herbs.

James Davidson *Courtesans and Fishcakes* (HarperCollins, UK). Not just a compendium of quirks – though attitudes and insults about consumption and consummation there are a-plenty – but wine, women and seafood in ancient Attica, placed in their social context.

Miles Lambert-Gócs *The Wines of Greece* (Faber & Faber). Comprehensive survey of the emerging and improving wines of Greece, with plenty of historical background; unfortunately few of these grace middle-of-the-road taverna tables as yet.

ARCHEOLOGY AND ART

John Beckwith *Early Christian and Byzantine Art* (Yale UP). Illustrated study placing Byzantine art within a wider context.

William R. Biers *Archeology of Greece: An Introduction* (Cornell UP). A recently revised and excellent standard text.

John Boardman *Greek Art* (Thames & Hudson, UK). A very good concise introduction: part of the "World of Art" series.

Chris Hellier *Monasteries of Greece* (Tauris Parke; St Martin's Press). Magnificently photographed survey of the surviving, active monasteries and their treasures, with insightful accompanying essays.

Reynold Higgins *Minoan and Mycenaean Art* (Thames & Hudson). A clear, well-illustrated round-up.

Sinclair Hood *The Arts in Prehistoric Greece* (Penguin; Yale UP). Sound introduction to the subject.

Roger Ling *Classical Greece* (Phaidon, UK). Another useful illustrated introduction.

Colin Renfrew *The Cycladic Spirit* (Thames & Hudson; Abrams). A fine, illustrated study of the meaning and purpose of Cycladic artefacts.

Gisela Richter *A Handbook of Greek Art* (Phaidon; Da Capo). Exhaustive survey of the visual arts of ancient Greece.

Suzanne Slesin et al *Greek Style* (Thames & Hudson; Crown). Stunning and stylish interiors from Corfu, Rhodes and Sérifos, among other spots.

R.R.R. Smith *Hellenistic Sculpture* (Thames & Hudson). Modern reappraisal of the art of Greece under Alexander and his successors.

Peter Warren *The Aegean Civilizations* (Phaidon, o/p; P. Bedrick Books, o/p). Illustrated account of the Minoan and Mycenaean cultures.

BYZANTINE, MEDIEVAL AND OTTOMAN HISTORY

Archbishop Kallistos (Timothy) Ware *The Orthodox Church* (Penguin). Good introduction to what is effectively the established religion of Greece, by the Orthodox archbishop resident in Oxford.

Averil Cameron *The Mediterranean World in Late Antiquity, AD 395–600* (Routledge). Essentially the early Byzantine years.

Nicholas Cheetham *Medieval Greece* (Yale UP, o/p in US). General survey of the period and its infinite convolutions in Greece, with Frankish, Catalan, Venetian, Byzantine and Ottoman struggles for power.

John Julius Norwich *Byzantium: The Early Centuries*; *Byzantium: the Apogee* and *Byzantium: The Decline* (all Penguin; Viking-Knopf). Perhaps the main surprise for first-time travellers to Greece is the fascination of its Byzantine monuments. This is an astonishingly detailed yet readable trilogy.

Michael Psellus *Fourteen Byzantine Rulers* (Penguin). A fascinating contemporary source, detailing the stormy but brilliant period from 976 to 1078.

Steven Runciman *The Fall of Constantinople, 1453* (Canto-Cambridge UP) is the standard account of the event; *The Great Church in Captivity* (Cambridge UP) follows the vicissitudes of the Orthodox Patriarchate in Constantinople up to the War of Independence. *Byzantine Style and Civilization* (Penguin, o/p in US) and *Mistra* (Thames & Hudson, o/p in US) are more slanted towards art, culture and monuments.

MODERN GREECE

Timothy Boatswain and Colin Nicolson *A Traveller's History of Greece* (Windrush Press; Interlink). Slightly dated (coverage ceases in early 1990s), but a well written overview of the important Greek periods and personalities.

Richard Clogg *A Concise History of Greece* (Cambridge UP). A remarkably clear and well-illustrated account of Greece, from the decline of Byzantium to 1991, with the emphasis on recent decades; there are numerous maps and lengthy feature captions to the artwork.

Douglas Dakin *The Unification of Greece, 1770–1923* (Ernest Benn, o/p; St Martin's Press, o/p). Benchmark account of the foundation of the Greek state and the struggle to extend its boundaries.

H. A. Lidderdale, trs and ed *The Memoirs of General Makriyannis 1797–1864* (Oxford UP, o/p). The "Peasant General", one of the few honest and self-sacrificing protagonists of the Greek uprising, taught himself to write at age 32 to set down this apologia of his conduct, in vivid demotic Greek. Heartbreaking in its portrayal of the incipient schisms, linguistic and otherwise, that tore the country apart until recently.

Michael Llewellyn Smith *Ionian Vision, Greece in Asia Minor, 1919–22* (Allen Lane, o/p; St Martin's Press, o/p). Standard work by the current UK ambassador to Greece, on the disastrous Anatolian campaign, which led to the exchange of populations between Greece and Turkey.

Yiannis Roubatis *Tangled Webs: The US in Greece 1947–67* (Pella Publishing, US). Chronicles growing American involvement in Greece during the lead-up to the military coup.

C. M. Woodhouse *Modern Greece, A Short History* (Faber & Faber). Woodhouse was active in the Greek Resistance during World War II. Writing from a more right-wing perspective than Clogg, this history (spanning from the foundation of Constantinople in 324 to the present), is briefer and a bit drier, but scrupulous with facts. *The Rise and Fall of the Greek Colonels* (Granada, o/p; Watts), recounts the (horror) story of the dictatorship.

WORLD WAR II AND ITS AFTERMATH

Mark Mazower *Inside Hitler's Greece: The Experience of Occupation 1941–44* (Yale UP). Somewhat choppily organized, but the standard of scholarship is high and the photos alone justify the price, though there's not much on the islands. Demonstrates how the complete demoralization of the country and the incompetence of conventional politicians led to the rise of ELAS and the onset of civil war.

George Psychoundakis *The Cretan Runner* (John Murray, o/p; Transatlantic Arts, o/p; Efstathiadis, Athens). Narrative of the invasion of Crete and subsequent resistance, by a participant who was a guide and message-runner for all the British protagonists –including Patrick Leigh Fermor, the translator of the book.

Marion Sarafis and Martin Eve *Background to Contemporary Greece, V. 1 & 2* (Merlin, UK). Papers and panel discussion from a late 1980s conference on the Civil War, with former belligerents confronting each other across podiums. Left-wing bias, but Sarafis herself – widow of an ELAS general – is impressive, especially in Volume 1.

Adrian Seligman *War in the Islands* (Allan Sutton, UK). Collected oral histories of a little-known Allied unit: a flotilla of kaïkia equipped to raid the Axis-held Dodecanese, Cyclades and northeast Aegean islands. *Boy's Own* stuff, with service-jargon-laced prose, but some pretty gripping tales, with lots of fine period photos and detail.

C. M. Woodhouse *The Struggle for Greece, 1941–49* (Hart-Davis, o/p; Beekman). A masterly and by no means uncritical account of this crucial decade, explaining how Greece emerged without a communist government.

ETHNOGRAPHY

Juliet du Boulay *Portrait of a Greek Mountain Village* (Oxford UP, o/p in UK). An account of the village of Ambéli, on Évvia, during the 1960s. The habits and customs of an all-but-vanished way of life are observed and evoked in an absorbing narrative.

John Cuthbert Lawson *Modern Greek Folklore and Ancient Greek Religion: A Study in Survivals* (University Books, New York; o/p). This is to Greece what *The Golden Bough* is to the world at large; well worth scouring libraries and antiquarian dealers for.

Clay Perry *Vanishing Greece* (Conran Octopus; Abbeville Press). Well captioned photos depict the threatened landscapes and relict ways of life in rural Greece, including several islands.

MODERN GREEK LITERATURE

Roderick Beaton *An Introduction to Modern Greek Literature* (Oxford UP). Chronological survey of fiction and poetry from independence to 1821, with a useful discussion on the "Language Question".

FICTION

Maro Douka *Fool's Gold* (Kedros, Athens*; Roundhouse, Oxford, UK). Describes an upper-class young woman's involvement, and subsequent disillusionment, with the clandestine resistance to the junta.

Eugenia Fakinou *The Seventh Garment* (Serpent's Tail). Greek history, from the War of Independence to the colonels' junta, as told through the life stories (interspersed in counterpoint) of three generations of women; it's a rather more successful experiment than Fakinou's *Astradeni* (Kedros, Athens*), in which a young girl — whose slightly irritating narrative voice is adopted throughout — leaves the island of Sými, with all its traditional values, for Athens.

Nikos Kazantzakis *Zorba the Greek; Christ Recrucified* (published in the US as *The Greek Passion*); *Report to Greco; Freedom or Death* (*Captain Mihalis* in the US); *The Fratricides* (all Faber & Faber; Touchstone). The most accessible (and Greece-related) of the numerous novels by the Cretan master. Even with inadequate translation, their strength — especially that of *Report to Greco* — shines through.

Artemis Leontis, ed *Greece: A Traveller's Literary Companion* (Whereabouts Press, San Francisco, US). An overdue idea, brilliantly executed: various regions of the country as portrayed in (very) short fiction or essays by modern Greek writers. A recommended antidote to the often condescending Grand Tourist accounts.

Stratis Myrivilis Life in the Tomb (Quartet; New England UP). A harrowing and unorthodox war novel, based on the author's experience on the Macedonian front during 1917–18, well translated by Peter Bien. Completing a loose trilogy are two later novels, set on the north coast of Lésvos, Myrivilis' homeland: *The Mermaid Madonna* and *The Schoolmistress with the Golden Eyes* (Efstathiadis, Athens). Translations of these are unhappily not as good, and tend to be abridged.

Alexandros Papadiamantis *The Murderess* (Writers & Readers). Landmark turn-of-the-century novel set on Skiáthos, in which an old woman, appalled by the fate that awaits them in adulthood, concludes that little girls are better off dead. Also available is a collection of Papadiamantis short stories, *Tales from a Greek Island* (Johns Hopkins UP).

Dido Sotiriou *Farewell Anatolia* (Kedros, Greece*). A classic since its initial appearance in 1962 (it is now in its 56th Greek printing), this epic chronicles the traumatic end of Greek life from World War I to the catastrophe of 1922, as narrated by a fictionalized version of the author's father; in the finale, he escapes across the narrow strait of Mycale to Sámos, as many did in those turbulent years.

Yiorgos Yatromanolakis *The History of a Vendetta* (Dedalus/Hippocrene). Greek magic realism as the tales of two families unravel from a murder in a small Cretan village.

* These books are part of a highly recommended "Modern Greek Writers" series, currently numbering nearly thirty titles, issued by the Athenian company Kedros Publishers.

MODERN GREEK POETRY

With two Nobel laureates in recent years — George Seferis and Odysseus Elytis — modern Greece has an extraordinarily intense and dynamic poetic tradition. Translations of all of the following are excellent.

C.P. Cavafy *Collected Poems* (Chatto & Windus/Princeton UP). The complete works, translated by Edmund Keeley and Philip Sherrard, of perhaps the most accessible modern Greek poet, resident for most of his life in Alexandria. For some, *The Complete Poems of Cavafy* (Harcourt Brace Jovanovich), translated by Rae Dalven, is a superior version.

Odysseus Elytis *The Axion Esti* (Anvil Press; Pittsburgh UP); *Selected Poems* (Anvil Press; Viking Penguin, o/p); *The Sovereign Sun* (Bloodaxe Books; Temple UP, Philadelphia, o/p). The major works in good English versions.

Modern Greek Poetry (Efstathiadis, Athens). Decent anthology of translations, predominantly of Seferis and Elytis.

Yannis Ritsos *Exile and Return, Selected Poems 1967–1974* (Anvil Press; Ecco Press). A fine volume of Greece's foremost leftist poet, from the junta era when he was internally exiled on Sámos.

George Seferis *Collected Poems, 1924–1955* (Anvil Press, o/p; Princeton UP, o/p). Virtually the complete works of the Nobel laureate, with Greek and English verses on facing pages. More recent, but lacking the facing Greek text, is *Complete Poems* (Anvil Press/Princeton UP).

GREECE IN FOREIGN FICTION

Louis de Bernières *Captain Corelli's Mandolin* (Minerva; Random House). Set on Kefalloniá mostly during the World War II occupation, this is a brilliant tragicomedy by an author best known for his South American extravaganzas. It has won praise from Greek intellectuals despite its sweeping disparagement of ELAS – quite an achievement.

John Fowles *The Magus* (Vintage; Dell). Fowles's biggest and best novel: a tale of mystery and manipulation – plus Greek island life – inspired by his stay on Spétses as a teacher, in the 1950s.

Mary Renault *The King Must Die, The Last of the Wine, The Mask of Apollo* (Sceptre; Random House) and others (all Penguin except *Masks*). Mary Renault's imaginative reconstructions are more than the adolescent's reading they're often taken for, with impeccable research and tight writing. The trio above retell, respectively, the myth of Theseus, the life of a pupil of Socrates, and that of a fourth-century BC actor.

The life of Alexander the Great is told in *Fire from Heaven, The Persian Boy* and *Funeral Games*, available separately or in one economical volume (all Penguin).

Evelyn Waugh *Officers and Gentleman* (Penguin). This volume of the wartime trilogy includes an account of the Battle for Crete and subsequent evacuation.

SPECIFIC GUIDES

ARCHEOLOGY

A.R. and Mary Burn *The Living Past of Greece: A Time Traveller's Tour of Historic and Prehistoric Places* (Herbert Press; HarperCollins). Unusual in extent, this covers sites from Minoan through to Byzantine and Frankish, with good clear plans and lively text.

Evi Melas ed *Temples and Sanctuaries of Ancient Greece: A Companion Guide* (Thames & Hudson, o/p). Excellent collection of essays on the main sites, written by archeologists who have worked at them.

Alexander Paradissis *Fortresses and Castles of Greece* (Efstathiadis, Athens). As it says, in three extremely prolix volumes, widely available in Greek bookshops. Volume III covers the islands.

REGIONAL GUIDES

Marc Dubin *The Rough Guide to Rhodes, the Dodecanese and the East Aegean* (Penguin). Exhaustive coverage of the islands described in Chapters Nine and Ten of this book by a part-time resident of Sámos.

John Fisher and Geoff Garvey *The Rough Guide to Crete* (Penguin). An expanded and practical guide to the island by two Cretophiles, who contributed the Crete chapter this book.

Lycabettus Press Guides (Athens, Greece). This series takes in some of the more popular islands; most, despite long intervals between revisions, pay their way both in interest and usefulness – in particular those on Páros, Kós, Pátmos, Ídhra, and the travels of St Paul.

Nikos Stavroulakis *Jewish Sites and Synagogues of Greece* (Talos Press, Athens). Lavishly illustrated alphabetical gazetteer of all Jewish monuments in Greece, including the islands, with town plans and full histories of the communities that created them. A few have been demolished since publication, however.

YACHTING

H. M. Denham *The Aegean* and *The Ionian Islands to the Anatolian Coast* (John Murray, UK, o/p). Long the standard references if you were out yachting; still found in second-hand book shops.

Rod Heikell *Greek Waters Pilot* (Imray, Laurie, Norrie and Wilson, UK). Rather better than the preceding, which it has superseded.

BOOKSHOPS

In **London**, the Hellenic Bookservice, 91 Fortess Rd, Kentish Town, London NW5 1AG (☎0171/267 9499), and Zeno's Greek Bookshop, 6 Denmark St, WC2H 8LP (☎0171/836 2522), are knowledgeable and well-stocked specialist dealers in new, secondhand and out-of-print books on all aspects of Greece.

HIKING

Marc Dubin *Trekking in Greece* (Lonely Planet). An excellent walkers' guide, expanding on the hikes covered in this book and adding others, both around the mainland and on the islands. Includes day-hikes and longer treks, plus extensive preparatory and background information. Look for a new version with a UK publisher in 1999.

Lance Chilton *Various Walking Pamphlets* (Marengo Publications, UK). Small but thorough guides to the best walks at various island charter resorts, accompanied by three-colour maps. Areas covered to date include: Áyios Yeóryios, Corfu; Yeoryioúpolis and Plakiás, Crete; Líndhos, Rhodes; and Kokkári, Sámos. Available in specialist UK shops or by mail order; catalogue from 17 Bernard Crescent, Hunstanton PE36 6ER, ☎ & fax 01485/532710.

LANGUAGE

So many Greeks have lived or worked abroad in America, Australia and, to a much lesser extent, Britain, that you will find someone who speaks English in the tiniest island village. Add to that the thousands attending language schools or working in the tourist industry – English is the lingua franca of most resorts, with German second – and it is easy to see how so many visitors come back having learned only half a dozen restaurant words between them.

You can certainly get by this way, but it isn't very satisfying, and the willingness and ability to say even a few words will transform your status from that of dumb *touristas* to the honourable one of *ksénos*, a word which can mean foreigner, traveller and guest all rolled into one.

LEARNING BASIC GREEK

Greek is not an easy language for English speakers but it is a very beautiful one, and even a brief acquaintance will give you some idea of the debt owed to it by western European languages.

On top of the usual difficulties of learning a new language, Greek presents the additional problem of an entirely separate **alphabet**. Despite initial appearances, this is in practice fairly easily mastered – a skill that will help enormously if you are going to get around independently (see the alphabet box overleaf). In addition, certain combinations of letters have unexpected results. This book's transliteration system should help you make intelligible noises but you have to remember that the correct **stress** (marked throughout the book with an acute accent) is crucial. With the right sounds but the wrong stress people will either fail to understand you, or else understand something quite different from what you intended.

Greek **grammar** is more complicated still: nouns are divided into three genders, all with different case endings in the singular and in the plural, and all adjectives and articles have to agree with these in gender, number and case. (All adjectives are arbitrarily cited in the neuter form in the following lists.) Verbs are even worse. To begin

LANGUAGE LEARNING MATERIALS

TEACH-YOURSELF GREEK COURSES
Breakthrough Greece (Pan Macmillan; book and two cassettes). Excellent, basic teach-yourself course – completely outclasses the competition.

Greek Language and People (BBC Publications, UK; book and cassette available). More limited in scope but good for acquiring the essentials, and the confidence to try them.

Anne Farmakides *A Manual of Modern Greek* (Yale/McGill; 3 vols). If you have the discipline and motivation, this is one of the best for learning proper, grammatical Greek; indeed, mastery of just the first volume will get you a long way.

PHRASEBOOKS
The Rough Guide to Greek (Penguin, UK/US). Practical and easy-to-use, the Rough Guide

phrasebooks allow you to speak the way you would in your own language. Feature boxes fill you in on dos and don'ts and cultural know-how.

DICTIONARIES
The Oxford Dictionary of Modern Greek (Oxford University Press, UK/US). A bit bulky, but generally considered the best Greek–English, English–Greek dictionary.

Collins Pocket Greek Dictionary (Harper Collins, UK/US). Very nearly as complete as the Oxford and probably better value for money.

Oxford Learner's Dictionary (Oxford University Press, UK/US). If you're planning a prolonged stay, this pricey two-volume set is unbeatable for usage and vocabulary. There's also a more portable one-volume Learner's Pocket Dictionary.

THE GREEK ALPHABET: TRANSLITERATION

Set out below is the Greek alphabet, the system of transliteration used in this book, and a brief aid to pronunciation.

Greek	Transliteration	Pronounced
Α, α	a	a as in father
Β, β	v	v as in vet
Γ, γ	y/g	y as in yes except before consonants or α, o or οι when its a breathy g as in gap.
Δ, δ	dh	th as in then
Ε, ε	e	e as in get
Ζ, ζ	z	z sound
Η, η	i	i as in ski
Θ, θ	th	th as in theme
Ι, ι	i	i as in ski
Κ, κ	k	k sound
Λ, λ	l	l sound
Μ, μ	m	m sound
Ν, ν	n	n sound
Ξ, ξ	x	x and in box
Ο, ο	o	o as in toad
Π, π	p	p sound
Ρ, ρ	r	rolled r sound
Σ, σ, ς	s	s sound, except z before μ
Τ, τ	t	t sound
Υ, υ	i	i as in ski
Φ, φ	f	f sound
Χ, χ	kh	harsh h sound, like ch in loch
Ψ, ψ	ps	ps as in lips
Ω, ω	o	o as in toad, indistinguishable from o

Combinations and dipthongs

ΑΙ, αι	e	e as in get
ΑΥ, αυ	av/af	av or af depending on following consonant
ΕΙ, ει	i	long i, as in ι or η
ΟΙ, οι	i	long i, as in ι or η
ΕΥ, ευ	ev/ef	ev or ef, depending on following consonant
ΟΥ, ου	ou	ou as in tourist
ΓΓ, γγ	ng	ng as in angle; always medial
ΓΚ, γκ	g/ng	g as in goat at the beginning of a word, ng in the middle
ΜΠ, μπ	b/mb	b at the beginning of a word, mb in the middle
ΝΤ, ντ	d/nd	d at the beginning of a word, nd in the middle
ΤΣ, τσ	ts	ts as in hits
ΤΖ, τζ	tz	j as in jam

Note: An umlaut over one of two adjacent vowels means they're pronounced separately; it often functions as the primary stress in this book. Thus kaïki is "ky-ee-key" not "cake-key", and Aóös is pronounced "Ah-ohs" not "Ah-oos".

with at least, the best thing is simply to say what you know the way you know it, and never mind the niceties. "Eat meat hungry" should get a result, however grammatically incorrect. If you worry about your mistakes, you'll never say anything.

KATHARÉVOUSSA, DHIMOTIKI AND DIALECTS

Greek may seem complicated enough in itself, but its impossibilities are multiplied when you con-

GREEK WORDS AND PHRASES

Essentials

Yes	*Néh*	Here	*Edhó*
Certainly	*Málista*	There	*Ekí*
No	*Ókhi*	This one	*Aftó*
Please	*Parakaló*	That one	*Ekíno*
Okay, agreed	*Endáysi*	Good	*Kaló*
Thank you (very much)	*Efkharistó (polý)*	Bad	*Kakó*
I (don't) understand	*(Dhen) Katalavéno*	Big	*Megálo*
Excuse me, do you	*Parakaló, mípos miláteh*	Small	*Mikró*
speak English?	*angliká?*	More	*Perisótero*
Sorry/excuse me	*Signómi*	Less	*Ligótero*
Today	*Símera*	A little	*Lígo*
Tomorrow	*Ávrio*	A lot	*Polí*
Yesterday	*Khthés*	Cheap	*Ftinó*
Now	*Tóra*	Expensive	*Akrivó*
Later	*Argótera*	Hot	*Zestó*
Open	*Anikhtó*	Cold	*Krío*
Closed	*Klistó*	With	*Mazí*
Day	*Méra*	Without	*Horís*
Night	*Níkhta*	Quickly	*Grígora*
In the morning	*Tó proï*	Slowly	*Sigá*
In the afternoon	*Tó apóyevma*	Mr/Mrs	*Kírios/Kiría*
In the evening	*Tó vrádhi*	Miss	*Dhespinís*

Other needs

To eat/drink	*Trógo/Píno*	Stamps	*Gramatosímata*	Police	*Astynomía*
Bakery	*Foúrnos,*	Petrol station	*Venzinádhiko*	Doctor	*Iatrós*
	psomádhiko	Bank	*Trápeza*	Hospital	*Nosokomío*
Pharmacy	*Farmakío*	Money	*Leftá/Khrímata*		
Post office	*Takhydhromío*	Toilet	*Toualéta*		

Requests and Questions

To ask a question, it's simplest to start with parakaló,
then name the thing you want in an interrogative tone.

Where is the bakery?	*Parakaló, o foúrnos?*	How many?	*Pússi or pósses?*
Can you show	*Parakaló, o*	How much?	*Póso?*
me the road to . . . ?	*dhrómos yiá . . ?*	When?	*Póteh?*
We'd like a	*Parakaló, éna dhomá-*	Why?	*Yatí?*
room for two	*tio yiá dhyo átoma?*	At what time . . . ?	*Ti óra . . . ?*
May I have a	*Parakaló, éna kiló*	What is/Which is . . . ?	*Ti íneh/pió íneh..?*
kilo of oranges?	*portokália?*	How much (does it cost)?	*Póso káni?*
Where?	*Poú?*	What time does it open?	*Tí óra aníyi?*
How?	*Pós?*	What time does it close?	*Tí óra klíni?*

Talking to People

Greek makes the distinction between the informal (*esí*) and formal (*esís*) second person, as French does
with *tu* and *vous*. Young people, older people and country people nearly always use esí even with total
strangers. In any event, no one will be too bothered if you get it wrong. By far the most common greeting, on meeting and parting, is yiá sou/yiá sas – literally "health to you".

Hello	*Khérete*	Goodbye	*Adío*
Good morning	*Kalí méra*	How are you?	*Ti kánis/Ti káneteh?*
Good evening	*Kalí spéra*	I'm fine	*Kalá ímeh*
Good night	*Kalí níkhta*		

Continued over

And you?	Keh esís?	I don't know	Dhen xéro
What's your name?	Pos se léneh?	See you tomorrow	Thá sé dhó ávrio
My name is . . .	Meh léneh . . .	See you soon	Kalí andhámosi
Speak slower, please	Parakaló, miláte pió sigá	Let's go	Pámeh
		Please help me	Parakaló, na me
How do you say it in Greek?	Pos léyeteh stá Eliniká?		voithísteh

Greek's Greek

There are numerous words and phrases which you will hear constantly, even if you rarely have the chance to use them. These are a few of the most common.

Éla!	Come (literally) but also Speak to me! You don't say! etc.	Po-po-po!	Expression of dismay or concern, like French "O la la!"
Orísteh?	What can I do for you?	Pedhí moú	My boy/girl, sonny, friend, etc.
Léyeyeh	Standard phone response	Maláka(s)	Literally "wanker", but often used (don't try it!) as an informal address.
Ti néa?	What's new?		
Ti yíneteh?	What's going on (here)?		
Étsi k'étsi	So-so	Sigá sigá	Take your time, slow down
Ópa!	Whoops! Watch it!	Kaló taxídhi	Bon voyage

Accommodation

Inn	Xenónes	hot water	zestó neró
Hotel	Xenodhokhío	Cold water	krío neró
A room . . .	Éna dhomátio . . .	Can I see it?	Boró na to dho?
for one/two/ three people	yiá éna/dhýo/tría átoma	Can we camp here?	Boróume na váloumeh ti skiní edhó?
for one/two/ three nights	ya mía/dhýo/trís vradhiés	Campsite	Kamping/Kataskínosi
		Tent	Skiní
with a double bed	méh megálo kreváti	Youth hostel	Xenónes neótitos
with a shower	méh doús		

On the Move

Aeroplane	Aeropláno	Taxi	Taksí
Bus	Leoforío	Ship	Plío/Vapóri/Karávi
Car	Aftokínito	Bicycle	Podhílato
Motorbike, moped	Mihanáki, papáki	Hitching	Otostóp

sider that for the last century there has been an ongoing dispute between two versions of the language: **katharévoussa** and **dhimotikí**.

When Greece first achieved independence in the nineteenth century, its people were almost universally illiterate, and the language they spoke – **dhimotikí**, "demotic" or "popular" Greek – had undergone enormous change since the days of the Byzantine Empire and Classical times. The vocabulary had assimilated count-less borrowings from the languages of the vari-ous invaders and conquerors, from the Turks, Venetians, Albanians and Slavs.

The finance and inspiration for the new Greek state, and its early leaders, came largely from the diaspora – Greek families who had been living in the sophisticated cities of central and eastern Europe, or in Russia. With their European notions about the grandeur of Greece's past, and lofty conception of Hellenism, they set about obliterating the mem-ory of subjugation to foreigners in every possi-ble field. And what better way to start than by purging the language of its foreign accretions and reviving its Classical purity.

They accordingly set about creating what was in effect a new form of the language, **katharévoussa** (literally "cleansed" Greek). The complexities of Classical grammar and syn-tax were reinstated, and Classical words, long

On foot	Meh ta pódhia	Far	Makriá
Trail	Monopáti	Left	Aristerá
Bus station	Praktorío leoforíon	Right	Dheksiá
Bus stop	Stási	Straight ahead	Katefthía
Harbour	Limáni	A ticket to . . .	Éna isistírio ya . . .
What time does it leave?	Ti óra févyi?	A return ticket	Éna isistírio me
What time does it arrive?	Ti óra ftháni?		epistrofí
How many kilometres?	Pósa hiliómetra?	Beach	Paralía
How many hours?	Pósses óres?	Cave	Spiliá
Where are you going?	Pou pas?	Centre (of town)	Kéndro
I'm going to . . .	Páo sto . . .	Church	Eklissía
I want to get off at . . .	Thélo na katévo sto . . .	Sea	Thálassa
The road to . . .	O dhrómos ya . . .	Village	Horió
Near	Kondá		

Numbers

1	énos/éna/mía	12	dhódheka	90	enenínda
2	dhýo	13	dhekatrís	100	ekató
3	trís/tría	14	dhekatésseres	150	ekatón penínda
4	tésseres/téssera	20	íkosi	200	dhiakóssies/ia
5	pénde	21	íkosiéna	500	pendakóssies/ia
6	éxi	30	triánda	1000	khíles/khília
7	eftá	40	saránda	2000	dhío khiliádhes
8	okhtó	50	penínda	1,000,000	éna ekatomírio
9	enyá	60	exínda	first	próto
10	dhéka	70	evdhomínda	second	dhéftero
11	éndheka	80	ogdhónda	third	tríto

The time and days of the week

Sunday	Kyriakí	What time is it?	Ti óra íneh?
Monday	Dheftéra	One/two/three o'clock	Mía óra, dhýo/trís (óres)
Tuesday	Tríti	Twenty minutes to four	Tésseres pará íkosi
Wednesday	Tetárti	Five minutes past seven	Eftá keh pénde
Thursday	Pémpti	Half past eleven	Éndheka keh misí
Friday	Paraskeví	Half-hour	Misí óra
Saturday	Sávato	Quarter-hour	Éna tétarto

out of use, were reintroduced. To the country's great detriment, katharévoussa became the language of the schools and the prestigious professions, government, business, the law, newspapers and academia. Everyone aspiring to membership in the elite strove to master it, and to speak it – even though there was no absolute and defined idea of how many of the words should be pronounced.

The katharévoussa/dhimotikí debate has been a highly contentious issue through most of this century. Writers – from Sikelianos and Seferis to Kazantzakis and Ritsos – have all championed the demotic in their literature. Meanwhile, crackpot right-wing governments forcibly (re)instated katharévoussa at every opportunity. Most recently, the **colonels' junta** of 1967–1974 reversed a decision of the previous government to teach in dhimotikí in the schools, bringing back katharévoussa, even on sweet wrappers, as part of their ragbag of notions about racial purity and heroic ages.

Dhimotikí returned once more after the fall of the colonels and now seems here to stay. It is used in schools, on radio and TV, in newspapers (with the exception of the extreme right-wing Estia) and in most official business. The only institutions which refuse to bring themselves up to date are the church and the legal professions – so beware rental contracts.

This is not to suggest that there is any less confusion. The Metaxas dictatorship of the 1930s changed scores of village names from Slavic to Classical forms and these official **place names** still hold sway on most road signs and maps – even though the local people may use the dhimotikí form. Thus you will see "Leonídhion" or "Spétsai" written, while everyone actually says Leonídhi or Spétses.

DIALECTS AND MINORITY LANGUAGES

If the lack of any standard Greek were not enough, Greece still offers a rich field of linguistic diversity, both in its dialects and minority languages. Ancient **dialects** are alive and well in many a remote area, and some of them are quite incomprehensible to outsiders. The dialect of Sfákia in Crete is one such. Tsakónika (spoken in the east-central Peloponnese) is another, while the dialect of the Sarakatsáni shepherds is said to be the oldest, a direct descendant of the language of the Dorian settlers.

The language of the Sarakatsáni's traditional rivals, the **Vlachs**, on the other hand, is not Greek at all, but a derivative of early Latin, with strong affinities to Romanian. In the Yugoslav and Bulgarian frontier regions you can still hear Slavic **Macedonian** spoken, while small numbers of Sephardic Jews in the north speak **Ladino**, a medieval form of Spanish. Until a few decades ago **Arvanitika** – a dialect of medieval Albanian – was the first language of many villages of inland Attica, southern Évvia, northern Ándhros, and much of the Argo-Saronic area; it is still widely spoken among the older generation. Lately the clock has been turned back as throngs of Albanian refugees circulate in Athens and other parts of the country. In Thrace there is also a substantial **Turkish**-speaking population, as well as some speakers of **Pomak** (a relative of Bulgarian with a large Greco-Turk vocabulary).

A GLOSSARY OF WORDS AND TERMS

ACROPOLIS Ancient, fortified hilltop.

AGORA Market and meeting place of an ancient Greek city.

AMPHORA Tall, narrow-necked jar for oil or wine.

ÁNO Upper; as in upper town or village.

APSE Polygonal or curved recess at the altar end of a church.

ARCHAIC PERIOD Late Iron Age period, from around 750 BC to the start of the Classical period in the fifth century BC.

ARKHONDIKÓ A stone mansion in the villages of the Zagóri.

ASTYKÓ (Intra) city, municipal, local; adjective applied to phone calls and bus services.

ATRIUM Open, inner courtyard of a house.

ÁYIOS/AYÍA/ÁYII Saint or holy (m/f/plural). Common place name prefix (abbreviated Ag. or Ay.), often spelled AGIOS or AGHIOS.

BASILICA Colonnaded, "hall-" or "barn-" type church, most common in northern Greece.

BEMA Rostrum for oratory (and later the chancel) of a church.

BOULEUTERION Auditorium for meetings of an ancient town's deliberative council.

BYZANTINE EMPIRE Created by the division of the Roman Empire in 395 AD, this, the eastern half, was ruled from Constantinople (modern Istanbul). In Greece, Byzantine culture peaked twice: in the eleventh century, and again at Mystra in the early fifteenth century.

CAPITAL The top, often ornamented, of a column.

CELLA Sacred room of a temple, housing the cult image.

CLASSICAL PERIOD Essentially from the end of the Persian Wars in the fifth century BC until the unification of Greece under Phillip II of Macedon (338 BC).

CORINTHIAN Decorative columns, festooned with acanthus florettes.

DHIMARKHÍO Town hall.

DHOMÁTIA Rooms for rent in private houses.

DORIAN Northern civilization that displaced and succeeded the Mycenaeans and Minoans through most of Greece around 1100 BC.

DORIC Primitive columns, dating from the Dorian period.

ENTABLATURE The horizontal linking structure atop the columns of an ancient temple.

EPARKHÍA Greek Orthodox diocese, also the smallest subdivision of a modern province.

EXONARTHEX The outer vestibule or entrance hall of a church.

FORUM Market and meeting place of a Roman-era city.

FRÁKHTES Dry-stone walls.

FRIEZE Band of sculptures around a temple. Doric friezes consist of various tableaux of figures (METOPES) interspersed with grooved panels (TRIGLYPHS); Ionic ones have continuous bands of figures.

FROÚRIO Medieval castle.

GARSONIÉRA/ES Studio self-catering apartment/s.

GEOMETRIC PERIOD Post-Mycenaean Iron Age era named for the style of its pottery; begins in the early eleventh century BC with the arrival of Dorian peoples. By the eighth century BC, with the development of representational styles, it becomes known as the ARCHAIC period.

HELLENISTIC PERIOD The last and most unified "Greek empire", created in the wake of Alexander the Great's Macedonian empire and finally collapsing with the fall of Corinth to the Romans in 146 BC.

HEROÖN Shrine or sanctuary, usually of a demigod or mortal; war memorials.

IERÓN Literally, "sacred" – the space between the altar screen and the apse of a church, reserved for a priest.

IKONOSTÁSI Screen between the nave of a church and the altar, supporting at least three icons.

IONIC Elaborate, decorative development of the older DORIC order; Ionic temple columns are slimmer with deeper "fluted" edges, spiral-shaped capitals, and ornamental bases.

CORINTHIAN capitals are a still more decorative development, with acanthus florettes.

IPERASTYKÓ Inter-city, long-distance – as in phone calls and bus services.

JANISSARY Member of the Turkish Imperial Guard, often forcibly recruited in childhood from the local population.

KAFENÍO Coffee house or café; in a small village the centre of communal life and probably serving as the bus stop, too.

KAÏKI (plural KAÏKIA) Caique, or medium-sized boat, traditionally wooden and used for transporting cargo and passengers; now refers mainly to island excursion boats.

KALDERÍMI Cobbled mule- and footpaths.

KÁMBOS Fertile agricultural plateau, usually near a river mouth.

KÁSTRO Any fortified hill (or a castle), but most usually the oldest, highest, walled-in part of an island KHÓRA.

KATHOLIKÓN Central chapel of a monastery.

KÁTO Lower; as in lower town or village.

KENTRIKÍ PLATÍA Central square.

KHOKHLÁKI Pebble mosaic.

KHÓRA Main town of an island or region; literally it means "the place". An island khóra may also be known by the same name as the island.

KOUROS Nude statue of an idealized young man, usually portrayed with one foot slightly forward of the other.

MACEDONIAN EMPIRE Empire created by Philip II in the mid-fourth century BC.

MEGARON Principal hall or throne room of a Mycenaean palace.

MELTÉMI North wind that blows across the Aegean in summer, starting softly from near the mainland and hitting the Cyclades, the Dodecanese and Crete full on.

METOPE see FRIEZE

MINOAN Crete's great Bronze Age Civilization, which dominated the Aegean from about 2500 to 1400 BC.

MONÍ Formal term for a monastery or convent.

MOREÁS Medieval term for the Peloponnese; the outline of the peninsula was likened to the leaf of a mulberry tree, *moreá* in Greek.

MYCENAEAN Mainland civilization centred on Mycenae and the Argolid from about 1700 to 1100 BC.

NAOS The inner sanctum of an ancient temple; also, any Orthodox Christian shrine.

NARTHEX Vestibule or church entrance hall.

NEOLITHIC Earliest era of settlement in Greece, characterized by the use of stone tools and weapons together with basic agriculture. Divided arbitrarily into Early (c. 6000 BC), Middle (c. 5000 BC), and Late (c. 3000 BC).

NÉOS, NÉA, NÉO "New" – a common part of a town or village name.

NOMÓS Modern Greek province – there are more than fifty of them. Village bus services are organized according to their borders.

ODEION Small amphitheatre, used for musical performances, minor dramatic productions or councils.

ORCHESTRA Circular area in a theatre where the chorus would sing and dance.

PALAESTRA Gymnasium for athletics and wrestling practice.

PALEÓS, PALEÁ, PALEÓ "Old" – again common in town and village names.

PANAYÍA Virgin Mary.

PANIYÍRI Festival or feast – the local celebration of a holy day.

PANDOKRÁTOR Literally "The Almighty"; generally refers to the stern portrayal of Christ in Majesty frescoed or in mosaic in the dome of many Byzantine churches.

PARALÍA Beach or seafront promenade.

PEDIMENT Triangular, sculpted gable below the roof of a temple.

PENDENTIVE Any of four triangular sections of vaulting with concave sides, positioned at a corner of a rectangular space to support a circular or polygonal dome; often adorned with frescoes of the four evangelists.

PERÍPTERO Street kiosk.

PERISTEREÓNES Pigeon towers.

PERISTYLE Gallery of columns around a temple or other building.

PINAKOTHIKI Picture gallery.

PÝRGOS Tower or bastion.

PITHOS (plural PITHOI) Large ceramic jar for storing oil, grain, etc. Very common in Minoan palaces and used in almost identical form in modern Greek homes.

PLATÍA Square, plaza.

PROPYLAION Portico or entrance to an ancient building; often used in the plural, propylaia.

SQUINCH Small concavity across a corner of a columnless interior space, which supports a superstructure such as a dome.

SKÁLA The port of an inland island settlement, nowadays often larger and more important than its namesake, but always younger since built after the disappearance of piracy.

STELE Upright stone slab or column, usually inscribed; an ancient tombstone.

STOA Colonnaded walkway in Classical-era marketplace.

TAVERNA Restaurant; see "Eating and Drinking" in Basics, p.42, for details of the different types of specialist eating places.

TÉMBLON Wooden altar screen of an Orthodox church, usually ornately carved and painted and studded with icons.

TEMENOS Sacred precinct, often used to refer to the sanctuary itself.

THEATRAL AREA Open area found in most of the Minoan palaces with seat-like steps around. Probably a type of theatre or ritual area, though this is not conclusively proven.

THOLOS Conical or beehive-shaped building, especially a Mycenaean tomb.

TRIGLYPH see FRIEZE

TYMPANUM The recessed space, flat or carved in relief, inside a pediment.

VOLTA Promenade.

ACRONYMS

ANEK Anonymí Navtikí Etería Krítis (Shipping Co of Crete, Ltd), which runs most ferries between Pireás and Crete, plus many to Italy.

EAM National Liberation Front, the political force behind ELAS.

ELAS Popular Liberation Army, the main resistance group during World War II and the basis of the communist army in the civil war.

EK Fascist party (Ethnikó Kómma), consisting mostly of adherents to the imprisoned junta colonel, Papadopoulos.

ELTA The postal service.

EOS Greek Mountaineering Federation, based in Athens.

EOT Ellinikós Organismós Tourismoú, the National Tourist Organization.

FYROM Former Yugoslav Republic of Macedonia.

KKE Communist Party, unreconstructed.

KTEL National syndicate of bus companies. The term is also used to refer to bus stations.

ND Conservative (Néa Dhimokratía) party.

NEL Navtikí Etería Lésvou (Lesvian Shipping Co), which runs most of the northeast Aegean ferries.

OSE Railway corporation.

OTE Telephone company.

PASOK Socialist party (Pan-Hellenic Socialist Movement)

SEO Greek Mountaineering Club, based in Thessaloníki.

INDEX